The Franz Boas Papers, VOLUME 1

Franz Boas as Public Intellectual — Theory, Ethnography, Activism

Edited by Regna Darnell, Michelle Hamilton,
Robert L. A. Hancock, and Joshua Smith

REGNA DARNELL, GENERAL EDITOR

University of Nebraska Press | Lincoln and London

© 2015 by the Board of Regents of the University of Nebraska. All rights reserved. Manufactured in the United States of America ∞

Frontispiece image: Franz Boas on the cover of *Time* magazine a few years before his death. Courtesy *Time* magazine, May 11, 1936, © 1936 Time Inc. Used under license.

Parts of chapter 4, "Franz Boas and the Conditions of Literature" by J. Edward Chamberlin, previously appeared in a different form as "'The Corn People Have a Song Too. It Is Very Good': On Beauty, Truth, and Goodness" in *Studies in American Indian Literatures* 21.3 (2009): 66–89, © J. Edward Chamberlin. Chapter 15, "Franz Boas's Correspondence with German Friends and Colleagues in the Early 1930s" by Jürgen Langenkämper, is based on "Ich fuerchte nur, wir verstehen einander nicht" and "Franz Boas' Briefwechsel mit deutschen Freunden und Kollegen 1932/33," which appeared in Friedrich Pöhl and Bernhard Tilg, eds., *Franz Boas—Kultur, Sprache, Rasse: Wege einer antirassistischen Anthropologie* (Wien: Lit, 2009), 2nd ed. (2011).

Library of Congress Cataloging-in-Publication Data

The Franz Boas papers / Regna Darnell, general editor.
volumes cm.—(Franz Boas papers documentary edition)
Contents: volume 1. Franz Boas as public intellectual: theory, ethnography, activism / edited by Regna Darnell, Michelle Hamilton, Robert L. A. Hancock, and Joshua Smith
Includes bibliographical references and index.
ISBN 978-0-8032-6984-2 (cloth: alk. paper)
ISBN 978-0-8032-7199-9 (pdf)
1. Boas, Franz, 1858–1942—Influence.
2. Boas, Franz, 1858–1942—Correspondence.
3. Ethnology. I. Darnell, Regna, editor of compilation.
GN21.B56F75 2015
301.092—dc23
2015011301

Set in Charis by L. Auten.

Contents

List of Figures	vii
Acknowledgments	ix
Historiographic Conundra: The Boasian Elephant in the Middle of Anthropology's Room REGNA DARNELL	xi

Part 1. Theory and Interdisciplinary Scope

1. Mind, Body, and the Native Point of View: Boasian Theory at the Centennial of *The Mind of Primitive Man*   3
REGNA DARNELL

2. The Individual and Individuality in Franz Boas's Anthropology and Philosophy   19
HERBERT S. LEWIS

3. The Police Dance: Dissemination in Boas's Field Notes and Diaries, 1886–1894   43
CHRISTOPHER BRACKEN

4. Franz Boas and the Conditions of Literature   65
J. EDWARD CHAMBERLIN

5. From Baffin Island to Boasian Induction: How Anthropology and Linguistics Got into Their Interlinear Groove   83
MICHAEL SILVERSTEIN

6. The Boasian Legacy in Ethnomusicology: Cultural Relativism, Narrative Texts, Linguistic Structures, and the Role of Comparison   129
SEAN O'NEILL

Part 2. Ethnography

7. Friends in This World: The Relationship of George Hunt and Franz Boas   163
ISAIAH LORADO WILNER

8. The Ethnographic Legacy of Franz Boas and
James Teit: The Thompson Indians of British Columbia   191
ANDREA LAFORET

Part 3. Activism

9. Anthropological Activism and Boas's
Pacific Northwest Ethnology   215
DAVID W. DINWOODIE

10. Franz Boas, Wilson Duff, and the Image of
Anthropology in British Columbia   237
ROBERT L. A. HANCOCK

11. Cultural Persistence in the Age of "Hopelessness":
Phinney, Boas, and U.S. Indian Policy   263
JOSHUA SMITH

12. Franz Boas's Correspondence with German
Friends and Colleagues in the Early 1930s   277
JÜRGEN LANGENKÄMPER

13. Franz Boas on War and Empire:
The Making of a Public Intellectual   293
JULIA E. LISS

Part 4. The Archival Project

14. Anthropology of Revitalization: Digitizing
the American Philosophical Society's
Native American Collections   331
TIMOTHY B. POWELL

15. "An expansive archive . . . not a diminished one":
The Franz Boas Papers Documentary Edition Project   345
MICHELLE HAMILTON

Contributors   363
The Franz Boas Papers Project Team   367
Index   369

Figures

1. "Kuē'qakila's heraldic column at Qumta'sqē" — 48
2. The Village of Nahwitti, Hope Island, British Columbia — 49
3. Front page of first lesson, Harper's Hebrew Correspondence School, Elementary course — 88
4. Genesis 1:1 Hebrew text with translation, explanatory notes, and further observations — 89
5. Exercises for students to submit via correspondence — 90
6. Harper's Manual: facing-page layout of Hebrew and English versions of Genesis — 91
7. Concordanced exemplification of syntactic forms in Harper's inductive syntax — 93
8. Grassmann's Rigvedic morpholexical concordance, by word roots and stems — 95
9. Kathlamet (Chinookan) text with notes keyed to grammatical sketch — 105
10. Dorsey's rendering of La Flèche's Omaha text, "How Rabbit Caught the Sun in a Trap" — 109
11. Boas's text of "Sednalo Qaxodlulo" as published — 110
12. Kathlamet (Chinookan) text with notes keyed to grammatical sketch — 111
13. Pages 20–21 of Boas's 1890 Lower Chinook notebook — 114
14. Pages 546–547 of Boas's 1894 Kathlamet notebook — 115
15. The text in figure 14 as rendered in Boas's "Kathlamet Texts," page 39 — 116
16. Edward Sapir's Kiksht ("Wishram") notebook 2, page 17 — 118
17. Sapir's Nootka notebook 19, page 29 — 119
18. The Franz Boas Papers Project Team — 366

Acknowledgments

The conference that gave rise to this volume of revisionist essays on Franz Boas was supported by a Workshop Grant from the Social Science and Humanities Research Council of Canada (SSHRC). The contributors served as an initial planning group for the documentary edition of the Boas Professional Papers that this volume inaugurates. A SSHRC Partnership Grant to General Editor Regna Darnell and the University of Western Ontario has supported the collaboration of the American Philosophical Society, holder of the Boas papers, the University of Nebraska Press, the University of Victoria, and the Musgamagw Dzawada'enuxw Tribal Council.

University of Nebraska Press senior acquisitions editor Matthew Bokovoy proposed a critical edition of Franz Boas papers to Darnell at the time of his appointment in 2008 and has worked tirelessly alongside the research team to obtain funding and to create a seminal resource for the social science and Indigenous communities.

Virtually the entire staff of the American Philosophical Society has become involved in "the Boas project" in some way. We single out Martin Levitt (librarian), his executive assistant Sandra Duffy, Timothy Powell (director, Center for Native American and Indigenous Research), Brian Carpenter (senior archivist, CNAIR), Bayard Miller (the archivist who has digitized the Boas Professional Papers), Richard Shrake (technical advisor extraordinaire), Annie Westcott (director of meetings), Linda Musumeci (director of grants and fellowships), and Keith Thomson (executive officer). The library's advisory committee on indigenous research has devised innovative protocols for the treatment of culturally sensitive materials that parallel the commitments of the Franz Boas Documentary Edition.

We are grateful for the diligence and commitment of our Indigenous Advisory Board: Ryan Nicolson (Kwakwaka'wakw), Deanna Nicolson (Kwakwaka'wakw), Marianne Nicolson (Kwakwaka'wakw), Johnny Mack (Nuu chah nulth), Rachel Flowers (Lyackson), Patricia Vickers (Haida, Tsimshian, Heiltsuk), Angie Bain (Union of British Columbia Indian Chiefs), Robert Hancock (Metis), Dean Jacobs (Anishinaabe), and especially IAC chair Susan Hill (Mohawk). The Musgamagw Dzawada'enuxw Tribal Council is a welcome partner in our efforts toward treatment of

culturally sensitive materials, return of intellectual property through Digital Knowledge Sharing (DKS), and training and mentoring of Native American and First Nations scholars.

We thank our graduate assistants, Paulina Johnson (Plains Cree, anthropology), Evan Habkirk (history), Jessica Knapp (public history), Jonathan Doering (theory and criticism), and Sarah Moritz (anthropology, McGill). Undergraduate work study students have been diligent in preparing initial transcriptions: Michael Cook, Dianne Le, Zachary Miller, Kristopher Connolly, Raquel Farrington, and Savroop Grewal. Rick Fehr, acting director of First Nations Studies at Western, supervised the work study students.

Anthropology Administrative Officer Jean M. Taylor went and continues to go beyond the call of duty despite an overwhelming workload of which this project is only a small part. We are humbly grateful.

Our invaluable project and office manager, Adair Harper, designed the website (www.franzboaspapers.uwo.ca). We have obtained invaluable assistance from the Society for Documentary Editing, particularly from Beth Luey and Bob Karachuk. Many thanks also to the Documents Compass team at the University of Virginia, whose Doctracker documentary editing database has become an integral part of our workflow. Special thanks go to Mary MacNeil, whose expertise, patience, and warmth were crucial to setting up our version of Doctracker.

Substantial changes in the documentary edition team are under way as we move into coming volumes. We will particularly miss Martin Levitt, librarian of the American Philosophical Society, and his ever-cheerful miracle-working executive assistant, Sandra Duffy, but wish them both well in retirement. Marty has generously lent his vision, gravitas, and long-term commitment. Our erstwhile project manager, Adair Harper, leaves an indelible mark on the shape of the documentary edition and its research team. M. Sam Cronk has joined the team and been critical to final preparation of the manuscript and Indigenous feedback on it.

Franz Boas is far too complicated for a single scholar to tackle either a biography or documentary edition, and many have contributed to the revisionist view of his work showcased in this volume. We dedicate the volume to the memory of George W. Stocking Jr., a major Boas scholar who passed on in 2013 and who will be sadly missed on our editorial advisory board. The thematic volumes that follow will provide an invaluable resource for academics, Native American and First Nations communities, and the general public.

Historiographic Conundra

The Boasian Elephant in the Middle of Anthropology's Room

REGNA DARNELL

For the twenty-first century as for the twentieth, anthropology has struggled to come to terms with the ongoing legacy of Franz Boas (1858–1942), indisputably the founder and dominant figure in the emergence of a professionalized academic discipline in North America. Boas has been eulogized and reviled, claimed as an ancestor and repudiated as having led anthropology astray. Despite the chaotic variability of the retrospective assessments, however, all practicing anthropologists have at some point struggled to position themselves in relation to the elephant in the middle of the room, the larger-than-life figure who defies simple definition or closure in any single perspective on his life, work, and stature as a public intellectual. Boas defies the boxes to which his successors have tried to confine him, leaving a legacy to which contemporary students of humankind can respond and have responded in multiple, not always commensurable ways. The challenge is simultaneously historiographic and intellectual, in the past and in the ongoing present.

This volume inaugurates *The Franz Boas Papers Documentary Edition* series and attests to the belief of the editors and contributors that Boas merits reassessment, indeed that there is some contemporary urgency to this task, both within anthropology and beyond. A conference in December 2010 at the University of Western Ontario, sponsored by a workshop grant from the Social Sciences and Humanities Research Council of Canada (SSHRC), framed this needed reassessment from a variety of disciplinary and thematic standpoints. Based in good part on the research reported in this volume, in March 2013 SSHRC awarded a substantial Partnership Grant to support research for the documentary edition, with Regna Darnell as project director and general editor and conference contributors (see the contributors section in the back) as its initial editorial board, since expanded to incorporate scholars unable to attend or who added new perspectives. (For the full editorial team, see the project website, www.franzboaspapers.uwo.ca.)

Participants came to this preliminary project through the Boasian

roots of their own scholarly preoccupations and began to build an interpretive mosaic with far greater potential to capture the complexity of Boas and his anthropology than could have been achieved by any one of them alone. The contributions included here do not, however, exhaust the potential to explore ongoing resonances of Boasian anthropology in North America and its adaptations by other national traditions and disciplinary discourses. Rather the papers open up directions for further endeavor, by these authors and by others. These forays do not aspire to instantiate a single monolithic revisionist Boas. Indeed the protean range of Boas's engagements with widening circles of anthropology, the social sciences, and public life by their very nature continue to evade comprehensive integration. The rich resources of the Franz Boas Papers held at the American Philosophical Society in Philadelphia allow Boas and his contemporaries to speak in their own words across professional generations. Publication of the Boas correspondence by the University of Nebraska Press, selected, annotated, and contextualized by a research team arising from the collaborations reported here and expanding to incorporate additional specializations and perspectives as the edition takes form, enables such reassessment and invites further scholarship.

Boas's career spanned interdisciplinary boundaries across the humanities and social sciences, encompassing aspects of disciplines we now separate out as at least potentially distinct from anthropology defined in terms of its four traditional subdisciplines of cultural, linguistic, biological, and archaeological inquiry: history (including ethnohistory), linguistics, literature, folklore, museum studies, philosophy, science studies, politics, law, education, and psychology. These disciplines spill over into public life in such domains as education, public policy, Native studies, Afro-American studies, women's studies, and antiracism activism. Boas was a pioneer in breaking down American isolationism, with its incumbent intolerance and misinformation about cultural, linguistic, and biological diversity. He argued passionately for academic and intellectual freedom and for science as a value transcending the short-term goals of nation-states. His work set a model for the capacity of the public intellectual to call the attention of citizens to social injustice, environmental degradation, systematic discrimination, and other ills of modern society. Boas's institutional base at Columbia University, fieldwork sites in Baffinland (now Baffin Island, Nunavut) and British Columbia, and his ongoing engagements with the Germany of his youth and education weave a complex and largely unexplored legacy.

The vast Boas scholarship emanating from within anthropology largely fails because it lacks Boas's intellectual range, ignores differentiation

over the six decades of his career, and provides insufficient historicism in linking his oeuvre to its present-day theoretical, methodological, and public implications. Boas's positions changed as he incorporated scientific advances that came to his attention. There were consistencies and continuities, to be sure, but a nuanced reading of the gradual development and elaboration of his ideas is called for.

The challenge to Boas's intellectual heirs has been to match his scope, both academically and as a public intellectual. Boas straddles the development of American academic life and public engagement in the context of his own times. His limitations as well as his pioneering contributions must be acknowledged. To build on the work of an earlier scholar is to move alongside an ongoing dynamic tradition, to select parts that are still significant, even prescient, and to move beyond those that no longer fit with the work we do or the society in which we live. This ongoing complexity of the biographical subject and his influence is directly reflected in both the strengths and weaknesses of Boasian historiography. Boas scholars do not all agree, and their standpoints do not mesh in a seamless narrative. We argue that this diversity is productive.

The Canadian historian Douglas Cole's posthumously published biography, *Franz Boas: The Early Years*, provides meticulous detail up to 1906, when Boas's career began to exceed the boundaries of anthropology as understood in his time. Unfortunately Cole died before completing the second volume, a project that had promised to become increasingly unwieldy in both scope and substance. In a parallel elision of Boas's later work, the historian turned anthropologist George W. Stocking Jr. focused on his views of race and evolution prior to the dual paradigm statements of 1911 before turning to the antecedents of British social anthropology.[1] *The Mind of Primitive Man* and the *Introduction to the Handbook of American Indian Languages* indeed set out the paradigm within which Boas and his students worked: the critique of evolution, the significance of history and environment, the standpoint of the individual grounded in culture. Nonetheless these seminal ideas, now largely taken for granted, did not emerge full-blown; they were tested and elaborated by Boasian anthropologists in the practice of what Thomas Kuhn called "normal science" over the ensuing three decades.[2] The centennial of *The Mind of Primitive Man* was the proximate occasion for the conference that underlies this volume. It also was celebrated by independent conferences organized at the New York Academy of Sciences by Neni Panourgiá at Columbia University and by Isaiah Wilner at Yale University. The year 1911 was indeed a watershed for the historiography of Americanist anthropology.

Book-length efforts to capture Boas's contribution have ranged from

hagiography to vilification for failure to underwrite the preoccupations of his successors.[3] Some have focused on limited domains of present-day import, particularly race and political engagement; others have emphasized professionalization, institutional growth, social networks, and theoretical preoccupations.[4] After World War II a new generation of anthropologists, led by veterans returning to newly expanding universities on the GI Bill, turned away from the study of the American Indian that had dominated the discipline in North America up to that time in favor of overseas field sites and a more global view of cultural diversity in relation to contemporary society. Further, postwar positivism deemed Boas retrogressively atheoretical, an attitude that has hindered consideration of his actual positions. The discipline as a whole failed to turn to Leslie White's or Marvin Harris's Marxist-tinged neo-evolutionary theory. Somewhat surprisingly, however, anthropologists for the most part have accepted without much reflexivity a jaundiced characterization of Boas's position as resolutely negative in theoretical terms, relegating his work to the past as being useful merely to undercut the now obvious foibles of Victorian unilinear evolution with its incumbent racism in support of colonialism.

Too many of those who accept latter-day dismissals of Boas's significance for contemporary anthropological practice rarely cite evidence, pursue archival research, or reassess the potential biases of inherited scholarship. Others create binaries where Boas himself was more nuanced—not materialist or idealist but responsive to multiple permutations of social life in different contexts. More measured assessment, however, has been under way for some time.[5] Complementary primary documents contributing to a potential synthesis are increasingly available. Archival resources abound. In addition to the source collection for this documentary edition, the Franz Boas Papers held at the American Philosophical Society in Philadelphia, extensive Boas materials are located in the archives of major universities and museums across North America, Mexico, and Europe. On the ethnographic side, Boas's Central Eskimo diaries have been edited by Ludger Müller-Wille and his Northwest Coast diaries by Ronald Rohner.[6] Pierre Swiggers is editing the Boas-Sapir correspondence, and Piero Matthey the correspondence of the core Boasians Edward Sapir and Robert Lowie.[7] There are book-length biographies, in some cases more than one, of Alfred Kroeber, Robert Lowie, Edward Sapir, Margaret Mead, Ruth Benedict, Melville Herskovits, Leslie White, Elsie Clews Parsons, Ruth Landes, and Julian Steward as well as autobiographical reflections by Boas's students and former students.

The epithet of public intellectual perhaps best captures the sense in which Boas did not, even in his own time, belong exclusively to anthro-

pology. Histories of anthropology from within the discipline have the advantage of insider perspective and attention to details of practice and evidence, but limitations of standpoint arise in relation to the larger intellectual history and context. For example, John Gilkeson,[8] with a baseline in American studies, assesses Boas's legacy from the viewpoint of American public understanding of culture and nation. Boas served as president of the American Association for the Advancement of Science as well as the American Anthropological Association, the Linguistic Society of America, and the American Folklore Society. He signed documents for human rights against Nazi oppression of Jews alongside Albert Einstein. His picture appeared on the cover of *Time* magazine in 1941 only a few years before his death. Many public accolades skirted engagement with Boas's narrowly anthropological work; instead they acknowledged his influence across disciplines, institutions, and domains of public life. He became a spokesperson for the legitimacy of American science, the optimism of American politics, and the conviction that the world could be made a better place.

This volume examines Boas's stature as a public intellectual in three crucial dimensions: theory, ethnography, and activism. In each case revisionism of anthropology's inherited view of Boas is overdue. The authors come from and move across many of the disciplines to which Boas himself contributed, bringing expertise in anthropology, history, linguistics, folklore, ethnomusicology, museum studies, Native studies, comparative literature, English literature, film studies, philosophy, and journalism. In addition to those whose papers are included here, participants in the 2010 conference also included the perspectives of the philosopher Barbara Saunders, Kwakw<u>a</u>ka'wakw knowledge keepers Ryan Nicolson and Marianne Nicolson, archaeologist Matthew Beaudoin, linguistic anthropologists Judith Berman and Tim Bisha, cultural anthropologists Aaron Glass and Marc Pinkoski, and historian Matthew Bokovoy.

Boas as theorist crossed disciplines and methodologies, with a few basic ideas to which he returned over and over again through his treatments of varied ethnographic data. In the binary posed by Isaiah Berlin, he epitomized the hedgehog, not the fox. Changes of emphasis and apparent inconsistencies in Boas's work reflect his return to long established problems from new angles. He tirelessly produced counterexamples to premature generalizations in evolutionary versions of the comparative method. His exemplars demonstrated that particular histories were influenced by environment and culture and did not proceed through a single sequence everywhere. His studies of the diffusion of cultural elements in art, language, and myth illustrate the capacity of anthropological

method to provide access to the past history of specific cultures despite the absence of written records extending into the deep past. Boas insisted on the importance of standpoint and the influence of Indigenous cultural as well as individual understandings on everything from phonology to worldview. He demonstrated the plasticity of human biological types and the inadequacy of race as a biological concept. Nonetheless his theories often remained implicit in his ethnographic reports, leaving it to his students to formulate them in more accessible form for broader disciplinary and public audiences—as Robert Lowie did for social structure and religion, Edward Sapir for language, A. L. Kroeber for the theory of culture and its relation to environment, Clark Wissler for material culture, Paul Radin for history and philosophy, and Margaret Mead and Ruth Benedict for culture and personality.[9] This classic first generation of Boas students filled in the pieces of the paradigm that would dominate Americanist anthropology at least up to World War II. The Boasian paradigm treated culture as a system of symbols rather than as a thing to be understood by observation alone, used native speaker texts in Native languages as a window to culture and standpoint, and emphasized the analytic autonomy of race, language, and culture as classificatory variables.[10]

Toward the end of his life, however, Boas turned to systematizing his legacy as he understood it. *Anthropology and Modern Life* claimed for anthropology a critical relevance to the understanding of contemporary North American society and the need for tolerance of cultural diversity. Thinking like an anthropologist would have positive consequences in the world. A revised edition of *The Mind of Primitive Man* appeared in 1938.[11] Although much of the text remained virtually unchanged, Boas smoothed out the gaps between chapters originally written for separate occasions, integrating his argument and honing it toward the defense of science and freedom in a world threatened by war. In 1940 he issued a selection from his published oeuvre in *Race, Language and Culture*, the same three classificatory domains he had argued varied independently in 1911. As in *The Mind of Primitive Man*, he began with race, acknowledged the methodological rigors of linguistic form, and insisted on the particularities of attested ethnographic diversity as a necessary precursor to understanding human nature or culture in general.

Several professional generations have intervened since Boas attempted to define his own legacy in a rapidly changing world. Today, therefore, we must reconstruct the context in which his views make sense and his social networks reflect the cultural and social history of his times. Because the documentary edition is not yet complete and the archival documents are not widely known, contributors to this volume have quoted exten-

sively from Boas and his interlocutors. Their style and rhetoric evoke the tenor of an academic milieu that now seems overly formal, even quaint. Participants in the various enterprises Boas touched upon are all quite capable of speaking for themselves, just as we assume our readers are able to assess the evidence presented and the persuasiveness of the interpretations arising from it. The same documents can be juxtaposed with diverse strands of contemporary scholarship and public discourse. We as editors have made no effort to normalize contradictory interpretations or minor repetitions from alternative standpoints.

Boas as theorist has received short shrift, both during his lifetime and in disciplinary memory. Part 1 counters that not only was Boas a theorist but also that approaching his legacy in revisionist terms through contemporary disciplinary perspectives and complementary perspectives within them requires a judicious balance between historicist method and presentist relevance. Papers are juxtaposed to emphasize the continuity of Boas's scholarship across subject matters, methodologies, and theories. Boas's theory, like that of Paul Radin's "primitive" philosopher, often was not systematic. But careful examination reveals the sophisticated theoretical questions underlying his superficially unmitigated descriptive exuberance.

The potential incommensurability of the material and the ideal or mental in Boas's thinking emerges in the papers by Regna Darnell and Herbert Lewis. Darnell follows Boas's movement from biology to environment or culture, encompassing texts and contexts, ideas and the environment in which they flourished or faded. Lewis emphasizes the material side of the argument, linking Boas to American pragmatist philosophy, and highlights the empiricism of his social analysis. Boas himself counterposed these methods, already arguing in "The Study of Geography" in 1887 that inductive and deductive methods were equally valid as long as they were applied to the appropriate phenomena. Geography, history, cosmology, and cultural anthropology or ethnology were interpretive sciences that nonetheless could reveal patterns of behavior and meaning-making. Physical anthropology and archaeology, in contrast, could be considered alongside what we now call the natural or physical sciences. The rigor of science properly accrued to both kinds of enterprise.

The two papers that arise from literary studies are quite different. Christopher Bracken explores the context of Kwakwaka'wakw response to rapid culture change through adaptation of ceremonial ritual to poke sly fun at the outsiders who opposed traditional rituals. Bracken's concern with the particulars of expressive culture and the ironic subversive wit of Kwakwaka'wakw (Boas's Kwaqiutl) performance reveals much

Historiographic Conundra   xvii

about the agency and self-confidence of the people with whom Boas did his most extensive research. It has taken a much later perspective on settler colonialism, in the language of contemporary British Columbia legal and political discourse, to recognize this agency and read it as ironic resistance. Boas's texts beg for a revisionist history of European and Aboriginal relations.

In contrast, J. Edward Chamberlin spreads a wide net based in comparative literature, evoking Boas's fine-tuned ear for language and translation in his ethnography and arguing for his methodological appropriation of the literary modernism of his day, that is, the New Criticism. Chamberlin reminds us that Boas saw beauty as well as ethnographic and historical documentation in the texts he collected. He approached his texts in terms of their own categories of genre and form, matter-of-factly eschewing ethnocentrism. Without suggesting anything more direct than the institutional copresence at Columbia of two powerful public intellectuals who were willing to challenge the morality of the academic world around them, Chamberlin draws Boas, the anthropologist, and Joel E. Spingarn, a significant figure in the history of race relations (a subject in which Boas had more than a passing interest), into a net of modernist reflection on form, meaning, and public relevance. It should not surprise us that modernism worked itself out similarly in parallel disciplines of the humanities and social sciences, without requiring documentation of direct interaction between particular figures at a given period in time, or that textual approaches in literary studies might provide fruitful models for ethnographic emulation.

Michael Silverstein and Sean O'Neill approach Boas as a linguist in very different modes. Silverstein demonstrates Boas's masterful capacity to borrow methods and perspectives useful for his ethnographic work. His texts drew on and integrated insights from Indo-European philology, medieval studies, and language pedagogy in remarkably canny though not always precisely original ways. Like Chamberlin, Silverstein sees Boas as a master bricoleur, using whatever he found at hand, perhaps a creativity of its own sort. Indeed twentieth-century anthropology fought long and hard for legitimacy to depict American Indian cultures using the methods of cultural analysis developed in post-Enlightenment European traditions. Boas accorded similar respect to the texts he recorded in Indian and Eskimo languages as to those of his own natal tradition. Edward Sapir and Leonard Bloomfield demonstrated that sound changes in language reflect prior historical relationships of cultures even in unwritten languages.

Sean O'Neill frames expressive culture in relation to linguistic form, drawing a parallel between Boas's ethnomusicology and his linguistics.

Boas's influence on the emergence of ethnomusicology, whether or not it has remained fundamental for anthropology at large, allows O'Neill to draw Boas's linguistics into larger considerations of cultural context and forms of expression that may include dance, ceremonial performance, and art as well as language and music. O'Neill speaks less about Boas's own linguistic work, distributed across almost his entire career, than about its legacy in the work of those he trained and inspired. The search for musical universals, as for linguistic universals, has drawn the ethnographically particular into juxtaposition with a larger methodological relativism.

Part 2 offers another kind of revisionism, revisiting Boas's fieldwork and its canonical status within the discipline of anthropology. Boas has been accused of mere descriptivism, of salvage ethnography oblivious to the realities of contemporary American Indian life. The papers in this section provide a more nuanced view of what he was up to and how he attempted to integrate his ethnography around "the native point of view" and the reconstruction of the history of the various peoples, languages, and cultures of the North Pacific Coast.

Boas as an ethnographer worked primarily among the people he called Kwakiutl and other Northwest Coast tribes in British Columbia from the mid-1880s until his death in 1942, visiting the area on multiple occasions (Dinwoodie, this volume, catalogues his long-term engagement) and working up his textual materials back home in New York, incorporating materials from his at-a-distance collaboration with George Hunt and other Native assistants he trained while in the field. Anthropologists based in the United States rarely acknowledge that Boas's fieldwork, including his 1883–1884 year among the Eskimo of Baffin Island (not yet called Inuit at that time), took place in Canada, not the United States. Indeed from a Canadian point of view, British Columbia is the *West* Coast, not the Northwest Coast, as Boas himself called it in writing for a primarily American audience. Although the national boundary was not a traditional one for the Native American groups in question, postcontact histories have diverged considerably because American and Canadian political, social, legal, and economic contexts were different.

Another kind of revisionist redress is at stake here. Much of Boas's work can be reassessed and drawn into contemporary debates without consideration of the location of his field research. Nonetheless there are times when place does matter, and little prior documentation focuses in this direction.[12] About half the contributors to this volume are Canadian, and several more did their own fieldwork in Canada. Much of the research describing Boas's ethnography is collaborative, drawing mem-

bers of the communities where Boas worked into the interpretation and contemporary uses of the texts, museum objects, and photographs that he collected.

In part 2 theory shades imperceptibly into ethnography. Isaiah Lorado Wilner proposes a very different reading of the relationship between Boas and Hunt than the one emergent from examination of their collaboration to produce a definitive corpus of linguistic texts. Wilner considers the personal relationship between Boas and Hunt as the basis of their co-constructed Kwakw_aka_'wakw ethnography (sometimes recognized by official coauthorship, unusual for the time). Wilner attributes the primary insight to Hunt as Boas's guide and go-between. In some very serious sense, nonetheless, Boas was the catalyst who lent significance to Hunt's knowledge and encouraged him to articulate it in nontraditional ways for a nontraditional audience.[13]

Andrea Laforet provides yet another dimension of contrast in dealing with a different Northwest Coast tribe and a different collaborative relationship. Hunt was not the only field assistant with whom Boas maintained a long-term relationship at a distance as he worked up his ethnographic materials and sought convergent evidence for history and standpoint. Laforet emphasizes the cultural documentation arising from Boas's collaborative relationship with James Teit in the ethnography of the Thompson Indians rather than the personal relationships involved; the biographical is secondary. Teit, notably, continued to publish independently after Boas's death and was recognized as an anthropologist in his own right.

The ethnographic specificity of part 2 enables a revision of the Boasian legacy in part 3, particularly in Canada, that draws heavily on contemporary collaboration with descendant communities holding ongoing interests in and claims to materials their ancestors shared with Boas, often by way of Hunt. The foundations of contemporary Canadian Indigenous activism are firmly grounded in Boasian engagement with Northwest Coast individuals and communities. The two papers in this section emphasize how the Boasian legacy has come to us today.

Some of Boas's critics have denied his activism and dismissed his American Indian studies as mere salvage ethnography that remained unaware of or uninterested in contemporary conditions and political constraints. Boas's documented legacy in terms of American Indian policy, training community members as anthropologists, and intervention on behalf of Native individuals and public issues paints quite a different picture. Without these contexts, we contend, understanding of what Boas was up to necessarily remains elusive.

Thus David W. Dinwoodie argues that Boas provides useful contemporary perspectives only when his ethnographic work is reframed in relation to its refractions in ongoing British Columbian political and legal debates. Dinwoodie contends that Boas's personal biography intersects at a critical juncture with the history of European contact on the North Pacific Coast. Reexamination of that intersection produces a history that extends to the present day and articulates the history of the peoples with whom Boas worked, alongside that of outsiders who settled among them. The antimonies implicit in the philosophical traditions to which Boas's ethnographic work responded are being reworked to new ends, although both the users and the uses to which anthropology is put have changed considerably since he did his fieldwork.

Following a historiographic thread, Robert L. A. Hancock focuses initially on the effective application of Boas's ethnographic work in British Columbia in political and legal as well as public discourse—again in a Canadian political context unfamiliar to many American readers—but he also situates it in a more global forum that has rendered it canonical for the discipline as a whole. Wilson Duff, whom Hancock identifies as the primary inheritor of Boas's Northwest Coast ethnographic mantle, aspired to bring Boasian interventions into the public domain, albeit on a more localized level than Boas himself. Anthropological interventions have in fact mattered, though not as often as many might wish.[14] Hancock documents some recent misreadings of anthropological insight and counters them in Boasian terms.

Boas's activism on behalf of Native Americans takes a U.S. turn as Joshua Smith explores his mentorship of Archie Phinney (Nez Percé) and how this Boas student and public intellectual in his own right provided ammunition for Boas's unsuccessful intervention in American Indian policy over the selection of John Collier as commissioner of the Bureau of Indian Affairs. Boas favored Phinney for the position and foresaw dangers in Collier's enthusiasm for one-size-fits-all Indian policy. In any case Boas's passion for attempting to influence Indian administration is far from the apolitical salvage ethnography among dying cultures of which he has often been accused.

Jürgen Langenkämper, a journalist based in Minden, where Boas was born, looks at his anthropology from the direction of his German homeland and his influence on anthropology there. He tells the story of Boas's interventions in the increasingly oppressive intellectual climate of Germany in the early 1930s with the immediacy of an unfolding news story. We know the ending, but Boas does not, as he tries to obtain accurate news on ongoing events in Germany, facilitate the professional affairs of

his colleagues there, and ensure that his personal library will end up in his homeland. Despite the increasing dangers of intervention, Boas did not back down from conflict over the morality of state actions. Just as he had paid a high price for accusing anthropologists of spying in Mexico for the U.S. government during World War I, his public letter to Reichs President von Hindenburg guaranteed that his reputation would not protect him in Germany from anti-Semitism or repression.

Julia E. Liss takes a more analytic tack, arguing that Boas's stature as a public intellectual arises primarily from the catalytic effect of war, empire, and the ambitions of nation-states in driving the focus of his work. She documents a remarkable range of Boas's public commitments in these areas, noting that he was consistently outspoken in defense of underdogs and his vision of individual freedom and social justice. She evokes the cultural relativism he engaged (without using the term) without compromising the necessity for moral judgment. Her analysis ties the Boasian legacy in British Columbia to his influence on contemporary global human rights discourses. In neither case do we do things today as Boas might have done them; nonetheless his example set the stage for contemporary ethical debates in anthropology and beyond.

Those who dismiss Boas as an activist tend to relegate him to a trash heap of so-called salvage ethnography of Native Americans and rarely consider the dynamic of his engagement with such hot-potato issues as immigration policy, anti-Semitism and antiracism more generally, or racial politics in the United States and support for Afro-American educational endeavors. Lee Baker, for example, treats Boas's American Indian and Afro-American researches as mirror images, reversing the role of culture and politics in their emphasis.[15] Moreover public engagement with Canadian society, in the absence of America's stark racial contrast of black and red, requires a different analysis that begs for equally serious investigation. We may perhaps conclude that effective activism, for us as for Boas, wields enormous potential to mobilize professional aspirations in the service of public discourse.

The two papers in part 4 reorient the emerging revisionist Boas of previous essays toward the emergence of the Boas documentary edition in terms of collaborative research with Native American communities in both the United States and in Canada. Timothy B. Powell, the director of the Center for Native American and Indigenous Research at the American Philosophical Society (APS), where the Boas papers are held, emphasizes the engagement of descendant communities in the adjudication of culturally sensitive materials and renewed access to ethnographic, linguistic, and photographic materials. The commitment of the APS to meeting

the needs of contemporary communities where Boas worked embodies a documentary stewardship that constitutes activism in the Boasian mode. APS protocols developed through Endangered Languages partnerships with community knowledge keepers and educators provide a model for the documentary edition initiated by this volume.

The public historian Michelle Hamilton contextualizes the forthcoming documentary edition in relation to documentary editing as it has developed in the United States and Canada and to the contexts in which a revisionist Boasian scholarship resonates with contemporary Native American and First Nations aspirations and agendas. Drawing on the motto of the APS, "useful knowledge" is produced when past achievements are rendered accessible physically and intellectually for ongoing application through Digital Knowledge Sharing (DKS). The revisionist Boas who begins to emerge in these pages foreshadows the insights and methodologies of the forthcoming volumes.

Notes

1. See the following by Stocking: *Race, Culture and Evolution, The Shaping of American Anthropology, The Ethnographer's Magic, Volksgeist as Method and Ethic.*
2. Kuhn, *The Structure of Scientific Revolutions.*
3. Goldschmidt, *The Anthropology of Franz Boas*; Herskovits, *Franz Boas: The Science of Man in the Making*; Norman Boas, *Franz Boas: 1848–1942*; White, *The Ethnology and Ethnography of Franz Boas*; White, "The Social Organization of Ethnological Theory"; Wax, "The Limits of Boas' Anthropology"; Harris, *The Rise of Anthropological Theory.*
4. Baker, *From Savage to Negro* and *Anthropology and the Racial Politics of Culture*; Hyatt, *Franz Boas: Social Activist*; Lewis, *In Defense of Anthropology*; Patterson, *A Social History of Anthropology*; Williams, *Rethinking Race*; Zumwalt and Willis, *Franz Boas and W. E. B. Dubois*; Stocking, *Race, Culture and Evolution*; Hinsley, *Savages and Scientists*; Darnell, *And Along Came Boas* and *Invisible Genealogies*; Müller-Wille, *The Franz Boas Enigma.*
5. Darnell, "The Importance of the Northwest Coast," *Invisible Genealogies*, and *Edward Sapir*; Darnell and Gleach, special issue of *American Anthropologist*; Valentine and Darnell, *Theorizing the Americanist Tradition*; Harrison and Darnell, *Historicizing Canadian Anthropology*; Lewis, *In Defense of Anthropology*; Müller-Wille, *The Franz Boas Enigma*; Stocking, *Volksgeist as Method and Ethic*; Bunzl, special "In Focus" section of *American Anthropologist*; Penny and Bunzl, *Worldly Provincialism*; Baker, *From Savage to Negro* and *Anthropology and the Racial Politics of Culture.*
6. Müller-Wille, *The Franz Boas Enigma*; Rohner, *The Ethnography of Franz Boas.*
7. Pierre Swiggers, personal communication.

8. Gilkeson, *Anthropologists and the Rediscovery of America*.
9. Darnell, *And Along Came Boas* and *Invisible Genealogies*.
10. Darnell, *And Along Came Boas* and *Invisible Genealogies*.
11. Darnell, "Franz Boas as Theorist."
12. See Harrison and Darnell, *Historicizing Canadian Anthropology*; Darnell, "The Importance of the Northwest Coast."
13. Berman, "'The Culture As It Appears to the Indian Himself.'"
14. Hancock, "Historiographical Representations of Materialist Anthropology."
15. Baker, *Anthropology and the Racial Politics of Culture*.

References

MANUSCRIPTS AND ARCHIVES

Franz Boas Papers. 2014. http://www.franzboaspapers.uwo.ca (accessed March 31, 2014).

PUBLISHED WORKS

Baker, Lee. *Anthropology and the Racial Politics of Culture*. Durham NC: Duke University Press, 2010.

———. *From Savage to Negro: Anthropology and the Construction of Race, 1896–1954*. Berkeley: University of California Press, 1998.

Berman, Judith. "'The Culture As It Appears to the Indian Himself': Boas, George Hunt and the Methods of Ethnography." In George Stocking ed., *Volksgeist as Method and Ethic. History of Anthropology 8*, 215–56. Madison: University of Wisconsin Press, 1996.

Boas, Franz. *Anthropology and Modern Life*. New York: Norton, 1928.

———. *Introduction to the Handbook of American Indian Languages.* Bureau of American Ethnology Bulletin 40. Washington DC: Smithsonian Institution, 1911.

———. *The Mind of Primitive Man*. New York: Macmillan, 1911.

———. *Race, Language and Culture*. New York: Macmillan, 1940.

———. "The Social Organization and the Secret Societies of the Kwakiutl Indians." 1897. In *Race, Language and Culture*. New York: Free Press, 1940.

———. "The Study of Geography." *Science* 9 (1887): 137–41.

Boas, Norman. *Franz Boas: 1848–1942*. Mystic CT: Seaport Autographs Press, 2004.

Bunzl, Matti, ed. Special issue of *American Anthropologist* 106.3 (2004).

Cole, Douglas. *Franz Boas: The Early Years, 1858–1906*. Vancouver: Douglas and McIntyre, 1999.

Darnell, Regna. *And Along Came Boas: Continuity and Revolution in Americanist Anthropology*. Amsterdam: John Benjamins, 1998.

———. *Edward Sapir: Anthropologist, Linguist, Humanist*. Lincoln: University of Nebraska Press, 2010.

———. "Franz Boas as Theorist: A Mentalist Paradigm for the Study of Mind, Body, Environment and Culture." Read at Indigenous Visions Conference, 2011.

———. "The Importance of the Northwest Coast in the History of Boasian Anthropology." *B.C. Studies*, nos. 125–126 (2000): 33–52.

———. *Invisible Genealogies: A History of Americanist Anthropology*. Lincoln: University of Nebraska Press, 2001.

Darnell, Regna, and Frederic W. Gleach, eds. Special centennial issue of *American Anthropologist* 104 (2002).Gilkeson, John. *Anthropologists and the Rediscovery of America, 1886–1965*. New York: Cambridge University Press, 2010.Goldschmidt, Walter, ed. "The Anthropology of Franz Boas: Essays on the Centennial of His Birth." Special issue of *American Anthropological Association Memoir* 89 (1959).

Hancock, Robert L. A. "Historiographical Representations of Materialist Anthropology in the Canadian Setting, 1972–1982." Ph.D. dissertation, University of Victoria, 2007.

Harris, Marvin. *The Rise of Anthropological Theory*. New York: Thomas Crowell, 1968.

Harrison, Julia, and Regna Darnell, eds. *Historicizing Canadian Anthropology*. Vancouver: University of British Columbia Press, 2006.

Herskovits, Melville. *Franz Boas: The Science of Man in the Making*. New York: Charles Scribner's Sons, 1953.

Hinsley, Curtis. *Savages and Scientists: The Smithsonian Institution and the Development of American Anthropology*. Washington DC: Smithsonian Institution Press, 1981

Hyatt, Marshall. *Franz Boas: Social Activist*. Westport CT: Greenwood Press, 1990.

Kuhn, Thomas S. *The Structure of Scientific Revolutions*. Chicago: University of Chicago Press, 1970.

Lewis, Herbert S. *In Defense of Anthropology: An Investigation of the Critique of Anthropology*. New Brunswick NJ: Transaction, 2014.

Müller-Wille, Ludger. *The Franz Boas Enigma: Inuit, Arctic and Sciences*. Montreal: Baraka Books, 2014.

Patterson, Thomas. *A Social History of Anthropology in the United States*. New York: Berg, 2001.

Penny, Glenn, and Matti Bunzl. *Worldly Provincialism: German Anthropology in the Age of Empire*. Ann Arbor: University of Michigan Press, 2003.

Rohner, Ronald P., ed. *The Ethnography of Franz Boas: Letters and Diaries of Franz Boas Written on the Northwest Coast from 1886 to 1931*. Chicago: University of Chicago Press, 1969.

Stocking, George W., Jr. *The Ethnographer's Magic and Other Essays in the History of Anthropology*. Madison: University of Wisconsin Press, 1992.

———. *Race, Culture and Evolution*. New York: Free Press, 1968.

———, ed. *The Shaping of American Anthropology, 1893–1911*. New York: Basic Books, 1974.

———, ed. *Volksgeist as Method and Ethic: Essays on Boasian Ethnography and the German Anthropological Tradition*. Madison: University of Wisconsin Press, 1996.

Valentine, Lisa, and Regna Darnell, eds. *Theorizing the Americanist Tradition*. Toronto: University of Toronto Press, 1999.

Wax, Murray. "The Limits of Boas' Anthropology." *American Anthropologist* 58 (1956): 63–74.

White, Leslie. *The Ethnology and Ethnography of Franz Boas*. Austin: University of Texas Memorial Museum 6, 1963.

———. "The Social Organization of Ethnological Theory." *Rice University Studies* 52 (1966): 1–66.

Williams, Vernon. *Rethinking Race: Franz Boas and His Contemporaries*. Lexington: University Press of Kentucky, 1996.

Zumwalt, Rosemary, and William Shedrick Willis. *Franz Boas and W. E. B. Dubois at Atlanta University*. Philadelphia: American Philosophical Society, 2008.

PART 1 Theory and Interdisciplinary Scope

1 Mind, Body, and the Native Point of View

Boasian Theory at the Centennial of
The Mind of Primitive Man

REGNA DARNELL

The Mind of Primitive Man, originally published in 1911, still stands as the primary theoretical manifesto of Boas's anthropology. Reassessment is overdue for at least two reasons: First, relational or abstract thought as a universal human capacity has come to be recognized as common sense in public as well as anthropological discourse and thus is dismissed as having ever been a theoretical position in need of articulation and defense. Second, postwar positivists in North America foregrounded descriptive ethnography of a nonmentalist variety and therefore insisted that Boas was atheoretical. "Mind" was as out of fashion as "primitive" was becoming. These self-confident empiricists dismissed Boas's cultural relativism,[1] which came into its own during his antiracist resistance to Nazi ideology, in favor of materialist and ecological perspectives that left no room for epistemological relativism in the sense of standpoint (a term Boas used alternately with *point of view*). Today this reading of Boas as atheoretical and his mentalism as nonempirical is more often applied in archaeology and physical anthropology than in the study of culture or society. Yet Boas's argument in 1911 is grounded in the study of mental phenomena, with surprisingly little attention to the physical anthropology for which he was best known at the time of its writing.

The theoretical climate in anthropology since the 1960s, however, reopens the possibility of returning to questions of what Boas called "the native point of view," which he understood to constitute the psychological aspect of culture and cultural experience. Anthropology, biology, geography, and psychology have all changed dramatically in the century since Boas wrote *The Mind of Primitive Man*. Therefore an exercise of deliberate historicism is required to make sense of his position today. Terms like *primitive* and *civilized*, reliance on "man" as generic human, and use of examples from European history without a clear statement about how they apply in the absence of written records prior to European contact all obscure the prescience with which Boas argued for a theory of mind that

could move back and forth between body and mind, the biological and the cultural, sometimes holding one constant and sometimes the other.

This essay assesses the commensurability between Boas's ideas about plasticity of human bodily form and the variability of mental or psychological forms of abstract thinking in relation to the diversity of human cultures, and explores how this alternation allowed him to devise a methodology in support of his theoretical position. Boas foreshadows here the potential synergy of the four subdisciplines that still constitute anthropology in the Americanist tradition. His position counters the internal fragmentation of natural science versus humanities and social science approaches to the study of humankind by reasoning analogically and comparatively across these traditional divides.

The rehabilitation of Boas as theorist has been ongoing for a long time,[2] although the critique it counters has been remarkably impervious to evidence (e.g., the late Douglas Cole's biography of Boas up to 1906). Nevertheless George W. Stocking Jr., in a selection of Boas's significant early essays, identified 1911 as the watershed of Boasian theorizing.[3] In that year Boas issued dual paradigm statements: *The Mind of Primitive Man* and the *Introduction to the Handbook of American Indian Languages*. He made two interrelated claims: First, all cultures, by virtue of being human, evince functionally equivalent capacities that are manifested differently due to environment and cultural context; as a corollary, variations in human biology do not constrain this cultural potential because it operates at the species level. Cultural relativism, although a term Boas did not use, follows from this position. His second point was that race, language, and culture must be understood as analytically separate, although they sometimes coincide in practice. These two principles seem so obvious today that they are hardly considered theoretical. The corollary of combining what the evolutionists called "the psychic unity of mankind" with the historical and geographical specificities of race, language, and culture as independent variables was at the core of Boas's critique of evolution but was included almost incidentally in the course of his argument in *The Mind of Primitive Man*. Nonetheless anthropology a century ago could not move forward in any kind of interpretivist framework without such a principled rejection of preordained evolutionary hierarchies of either culture or race. Boas's critique, then, stands as the third prong of his theoretical edifice.

I identify the anthropology that Boas built on these foundations as "the Americanist tradition," distinguishing it from other anthropologies practiced in North America, including that of his latter-day critics.[4] Boas's anthropology took for granted a symbolic rather than material defini-

tion of culture, a text-based approach to cultural knowledge through the recorded words of members of culture, and the inextricability of language, thought, and reality (i.e., the external world). This position entailed a robust standpoint-based epistemology that underwrote later culture and personality, ethnoscience, social interactionist, and interpretivist approaches constructed on Boasian foundations.

Somewhere along the way, however, Boas's physical studies of race were disarticulated in disciplinary memory from the antiracist activism that came to a head in his later years in response to Nazi atrocities. The study of race, perhaps because Boas's biological studies were superseded in data and method by subsequent scientific breakthroughs, became for his intellectual heirs rac*ism* and was approached by his successors primarily through cultural analysis.[5] Much recent Boas scholarship has been preoccupied with his interaction with the Afro-American community and his activist role in anti-Nazi critiques of race, eugenics, and genocide.[6]

This is not, however, the position Boas took in *The Mind of Primitive Man*, and it behooves us to return to the details of his argument, dissolve the artificial dichotomy of mind and body, and explore how human biology provided him with a method to approach culture as its analogue. Biological plasticity gave Boas a viable approach for reasoning about the apparently limitless variability of culture. A close reading of the 1911 text reveals that he foregrounded the relatively robust methods of the biological science of his day in his search for an entrée to situate mental phenomena within the broad scope he already had delineated for anthropology as the holistic science of humankind. He hypothesized a similar normal curve for "body measurements, physical phenomena [environment], and socio-economic life," thus inviting generalization of methodology and inference across these domains. Mental development had been much less studied, but he believed that it would produce "laws . . . quite analogous" to those of physical development. Although "actual observation" was not yet available, every explanation for differences of body and mind other than environment was rendered "improbable" by virtue of its "complexity."[7] The argument for heredity as an alternative to environment received considerably less attention.

The Mind of Primitive Man was based on a series of lectures at Boston's Lowell Institute, founded in 1836 as a family bequest to sponsor public lectures on diverse scientific and popular topics. The Lowell Institute remained firmly within the nineteenth-century institutional framework of elite learned societies of which Philadelphia's American Philosophical Society was the most distinguished. By 1911 Boas had established himself at Columbia University and already was producing a distinguished cohort

of academically credentialed students who would populate the anthropology departments springing up around North America and beyond. The same lectures were repeated at the National University of Mexico, where Boas had established a working collaboration with Manuel Gamio. On the one hand, he aspired to "organize anthropological research in America" according to his own vision and under his personal control; on the other, he was deeply committed to public pedagogy, largely museum-based at this time, to disseminate the anthropological point of view beyond the academy in the interests of science as "freedom from tradition." His pedagogical goal was to "improve human mental operations."[8]

Boas's arguments did not spring full-blown from the pages of his theoretical magnum opus. The only new material in the *The Mind of Primitive Man*, reflecting his pedagogical intention and new public audience, is the introduction on "racial prejudices" and the capacity of the anthropological standpoint to transcend them. Nor did he cease to revisit and refine these positions over the ensuing three decades. To appropriate the metaphor of Isaiah Berlin, Boas was more hedgehog than fox, with a small number of key ideas that he returned to from different angles, contexts, and data sets. His 1911 preface cites six previously published articles as underpinning his arguments. Interestingly enough, none were published in the *American Anthropologist*, ostensibly the flagship journal of Boas's adopted discipline. Their titles—"Human Faculty as Determined by Race," "The Limitations of the Comparative Method of Anthropology," "The Mind of Primitive Man," "Some Traits of Primitive Culture," "Race Problems in America," and "Psychological Problems in Anthropology"—illustrate the complexity of these standpoints that Boas developed separately but now sought to integrate into a single framework targeting a public audience in need of the methods and insights of anthropological science.

Nor is it accidental that *The Mind of Primitive Man,* in both the 1911 and 1938 editions, and in Boas's late-life selection of his own seminal essays—entitled *Race, Language and Culture,* still in accordance with his 1911 priorities in distinguishing these as independent analytic variables—begins with biology and moves on to culture. To appropriate a favorite metaphor of Boas's preeminent linguistic student, Edward Sapir, they remained sides of the same coin, such that moving from one to the other would reveal contrasting dimensions to clarify both.

The structure of *The Mind of Primitive Man* reflects this stereoscopic method. Boas's dual argument requires historicist recontextualization today because its biological thesis is largely taken for granted despite vestiges of a discredited but persistent scientific racism. Conversely, contemporary studies of cultural variation are wont to remove race from its

biological context to argue for human rights and identity politics and thereby also to miss Boas's synthetic point.[9]

Boas's discussion of "human types," his intentionally neutral term for what at the time were normally called races, characterized "racial prejudices" as the "naïve," unconscious "basis of our opinions." The insights of anthropological science reveal that, due to the unique "genius of a single people," "a culture of equal value" might develop in unfamiliar times and places; indeed several are known to have developed in the New World. The "vicissitudes" of the history of a people, particularly its contacts with other peoples, rather than innate biological capacity, determine the rate of its progress. Boas poses a high evidentiary standard for the argument that any particular "race" has less capacity for civilization given the complications introduced by the diverse conditions of its contact history and geographical location. Civilization "is taken up, now by one people, now by another." He noted that ancient European societies incorporated "more primitive people" but that Old World expansion brought epidemic diseases and population decimation to the Americas. "In short, historical events appear to have been much more potent in leading races to civilization than their faculty."[10] Moreover no single index of relative value could be determined.

"Modern biological concepts" further suggest a great divergence of humans from animals and "varying intensity" (i.e., distribution) of uniquely human features across conventional races. Boas contends that the anatomical peculiarities of the usual racial groupings show no necessary relationship to "mental aptitude." He is far more interested in the complexity of the human central nervous system, accessible to scientific study only under experimental conditions that have yet to be met. He aspires to compare individuals and groups "on equal terms," citing nutrition, gender, and intragroup variation as confounding variables to permanent discreteness of human types. Multiple explanations working in tandem and including bodily measurements, "social and economic phenomena," and environment are sufficient to explain observed variability.[11] "Human types" are not necessarily stable across environments. The degree rather than the existence of their plasticity is therefore the pressing scientific question. Bodily form is not permanently stable and reflects the past history of an organism.

Despite its meaninglessness in delimiting stable racial types, however, Boas clings to anthropometry as a method to trace the movement of groups within a given environment over time. This provides him with a necessary proxy for the history of peoples without writing. Without some such method to access unwritten history, he would be unable to

demonstrate how rate of development is dependent on environmental stimulus. After provisionally accepting evidence that "mental development follows laws quite analogous to those of physical development," Boas turns to his own studies of immigrant head form then in progress for the U.S. Census Commission.[12] The priority he gives to the explanatory value of biological over mental variation is reflected in his choice to study head form and other anthropometric features despite the Dillingham Commission's explicit preference for research-based advice on the cultural non-assimilability of a new wave of immigrants from southern and eastern Europe, many of them Jewish ("Hebrew" in Boas's terminology). Boas excludes himself and other assimilated German Jews from these categories and unequivocally claims a personal identity as a scholar working within "our" mainstream American, white, northern European heritage; Judaism was merely a religious category that could be shed along with other "trammels of culture."[13]

Boas declines to evoke natural selection without extensive evidence from "definite families" and sets out to obtain such evidence. Moreover he concludes that correlation of head form with such overtly Darwinian factors as mortality and fertility is "improbable." Through his research in New York City he acknowledges his "good fortune" to be able to show "direct influence of environment upon the bodily form of man" by comparing immigrants born in Europe and their American-born descendants within specific family lines. He describes the results as "unexpected." American-born developed differences in childhood that persisted throughout life. Sicilians, Neapolitans, Bohemians, and Hebrews all changed head form but in patterns unique to each of these groups, thus militating against the existence of an emerging "uniform general type" in America.[14]

Boas cautions that "the instability or plasticity of types" is not unlimited. Nonetheless he goes on to infer the "great plasticity of the mental make-up of human types," especially those correlated with bodily condition and developed over the life cycle. He has "succeeded in proving that bodily changes [do] occur" and places "the burden of proof" on those who reject the parallelism he attributes to the mental. His argument for the salience of environment in the emergence of plasticity is indirect and relies heavily on evidence of "alternating heredity" on combinations of parental types under domestication.[15] This evidence supplements the limited longitudinal data available for changes in human bodily form and justifies the inference back to the human and, for Boas, from physical to mental form.

Crucially his argument does not identify culture as mediating between individual bodily and psychological processes. Indeed the term *social*

occurs far more frequently than *cultural*. The critical environmental influence, moreover, is limited by heredity, that is, the biological rather than the cultural. Retrospective discussion of Boas on geography and environment has emphasized the limiting but also limited impact of natural environment on cultural forms. According to this reading, Boas experienced a conversion against environmental determinism during his 1883–1884 fieldwork among the Eskimo of Baffin Island (now called Inuit in Canada). Stocking argues persuasively for greater complexity, with Boas combining a geographical problem and its epistemological entailments from the outset.[16] As early as 1887, in "On the Study of Geography," Boas already placed geography within the human sciences alongside history, ethnology, and cosmology. His comparative method eschewed the apples and oranges of evolutionary typologies based on typological form in favor of comparing peoples with comparable livelihoods, thereby rendering environment a historically particular intersection of the natural, the social, and the technological.

In *The Mind of Primitive Man* Boas identifies domestication as an index of civilization and attributes the vitality of modern European and American civilizations to "their unstable population," which increased plasticity. Historical conditions of intermarriage and variable origin compound the internal variability of "a people." "Distinct local types" are more likely to develop "in primitive races" as exemplified by the diversity of Native American cultures and adaptations to environment. Variation within groups is greater than across types, thereby facilitating further plasticity.[17]

Reasoning "from a purely psychological point of view" necessitates "the same lines of thought" as does anatomical variability or stability. But psychological problems are more complex because of the need for the observer to transcend personal bias. The student must take seriously and adapt to the "inner life" of the primitive. "Confusion" abounds in psychology, however, because racial and social problems, heredity and environment, can never be fully disambiguated. There is a chicken-and-egg character to this inextricability. Boas distinguishes the universal "organization of the mind," the species capacity or the characteristic "modes of thought," from "the diversity produced by the variety of contents of the mind as found in the various social and geographical environments."[18] He predicts that the underlying mental attitudes will prove remarkably similar across time and space. Both Noam Chomsky and Claude Lévi-Strauss would appreciate the theoretical stance; the latter, like Boas, turned also to the local instantiations of universal products of the human mind.

Boas begins to establish the pan-human capacity by drawing a firm

line between human and animal, with the latter encapsulated in instinct and lacking "freedom of use," as in human inventions. Human minds are slippery things to study because of their "infinite variety of form," which is greater than the variety of bodily form. Thus the investigator must set aside the assumptions of his own culture "and observe the manifestations of the mind of man under varying conditions." Anthropologists are ideally situated to do this, although none has yet succeeded in describing "the psychological characters of races independent of their social surroundings."[19] Boas presents considerable evidence that such psychological character is inseparable from environmental, historical, and social context. He explores the purportedly primitive mental characteristics of fickleness of mind, inability of concentration, and lack of originality—in each case proposing adequate explanations other than inherent inferiority of mental process.

The observed differences are more apparent than real. Boas has observed firsthand the "mental attitude" of the "civilized philosopher" in primitive cultures, an argument taken up later by his student Paul Radin. The methods for the biological study of psychology, however, are necessarily different from those of the biologist: "Differences of structure must be accompanied by differences of function, physiological as well as psychological; and, as we found clear evidence of difference in structure between the races, so we must anticipate that differences in mental characteristics will be found."[20]

Boas anticipates quantitative structural differences in mental phenomena because he already has found them in physical phenomena. He laments that data do not exist to specify the anatomical or mental changes accompanying civilizations, although some cases of the same people living under different conditions do exist. He cites Freud for evidence that some traits seem inherited but actually may be acquired in early childhood and persist at unconscious levels. In any case he concludes that the mental faculties of all present races of mankind are "highly developed," and all have the capacity to "reach the level of civilization represented by the bulk of our own people."[21]

Boas castigates Nietzsche, long before Nazi domination of Germany, for "the modern doctrine of prerogatives of the master-mind." He equates the Aryan race argument with the evolutionary overtones of linguistic typology as correlated with race.[22] His argument for the separation of race, language, and culture, then, arises from his characteristic activism based in privileging science over prejudice. The two theoretical manifestos of 1911 are of a piece and not discontinuous with his later and better known politics of race.[23]

Classifications, to which heirs of Enlightenment science are much prone, produce artificial explanations that require empirical demonstration in particular cases. Boas accepts that classification is necessary to the exercise of the human faculty, but it must be applied in self-conscious and nonethnocentric ways. Indeed different "points of view" would inevitably produce different classifications. The argument for the mental capacity of primitive peoples as parallel to that of the "bulk of individuals" "in our own civilization," however, must proceed by inference because of the absence of direct historical evidence for the intermingling of peoples.[24]

Boas applies his argument about the discreteness of race, language, and culture from the *Introduction to the Handbook of American Indian Languages* to the contentious issues of race/biology and environment/culture. Language is the piece of the classificatory triad that renders mind rather than body the centerpiece. The "genius of a people as reflected in its language" is the primary key to the "mind of primitive man." This "genius" can be modified by diffusion, migration, culture contact and other variables that "without historical evidence . . . cannot . . . be proved" but must remain a question of inference.[25] Documented diffusion of cultural elements constitutes the "proof" that is needed; Boas was already amassing a database of such evidence on the North Pacific Coast.

Boas cautions, however, that different "types" of society, beliefs, social organizations, inventions, and so on would produce different classifications and that "the general term 'culture' . . . may be subdivided from a considerable number of points of view." That is, variations within races, languages, and cultures will prove at least as variable as those across them. Boas cites his 1889 paper "On Alternating Sounds" to illustrate that familiarity guides perception "according to the classifications of our own language."[26] For the member of culture "articulate speech" forms the link between the "infinitely varied" "range of personal experience" and an "underlying extended classification of experience" in the language of a people.[27]

Boas assumes that change in racial type proceeds more slowly than linguistic change; ample evidence of diffusion exists. His analysis is parallel in its logic to Sapir's *Time Perspective in Aboriginal American Culture: A Study in Method*.[28] Both works presented extensive illustrative ethnographic details out of context to confirm each logical hypothesis. Archaeology, the only direct method of accessing the history of "people that have no history," could in 1911 offer little specific evidence.[29]

Comparison of civilization's own past with contemporary primitive peoples is a flawed method for inference because domains of culture develop independently; sequences from simple to complex develop out of

order or skip stages; convergence or borrowing cannot be distinguished reliably from independent invention. Boas, citing his student Alexander Goldenweiser's analysis of totemism as a diverse set of psychological phenomena in variant contexts, sees no principled reason to assume that similar surface traits of culture must reflect the same psychological processes.[30]

The domains of culture are variable and must be approached "from a considerable number of points of view." Particular forms always appear arbitrary from the standpoint of another language or culture. Language therefore provides Boas with a methodological hook, a way of approaching psychological questions empirically. In culture as with language, he emphasizes universal functions, what we would now call design features of language, rather than particular forms. A small number of universal cultural ideas are noted by analogy from linguistic evidence, demonstrating that a few essential ideas turn up over and over. Folklore provides proof that such ideas are subject to wide transmission and adaptation. Nevertheless Boas considers Adolf Bastian's "elementary ideas" somewhat mystical because the ideas are intangible and not accessible to empirical investigation. He also worries that the student of such mental phenomena is "compelled to think in terms of these [same] elementary ideas," a telling though unacknowledged evocation of the hermeneutic circle.[31]

Boas pulls no punches: "the evolutionary viewpoint" must yield to "unbiased research" rather than premature generalization. What is now called social evolution "can be understood only as an application of the theory of biological evolution to mental phenomena." The whole "grand structure" rests uneasily on "our present civilization as the necessary outcome of all the activities of all the races of man."[32]

Nonetheless there remains a real difference that begs for investigation. Here and elsewhere Boas uses the terms *civilized* or *modern* and *primitive* matter-of-factly and without irony—despite having demonstrated the biological plasticity of human types—and extends their referents into the psychological domain. "The whole classification of experience among mankind living in different forms of society follows entirely distinct lines."[33] The classifications provided by culture come under increasing reflexive consciousness in civilization. Boas cautions, however, that modern man retains much of this inertia, bowing to forces of tradition through what Benjamin Whorf would later call "habitual thought." He argues that mythology is the conventional tool with which "primitive man as philosopher" thinks—anticipating both Radin and Lévi-Strauss.

Although traditional elements often get in the way of logic, civilization allows more people to "free themselves from the fetters of tradition."[34] Drawing on an older, nonanthropological concept of culture as the property of an educated elite, Boas aspires to expand the number of his fellow citizens who achieve "freedom" from the "shackles" of tradition, to raise them above the "habitual" level of "primitive mind."

Boas claims a "general theory of valuation of human activities" as anthropology's potential contribution to social thought (again without using the term *cultural relativism*). Differences of social etiquette must not be equated with moral lapses. Our rational explanation is highly influenced by "associated ideas" and their emotional effects. "Secondary explanations," "inferences based on the general knowledge possessed by the people," do not reflect historical origins, although most of us try to "justify our standpoint" by postulating the absolute truth of our own principles. Contact with other ways of life is in itself a method to enhance consciousness of diversity of customs (i.e., "defamiliarization"). "Gradual elimination" of the irrational, however, will never be fully successful, although it is the ultimate goal of science. In sum, "the change from primitive to civilized society includes a lessening of the number of the emotional associations, and an improvement of the traditional material that enters into our habitual mental operations."[35]

After his summary Boas turns to the more immediate and practical question of "race problems in the United States." He speaks as an American intellectual, without acknowledging his own status as immigrant, German, and Jew. Approaching the problem "from a biological standpoint" only after analysis of "the historical relations of our problem," he assumes that changes occur in both physical and mental traits. Nonetheless he confines himself "entirely" to the biological because "mental life is so plastic, that no hereditary inability can be assumed to exist in any of the peoples of Europe." In any case "the data of anthropology teach us a greater tolerance of forms of civilization different from our own."[36] This, rather than the impossibility of universal standards, was the essence of the now often maligned concept of cultural relativism.

Boas's motives for foregrounding the biological side of the mind-body equation return rapidly to the racial prejudices and stereotypes with which *The Mind of Primitive Man* began, and he emphasizes that anthropology provides method to transcend them. His text devotes much more time to considering how environment leavens the effects of heredity than how culture plays into the argument; the term *culture* usually appears in *The Mind of Primitive Man* as "culture and environment." This historical and contextual framing of the biological and the mental is, for Boas, the sine

qua non of gaining access to "the native point of view," the ultimate psychological phenomenon—the individual writ large as spokesperson for the universal in one of its culture-specific and empirically attested forms.

Boas apparently felt that his 1911 synthesis stood the test of time. *Race, Language and Culture*, his 1940 collection of his own seminal papers, took for granted and thus did not reiterate the integrated paradigmatic statements of *The Mind of Primitive Man*. Only the paper "The Limitations of the Comparative Method of Anthropology" is included; in *The Mind of Primitive Man* this key critique of human evolution is retitled "The Evolutionary Viewpoint." Evolution, then, was a matter more of standpoint than of proven theory. The theory of evolution suffered from "lack of comparability of the data" and the "logical error" of assuming that simple phenomena inevitably developed into complex ones.[37] In 1940 Boas exemplified his work in the three independent modes of anthropological classification—the biological, the linguistic and the ethnographic or ethnological—according to the respective established subdisciplines. The arrangement of papers echoed the methodology of *The Mind of Primitive Man* in beginning with physical anthropology, then turning to language and finally to the fuzzier domain of culture. The revised edition in 1938 did not change this fundamental organization.

Changes in data, method, and theory over the past century have yet to surpass Boas's challenge to anthropology to claim a key role in increasing human capacity for reflexivity and movement toward freedom, understood as individual personal fulfillment.

Acknowledgments

An early version of this essay was presented at a symposium organized by Neni Panourgiá in 2011 in honor of the centennial of *The Mind of Primitive Man*. I also draw on a related paper for the centennial conference organized at Yale by Isaiah Wilner. I am grateful for these opportunities to revisit the integration and ongoing relevance of Boas's thought. In addition I would like to thank Michael Asch, Lee Baker, Tim Bisha, Matt Bokovoy, Ray DeMallie, Ray Fogelson, Fred Gleach, Rob Hancock, the late Dell Hymes, Martin Levitt, Steve Murray, Marc Pinkoski, Tim Powell, Joshua Smith, the late George W. Stocking Jr., and A. F. C. Wallace.

Notes

1. For example Harris, *The Rise of Anthropological Theory*; White, *The Ethnography and Ethnology of Franz Boas* and *The Social Organization of Ethnological Theory*.

2. Darnell, *And Along Came Boas* and *Invisible Genealogies*; Darnell and Gleach, eds., special centennial issue of the *American Anthropologist*.
3. Stocking, *The Shaping of American Anthropology*.
4. Darnell, *And Along Came Boas* and *Invisible Genealogies*; Valentine and Darnell, *Theorizing the Americanist Tradition*.
5. See Darnell, *Invisible Genealogies* and "Franz Boas: Scientist and Public Intellectual."
6. Baker, *From Savage to Negro* and *Anthropology and the Racial Politics of Culture*; Shedrich and Zumwalt, *Franz Boas and W. E. B. DuBois*; Hyatt, *Franz Boas: Social Activist*; Patterson, *A Social History of Anthropology*; Williams, *Rethinking Race*.
7. Boas, *The Mind of Primitive Man* (1911), 36, 49, 64.
8. Boas to Zelia Nuttall, May 16, 1901, APS; Boas, *The Mind of Primitive Man* (1911), 250.
9. Darnell, *Invisible Genealogies* and "Franz Boas: Scientist and Public Intellectual."
10. Boas, *The Mind of Primitive Man* (1911), 1, 7, 9, 10, 6, 11, 17.
11. Boas, *The Mind of Primitive Man* (1911), 22, 19, 28, 36.
12. Boas, *The Mind of Primitive Man* (1911), 49; Boas, *Changes in Bodily Form of Descendants of Immigrants*.
13. See Glick, "Types Distinct from Our Own."
14. Boas, *The Mind of Primitive Man* (1911), 52, 51, 53, 54, 6.
15. Boas, *The Mind of Primitive Man* (1911), 65, 83.
16. Stocking, *Race, Culture and Evolution*, 144.
17. Boas, *The Mind of Primitive Man* (1911), 87, 93, 89, 94.
18. Boas, *The Mind of Primitive Man* (1911), 95, 99, 101, 104.
19. Boas, *The Mind of Primitive Man* (1911), 97, 98, 100.
20. Boas, *The Mind of Primitive Man* (1911), 113, 115.
21. Boas, *The Mind of Primitive Man* (1911), 122–23.
22. Boas, *The Mind of Primitive Man* (1911), 100, 124.
23. Baker, *Anthropology and the Racial Politics of Culture*.
24. Boas, *The Mind of Primitive Man* (1911), 123.
25. Boas, *The Mind of Primitive Man* (1911), 125, 131.
26. Boas, *The Mind of Primitive Man* (1911), 139, 142.
27. Boas, *The Mind of Primitive Man* (1911), 145.
28. Darnell, *Edward Sapir* and *Invisible Genealogies*.
29. Boas, *The Mind of Primitive Man* (1911), 182.
30. Boas, *The Mind of Primitive Man* (1911), 182, 190–91.
31. Boas, *The Mind of Primitive Man* (1911), 139, 142, 172.
32. Boas, *The Mind of Primitive Man* (1911), 174, 175, 181.
33. Boas, *The Mind of Primitive Man* (1911), 198.
34. Boas, *The Mind of Primitive Man* (1911), 206.
35. Boas, *The Mind of Primitive Man* (1911), 208, 219, 225, 226, 241, 243, 250.
36. Boas, *The Mind of Primitive Man* (1911), 262, 268, 278.
37. Boas, *The Mind of Primitive Man* (1911), 188, 195.

References

MANUSCRIPTS AND ARCHIVES

APS. Franz Boas Papers, Mss.B.B61. American Philosophical Society, Philadelphia.

PUBLISHED WORKS

Baker, Lee D. *Anthropology and the Racial Politics of Culture*. Durham NC: Duke University Press, 2010.

———. *From Savage to Negro: Anthropology and the Construction of Race, 1896-1954*. Berkeley: University of California Press, 1998.

Boas, Franz. *Changes in Bodily Form of Descendants of Immigrants*. New York: Columbia University Press, 1912.

———. "Human Faculty as Determined by Race." *Proceedings of the American Association for the Advancement of Science* 43 (1894): 301-27.

———. *Introduction to the Handbook of American Indian Languages*. Washington DC: Smithsonian Institution, 1911.

———. "The Limitations of the Comparative Method of Anthropology." *Science* 4 (1896): 901-8.

———. "The Mind of Primitive Man." *Journal of American Folklore* 14 (1901): 1-11.

———. *The Mind of Primitive Man*. New York: Macmillan, 1911.

———. *The Mind of Primitive Man*. 2nd ed. New York: Macmillan, 1938.

———. "On Alternating Sounds." *American Anthropologist* 2 (1889): 47-53.

———. "On the Study of Geography." *Science* 9 (1887): 137-41.

———. "Psychological Problems in Anthropology." *American Journal of Psychology* 21 (1910): 371-84.

———. *Race, Language and Culture*. New York: Free Press, 1940.

———. *Race Problems in America. Science* 29 (1909): 839-49.

———. "Some Traits of Primitive Culture." *Journal of American Folklore* 17 (1904): 243-54.

Cole, Douglas. *Franz Boas: The Early Years, 1858-1906*. Vancouver: Douglas and McIntyre, 1999.

Darnell, Regna. *And Along Came Boas: Continuity and Revolution in the History of Americanist Anthropology*. Amsterdam: John Benjamins, 1998.

———. *Edward Sapir: Linguist, Anthropologist, Humanist*. 1990. Lincoln: University of Nebraska Press, 2010.

———. "Franz Boas: Scientist and Public Intellectual." In Jill Cherneff and Eve Hochwald, eds., *Visionary Observers: Anthropological Inquiry and Education*, 1-24. Lincoln: University of Nebraska Press, 2006.

———. "Franz Boas: The Elephant in Anthropology's Room." Paper read at the Franz Boas: Ethnographer, Theorist, Activist, Public Intellectual Conference, London ON, 2010.

———. *Invisible Genealogies: A History of Americanist Anthropology*. Lincoln: University of Nebraska Press, 2001.

Darnell, Regna, and Frederic W. Gleach, eds. Special centennial issue of *American Anthropologist* 2004 (2002).

Glick, Leonard B. "Types Distinct from Our Own: Franz Boas on Jewish Identity and Assimilation." *American Anthropologist* 84 (1982): 545–65.

Harris, Marvin. *The Rise of Anthropological Theory*. New York: Thomas Crowell, 1968.

Hyatt, Marshall. *Franz Boas: Social Activist*. Westport CT: Greenwood Press, 1990.

Patterson, Thomas C. *A Social History of Anthropology in the United States*. New York: Berg, 2001.

Sapir, Edward. *Time Perspective in Aboriginal American Culture: A Study in Method*. Geological Survey, Memoir 90, Anthropological Series 13. Ottawa: Canadian Department of Mines, 1916.

Saunders, Barbara. "Franz Boas, John Dewey on 'Transitional Situations.'" Paper presented at Franz Boas as Theorist, Ethnographer, Activist, Public Intellectual Conference, London ON, 2010.

Shedrich, William, and Rosemary Levy Zumwalt. *Franz Boas and W. E. B. DuBois at Atlanta University, 1906*. Philadelphia: American Philosophical Society, 2008.

Stocking, George W., Jr. *Race, Culture and Evolution: Essays in the History of Anthropology*. New York: Free Press, 1968.

———, ed. *The Shaping of American Anthropology, 1883–1911*. New York: Basic Books, 1974.

Valentine, Lisa, and Regna Darnell, eds. *Theorizing the Americanist Tradition*. Toronto: University of Toronto Press, 1999.

White, Leslie. *The Ethnography and Ethnology of Franz Boas*. Austin: University of Texas Press, 1963.

———. *The Social Organization of Ethnological Theory*. Houston: Rice University Press, 1966.

Williams, Vernon J. *Rethinking Race: Franz Boas and His Contemporaries*. Lexington: University Press of Kentucky, 1996.

2 The Individual and Individuality in Franz Boas's Anthropology and Philosophy

HERBERT S. LEWIS

> We all learned to study culture as Boas and his followers conceived of it, as that which is unchanging and unique, but we note the implicit conservatism in this conception. After all, if culture is that which doesn't change, then how can anthropologists ever understand how change works, or be participants in change? We all know of the *Boasian* emphasis on intra-cultural uniformity and integration. But doesn't this emphasis deny the actions of individuals within cultures, especially those cultural dissidents who are so often the proponents of change?
>
> "AIMS OF ANTHROPOLOGICAL RESEARCH: New Ideas for the Twenty-first Century," session abstract, American Anthropological Association meeting, 2010

It is ironic and sad that what is called "Boasian anthropology" should so often be characterized as presenting "cultures" as "holistic" and "reified" and "unchanging," "homogeneous . . . closed systems of 'collective representations,'" with "identical, homogeneous individuals," a "'totalitarian' concept of culture" that "exercises total determining power over the identity of its members."[1]

Franz Boas himself was deeply concerned about individuals and individuality—in every aspect of his thinking. Indeed it might be said that he was obsessed by the need to recognize and give individuals their due. Perhaps Boas's early concern for tracing the origins of traits in cultures, and his later identification with Ruth Benedict, whose *Patterns of Culture* was so widely disseminated and debated, has been conducive to this widespread and unexamined belief, but it is unfortunate for our understanding of Boas and his anthropology, and that of some of his prominent early followers.[2] From the beginning of his anthropological work in the United States, Boas was interested in questions of individuality, variation, and the interaction between individuals and their societies and cultures, just as his studies in biological anthropology were also focused on individuals.[3]

In this paper I argue that Boas was not only acutely aware of the significance of individual differences but his whole way of thinking gave precedence to individuals, individuality, and variability—when appropriate to the case. And there were very many domains in which concern with individuals was appropriate. Furthermore the fact that his students Herman K. Haeberlin, Edward Sapir, Paul Radin, Alexander Goldenweiser, Ruth Bunzel, and Alexander Lesser, among others, focused on individuals in culture in their work at one time or another is largely the result of Boas's teaching and concerns.

If we consider some of the major influences on Boas's thinking it might even seem that his concern with the individual was overdetermined.

Family and Cultural Background

Boas credited his family as the major influence on his thinking: "The background of my early thinking was a German home in which the ideas of the revolution of 1848 were a living force."[4] For the Boas and Meyer families (his mother was Sophie Meyer), as for many other German Jews of the period, the spirits of both the Enlightenment and the Romantic-Liberal era as they coalesced in the abortive revolutions of 1848 formed the basis of an intellectual and political life that celebrated reason, freedom, free speech and thought, "truth," and human rights, especially the rights of the individual versus the state. Young Franz got a particularly strong dose of this ideology through his mother and her circle of revolutionary friends, especially her sister and her sister's husband, Dr. Abraham Jacobi, Franz's uncle and sometime patron and advisor.[5]

The Romantic era also featured the celebration of the individual artist struggling against patrons or an uncomprehending public and the struggle of the free-thinking individual for truth, embodied and personified in that most famous and most popular German masterpiece, Goethe's *Faust*, so well known to Boas and his society.[6] As we might expect, he was frequently wont to quote bits of Goethe. Here is a particularly apposite statement from Goethe from "The Study of Geography": "It seems to me that every phenomenon, every fact, itself is the really interesting object. Whoever explains it, or connects it with other events, usually only amuses himself or makes sport of us, as, for instance, the naturalist or historian. But a single action or event is interesting, not because it is explainable, but because it is true."[7] Julia Liss writes, "What concerned Boas primarily were his efforts to fulfill himself as an individual."[8] The search for "truth" was a frequent theme in young Franz's correspondence with his family. He wrote, "First and last, what is demanded of genius is love of truth".[9] And, no surprise, Beethoven,

the individualist genius and champion of truth and freedom, was his favorite composer.

Boas summed up his political philosophy in a letter to John Dewey on November 6, 1939: "There are two matters to which I am devoted: absolute intellectual and spiritual freedom, and the subordination of the state to the interests of the individual; expressed in other forms, the furthering of conditions in which the individual can develop to the best of his own ability—as far as it is possible with a full understanding of the fetters imposed upon us by tradition; and the fight against all forms of power policy of states or private organizations."[10] This neatly states his credo and gives us the code by which he lived until the end, as he worked to further what he thought would best serve the interest of intellectual and spiritual freedom and the interests of individuals.[11]

Boas has sometimes been criticized for his apparent discomfort with ethnic and national causes, as for instance his preference for the assimilation of the Jewish people within American society as well as his belief that the end of racism in America would come when America's Negroes would blend into the rest of the population through interbreeding—a proposition that thrilled neither white racists nor black nationalists. As he put it on one occasion, "Thus it would seem that man being what he is, the Negro problem will not disappear until the Negro blood will be so much diluted that it will no longer be recognized just as anti-Semitism will not disappear until the last vestige of the Jew as a Jew has disappeared."[12]

This approach is consonant with his deeply felt desire to avoid categorizing individuals against their will and with his hatred of chauvinism. A case can be and has been made that these attitudes derive in no small part from his cultural background and personal experience as a Jew in Germany and with the attitude to Judaism and Jewishness that characterized his home. In "Types Distinct from Our Own" Leonard B. Glick wrote in some detail about the cultural and historical background of Boas's experience as a German Jew and makes a strong case to explain Boas's expressed feelings about the future of the Negro and the Jew.

The strong assimilationist trend in the Boas and Meyer families was only one of several possibilities for German Jews at that time. Some chose the route of Jewish nationalism (Zionism), while others chose to remain "orthodox" or "traditional." Boas wrote, "My father had retained an emotional affection for the ceremonial of his parental home without allowing it to influence his intellectual freedom," and nothing of the beliefs and practices of Judaism seem to have been imparted to young Franz.[13] (This does not necessarily apply to his ethics and values, however, for those he embraced clearly bore a distinctly German *Jewish*

character.) Nor does his Jewishness—which he never denied—seem to have been much of an element in his life once he left the anti-Semitic environment of his university days in Germany. He happily married a Catholic woman, and the Boas circle of friends and relatives in America was quite mixed in ethnic and religious (or irreligious) origin.[14] In New York he joined the Society for Ethical Culture, a movement founded on the notion of abandoning religious belief and ritual in favor of rational and secular universalistic humanism—founded, of course, by a German Jewish son of a rabbi. (His student A. L. Kroeber, of German Lutheran origins, attended the Ethical Culture School.)

Thus Boas was obsessed by the notion that each person should be treated as an individual, not as a member of a "class." Given the choices of his family of orientation and of procreation, this is not a surprise.[15]

Darwin and the Individual

Another early source of Boas's awareness of and concern for individuality must have been the work of Charles Darwin. Although there is no end to the debate about Darwin and "group selection," there is no question that the primary focus of natural selection, for Darwin and Darwinians, is the individual organism. The key to Darwin's great contribution is the notion of "blind variation" producing diversity among the individuals in any population and the "selective retention" of certain individuals who will reproduce and produce changes in their genetic community. Until recently, fueled by Leslie White's antagonism to Boas and reinforced by the almost total lack of references to Darwin in Boas's writings, there was skepticism about his knowledge of and respect for Darwin, but this doubt can be laid to rest, as we shall see.

Young Franz, who began his scientific explorations with botanical and zoological field trips at the age of four, before kindergarten, and who was already critical of his own naïve collecting and classification by the age of seven—six years after the heralded publication of *Origin of Species*—had to have been well acquainted with Darwin. On February 12, 1877, when he passed his finals at Gymnasium, young Franz wrote to his sister Tony, "I will never forget Darwin's birthday—the day of our examination."[16] By the time of his death Boas was considered one of the most prominent scientists of his time, a member of the National Academy of Science and the American Philosophical Society, conversant with all the sciences (mathematically sophisticated, having produced a dissertation in psychophysics, a geographer, biological anthropologist, linguist, student of culture and history), and recognized as such. It is impossible that he could not have known and appreciated Darwin. And yet such was the

air of skepticism about Boas as a scientist after his death that this obvious point was doubted.[17]

If not for the prevailing attitude that rejected Boas as a scientist shortly after his death—a movement led by White—it would have been obvious that these brief statements in his debate with Mason in 1887 over museum arrangement were directly from the heart of Darwin: "It is only since the development of the evolutional theory that it became clear that the object of study is the individual, not abstractions from the individual under observation." This is a key point about the Darwinian revolution, and Boas builds on it in one of his earliest anthropological papers. To further confirm the Darwinian connection, in the same short piece he writes:

> Former events . . . leave their stamp on the present character of a people. *I consider it one of the greatest achievements of Darwinism* to have brought to light this fact, and thus to have made a physical treatment of biology and psychology possible. The fact may be expressed by the words "the physiological and psychological state of an organism is a function of its whole history"; that is, the character and future development of a biological *or an ethnological phenomenon* is not expressed by its appearance, by the state in which it *is*, but by its whole history.[18]

Typically the first statement has been taken as proof of Boas's supposed "particularism" rather than recognized as Darwinian in origin. The second seems to have been completely ignored.

There is now a firm link between Boas and Darwin since the discovery of the text of the lecture that Boas delivered at the celebration of Darwin's hundredth birthday and the fiftieth anniversary of the *Origin of Species* in March 1909—a celebration similar to those of 2009. In his paper "The Relation of Darwin to Anthropology" Boas leaves no doubt about his complete understanding, appreciation, and agreement with the scientist he calls "the immortal Darwin."[19] Boas's lecture went to the core of Darwin's thinking about process, about natural selection, and especially about the importance of variation and individuality, in all aspects of life, including culture, language, and society.

Expanding on one of Darwin's major themes, the accidental and unplanned nature of variation, Boas wrote:

> Although the idea does not appear quite definitely expressed in Darwin's discussion of the development of mental powers, it seems quite clear that his main object has been to express his conviction that the mental faculties developed essentially without a purposive end, but that

The Individual and Individuality 23

they originated as variations and were continued by natural selection. This idea was also brought out very clearly by [Alfred Russel] Wallace, who emphasized that apparently reasonable activities of man might very well have developed with an actual application of reasoning.[20]

Boas adopts the Darwinian notion that variations occur randomly ("blind variation"), without plan or purpose, and are subsequently "selected" by the environment. He uses Darwin to support his own idea about the unconscious nature of cultural and linguistic innovations that arise and are later selected, retained, and eventually reinforced through elaboration and rationalization. And he reiterates a central idea from Darwin: that change, descent with modification, begins with individuals.[21]

Lazarus and Steinthal

It is often said that Boas's anthropology was influenced by the work and ideas of Moritz Lazarus and H. Steinthal, philosopher-psychologist-linguists a generation his seniors, who established a new field they called *Völkerpsychologie*, best translated as "cultural psychology." Although this claim is often made, it is barely discussed, and since hardly any of their work has been translated into English it is difficult to judge their possible influence on Boas.

Matti Bunzl frequently refers to these two and their use of the term *Volksgeist*.[22] His point is that Boas was "grounded in a German anthropological tradition extending back through Bastian and Ritter, through Steinthal and Waitz, to the brothers Alexander and Wilhelm von Humboldt."[23] Although Boas mentions Lazarus and Steinthal occasionally, it is not clear how large a role they played in his thinking. However, Boas wrote to Robert Lowie that, "in his own opinion . . . [he] had contributed to 'just three things,'—a reexamination of the basis of physical anthropology; a presentation of languages on Steinthal's principles, i.e., from their own, not an outsider's point of view; and 'a more thorough empirical understanding of cultural life.'"[24]

Since Boas credits Steinthal with an important contribution to his own work (though without mention of *Volksgeist*) I shall borrow heavily from the fullest account of the work of Steinthal and Lazarus in English in order to point to another possible source of Boas's recognition of the individual in the context of culture. Ivan Kalmar makes the case that the "modern" concept of culture "was in its essentials present in the work of [these] two now largely forgotten scholars. . . . In 1860 they founded the *Zeitschrift für Völkerpsychologie und Sprachwissenschaft*, where they developed their concept of *Volksgeist*, a precursor of culture."[25]

Although they called their field *Völkerpsychologie* it "was to be, in the modern sense, more anthropological than psychological," covering "language, mythology, religion, cult, oral literature, writing, and art forms as 'elements of *Volksgeist*;' and customs, written law, labor, and occupations, and home and family life as a part of 'practical life.'" *Volksgeist* was their idea of a "group spirit," "'a system, consistent even as it is embedded in ever developing activity, of opinions, concepts, understandings, and ideas by which the particular objective *Volksgeist* is distinguished from all others.'" But they also wrote of other forms of group spirit (*Gesamtheitsgeister*): "There are also the *Geister* of religious communities, of social estates, of scientific and artistic schools and others." Kalmar writes, "*Volksgeist* thus corresponded to the usual modern use of culture as the social heritage of an ethnic group. The other *Gesamtgeister* corresponded to *subcultures*."[26]

The term *group mind* strikes a discordant note in a paper on Boas and the individual. But when Lazarus and Steinthal spoke of the "group mind" or Boas spoke of the *Geist* of a culture or people, they—and he—did not mean that the individual was only carrying out a group function in some simple-minded or automatic fashion. Despite their insistence that an individual cannot live and function without partaking fully in the *Volksgeist*—the culture—of his surroundings, "

> even a "fully developed" *Volksgeist* permits an individual to "rise above" it and to contribute something new. . . . Each and every mental activity of an individual, much as it may rise above that of the others, and above the whole prevailing temporal point of view, is nevertheless rooted in the *Geist* of the people [*Volk*]. . . . On the other hand, such nonconformist acts by individuals do not remain isolated, but react—directly or indirectly—on the *Volksgeist*; they become the property and a formative element of the same.[27]

Compare Boas (and James, below) when he writes of "the important problem of the relations of the individual to society, a problem that has to be considered whenever we study the dynamic conditions of change. The activities of the individual are determined to a great extent by his social environment, but in turn his own activities influence the society in which he lives, and may bring about modifications in its form." He speaks of "the differences of opinion and of mode of action that occur in primitive society and which are the causes of far reaching changes"[28]—stressing the individual and variation, even in "primitive society." The next figure was even more insistent on the importance of individuals.

Gabriel Tarde: Innovation, Imitation, and Unconscious Creation of Culture

Gabriel Tarde flourished as a writer, thinker, and sociologist in Paris in the 1880s and 1890s, but he did not have academic followers and could not establish a scholastic following the way his intellectual rival, Emile Durkheim, was able to. Individuals have appreciated him over the years, but, in what seems like a sad paradox, this inventor of the notions of invention and imitation had few imitators. Boas was among those who *did* appreciate Tarde, as did his friend and supporter, Elsie Clews Parsons. More than a decade before she joined the ranks of the Boasians, Parsons published the first English translation of any book by Tarde: *Les Lois d'Imitation*.[29]

As a sociology student in 1894, Parsons had been attracted by Tarde's "respect for individual difference and autonomy."[30] In contrast to Durkheim's insistence on the external power of society and all its symbols, its forces, its collective sentiments, its "conscience collectif" pressing upon and constraining individuals to do its impersonal bidding, Tarde envisioned a world of active individuals of varying interests and endowments, initiating, innovating, and inventing, and others imitating and/or rejecting the new, inventing still other ways. "In discussing the general bases for social change, Tarde stressed the centrality of the creative individual in suggesting new lines of development which the collectivity would subsequently adopt."[31]

For Boasians, Tarde offered a view of psychological processes that gave insight into the growth of cultures and changes in cultures. An individual, for various personal and psychological reasons, invents or innovates, and for their own reasons others imitate him or her, and in time the circle of imitation radiates outward like the ripples on a pond. Thus a process sometimes called "borrowing" and, in its larger dimension, "diffusion" or "dissemination," could be explained by universal psychological processes. This was relevant for Boas as he tried to make sense of the processes by which folk tales, secret societies, rituals, all manner of culture arose and spread beyond their origins. Boas rarely mentioned Tarde in his writings, but we know from his students (e.g., Lowie, Benedict, and Mead) that he thought highly of Tarde's ideas.[32]

Pragmatism

In the words of the historian Carl Resek, discussing the decline of social and cultural evolutionism, "In almost every field of learning, pragmatism effected a turn from all rigid systems and social laws that presumed

to reflect reality. It replaced certainty with probability, causality with choice."[33] And the founders of pragmatism (Chauncey Wright, Charles Peirce) were directly stimulated by Darwin.

Boas was born twenty years after Peirce, sixteen years after James, one year before Dewey, and five before George Herbert Mead. While his university studies were in Europe rather than in the United States, home of the pragmatist movement, similar ideas were circulating in Europe (e.g., Henri Bergson, Ernst Mach) and were at the forefront of progressive thought in America during Boas's first decades here.[34] At the turn of the twentieth century Columbia University and New York City were leading centers for pragmatism in philosophy and history, but Boas's approach was formed well before he began teaching at Columbia.

For the pragmatists variation, diversity, history, and individual persons and individual phenomena were basic, just as they were for Darwin. James, in particular, presents the closest parallel with Boas. Drawing a contrast between "rationalism" and his own *Weltanschauung*, "radical empiricism," James writes, "Rationalism tends to emphasize universals and to make wholes prior to parts. . . . Empiricism, on the contrary, lays the explanatory stress upon the part, the element, the individual, and treats the whole as a collection and the universal as an abstraction. My description of things, accordingly, starts with the parts and makes of the whole a being of the second order."[35] Elsewhere he adds, "Surely the individual, the person in the singular, is the more fundamental phenomenon, and the social institution, of whatever grade, is but secondary and ministerial."[36]

Boas expressed the same contrast in his famous paper "The Study of Geography," distinguishing two types of scientists. One type considers individual phenomena worthy of study not for their own sake but only as "a proof or a refutation of their laws, systems, and hypotheses. Losing sight of the single facts, [this type of scientist sees] only the beautiful order of the world." The other prefers to study a particular phenomenon, "may it occupy a high or a low rank in the system of physical sciences, and lovingly tries to penetrate into its secrets until every feature is plain and clear. This occupation with the object of his affection affords him a delight not inferior to that which the physicist enjoys in his systematical arrangement of the world."[37]

We can find many parallels between these two leading scientists of their time, but one particularly striking example is worth citing. In "Great Men and Their Environment," James propounded an explicitly Darwinian theory of social and cultural change—in direct opposition to a Spence-

rian one. Where Herbert Spencer sees the forces of change in environment, physical geography, and the great "laws of history," for James the source of change "is due to the accumulated influences of individuals, of their examples, their initiatives, and their decisions." As for Darwin, the process begins with individual variation: "Thus social evolution is a resultant of the interaction of two wholly distinct factors,—the individual, deriving his peculiar gifts from the play of physiological and infrasocial forces, but bearing all the power of initiative and origination in his hands; and, second, the social environment, with its power of adopting or rejecting both him and his gifts. Both factors are essential to change."[38] As we shall see, Boas approaches the problem of change in a similar way. Both he and James were presenting the notion of "structure and agency," as it would be called by social theorists a century later. "The historical process is seen as agential accomplishment, the accumulated effect of productive and reproductive efforts of human actors, undertaken in the structural conditions shaped by earlier generations."[39]

As with Boas, James's stress on individualism and individuality had both a scientific or philosophical and epistemological dimension and a political and personal one. Here is one small but telling example: in a talk titled "The True Harvard" he spoke of Harvard's "outsiders," the students without money, the graduate students, "scientific students," who come to Harvard not for the clubs or "because she is a club" but "because they have heard of her persistently atomistic constitution, of her tolerance of exceptionality and eccentricity, of her devotion to the principles of individual vocation and choice."[40]

Other Influences

Of course many other individuals in Germany, and perhaps some in the United States, added to Boas's deep scientific and philosophical background and may also have reinforced his focus on variability and the individual. Among those most often mentioned in the literature are Adolph Bastian, Rudolph Virchow, Theodor Waitz, Wilhelm Wundt, Gustav Fechner, Hermann Helmholtz, Benno Erdmann, Wilhelm Dilthey, Karl Ritter, and, it seems, every philosopher and scientist from Herder and Kant through Alexander and Wilhelm von Humboldt and beyond.[41] But these associations with Darwin, Lazarus and Steinthal, Tarde, and James and the pragmatists demonstrate that important figures in Boas's intellectual environment were those who never lost sight of individuals and rejected the metaphors of society as an organism and culture as superorganic. How did this work out in Boas's practice?

Boas, the Individual, and "Race"

In his physical anthropology Boas was always conscious of the differences between individuals. In Worcester, Massachusetts, in 1891 Boas initiated the first substantial longitudinal study of the growth of children. By following the same individual children through successive classes instead of comparing different cohorts of children at different ages, "[Boas] was largely responsible for the discovery that some individuals are throughout their childhood more advanced on the road to maturity than others, and for the introduction of the concept of physiological or developmental age." Others had been studying child development from the 1870s, but neither of the leading researchers had "stumbled on the idea of one child being more advanced in his growth than another. This was Boas' great and fundamental discovery in human growth—a discovery summed up in his own phrase, 'tempo of growth.'"[42]

When Boas learned his physical anthropology in the 1880s the burning issue was that of monogenesis versus polygenesis of races, and well into the twentieth century prevailing attitudes among most students of physical anthropology were still pre-Darwinian. They "had their basis in the polygenist attempt to apply pre-evolutionary concepts of species as absolute, supra-individual, essentially distinct and hierarchical entities to the study of mankind."[43] With his concern for and understanding of individual differences and physical variations, Boas never accepted this view. He understood the impossibility of classifying people into fixed racial groups, the changing nature and the variability of family lines, and pointed to the inescapable fact of variation—the significance of individual biological, temperamental, and intellectual variability.

Boas grew more and more skeptical of the concept of race over the years, and although he used that term to the end of his life—even in the last sentence he spoke—he was clear about the limited meaning he gave it. In 1943 he said of race, "As a matter of fact we have no such purebred groups. All we can observe are individuals and populations. Populations may be groups of blood relatives, local or social groups.[44] *Race* as he understood it was not the fixed, bounded, unchanging pre-Darwinian entity that was—and for many still is—meant by that term, nor did he believe individuals could validly be fit into subjectively created "racial" slots.

The sociologist Bernhard Stern published a useful summary of Boas's ideas about race, drawing on his statements. It is a long list, but here are several key points:

> —A racial type is based on averages and so has no actual reality. Individual variability is characteristic of all human types.... No individual can be considered as representative of any existing group, because the members of all groups vary markedly among themselves. —Because of differences between family lines, and fraternal differences within families, there is no limit to the number of subtypes that can be distinguished within each of the major divisions of mankind, depending upon the criteria used. —The criteria used to define types are selected arbitrarily.[45]

Boas understood a fundamental fact about heredity and populations that escapes some of today's enthusiasts for the genome who believe that they can finally classify the races—into the same five categories as Linnaeus did! "The error of modern [*sic*] theories is due largely to a faulty extension of the concept of individual heredity to that of racial heredity. Heredity acts only in lines of direct descent" rather than in some supposed regional or continental population.[46]

Ruth Bunzel summarized this aspect of his thinking:

> In his emphasis on family lines, rather than race, as the mechanism of inheritance, he was *establishing the scientific basis of individualism.* Equality of races did not mean equality of individuals. [*Pace* Goldschmidt. See note 1.] Each individual being is unique, the product of his own particular heredity, shared only by an identical twin, and of his life experience, including his culture. In a truly democratic society each individual, regardless of color, class, or sex is entitled to equal participation in the rewards of his culture, and the fullest development of his unique potentialities. Boas made his declaration of human rights in the name of science.[47]

In Boas's own words: "The habit of identifying an individual with a class, owing to his bodily appearance, language, or manners, has always seemed to me a survival of barbaric, or rather of primitive, habits of mind.... There are too few among us who are willing to forget completely that a particular person is a Negro, a Jew, ... and *to judge him as an individual.*"[48]

Boas and the Individual in Culture

Boas's ethnography has frequently been satirized with reference to the collection of Kwakiutl (Kwakw<u>aka</u>'wakw) texts containing a great number of undigested berry recipes, and it is hard to climb out from under this burden. His early research, in which he tried to understand Northwest

Coast history through the distribution of traits and institutions ("social organization, secret societies, the spread of art forms, of folktales"), may be difficult to see in terms of living, breathing, acting individuals. At a certain point in his long career, however, he began to speak in terms of individuals in culture and "the dynamics of life," at least in his more programmatic statements.[49] It is worthwhile looking at some of these statements, then considering some examples of his concern with individuals in actual studies.

In 1936 Boas wrote an animated reply to "Dr. Kroeber's analysis not only of my scientific work but also of my personality."[50] In this brief but rich piece he states, "In my early teaching, when I fought 'the old speculative theories,' . . . I stressed the necessity of the study of acculturation . . . and dissemination. When I thought that these *historical* methods were firmly established I began to stress, about 1910, the problems of cultural dynamics, of integration of culture and of *the interaction between individual and society*."[51] Bearing out this claim, in his lecture notes for May 8, 1917, we find the following: "There are certain customs of individuals, actions of individuals that differ considerably. We cannot be confined to the stereotyped and generalized description which is characteristic of most descriptions of primitive people. Dynamic conditions become known to us only if we take the characteristic type in this individual way, not as expressed in the actions of the whole mass. The necessity of a study of the individual, in the social setting in which he is found."

This passage can be compared with the one from 1920 in "The Methods of Ethnology," cited earlier, in which he writes of "the important problem of the relation of the individual to society, a problem that has to be considered whenever we study the dynamic conditions of change." Finally, in the piece where he declared his (infamous) belief "Cultural phenomena are of such complexity that it seems to me doubtful whether valid cultural laws can be found":

> The problems of the relation of the individual to his culture, to the society in which he lives have received too little attention. The standardized anthropological data that inform us of customary behavior give no clue to the reaction of the individual to his culture, nor to an understanding of his influence upon it. Still, here lie the sources of a true interpretation of human behavior. It seems a vain effort to search for sociological laws disregarding what should be called social psychology, namely, the reaction of the individual to culture. They can be no more than empty formulas that can be imbued with life only by taking account of individual behavior in cultural settings.[52]

The Individual and Individuality 31

Boas would publish variations on this theme over and over, making the same case as James, Lazarus and Steinthal, and Tarde. It is a notion that would later underlie the short-lived "actor-oriented" or "nongroup" approach that began to develop in the 1960s (before being overtaken by world events and Marxist approaches) and later reappeared as "structure and agency" in sociology.

How did Boas act on his concern about individuals and culture beyond these programmatic statements? There isn't too much evidence that I have found.

Boas apparently encouraged his collaborators and students to observe individual artists working with traditional materials and within culturally prescribed styles and conventions. These formed something like natural experiments, where the observer could look for variation, innovation, conformity, and the expression of individuality in an activity engaged in by a number of performers. In 1916 he urged his student Herman Haeberlin and his collaborator James A. Teit "to study the personal distribution of (basketry) designs among the women of Puget Sound" because he "was interested in the designs made by each woman, how designs are criticized, and how they are taught to young girls."[53] We know from Ruth Bunzel's account that he would suggest something similar to her in 1924, recommending she look at the huge manuscript by Haeberlin et al. before she went to Zuni that summer.[54] The result was her book, *The Pueblo Potter: A Study of Creative Imagination in Primitive Art*.

In "The Growth of the Secret Societies of the Kwakiutl" Boas calls on the social psychology of Tarde's "imitation" and Otto Stoll's "suggestion" to try to explain the efflorescence of secret societies in relatively recent times.[55] He makes no attempt to speak of particular individuals who might have been innovators but invokes the sense of excitement derived from the ceremonials of cannibal societies and the desire for the advantages and prerogatives enjoyed through membership in secret societies that led individual young men to either "acquire memberships in existing societies, or, where these were not sufficient, for the people to invent new ones."[56]

In *The Mind of Primitive Man* he offers a brief discussion of originality versus conservatism among primitive people and writes of "the appearance of prophets among newly converted tribes as well as among pagan tribes":

> Among the latter we learn quite frequently of new dogmas which have been introduced by such individuals. It is true that these may often be traced to the influence of the ideas of neighboring tribes, but they

are modified by the individuality of the person, and grafted upon the current beliefs of the people. . . . Undoubtedly this has often been accomplished by the independent thought of individuals, as may be observed in the increasing complexity of *esoteric doctrines* intrusted to the care of a priesthood.

He offers the ghost dance as a prime example "of such independent thought." He goes on, "It seems to my mind that the mental attitude of individuals who thus develop the beliefs of a tribe is exactly *that of the civilized philosopher.* The student of the history of philosophy is well aware how strongly the mind of even the greatest genius is influenced by the current thought of his time."[57] (This was published sixteen years before Paul Radin's *Primitive Man as Philosopher.*) Twenty-five years earlier Boas had already made the point that what he calls "esoteric doctrines," the elaborated teachings and rituals found among North American tribes, were undoubtedly rarefied and special. Such a doctrine is "[a] product of individual thought. It expresses the reaction of the best minds in the community to the general cultural environment. It is their attempt to synthesize the knowledge that underlies the culture of the community. In other words, this doctrine must be treated like any other system of philosophy, and its study has the same aims as the study of the history of philosophy." It is the product of the minds of "the priest, the chief, the leader."[58]

Finally he devotes some pages of *Anthropology and Modern Life* to a discussion of the individual, conformity to culture, diversity versus homogeneity, mass society, and independence and innovation. There he speaks of innovators in architecture and art styles, in religious belief and ritual, and political leadership. "Thus the famous League of the Iroquois which in all probability was in its main outlines the creation of an individual," although it "was based on the ancient social organization of the tribes." Perhaps the most outstanding example of this kind is the reorganization of the Zulu by Chaka who created a rigid military government."[59] These few references may not add up to an impressive demonstration of the ringing statements quoted earlier, but they are evidence of his desire to address this subject.

Conclusions

I hope I have succeeded in demonstrating that the stereotype of Boas's approach to culture as integrationist, uniformitarian, essentializing, and blind to individuals is quite inaccurate. To conclude, here is one of his political and ethical pronouncements that I hope will convince a doubter not only of his overwhelming concern for the individual but

also his awareness of the structures of inequality that he has frequently been accused of ignoring:

> It is not true that all men are created equal. On the contrary, their natural gifts are immensely diverse; but each should be given the fullest opportunity to develop his natural endowment. We like to point with pride to our system of education, that assures this privilege to every child; but we should not deceive ourselves. Free schools are not equal opportunities. The well-to-do can select a school, his children are well nourished and well cared for. They do not need to help the family income. . . . A necessary correlate of justice to all is the freedom of individual development. This freedom implies two fundamental ideas—one, that each man is to be treated according to his individual worth, no matter what his racial, national, or religious affiliations may be; the other, that there should be no tyranny of public opinion that may shackle the freedom of individual thought. Here also is room for progressive Americanism.[60]

Or we may conclude as Boas ended the 1938 (revised) edition of *The Mind of Primitive Man*, speaking of individuals: "Our tendency to evaluate an individual according to the picture that we form of the class to which we assign him, although he may not feel any inner connection with that class, is a survival of primitive forms of thought. . . . Freedom of judgment can be attained only when we learn to estimate an individual according to his own ability and character."[61]

Notes

1. Turner, "Representing, Resisting, Rethinking," 308; Wright, "The Politicization of 'Culture,'" 8; Hann, "All Kulturvölker Now?," 260.
2. It is possible that Boas may be identified with the notion of the "superorganic," the guiding principle for A. L. Kroeber, Boas's successor as "dean" of anthropology, but Boas never accepted Kroeber's view, and they had fundamental differences in their approaches to culture and history. See Boas, "History and Science in Anthropology." Walter Goldschmidt made a different suggestion. He wrote of Boas, "It is curious that this quintessentially liberal man should have had so little understanding of the individual. It is as if his belief that all people were equal rendered them all the same" (introduction to *The Anthropology of Franz Boas*, 2). But on this occasion Goldschmidt was wrong.
3. See Darnell, *Invisible Genealogies*, for a moderating view and Morris, *Western Conceptions of the Individual*, for an appreciation of Boas's concern for the individual in culture.

4. Quoted in Stocking, *Race, Culture, and Evolution*, 41. It is interesting and by no means irrelevant that he did not write "a German Jewish home," which would have been more accurate and revealing. See Mosse, *German Jews beyond Judaism*.
5. Others in the circle included Carl Schurz and his father-in-law, Ernst Krackowizer, a physician and Lincoln's supervisor of hospitals, who died before Boas and his wife, Marie, met.
6. See Liss, "German Culture and German Science," 167.
7. Boas, "The Study of Geography," 644.
8. Liss, "German Culture and German Science," 164.
9. In Liss, "German Culture and German Science," Letter-Diary.
10. Interestingly Roman Jakobson wrote, "The only linguist he met in his student years was Steinthal, but Boas was not yet interested in language and afterwards he regretted never to have attended the lectures of that enquiring thinker" ("Franz Boas' Approach to Language," 188).
11. See Lewis, "The Passion of Franz Boas," for examples.
12. Boas, "The Problem of the American Negro," 395.
13. Boas, "An Anthropologist's Credo," 201.
14. See Boas and Meyer, *Alma Farm*.
15. Murray Wax writes that it followed for Boas that, ethically, "each individual should be judged by his actions, not by his nonvoluntary membership in some group or placement in some physical or historical situation" ("The Limitations of Boas' Anthropology," 69).
16. Quoted in Cole, *Franz Boas: The Early Years*, 27.
17. Kluckhohn and Prufer have a brief discussion of Boas and Darwin and suggest that Boas might have been influenced by Rudolph Virchow's reservations about Darwin ("Influences During the Formative Years," 22). George Stocking expresses doubt about Boas's status as a "Darwinian" based on what appears to be rather slender evidence—or lack of evidence (*Race, Culture, and Evolution*, 184–85).
18. Quoted in Stocking, "The Principles of Ethnological Classification," in *The Shaping of American Anthropology*, 62, 66, emphasis added.
19. This lecture was evidently completely forgotten until June 1996, when I had the good fortune to discover it in the library of the American Philosophical Society, not in the archives where researchers normally work. A transcription of the original can be found online with the article in *Current Anthropology* (Lewis, "Boas, Darwin, Science, and Anthropology").
20. Boas, "The Relation of Darwin to Anthropology," 19.
21. I have published a fuller discussion of Boas's exposition of the relation of Darwin to anthropology in Lewis, "Boas, Darwin, Science, and Anthropology."
22. Bunzl, "Franz Boas and the Humboldtian Tradition" and "*Volkerpsychologie* and German-Jewish Emancipation."
23. Bunzl, "Franz Boas and the Humboldtian Tradition," 73.
24. Lowie, "Franz Boas, Anthropologist," 184. Lest one fear that Boas was a "libertarian," however, he went on to write, "In our complex economic

system absolute freedom of the individual to reach his own ends must be restricted by a consideration of the effects of his actions upon his fellow citizens, even upon the rest of mankind. Whenever his activities threaten the welfare of others the general interests of society demand that his freedom of action be controlled, the more so as economic exploitation is made possible only by the existence of our society. The developments of the last century prove that the necessity of such restrictions and of the protection of the individual against the effects of our modern methods of production is being recognized. *I agree to the necessity of economic control, but this has no relation to intellectual and spiritual freedom*" (letter to John Dewey, November 6, 1939, my emphasis).

25. Kalmar, "The Völkerpsychologie of Lazarus and Steinthal," 671. See Stocking, *Race, Culture, and Evolution*.
26. Kalmar, "The Völkerpsychologie of Lazarus and Steinthal," 674, 676, 675.
27. Lazarus and Steinthal, *Einleitende Gedanken*, translated in Kalmar, "The Völkerpsychologie of Lazarus and Steinthal," 677.
28. Boas, "The Methods of Ethnology," 316.
29. Even today very little of Tarde's large corpus has been translated, although there is a potential for a revival because at this time Bruno Latour is carrying out a campaign to revivify Tarde, especially for economic anthropology.
30. Deacon, *Elsie Clews Parsons*, 36.
31. Clark, introduction, 17–18. In fact Tarde envisioned a future of cultural globalization—not enforced by one or a few powers but resulting from "the purest and most potent individualism and of consummate sociability" (*The Laws of Imitation*, xxiv). In his view it would be a democratic process of social leveling.
32. Mead, "Apprenticeship under Boas."
33. Resek, *Lewis Henry Morgan*, 156.
34. James studied for some time in Germany, and two important figures familiar to both him and Boas were Wilhelm Wundt and Gustav Fechner. Murray Wax saw this parallel long ago and wrote, "It fitted with his adherence to *radical empiricism* that Boas emphasized the reality of the individual and warned against reifying culture" ("The Limitations of Boas' Anthropology," 68, my emphasis).
35. James, "Essays in Radical Empiricism," 24.
36. James, *Memories and Studies*, 102–3. In a further resemblance to Boas, he later refers to "G. Tarde's book (itself a work of genius) . . . the best commentary on this text,—'Invention' on the one hand, and 'imitation' on the other, being for this author the two sole factors of social change" (James, "The Importance of Individuals," 261).
37. Boas, "The Study of Geography," 644–45.
38. James, "Great Men and Their Environment," 218, 232.
39. Sztompka, *Agency and Structure*, 54. See Joas, *Pragmatism and Social Theory*; Lewis, "The Passion of Franz Boas."

40. Quoted in Perry, *In the Spirit of William James*, 12.
41. See Kluckhohn and Prufer, "Influences During the Formative Years."
42. Tanner, "Boas' Contributions," 76, 77. Among the results of these studies of children's growth was the replacement of the terms *bright* and *dull* with *advanced* and *retarded*. As Walter Goldschmidt put it, "Boas insisted on the potential worth, the ultimate equality, of the retarded boy" (introduction to *The Anthropology of Franz Boas*, 2).
43. Stocking, *Race, Culture, and Evolution*, 42.
44. Boas, "Individual, Family, Population, and Race," 161.
45. Stern, "Franz Boas as Scientist and Citizen," 210.
46. Boas, "Some Problems of Methodology in the Social Sciences," 91.
47. Bunzel, introduction, 8. See Wax, "The Limitations of Boas' Anthropology."
48. Boas, "An Anthropologist's Credo," quoted in Smith, "Boas' 'Natural History' Approach," 59, my emphasis.
49. Boas, *Race, Language and Culture*, 307, v.
50. Boas, "History and Science in Anthropology," 137; Boas, *Race, Language and Culture*, 305.
51. Boas, *Race, Language and Culture*, 311, my emphasis. By "acculturation" Boas apparently means the process of borrowing and adopting material from other groups. It seems to be an early use of that term (see "The Growth of Indian Mythologies") that will become much more prominent several decades later.
52. Boas, *Race, Language and Culture*, 258–59. He writes, "Integration is not often so complete that all contradictory elements are eliminated. We rather find in the same culture curious breaks in the attitudes of different individuals, and, in the case of varying situations, even in the behavior of the same individual" (Boas, "The Aims of Anthropological Research," in *Race, Language and Culture*, 256).
53. In Miller, *Regaining Dr. Herman Haeberlin*, 55.
54. In Mead, "Apprenticeship under Boas."
55. Stoll, *Suggestion und Hypnotismus in der Völkerpsychologie*.
56. Boas, "The Growth of the Secret Societies of the Kwakiutl," 382.
57. Boas, *The Mind of Primitive Man*, 112, 113, my emphasis.
58. Boas, *Race, Language and Culture*, 313–14, 315.
59. Boas, *Anthropology and Modern Life*, 153–67, 163.
60. Boas, *Race and Democratic Society*, 166.
61. Boas, *The Mind of Primitive Man* (1938), 272.

References

MANUSCRIPTS AND ARCHIVES

Franz Boas Papers, Mss.B.B61. Letter to John Dewey, November 6, 1939. American Philosophical Society, Philadelphia.

———. Lecture notes, May 8, 1917. American Philosophical Society, Philadelphia.

———. "The Relation of Darwin to Anthropology." Unpublished lecture, 1909. American Philosophical Society, Philadelphia.

PUBLISHED WORKS

American Anthropological Association. "Aims of Anthropological Research: New Ideas for the Twenty-first Century." Session abstract. 2010.

Boas, Franz. "The Aims of Anthropological Research." 1932. In *Race, Language and Culture*, 243–59. New York: Free Press, 1940.

———. "An Anthropologist's Credo." *Nation* 147 (1938): 201–4.

———. "An Anthropologist's View of War." In *International Conciliation*, 5–15. New York: American Association for International Conciliation, 1913.

———. *Anthropology and Modern Life*. New York: Norton, 1928.

———. "The Ethnological Significance of Esoteric Doctrines." *Science*, n.s., 16 (1902): 872–74.

———. "The Growth of Indian Mythologies." *Journal of American Folklore* 9 (1895): 1–11.

———. "The Growth of the Secret Societies of the Kwakiutl." 1897. In *Race, Language and Culture*. New York: Free Press, 1940. (Originally "The Social Organization and the Secret Societies of the Kwakiutl Indians")

———."History and Science in Anthropology: A Reply." 1936.In *Race, Language and Culture*, 305–11. New York: Free Press, 1940.

———. "Individual, Family, Population, and Race." *Proceedings of the American Philosophical Society* 87.2 (1943): 161–64.

———. "The Methods of Ethnology." *American Anthropologist* 22 (1920): 311–22.

———. *The Mind of Primitive Man*. New York: Macmillan, 1911.

———. *The Mind of Primitive Man*. Revised ed. New York: Macmillan, 1938.

———. "The Occurrence of Similar Inventions in Areas Widely Apart." *Science* 9 (1887): 485–86.

———. "The Problem of the American Negro." *Yale Quarterly Review* 10.2 (1921): 384–95.

———. *Race and Democratic Society*. New York: J. J. Augustin, 1945.

———. "Race and Progress." 1931. In *Race, Language and Culture*, 3–17. New York: Free Press, 1940.

———. *Race, Language and Culture*. New York: Free Press, 1940.

———. "Some Problems of Methodology in the Social Sciences." In Leonard D. White, ed., *The New Social Science*, 84–98. Chicago: University of Chicago Press, 1930.

———. "The Study of Geography." 1887. In *Race, Language and Culture*, 639–47. New York: Free Press, 1940.

Boas, Norman F., and Barbara L. Meyer. *Alma Farm: An Adirondack Meeting Place*. Mystic CT: Boas & Meyer, 1999.

Bunzel, Ruth. Introduction to *Anthropology and Modern Life*, by Franz Boas. New York: Norton, 1962.

———. *The Pueblo Potter: A Study of Creative Imagination in Primitive Art*. Columbia University Contributions to Anthropology 8. New York: Columbia University Press, 1929.

Bunzl, Matti. "Franz Boas and the Humboldtian Tradition: From *Volksgeist* and *Nationalcharakter* to an Anthropological Concept of Culture." In George W. Stocking, ed., *Volksgeist as Method and Ethic*, 17–78. Madison: University of Wisconsin Press, 1996.

———. "*Volkerpsychologie* and German-Jewish Emancipation." In H. Glenn Penny and Matti Bunzl eds., *Worldly Provincialism: German Anthropology in the Age of Empire,* 47–85. Ann Arbor: University of Michigan Press, 2003.

Clark, Terry N. Introduction. In Terry N. Clark, ed., *Gabriel Tarde on Communication and Social Influence*, 1–69. Chicago: University of Chicago Press, 1969.

Cole, Douglas. *Franz Boas: The Early Years, 1858–1906*. Seattle: University of Washington Press, 1999.

Darnell, Regna. *Invisible Genealogies: A History of Americanist Anthropology.* Lincoln: University of Nebraska Press, 2001.

Deacon, Desley. *Elsie Clews Parsons: Inventing Modern Life.* Chicago: University of Chicago Press, 1997.

Glick, Leonard B. "Types Distinct from Our Own: Franz Boas on Jewish Identity and Assimilation." *American Anthropologist* 84 (1982): 545–65.

Goldschmidt, Walter. Introduction. In Walter Goldschmidt, ed., *The Anthropology of Franz Boas: Essays on the Centennial of His Birth*, 1–3. American Anthropological Association Memoir 89. San Francisco: Howard Chandler, 1959.

Hann, Christopher M. "All Kulturvölker Now? Social Anthropological Reflections on the German-American Tradition." In Richard G. Fox and Barbara J. King, eds., *Anthropology Beyond Culture*, 259–76. New York: Berg, 2002.

Jakobson, Roman. "Franz Boas' Approach to Language." *International Journal of American Linguistics* 10.4 (1944): 188–95.

James, William. "Essays in Radical Empiricism." 1912. In *Essays in Radical Empiricism and a Pluralistic Universe*, 3–120. New York: E. P. Dutton, 1971.

———. "Great Men and Their Environment." 1880. In *The Will to Believe and Other Essays in Popular Philosophy [and] Human Immortality*, 216–54. New York: Dover, 1956.

———. "The Importance of Individuals. Open Court." 1890. In *The Will to Believe and Other Essays in Popular Philosophy [and] Human Immortality*, 255–62. New York: Dover, 1956.

———. *Memories and Studies*. New York: Longmans, Green, 1911.

Joas, Hans. *Pragmatism and Social Theory*. Chicago: University of Chicago Press, 1993.

Kalmar, Ivan. "The Völkerpsychologie of Lazarus and Steinthal and the Modern Concept of Culture." *Journal of the History of Ideas* 48.4 (1987): 671–90.

Kluckhohn, Clyde, and Olaf Prufer. "Influences During the Formative Years." In Walter Goldschmidt, ed., *The Anthropology of Franz Boas: Essays on the Centennial of His Birth*, 4–28. American Anthropological Association Memoir 89. San Francisco: Howard Chandler, 1959.

Lewis, Herbert. "Boas, Darwin, Science, and Anthropology." *Current Anthropology* 42.3 (2001): 381–406.

———. "The Passion of Franz Boas." *American Anthropologist* 103.2 (2001): 447–67.

———. "Review Essay: Franz Boas: Boon or Bane?" *Reviews in Anthropology* 37.2–3 (2008): 169–200.

Liss, Julia E. "German Culture and German Science in the *Bildung* of Franz Boas." In George W. Stocking, ed., *Volksgeist as Method and Ethic*, 155–84. Madison: University of Wisconsin Press, 1996.

Lowie, Robert H. "Franz Boas, Anthropologist." *Scientific Monthly* 56.2 (1943): 182–84.

Mead, Margaret. "Apprenticeship under Boas." In Walter Goldschmidt, ed., *The Anthropology of Franz Boas: Essays on the Centennial of His Birth*, 29–45. American Anthropological Association Memoir 89. San Francisco: Howard Chandler, 1959.

Miller, Jay. *Regaining Dr. Herman Haeberlin: Early Anthropology and Museology in Puget Sound, 1916–17*. N.p.: Lushootseed Press, 2007.

Morris, Brian. *Western Conceptions of the Individual*. New York: Berg, 1991.

Mosse, George. *German Jews beyond Judaism*. Bloomington: University of Indiana Press, 1985.

Perry, Ralph Barton. *In the Spirit of William James*. New Haven CT: Yale University Press, 1938.

Radin, Paul. *Primitive Man as Philosopher*. New York: Appleton, 1927.

Resek, Carl. *Lewis Henry Morgan: American Scholar*. Chicago: University of Chicago Press, 1960.

Smith, Marian W. "Boas' 'Natural History' Approach to Field Method." In Walter Goldschmidt, ed., *The Anthropology of Franz Boas: Essays on the Centennial of His Birth*, 46–60. American Anthropological Association Memoir 89. San Francisco: Howard Chandler, 1959.

Stern, Bernhard J. "Franz Boas as Scientist and Citizen." In *Historical Sociology: The Selected Papers of Bernhard J. Stern*, 208–41. New York: Citadel Press, 1959.

Stocking, George W., Jr. *Race, Culture, and Evolution: Essays in the History of Anthropology*. New York: Free Press, 1968.

———, ed. *The Shaping of American Anthropology, 1883–1911 A Franz Boas Reader*. New York: Basic Books, 1974.

Stoll, Otto. *Suggestion und Hypnotismus in der Völkerpsychologie*. Leipzig: K. F. Koehler's Antiquarium, 1894.

Sztompka, Piotr, ed. *Agency and Structure: Reorienting Social Theory*. Langhorne PA: Gordon and Breach, 1994.

Tanner, J. M. "Boas' Contributions to Knowledge of Human Growth and Form." In Walter Goldschmidt, ed., *The Anthropology of Franz Boas: Essays on the Centennial of His Birth*, 77–111. American Anthropological Association Memoir 89. San Francisco: Howard Chandler, 1959.

Tarde, Gabriel. *The Laws of Imitation*. Trans. Elsie Clews Parsons. New York: Henry Holt, 1903.

Turner, Terry. "Representing, Resisting, Rethinking: Historical Transformations of Kayapo Culture and Anthropological Consciousness." In George W. Stocking, ed., *Colonial Situation: Essays on the Contextualization of Ethnographic Knowledge*, 285–313. Madison: University of Wisconsin Press, 1991.

Wax, Murray. "The Limitations of Boas' Anthropology." *American Anthropologist* 58 (1956): 63–74.

Wright, Susan. "The Politicization of 'Culture.'" *Anthropology Today* 14.1 (1998): 7.

3 The Police Dance

Dissemination in Boas's Field Notes and Diaries, 1886–1894

CHRISTOPHER BRACKEN

What is lost . . . is therefore the myth of the simplicity of origin.

—JACQUES DERRIDA, "Writing before the Letter"

Writing home in October 1886, a twenty-eight-year-old Franz Boas tells his parents about his recent journey north from Victoria aboard the *Barbara Boskowitz*, a steamer with "schooner rigging" but "none of the elegance" of "an ocean liner."[1] The *Boskowitz* stops at Alert Bay on the afternoon of the 6th and then continues northward, arriving at X̱wa̱mdasbe' (Humdaspe), on Hope Island, half an hour before midnight. The village was a traditional home of the T'ɬat'ɬaikwa̱la (Tlatlasikwala) band of the Kwakwa̱ka'wakw (Kwakwahkyah'wakw) peoples; the Nkomgilisala band had joined them there earlier in the nineteenth century after merging with the Yutlinuk.[2] Boas calls it both "Qumta'spē" and "Nahwittee." Later he describes it as a zone for the dissemination of discourses.[3]

Even the name of the village disseminates itself, proliferating sense and reference every time it is repeated. Traders, whalers, missionaries, and government agents called it Nahwitti, spelling it various ways: Newette, Newitti, Nooweetee. Roger Galois warns, however, that Nahwitti (or Newettee or Nawitty) is "probably the most confusing word" in the Kwak'wala "lexicon." It refers to too many things, conjures up too many ideas, takes too many forms. "After entering the White documentary record in 1800," he explains, "Nahwitti soon acquired a perplexing variety of referents and spellings" and, more "perplexing" still, acquired "new meanings" throughout the nineteenth century. It was the name for a T'ɬat'ɬaikwa̱la chief, for the T'ɬat'ɬaikwa̱la band, for the union of the T'ɬat'ɬaikwa̱la with the Nkomgilisala and Yutlinuk bands, for certain features of the surrounding landscape, and for two villages: X̱wa̱mdasbe' on Hope Island and Na̱'witi on Cape Sutil at the adjacent northern end of Vancouver Island. Significantly Europeans attacked Na̱'witi twice. The Salem-registered ship *New Hazard* fired on the village in 1812 while en

route to China; the crew of the HMS *Daphne* burned it down in 1853 to punish, or just terrorize, "the Nahwitti" for allegedly murdering three white miners, an allegation they denied.[4]

It is in this zone of dissemination and excess, with its connotations of murder and revenge, that Boas disembarks, and it is here, "cut off from the world for an *endlessly* long time" that he witnesses "*so incredibly much* that is new." He hears his hosts discussing him as they paddle him ashore. They are not sure why he has come. He is a sign in need of a referent, out of place, a catachresis. "Since I looked respectable," he decides, "they took me for a missionary." He tells them he wants to stay in "an Indian home"—in 1888 he will publish a paper about the houses at Qumta'spē—so they take him to a chief's house, where "a large group" comes to greet him. The next evening he attends a feast, "a great potlatch festival," in a "neighboring house." He finds the people "very friendly" toward him. They no longer think he is a priest. They worry he is "a government agent come to put a stop to this festival."[5]

It was a reasonable assumption. Section 114 of the Indian Act, the law against the feast system, had come into force on the first day of 1885, less than two years earlier. Boas remarks that the "Indian agent" has threatened to send a gunboat if the people of the village do not put a stop to their feasts. The "Indian agent" was in fact Israel Wood Powell, the federal Indian superintendent for British Columbia. And he was not making an idle threat. In the summer of 1881 he had toured the coast in HMS *Rocket*, a Beacon-class gun vessel armed with four heavy cannon.[6] Nor did he travel alone. The *Rocket* dropped George Blenkinsop at "Nooweettee" at the end of June 1881, where he took up his duties as the first Indian agent in charge of the Kwawkewlth Agency, which was established the previous April. In his annual report to the Department of Indians Affairs in Ottawa, Powell smugly remarks that transporting Blenkinsop to his post on a gunboat was "of great service for the purpose of obtaining his status and influence among these people."[7]

In 1886 the T'łat'łaik̲wala are aware of Powell's threats, though they are actively ignoring them. Boas decides to dispel any lingering suspicion about his own motives. Speaking through an interpreter, he makes a classically Boasian declaration of individual sovereignty. "The commands of the Queen do not affect me," he assures his hosts, "I am a chief and no one may command me." He adds that he has come simply to see how they live. He promises to hold a feast for them if they agree to dance for him. Afterward an elder informs him that the people do not usually dance when a chief pays a visit, but since Boas is a "chief from a distant land," they have decided to break with tradition and stage a dance espe-

cially for him. The house is prepared, a fire is made, and a drum begins to sound. Boas protests it is "impossible to describe" what he saw next: "The whole presented an indescribably wild picture." But by then he has already described it: "Loud screeching was heard outside and a wild horde entered dancing. In the lead was the chief, a man certainly over sixty. He had been given a uniform by the Indian agent so that he could serve as policeman and keep order, and especially, prevent the holding of large festivals. In order to carry out this duty he wore the uniform and carried the British flag, which he declared with the greatest pride had been given him by the king. A second chief followed, carrying a large flag."[8]

The police dance frames everything Boas is about to witness. It includes what it is supposed to exclude, just as it permits what it is supposed to forbid. The chief dresses in the authority of the law in order to lend his authority to a breach of the law, "especially" the law banning "large festivals" like the one he is leading. He waves the flag in order to waive the flag. He says the king gave it to him, but everybody knows there is no king. Queen Victoria has reigned since this man, "over sixty," was a boy. It is as if he were offering Boas a lesson that the prohibition of dancing facilitates its performance.[9]

The next day Boas fulfills his promise. "I held my own 'potlatch,'" he writes, "to pay for the dance yesterday." His feast consists of a humble distribution of rice. In giving his "potlatch," of course, he is knowingly breaking the law against the "Potlach."[10] His hosts take it as a sign that he is not "like the other whites." Just as the dancers imitated Euro-Canadian law the night before, so the European imitates the dancers' law today. Each copies the other, but each copy misrepresents the original, like a letter that reaches its destination by going astray.[11] In this way one tradition grows out of contact with another.

A few months later, in a letter to John Wesley Powell, director of the Bureau of Ethnology in Washington, Boas explains that when he decided to travel to the Northwest Coast for the first time, he was acting on the hypothesis that the "origins" of any culture's practices are "far too complex" to be studied from a single disciplinary perspective.[12] In doing so he was breaking with evolutionary ethnology (he calls it "psychology" here), which assumes the development of culture obeys identical laws and follows an identical sequence of stages at all times and in all places, as if like causes necessarily produce like effects.[13] Boas wanted to ask how differences of place and time, geography and history, drive a society's development. He decided he could not measure the impact of "geographical surroundings" on "migrations" and "stages of ideas" without "practical experiences." So he traveled to Baffin Island to study an Inuit

community, "the best race for these studies," "on the spot." Afterward he concluded that if he was to renounce the evolutionary law that is valid for all times and places, he would have to amass "a thorough knowledge" of historical causality. What he needed next, therefore, was a group of societies that could personify history for him. He found them on the west coast of British Columbia. As if answering a conjuration, a call for theory, the societies of the coast would speak to him of the possibility that every culture grows out of its contact with its neighbors.

The theory of complex growth would remain a constant of Boas's thought from 1887 onward. In 1911, in *The Mind of Primitive Man*, a book that, despite its unfortunate title, actually debunks the racial prejudices of "civilized" science, he exhorts anthropologists not just to measure a society's "inner growth" but also to study "its relation to the culture of its near and distant neighbors, and the effect they may have exerted."[14] In 1928, in *Anthropology and Modern Life*, he explains that it is the relation to neighbors that makes complex growth complex. Societies do not grow by law, moreover, but by accident. Paradoxically "accidents" for Boas "are the rule." But they tend to befall a culture from the outside. "Every culture is a complex growth," he maintains, because "it is determined to a great extent by outer occurrences that do not originate in the inner life of the people" and are "in no way related to the inner working of the society itself." Societies develop "by contact with their neighbors." Boas cites the imaginary example of a group that is displaced by a more powerful neighbor and migrates to "new surroundings," where they develop "new ideas" and "new forms of life." Social scientists can arrange the accidents of contact into general patterns, but they cannot isolate regular laws of historical development, nor can they predict where social life is tending at a given moment on the basis of their generalizations. In the beginning, says Boas, there were neighbors, and the only logical relation between them was nonrelation: "The varied activities of society and its relation to the outer world are logically unrelated."[15]

By locating the principle of change outside the social organism, Boas displaces the theory of growth from the conventional interpretation of nature in the Western-European tradition. According to Heidegger, this interpretation achieves systematic expression in book 2 of Aristotle's *Physics*. Aristotle argues that the essence of nature (*phūsis*) is being moved or "movedness" (*kinēsis*).[16] Change is a species of movedness, and growth is a species of change. A living thing has its source of change within itself. When a tree grows from a seed, it realizes a form that was already its own. A product of labor, in contrast, has its source of change outside itself. A carving made from the wood of the tree "grows" by the skill (*technē*)

of the artist.[17] It takes its form from something outside itself. Boas proposes that social life has its principle of change neither inside nor outside itself. Since a society grows in relation to its neighbors, change is an impulse communicated between zones that simultaneously join and separate along a limit.

It is tempting to infer that the theory of complex growth grew out of Boas's encounter with the police dancers at X̱wa̱mdasbe'. After all, the first thing the dancers show him, indeed what they wave in his face like a flag, is a dance that arrived in the village from somewhere else. But Boas takes particular care to warn his readers that the leader of the dance, the chief with the uniform and the flag, is not to be trusted. He issues this warning in "The Houses of the Kwakiutl Indians," published in the *Proceedings of the United States National Museum* in 1888. There he reveals that the chief's English name is "Mr Cheap" and his "proper," Kwak'wala name is Komena'kulu. He doesn't say why Cheap cannot be trusted. The answer, however, might have something to do with his house. A sketch of it appears as figure 13 in Boas's paper. A tall, carved pole rises in front. The outer walls are largely undecorated, but two boards bearing "English inscriptions" appear over the doorframe (fig. 1). Boas reports that "a white trader" nailed them there.[18] But what about the house suggests that Cheap is a "liar"?

I. W. Powell stopped at "Newettee" on the last leg of his gunboat tour in 1881, and he makes a point of describing Cheap's house in his annual report. Powell suggests that Cheap posted the signboards as a carefully considered act of diplomacy. Nor was he the only one to do so: "Two chiefs at this village, 'Cheap' and 'Boston,' seem most desirous of cultivating friendship with the whites, giving prominent evidence of their pacific intentions by a sign board to this effect over their respective residences."[19] At the time of his visit Powell was actively collecting artifacts for the American Museum of Natural History at the request of Hebert R. Bishop, a friend of the museum who made his fortune in sugar, gas, iron, and railroads.[20] Edward Dossetter accompanied Powell and took a posed photograph that offers an oblique frontal view of the houses of Cheap, on the left, and Boston on the right. Two signboards are fixed over the door of Cheap's house. On the upper board the name "CHEAP" appears in white letters. On the lower board a is inscribed in black letters: "Hes one of the head chief / of al tribes in this country / white man can get information." Two signboards are similarly fixed over the door of Boston's house. One displays his English name, "BOSTON," while the other carries a competing testimonial: "He is the head chief of / Naweeti He is true and / honest He don't give no / trouble to no white man." Signifi-

Fig. 1. "Kuē′qakila's heraldic column at Qumta′sqē," from Franz Boas, "The Houses of the Kwakiutl Indians," in *Proceedings of the United States National Museum, 1888* (Washington DC: Smithsonian Institution Press, 1888), 207.

cantly the fronts of both houses are painted with striking designs. Over Cheap's door, and descending with the slope of the roof, there appears the stylized image of the sisiutl; a flag, apparently the Red Ensign and possibly the flag mentioned in Boas's diary, hangs limply from a pole mounted above the door. An image of the moon surrounds Boston's door; the images of two grizzly bears frame it on the left and right (fig. 2).[21] Powell sent Dossetter's portfolio to New York in 1885.[22]

Although Cheap's sign assures visitors that they can "get information" at his house, Boas cautions that "Mr Cheap" does not always say what he means, unlike his neighbor, the "true and honest" Boston. The signature over Cheap's door is no guarantee of the house's contents. It may be a false front. Nor can the "sign" fixed under his signature be taken, as Powell claims, as reliable "evidence" of his "intentions." On the con-

48 BRACKEN

Fig. 2. The Village of Nahwitti, Hope Island, British Columbia. Photograph by Edward Dossetter (1881). Image 42298, American Museum of Natural History Library.

trary, complains Boas, "I should advise future explorers not to trust the man 'Cheap' (a corruption of 'chief'), as he is the 'greatest liar' on the whole coast. Formerly the sisiutl was painted on the front of the house, but at the request of the Indian agent, Mr Cheap, whose proper name is x̱omena'kulu, whitewashed it, and unfortunately I could only see a few faint traces of the painting."[23]

In the "Study of Geography," published the year after his visit to X̱wamdasbe', Boas proposes that the physical sciences are motivated by an "aesthetic desire" for arrangement and system, whereas the historical sciences are driven by an "affective impulse" that measures the observer's feelings about the object of study.[24] So what "affective impulse" compels Boas to call Cheap the "'greatest liar'" not just in the village but "on the whole coast"? Why does the scientist single out his information for suspicion? What about Boston? Sometime between the moment when Dosseter exposed his plate in the summer of 1881 and the moment when Boas made his sketch in the fall of 1886, Cheap whitewashed the

house front that bears his signature. "In consideration of this action," Boas continues, "he was appointed constable and presented with an old uniform and a flag. It was made his special duty to prevent dances and feasts, and since that time he dances in this uniform with the flag."[25] The issue apparently is that Cheap has cheated Boas of a view of the sisiutl, hiding a superbly executed T'łat'łaikwala design under the bland, white veneer of Euro-Canadian propriety. He has cast a veil over precisely the kind of object that the historical scientist, in Boas's remarkable phrase, "lovingly tries to penetrate . . . until every feature is plain and clear."[26] Cheap is an obstacle to scientific penetration. What is worse, although he concealed the sisiutl in return for the constable's uniform and the Dominion flag, he does not use these settler regalia as promised. He was supposed to wear the uniform while suppressing dances, but instead he wears it while inventing them. He carries the flag but does not uphold the law it signifies. Audrey Hawthorn associates the sisiutl with the themes of "warrior power, strength, and invulnerability."[27] Did Cheap make himself invulnerable through concealment—concealing the sisiutl to conceal his opposition to the law? Who better than an officer of the law to ensure the law is never enforced?

It is his ambiguity that seems to make Cheap a "liar," indeed a cheat, in Boas's eyes. Cheap, he alleges, says one thing but means another. He affixes his signature with one hand and erases it with the other. But doesn't Boas do the same? Isn't he cheating a little, really, when he calls Cheap "the 'greatest liar'" on the coast? He doesn't level his accusation directly. He puts it in quotations marks, as if to suggest the phrase is not his own, as if he is not stating an opinion but citing one. Hence it is not quite true that Cheap *is* a liar. The fact is that someone has called him one, and this anonymous source could be lying too. The greatest lie may well be that Mr. Cheap is the "greatest liar." The quotation marks arouse the suspicion that Boas is not telling the "whole" story, that he is holding something back.

The irony of Boas's indictment is that the "greatest liar" is telling the greatest Boasian truth. Cheap personifies the hypothesis that societies grow by contact with their neighbors in accidental ways. He confirms that every society speaks of its neighbors even when it is speaking only of itself. A society that claimed to be more original than its neighbors, as if it developed independently of them, would be the greatest liar in the neighborhood. "It seems true to me," Scott Lyons remarks in a recent effort to revive the theory of complex growth, "that our cultures, like all cultures, are constantly changing, adapting, and evolving as time goes by; that they are doing so largely as a direct result of contact with other

cultures; and that they are changing precisely as Franz Boas said they would—through adaptation to the historical and environmental conditions of our lives."[28]

Boas replays the scene of contact between neighbors ten years later in chapter 10 of *The Social Organization and the Secret Societies of the Kwakiutl Indians*, where he describes the dances he witnessed at Fort Rupert (Tsaxis) in the fall of 1894. He arrives on November 15 to find three groups assembled for feasts and dances: the Kwakiutl (Kwagu'ł), the Koskimo (G̱usg̱imukw), and the Nakwoktak ('Nak'waxda'x̱w). He relies on George Hunt to "explain everything" to him.[29] On Wednesday, November 21, the speaker of the Nakwoktak announces that a group of white men have landed on the beach and are asking for permission to enter the house. "The speaker sent for them," Boas recalls, but instead of bringing "white men" to the house, as might be expected, "the messengers came back leading a young Indian girl, who was dressed up in European costume, with a gaudy hat, a velvet skirt, and a silk blouse." They ask a chief named Nō'Lq'auLEla what he thinks of her, urging him "to send her back" if he decides she is poor: "He looked at her and said: 'I can easily distinguish rich and poor and I see she is wealthy. Let her stay here.'" After the chief approves of her, the speaker suddenly recognizes her and calls her by her name. "Oh," he says, "that is Mrs. Nū'lē." She produces a roll of silver quarters and the speaker distributes them among the assembled guests.[30]

The drama of Mrs. Nū'lē echoes an event mentioned briefly in the letter-diary Boas wrote to his wife during his visit. In an entry dated Wednesday, November 21, the same day that Mrs. Nū'lē makes her appearance, Boas reports that two "little steamers" stopped at the village on the morning of the previous day: "The first was a seal hunter which came to hire Indians for the trip, and the second was an Indian agent." The agent personifies settler law. His arrival leaves Boas "trembling with fear," not because he might interfere with the "feasts and dances," though, but because he might want "to engage Hunt."[31] The Indian agent left the next morning, apparently without incident. The drama of Mrs. Nū'lē was staged in the evening as a commentary on his visit. The dancers seem to be offering him a lesson, though he does not stay to see it, about how a visitor ought to behave when the feasts and dances are in progress: he was "poor" where Mrs. Nū'lē was "rich."

Boas more than once comments on the plasticity of gender roles in the performances he witnesses at Fort Rupert. It is difficult to ignore, therefore, that Mrs. Nū'lē takes over the role that Boas himself played ten years earlier at X̱wa̱mdasbe'. She arrives on the beach, where she

instantly becomes a topic of discussion. Her hosts and their guests try to assess whether she means to join the dance or oppose it. She gains entry by signaling her intention to break the law. When Nō'Lq'auLEla declares that she is wealthy, presumably he does not mean that she has a lot of quarters but that she means to distribute them, just as a decade earlier Boas's hosts praised his rice feast not because it was lavish but because it distinguished him from the "English" and "American" visitors who give nothing away.[32] The drama stages the inclusion of the stranger. The local people adopt the neighbor, and the neighbor adopts local practice. Each is transformed by contact with the other.

The Kwakiutl hold a festival the next evening, November 22. First a dancer named K·ēx displays the dance that Mink performed after killing the son of the wolves. Then the door opens and four men dressed as police officers enter. The last carries a book and plays the part of a judge. He instructs one of his officers to ask if everybody is present. The other two officers scan the crowd and report that somebody is missing. They go out and return, leading an elderly woman named Gudō´yō. She is in handcuffs. "Then," says Boas, "they pretended to hold court over her on account of her absence. The judge pretended to read the law on the case, and fined her $70." While one of the officers plays the role of translator, Gudō´yō tells the judge that "she was able to pay in blankets," says Boas, "but had no ready money." The "judge" agrees to accept payment in kind. The friends of the accused respond by heaping ridicule on the court: "That is always your way policemen. As soon as you see anyone who has money, you arrest him and fine him." Afterward the blankets are distributed in Gudō´yō's name.[33]

As at X̱wamdasbe' in 1886, the police dance staged at Fort Rupert in 1894 is a self-conscious satire of the Indian Act. The dancer who plays the judge literally "reads" the law, as if to encourage the members of the audience to read it too, and they do, since they criticize "the policemen" who enforce it. No doubt both the dancers and the audience were aware that when Section 114 was enforced for the first time in 1889, the chief justice of the Supreme Court of British Columbia, after a careful reading, pointed out that the statute did not define what it purported to ban, which made it impossible to explain the charge to anyone arraigned under it, so that no plea could be entered. A revised statute came into force in July 1895, seven months after Boas left Fort Rupert, and explicitly banned a long list of practices, including any festival, dance, or ceremony that featured the giving away or giving back of money, goods, or any other articles.[34] The next time the police dancers decided to act out the drama of arrest and trial "on stage," they would risk arrest and trial "off stage."

As in 1886 the dance that Boas witnessed in 1894, a day after the law's representative came and went, makes the law do the opposite of what it says. The enforcement of the law turns into a violation of the law. The judge-dancer does not try the accused for attending an illegal dance; he tries her for not attending one. He does not fine her for breaking the law; he fines her for not breaking it. Her sentence, moreover, requires her to do what the Indian Act is supposed to forbid. She is "forced" to distribute property. The police dancers affirm customary law by clothing it, literally, in the regalia of settler law. They incorporate Section 114 into the acts it bans. The foreign is neither excluded nor shunned; it is brought inside and tamed.

In the days that follow, the performers repeatedly affirm the necessity of keeping the laws of the dancing societies in defiance of settler law. When a double mask breaks during a fool dancer's initiation, some of the other dancers respond by throwing "burning coals and firebrands" at the audience. Afterward Lō´Xoaxstaaku attributes the mistake to the influence of "strangers": "Friends, if you have a mask . . . which you want to show, do not let a stranger show it; teach your own people to show it, that no mistakes may occur." Significantly in sheltering the mask from the stranger, he seems to contradict Boas's hypothesis of complex growth, which assumes that every cultural form is borrowed from neighbors. The next day, for example, when he announces his intention to dance with the Hamatsa, he stresses that in taming the cannibal he is upholding the laws of his own ancestors. Tō'qoamalis praises him for keeping the laws and urges the other dancers not to make mistakes. Other speakers recall that the laws were more strictly enforced in "olden times." Even as they exhort each other to uphold their own laws, however, they are careful to acknowledge the existence of their neighbors' laws. "Be very careful," Tō'qoamalis warns the Koskimo dancers, "for the Kwakiutl tribes will watch us closely. They will try to find fault with our laws, for they have ways of their own which differ widely from ours." The encounter with the neighboring law puts the authority of local law in doubt. "We have traditions which teach us our laws," Lā'gulag·ilis maintains. "We are not like our rivals, the Kwakiutl. I tried to discover the origin of their names which they use in the winter ceremonial, but no one could tell me, for they have no traditions." Later, though, one of the Kwakiutl dancers teases the Koskimo for distributing blankets at the wrong time, in violation of the law. "It is not customary to do so," says Hä'masaqa, "but now I will show you what I can do." Everyone is exhorted to uphold the law and everyone is accused of breaking it, as if to suggest that nobody possesses the law absolutely. One law is affirmed in the knowledge that there are

other laws. An inner law asserts itself only in relation to an outer law. There is no law that does not exist in tension with "strangers."[35]

But hasn't Boas already lost his faith in the law? Hasn't he given up especially on the idea that there can be a law of laws? Isn't that what brought him to the coast in 1886? He set out to bring down the law of evolutionary ethnography, the law that dictates that every culture develops according to the same laws. Giving the lie to the law is the law of his discourse.

In December 1895, a year after his visit to Fort Rupert, Boas delivered "The Growth of Indian Mythologies" to the American Folk-Lore Society in Philadelphia. He bases his argument, in part, on the "traditions" he collected at Nahwittee in 1886.[36] He admits that when he first arrived, he assumed he would be able to distinguish one cultural group from another by studying the differences between their stories. What he found was different groups reciting the same stories in different languages.[37] Stories about the raven, for example, recur just about everywhere. He could not tell what was original from what was borrowed: "The arts of the tribes of a large portion of the territory are so uniform that it is almost impossible to discover the origin of even the most specialized forms of their productions inside of a wide of territory." How can communities so "diverse in language" be so "alike" in literary culture? "The phenomena of distribution can be explained," he answers, "only by the theory that the tales have been carried from one tribe to its neighbors, and by the tribe that has newly acquired them in turn to its own neighbors"—just as the police dances at Fort Rupert were modeled on the ritual process of the settler courtroom. Stories grow by "dissemination," and dissemination proceeds along avenues of contiguity. "The identity of a great many tales in geographically contiguous areas has led me," he concludes, "to the point of view of assuming that wherever considerable similarity between two tales is found in North America, it is more likely to be due to dissemination than to independent origin."[38] When he presented his paper in 1895, the theory of "independent origin" was one of the conceptual pillars of evolutionary ethnology. The theory holds that different peoples will eventually invent the same ideas and practices if placed in similar circumstances.[39] But Boas questions "the sweeping assertion that sameness of ethnical phenomena is *always* due to the sameness of the working of the human mind."[40] Cultures, by this argument, grow apart from one another. He insists that they grow toward one another. "The same ethnical phenomena," he argues the following year in "The Limitations of the Comparative Method," "may develop from different sources."[41] What is most central to a culture is external to it. Its inside

is its outside. Similarities emerge only after distinct cultural forms have "disseminated" between neighboring fields.

Hayden White remarks that at the core of every strategy of interpretation there lies a tropological wager.[42] Every tropological wager, he adds, carries unique epistemological risks. Boas agrees. "When studying the culture of any one tribe," he observes in "Limitations," "more or less close *analoga* of single traits of such a culture may be found among a great diversity of peoples. Instances of such *analoga* have been collected to a vast extent by Tylor, Spencer, Bastian, Andree, Post and many others."[43] Aristotle classes analogy as a species of metaphor; Boas identifies it as the tropological wager of evolutionary ethnology.[44] E. B. Tylor and "others" aim to prove the theory of cultural evolution by discovering unexpected similarities between dissimilar and disparate cultural forms. Analogy, however, is a notoriously unreliable mode of reasoning. In *Primitive Culture* Tylor admits that "the great doctrine of analogy" sometimes produces "misleading results," but, despite its risks, he bets everything on it: "It is still . . . a chief means of discovery and illustration." For example, in a single paragraph in the first of three chapters on mythology, he grafts together stories from Germany, India, Turkey, Brazil, and "Slavonia," classifying all of them as "specimens of a widespread" but unified "mythic group." What justifies him in amassing a collection that, by his own admission, is as likely to "mislead" his readers as to enlighten them? "The treatment of similar myths from different regions," he argues, "by arranging them in large compared groups, makes it possible to trace in mythology the operation of imaginative processes recurring with the evident regularity of mental law; and thus stories of which a single instance would have been a mere isolated curiosity, take their place among well-marked and consistent structures of the human mind."[45] Boas counters that "recent researches," notably his own studies of "the Indians of the North Pacific Coast," point to the opposite conclusion: "the same phenomena may develop in a multitude of ways" and from "a variety of sources." In breaking with evolutionary ethnography, moreover, he rejects the tropological wager that sets it in play. "We cannot say that the occurrence of the same phenomena is always due to the same causes," he concludes, "and that thus it is proved that the human mind obeys the same laws everywhere."[46] Tylor's error was to mistake indications of similarity for relations of causality.

Boas bets instead on metonymy, the trope that grafts together dissimilar but contiguous things. The "sameness" of cultural forms, he explains in "The Growth of Indian Mythologies," results from the "dissemination" of "elements" among neighboring geographical "areas." He points out that

there are societies on the Northwest Coast where even the "most fundamental" stories are "not of native growth, but partly, at least, borrowed." Within this zone of "dissemination" what is most proper to a society is thoroughly improper to it. Every seemingly original form is the repetition of a neighboring one: "A great many other important legends prove to be of foreign origin, being *grafted* upon more ancient mythologies. This being the case, I draw the conclusion that the mythologies as we find them now are not organic growths, but have gradually developed and obtained their present form by *accretion* of foreign material." The act of "borrowing," moreover, is wholly "involuntary."[47] Stories grow by "grafting" and "accretion." They spread like living organisms, and yet they are pieced together as if they were machines. In Aristotle's terms, they belong to *phūsis* and *technē* simultaneously.

Ironically, then, although he bets everything on metonymy, Boas backs his wager with all the resources of metaphor. To describe an inorganic and metonymic process he sows a rich field of organic, even agricultural analogies: culture is a zone of growth and dissemination, grafts, and roots. Stories spread like seeds between contiguous terrains and take root in soils where they do not properly belong. Yet they are the opposite of seeds. According to Aristotle, seeds grow out of themselves, toward themselves. They carry their principle of change within themselves. According to Boas, stories grow by being repeated. They acquire their principle of change from outside themselves. They disseminate by citation. In order to begin here, right now, then, they must already be going on somewhere else. "Everything," Derrida confirms in his 1969 essay, "Dissemination," which can be read as philosophical justification of Boasian relativism, "begins in the folds of citation." Each text, or each "myth," to use Boas's term, grows out of the repetition of some other text. There is no proper, self-present origin lying behind the uniformity of stories, but only an open series of grafts conducted from one textual organism to another. A story proliferates not by growing into a form that is already its own but by adding to itself from the stories that are already being told elsewhere. If we continue to speak of an origin we can no longer locate, it is because we tend to lose sight of a graft once it takes. "There is no first insemination," Derrida explains, extending the organic analogy past its proper limits; "the 'primal' insemination is dissemination. A trace, a graft whose traces have been lost."[48]

It is therefore only fitting that when he discovers citation at the origin, Derrida is, without acknowledging it, presumably without knowing it, citing a hypothesis that Boas posited several decades earlier. Derrida's hypothesis about citation is itself a citation. Its citability, however, only

enhances its force. "In most cases," Boas writes in 1895, as if echoing Derrida in advance, "the present form [of a 'specific myth'] has undergone material change by disintegration and by accretion of foreign material, so that the original underlying idea is, at best, much obscured."[49] Boas and Derrida agree that a cultural form, or sign, is the chance product of a graft that effaces its traces as it drifts between neighboring fields. This "foreign material," however, is itself the result of a prior graft. There is no origin of accretion; there is only the accretion of accretion. "There is nothing before the text," Derrida insists, "there is no pretext that is not already a text," and a text is an organism that has "no proper, unified, present origin."[50] But once again he is citing a claim articulated by Boas thirty years before. "Here," Boas writes in 1938, in "Methods of Research," "the question arises whether we can determine the place of origin. Many ethnologists hold to the opinion that wherever a certain cultural feature shows its strongest development, decreasing in complexity and importance as distance from the center increases, there must be its origin." Boas disputes the assumption that grafting weakens the "cultural feature." Sometimes, he argues, grafting makes it stronger: "It may even be that a foreign importation took root and developed vigorously in a new soil."[51] The sign grows by cutting itself off from its missing origin.

Some historians have argued that Boas was a "historical particularist."[52] It might also be said that he was a textualist before the emergence of textualism. His discourse therefore comes before its origin. As Derrida points out, the structural nonbelonging of a text to its context, or, as Boas puts it, of the "cultural feature" to its "soil," exposes it as an essential drift. It is this drift that defines "textuality as such." Textuality unfolds as a process of scission. Scission, however, originates nothing. It transforms an existing text, cutting across the distinction between "original" and "quotation" and uncoupling the long series of conceptual oppositions that radiate out from that distinction, such as the opposition between "the original and the derived, the simple and the repeated, the first and the second." As soon as it is granted that "everything 'begins' by following a vestige, *i.e.* a certain repetition or text," it is no longer possible to decide what properly belongs at the center of a culture and what belongs to its margins.[53]

Boas maintains, in terms that anticipate Derrida's, that the "accretion" of "traditions" takes place on the scission between contiguous "soils," a scission that brings traditions together even as it holds them apart. "When we compare the legends as told by the various tribes of the coast," he notes in *The Social Organization and the Secret Societies of the Kwakiutl Indians*, "we find that the [winter] ceremonial is derived from a variety

of myths." Some say they obtained it from the cannibal; "others from the wolves"; still others that they "brought it down from heaven." One story recounts how a hunter got it from a bear. "Traditions which are entirely distinct in character and origin," he continues, "are brought forward to explain the origin of the same ceremonial."[54] At the origin lies an accretion of grafted elements. There is no way to know which is earlier and which is later, for the graft transforms both the tradition from which it was lifted and the one to which it is sutured, just as Boas's assertion of difference at the origin grafts almost seamlessly with Derrida's: "Each grafted text continues to radiate back toward the site of its removal, transforming that, too, as it affects the new territory."[55]

In *Primitive Art*, published in 1927, about thirty years after "The Growth of Indian Mythologies," Boas points out that the form of a text remains remarkably constant as it disseminates itself among contiguous societies, but its interpretation inevitably grows by the accretion of the "foreign element":

> As a geometric form often receives a secondary meaning that is read into it, so the narrative is given an interpretive significance that is quite foreign to the original tale.... We have found that art styles are apt to be disseminated over wide areas while the explanatory meaning of art forms shows much greater individuality. Precisely in the same manner, tales are apt to travel over enormous areas but their significance changes according to the various cultural interests of the tribes.[56]

Boas is in fact repeating a claim he made in 1911, in *The Mind of Primitive Man*: "Form tends to associate itself with ideas entirely foreign to it."[57] He is in effect citing himself. Indeed his discourse is a fabric of grafts and accretions, some borrowed, consciously or not, from neighboring discourses, some from his own writings. The notion of secondary interpretation, for example, is a graft of Freud's "secondary revision," that final phase of the dream work that inserts connecting thoughts between unconnected dream contents.[58] Similarly when Boas defines "primitive thought" as the art of discovering relations between "groups" of "apparently unrelated" ideas, he is echoing Nietzsche's "genealogical" hypothesis "that anything in existence, having somehow come about, is continually interpreted anew, requisitioned anew, transformed and redirected to a new purpose."[59] If formerly related ideas seem unrelated today, it is because they have lost their previous significations and acquired new ones. Boas says this is how "primitive" societies build systems of signi-

fication. But isn't this what he means by "complex growth"? In seeking a definition of "primitive thought," he arrives at a definition of his own.

There are no "necessary correlations" between the fragments that cultural accretion grafts together. What Boas is proposing, therefore, is "something like" an originary complexity, though it can no longer properly be called originary since in the Western-European tradition the value of origin denotes simplicity.[60] Instead a complex origin is the retention of the other as other in the same.[61] To state the problem in the words of another of Boas's contemporaries, Ferdinand de Saussure, culture is a system of differences without positive terms.[62] According to Derrida, Saussure's formula entails that a concept, or indeed any "cultural feature" or sign, "is never present in and of itself" but rather is "inscribed in a chain or in a system within which it refers to the other, to other concepts."[63] Derrida's gloss grafts well with Boas's assertion, in "The Aims of Anthropological Research," that "the various expressions of culture are closely interrelated and one cannot be altered without having an effect upon all the others." Boas adds that the system of cultural differences is a global one: "the study of geographical distribution of cultural phenomena" therefore makes it possible for the anthropologist to grasp "the intricate interrelation of people of all parts of the world. Africa, Europe and the greater part of Asia appear to us as a cultural unit in which one area cannot be separated from the rest."[64]

As early as 1911 Boas concluded that the globalizing force of interrelation was transforming the United States into "a 'mongrel' nation." There is no racial purity among Americans, he says, there is only a contiguity of grafted cultures.[65] By this time Boas had been calling himself a "mongrel" for more than two decades. "I am as well known here in Victoria," he confides to his diary in June 1888, "as a mongrel dog. I look up all kinds of people without modesty or hesitation."[66]

Notes

1. Boas, *The Ethnography of Franz Boas*, 31.
2. Galois, *Kwakwaka-wakw Settlements*, 285–86, 290, 303.
3. Boas, "The Growth of Indian Mythologies," 426.
4. Galois, *Kwakwaka-wakw Settlements*, 188–205, 277, 423–26. Galois joins a long tradition of observers who frame the Kwakwaka'wakw peoples as a problem of excess. See Bracken, *Magical Criticism*, 188–205.
5. Boas, *The Ethnography of Franz Boas*, 36, 40, 32–33, emphasis added.
6. Gardiner et al., *Conway's All the World's Fighting Ships*, 109.
7. Dominion of Canada, *Annual Report of the Department of Indian Affairs*, 139, 149.

8. Boas, *The Ethnography of Franz Boas*, 33.
9. Boas, *The Ethnography of Franz Boas*, 35–36.
10. Bracken, *The Potlatch Papers*, 83.
11. Boas, *The Ethnography of Franz Boas*, 37.
12. Boas, *Indian Myths and Legends*, 31–32, June 12, 1887.
13. Stocking, "Franz Boas and the Culture Concept," 205, 208; Stocking, "The Basic Assumptions of Boasian Anthropology," 28.
14. Boas, *The Mind of Primitive Man*, 168–69; Lewis, "Boas, Darwin, Science, and Anthropology," 385.
15. Boas, *Anthropology and Modern Life*, 211, 215.
16. Heidegger, "On the Essence and Concept of Φύσιζ," 186–97.
17. Bracken, *Magical Criticism*, 17-18, 57, 82; Aristotle, *Physics*, 193a–b.
18. Boas, "The Houses of the Kwakiutl Indians," 206–7. I thank Aaron Glass for drawing my attention to the connection between the dancer described in Boas's diary and the chief named in "The Houses of the Kwakiutl Indians."
19. Dominion of Canada, *Annual Report of the Department of Indian Affairs*, 154.
20. Cole, *Captured Heritage*, 82–83.
21. See Glass, *Objects of Exchange*, 197–201.
22. Cole, *Captured Heritage*, 83.
23. Boas, "The Houses of the Kwakiutl Indians," 206.
24. Boas, "Study of Geography," 643–44.
25. Boas, "The Houses of the Kwakiutl Indians," 206.
26. Boas, "Study of Geography," 645.
27. Hawthorn, *Kwakiutl Art*, 29.
28. Lyons, *X-Marks*, 104.
29. Boas, *The Ethnography of Franz Boas*, 179.
30. Boas, *The Social Organization and the Secret Societies of the Kwakiutl Indians*, 559–60.
31. Boas, *The Ethnography of Franz Boas*, 182.
32. Boas, *The Ethnography of Franz Boas*, 37.
33. Boas, *The Social Organization and the Secret Societies of the Kwakiutl Indians*, 562, 563.
34. Bracken, *The Potlatch Papers*, 91–93, 118–19.
35. Boas, *The Social Organization and the Secret Societies of the Kwakiutl Indians*, 565, 567, 568, 588–90, 592, 602.
36. Boas, "The Growth of Indian Mythologies," 426.
37. Stocking, "Franz Boas and the Culture Concept," 206.
38. Boas, "The Growth of Indian Mythologies," 425, 428.
39. Stocking, "Franz Boas and the Culture Concept," 205.
40. Boas, "The Growth of Indian Mythologies," 434.
41. Boas, "The Limitations of the Comparative Method," 275.
42. White, "Interpretation in History," 74. See Krupat, "Anthropology in the Ironic Mode," 106, 115.

43. Boas, "The Limitations of the Comparative Method," 271, emphasis added.
44. Aristotle, *Poetics*, 1457b.
45. Tylor, *Primitive Culture*, 1: 297, 282.
46. Boas, "The Limitations of the Comparative Method," 273, 275.
47. Boas, "The Growth of Indian Mythologies," 434, 429, 432, emphasis added.
48. Derrida, "Dissemination," 316, 323, 328, 304.
49. Boas, "The Growth of Indian Mythologies," 429–30.
50. Derrida, "Dissemination," 328.
51. Boas, "Methods of Research," 669–70.
52. Darnell, *Invisible Genealogies*, 34.
53. Derrida, "Dissemination," 329, 333.
54. Boas, *The Social Organization and the Secret Societies of the Kwakiutl Indians*, 663.
55. Derrida, "Dissemination," 355.
56. Boas, *Primitive Art*, 36–37.
57. Boas, *The Mind of Primitive Man*, 235.
58. Freud, *The Interpretation of Dreams*, 4: 319.
59. Boas, *The Mind of Primitive Man*, 235; Nietzsche, *On the Genealogy of Morality*, 2.12.
60. Derrida, "Différance," 9.
61. Derrida, "Writing before the Letter," 62.
62. Saussure, *Course in General Linguistics*, 118.
63. Derrida, "Différance," 10–11.
64. Boas, "The Aims of Anthropological Research," 256, 252.
65. Boas, *The Mind of Primitive Man*, 255, 260.
66. Boas, *The Ethnography of Franz Boas*, 88.

References

Aristotle. *Physics*. Trans. Robin Waterfield. Oxford: Oxford University Press, 1996.

———. *Poetics*. Trans. Richard Janko. Indianapolis: Hackett, 1987.

Baehre, Rainier. "Early Anthropological Discourse on the Inuit and the Influence of Virchow on Boas." *Études/Inuit/Studies* 32.2 (2008): 13–34.

Berman, Judith. "'The Culture as It Appears to the Indian Himself': Boas, George Hunt and the Methods of Ethnography." In George Stocking Jr., ed., *Volksgeist as Method and Ethic: Essays on Boasian Ethnography and the German Anthropological Tradition*, 215–56. Madison: University of Wisconsin Press, 1996.

Boas, Franz. "The Aims of Anthropological Research." 1932. In *Race, Language and Culture*, 243–59. New York: Macmillan, 1940.

———. *Anthropology and Modern Life*. New York: Norton, 1928.

———. *The Ethnography of Franz Boas: Letters and Diaries of Franz Boas Written on the Northwest Coast from 1886 to 1931*. Ed. Ronald P. Rohner. Chicago: University of Chicago Press, 1969.

———. "The Growth of Indian Mythologies." 1895. In *Race, Language and Culture*, 425–36. New York: Macmillan, 1940.

———. "The Houses of the Kwakiutl Indians, British Columbia." In *Proceedings of the United States National Museum, 1888*, 197–213. Washington DC: Smithsonian Institution Press, 1888.

———. *Indian Myths and Legends from the North Pacific Coast of America*. 1895. Ed. Randy Bouchard and Dorothy Kennedy. Trans. Dietrich Bertz. Vancouver: Talonbooks, 2002.

———. "The Limitations of the Comparative Method." 1896. In *Race, Language and Culture*, 270–80. New York: Macmillan, 1940.

———. "Methods of Research." In Franz Boas, ed., *General Anthropology*, 666–86. New York: D. C. Heath, 1938.

———. *The Mind of Primitive Man*. New York: Macmillan, 1911.

———. *Primitive Art*. 1927. New York: Dover, 1955.

———. *The Social Organization and the Secret Societies of the Kwakiutl Indians*. In *Report of the United States National Museum for 1895*, 311–738. Washington DC: Government Printing Office, 1897.

———. "Study of Geography." 1887. In *Race, Language and Culture*, 243–59. New York: Macmillan, 1940.

Bracken, Christopher. *Magical Criticism: The Recourse of Savage Philosophy*. Chicago: University of Chicago Press, 2007.

———. *The Potlatch Papers: A Colonial Case History*. Chicago: University of Chicago Press, 1997.

Cole, Douglas. *Captured Heritage: The Scramble for Northwest Coast Artifacts*. Vancouver: UBC Press, 1985.

———. *Franz Boas: The Early Years, 1858–1906*. Vancouver: Douglas & McIntyre, University of Washington Press, 1999.

Darnell, Regna. *Invisible Genealogies: A History of Americanist Anthropology*. Lincoln: University of Nebraska Press, 2001.

Derrida, Jacques. "Différance." In *Margins of Philosophy*, trans. Alan Bass, 1–27. Chicago: University of Chicago Press, 1982.

———. "Dissemination." In *Dissemination*, trans. Barbara Johnson, 287–366. Chicago: University of Chicago Press, 1981.

———. "Signature, Event, Context." In *Margins of Philosophy*, trans. Alan Bass, 307–30. Chicago: University of Chicago Press, 1982.

———. "Writing before the Letter." In *Of Grammatology*, trans. Gayatri Chakravorty Spivak, 1–93. Baltimore: Johns Hopkins University Press, 1974.

Dominion of Canada. *Annual Report of the Department of Indian Affairs for the Year Ended 31st December 1881*. Ottawa: Maclean, Roger, 1882.

Freud, Sigmund. *The Interpretation of Dreams*. Vols. 4 and 5 in *The Standard Edition of the Complete Psychological Works of Sigmund Freud*. Trans. James Strachey et al. London: Hogarth Press, 1955.

Galois, Roger. *Kwakwaka-wakw Settlements, 1775–1920: A Geographical Analysis and Gazetteer*. Vancouver: UBC Press, University of Washington Press, 1994.

Gardiner, Robert, et al., eds. *Conway's All the World's Fighting Ships, 1860–1905.* London: Conway Maritime Press, 1979.

Glass, Aaron. "Conspicuous Consumption: An Intercultural History of the Kwakwa̱ka'wakw Hamat'sa." Ph.D. dissertation, New York University, 2006.

———, ed. *Objects of Exchange: Social and Material Transformation on the Late Nineteenth-Century Northwest Coast.* New York: Bard Graduate Center for Decorative Art, Design History, Material Culture, 2011.

Hawthorn, Audrey. *Kwakiutl Art.* Seattle: University of Washington Press, 1967.

Heidegger, Martin. "On the Essence and Concept of Φύσιζ in Aristotle's *Physics* B, I." Trans. Thomas Sheehan. In William McNeill, ed., *Pathmarks* 183–230. Cambridge, UK: Cambridge University Press, 1998.

Koelsch, William A. "Franz Boas, Geographer, and the Problem of Disciplinary Identity." *Journal of the History of the Behavioral Sciences* 40.1 (2004): 1–22.

Krupat, Arnold. "Anthropology in the Ironic Mode: The Work of Franz Boas." *Social Text* 19–20 (1988): 105–18.

Lewis, Herbert S. "Boas, Darwin, Science, and Anthropology." *Current Anthropology* 43.3 (2001): 381–406.

———. "The Passion of Franz Boas." *American Anthropologist* 103.2 (2001): 447–67.

Liss, Julia E. "German Culture and German Science in the *Bildung* of Franz Boas." In George Stocking Jr., ed., *Volksgeist as Method and Ethic: Essays on Boasian Ethnography and the German Anthropological Tradition.* Vol. 8 of *History of Anthropology*, 155–84. Madison: University of Wisconsin Press, 1996.

Lyons, Scott. *X-Marks: Native Signatures of Assent.* Minneapolis: University of Minneapolis Press, 2010.

MacLean, Bruce. "The Reduction of Kwakiutl Symbolic Activity Subsequent to European Colonization." Ph.D. dissertation, New School for Social Research, 1983.

Nietzsche, Friedrich. *On the Genealogy of Morality.* Ed. Keith Ansell-Pearson. Trans. Carol Diethe. Cambridge, UK: Cambridge University Press, 1994.

Orta, Andrew. "The Promise of Particularism and the Theology of Culture: Limits and Lessons of 'Neo-Boasianism.'" *American Anthropologist* 106.3 (2004): 473–87.

Saussure, Ferdinand de. *Course in General Linguistics.* Trans. Roy Harris. Ed. Charles Bally and Albert Sechehaye with Albert Riedlinger. La Salle IL: Open Court, 1983.

Stocking, George W., Jr. "The Basic Assumptions of Boasian Anthropology." In *Delimiting Anthropology: Occasional Inquiries and Reflections*, 24–48. Madison: University of Wisconsin Press, 2001.

———. "Franz Boas and the Culture Concept in Historical Perspective." In *Race, Culture, and Evolution: Essays in the History of Anthropology*, 195–233. Chicago: University of Chicago Press, 1968.

Suttles, Wayne. "Streams of Property, Armor of Wealth: The Traditional Kwakiutl Potlatch." In Aldona Jonaitis, ed., *Chiefly Feasts: The Enduring Kwakiutl Potlatch*, 71–133. Seattle: University of Washington Press, 1991.

Tylor, Edward B. *Primitive Culture: Researches into the Development of Mythology, Philosophy, Religion, Language, Art and Custom.* 2 vols. London: John Murray, 1871.

White, Hayden. "Interpretation in History." In *The Tropics of Discourse*, 51–80. Baltimore: Johns Hopkins University Press, 1978.

4 Franz Boas and the Conditions of Literature

J. EDWARD CHAMBERLIN

When Franz Boas's student Ruth Benedict paid tribute to him in her presidential address to the American Anthropological Association five years after his death in 1942, she reminded her audience of the importance of Boas's approach to his subject by quoting a literary critic, the Shakespeare scholar A. C. Bradley: "We watch what is, seeing that so it happened and must have happened."[1]

In his book *Shakespearean Tragedy*, Bradley, writing in 1905, was referring to our experience of drama—about which he wrote with formidable authority—and cautioning against bringing notions of morality or utility to bear on that experience. A hundred years earlier the great German writer Johann Wolfgang von Goethe counseled along the same lines in a passage that Boas quoted in his 1887 essay "The Study of Geography."[2] We pay attention to an action or event, Goethe advised, not because it is explainable but because it is true. And that advice wasn't just a holdover from the Romantic period. It was up to date, chiming with the modernist principles of what would become known in literary studies as New Criticism and with the renewed awareness in science of subjective bias and the authority of the observed event—and, where the event could not be observed (because either too small or two large, too fast or too slow, too long ago or too uncertain in time) the authority of indirect or "hearsay" evidence. And so scientists such as the widely read Karl Pearson insisted, in his influential (and resolutely antimetaphysical) *Grammar of Science*, that there was nothing but hearsay, using the latest technology as a metaphor to propose that scientists, like everyone else,

> are like the clerk in the [new] central telephone exchange [in London] who cannot get nearer to his customers than his end of the . . . wires. We are indeed worse off than the clerk, for to carry out the analogy properly we must suppose him never to have been outside the telephone exchange, never to have seen a customer or any one like a customer—in short, never, except through the telephone wire, to have come in contact with the outside universe. . . . The real universe for

him would be the aggregate of his constructs from the messages which were brought by the telephone wires in his office. . . . We are cribbed and confined in this world of sense impressions like the exchange clerk in his world of sounds, and not a step beyond can we get.[3]

I would like to suggest some ways in which Boas, in his own modernist way and with his belief in the determinisms of language, shared—or in some instances possibly sponsored—many of the tenets that characterized both the literary principles of New Criticism and the phenomenological practices of the natural and physical sciences, acutely conscious of the ways modes of perception condition interpretation and evaluation.

Let me begin with a short poem, set down by Boas in the 1920s and made widely available a half century later by Jerome Rothenberg as his opening selection in *Shaking the Pumpkin: Traditional Poetry of the Indian North Americas*. Here it is, in translation from the western Pueblo dialect of Keresan.

> long ago her mother
> had to sing this song and so
> she had to grind along with it
> the corn people have a song too
> it is very good
> I refuse to tell it.[4]

In one sense Rothenberg's anthology represents the kind of museum display that Boas argued against, setting artifacts from different cultures in the same general display rather than grouping them according in their specific cultural settings. But it also represents Rothenberg's ethnopoetic ambition to follow Boas's lead, countering a developmental account of Indigenous creativity by confirming literary texts as *monuments* of the human imagination rather than as *documents* of progress toward civilized expression. It was, in its way, an exercise in canon formation. For Rothenberg this poem was not a simple Aboriginal expression but a sophisticated poetic revelation, belonging with the best of the world's poetic forms. Rothenberg's texts are mostly offered in translation, though with self-conscious attention to the relativity of linguistic forms and functions, in the same way that the architects of the modernist understanding of the role of oral traditions in written literatures (such as Milman Parry, Eric Havelock, and later Albert Lord) brought New Critical principles to their interpretation of languages (like classical Greek) that were no longer spoken. Given Boas's role in nourishing the work of Edward

Sapir and Benjamin Lee Whorf, and his confidence in the importance of story and song (to which we sometimes give the fancier name of literature) in representing a people's sense of who they are and where they belong, he would have paid close attention to these fellow New Critical travelers. And his conviction (as interpreted by an argumentative Walter Ong) that "primitive peoples thought as we do but used a different set of categories" provided a useful point of departure for the speculations of Ong and others,[5] including Ong's mentor Marshall McLuhan, who had a considerable (and not always salutary) influence on the development of comparative literary practices in the second half of the twentieth century with their emphasis on the cognitive as well as cultural implications of literacy. Boas, for his part, privileged what the anthropologist Julie Cruikshank calls a "thoroughly modernist practice—preservation and protection—while continuing to burnish them as authentic replications of 'the native point of view.'"[6]

New Critics were, of course, well aware of the element of translation involved in reading texts not only in other languages but also from that foreign country called the past, and certainly they were acutely conscious of cultural differences between imperial Britain, where many of their canonical texts came from, and revolutionary America, where many modernist critics found themselves at home. This poem that Boas collected embodied his modernist custodial and conservationist principles, and reading it with New Critical instincts in mind may give a sense of how congenial he would have found their method. Paying close attention to how the text itself takes charge illuminates something of this. Its last line, for instance, catches the character of poetic tricksters from the Greek Hermes to the Pueblo Coyote, full of malice and mystery and also something of a thief, fashioning a song out of someone else's (which is exactly what literary traditions specifically—and cultures generally—encourage) and wrapping a storyteller's habit around an ancient heritage. "Long ago," the poet begins, conjuring up both time immemorial and the familiar story-time invitation "Once upon a time"—both signaling "right now"—with a ritual incantation echoing an artist's compulsion. "Had to" is repeated twice in six lines, as the singer becomes inseparable from the song and together they claim material and spiritual agency, finessing the age-old question of whether we believe the teller or the tale and both bringing the corn people into the material sustenance of community and placating the sovereign spirits of place without whom there can be no community and no culture. The song, sung or silent, creates a covenant of words and ceremonies that fortify the people; like language itself, the song holds them together even as, in its final refusal, it keeps others apart.

Indeed the end of this Pueblo poem is very much like the beginning of many of the poems we credit in our literatures—I'll stick with English for convenience here—defying interpretation even as they demand belief. "I saw eternity the other night," says the seventeenth-century mystic Henry Vaughan at the beginning of his poem "The World." Didn't all of you? "I like a look of agony," says Emily Dickinson. Don't you? "So much depends upon a red wheelbarrow," says William Carlos Williams, "glazed with rain water beside the white chickens." What exactly is it that depends on that red wheelbarrow, we ask? I refuse to tell you, replies—or implies—the poet, sending us both on to the end and back to the beginning.

This Pueblo poem has the mischief of riddle and the magic of charm. It posits knowledge and presumes belief, both private (in thought and feeling) and public (in ceremony). It claims clarity while creating mystery. Picking up Bradley's line, it reminds us that we never know exactly what happened, or whether anything happened, in a story or song or performance. "*Garube*," say the Indigenous Khoikhoi herders of southern Africa when they start a story or a song. It means "the happening that is not happening."[7] "It was, and it was not," say storytellers on the island of Majorca when they begin.[8]

These are the tricks of the trade for singers and storytellers all over the world. Those of us in literary studies have developed a critical currency to account for this and to make it comfortable, but it is its *un*comfortability, its strangeness, what Bronislaw Malinowski called its "weirdness," that is crucial.[9] So we find words like *defamiliarization, alienation, incompleteness, indeterminacy, ungrammaticality* to account for the beauties and truths and goodnesses that we recognize in a literary, or a cultural, text. And we do so with a sense of the artifice of ceremony within which we "believe" a story or a song. T. S. Eliot called his seminal collection *The Sacred Wood*, in which he published, *inter alia*, his famous essay "Tradition and the Individual Talent," to catch the sense of ceremonial place and practice that he associated with literature, as Boas did with culture. This is where early twentieth-century comparative literary studies and the anthropology of Franz Boas come into conversation.

Even if we, being postmodern skeptics, think that there's really no such thing as beauty and truth, and certainly not goodness, we must recognize that the Pueblo poet seemed to think there was—"the corn people have a song / it is very good"—and that it was as "real" as anything else. Boas certainly celebrated this in the texts he heard, in company with the literary historians of oral traditions and the creators of the discipline we now know as comparative literature. Furthermore he insisted that literate and nonliterate societies should be analyzed in the same way, and

although there are those who would quarrel with my use of the term *literature* to include oral performances, no other word quite catches the way language, the medium of literature after all, figures in both. I like John Miles Foley's maxim "Oral traditions work like language, only more so."[10] Ironically there is no word other than *literature* that respects the writing *without* words in woven and beaded fabric,[11] in carved wood and stone, and in the intricate choreographies of dancing and drama, which are a central part of many performances in the languages of gesture and form and texture and movement and melody and rhythm. Many scholars now use the word *literature* not in order to appropriate the character of these texts to European models but to remind themselves and us that all such texts deserve an attention that acknowledges their aesthetic character, crafted out of language and discovered — or divined — in language.[12] These texts may also provide evidence of cultural, historical, political, or psychological conditions. But they are first and last made of language, language that, as Boas constantly reminded his colleagues, determines thoughts and feelings as much as it conveys them.

Modernist philologists and philosophers such as Sapir and Whorf and Ernst Cassirer were rediscovering this in the writing of their German predecessors Johann Gottfried Herder and Wilhelm von Humboldt (whose brother Alexander proposed the idea of virtual "islands" of biological integrity, a notion that intrigued Darwin). Meanwhile another scholar, a Frenchman named Marcel Jousse, was teaching about oral traditions at the Sorbonne in the decades following Ferdinand de Saussure. Jousse's interests were in the styles rather than the structures and norms of language, but he used the word *style* in a nineteenth-century way to refer to the essential qualities of a tradition, the elements that make it what it is, as when we refer to a "renaissance style." *Hexis*, Aristotle would have said, a word that came into Latin as *habitus*; so in medieval times, when you learned a language it was said that you had the habit of it.[13] Jousse was convinced that the habits of reading gestures and of listening to words and phrases developed very early in human society, in something that he called "oral style," which has shaped literary traditions from time immemorial.

There were other prominent scholars with whom Boas shared a commitment to language and gesture as conditions of imaginative expression. During the late nineteenth and early twentieth century, many literary critics in the Americas and Europe were returning to what Hugh Kenner once called our central intellectual concern: language. Especially the so-called New Critics, who advocated close attention to the autonomous text and to the ways beauty *reveals* rather than *expresses* truth and

nourishes the spirit. The emphasis on revelation rather than expression echoes Boas's belief that stories and songs reveal elements of culture, including ideas of right and wrong, even when singers and storytellers are not consciously expressing them.

New Criticism eventually became a parody of itself and party to various retreats from the colonial context of many Indigenous imaginative forms. But even at its most irresponsible, New Criticism kept its eye and ear on those very forms, looking and listening for their poetic and polemical character while insisting that ultimately these are inseparable, so it is worth revisiting its early advocates and considering the company they kept.

Let's listen, for a start, to John Crowe Ransom, one of the critics most closely associated with New Criticism and a member of the misremembered group who gathered together in Nashville at Vanderbilt University in the midst of the Great Depression, resisting what they referred to as "the high caste Brahmins of the old south" and vesting authority in the text, not in the critic.[14] Their journal was called *The Fugitive,* and their ideal was wandering Ishmael. Like Boas they believed that literary texts are conditioned—or more precisely, underwritten—by tradition as much as they are determined by talent. Ransom's definition of a poem was "a loose logical structure with a good deal of local texture,"[15] which in its nonchalant assumption of the interdependence of language and culture would have, indeed may have appealed to Boas. Furthermore New Critical unease over intention—which has its roots in nineteenth-century ideals of impersonality, and (for Boas) in the caution expressed by Goethe about seeking explanation—signaled a belief in the essential stability of texts through time and place.[16] For the New Critics texts were, as Eliot pointed out, the product of tradition—a.k.a. nurture, or what Ransom called local texture—as much as of individual talent—which is to say nature, Ransom's loose logic. Eliot's writing in *The Sacred Wood* caught his fascination with the verandah anthropology of Edward Tylor and James Frazer, but his own critical inclinations—and Eliot was a fine critic—put him much closer to the fieldwork of Boas and Malinowski.

In a more difficult statement, Ransom identified literary texts—texts worth the attention of reader and critic, analogous to the cultural texts to which Boas paid attention—as ones that reveal "the kind of knowledge by which we must know what we have arranged that we shall not know otherwise."[17] It is an academic version of "the corn people have a song too / it is very good / I refuse to tell it." It is Paul Ricoeur's hermeneutic circle, wherein there is no interpretation without belief and no belief without interpretation.[18] It is George Steiner's fourth and final type

of difficult, which he calls ontological.[19] It is that old trickster Jacques Derrida, saying "Il n'y a pas d'hors-texte"—there is nothing outside the text;[20] all we have is the text, which if it is good will reveal truth. And it is Franz Boas, insisting that we understand things on their own terms, not those we bring to the party. This is Boas's answer, and New Criticism's answer, to the question of ethnocentric standards. The standards are to be found in or emerge out of the texts themselves, which properly interpreted and evaluated create the conditions in which they are to be appreciated, with the texts (along with the talents that produced them) being ultimately inseparable from the tradition.

Ransom is often credited with the phrase *new criticism*, from the title of a book he published in 1941, but in fact the New Criticism was first announced thirty years earlier (*pace* the self-promotion of the Vanderbilt boys) in a lecture with that title published in 1911 (the same year that Boas published *The Mind of Primitive Man*) within the community that Boas was part of at Columbia University. It was written by Joel Elias Spingarn, at the time chair of the Comparative Literature Department at Columbia, and cofounder in 1903 of the first academic *Journal of Comparative Literature* in the English-speaking Americas. This was of course the time that Boas was consolidating his own position at Columbia, and although not much attention has been paid to his colleagues outside his field(s), the strength of the faculties in sociology and history there would certainly have caught his attention, and it is inconceivable that he would not have consorted with those in literary studies, if only—though not only—because they too were at the center of an intellectual revolution. Especially Spingarn. Who was he? Well, he was a somebody, and Boas courted those during these years. When the literary critic M. H. Abrams published his magisterial work on the history of eighteenth- and nineteenth-century ideas titled *The Mirror and the Lamp* in 1953, it was praised by the formidable Rene Wellek as "the most distinguished contribution of American scholarship in [the history of criticism] since the work of J. E. Spingarn."[21] In E. B. Burgum's defining collection titled *New Criticism*, published in 1930, Spingarn's was the lead essay. Earlier he had joined with the anthropologist Elsie Clews Parsons in the collection *Civilization in the United States: An Inquiry by 30 Americans*, edited by Harold Stearns. Parsons was a student of Boas at Columbia, and Ruth Benedict, in turn, was a student of hers in 1919 at the New School for Social Research.

In 1911 Spingarn was an unruly somebody, a type that also appealed to Boas. He proposed the new criticism to replace the grab bag of sociology, psychology, dogmatic historicism, reactionary idealism, and dec-

adent impressionism that passed for literary criticism in his day. H. L. Mencken called Spingarn "magnificently unprofessorial, fly[ing] violently in the face of the principles that distinguish the largest and most influential group of critics" (whom Mencken went on to describe as grown-up sophomores who lack the intellectual resilience for taking in new ideas and who exhibit alarm in the presence of anything not packaged and labeled by their predecessors).[22]

So in 1911, the year his essay "The New Criticism" was published by Columbia University Press, Spingarn was fired from the university. But it wasn't for advocating this New Criticism; instead it was because he defended a colleague, one Harry Thurston Peck. Peck, it seems, had sent some candid love letters to a young lady, clearly hoping for something more than a correspondence, but in the wacky way of the world, when things didn't work out she turned around and sued him for breach of promise. Peck was quickly deserted by his wife and his friends, and then by his university, which fired him. But he was not deserted by Spingarn, who hardly knew him but as a matter of principle moved a resolution in his favor at the faculty council. The president of the university suggested that Spingarn should follow Peck into the sunset since he obviously didn't belong in their club. Spingarn refused, forcing the president to fire him and sending the story to the front page of the *New York Times*. Boas would have liked his anti-authoritarian instincts, as well as the antiracist implications of his gesture, for Spingarn was Jewish and Columbia was moving toward discriminatory admissions policies. As Wade Davis remarked in *The Wayfinders*, everything Boas proposed ran against orthodoxy, including the racism that was becoming conventional in American and European life.

Fortunately Spingarn went on to a distinguished career. He cofounded the publishing house of Harcourt Brace and Company, and he used his not particularly clubbable ways to settle a long-standing dispute between the disciples of W. E. B. DuBois and those of Booker T. Washington, who had frustrated every other attempt. This was not so long after Boas had given a lecture in Atlanta that surprised DuBois by celebrating the heritage of African Americans.[23] Then, in an astonishing initiative for anyone at that time, much less a New York Jew—like Boas—Spingarn helped establish the National Association for the Advancement of Colored People, the NAACP, born in the grim shadow of lynchings but based on the inspiring idea of a unified black movement that might change American society. Spingarn was its second president and the chairman of its board for twenty-seven years, from its founding in 1913 right up until his death in 1939. He is still remembered for the Spingarn Medal, awarded annu-

ally for outstanding achievement by an African American, with recipients that include DuBois himself, Marian Anderson and Paul Robeson, Langston Hughes and Richard Wright, Jackie Robinson and Hank Aaron, Rosa Parks, Martin Luther King Jr. and Jesse Jackson, Alvin Ailey and Jacob Lawrence. Quite apart from the Columbia connection, Spingarn's celebration of African American traditions would certainly have caught Boas's attention, as it did many of his most famous students, such as Zora Neale Hurston and Melville Herskovits. Hurston's tribute to the powers of friendship and love, published in Mencken's *American Mercury*, catches a contradiction that Boas embraced all his life: "Dr. William E. Burkhardt [sic], the bitterest opponent of the white race that America has ever known, loved Joel Spingarn and was certainly loved in turn by him. The thing doesn't make sense. It just makes beauty."[24]

Spingarn wrote elegant essays on writers from Dante to Milton and Bacon to Boccalini, and he edited the literary essays of Goethe; he also celebrated and supported the work of African American writers during the Harlem Renaissance, acknowledging their struggles in the same way he did those of the artists during the troubled times of the European Renaissance. He insisted that literary criticism needed to "wipe out"—that was his phrase—the old classical rules and the old European themes, which were narrowing the field of imaginative force that texts offered. He rejected any analysis that derived from arbitrary rules that did not emerge from the text and suggested that determinations of genre—crucial in anthropology as well—should be made only from within a tradition, not imposed on it, and that false dichotomies of form and content, or style and subject, only obscure meaning and obliterate value. Boas could have sung the chorus; indeed the echoes and choruses around these ideas formed the basis of twentieth-century comparative literary studies that was taking shape at the institutions and in the communities that Boas frequented. For comparative literature was premised on the idea that there were commonalities across national boundaries, universals of literary production and reception that illuminated rather than eliminated the particularities of culture and heritage. And although comparative literature did not (until later encouraged by postcolonial polemic) become preoccupied with race, its founding principles, which were based in opposition to the influence of discredited dichotomies on our appreciation of national literary traditions, offered a counterpart to Boas's stern warning (originally uttered in 1914) that "the term race is only a disguise of the idea of nationality, which has really very, very little to do with racial descent."[25]

Though meaning and value are the basis of any theory of interpreta-

tion and evaluation and the staples of comparative literature, they sound suspiciously—and contentiously—old-fashioned, like beauty and truth and goodness. I'd prefer to call them retro, hoping for a revival. But whatever we call them I'm wary of throwing them away. Old-fashioned is what Aboriginal traditions often are, and maybe, just maybe—and here again we might hear Boas's voice—they could generate respectful and rigorous attention to texts rather than patronizing concern about everything else. Beauty and truth and goodness, with different names but a similar hold on the imagination, have been talked about and turned over among Aboriginal peoples for millennia, and their response has been as complex, and occasionally as contentious, as it has been in non-Aboriginal society. So we don't want to, and Boas certainly didn't want us to, run the risk of behaving as though beauty is for Europeans and Asians and maybe some Africans, the way courts sometimes behave as though truth is something Aboriginals don't tell.

Let me use an event familiar to many Canadians to illustrate how forgetting this can cause trouble. During the *Delgamuukw* trial, a major Aboriginal rights case (named after the elder in whose inherited name the action was brought) seeking recognition of the traditional territory of the Gitxsan and Wet'suwet'en peoples in northern British Columbia, one of the other elders, named Antgulilibix (Mary Johnson), was telling her *ada'ox*—the cycle of stories and songs that were in her custody—to the court. At a certain point she said that she must sing a song. The judge (Allan McEachern) balked, for the request seemed to flout the protocols of his court. He tried to explain how uncomfortable he felt having someone sing in his court. He said that it was unlikely to get him any nearer the truth that he was seeking. He asked the lawyer for the Gitxsan whether it might not be sufficient to have just the words written down and avoid the performance. Met with a dignified intransigence, he finally agreed to let Antgulilibix sing her song, but just as she was about to start he fired his final salvo. "It's not going to do any good to sing it to me," he said. "I have a tin ear."[26]

Judge McEachern was roundly criticized for his comments, both by the wider community and by the Supreme Court of Canada, which later heard the case on appeal and reversed his decision in favor of the plaintiffs; he became known locally as Old Tin Ears. It *was* a stupid thing for him to say since he wasn't the least bit interested in the song or its music anyway, having decided, perhaps reasonably, to keep himself immune from charm, or song, and from beauty. He was after truth.

But in another sense it was also a smart thing to say, for he *did* have a tin ear, and he could not have heard the music of the song, or appre-

ciated its beauty, even if he were interested in doing so. Most of us go through life assuming that we could make music as well as meaning out of Mary Johnson's song. For the Antgulilibixes of the world it is a sinister assumption. It is an assumption that understanding artistic performance comes naturally to the sympathetic eye and ear. It does not. It requires what Frye used to call an educated imagination, the kind of imagination that Boas spent his life nourishing in his students and colleagues. Like the judge, we often come to such texts uneducated. Increasingly we also come looking for truth and forgetting about beauty.

And Mary Johnson's song *was* a thing of beauty. In it the drumming of the wings of a ruffed grouse is transformed into a lament for the dead and becomes an occasion for remembering a totem pole carved and raised in their honor. The music—the drumming, the dissolving of the distinction between sound and sense, what Coleridge (referring to Plato) called the dear gorgeous nonsense of imaginative figuration—may be unfamiliar to many of us, but we can recognize its elegiac power. And if we remember our own ceremonies of belief we can understand why Mary Johnson needed a moment of haunting beauty at the center of historical truth: not as a relief from that truth but as an intensification of it and, within the tradition of literary performance to which it belongs, a verification of it. This is pure New Criticism. Beauty is truth, truth beauty, John Keats said of the Grecian urn. The judge couldn't acknowledge this, dedicated as he was to an unmediated truth. But we have no such excuse; indeed Boas tried to teach us to recognize the inseparability of form and content, of beauty and truth. After listening as best he could to Antgulilibix, the judge said he believed her but not her story. He believed individual talent, not the tradition. Such a dichotomy is always untenable, just as it is unreasonable to expect anyone, in any culture, to define beauty and truth and goodness. But everyone, in all cultures, learns to know them, and believe them, when they encounter them. And that happens most compellingly, as Boas knew, in works of art. Which was why he treasured them, like texts in a literary canon.

Within any tradition there will be standards. That is what traditions are all about, and those standards of beauty and truth and goodness are custodians of the experiences these traditions sponsor. The right things in the right order performed by the right people to the right people in the right place and time. In every culture these standards are embodied in the idea of a canon, an idea that was very much under debate at Columbia in Boas's time and represented an institutional culture that shaped his thinking. The debate was promoted by another of his colleagues, Charles Sprague Smith, who is little remembered these days but

who brought the idea of the canon into the literary academy, and into the Americas, just as Boas brought the idea of canonical artifacts into American anthropology, and into its museums—artifacts like the Nuhchal-nulth whaler's shrine from Jewitt island, taken for display at the American Museum of Natural History in New York.[27] Without excusing the taking of it by Boas and George Hunt, his Tlingit/Kwakwaka'wakw broker, we should acknowledge that it was gathered up not in a demonstration of white superiority but as a celebration of what Boas considered truly great Indigenous art, from a tribal community that he thought was on its last legs. He was wrong in both his practice and his prediction. But perhaps not in his motive, for he was caught up in the business of putting together a canon. The fact that it did not become a canonical "text" in the art of the Northwest Coast—or at least has not yet become canonical—may have as much to do with its material history as with its spiritual power and aesthetic authority. Contemporary scholars are reminding us of what Boas understood, that meaning and value may be inscribed in a very wide and often bewildering range of texts and artifacts.[28] Whatever the case, Boas certainly didn't get everything right. But he would have been intrigued by Smith's canon-making initiative, just as he was later appalled by Columbia's discriminatory practices.

Smith was a predecessor of Spingarn's and the founder of the Comparative Literature Society in 1895, the year before Boas came to Columbia. Smith began it not in order to nourish academic careers but to foster understanding across the new linguistic and cultural communities in New York through the shared reading of books. Indeed Smith's Comparative Literature Society was the forerunner of the People's Institute in New York, which Smith also founded and where John Collier (who had graduated from Columbia) worked from 1909 to 1919, later becoming commissioner of the Bureau of Indian Affairs, responsible both for the Indian Reorganization Act of 1934 and for bringing a number of anthropologists into the Bureau. The People's Institute sponsored lectures through the 1920s to complement the adult education seminars put on by the public library system, also organizing discussions at the Cooper Union, the Manhattan Trade School, and across town at the Labor Temple, where the philosopher Will Durant taught. Their foundational texts came from a canonical list that constituted what were eventually referred to as "great books," the nineteenth- and twentieth-century version of the good songs that the Pueblo poet identified in the corn field.

The specific list of books that they started with came from the British Working Men's Colleges (which included women from their beginnings in the middle of the nineteenth century) and Mechanics' Institutes, old-

fashioned reading and recreation clubs. John Lubbock edited a series of a hundred books for such readers, advertised as "Sir John Lubbock's Hundred Books" and published during the 1890s by George Routledge in sturdy bindings, priced from 1 shilling to 3 and six. Lubbock was known to Boas in another capacity, as the founder of prehistoric archaeology who coined the terms *Paleolithic* and *Neolithic*. His book *Pre-Historic Times, As Illustrated by Ancient Remains and the Manners and Customs of Modern Savages* was a nineteenth-century standard, and was followed by *The Origin of Civilization and the Primitive Condition of Man*. The title phrases may be disconcerting to a contemporary ear (though they are echoed in Boas's *The Mind of Primitive Man*), but the material is surprisingly modern and directed toward field study rather than verandah speculation, for Lubbock was also a naturalist dedicated to the yard rather than the tower, and his work was acknowledged by Darwin in *The Origin of Species*. And as a politician he saw more progressive legislation through the British Houses of Parliament than anyone else in the second half of the nineteenth century. The books he chose covered a wide range of cultures and traditions, including classical and contemporary European literary, historical, philosophical, natural and social scientific texts, as well as a translation of the Qur'an, the Shi King from the Chinese, the Shah Nameh of the Persian poet Firdausi, and the Indian drama *Sakoontala*. Each text was to be its own teacher, an idea that has never endeared itself to those who want to be superior to the text but which was the literary counterpart to Boas's anthropological approach.

The connection to American intellectual life in the humanities was precise and profound and as revolutionary as the transformation that Boas inspired in the social sciences. It all began with Charles Sprague Smith's Comparative Literature Society and People's Institute, where educators such as Mortimer Adler, Robert Hutchins, Mark Van Doren, Scott Buchanan, Stringfellow Barr, and Richard McKeon gave lectures and participated in seminars. In due course Buchanan left to join Barr at the University of Virginia, while Adler and McKeon were brought by Hutchins to the University of Chicago. And so began a radical reform of North American higher education. Buchanan and Barr went on to revive and restructure St. John's College in Annapolis, which eventually extended a campus to Santa Fe; it remains one of the most challenging educational experiments on the continent, unlike the authoritarian models developed elsewhere and dedicated to transforming students into their own teachers by getting them to read a list of books deemed monuments of human intelligence and imagination, of material enterprise and spiritual revelation.

In his study of geography written in 1887, Boas had insisted that cultural phenomena too are worthy of being studied for their own sake—not for our sake but for *their own* sake, serving their own ends (which of course have to be discovered by the diligent listener, reader, or observer). This phrase echoes the call of art for art's sake, a fin de siècle motto that inspired both New Criticism and those "great books" programs, and insisting on it is as important—and as controversial—now as it was then.

Notes

1. Bradley, *Shakespearean Tragedy*, 33. See also Chamberlin, "The Corn People Have a Song Too."
2. Boas, "The Study of Geography," 137–41.
3. Pearson, *The Grammar of Science*, 61–63.
4. Rothenberg, *Shaking the Pumpkin*, 3.
5. Ong, *Orality and Literacy*, 50.
6. Cruikshank, *Do Glaciers Listen?*, 59.
7. I am indebted to Levi Namaseb, professor of linguistics and African literature at the University of Namibia, for this translation.
8. Jakobson, "Linguistics and Poetics." See also Jakobson, "On Linguistic Aspects of Translation."
9. Malinowski, "Coefficient of Weirdness," 218–23.
10. Foley, *Oral Tradition and the Internet*, 176, 251.
11. Boone and Mignolo, *Writing without Words*.
12. For example, see Dauenhauer and Dauenhauer, *Classics of Tlingit Oral Literature*.
13. Frye, *Some Reflection on Life and Habit*, 14.
14. Ransom, foreword to the inaugural issue of the *Fugitive* magazine, April 1922.
15. Ransom, "Wanted: An Ontological Critic" (1941), quoted in Young, *The New Criticism and After*, 24.
16. The ideal of impersonality received sustained attention in a correspondence between C. S. Lewis and E. M. W. Tillyard that originally appeared in *Essays and Studies* between 1934 and 1936 and was published as *The Personal Heresy: A Controversy*, preceding by a decade W. K. Wimsatt and Monroe Beardsley's essay "The Intentional Fallacy."
17. Ransom, *The World's Body*, 10.
18. Ricoeur, *Hermeneutics and the Human Sciences*.
19. Steiner, *On Difficulty and Other Essays*.
20. Derrida, *De la grammatologie*.
21. Wellek, review of *The Mirror and the Lamp*, 178.
22. Mencken, "Criticism of Criticism of Criticism," 9–21.
23. In his preface to *Black Folk Then and Now: An Essay in the History and Sociology of the Negro Race*, DuBois recalled, "Franz Boas came to Atlanta Uni-

versity where I was teaching history of the black kingdoms south of the Sahara for a thousand years. I was too astonished to speak. All of this I had never heard" (vii). Bornstein, *The Colors of Zion*, 62.
24. Quoted in Bornstein, *The Colors of Zion*, 201.
25. Boas, *Race and Democratic Society*, 109.
26. See *Delgamuukw v. British Columbia*. Judge McEachern's comments are recorded in the transcripts of the *Delgamuukw* trial (1987–1991), finally decided (in favor of the plaintiffs) by the Supreme Court of Canada on December 11, 1997. Richard Overstall and Susan Marsden played a key role during the trial (and afterward) in providing a context for the stories and song presented and performed by Gitxsan and Wet'suwet'en elders.
27. Jonaitis and Inglis, *The Yuquot Whaler's Shrine*.
28. For example, see Kreamer et al., *Inscribing Meaning*; Fienup-Riordan, *Yuungnaqpiallerput*.

References

Boas, Franz. *Race and Democratic Society*. 1914. New York: J. J. Augustin, 1945.
———. "The Study of Geography." *Science* 9.210 (1887): 137–41.
Boone, Elizabeth Hill, and Walter D. Mignolo. *Writing without Words: Alternative Literacies in Mesoamerica and the Andes*. Durham NC: Duke University Press, 1994.
Bornstein, George. *The Colors of Zion: Blacks, Jews, and Irish from 1845 to 1945*. Cambridge MA: Harvard University Press, 2011.
Bradley, A. C. *Shakespearean Tragedy*. London: Macmillan, 1905.
Chamberlin, J. Edward. "The Corn People Have a Song Too. It Is Very Good. On Beauty, Truth, and Goodness." *Studies in American Indian Literatures* 21.3 (2009): 66–89.
Cruikshank, Julie. *Do Glaciers Listen? Local Knowledge, Colonial Encounters and Social Imagination* Vancouver: University of British Columbia Press, 2005.
Dauenhauer, Richard, and Nora Marks Dauenhauer. *Classics of Tlingit Oral Literature*. 4 vols. Seattle: University of Washington Press, 1987–2008.
Davis, Wade. *The Wayfinders*. Toronto: House of Anansi Press, 2009.
Delgamuukw v. British Columbia. 3 S.C.R. 1010 (1997).
Derrida, Jacques. *De la grammatologie*. Paris: Les Éditions de Minuit, 1967.
DuBois, W. E. B. *Black Folk Then and Now: An Essay in the History and Sociology of the Negro Race*. London: Octagon Books, 1939.
———. *Dusk of Dawn: An Essay toward an Autobiography of a Race Concept*. New York: Harcourt, Brace, 1940.
Eliot, T. S. *The Sacred Wood: Essays on Poetry and Criticism*. London: Methuen, 1920.
Fienup-Riordan, Ann. *Yuungnaqpiallerput: The Way We Genuinely Live*. Seattle: University of Washington Press, 2007.
Foley, John Miles. *Oral Tradition and the Internet: Pathways of the Mind*. Urbana: University of Illinois Press, 2012.

Frye, Northrop. *Some Reflection on Life and Habit*. Lethbridge, Canada: University of Lethbridge Press, 1988.

———. Editorial. *The Fugitive* 1 (1922).

Jakobson, Roman. "Linguistics and Poetics." In Thomas Sebeok, ed., *Style in Language*, 350–77. Cambridge MA: The MIT Press 1960.

———. "On Linguistic Aspects of Translation." 1959. In Krystyna Pomorska and Stephen Rudy, eds., *Language in Literature*, 428–35. Cambridge MA: Harvard University Press, 1987.

Jonaitis, Aldona, with research contributions by Richard Inglis. *The Yuquot Whaler's Shrine*. Seattle: University of Washington Press, 1999.

Jousse, Marcel. *The Anthropology of Geste and Rhythm*. Ed. and trans. Edgard Sienaert and Joan Conolly. Durban, South Africa: Mantis, 2000.

———. *The Oral Style*. Trans. Edgar Sienaert and R. Whitaker. New York: Garland, 1990.

Kreamer C. M., M. N. Roberts, E. Harvery, and A. Purpura. *Inscribing Meaning: Writing and Graphic Systems in African Art*. Washington DC: Smithsonian, 2007.

Lubbock, John. *The Origin of Civilization and the Primitive Condition of Man*. London: Longmans, Green, 1870.

———. *Pre-Historic Times, As Illustrated by Ancient Remains, and the Manners and Customs of Modern Savages*. London: Williams & Norgate, 1865.

Malinowski, Bronislaw. "Coefficient of Weirdness in the Magic of Language." In *The Language of Magic and Gardening*. Vol. 2 of *Coral Gardens and Their Magic: A Study of the Methods of Tilling the Soil and of Agricultural Rites in the Trobriand Islands*. London: George Allen & Unwin, 1935.

Mencken, H. L. "Criticism of Criticism of Criticism." In *Prejudices: First Series*. New York: Knopf, 1919.

Ong, Walter J. *Orality and Literacy: The Technologizing of the Word*. London: Methuen, 1982.

Pearson, Karl. *The Grammar of Science*. London: J. M. Dent & Sons, 1937.

Ransom, John Crowe. *The World's Body*. New York: Charles Scribner's Sons, 1938.

Ricoeur, Paul. *Hermeneutics and the Human Sciences: Essays on Language, Action and Interpretation*. Trans. John B. Thompson. Cambridge, UK: Cambridge University Press, 1981.

Rothenberg, Jerome. *Shaking the Pumpkin: Traditional Poetry of the Indian North Americas*. Albuquerque: University of New Mexico Press, 1991.

Spingarn, Joel. "The New Criticism." In E. B. Burgum, ed., *The New Criticism: An Anthology of Modern Aesthetics and Literary Criticism*, 3–27. New York: Prentice-Hall, 1930.

Stearns, Harold, ed. *Civilization in the United States: An Inquiry by 30 Americans*. New York: Harcourt, Brace, 1922.

Steiner, George. *On Difficulty and Other Essays*. Oxford: Oxford University Press, 1978.

Tillyard, Eustace Mandevile Wetenhall, and Clive Staples Lewis. *The Personal Heresy: A Controversy*. London: Oxford University Press, 1939.

Wellek, Rene. Review of *The Mirror and the Lamp*. *Comparative Literature* 6 (Spring 1954).

Wimsatt, William, and Monroe C. Beardsley. *The Intentional Fallacy. The Verbal Icon: Studies in the Meaning of Poetry*. Lexington: University of Kentucky Press, 1954.

Young, Thomas Daniel. *The New Criticism and After*. Charlottesville: University Press of Virginia, 1976.

5 From Baffin Island to Boasian Induction

How Anthropology and Linguistics Got into Their Interlinear Groove

MICHAEL SILVERSTEIN

Oral texts, elicited at fluent dictation speed from the lips of native speakers, carefully recorded in handwritten form, then rendered into print in both original form and translation, constituted, for Boas, the cultural material of an anthropological philology for unlettered peoples' cultures. He promoted and defended this approach as the equivalent of studying ancient civilizations from their literary monuments. Such texts, like those of premodern European traditions, constitute indeed the record of cultures expressed "from the native's point of view," to use the Malinowskian phrase, for Boas the sine qua non of being able to know another culture. What classicist could claim to illuminate the cultural history of Rome and its imperial expansion, Boas in effect asked, without having Latin-language textual material of both imaginative works of literature and narrative, expository, and other daily communication? Like archaeological remains of those civilizations, like their "material culture" cumulated—and imitated—over the centuries down to the present day, texts were the verbal counterpart of a people's material cultural production that constituted, for Boas and his students, the primary data for ethnology as well as for linguistics.[1]

Boas himself was indefatigable over decades in bringing to publication the textual results of his own fieldwork as well as those of his students. Whether under the imprint of the Bureau of American Ethnology, the American Museum of Natural History's Jesup North Pacific Expedition, the American Ethnological Society, Columbia University, the universities of California or Pennsylvania or Washington, or the American Folklore Society, Boasian text collections cumulated in publication series into a veritable *Loeb Classical Library* for the peoples and cultures of North America, whenever possible published, as were the *Loeb* texts, in both original and translated versions (though the bilingual format and layout vary widely). As Regna Darnell points out in her biography of Edward Sapir (1884–1939), by the 1930s the new "social anthropological" trend

in American anthropology, influenced by the British-derived comparative structural-functionalism that A. R. Radcliffe-Brown (1881–1955) had newly brought to Chicago, essentially marked an end to this conception of the central role of primary textual documentation of a culture.[2]

Yet, in a countervailing move, the practice was resuscitated in the context of a different discipline in 1953 at the University of California, Berkeley, with the founding of the Department of Linguistics and its graduate training research project, the Survey of California Indian Languages, by two scholars mentored by Sapir, the noted Americanist Mary R. Haas (1910–1996) and the great Indo-Aryan and Dravidian scholar Murray B. Emeneau (1904–2005). For a couple of generations most linguistics PhD dissertation projects done at Berkeley consisted of documenting an Indigenous language by extensive fieldwork, resulting in a grammar, a bilingual text collection, and a dictionary regularly published in the series *University of California Publications in Linguistics*, issued by the institution's press. This definitively revivified the practice of the earliest days of the university's anthropological work, when A. L. Kroeber (1876–1960), Boas's first Columbia PhD student, regularly included several Boas-style text collections—among them, in 1910, one by Sapir himself—in the series *University of California Publications in American Archaeology and Ethnology*, which he oversaw from 1903 forward.

But my purpose here is not merely to discuss the intellectual rationale within anthropology, for Boas and his students, for collecting and publishing such important primary cultural material, nor the obvious role of such material as exemplary linguistic data. My purpose is to contextualize the emergence of Boas's own practices with respect to texts in the broader nineteenth-century philological sciences, in which he had not in fact been specifically trained, having received his Kiel PhD in 1881 for a physics project on the optical properties of seawater. His earliest efforts with textual cultural materials during his Baffinland trip of 1883–1884, revealed in his earliest publications both in German and English, are distinctly ad hoc. And yet by September 1886, when he began his self-funded systematic Northwest Coast research in British Columbia,[3] what we have come to know as Boasian textual practice is full-blown from the very first pages in his notebooks, let alone the later published accounts derived from them. It is this transformative absorption into the very practices of philological science—as well as his sense of their centrality to a linguistics and an ethnology of the technologically pregraphic peoples—that makes Boas seem at once an autodidact coming to an already fully formed discipline and, retrospectively from the later

history of anthropology and linguistics, a transformative ancestor figure who revolutionized an area of study and created the North American disciplines of ethnology and anthropological linguistics as they came to be normal text-based science.

At once a Franz-come-lately to the flourishing field of philology as an "inductive" human science and yet the individual who is widely credited with instilling the very relativist philological flavor of American cultural anthropology and descriptive linguistics down to the mid-twentieth century. How can this be? My purpose here is to resolve this seeming historical paradox by showing that Boas's enthusiastic adoption of traditional philological inductivism as the epistemological stance for his own fieldwork in North America turned out to provide the empirical foundation for his transformative role in several ontological crises of late nineteenth-century human sciences that emerged as theorists sought to define the distinctiveness of language and of culture as frameworks of social collectivities. In turn his anti-social evolutionist, relativist stance on the latter proved critical to the transition to synchronic views of language and of culture in succeeding generations of linguists and anthropologists, for whom Boas embodied in his own work and inculcated in his teaching the essential connection between inductive epistemology and relativist ontology.

Nineteenth-century comparative philology—comparative and historical linguistics, as we now retrospectively term it, plus the text-critical practices underlying the editing and utilization of ancient manuscripts to reveal cultures—effloresced and culminated in the Germany of Boas's youth, interestingly enough, as the very prototype of true, inductively based historical science applied to human sociocultural phenomena. This is what in effect Boas brought in 1886 to his emerging anthropology. What are the foundations of philological science in textuality, and how do the epistemic paraphernalia of Boasian ethnology and linguistics emerge from them? And, most interesting, what is the route by which Boas and all those he influenced as a teacher came to be the philologists of the unlettered? To understand these matters we must see the broader picture of philology in its epistemological aspect.

An intellectual consequence of the Enlightenment set in irreversible motion by Lord Bacon, the prestige of "induction" cumulated during the nineteenth century and spread from the natural to the human sciences. It had three effective faces or avatars in the world of learning, a pedagogical, an epistemological, and an ontological. Certainly beginning in the third quarter of the nineteenth century there was no question among the

linguistically sophisticated but that the innovative method of language teaching was "inductive," direct student experience of actual language in use, thus to be preferred over having them memorize grammatical rules and then trying to apply them—paralleling the pedagogical advances in giving priority to students' laboratory and field experience with natural phenomena of the physical and biological worlds. There was as well no question but that comparative philology—linguistics, to the more terminologically aspiring—ranked in the vanguard of the human sciences because it was an "inductive science," sifting, sorting, classifying, and then explanatorily generalizing about its data, meaningful words isolated from textual contexts, just as botany, zoology, and geology treated the data of their concern. And there was no question but that underlying all of these enterprises was the human mental faculty of induction, or inductive conceptual reasoning, the faculty that allowed us both to learn languages and to make useful and thus pragmatically valid scientific generalizations—Charles Sanders Peirce (1839–1914) would call them "abductive" syllogistic leaps—about the phenomena in the world. When we look at the early career of Boas, and its efflorescence in the next generation of anthropologists and linguists he trained and/or influenced, we see how integrally his acquired philological practices came to fit within this scientific order.

We can do so, I would claim, by looking at Boas's practices in relation to texts and the inscriptional methods through which "the native's point of view" is made to emerge through them. Here Boas, the autodidact in matters cultural, early on caught the empirical spirit of last-quarter nineteenth-century philology and linguistics and sought to create materials for the American Native languages, as he termed them, in the image of those on which students of Indo-European, Semitic, and other language families had already long been laboring.

My research has thus sought to contextualize Boas's archive and oeuvre as a corpus of scholarly text artifacts that link his career to the late nineteenth-century emergence of professionalized disciplinary linguistics itself, an intellectual context that by then had already been maturing over more than a hundred years. My claim here is that there is causal continuity in the diffusion of inductive technique across both geographical and conceptual space: from the eastern to the western shores of the Atlantic; from Indo-European, Semitic, Finno-Ugric, and so on to Algonquian, Wakashan, Uto-Aztecan, and so on; from theorizing at first driven by linguistic comparison and history to the theoretical priority of structural or descriptive approaches; from found text artifacts in ancient scripts

requiring decipherment, transliteration, and—mediated by grammatical and lexical study—translation, to field notebook inscriptions capturing spoken textualities with the then graphic tools of the trade, a close "phonetic" transcription that served as the basis for phonological and lexicogrammatical analysis. Boas was the key figure in this transformative diffusion.

So I wish to elaborate somewhat on the sources of Boasian text-focal inductivism, starting with language pedagogy as a species of more general pedagogical inductivism, and then moving to comparative-historical linguistics and its transition to thinking about so-called synchronic—structural and functional—aspects of language, a transition in which Boas himself played a major role.

Pedagogical Inductivism and Inductive Philology

Pedagogical inductivism is well illustrated in *Elements of Hebrew by an Inductive Method*, created in the 1870s by the founding president of the University of Chicago, William Rainey Harper (1856–1906). Harper had, to be sure, made a scholarly name for himself early in life as a Yale Semiticist and expert in the field of biblical Hebrew. But perhaps more importantly he was an academic entrepreneur who had earlier invented the Hebrew Correspondence School (among many ventures that constituted his American Institute of Hebrew), which he continued to manage while serving as professor and president of the Baptist Union's Theological School in Morgan Park, just south of Chicago city limits at the time.[4] Each fortnight or so the paying students received a booklet that comprised the lesson (see fig. 3), which was essentially a set of word-by-word glossing and related grammatical notes to a verse of the Old Testament (fig. 4), together with further "observations" referenced to a grammar, and followed by a set of reading-recitation and back-and-forth translation exercises based cumulatively on the material thus far (fig. 5). Harper, familiar to the Chautauqua circuit of quick tent-sales as well as Baptist revivalism, also sold to the Correspondence School students the *Manual* on which the lessons were based, namely, a book of the Bible done up as texts in facing-page Hebrew and word-by-word English translation (fig. 6),[5] as well as his own reference grammars, *Elements of Hebrew by an Inductive Method* and later *Elements of Hebrew Syntax by an Inductive Method*, to the paragraphs of which are keyed the explanatory remarks in each of the individual lessons sent out to the students, and whose captioned sections collect references to the chapters and verses of the Bible text in the *Manual* where a particular phenomenon is illustrated.

THE HEBREW STUDENT

THE HEBREW SUMMER SCHOOL

THE HEBREW BOOK EXCHANGE

AMERICAN INSTITUTE OF HEBREW

CONDUCTED BY

WILLIAM R. HARPER, Ph. D.,
MORGAN PARK, CHICAGO.

The Hebrew Correspondence School

דְּבָרִים בְּיוֹמוֹ

I. Elementary Course.   III. Progressive Course.
II. Intermediate Course.   IV. Advanced Course.

Entered, according to act of Congress, in the year 1882 in the office of the Librarian of Congress, by WILLIAM R. HARPER.

Elementary Course.   **Lesson 1.**

❧ SUGGESTIONS. ❧

1. Master absolutely the entire lesson; not a needless word or statement is inserted.

2. The greatest difficulties in acquiring Hebrew are (1) the pronunciation and (2) the vocabulary; therefore *never* pass a word without pronouncing it, and *never* pronounce a word without immediately ascertaining its meaning.

3. Do not suppose that everything will be clear at a glance. Many points of difficulty will arise. Feel perfectly free, however, to ask concerning any matter that may be obscure.

4. Make it a principle to do *exactly* the amount of work assigned,—no more, *no less*.

5. The "Notes" and "Observations" are to be carefully studied and compared. The "Recitation-lesson" is to be written out and sent to the Instructor for correction.

Fig. 3. Front page of first lesson, Harper's Hebrew Correspondence School, Elementary course.

Elementary Course.

1. Notes.—Genesis 1. 1.

וְאֵ֥ת   אֵ֖ת   הָאָֽרֶץ׃   הַשָּׁמַ֖יִם   אֵ֥ת   בָּרָ֣א   אֱלֹהִ֑ים   בְּרֵאשִׁ֖ית
v'ēth   ēth   hā-ā́-rĕts   hash-shā-ma̅-yı̆m   ēth   bā-rā́   'lō-hı̄m   bĕrē-shīth
and   —   the-earth   the-heavens   —   created   God   In-beginning

1. בְּרֵאשִׁית—b'rē̄-shīth (two syllables)—*In beginning.*
   1) *Six letters*: —ב (b); ר (r); א, called 'Āleph,' which is not pronounced, but represented in transliteration by '; שׁ (sh); י (y), here silent after ֵ; ת (th).
   2) *Three vowel-sounds*: —ֵ under ר, represented by a so-called italicized superior letter ᵉ, and pronounced like *e* in *below*, a very quick, short sound; ֵ (ē), like *ey* in *they*; ִ (ı̆), like *i* in *machine*.

2. בָּרָא—bā-rā́ (two syllables)—*(he) created.*
   1) *Three letters*: —ב (b); ר (r); א (') called 'Aleph.—See above.
   2) *Two vowel-sounds*: —ָ (ā), like *a* in *father.*

3. אֱלֹהִים—'lō-hı̄m (two syllables)—*God.*
   1) *Five letters*: —א ('); ל (l); ה (h); י (y), here silent after ֹ; ם (m).
   2) *Three vowel-sounds*: —ֱ (ᵉ), a very quickly uttered *e*-sound, as in *art*; ֹ (ō), a point *above* the line, like *o* in *note*; ִ (ı̄).

4. אֵת—ēth (one syllable)—[no translation].

5. הַשָּׁמַיִם—hash-shā-ma̅-yı̆m (four syl's.)—*the-heavens.*
   1) *Five letters*: —ה (h); שׁ (sh), but שּׁ (with a point in its bosom) is sh doubled; ל (m); י (y), here pronounced as *y* in *year*; ם (m).
   2) *Four vowel-sounds*: —ַ (ă), like *a* in *hat*; ָ (ā), like *a* in *father*; ֵ (ā); ִ (ı̆), like *i* in *pin.*

Remark 1.—ל represents the *m*-sound at the beginning or in the middle of a word; ם at the end of a word.

Remark 2.—The sign ⸱ indicates that the accent is on the syllable ל *the penult.*

---
¹ This word is pronounced as if spelled Ah-leph, the *ah* having the sound of *a* in *father.*

Elementary Course.

6. אֵת—v'ēth (one syllable)—*and*)(.
   1) *Three letters*: —ו (v); א ('); ת (th).
   2) *Two vowel-sounds*: —ְ (ʾ), compare ː () under ר (1); ֵ (ē).

7. הָאָרֶץ—hā-ā́-rĕts (three syllables)—*the-earth.*
   1) *Five letters*: —ה (h); א ('); ר (r); צ (ts), like *ts* in *gets.*
   2) *Three vowel-sounds*: —ָ (ā); ֶ (ĕ), like *e* in *gets.*

Remark.—The accent ◌֥ with אֱלֹהִים (*God*), marks the middle of the verse; the accent ◌֖, with הָאָֽרֶץ (*the-earth*), marks the end of the verse. ׃ is equivalent to a period.

II. Observations.—Gen. I. 1.

1. The letters in this verse:
   (1) ב, (2) ר, (3) א, (4) שׁ, (5) י, (6) ת, (7) ל, (8) ה, (9) ם, (10) ע, (11) צ, (12) ו, (13) ץ.

2. The vowel-sounds in this verse:
   (1) ֵ, (2) ◌ֱ, (3) ֱ, (4) ָ, (5) ◌ׁ, (6) ִ, (7) ◌ֶ, (8) ◌ַ, (9) ◌ֹ.

3. To be carefully distinguished in pronunciation are
   1) ֻ ; ◌ֶ ֵ ; ◌ֶ ◌ֲ;
   2) ֹ ŏ, ◌ָ ā; likewise ◌ִ i and ◌ִי ī.

4. A dot *above* the line is ō (*note*); *below* the line it is ū (*pin*).

5. Hebrew is written and pronounced *from right to left.*

6. The plural ending of masculine nouns is ים (im), see אֱלֹהִים, (*literally, Gods*); compare *cherub, cherubim,* and *seraph, seraphim.*

7. אֵת (ēth) is not translatable; it is a sign placed before the direct object of a verb, when that object is definite.

8. The preposition *in* (ב), and the conjunction *and* (ו) are always prefixed to the following word; they are never written separately.

9. When a letter is to be pronounced *twice in succession,* it is written but *once* and a point inserted (see שּׁ) in its bosom.

10. The *letter* of the Definite Article is ה (h).

11. Words, as a rule, are accented on the ultima; those accented on the penult are always so marked.

12. Every syllable begins with a consonant.

Fig. 4. Genesis 1:1 Hebrew text with translation, explanatory notes, and further observations.

3. Recitation-lesson.

General Remark.—Everything in this work depends upon the absolute mastering (1) of the individual words which come up in the lesson, and (2) of the words in their connection in the verse. The following suggestions are offered:

1. Study *one* word at a time: *first*, comparing with the Hebrew form its transliteration and translation; *secondly*, copying it repeatedly until it can be written easily and correctly; *thirdly*, pronouncing it repeatedly until it can be uttered without hesitation.
2. After mastering a new word, go back each time and review all the old words.
3. After mastering all the words of the verse separately, learn, by practicing, to write the entire verse. This is to be done with the translation, *but not with the transliteration*, before the eye. It is not expected, nor even desired, that the verse be committed; but it is *necessary* that, in every case, the student shall be able to write the verse without *the aid of the Hebrew text*.
4. Do not master the transliteration but the *Hebrew text*. No greater mistake can be made than that one, so common, of relying entirely upon the transliteration.

If these directions shall be faithfully carried out, the student will gain, in addition to the knowledge of Hebrew, considerable in the way of mental discipline.

1. Write the *Hebrew* of this verse.
2. Write the *Hebrew* of (1) *God*; (2) *and*; (3) *the-earth*; (4) *in*; (5) *he created*.
3. Write the *English* translation of (1) הַשָּׁמַיִם; (2) וְהָאָרֶץ; (3) וְשָׁמַיִם; (4) שָׁמַיִם.
4. Transliterate, that is, put into English letters: (1) הַשָּׁמַיִם; (2) וְאֵת; (3) בָּרָא.
5. Write in Hebrew letters: (1) hîm; (2) yĭm; (3) rĕts; (4) hā; (5) hăsh.
6. What do you understand to be the force of the word אֵת?
7. What is the difference between the sign which represents ĭ, and that which represents ō or ô?
8. How is the *doubling* of a letter indicated?
9. What is the *letter* of the Definite Article?
10. What is the difference between ָ, ֳ, ֲ and ֱ?

Fig. 5. Exercises for students to submit via correspondence.

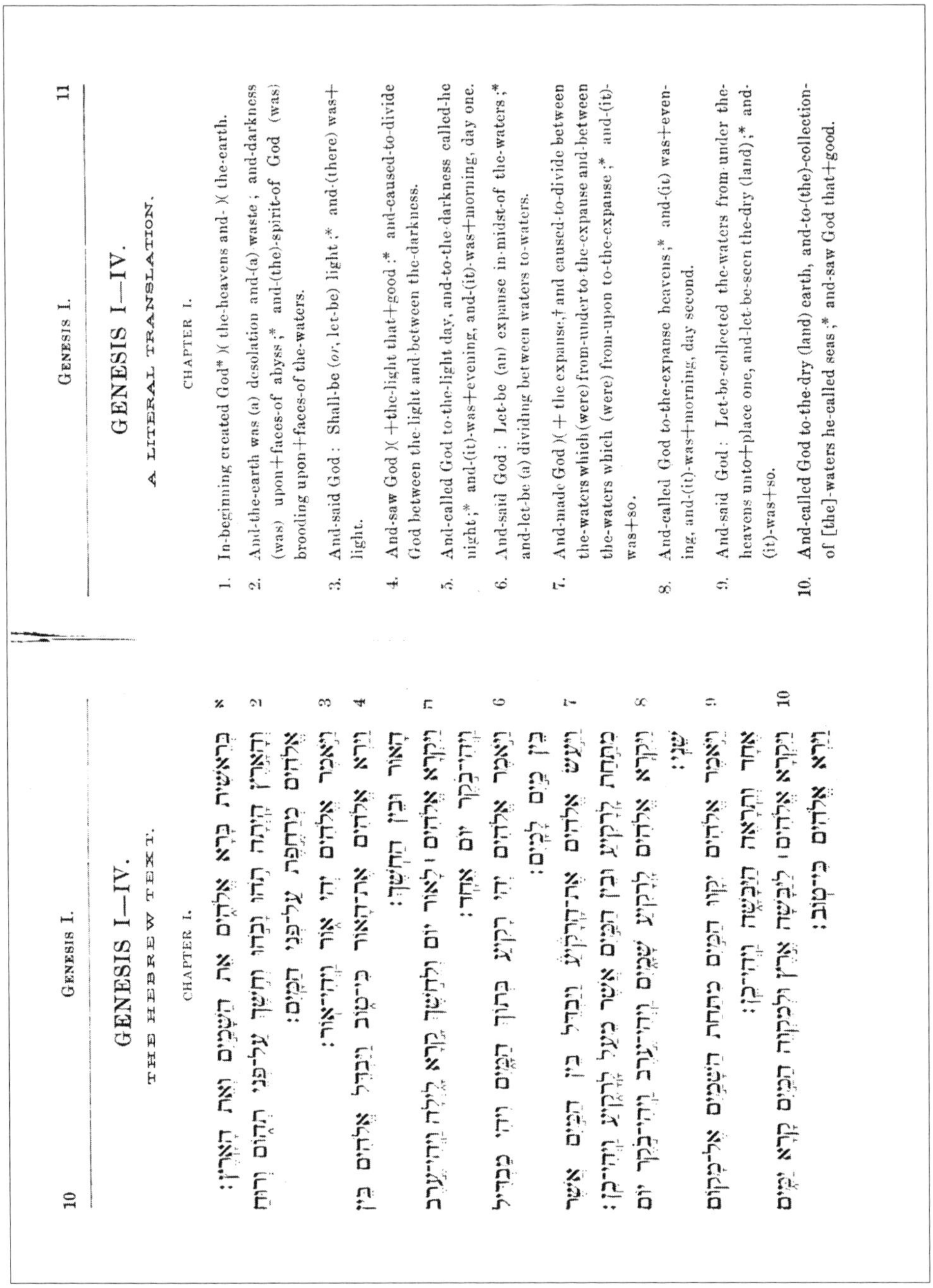

10 Genesis I.

GENESIS I—IV.

THE HEBREW TEXT.

CHAPTER I.

א בראשית ברא אלהים את השמים ואת הארץ׃
2 והארץ היתה תהו ובהו וחשך על־פני תהום ורוח אלהים מרחפת על־פני המים׃
3 ויאמר אלהים יהי אור ויהי־אור׃
4 וירא אלהים את־האור כי־טוב ויבדל אלהים בין האור ובין החשך׃
ה ויקרא אלהים ׀ לאור יום ולחשך קרא לילה ויהי־ערב ויהי־בקר יום אחד׃
6 ויאמר אלהים יהי רקיע בתוך המים ויהי מבדיל בין מים למים׃
7 ויעש אלהים את־הרקיע ויבדל בין המים אשר מתחת לרקיע ובין המים אשר מעל לרקיע ויהי־כן׃
8 ויקרא אלהים לרקיע שמים ויהי־ערב ויהי־בקר יום שני׃
9 ויאמר אלהים יקוו המים מתחת השמים אל־מקום אחד ותראה היבשה ויהי־כן׃
10 ויקרא אלהים ׀ ליבשה ארץ ולמקוה המים קרא ימים וירא אלהים כי־טוב׃

Genesis I. 11

GENESIS I—IV.

A LITERAL TRANSLATION.

CHAPTER I.

1. In-beginning created God*)(the-heavens and-)(the-earth.
2. And-the-earth was (a) desolation and-(a) waste; and-darkness (was) upon+faces-of abyss;* and-(the)-spirit-of God (was) brooding upon+faces-of the-waters.
3. And-said God: Shall-be (*or*, let-be) light;* and-(there) was+light.
4. And-saw God)(+the-light that+good;* and-caused-to-divide God between the-light and-between the-darkness.
5. And-called God to-the-light day, and-to-the-darkness called-he night;* and-(it)-was+evening, and-(it)-was+morning, day one.
6. And-said God: Let-be (an) expanse in-midst-of the-waters;* and-let-be (a) dividing between waters to-waters.
7. And-made God)(+ the expanse,† and caused-to-divide between the-waters which (were) from-under to-the-expanse and-between the-waters which (were) from-upon to-the-expanse;* and-(it)-was+so.
8. And-called God to-the-expanse heavens;* and-(it) was+evening, and-(it)-was+morning, day second.
9. And-said God: Let-be-collected the-waters from-under the-heavens unto+place one, and-let-be-seen the-dry (land);* and-(it)-was+so.
10. And-called God to-the-dry (land) earth, and-to-(the)-collection-of [the]-waters he-called seas;* and-saw God that+good.

Fig. 6. Harper's Manual: facing-page layout of Hebrew and English versions of Genesis.

As can be seen, the whole "inductive method" here is text-centered, with the pupils encountering and at least parroting and trying to use "real biblical Hebrew" from day one—appropriately, of course, the day of the Creation! They thus learn any rules or generalizations about Hebrew in the order in which such features of the language are illustrated by the particulars of usage in the text. Each such usage encountered is paradigmatically embedded in the referenced paragraphs of the *Elements*, in its declensional or conjugational frame, as well as in its frame of syntagmatic particulars, how it co-occurs with other forms in certain phraseological configurations. There is no Saussurean *langue* learned, we might say, outside of its proper (con)text of *parole*; here that context in which instances of forms appear is the very text of Genesis, studied (and indeed memorized with comprehension) verse by verse.

This feature is pervasive. Even Harper's *Hebrew Syntax* itself is organized by a table of contents as a systematic discussion of the syntactic particulars of various kinds of phrase-defining lexical forms, from major (nouns, verbs) to minor (prepositions); note for example sections 14 on "other pronominal expressions" and 15 on the syntax of numerals (see fig. 7). Yet each captioned topic is essentially organized as a set of actual textual examples, each of which is keyed back to the book—chapter—verse loci of the Old Testament, with cautionary remarks on any peculiarities and then a whole set of further textual "references for study" left for the reader to pursue so as to clinch the generalization by relying on the inductive capacity of the student to find the particular phenomenon as classified at the indicated textual locus.

It can be immediately seen that this is essentially a *lexicogrammatical concordance to the original text*. It collects multiple examples in the original text—here the Old Testament—of a given form or type of form, depending on the level of abstraction, and, listing each form or form type, gives us an index to the textual occurrences of prominent examples. In a full concordance the lists would exhaustively include each and every instance of every captioned grammatical form type. Theoretically, at least, were Harper's *Syntax* an exhaustive concordance, if we collected all of the examples tagged by location in the original text, liberating them from under the generalizing rubrics where they are gathered, we should be able painstakingly to reconstruct the text of the Bible like solving a verbal jigsaw puzzle, since every element of every verse will come with its numerical label of place from which it was excerpted. To produce the *Syntax* the original text has been segmented into chunks of form that can be extracted and multiply aggregated. And, collected and gathered in one place, that is, under a descriptive caption such as "Nouns in Con-

14. OTHER PRONOMINAL EXPRESSIONS.

1. *a.* וָאַחְבֵּא[1] *and I hid myself;* וַיֵּחָבֵא[2] *and he hid himself.*

   b. אֲנִי יְהוָה[3] *the Lord himself;* וְהוּא הַיְהוּדִים[4] *the Jews themselves.* וְאֵהוּד עָשָׂה לוֹ חֶרֶב[5] *and Ehud made for himself a sword.* וַתִּקָּחֵהוּ[6] *and she took him up with herself.*

   c. לֹא יָדַעְתִּי נַפְשִׁי[7] *I know not myself* (lit, *my soul*). וַתִּצְחַק שָׂרָה בְּקִרְבָּהּ[8] *and Sarah laughed within herself.*

2. *a.* אִישׁ ... אֶחָיו[9] *and they dreamed . . . each his dream.* לַבֹּקֶר לַבֹּקֶר[10] *every morning;* שְׁנֵי עֹמְרִים לָאִישׁ[11] *two omers for each;* יוֹם בְּיוֹם[12] *in every day;* כָּל־חָי[13] *every one living.*

   b. אַל־יוֹצֵא אִישׁ מִמְּקֹמוֹ[14] *let not any one go forth from his place.* הֲיִפָּלֵא מֵיְהוָה דָּבָר[15] *Is anything too difficult for Yahweh?* כָּל־חֵפֶץ[16] *anything;* כָּל־אֲשֶׁר־לְךָ[17] *anything evil.*

   " כָּל־אֲשֶׁר־לִי [16] *any of Y.'s commandments;* כָּל־אֲשֶׁר־לְךָ[18] *whoever belongs to thee in the city.* כָּל־אֲשֶׁר יַחְפֹּץ[19] *whatever Y. pleases, he does.*

   c. קְחוּ ... מִזִּקְנֵי[20] *take . . . some of the elders of Israel.* מִן־הָעָם[21] *some of the people went out.*

   d. לֹא טוֹב כִּי[22] *it is good for nothing;* לֹא עָשׂוּ מְאוּמָה[23] *nobody takes it to heart;* וְאֵין אִישׁ בָּאֹהֶל[24] *do nothing;* אֵין אִישׁ בַּבַּיִת[25] *nobody shall be in the tent.*

   e. עַם כָּזֶה[26] *such a people;* אִישׁ כָּזֶה[27] *such a man;*
   וְאֵין אִישׁ כָּמוֹהוּ[28] *there were no such locusts as they.*

   f. אֶחָד מִזֶּה וְאֶחָד מִזֶּה[29] *the one on the one side, the other on the other.* וַיַּפְרִידוּ בֵּין שְׁנֵיהֶם[30] *and they separated the one from the other.* לֹא קָרַב זֶה אֶל־זֶה[31] *and the one did not draw near the other.* עִיר בְּעִיר וּמַמְלָכָה בְּמַמְלָכָה[32] *one city against another, one kingdom against another.*

[1] Gen. 3:10. [2] Gen. 3:8. [3] Isa. 7:14. [4] Est. 9:1. [5] Judg. 3:16. [6] 1 Sam. 1:24. [7] Job 9:21. [8] Gen. 18:12. [9] Gen. 40:5. [10] Ex. 16:21. [11] Ex. 16:22. [12] Ps. 7:12. [13] Gen. 3:20. [14] Ex. 16:29. [15] Gen. 18:14. [16] Lev. 4:2. [17] Isa. 56:2. [18] Gen. 19:12. [19] Ps. 135:6. [20] Ex. 17:5. [21] Ex. 16:27. [22] Jer. 13:7. [23] Isa. 57:1. [24] Gen. 19:3. [25] Lev. 16:17. [26] Jer. 5:9. [27] Gen. 41:38. [28] Ex. 10:14. [29] Ex. 17:12. [30] Gen. 13:11. [31] Ex. 14:20. [32] Isa. 19:2.

BY AN INDUCTIVE METHOD.

Certain ideas, expressed in English by means of pronouns, are otherwise expressed in Hebrew. The more important of these are the following:—

1. The *reflexive* pronoun is expressed,

   a. By the Niph'al and Hithpa'ēl stems.

   b. By the personal pronoun of the third person and by pronominal suffixes.

   c. By the use of certain nouns like נֶפֶשׁ, עֶצֶם, עַצְמוֹ (§ 8, 2, *c*), לֵבָב, and לֵב.

2. The *indefinite* pronouns are expressed variously:—

   a. *Each, every,* by כֹּל, or the repetition of a word (§ 3. 1. *c*), or אִישׁ, or כֹּל.

   b. *Any, anyone, anything, whoever, whatever,* by אִישׁ, כֹּל, כֹּל־אֲשֶׁר.

   c. *Some of,* by the preposition מִן *from.*

   d. *Nothing, nobody,* by כֹּל ... לֹא, אִישׁ אֵין, כֹּל ... אֵין (or אַל), לֹא כָל־דָּבָר.

   e. *Such,* by כָּזֶה, כֵּן.

   f. *The one—the other,* by אֶחָד—אֶחָד, אִישׁ—אִישׁ, אִישׁ—אֶת־אִישׁ or אִשָּׁה—אֲחוֹתָהּ, זֶה—זֶה, זֶה—זֶה, or the repetition of a noun.

REFERENCES FOR STUDY.

Gen. 8:9; 22:3; 33:17	1b.
Gen. 9:5; 13:11	27.
Gen. 30:14	2c.
Gen. 29:23	2a.
Ex. 4:9	2a.
Ex. 35:24	2a.
Lev. 5:9	2a.
Lev. 11:32	2b.
Num. 20:19	2c.
Num. 35:22	2b.
Deut. 2:7	2d.
Judg. 6:29	2d.
Judg. 13:23	2c.
1 Sam. 10:3	2f.
2 Sam. 12:1	1b.
1 Kgs. 3:23	2f.
1 Kgs. 10:12	2a.
Isa. 6:3	2a.
Isa. 66:8	2a.
Jer. 7:18	2b.
Jer. 9:3	2d.
Jer. 37:9	1c.
Ezek. 15:3	1b.
Ezek. 34:2	2d.
Eccles. 8:5	2f.
Hab. 2:19	2a.
1 Chron. 9:28	2a.
1 Chron. 17:15	2f.

15. NUMERALS.

1. יוֹם אֶחָד[1] *one day;* תּוֹרָה אַחַת[2] *one law;* יָמִים אֲחָדִים[3] *single days.*

2. *a.* שְׁלֹשֶׁת יָמִים[4] *triad of days* = *three days;* שְׁנֵי הַלֻּחֹת[5] *the two l.*

   b. שֶׁבַע שָׁנִים[6] *seven years;* שִׁבְעַת פָּרִים[7] *seven bullocks.*

[1] Gen. 27:45. [2] Ex. 12:49. [3] Gen. 27:44. [4] Josh. 2:22. [5] Gen. 1:16. [6] Gen. 5:7. [7] Num. 23:1, 29.

Fig. 7. Concordanced exemplification of syntactic forms in Harper's inductive syntax.

struct Case," sets of such chunks of text consist of exemplifications of a single grammatical fact—an inductive generalization—about the language, which thus, stated in the grammatical treatise, indexes (points to) its multiple occurrences in the original text. We might say in the register of philosophy of scientific language, that the intensional statement of the (inductive) generalization is extensionalizable as, realizable as, the original set of textual exemplifications, locatable numerically by chapter and verse, which are theoretically exhaustive in a finite—even if, to believers, inspired!—corpus such as the Bible was believed to be in the 1880s (especially by religious folk).

The concept is exactly the same for Hermann Grassmann's (1809–1877) *Wörterbuch zum Rig-Veda*, originally published in 1873, though the arrangement is based on intensionalization at the word-morphology (rather than syntactic) level, organized into lemmata by grammatical word root rather than by construction type. I recall my humbling sense of unbounded admiration when, as a student in second-year Sanskrit (Vedic), I encountered this incredible work all done by hand in which, as exemplified in figure 8, every declensional or conjugational form of every root in its different forms and senses—including, vacuously, indeclinables—is classified, grouped, and keyed to the place in the standard numbering of the Rigveda by hymn and the poetic line or *śloka* in that hymn where the form occurs. From the data in this work too one can reconstruct the entire Rigvedic corpus up to but not determining the exact order of words in each *śloka* (for which one would have to use the guidance of syntax and metrics).

So the concordance, that indispensable product of and tool for the inductive philology of all the ancient languages, is an intermediate shuffling, a cross-cutting sort of the data of textual occurrences according to particular generalizations over the data—the principles of what we now call the grammar of the language of the text—that permit identification of each specific textual example as an instantiation "in nature," as it were, of multiple intersecting regularities (and some irregularities!) according to which it is formed. Concordances are a meeting point of both President Harper's "inductive method" of language teaching and of Herr Grassmann's textual criticism in the service of Indo-European philology and comparative-historical linguistics—and that of all our other great predecessors of the time. The pedagogical "inductivism" of Harper's Hebrew course is anchored in practice *in precisely the same kind of text artifacts* as the epistemological "inductivism" of high-water neogrammarianism, the crowning achievement of the previous hundred years of linguistics. For the ancient languages in particular, then, the procedures

Fig. 8. Grassmann's Rigvedic morpholexical concordance, by word roots and stems.

by which text, translation, lexicogrammatical concordance, and teaching lessons are used by students inculcate them into the inductive world of philology itself, just as this very world produced such artifacts as the instruments of furthering scholarly induction.

Facts first, principles later. But of course William Dwight Whitney (1827–1894), under whom Harper had studied for his PhD at Yale (1875), had been doing this not only for Sanskrit but for modern languages as well (French, German, English).[6] It seems clear that Harper must have been exposed to the paraphernalia at the heart of the philological program for modern as well as ancient languages when he did his PhD work at Yale (1873–1875), principally under Whitney, who was the great Yankee apostle of the inductive science of language. "It was Whitney," recalled Harper's longtime friend and colleague, the Latinist Charles Chandler, "who had pointed out to him that the Semitic languages were a very promising field for exploitation by an enterprising man, both text-books and methods here and abroad being antiquated, unscientific, and in America notoriously futile."[7] Antiquated and unscientific meant noninductive, of course. This is what Harper undertook to undo with his inductive language courses in Hebrew. The genius here is the reshuffling, the reorganization of all the philological material around the text itself as a stimulus to the process of learning the language, which becomes for the student a recapitulation of philological induction. This was exactly what Harper had been doing in Whitney's introductory and Vedic Sanskrit classes, of course.

I will return to the epistemology of philological induction later but wish now to point out that there was in fact a second strand of inductivism leading to Harper's lessons and to Boas's anthropology. It is the whole tradition of pedagogical inductivism that is, like the scientific, ultimately sprung from the great Baconian instauration and its Continental congeners. As a pedagogical theory, it was vigorously and influentially advocated by Comenius (Jan Komenský, 1592–1670) and taken up as a practical program with extraordinary effect during the late eighteenth and early nineteenth century by Johann Heinrich Pestalozzi (1746–1827), the Swiss educator.[8] Pestalozzi ran several of what we would today call demonstration or "laboratory" schools for young children, in which subjects like natural philosophy, mathematics, and language were induced as knowledge in the young through a kind of step-by-step, prioritized exposure crafted on the basis of the era's developmental theories.

Pestalozzi's ideas influenced generations of reformers as well as designers of curricula, in which the adjective *Pestalozzian* became synonymous with *inductive*. Among his followers were, in the United States, the great

educational reformer Horace Mann (1796–1859), who created the idea of the normal school—that is, the teacher-training college—to create a corps of Pestalozzians, and in Europe such figures as Friedrich Wilhelm August Fröbel (1782–1852), who was central to Prussian elementary educational reform along inductive lines. (I will pick up this story later in reference to Boas, whose mother, Sophie Meyer Boas [1828–1916] started a Fröbel kindergarten in Minden, Westphalia, in 1860.)

After Pestalozzi "inductive" courses for elementary phases of subjects were all the rage. The pedagogy of guided inductive discovery allied a subject taught with the most prestigious of post-Romantic ideas of pedagogy for the epistemological growth of the student; indeed the "inductive sciences"—what we today call the empirical natural sciences—were at the center of nineteenth-century philosophizing about and consideration of the history of science. What is this method like when transferred to languages? It is precisely the encounter with usage itself, as for example texts that stimulate the inductive discovery of the "principles and laws"—grammatical structure—underlying.

Transitioning from Diachrony to Synchrony in the Philological Sciences

Let us focus now on the context of scholarly and scientific work that seemed to attract Boas during his 1885–1886 apprenticeship in Berlin: the enterprise of German comparative philology as the foundation of the study of cultures. The professionalization of this field involved the gradual emergence and Kuhnian "normalizing" of the inductive study of the Indo-European languages and their textual forms, both individually and as members of the inclusive language family, and the study of other languages and their familial relationships by the same methods: Semitic, Finno-Ugric, Dravidian, and so on. Little by little a central factor in the institutionalization of the field among its practitioners was an emerging shared consciousness that such comparative-historical work depended on the facticity of what we now term autonomous phonological change, a.k.a. *Lautgesetz* (sound law).[9] *Lautgesetze* had both an epistemological and an ontological manifestation, not carefully enough distinguished either in the instance or in the later historiographic accounts of the late nineteenth century.

What gradually emerges, then, in the context of German *Sprachforschung* and becomes reflexively obvious to its practitioners around 1875–1880 is the mutual necessity of (1) the ontological presumption of uniformitarian regularity of autonomous "sound change," the great scientific discovery of the era about language history, and (2) the epistemology of "the method of residues," one of the chief modes of "induc-

tive" reasoning set out by all the philosophers of science of the time that involves iterated generalizing inferences over multidimensional or multifactorial sets of data.[10] Whether operating in the realm of a single language or across multiple languages, in this "comparative" approach to etymological investigation one gathers textual examples, and one segments and sifts them by postulating a generalization that would apply to all the forms, thus hypothesized to be members of a class by their common class characteristic(s). The generalization for historians of language is achieved in two phases. First is remarked a particular "correspondence of form" across several languages or across stages of a single language in which there is observed recurrent and systematically equivalent (if not same) features. In turn, second, each such correspondence set is referred to a postulated earlier form that must have altered under sound laws specific to each of the corresponding languages or stages, producing, it would appear, the multiple attested forms gathered and systematized as a correspondence set.

Note that by following this logic iteratively in applying the inductive method of residues to its conclusion, exceptions under one pass of reconstructive generalizing become special cases, the exceptionless regularity of which at their own, more circumscribed level one can come to understand when the exceptions too are segmented and sifted so as to be seen as their own class or category. (Think of Grassmann's Law of de-aspirating the first of two aspirate stops in syllabic sequence in Indo-European roots [*DH . . . DH . . . > D . . . DH . . .] that explains certain otherwise glaring exceptions to Grimm's Law regularities of how Indo-European stop types are realized in Germanic; or Verner's Law of the apparently double shift of manner of articulation of Indo-European stop consonants that follow the word stress in Germanic [* . . . V′T . . . > . . . V′D . . .], rather than the one predicted by Grimm's Law [*T > Θ]. Each of the "laws" covering a comparative residue of forms, it was concluded, must have been sound changes that took place before the more general and unrestricted sound change, in effect making the latter inapplicable to forms now altered in their shapes. Leonard Bloomfield's (1887–1949) admiring account of these generalizations is classic as a historiographic conflation of the logic of the method of residues with the actual history of discovery by Rask and Grimm, Grassmann, and Verner.)[11] This mutual implication of the covering-law regularity of sound change and the logical method of residues is what came to acute reflexive consciousness in pronouncements by August Leskien (1840–1916), Wilhelm Osthoff (1847–1909), and Karl Brugmann (1849–1919) during the 1870s as they formulated their dicta about method and theory.

Hence two important corollary investigations emerged both for neogrammarians and for their critics to give support (or not) to the ontological presumption that *Lautgesetze*, "sound laws," posited as applying in chronological order to get from original stage *1* to later stage *n* in the historical trajectory of a linguistic form passed on over time, should be truly "law"-like, *Ausnahmslos* (exceptionless); that is, that such "laws" should apply purely as a function of the sonic shape of linguistic forms—and independent of anything about their meaning, grammatical function, or salience to the community of users of the words or expressions—at the moment at which a change of sonic shape occurs in the community.

Studying living, especially "exotic" languages, it was realized, may reveal the phonetic and other tendencies in pronunciation when various sounds are produced and heard in rapid succession. Thus we might investigate the slight perturbations of the sonic realization of particular sounds when they occur in words in sequence with other sounds, if we had access to laboratory instruments for making repeated measurements of the phonetic characteristics of speech as physiologically articulated, physically transmitted, and/or psycho-acoustically perceived. Such phenomena, it was thought, when demonstrated to be statistically robust, constitute a realm of microdiachrony, the leading edges of precisely the kind of inductively inferred changes that were posited to have occurred in the undocumented, prehistoric past of the ancient languages. For example, a target *k* sound in English is inevitably produced slightly differently, and sounds generally different to an auditor, when it is followed by an *i* sound as compared to when it is followed by an *a* sound; the *k* is pronounced with a momentary closure of the articulators inevitably somewhat farther forward in the mouth before *i*. Sure enough, among the sound laws of the world's linguistic (pre)histories are many historical cases of so-called palatalization and even accompanying affrication of velar sounds like *k* or *g*, when they earlier preceded high and front vowels like *i* and *e*, resulting in sound segments with more forward places of closure, as in *ky* or *č* (tsh), *gy* or *ǰ* (dzh) in historically later forms deriving from earlier ones with *k* or *g*.

Such laboratory investigations seemed to support the neogrammarian position of physico-physiologically motivated sound change so long as one could depend on having a firm sense of the difference between what we may pretheoretically call a "target sound" with respect to which some large number *n* of trial pronunciations or transmissions or perceptions of speech can be grouped for relevant measurement and statistical analysis. But the really difficult question, one the neogrammarians were hard-pressed to face, is: How does one—inductively!—*find* the units of "sound"

of exotic, nonstandardized and only oral-aural, not graphic, exemplars of Indo-European languages, let alone those of languages of non-European peoples in small language communities that have no experience of an orthographically fixed register? In the ancient languages philologists could simply rely on the apparent *Buchstaben* (letters) of the alphabetic graphic modes of inscription or their syllabary-script equivalents. Transcriptional work from such syllabaries on several Asian languages such as Sanskrit had, as well, "reduced" them (in the phrase of the day) to representation in alphabetic letters. But notice how this practical matter—essentially inventing an alphabetic script for the "true" or "real" sounds—presents a whole new epistemological problem for contemporary, "living" linguistic phenomena in their spoken manifestation. Can we find help in achieving what we now term the "phonemicization" of a sound system and its representation in alphabetic graphic signs through the methods of philology as it had been constituted—to be sure, for comparative-historical investigation—as an inductive science?

Notice, then, what was at issue in the last quarter of the nineteenth century. As an inductive intellectual project, neogrammarianism—and with it nineteenth-century linguistics more generally, note—was sent, respectively, to the natural science laboratories of the psychophysicist and the physiologist to investigate the phenomenon of "sound" in people's production and reception of language, and to the ethnologist's and folklorist's field, where languages lived in the spoken actualities of discursive communication. In short, the task of shoring up the foundations of linguistic theory, notwithstanding its historical focus on reconstruction and classification in the heyday of neogrammarianism, fell to the phonetician and to the field worker. We must observe that in the history of linguistics, it has been the second, the empirical fieldwork track seeking out and describing "exotic" languages such as those of the erstwhile colonial hinterlands of Asia and of the Indigenous Americas, that led to synchronic descriptive and structural linguistics as we know it, built on continuity of methods that essentially survive the transition. The first, the instrumentally refined micromeasurement of articulated and audible phonetic sound for its own sake, was eventually provided a new raison d'être once it had been reincorporated in the framework of structural linguistics, that is, when statistical variation could be seen through the ontological perspective that identified "target sounds" with the phoneme segments of phonological theory. This breakthrough ontological reimagination of what in fact *are* the "sounds" of languages thus played the central role in the birth of a new kind of inductivist linguis-

tics in which phonetics—now in relation to phonology or phonemics—can take its place in relation to language structure.

Boas was unavoidably drawn into the intellectual field of this transition from comparative-historical philology to descriptive-structural linguistics as a researcher of the Indigenous languages and cultures of North America. And yet, given his background in laboratory psychophysics and statistics, he clearly understood the problem of variation-around-means in phonetic space, presented even by the practical problem of transcribing texts and other linguistic material in the field rather than measuring their parameters in the lab. It turned out that he was in a privileged position with respect to the disciplinary transition, since the conceptual breakthrough into synchrony integrally depended on the continued focus on the plane of phonology, the sound structure of language and its perceptible matrix in sonic materiality, and on the extraordinary continuity of the methods for its study across such profound metatheoretical refocusing of what in fact was the object of explanation and generalization in philological science.[12]

The transition culminated in his intellectual progeny dealing with living languages, those who worked out the ontology and epistemology of the phoneme, for them the foundational scientific entity of modern linguistics as a science of implicit cognitive norms in a community of speakers, as Bloomfield noted in his commentary of 1927, "On Recent Work." By this time the substantive problem of the (pre)historical provenance and chronological development of the "sounds" of the words in languages with written records had morphed into the substantive problem of what, precisely, *are* the "sounds" of a given language and how they are organized in language in structures of mutual relationships. When we examine the work of the key figures of the Boasian tradition, we can observe that across the transition of theoretical focus from diachronic comparative philology to synchronic descriptive-structural linguistics *precisely the same methods carried over to create epistemologically corresponding but ontologically different theoretical entities*. Scientific practices about etymological sounds become those concerning phonemic segments; phonetic changes or "sound laws" thus become structural (morpho)phonological rules; earlier versus later forms becomes "inner/organic" versus "outer/inorganic"; chronological order of occurrence of changes becomes logical order of application of rules; and so on. (Notice, please, the Haeckelesque recapitulationism in all this in which synchronic derivation by ordered rules must, of necessity, resemble historical provenance via chronologically ordered sound changes.)[13]

Boas Assimilated Specifically Philological Inductivism

Let us return to Boas's professional development. As historical studies by my late colleague George Stocking, Regna Darnell, and others have discussed, Boas was not trained in any real sense in anthropology; his university background was in mathematics, physics, philosophy, and geography.[14] His biographer Douglas Cole makes clear the personal reasons why he attended an inferior university, Kiel, for his 1881 doctorate.[15] There, however, he came under the influence not only of the geographer Theobald Fischer (1846–1910) but also of a neo-Kantian and Helmholtz and Steinthal student, the philosopher Benno Erdmann (1851–1921), just seven years older than Boas, whose work, among other things, focused on epistemological aspects of logic and inductive science. This affiliation is central, it seems to me, in Boas's turn from physics to psychophysics to his key epistemological position on what we might term, with him—echoing Alexander von Humboldt—the "cosmographic" nature of culture, a phenomenon of the human mind in sociohistorical context. Retrospectively we see that this cultural psychology was initially articulated in a paper titled "On Alternating Sounds," which situates his thought at the intersection of phonetics and fieldwork. It is a paper aimed directly at the work and linguistic views of Major John Wesley Powell (1834–1902), head of the Smithsonian Bureau of American Ethnology, and others whose views of American Native languages were couched in a widely held social evolutionary framework on language and "primitive mentality" that, echoing others, Powell laid out in his *Introduction to the Study of Indian Languages*.

The critical problem Boas takes up is how to ensure the accurate, inductive scientific discernment of the sound system—and hence the proper means of transcribing and spelling—of languages such as the exotic-sounding ones of the North American Arctic and Northwest Coast, on which he had already begun to work in the field in 1886. In an evolutionary view of the universal history of the human mind, Powell and others took their own reflexive consciousness of Indo-European sounds, as written alphabetically, as the endpoint of an evolutionary development of clear mental categories out of primitive confusion. They reported hearing the sound categories of other languages as "fluctuating" or "alternating" across categorical boundaries of their own distinct sound types, or as "compounded," a conflation of two or more of these "distinct" sounds. This was seen to be consistent with the putative lack of abstraction and lack of fixity of the categories of so-called primitive thought.

In this paper, widely commented upon by a range of writers from Stocking to Rulon Wells and Michael Mackert, the solution that Boas

proposes relativizes the very perception of the sounds of a language and thus, we can infer, proposes a sociocultural psychology of sound.[16] He points to what we now term the underlying phonological system of any perceiver's—and would-be transcriber's—language as a biasing filter on the perception of intensional category boundaries through which, in processing a spoken language signal, one comes to identify the elements in the sound stream one hears as segments of this or that particular type, notwithstanding statistical variance of tokens, and thus allowing recognition of meaningful units like words. Such a system of categories is in essence a structure of (Herbartian) *apperceptional norms* for the special psychophysics of language, relative to which a speaker has been trained to hear not only his or her language, but—key to the *mis*perception of the phonologies of so-called primitive languages—other languages as well, without special training to overcome the bias.

And as goes phonology, so also categories coded in grammaticosemantic forms of the higher, meaning-bearing planes of language. You can see the epistemological—and ultimately ontological—revolution that this implies for linguistics as an inductive, generalizing and comparative science. Suddenly we know that mere phonetic form, a physical fact, is not the proper framework for the determination of what in the spoken/ heard stream of the signals of language count as the "sounds," just as the most accurate and painstaking scientific descriptive appreciation of mere physical phenomena of experience in all their statistical variation is not the useful framework for determining how grammatical categories are associated with our ability to pick out an infinite number of new experiences in the world. A stunning analogical, inductive transfer, this, from Boas's cumulated research experience and training in his increasingly psychologically oriented fields of study—not, however, from philological training as such, and surely not from having encountered Heymann Steinthal (1823–1899) while an assistant at the Königliches Museum für Völkerkunde in Berlin in 1885–1886.[17]

This relativistic ontology emerged early in Boas's own scholarly practice of investigating languages and cultures in the field; in the view of his Columbia students, widely repeated, it seemed to be linked essentially to his method of work, with ontology and epistemology a seamless whole. Yet his method turns out to be precisely assimilated from the philological inductivism that I have already described as convergent in both of the realms of language pedagogy and comparative-historical linguistic research. We have only to look at examples of the Boasian published corpus to realize that his anthropological linguistics is a philology of the unlettered, the practice of the inductive science of language of the times

transferred to the languages of North America. In the *Handbook of American Indian Languages*, the first volume of which appeared in 1911, each grammatical sketch, done up in numbered and captioned sections, is followed by a text; here figure 9 is the sample Kathlamet dialect text from Boas's own "Chinook" sketch. Observe the apparatus: an interlinear translation of a word-by-word close rendition, with the fluent and idiomatic translation reserved for distinct printing; superscript-indexed notes to the text, giving the analysis of the elements of each word as it occurs in the published text, together with explanations keyed to the general statements that apply from the sections of the grammar. Haven't we seen this before, in the teaching materials of Harper in relation to the philological inductivism of Whitney, Grassmann, and others? But where did Boas learn this? Surely he did not invent, or reinvent, philological inductivism himself.

He might well have read various works in the realm of philology; for example he makes reference to Richard Lepsius (1810–1884) in some of his explanations of his use of phonetic signs, and Steinthal is, to be sure, referred to, but only in later, general writings. But it is the specific philological inductivism common to all serious Indo-European and nearby linguistic research that is so startling in this autodidact. Here are some considerations to pinpoint the historical connections.

First, that Boas was committed, almost religiously, to inductive science is something that appears in his youthful letters to family and friends and is part of the multigenerational commentaries of all of his students and their interlocutors.[18] There is no question but that the patient gathering of facts of whatever sort—in language, of course, in the form of spoken word forms and texts—must for Boas be the starting point for all anthropological research. Hence his publication of hundreds of pages in Kwak'wala (Kwakiutl) not only of "mythology" but of directions for preparing foodstuffs, for engaging in certain daily craft activities, and so on, that his critics have long pointed to as a sign of a disordered—even absent—ethnographic sensibility. Boas truly believed as well that the anthropologist ("ethnologist") is the culture historian on behalf of peoples without such a scholarly tradition in the Western sense—anthropology as the philology of the oppressed. As noted earlier, for Boas the foundation of culture history is composed of great bodies of texts and other art forms, precisely the orientation of the nineteenth-century philologists and museum curators of the great, writing-based "civilizational" cultures so central to European, and especially German, scholarship.

But Boas came to operationalize this position in his own linguistic and ethnographic work long before he articulated it as a general conceptualization of ethnology as such (see note 1). Looking to reconstruct the

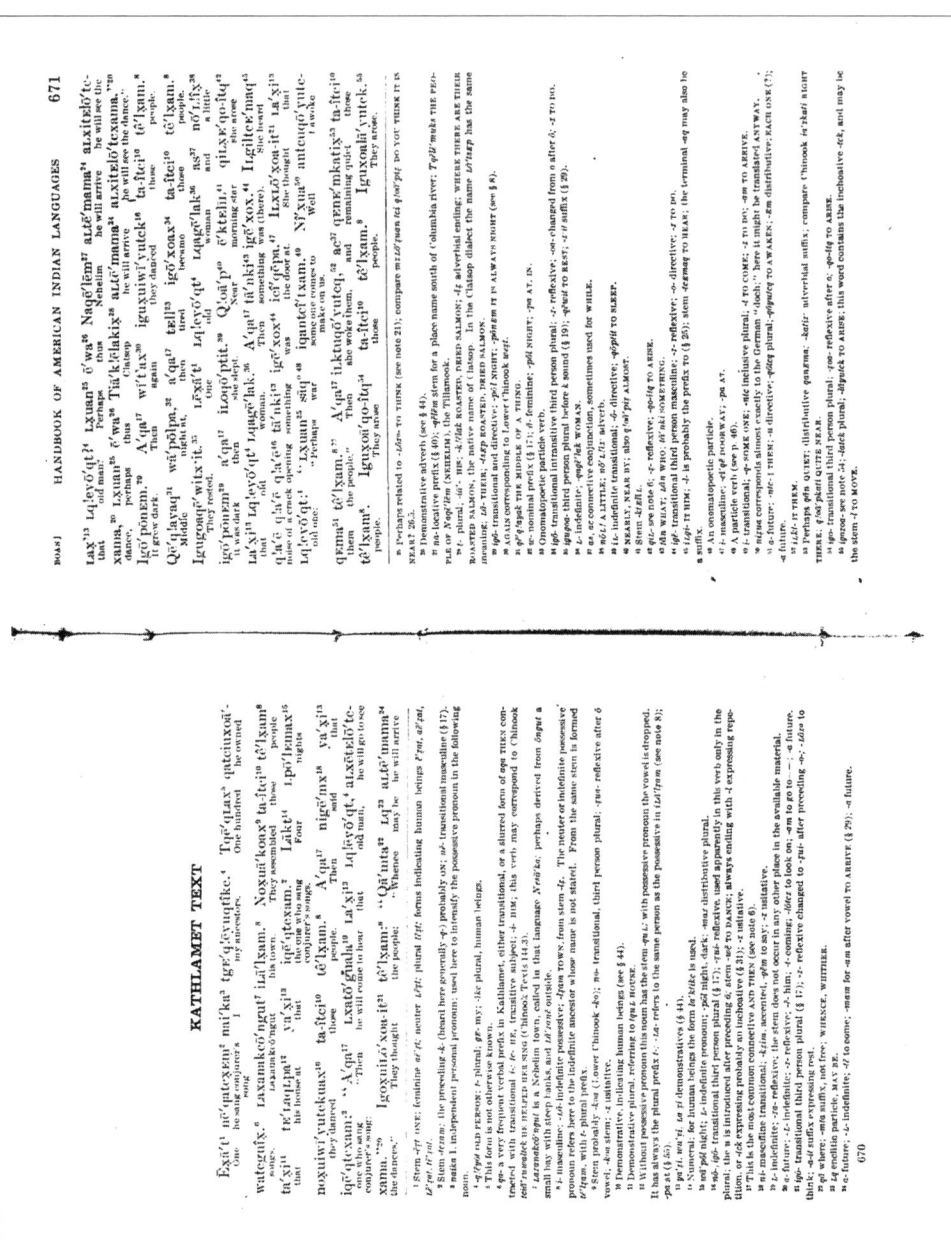

Fig. 9. Kathlamet (Chinookan) text with notes keyed to grammatical sketch, from Boas's "Chinook" grammatical sketch, in Franz Boas, ed., *Handbook of American Indian Languages*, part 1, 559–677, Bureau of American Ethnology, Bulletin 40 (Washington DC: Government Printing Office, 1911), 670–71.

chronology of his practice, we can be guided by the manuscript evidence that survives. The first thing one notes is that in the surviving scientific materials from his 1883–1884 fieldwork among the Inuit of Baffin Island, other than maps in the National Anthropological Archives there is some text material in the American Philosophical Society on loose sheets, many of which appear to have been removed from notebooks.[19] Several of these are the texts of songs that Boas later published in the *Journal of American Folklore*.[20] Some of the material matches exemplary small texts that eventually appeared in his monographic presentations, such as "The Central Eskimo," an accompanying paper in the *Sixth Annual Report* of the Bureau of American Ethnology (BAE) that, in a letter of July 27, 1886, Boas proposed personally to deliver to Major Powell, its first director.[21] But none of the material is systematically treated in a philological manner such as I have been discussing. Indeed I will suggest later how this material underwent "philologizing" in the hands of a master.

When, by contrast, we examine the earliest Northwest Coast field notebooks thus far available in the American Philosophical Society collection, in particular notebook no. 1, beginning on September 18, 1886 (through October 3), a field trip undertaken immediately after the delivery of the Eskimo manuscript to the BAE, the layout is already designed for this philological linguistic intervention: beginning on page 4 facing pages of recto Tsimshian text with interlinear English and German, and verso keyed notes with contrastive vocabulary of semantic sets, paradigmatic and derivational material, and so on that pinpoint each form at that point needing elaboration for the researcher. Thus the text beginning on page 5 opens as follows:

Tlkuanáax tlkuótlka šimójit Tlánila
Little girl child chief only

And on page 4 is found explanatory paradigmatic material to help segment and gloss the Tsimshian forms in the text, for example:

Tlkuótlkōt my child
Tlkuótlkatkaa his child

and so forth. It is as though Boas too, like Harper, had been seated *zu Füße Whitneys*, learning the philologically sound way of taking down primary cultural documents for later interlinear publication, concordancing, sifting into grammar and lexicon, and so on. It is particularly interesting in these earliest eight philologically arranged notebooks, recording work on

various field trips from 1886 through 1889, that Boas clearly distinguishes texts for dictation and full apparatus and other systematic linguistic and ethnographic material—seemingly everything from vocabulary elicitation to place-names to current events and experiences of the person dictating to explanations of customs mentioned in the texts. These other materials are taken down in shorthand, sometimes interspersed with longhand English or German (clues as to what was being talked about at that point). There is, then, a kind of connoisseurship that dictates Boas's differentiation of texts like "myths" and "tales," worthy of full philological treatment, and all this other ethnographic material that, it must be noted, would indeed also have provided "the native's point of view" on contemporary cultural experience.

What is important to observe in Boas's mature treatment is his systematic absorption of the texts-to-concordance-to-lexicon-and-grammar methods of working up his language material. The Chinookan notebooks now in the American Philosophical Society, with their pages numbered, are referenced by number both in the lexicon-concordance ledgers sorted by word roots and semantic fields now in the Manuscripts and Archives Division of the Columbia University Libraries, and in the slip-file lexicon in the National Anthropological Archives. As well the very notebook pages of text, written for the most part in regular pencil, are overwritten with colored pencil indications of which page and line of the printed versions correspond to every stretch of text in the notebooks.[22] The concordances and lexicons too show dual numbering systems, as though a reference to the notebooks, when superseded by the edited, printed version, was itself now superseded as Boas thought of future publication of these worked-up materials as part of a complete philological suite of documentary works—texts, grammar, lexicon, interpretative thematic studies. While, to be sure, not all of Boas's field materials got to have the full elaboration of philological treatment, the various stages of the process in which we find each of the respective ethnographic and linguistic corpora show that his goal was similar even where, in his later career, he gave primary documents to a student or colleague to continue the scholarly work.

To be sure, the publication of texts as such in this philologically suitable style had already been presented as part of Major Powell's paper accompanying his *First Annual Report* (for 1879–1980) of the Bureau of Ethnology, "Illustration of the Method of Recording Indian Languages," reprinting textual materials by A. S. Gatchet, J. O. Dorsey, and S. R. Riggs previously published in the *Contributions to North American Ethnology*, while Powell was still connected to the U.S. Geological Survey. Observe the illustrative format in figure 10, with its interlinear original and trans-

lation, followed by explanatory and elaborating notes keyed to the lines of the original text and by an idiomatic running translation into English. This paper was probably not available to Boas when he undertook his first field trip from Germany, and had it become available afterward when he traveled to the United States, it is certainly not reflected in any of his published ethnographic material on that fieldwork, not even in the Bureau's publication of his report, in process from summer 1886 to its appearance in 1888. Nor can the model of this method of printing text material by itself stimulate his full philological enterprise as described earlier.

A second consideration in Boas's inductivist philological orientation is this: Boas may have become familiar with specifically linguistic pedagogical inductivism from inductive study of Latin and Greek languages in his youth at the Minden Gymnasium, a school then highly influenced by Pestalozzian pedagogical technique through its late former director, Siegmund Imanuel (1792–1847). One would have to explore the specific texts in the curriculum at that time, and perhaps there are some Boas juvenilia as yet unexamined that reveal how he was exposed to the study of languages, in which he apparently did not excel![23] But that would still not explain why his Baffin Island textual material is rather ad hoc in its treatment and why, at the precise moment he undertakes his Northwest Coast work, it is regimented and organized by a clear philological methodology.

What, I argue, is a third and more convincing source of Boas's transformation into a philological scientist of language and culture is his immersion in 1885–1886 in the milieus of philologically trained ethnologists and folklorists. For example, in respect of the Inuktitut language textual material from his earliest fieldwork in Baffin Island in 1883–1884, we can observe his publications after "The Central Eskimo" evolving under the influence of his collaborator, Hinrich Rink (1819–1893). Rink was a high-ranking Danish colonial official in Greenland, a geologist by training (PhD Kiel, 1844), whose expertise on Greenland included long-term interest in the linguistics of Greenlandic and of the dialectology and narrative expression of the Inuit peoples. He was interested in the Baffin Island correspondents in language and mythology that Boas could provide after his explorations there. To judge from the extensive correspondence and enclosures of material that Boas initiated in November 1884,[24] it was Rink who put many of Boas's early published texts into canonical philological shape with interlinear translation, linguistic and dialectological explanatory notes, and so on, Boas supplying cultural commentary on the significance of the texts (see figs. 11 and 12). Illustrated here are pages that come from the *Journal of American Folklore* published in 1889, but the influence was several years earlier.

582   METHOD OF RECORDING INDIAN LANGUAGES.

ě′di a¢á-biamá.   Kĭ ecaⁿ′-qtci ahí-biamá.   Pĭäjĭ ckáxe.   Eátaⁿ égaⁿ
there went, they say.   And near very ar- they say.   Bad you did.   Why so
                                  rived

ckáxe ă.   Ĕ′di gí-adaⁿ′ iⁿ′¢ická-gă hă, á-biamá miⁿ′ aká.   Mactciñ′ge
you did ?   Hither come and for me untie it , said, they say sun the sub.   Rabbit

3 aká ě′di a¢á-bi ctěwaⁿ′ naⁿ′pa-bi egaⁿ′ hébe ĭhe a¢é-hnaⁿ′-biamá.   Kĭ
the there went they notwith- feared they having partly passed went habitu- they say.   And
sub.   say standing   by.   ally

ɥu′ě′ a¢á-bi egaⁿ′ mása-biamá man′dě-ɥaⁿ ¢aⁿ′.   Gañ′ki miⁿ′ ¢aⁿ maⁿ′-
rushed went they having cut with they say bow string the ob.   And sun the on
             a knife   cv. ob.

ciáha áia¢a-biamá.   Kĭ mactciñ′ge aká ábáɥu hiⁿ′ názi-biamá
high had gone, they say. And   Rabbit   the sub. space bet. hair the ob. burnt they say
                                          the shoulders   yellow

6 ánakadá-bi egaⁿ′. (Mactciñ′ge amá akí-biamá.)   Ítctci+, ɥaⁿhá,
it was hot they having.   (Rabbit   the   reached home,   Itctci+!!   grand-
on it say   mv. sub.   they say.)   mother,

ná¢iñgě-qti-maⁿ′ hă, á-biamá.   Ṭúcpa¢aⁿ+, iⁿ′na¢iñgě′-qti-maⁿ′ eskaⁿ+,
burnt to very I am .   said, they say.   Grandchild!!   burnt to nothing very I am   I think,
nothing   for me

á-biamá.   Cetaⁿ′.
said, they say.   So far.

NOTES.

581. 1. Mactciñge, the Rabbit, or Si¢e-makaⁿ (meaning uncertain), is the hero of numerous myths of several tribes. He is the deliverer of mankind from different tyrants. One of his opponents is Ictinike, the maker of this world, according to the Iowas. The Rabbit's grandmother is Mother Earth, who calls mankind her children.

581, 7. a¢ai te aⁿ. The conclusion of this sentence seems odd to the collector, but its translation given with this myth is that furnished by the Indian informant.

581, 12. haⁿ+egaⁿtcě-qtci, "ve--ry early in the morning." The prolongation of the first syllable adds to the force of the adverb "qtci," very.

582, 3. hebe ihe a¢e-hnaⁿ-biama. The Rabbit tried to obey the Sun; but each time that he attempted it, he was so much afraid of him that he passed by a little to one side. He could not go directly to him.

582, 4. 5. maⁿciaha aia¢a-biama. When the Rabbit rushed forward with bowed head, and cut the bow-string, the Sun's departure was so rapid that "he had *already* gone on high."

ABBREVIATIONS USED IN THIS MYTH.

cv.	curvilinear.	sub.	subject.
mv.	moving.	ob.	object.
st.	sitting.		

TRANSLATION.

Once upon a time the Rabbit dwelt in a lodge with no one but his grandmother. And it was his custom to go hunting very early in the morning. No matter how early in the morning he went, a person with

Fig. 10. J. Owen Dorsey's rendering of Francis La Flèche's Omaha text, "How Rabbit Caught the Sun in a Trap," illustrating interlinear, notes, and running translation. BAE-AR 1.582.

expedition to Frobisher Bay, without any additions. It is, on the other hand, entirely in accord with known facts, that the report of the advent of the whites coming from beyond the sea should be confounded with an old legend treating of a tribe of this kind, and it is easily understood how such a legend spread from one tribe to the other. It is worth remarking, that the song given above does not refer to the whites expressly, although it is understood that "the little things" the children make are the whites.

The fuller account of the tradition as given above shows a marked resemblance to the Sedna legend, which I have treated at another place (Petermann's "Mittheilungen," 1887, p. 303). Evidently the story of the transformation of her fingers into sea animals is the same in both. Petitot's tale also indicates a certain connection between the legend of the sea animals and of the whites.

It would be of the greatest interest to know the version in which this legend is told in Alaska, as it would probably give a clue to its history, more particularly to the question, how the legend came to be applied to the whites.

We give here the text of the Sedna legend: —

SEDNALO[1] QAXODLULO.[1]
SEDNOR AND THE FULMAR.

Nautaima   Uinigumissuitoq?[2]   Qajarmut[3]   kangenut[4]   audlirtoq.
Where then   She who never would marry?   In a kayok   to the mainland   going off.

Sikoqa'ngenut[5]   ikurika'.[6]   Takuvigit   ijika,[7]   takuvigit?
Over the ice   crossed.   Doest thou see   my eyes,   Doest thou see them?

ia ha ha ha ha!
ia ha ha ha ha!

Tupirmut   itelingmut[8]   aidniedliranuk[9]   qietaronivik.[10]   Angutā'
To a tent   of ragged skins   as he had brought her   crying.   Her father

angninga   umiarmut   tikitoq.   Paningminik   aitirtoq.[11]   Umiarmut
her elder brother   in a boat   coming.   His daughter   going for.   In the boat

paninga   ikivoq.   Uinga[12]   qaxodluk   qiessivoq.   Qaxodluk
his daughter   embarked.   Her husband   the fulmar   cried.   The fulmar

oxapoq: agartsorutika[13]   takuleka   taimaitjut   ijingit
says: my means for transforming   let me see them   being thus   the eyes

takudnejukpat.   Tupirmut   angiqatut[14]   qaxodluk   madlilirpoq.
they see once more (?).   To the tent   going home   the fulmar   followed.

Anure   agsualuk   kanipoq;   umiavat[15]   kanipoq.   Panine
Wind   very strong   was near;   they were wrecked   nearly.   His daughter

singipa.   Umiarmut   igdliuktut[16]   umiarmut   ajeqpurpoq.[17]
he pushed into the sea.   To the boat   on both sides   to the boat   she clings.

Savingmut   anauva: aqbirit[18]   puiva.[19]   Ate'dlo   anauva: ugjuk
With a knife   he struck her: whales   emerged.   Again   he struck her: a thongseal

puiva.   Atedlo   anauva: netiq   puiva.   Tamarme[20]   ajeqpurpa
emerged.   Again   he struck her: a fiord seal   emerged.   Her whole body   she leaned:

Fig. 11. Boas's text of "Sednalo Qaxodlulo" as published in Hinrich Rink and Franz Boas, "Eskimo Tales and Songs," *Journal of American Folklore* 2.5 (1889): 127–28.

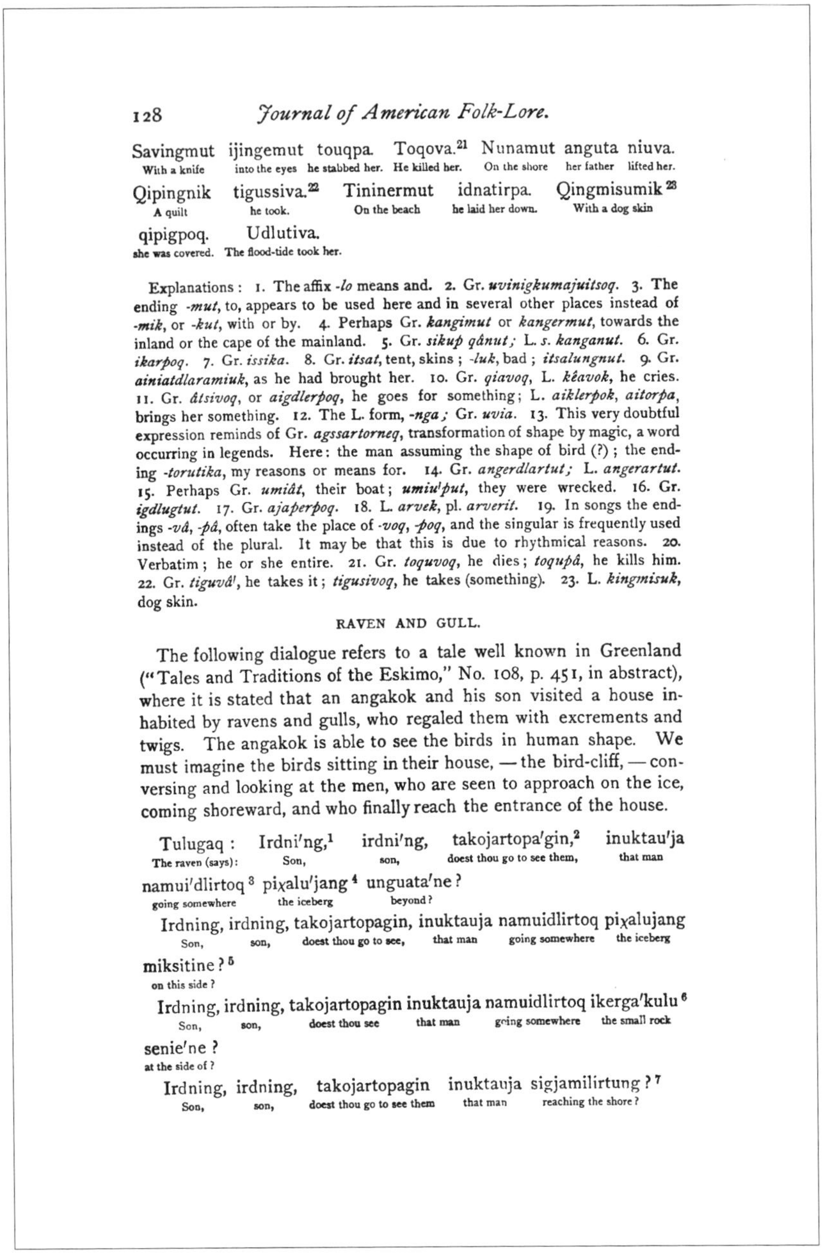

Savingmut ijingemut touqpa. Toqova.²¹ Nunamut anguta niuva.
With a knife into the eyes he stabbed her. He killed her. On the shore her father lifted her.

Qipingnik tigussiva.²² Tininermut idnatirpa. Qingmisumik²³
A quilt he took. On the beach he laid her down. With a dog skin

qipigpoq. Udlutiva.
she was covered. The flood-tide took her.

Explanations: 1. The affix -*lo* means and. 2. Gr. *uvinigkumajuitsoq*. 3. The ending -*mut*, to, appears to be used here and in several other places instead of -*mik*, or -*kut*, with or by. 4. Perhaps Gr. *kangimut* or *kangermut*, towards the inland or the cape of the mainland. 5. Gr. *sikup qánut;* L. *s. kanganut*. 6. Gr. *ikarpoq*. 7. Gr. *issika*. 8. Gr. *itsat*, tent, skins; -*luk*, bad; *itsalungnut*. 9. Gr. *ainiatdlaramiuk*, as he had brought her. 10. Gr. *qiavoq*, L. *kěavok*, he cries. 11. Gr. *átsivoq*, or *aigdlerpoq*, he goes for something; L. *aiklerpok, aitorpa*, brings her something. 12. The L. form, -*nga;* Gr. *uvia*. 13. This very doubtful expression reminds of Gr. *agssartorneq*, transformation of shape by magic, a word occurring in legends. Here (?): the man assuming the shape of bird (?); the ending -*torutika*, my reasons or means for. 14. Gr. *angerdlartut;* L. *angerartut*. 15. Perhaps Gr. *umiát*, their boat; *umiu'put*, they were wrecked. 16. Gr. *igdlugtut*. 17. Gr. *ajaperpoq*. 18. L. *arvek*, pl. *arverit*. 19. In songs the endings -*vá*, -*pá*, often take the place of -*voq*, -*poq*, and the singular is frequently used instead of the plural. It may be that this is due to rhythmical reasons. 20. Verbatim; he or she entire. 21. Gr. *toquvoq*, he dies; *toqupá*, he kills him. 22. Gr. *tiguvá'*, he takes it; *tigusivoq*, he takes (something). 23. L. *kingmisuk*, dog skin.

RAVEN AND GULL.

The following dialogue refers to a tale well known in Greenland ("Tales and Traditions of the Eskimo," No. 108, p. 451, in abstract), where it is stated that an angakok and his son visited a house inhabited by ravens and gulls, who regaled them with excrements and twigs. The angakok is able to see the birds in human shape. We must imagine the birds sitting in their house, — the bird-cliff, — conversing and looking at the men, who are seen to approach on the ice, coming shoreward, and who finally reach the entrance of the house.

Tulugaq: Irdni'ng,¹ irdni'ng, takojartopa'gin,² inuktau'ja
The raven (says): Son, son, doest thou go to see them, that man

namui'dlirtoq³ pixalu'jang⁴ unguata'ne?
going somewhere the iceberg beyond?

Irdning, irdning, takojartopagin, inuktauja namuidlirtoq pixalujang
Son, son, doest thou go to see, that man going somewhere the iceberg

miksitine?⁵
on this side?

Irdning, irdning, takojartopagin inuktauja namuidlirtoq ikerga'kulu⁶
Son, son, doest thou see that man going somewhere the small rock

senie'ne?
at the side of?

Irdning, irdning, takojartopagin inuktauja sigjamilirtung?⁷
Son, son, doest thou go to see them that man reaching the shore?

Fig. 12. Kathlamet (Chinookan) text with notes keyed to grammatical sketch, from Franz Boas, "Chinook," in *Handbook of American Indian Languages*, 1: 670–71. Bureau of American Ethnology, Bulletin 40. Washington DC: Government Printing Office, 1911.

From the long and intense correspondence between the two men during the 1880s, we know that Boas relied on the older scholar's Eskimological expertise as much as the latter appreciated the younger man's willing collaboration. Boas wrote to Powell in his German-accented English on October 3, 1885, "I saw this summer the excellent Eskimo scholar, Dr Rink, with whom I zealously studied my text."[25] Indeed, as noted earlier, what remains at the American Philosophical Society of Boas's Baffin Island notebooks from 1883–1884, pages cut apart and paginated in another hand, contains the song texts that later would appear in the jointly and singly published *Journal of American Folklore* reports of 1889 and 1894. The songs are glossed as well in another hand, in English, and indeed they need confirmatory study against any Rink papers in the Royal Copenhagen Library to see if these are the master's interlinears.

By 1894 Boas himself, without Rink, was republishing texts in canonical philological format that he had previously included in his Bureau of American Ethnology report submitted before his 1886 field season, but now with essentially identically formatted translation, annotation, and so on, as appears in their joint publication that came out in 1889, no doubt based on work in the summer of 1885. This is not to say that Rink had a magic method; he was merely doing what was being done by all European ethnological philologists, even missionaries like the great Samuel Kleinschmidt, whose Greenlandic grammar, *Grammatik der Grönländischen Sprache,* Boas too used. Given the fact that Boas personally delivered his pre-interlinear Eskimo manuscript to Powell in summer 1886, before leaving for the Northwest Coast, it is unlikely that he was influenced directly by the interlinear texts by Messrs. Gatschet, Dorsey, and Riggs that Powell published as samples in his *First Annual Report* for 1879–1880. But seeing this arrangement in Bureau publications could not but have reinforced the method of arrangement, at least in publication, that he adopted in all his own early BAE publications (though his later publications also use facing-page versions or vertically split-page versions). What is extraordinary is that beginning in September 1886 his very notebooks are arranged in perfect philological form, the first, inscription stage of producing a properly worked archive of ethnographically and linguistically disciplined text.

Rink was not, however, the only philological sophisticate of Boas's acquaintance during this period. In September 1885 he began a temporary appointment at the ethnological section of the Kaiserliche Museum in Berlin under the direction of Adolf Bastian (1826–1905), where he had the good fortune to land among three friendly and well-disposed agemates of great philological sophistication: Felix von Luschan (1854–1924),

who became a noted explorer and archaeologist; Wilhelm Grube (1855–1908), who became noted as a Sinologist, a linguist and ethnographer of peoples of the Russian Far East; and Albert Grünwedel (1856–1935), an Indo-Iranianist and art historian of Buddhism. In particular, Grube had studied at St. Petersburg and later at Leipzig under the linguist Georg von der Gabelentz (1840–1893), and Grünwedel had studied art history and Indo-Iranian philology at Munich and had become Bastian's deputy in 1883. Cole quotes Boas's fond and admiring reminiscences of some twenty years later on the impact their ethnographically oriented philology had on him.[26] They surely provided a detailed working role model shared among coevals about how to philologize in the already highly professionalized traditions of study of South and East Asian peoples.

My point, then, is that in matters linguistic, Boas the empirical, inductive scientist of language and culture had moved into the workspace of philologists of texts, where the classificatory generalizations implicit in the grouping of examples within a concordance are essentially the next step of generalization over these texts. The grammaticosemantic aspect of concordancing is the grammar; the lexicosemantic and lexicopragmatic aspect of concordancing is the text apparatus and dictionary or lexicon; the thematic aspect of concordancing is the ethnographic notes (perhaps incorporating material such as Boas took down in shorthand), eventually resulting in thematic interpretative works. Documenting a language and culture inductively starts from the texts and anchors all rearrangements of the data, including generalizations over it, to them. Methodologically, as we have seen for the Euro-American philological tradition, how language is observed, analyzed, and presented in its synchronic aspect is precisely continuous with its treatment in its diachronic aspects. Theoretical frameworks of explanation change; method continues.

In the American anthropological linguistic tradition, this is obvious in the field notebooks of both Boas and all his real and fancied students. It is the method of Edward Sapir and of Leonard Bloomfield.[27] And it is the method in turn of every one of their students whose notebooks I have examined.

Observe images of some pages of Boas's Chinook and Kathlamet notebooks, courtesy of the Library of the American Philosophical Society. The first (fig. 13) shows a whole set of numbered micro-elicitations that give paradigmatic and semantically related lexical material. The next (fig. 14) gives a good view of a verso and recto of text dictation in Kathlamet in the 1894 field season; note how few words are glossed in the notebook version, though the image of the published text (fig. 15) shows it fully

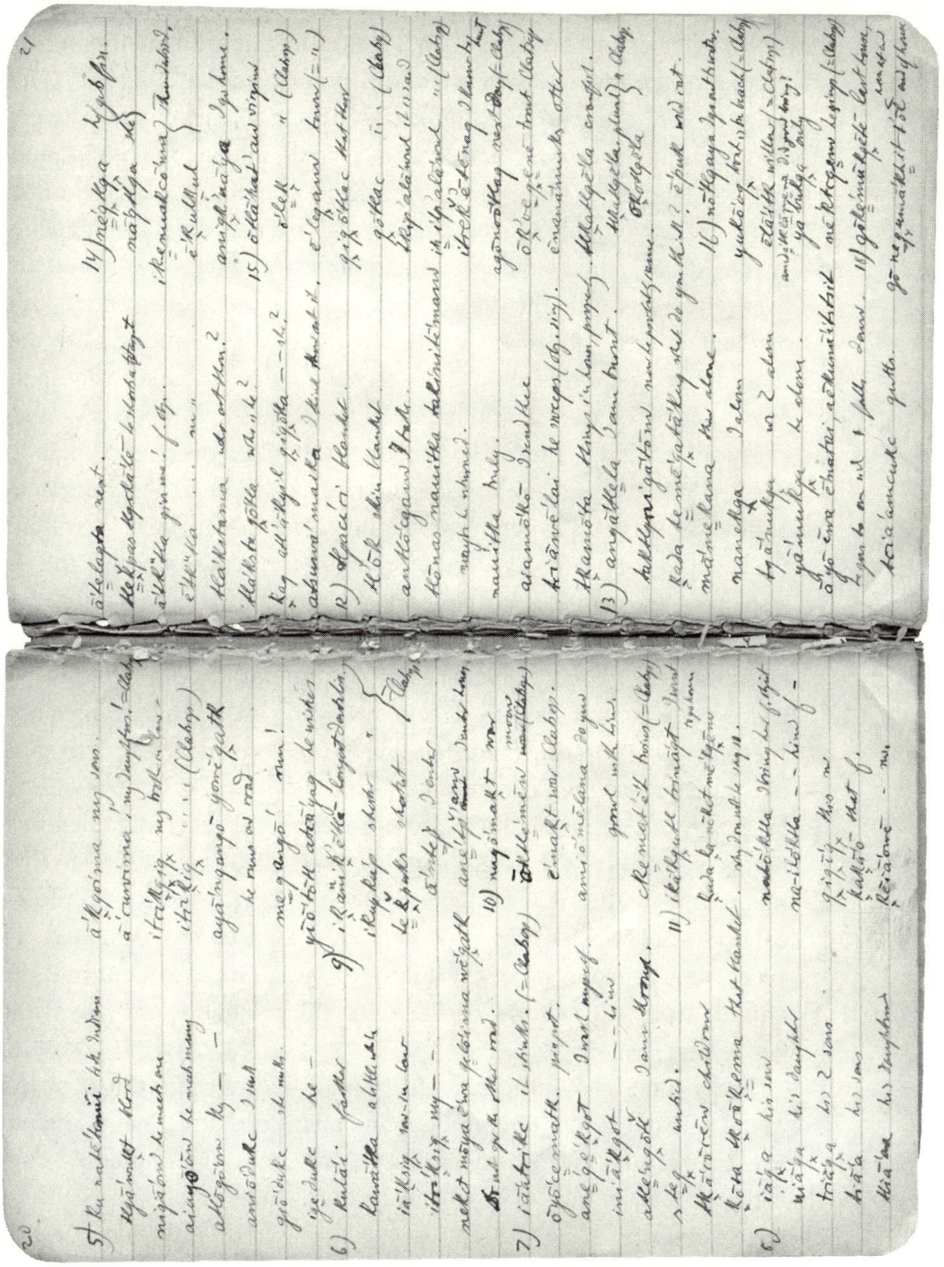

Fig. 13. Pages 20–21 of Boas's 1890 Lower Chinook notebook, APS Pn4b.5.

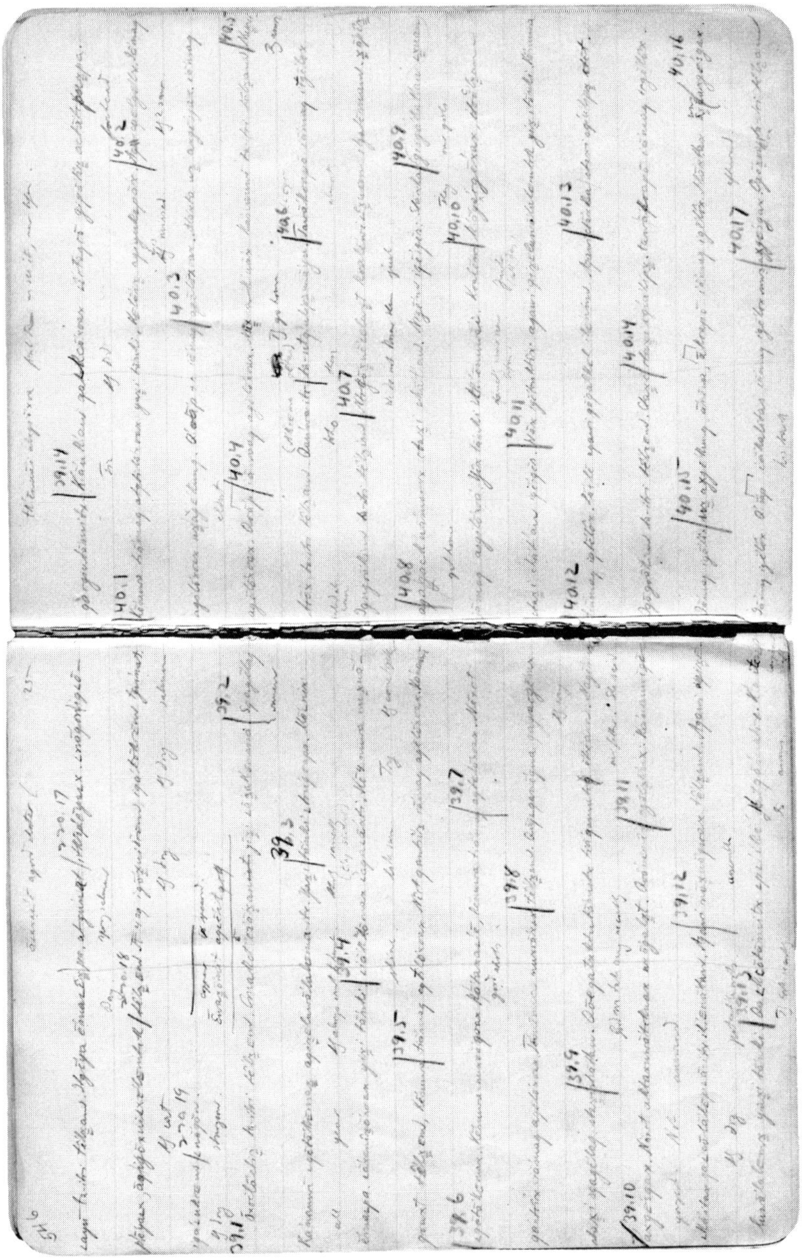

Fig. 14. Pages 546–547 of Boas's 1894 Kathlamet notebook, APS Pn4a.8.

The Copper is Speared (told 1894)

There were many people. Their chief had two children—two girls. All the year round they went hunting a thing that was on the water. That thing was far out at sea. It shone like the sun. The people came together and tried to shoot it, but they could not hit it. They did so all the year round. Their best marksmen tried to hit it, but they could not hit it. Then the people gave it up.

One day these girls said: "Let us take our father's arrows secretly." Thus said the younger one. The elder one did not reply. She spoke to her five times. All day long they were digging potentilla roots. The people came together and always tried to shoot that something. The girls took secretly the bow and arrows and the harpoon shaft. They tied their hair here on the forehead.

ĒwaXō'mit AqLē'itqcq
COPPER IS SPEARED

1. Oxoelā'etiX ta-îtci tê'lXam. Cmôket ciā'Xan yaXi iLā'Xak¡ɛmana
   There were   those   people.   Two   his children   that   their chief

2. sqagē'lak. Ka'nauwē LqētāʹkɛmaX aqiXɛluwāʹlalɛma-îtx yaXi
   girls.   All   years   they always went to hunt   that

3. tā'nki Ltcu'qoapa. Mā'LniX ē'maLpa, Lāʹxaníx ōʹxoax yaXi tāʹnki.
   something   water on.   At sea   sea on,   outside   it was   that   something.

4. Liā'kʷt¡ōmax Lʼa aqaLā'xti. Kēʹnuwa nuXuā'qoaxt têʹlXam, kēʹnuwa
   Shining   like   the sun.   Try   they assembled the people,   try

5. tiā'maq aqtilōʹxoax, nîct qantsîʹx iā'maq aqelōʹxoax. Ka'nauwē
   shooting it   it was done,   never   hit   it was.   All

6. LqētāʹkɛmaX kēʹnuwa nuxoñāʹqoax gāʹtaxaL¡ē, kēʹnuwa tiā'maq
   years   try   they assembled   the best archers,   try   hit

7. aqtelōʹxoax. Nē2ct qantsîʹx iā'maq aqelōʹxoax. Tē'menua nuxoāʹxax
   they did it.   Never   hit   it was.   Give up   they did

8. têʹlXam. Qāqlqanēʹgua aqa qacgēʹmx staʹXi sqagēʹlak staXi
   the people.   One day   then   they spoke   those   women   those

9. shāʹt¡au: "Qoē qatxktutāʹmitx tiāʹqamatex ēʹtxam," nagēʹmx wuX
   virgins: "Must   we take away   his arrows   our father's,"   she said   that

10. axgɛʹsqax. Nā2ct aktaxuwāʹtekuax wuX ā'galXt. QoāʹnɛmiX
    younger one.   Not   she answered   that   elder sister.   Five times

11. agōlXāʹmx. Ka'nauwē Lkāʹetax qaLcolā'lɛpLa-îtx ik¡ɛnāʹtan. Aqa
    she spoke.   All   days   they always gathered   potentilla roots.   Then

12. wi nōXuāʹqoax têʹlXam. Aqa wi aqiXɛluwāʹlalɛmX yaXi tāʹnki.
    again   assembled   the people.   Then again   they went to hunt   that   something.

13. QaLkcōtāʹmitx LpL¡ikēʹ k¡a tqāʹmatex k¡a itcōʹLq qacgiutāʹmitx.
    They took away   the bow   and   the arrows   and the harpoon   they took them away from him.

14. K¡au'k¡au qaLkeōʹxoax Lîʹetaqcō gipāʹtîX actāʹtepuXpa.
    Tie   they did it   their hair   here   their foreheads on.

39

Fig. 15. The text in figure 14 as rendered in Boas, "Kathlamet Texts," in *Bureau of American Ethnology*, Bulletin 26 (Washington DC: Government Printing Office, 1901), 39.

glossed interlinearly as well as in running English. (Boas had inductively mastered much of the language by this time.)

Precisely the same method is revealed in Sapir's notebooks, with halting consistency at first in his maiden-flight Wishram (Kiksht) notebooks of the summer of 1905 (fig. 16), and with a masterly orderliness in his 1914 Nootka notebooks, here a dictation on January 3–4 of that year, confidently written out by Sapir with few corrections directly in black ink, not pencil (fig. 17), on the recto side of the fold, with superscript-indexed clarifying notes on the verso. The physical medium through which language was investigated, as well as learned, is continuous across all theoretical revolutions, across all schools of inductive science.

By the mid-nineteenth century William Dwight Whitney delighted in the fact that linguistics—comparative philology—had become an inductive science, its maximal efflorescence in Germany. Boas was brought to it and to the text-anchored ethnography it projected from physical and psychophysical science in precisely this spirit as well. And it was Boas the German immigrant and his linguistic and anthropological successors who, metaphorically speaking, took the baton of philological inductivism and ran with it.

Acknowledgments

Thanks to Regna Darnell not only for her patience during the revision of this paper but also for her "groovy" title for it, created for the program of the conference at which it was delivered in highly abbreviated form. An earlier version, "Inductivism and the Emergence of Modern Descriptive Linguistics," stimulated by a query of Jan Blommaert, then visiting at the University of Chicago, was a keynote address presented at the kind invitation of Douglas Kibbee of the University of Illinois, Urbana-Champaign to the Tenth International Congress on the History of the Language Sciences, September 1, 2005. For access to manuscript archival material, I am grateful to the staffs at the Library of the American Philosophical Society and the Rare Books and Manuscripts Division of the Columbia University Libraries.

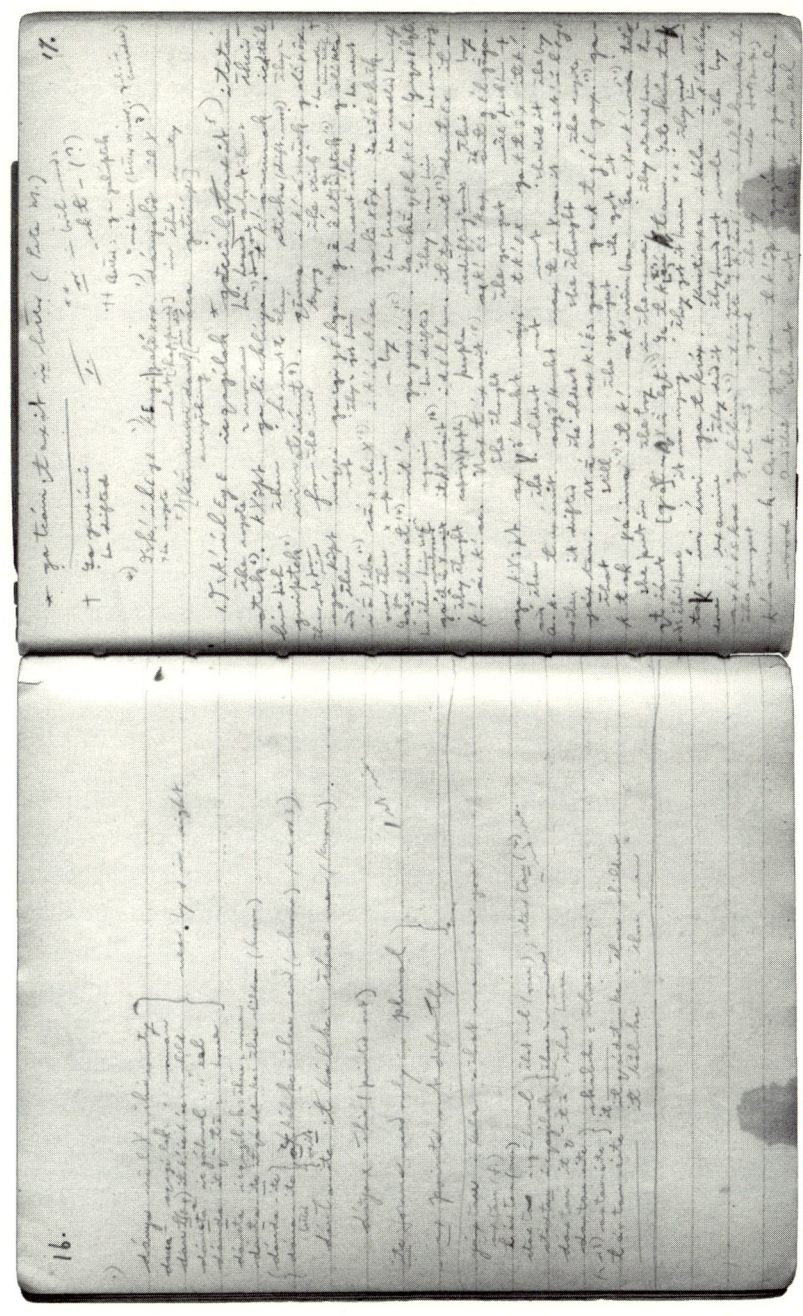

Fig. 16. Edward Sapir's Kiksht ("Wishram") notebook 2, p. 17, APS 497.3 Sa63w.

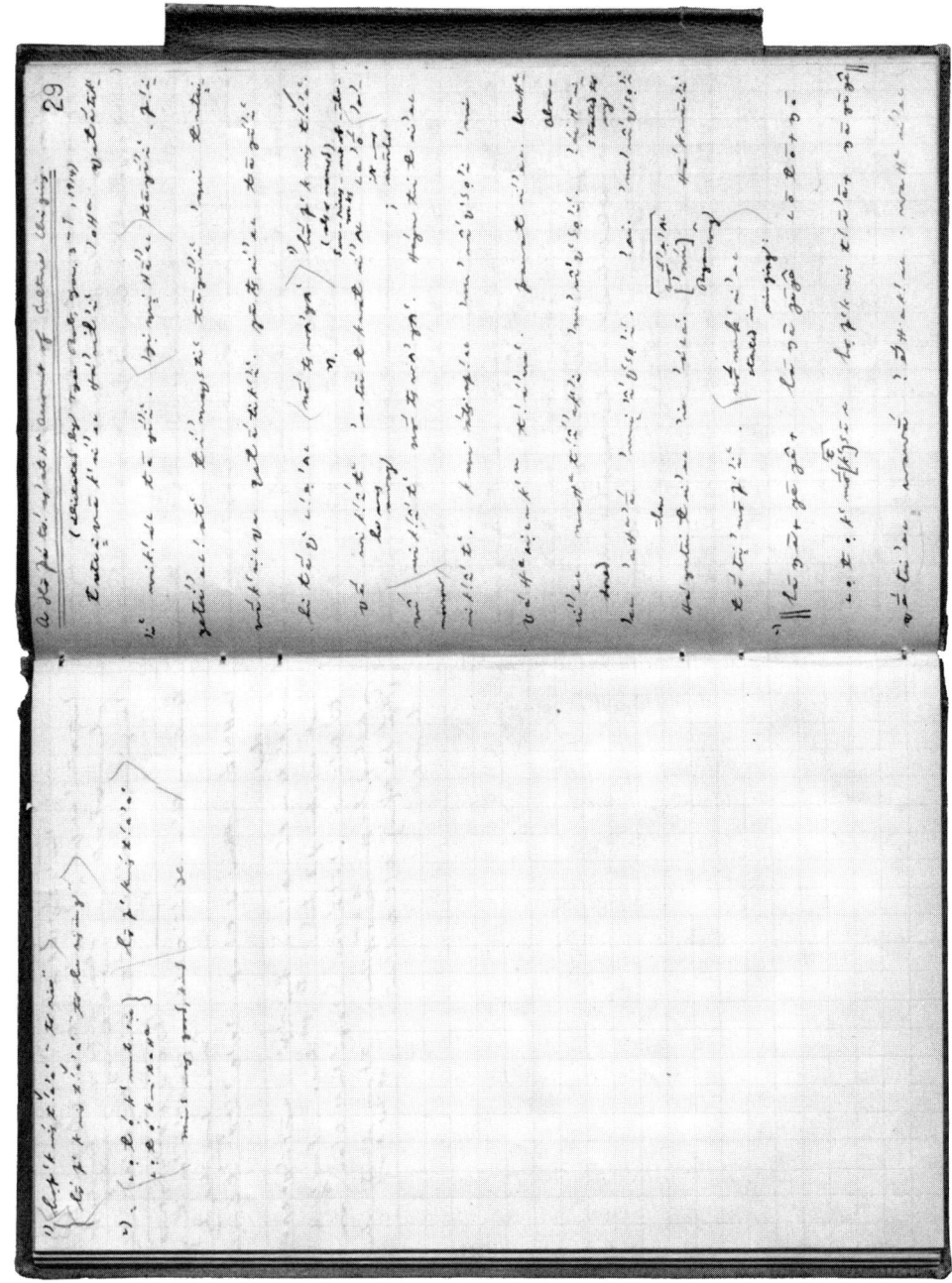

Fig. 17. Sapir's Nootka notebook 19, p. 29, APS W2a.18.

Notes

1. In reviewing "Kwakiutl Tales" (1910), the fourth in Boas's series of text publications from his and George Hunt's investigations, Edward Sapir, writing in the short-lived periodical *Current Anthropological Literature*, observes:

> Some may feel inclined to apply to the publication of texts, beyond a certain point, the law of diminishing returns, but this should seem far from justified from the standpoint of either the linguistic or the ethnologic student. . . . The ethnological data that are to be gleaned from native texts generally acquire an added interest from the fact that they are presented in a specifically native setting. . . . One may well believe, then, that future students of language and culture will complain of a paucity rather than a superabundance of Kwakiutl text, just as students of earlier cultures find what seems at first sight a vast mass of source material all too scanty for the satisfactory treatment of many a problem. (review of Boas 1910, 194)

This echoes Boas's own defense of his textually centered approach to ethnography and linguistics, as for example articulated in his letter to W. H. Holmes, the director of the Bureau of American Ethnology (July 24, 1905), to justify printing all the originals of John Swanton's Skidegate Haida texts:

> I do not think that anyone would advocate the study of antique civilizations or, let me say, of the Turks or the Russians, without a thorough knowledge of their languages and of the literary documents in these languages; and contributions not based on such material would not be considered as adequate. In regard to our American Indians we are in the position that practically no such literary material is available for study, and it appears to me as one of the essential things that we have to do, to make such material accessible. My own published work shows, that I let this kind of work take precedence over practically everything else, knowing it is the foundation of all future researches. . . . What would Indo-European philology be, if we had only grammars made by one or two students and not the live material from which these grammars have been built up, which is, at the same time, the material on which philosophic study of language must be based. (in Stocking, *The Shaping of American Anthropology*, 122–23)

Later in 1905 Boas similarly addressed a joint meeting of the American Anthropological Association, the Archaeological Institute of America, and the American Philological Association in Ithaca, New York, on December 28:

> According to the canons of philological research, would not the investigator who is not able to read the classics be barred from the number of serious students? . . . Still, this is the position which has confronted anthropology up to the present time. There are very few students who

have taken the time and who have considered it necessary to familiarize themselves sufficiently with native languages to understand directly what the people whom they study speak about, what they think and what they do. There are fewer still who have deemed it worth while to record the customs and beliefs and the traditions of the people in their own words, thus giving us the objective material which will stand the scrutiny of painstaking investigation. I think it is obvious that in this respect anthropologists have everything to learn from you; that until we acquire the habit of demanding such authenticity of our reports as can be guaranteed only by philological accuracy of the record, we can hope to accumulate material that will be a safe guide to future studies ("Some Philological Aspects of Anthropological Research," 642–43, reprinted in Stocking, *The Shaping of American Anthropology*, 184–85).

2. Darnell, *Edward Sapir*, 247–52.
3. Cole, *Franz Boas: The Early Years*, 99–103.
4. See the compilation of lessons in Harper, *Lessons of the Elementary Course*.
5. We should take note of the apparatus that Harper used in "word-by-word translation" when the various syntactic function words of the two languages do not correspond. When multiple English words translate a Hebrew one, they are joined by hyphens. Where, conversely, the Hebrew grammatical proclitic '*et* occurs, indicating that a direct object of a verb follows, the corresponding English indicates the absence of a lexical translation by using contraverted parentheses, thus ")(". Where, by contrast, English demands an additional syntactic marker, as an indefinite article before a noun or a copular form of the verb *be*, Harper puts it in parentheses to indicate it is not present as lexical material in the Hebrew from which it is translated. The idea is to render in English as precisely corresponding a surface segment—by—surface segment version as possible, preserving in the quasi-English even the verb-first order of Hebrew clauses in the face of normal English subject-first order. The translation with such apparatus hovers somewhere between our current practice of using two renderings: one a morpheme-by-morpheme interlinear gloss and the other an attempted idiomatic and grammatical closest equivalent. As will be seen in illustrative material later, Americanist practice, including Boas's, has long used this double system.
6. Roth and Whitney, *Atharva-Veda-Sanhitā*; the following by Whitney: *Sanskrit Grammar, Index Verborum, The Roots, Verb-Forms, and Primary Derivatives of the Sanskrit Language, Atharva-Veda-Samhita*.
7. Quoted in Goodspeed, *William Rainey Harper*, 39.
8. On Pestalozzi and his impact, see Biber, *Henry Pestalozzi and His Plan of Education*; Krüsi, *Pestalozzi: His Life, Work, and Influence*; Silber, *Pestalozzi: The Man and His Work*.
9. See Jankowsky, *The Neogrammarians*; Wilbur, *The Lautgesetz-Controversy*; Morpurgo Davies, "The Nineteenth Century."

10. On the emergence of the concept of sound law, see Pedersen, *Linguistic Science in the Nineteenth Century*; and Bloomfield, *Language*, 346–68. On induction, especially by the method of residues, see Mill, *A System of Logic*; Wundt, *Logik*; Venn, *The Principles of Empirical or Inductive Logic*; Fowler, *The Elements of Inductive Logic*; Hibben, *Logic, Deductive and Inductive*.
11. Bloomfield, *Language*, 357–59.
12. The retrospectively bestowed patron sainthood of Saussure in this ontological revolution about the sounds of language, evidenced by the reception of the posthumous *Cours de linguistique générale*, is all the more ironic, in that the Ascended Master had nothing of interest to say directly about phonology in the *Cours*, a plane of structure in language that is outside his concern in theorizing the actual "linguistic sign" at the lexicogrammatical plane, where language forms, identifiable by their differential privileges of combination and contrast with one another, can be associated with specific conceptual meanings, that is, differential denotational values. Saussure's actual "structuralist" breakthrough at the level of phonology had come much earlier, when, as a student at Leipzig, his self-published *Mémoire sur le système primitif des voyelles dans les langues indo-européenes* justified at elaborate length his reconstruction of the abstract phonological system of the Indo-European family's proto-language that he posited to be ancestral to various until then "irregular" vowel correspondences—suggesting chaos instead of *Lautgesetze*—among the ancient daughter languages. Indirectly Saussure's key reconstructive hypothesis, the existence of a whole class of phonological units with a characteristic syllabic and morphological distribution, was confirmed with the decipherment of a "new" Indo-European language, Hittite, which preserves some of them in graphic form, as Jerzy Kuryłowicz (1895–1978) was able to demonstrate in a 1927 festschrift publication, "ə indoeuropéen et ḫ hittite." For a summary of the *Mémoire* and its context of appearance, see John Joseph's biography of Saussure (*Saussure*, 221–49).
13. A justly famous observation of Bloomfield's ("Menomini Morphophonemics," 105–6) is to the effect that the synchronically immanent and "underlying" morphophonemic forms of his Menomini (Algonquian) phonological description appear to recuperate the reconstructed prehistorical forms one would postulate on the basis of the comparison of this language with other Algonquian languages. The morphophonological rules, applied in stipulated logical order in order to derive the actually pronounced "surface" forms of Menomini words, in large measure duplicate the inferred "sound laws" that, applied in their inferred chronological order, would derive current Menomini from its earlier linguistic form, known as "Proto-[Central-]Algonquian." Later self-styled "generative phonologists" such as Chomsky and Halle (*The Sound Pattern of English*, 251), took note of Bloomfield's observation and celebrated it as an adumbration of their own recapitulationist sense—a position still not worked out in all its presumptions and entailments.
14. Stocking, *Race, Culture, and Evolution*, *The Shaping of American Anthropology*, and "*Volksgeist* as Method and Ethic"; Darnell, *And Along Came Boas*.

15. Cole, *Franz Boas: The Early Years*, 51–57.
16. Stocking, *Race, Culture, and Evolution*, 157–60; Wells, "Phonemics in the Nineteenth Century"; Mackert, "The Roots of Franz Boas' View of Linguistic Categories" and "Franz Boas' Theory of Phonetics."
17. Bunzl, "Franz Boas and the Humboldtian Tradition," 63.
18. See Cole, *Franz Boas: The Early Years*; Müller-Wille, *Franz Boas among the Inuit of Baffin Island*; retrospectively, Boas, "[An Anthropologist's Credo]"; Kroeber et al., "Franz Boas 1858–1942."
19. I have examined several packets of such notes in the library of the American Philosophical Society, catalogued under the call numbers ACLS 497.3 B63c E1a.1/2/4 and A497.3 B63c 26, termed "Eskimo ethnographic notes from Baffinland 1885" (*sic*; the date, if correct, suggests that perhaps they are copies made after Boas's return from fieldwork).
20. For example Rink and Boas, "Eskimo Tales and Songs"; Boas, "Eskimo Tales and Songs."
21. Boas, "The Central Eskimo."
22. Lower Chinook in *Bulletin 20* of the Bureau of American Ethnology (Boas, *Chinook Texts*); Kathlamet in *Bulletin 26* (Boas, *Kathlamet Texts*).
23. See Cole, *Franz Boas: The Early Years*, 27.
24. APS. Boas Papers, Boas to Rink, November 12, 1884.
25. APS. Boas Papers, Boas to Powell, October 3, 1885. Cole notes as well a trip to Copenhagen for "a long session" of consultation during Boas's temporary residence while habilitating in Berlin (*Franz Boas: The Early Years*, 87).
26. Cole, *Franz Boas: The Early Years*, 96.
27. In an extraordinary letter of December 23, 1919, I discovered, copied, and circulated in 1966 from the then BAE archive (since published by Hockett, "Letters from Bloomfield to Michelson and Sapir," 40–41), Bloomfield, writing to the distinguished BAE Algonquianist Truman Michelson (1879–1938), claimed that his own working methods were modeled on Pāṇini (!) and on those of his one-time teacher, the great Sanskrit philologist and Indo-Europeanist Jacob Wagernagel (1853–1938), with whom he had studied during his academic year in Germany, 1913–1914. By this time Bloomfield had already produced a fieldwork-based text—grammar—lexicon of Tagalog (*Tagalog Texts with Grammatical Analysis*), done and presented indeed in the proper philological mode from primary data taken by dictation from an engineering student, Alfredo V. Santiago, then studying at the University of Illinois. Nevertheless Bloomfield in later years referred to Boas as the Ur-figure of inductive linguistics.

References

MANUSCRIPTS AND ARCHIVES

Franz Boas. Chinookan Notebooks. Rare Books and Manuscripts Division, Butler Library, Columbia University, New York.

———. Franz Boas Papers, Mss.B.B61. American Philosophical Society, Philadelphia.

———. "Eskimo ethnographic notes from Baffinland 1885."A497.3 B63c 26. American Philosophical Society, Philadelphia.

PUBLISHED WORKS

Biber, [George] Edward. *Henry Pestalozzi and His Plan of Education: Being an Account of His Life and Writings.* London: John Souter, School Library, 1831.

Bloomfield, Leonard. *Language.* New York: Henry Holt, 1933.

———. "Menomini Morphophonemics." *Etudes phonologiques dédiées à la mémoire de M. le Prince N. S. Trubtezkoy.* Travaux du Cercle Linguistique de Prague 6 (1939): 105–15.

———. *On Recent Work in General Linguistics. Modern Philology* 25.2 (1927): 211–30.

———. *Tagalog Texts with Grammatical Analysis. Studies in Language and Literature* 3.2–4 (1917). University of Illinois.

Boas, Franz. "[An Anthropologist's Credo.]" In Clifton Fadiman, ed., *I Believe: The Personal Philosophies of Certain Eminent Men and Women of Our Time,* 19–20. New York: Simon and Schuster, 1939.

———. "The Central Eskimo." In *Bureau of American Ethnology, Annual Report,* no. 6, 399–669. Washington DC: Government Printing Office, 1888.

———. "Chinook." In Franz Boas, ed., *Handbook of American Indian Languages,* part 1, 559–77. Bureau of American Ethnology, Bulletin 40. Washington DC: Government Printing Office, 1911.

———. "Chinook Texts." In *Bureau of American Ethnology,* Bulletin 20. Washington DC: Government Printing Office, 1894.

———. "Eskimo Tales and Songs." *Journal of American Folklore* 7.24 (1894): 45–50.

———. "Kathlamet Texts." In *Bureau of American Ethnology,* Bulletin 26. Washington DC: Government Printing Office, 1901.

———. "Kwakiutl Tales." In *Columbia University Contributions to Anthropology,* no. 2. New York: Columbia University Press, Brill, 1910.

———. "On Alternating Sounds." *American Anthropologist,* o.s., 2.1 (1889): 47–53.

———. "Some Philological Aspects of Anthropological Research." *Science,* n.s., 23 (1906): 641–45.

Bunzl, Matti. "Franz Boas and the Humboldtian Tradition: From *Volksgeist* and *Nationalcharakter* to an Anthropological Concept of Culture." In George W. Stocking, ed., *History of Anthropology,* 8: 17–78. Madison: University of Wisconsin Press, 1996.

Chomsky, Noam, and Morris Halle. *The Sound Pattern of English.* New York: Harper & Row, 1968.

Cole, Douglas. *Franz Boas: The Early Years, 1858–1906.* Vancouver: Douglas and McIntyre, University of Washington Press, 1999.

Darnell, Regna. *And Along Came Boas: Continuity and Revolution in Americanist Anthropology*. Amsterdam: John Benjamins, 1998.

———. *Edward Sapir: Linguist, Anthropologist, Humanist*. Berkeley: University of California Press, 1990.

Fowler, Thomas. *The Elements of Inductive Logic*. 4th ed. Oxford: Clarendon Press, 1893.

Goodspeed, Thomas Wakefield. *William Rainey Harper, First President of the University of Chicago*. Chicago: University of Chicago Press, 1928.

Grassmann, Hermann. *Wörterbuch zum Rig-Veda*. Leipzig: Brockhaus, 1873.

Harper, William Rainey. *Elements of Hebrew by an Inductive Method*. 2nd ed., revised and enlarged. Chicago: Hebrew Book Exchange, 1882.

———. *Elements of Hebrew Syntax by an Inductive Method*. New York: Charles Scribner's Sons, 1888.

———. *A Hebrew Manual*. Chicago: Hebrew Book Exchange, 1883.

———. *Lessons of the Elementary Course: The Hebrew Correspondence School, Morgan Park*. Chicago: American Publication Society of Hebrew, 1883.

Hibben, John Grier. *Logic, Deductive and Inductive*. New York: Charles Scribner's Sons, 1912.

Hockett, Charles F. "Letters from Bloomfield to Michelson and Sapir." *Historiographia Linguistica* 14.1–2 (1987): 39–60.

Jankowsky, Kurt R. *The Neogrammarians: A Re-evaluation of Their Place in the Development of Linguistic Science*. The Hague: Mouton, 1972.

Joseph, John E. *Saussure*. Oxford: Oxford University Press, 2012.

Kleinschmidt, Samuel. *Grammatik der Grönländischen Sprache, mit theilweisem Einschluss des Labradordialects*. Berlin: G. Reimer, 1851.

Kroeber, Alfred L., et al. "Franz Boas 1858–1942." *Memoirs of the American Anthropological Association*, no. 61, 1943.

Krüsi, Hermann. *Pestalozzi: His Life, Work, and Influence*. Cincinnati: Wilson, Hinkle, 1875.

Kuryłowicz, Jerzy. "ə indoeuropéen et ḫ hittite." In Witold Taszycki et al., *Symbolae Grammaticae in Honorem Ioannis Rozwadowski*, 1: 95–104. Cracow: Drukarnia Uniwersytetu Jagiellońskiego, 1927.

Mackert, Michael. "Franz Boas' Theory of Phonetics." *Historiographia Linguistica* 21.3 (1994): 351–84.

———. "The Roots of Franz Boas' View of Linguistic Categories as a Window to the Human Mind." *Historiographia Linguistica* 20.2–3 (1993): 331–51.

Mill, John Stuart. *A System of Logic, Ratiocinative and Inductive, Being a Connected View of the Principles of Evidence, and the Methods of Scientific Investigation*. London: John W. Parker, 1843.

Morpurgo Davies, Anna. "The Nineteenth Century." In Giulio Lepschy, ed., *History of Linguistics*, vol. 4. London: Longman, 1994.

Müller-Wille, Ludger, ed. *Franz Boas among the Inuit of Baffin Island, 1883–1884: Journals and Letters*. Trans. William Barr. Toronto: University of Toronto Press, 1998.

Pedersen, Holger. *Linguistic Science in the Nineteenth Century: Methods and Results*. Trans. John W. Spargo. Cambridge MA: Harvard University Press, 1931.

Powell, John Wesley. "Illustration of the Method for Recording Indian Languages." In *First Annual Report of the Bureau of Ethnology to the Secretary of the Smithsonian Institution, 1879–1880*, 579–89. Washington DC: Government Printing Office, 1881.

———. *Introduction to the Study of Indian Languages, with Words, Phrases, and Sentences to by Collected*. 1877. 2nd ed., revised and expanded. Washington DC: Government Printing Office, 1880.

Rink, Hinrich, and Franz Boas. "Eskimo Tales and Songs." *Journal of American Folklore* 2.5 (1889): 123–31.

Roth, Rudolf von, and William Dwight Whitney, eds. *Atharva-Veda-Sanhitā*. Berlin: Ferdinand Dümmlers Verlagsbuchhandlung, 1855–1856.

Sapir, Edward. Review of Boas 1910. *Current Anthropological Literature* 1 (1912): 193–98.

———. "Yana Texts (Together with Yana Myths, Collected by Roland B. Dixon)." *University of California Publications in American Archaeology and Ethnology* 9.1 (1910): 1–235.

Saussure, Ferdinand de. *Cours de linguistique générale*. Ed. Charles Bally and Albert Sechehaye. Lausanne: Payot, 1916.

———. *Mémoire sur le système primitif des voyelles dans les langues indo- européennes*. Leipzig: B. G. Teubner, 1879.

Silber, Kate. *Pestalozzi: The Man and His Work*. London: Routledge & Kegan Paul, 1960.

Stocking, George W., ed. *History of Anthropology*. Vol. 8: *Volksgeist as Method and Ethic: Essays on Boasian Ethnography and the German Anthropological Tradition*. Madison: University of Wisconsin Press, 1996.

———. *Race, Culture, and Evolution: Essays in the History of Anthropology*. New York: Free Press, 1968.

———. *The Shaping of American Anthropology, 1883–1911: A Franz Boas Reader*. New York: Basic Books, 1974.

Venn, John. *The Principles of Empirical or Inductive Logic*. London: Macmillan, 1889.

Wells, Rulon S. "Phonemics in the Nineteenth Century, 1876–1900." In Dell Hymes, ed., *Studies in the History of Linguistics: Traditions and Paradigms*, 434–53. Bloomington: Indiana University Press, 1974.

Wilbur, Terence H., ed. *The Lautgesetz-Controversy: A Documentation*. Amsterdam: John Benjamins, 1977.

Whitney, William Dwight. *Atharva-Veda-Samhita: Translated with a Critical and Exegetical Commentary*. Edited and revised by Charles Rockwell Lanman. Cambridge MA: Harvard University Press, 1905.

———. *A Compendious German Grammar*. 1869. 6th ed., revised. New York: Henry Holt, C. Schoenhof, 1888.

———. *Index Verborum to the Published Text of the Atharva-Veda.* New Haven CT: American Oriental Society, 1881.

———. *The Roots, Verb-Forms, and Primary Derivatives of the Sanskrit Language: A Supplement to His Sanskrit Grammar.* Leipzig: Breitkopf & Härtel, 1885.

———. *Sanskrit Grammar: Including both the Classical Language and the Older Dialects, of Veda and Brâhmana.* Leipzig: Breitkopf & Härtel, 1879.

Wundt, Wilhelm. *Logik: Eine Untersuchung der Principien der Erkenntniss und der Methoden Wissenschaftlicher Forschung.* Vol. 2: *Methodenlehre.* Stuttgart: Verlag von Ferdinand Enke, 1883.

6 The Boasian Legacy in Ethnomusicology

Cultural Relativism, Narrative Texts, Linguistic Structures, and the Role of Comparison

SEAN O'NEILL

In telling our own origin story in the field of anthropology, anthropologists often credit Franz Boas with giving the discipline an all-encompassing vision of humanity that engages with biology, history, language, and culture—more or less the four fields we know today. At the core we might recognize the principles of *holism* and *cultural relativism*, which eventually came to define the American approach to anthropology. These are the familiar hallmarks of the Boasian school, in the mainstream view, even if *music* is rarely granted a major place in fieldwork or anthropological theory for most working professionals today.

Central to the entire Boasian mission was the premise of cultural relativism, or the strong methodological assertion that each culture must be understood on its own terms, not merely in relation to other cultures, as the "comparative method" once dictated in earlier lines of anthropological thought. Even among the first generation of Boasian anthropologists, this premise quickly led to the production of many copiously detailed ethnographic accounts, developed in consultation with knowledgeable consultants in their native languages and only secondarily translated into English, without much margin separating the cultural and linguistic subdisciplines.[1] For specialists in ethnomusicology today it is especially significant that Boas encouraged his students to transcribe *song texts*,[2] which often included an analysis of their linguistic elements and narrative structures, knowing that such musical performances constituted a major part of human life the world over. By the mid-twentieth century this approach set the stage for the emerging field of *ethnomusicology* by placing music squarely within its proper ethnographic setting, with a focus on the cultural meanings of the musical performances and without extraneous comparisons to outside traditions.[3]

While the field of ethnomusicology in particular still bears the marks of the Boasian approach, with its emphasis on social context and the fundamental axiom of cultural relativism,[4] the regular practice of musical

analysis has not been absorbed into mainstream anthropology. Instead the study of music has become a specialty within the field of anthropology—a secondary focus for a small group of scholars, entering mainstream anthropological work mostly as an afterthought. In moving music to the periphery—in relegating it to a specialty—it seems that the field has potentially turned away from one of the most important hallmarks of our species, which stands alongside other human universals, such as language, politics, economics, and other art forms. Probably anyone who has recently returned from the field can talk at length about the countless hours they spent listening to music—the most enjoyable moments of their stay, perhaps, and their deepest moments of engagement with the community where the work was carried out. However, when it comes to capturing the experience on the printed page, who can do justice to music in mere words, even among those who have specialized training in musical analysis? Who among anthropologists has that training, even the musicians among our ranks?

In the received conception of the profession today, Boas is rarely credited with granting music a central role in the development of anthropology, nor is he usually credited with having had a seminal impact on the development of *comparative musicology* worldwide. For that matter cross-cultural comparison and the search for universals are not often associated with the legacy of Boas either, though he had much to say about both areas of inquiry, particularly in relation to music.

This familiar narrative is somewhat off the mark, however, which only underscores the importance of reexamining the historical record. Received history, as is so often the case, tells only part of the story, and it is usually more a reflection of current ideology than of the actual past, which is generally more complex. In taking a closer look at the development of the field, Boas appears to have stood at the center of the many debates that led to the development of ethnomusicology as a profession.[5] Yet outside of the literature of ethnomusicology, his impact on the study of music across cultures remains one of the lesser known trajectories of his pervasive intellectual legacy. Among cultural anthropologists and linguists in particular, the central place of music in the Boasian vision of anthropology is not well known, nor has music been integrated very thoroughly into our discourses about humanity since the time of his death. Instead the study of music in relation to culture has become a specialization, one that is more underrepresented even than linguistics since the passing of the Boasian era.

One of the primary goals of this chapter is to explore the many Boasian contributions to the anthropological study of music, with an emphasis

on both the descriptive and theoretical nature of this line of research, in relation to his characteristically holistic approach, where music sits comfortably alongside ethnography and linguistic analysis. This chapter also revisits the question of comparison in relation to the school of Boasian anthropology; the study of ethnic music was in fact known as the disciple of *comparative musicology* in the early twentieth century,[6] when Boas and his students published their most important work in this field. As was the case in linguistic research, the goal of comparison was to show historical relationships among related traditions, or to reveal contact, while uncovering general principles along the way, such as the presence of rhythms or melodic passages that roughly parallel those of standard Western notation and can be captured with slight modifications to the system.[7] Despite Boas's many cautions on the subject, the comparative approach continued to hold sway in the work of many his students—including George Herzog, Edward Sapir, Helen Roberts, Margaret Mead, and Alfred Kroeber—though in each case these comparisons were tempered by a detailed knowledge of the cultures in question. In this sense Boas and his students contributed to the development of more nuanced comparisons in anthropological theory, as became the hallmark of Claude Lévi-Strauss's work, who in fact came under the influence of Boas and contributed to the study of music across cultures. Thus through these many primary and secondary influences the influence of Boasian anthropology can still be felt throughout the entire field of ethnomusicology. Toward the end of this chapter I explore the secondary influence of Boasian anthropology on other pioneers of ethnomusicology, including such figures as Charles Seeger and Alan Lomax, with whom Boas had personal contact.

"No Other Art Moves Me as Deeply as Music": The Place of Music in Boas's Work

The historical record reveals that Boas was deeply committed to music, both professionally and in his private life. He wrote extensively about musical themes, publishing at least thirty papers on topics related to music over the course of his career, probably enough to earn tenure on the basis of his work in ethnomusicology alone. In his private life his diaries reveal that music was often on his mind even in his earliest days of fieldwork while doing his apparently unrelated work on the color of seawater, starting in 1883 on his voyage to Baffin Island. The notes from that period contain handwritten transcriptions of classical music, with several lines from Beethoven's Ninth Symphony appearing on July 20, 1883, just before one of his entries. In a note to his fiancée, Marie Krack-

owizer, later that day, he wrote, "No other art moves me as deeply as music."[8] Later that year he transcribed some of the Inuit songs he heard on that auspicious voyage;[9] thus his first fieldwork and entire career in anthropology began on a very musical note.

Throughout his professional career music continued to be a source of both inspiration and distraction, as he went on to transcribe nearly any song that passed through his head when conducting fieldwork or simply reflecting on music in an inner auditory stream; later, phonographs would allow him to replay and carefully transcribe music that he once asked his consultants to repeat syllable by syllable.[10] As a matter of distraction, Boas was often called on to perform music in local venues, even when conducting fieldwork, given that he was a gifted performer on both piano and organ.[11] As Douglas Cole notes, Boas's passion for music was both aesthetic and intellectual; even as a teenager he worked hard to understand the music he played, presaging his professional interest in ethnic music with these words: "I wanted to learn only in order to understand, and to listen. I want to learn the playing of music only in so far as it allows me to appreciate it" (F. Boas to Toni Boas, October 6, 1876).[12] Cole tells us that even after turning to anthropology, he continued to play piano at home and attended concerts frequently, going so far as to hang portraits of classical icons, such as Beethoven and Mozart, throughout this home.[13] This deep, personal love of music, beginning with training as a classical pianist, provided him a platform for understanding the sound patterning of the Indigenous music that he strove to understand at its deepest structural and social layers of significance.

Consistent with the principle of holism, whereby any single element of culture is analyzed in relation to the entire social system around it, most of his writings on musical themes touched on related cultural topics, such as narrative, poetry, and dance, as well as the artistic use of metaphor, grammar, and even vocabulary.[14] In this way music frequently found a way into his publications and field research, following him in his broad range of interests. Consistent with the principle of cultural relativism, whereby each culture is understood within its own internal framework, Boas tapped into music, alongside language and folklore, as a way of understanding the intimate details of life in the field, even drawing on songs to grasp local traditions in aesthetics or humor. In speaking of his first field experience among the Inuit of Baffin Island in 1883, Boas makes it clear that learning the language well enough to understand the music was an integral part of his initiation into professional anthropology: "As I learned the language of this people, I was able to understand the old songs and tales, which are handed down from their ancestors. As I lived

amongst them as one of them, I learned their habits and ways, I saw their customs referring to birth and death, their feasts, etc."[15] From the outset of his career Boas carved out a major place for music in anthropological field methodology, even drawing on the resource of song to provide a key to the worldview or a sense of the insider's point of view. In another sense his approach contributed to ethnography from the native point of view since cultural institutions, such as the tale and songs, were described primarily by local experts in the Native language.

Several years later Boas wrote his first major piece on music, "Poetry and Music of Some North American Tribes.". In this general comparative piece he goes to great lengths to illustrate the diversity of Indigenous music, which many members of the public took to be uniform in expression, by juxtaposing Inuit chants, which are normally done alone, with the polyphonic, choral music of the Northwest Coast, which is sung in larger groups.[16] Wishing to establish poetry and music as universal categories of artistic expression, present in all societies and therefore worthy of scholarly attention, he declared, "Ethnologists are well acquainted with the fact that there is no people and no tribe that has not some kind of poetry and music but the study of this branch of aboriginal literature has hardly been begun."[17] Significantly in terms of teasing out universals, he found common ground in the social functions these songs serve, which range from celebration to mourning, humor, and even outright satire. These ventures into the realm of comparison are worth remembering, since I wish to establish a place for comparative thought in Boasian anthropology.

The timing of this 1887 piece is significant for the then-fledgling field of ethnomusicology, since Boas's article appeared just two years after the German scholar Guido Adler called for a new field of ethnomusicology, with the publication of his own programmatic paper on the comparative study of music across cultures.[18] Whether this paper by Boas was written in response to the famous piece by Adler, we'll never know. Given that Boas, a product of the German academy, was very much in touch with German scholarly tradition, there is a chance he read Adler's work, perhaps entering the historical record as one of the first to respond to his call for a global study of music in cultural context. To echo his early student Alfred Kroeber on the concept of the "superorganic," perhaps this parallel development is something like the "simultaneous invention" of calculus by Newton and Leibniz within a year or two of one another.[19] Something was in the air, and as Kroeber often pointed out, the seeds of greatness are sown by culture, that is, by the society that in part shapes the creative individual. However, several years before Adler published

his visionary piece on ethnomusicology, Boas had already started studying music in an anthropological vein, making music a serious focal point in his first fieldwork. In fact almost the moment he became an anthropologist, during his stay in Baffin Island in 1883, Boas began transcribing Inuit songs, publishing the results the following year in one of his first field reports, "A Journey in Cumberland Sound on the West Shore of Davis Strait in 1883 and 1884."

The following year, in his first published ethnography, Boas included nearly a dozen musical scores, not only transcribing the melodies of the songs but also placing them squarely in their proper linguistic and cultural context, giving the lyrics in the original language and also giving an indication of when the songs were sung.[20] This work created a model for his students, including Edward Sapir, his most gifted pupil in linguistics, who frequently transcribed songs in his many field excursions. Among his other prominent students, Helen Roberts and George Herzog also continued this tradition of meticulous transcription, often aided by the use of the phonograph as a means of reviewing the material until a satisfactory sense of the melodic flow and rhythm could be established.[21]

In first ethnographic work Boas discussed remarkably prescient topics, such as the use of "voice" in song, when the singer modulates his or her normal voice to take on the distant persona of another character, either mythic or human, within the social imagination of the audience. In this first major entry of the topic within the Americanist tradition, he moves from technical and structural topics, such as the use of particular scales and modes, to the discussion of more social topics, such as song ownership and personal compositions. He made a few careful comparisons, finding structural parallels in Gregorian chant as well as in Chinese and East Indian musical traditions,[22] which also demonstrates his deep familiarity with the range of musical structures.

In the decade that followed, Boas continued to publish extensively on musical themes, writing about song among the Kwakiutl, Inuit, Chinook, and Salish, among others.[23] From these early essays it is clear that he understood the role of the creative individual and the shifting meanings of a given text as it finds its way into ever new situations. Rather than seeing the song text as fixed—as a mere product of tradition—Boas often took great pains to demonstrate how music may be used solemnly or even in parody and also that humor and beauty play a role in Indigenous aesthetics.[24] In his earlier works he discusses song composition and individual style, and even what we would now call "registers" of language, that is, specialized vocabularies, grammatical features, and even styles of delivery that are associated with a particular group with

the society. Consider, for instance, his essay "Eskimo Tales and Songs," where he identifies a song register associated with shamanism, one that has its own sacred vocabulary and style of delivery, namely, a distinctive choral style.[25] In this sense it is clear that Boas did not see each culture simply as a frozen historical product, beyond comparison with other developments elsewhere on the planet, as is so often suggested in caricatures of his work that arose in later generations.[26]

Over the course of his career Boas continued to grant an important place to music in his overall vision of anthropology, publishing several articles a decade on the topic and training some of the finest students in the history of the ethnomusicology. Even in the inaugural article for the *International Journal of American Linguistics*, Boas urges all serious students of language to consider the place of music in their studies: "Undoubtedly problems of native poetry have to be taken up in connection with the study of native music, because there is practically no poetry that is not at the same time song. The literary aspects of this subject, however, fall entirely within the scope of a linguistic journal."[27] Clearly he expected students of language to study music as well, especially songs. Elsewhere in his writings he often seems to imply that an understanding of music is one way to gauge the fieldworker's competence in the minutiae of the local culture.

Generally speaking Boas made significant contributions to the study of music in each of the culture areas where he conducted fieldwork. In his formative experiences among the Baffin Island Inuit, he was able to draw upon his musical training to transcribe songs, intuitively understanding that the notation could capture features of sound that only loosely fit the standard Western system, limning the overall melodic contours and sense of rhythm, much as he used a modified Roman alphabet to represent the sounds of Inuit speech.[28] Based in part on these experiences with the language and music of the Inuit, Boas went on to write insightfully about an observer bias in sound patterning, laying the groundwork for the phonemic effect in speech, which has a parallel in music, as he observed when a note may be sung (in a given tradition) a little higher or lower than the standard notated pitch.[29] Furthermore, as a student of material culture, Boas also contributed to the study of musical instruments, or organology, frequently taking careful notes on the comparative status of an instrument when seen through different cultural lenses. He even notes that the rattle (both as art object and as instrument) may take on different religious meanings, based on tribe:

> The rattle, for instance, is not merely the outcome of the idea of making noise, and of the technical methods applied to reach this end: it is,

besides this, the outcome of religious conceptions, as any noise may be applied to invoke or drive away sprits; or it may be the outcome of the pleasure children have in noise of any kind; and its form may be characteristic of the art of a people. Thus, the same implement belongs to very different departments of the psychological museum.[30]

During the Chicago World's Fair in 1893 Boas managed to record some Kwakiutl songs, making some of the first sound recordings in the history of the profession, though, surprisingly, in a nontraditional context.[31] A few years later he joined the Jesup Expedition to the Pacific Northwest (1897–1902), where he pioneered the use of sound recordings, both as a means of making more accurate transcriptions (by listening repeatedly and checking one's observations) as well as a way of preserving sound for future generations. In this period he also recorded dance, gesture, and musical performances, principally among the groups known at the time as the Kwakiutl (Kwakwaka'wakw), Bella Coola (Nuxalk), and Thompson River Indians (Nlaka'pamux). Realizing the limitations of the phonograph, which captures only sound but not the underlying meaning or even the social context, Boas was quick to catalogue these other features when recording a given performance, including the gender and tribal affiliation of the performer, the genre (e.g., religious songs, love songs), as well as the general cultural significance of the central characters.[32] Toward the end of his career he was collaborating with his daughter, Franziska, on relationships between music and dance, returning to a theme he had first explored at the start of his career.[33]

Though Boas published consistently on a range of musical themes, his most widely read piece appeared in the final chapter of *Primitive Art*, originally published in 1927, with many reprints afterward. In this final chapter he presents a portrait of music in society, giving it a place alongside oral literature, poetry, and dance as one element of what we now call "expressive culture." Rather than speaking for a single tribe, or even strictly working from his own field experience, Boas paints a composite picture of music in preliterate (or "primitive") societies, based on many concrete cases, with examples of linguistic texts and even a detailed musical score at the close. At the outset he announces that poetry and music are perhaps the most prolific of the many arts found among all human groups, both having their roots in the creative or expressive side of social life:

> It is a noticeable fact that a rich literary art is more universally distributed than a well developed decorative art. While among tribes like

> the Bushman and eastern Eskimo very few manufactured objects of artistic value are found, these same tribes produce an abundance of literary work. Volumes of Eskimo lore have been collected and if it did not require a most intimate knowledge of the people and an endless amount of patience to collect songs and poems, their number would undoubtedly equal that of the tales. The collections of Bushmen lore are quite extended. I believe the reason for this difference is not far to seek. Decorative art requires rest and quiet, a stationary abode. . . . The life of hunters is not favorable to the prosecution of such work. . . . Quite different are conditions under which literary work and music develop. . . . He is not all the time following strenuously the tracks of the game, but often he resorts to trapping or he sits still, waiting for the game to appear. During such time his fancy is free to wander and many of his songs take shape during these moments.[34]

As this passage illustrates, Boas did not shy away from comparison, historical speculation, or even making cautious inferences about widespread tendencies, such as the profuse flowering of oral literature in hunting and gathering societies. As he points out later in the chapter, there is a deep relationship between poetry and music, one that is perhaps found all human societies, given that both of these arts rely on measuring vocalizations in accordance with an established rhythm. As frequently occurs, the formal linguistic aspect drops out, leaving vocalizations with no clear conceptual meaning beyond the sheer emotion of the voice; such a tendency gives rise to the widespread occurrence of "vocables," or meaningless syllables, which he documents in many cultures, our own included (consider jazz scat singing). In other cases it is the melodic element that is lost, giving rise to lyrical types of poetry, which are no longer purely musical, despite the obvious rhythmic aspect and deep historical connection to music. Boas also notes that as a general human situation, found across cultures, poetry and music are often fused, in lyrics for instance, and that stories are frequently set to music, as in the case of epic poetry. As we know, this is the case even for *Beowulf* in Old English and the precursors to the *Odyssey* and *Iliad* in ancient Greek, which in all probability combined lyrics and instrumental music as epic poems.[35]

Music played a significant role in his lifelong campaign against racism, as he frequently sought to reveal the complexity, beauty, and diversity of Indigenous musical traditions. In several key articles he took on racist stereotypes associated with music, such as those that credited African Americans with great musical gifts that were considered lacking among other peoples, such as the Native North Americans. As he explained in

an early review on the complexity of Native music, "These facts may appear startling when compared to the often repeated statement that the Indian has no sense for music, and that particularly as compared to the negro, he is entirely lacking in musical genius."[36] Of course Boas wanted to demonstrate the opposite through careful comparison, systematically contradicting these racist discourses. When discussing the scope of Indigenous music, he is quick to point out the sheer volume of musical lore in Indigenous societies, clearly showing that there is no deficiency within this realm of culture, as so often suggested in popular discourse about non-Western music. By drawing on music as one of the fundamental features of culture, Boas built a case for why music belonged at the heart of anthropology, with an important a role to play in many of his intellectual projects, from combating racism to documenting languages or even understanding the theater of everyday life while conducting fieldwork.

Music among Boas's Students

Given that Boas engaged with music from the very start of his career, if not from long before, he most likely expected his students to take music seriously in their own studies.[37] One can begin to get a sense of the man—his tastes, his approach, and his convictions—from his inner circle of students. In this sense his strong musical predilection was reflected in nearly everyone who crossed his path.

Margaret Mead, for instance, mentions music in the context of child rearing and adolescence, paving the way for what we now call "socialization" in a pioneering sense that encompassed both language and music as elements of expressive culture. In her first two books she devoted a great deal of attention to the role of music in everyday life, especially in the formation of childhood gender roles. In *Coming of Age in Samoa* she discusses the role of music in adolescent courtship, where original songs were sometimes composed to mock or ridicule those who step out of line with the cultural mores.[38] In her subsequent book, *Growing Up in New Guinea*, she focuses more explicitly on the role of music in shaping gender roles, even drawing on musical events to show how boys and girls learn their place in society:

> Whenever there is a dance there is an orchestra of slit drums of all sizes played by the most proficient drummers in the village. The very small boys of four and five settle themselves beside small hollow log ends or pieces of bamboo and drum away indefatigably in time with the orchestra. This period of open and unashamed imitation is followed by a period of embarrassment, so that it is impossible to persuade a

boy of ten or twelve to touch a drum in public, but in the boy's house when only a few older boys are present, he will practice, making good use of the flexibility of the wrist and sense of rhythm learned earlier. Girls practice less, for only one drumbeat, the simple death beat, falls to their hands later in life.[39]

Later in the book Mead gives many detailed ethnographic sketches illustrating the role that music plays over the course of life, including a specialized drum language and the use of incantation in performing puberty rites for girls and boys.[40] Toward the end of the book she considers the role of education in broad comparative terms, contrasting formal Western modes of schooling with the more relaxed and playful mode found among the Manus of New Guinea and many other Indigenous societies around the planet, ultimately claiming that even a relatively unstructured childhood can produce great artistic talent.[41] Later in her career she mentored the great ethnomusicologist Alan Lomax, who shared an office with her at Columbia University, where they both taught, giving him further background in Boasian anthropology.

Turning to another prominent student, the remarkable story of Zora Neale Hurston has attracted popular attention in recent years—especially her early encounter with Boas, before going on to inscribe the living history of African American folklore and music—not merely in folklore and musicology, but also in novels and sound recordings made at the Library of Congress, documenting the oral folklore of the American South in hundreds of songs, stories, and instrumentals.[42] Given that she was also a novelist, a composer, and a poet, her contributions to American culture are inestimable, and few of Boas's students had such a lasting impact on the world of arts and literature. Recently it has come to light that she was also a playwright, having composed several musical scores representing the American blues tradition—not merely on the printed page but in performance as well. In our own era, when performance and literary modes of representation have received renewed attention, this work would certainly represent a profound contribution to postmodern ethnography. Again Boas and his students were often ahead of the mark, making contributions that sometimes took decades to achieve full recognition.

Melville Herskovits, the most prominent Africanist among Boas's students, made frequent use of musical material in tracing the African roots of American folklore in a long series of publications employing a sophisticated iteration of the comparative method.[43] In these comparative studies, which sometimes featured his own sound recordings and films, Herskovits often uncovered striking similarities between the cultural tra-

ditions of African Americans and Native Africans, most evident in folklore and musical motifs, even including such structural features as counterpoint and polyrhythm. In many ways his entire career was based on the premise that one could not understand a culture without understanding its historical roots as reconstructed through comparative inference, including fieldwork at multiple, even far-flung sites. For this reason he often asserted that one could not understand African American culture without also having a deep knowledge of its roots in Africa and its parallel developments elsewhere in the Americas, including the Caribbean and Brazil. In this sense Herskovits was a comparativist in method and theory alike, though in a Boasian sense he was cautious with his inferences, which were always rooted in careful fieldwork.

Perhaps less well-known is Sapir's lifelong commitment to music as a subject he pursued largely in private, spending much of his spare time composing original scores and thinking about musical themes. In Regna Darnell's biography of Sapir, we learn that he devoted an enormous amount of time to music. In a personal letter to Robert Lowie dated August 12, 1916, Sapir wrote:

> I do practically no anthropology out of office hours, most of my time being taken up with music—reading and composing. Circumstances being what they are, it is more than unlikely that I should ever be able to give up anthropology and switch over frankly to music. Still, the impulse tending in that direction is certainly there. Some of my happiest moments of late have been due to the pleasure of hitting upon what seem to me to be exquisite bits of melody or rhythm or chordal progressions. I find that what I most care for is beauty of form, whether in substance or, perhaps, even more keenly, in spirit. A perfect style, a well-balanced system of philosophy, a perfect bit of music, the beauty of mathematical relations—these are some of the things that, in the sphere of the immaterial, have most deeply stirred me.[44]

These could well have been the words of Lévi-Strauss, who, like Sapir, also maintained a lasting affection for music, which seemed to strengthen his insights into the structures of language and even cognition.

Over the course of his career Sapir published extensively on music. Following Boas, he incorporated musical studies into his ethnographic work in a major way. Also like his mentor, Sapir regularly conducted musical fieldwork not as a specialist but merely as an ordinary facet of Boasian anthropology. Sapir's father was a cantor and sometimes helped him with the analysis of recorded songs. Later the ethnomusicologist George Her-

zog, who was also trained by Boas, sometimes accompanied Sapir to the field as a transcriber and expert in musical notation.

Music makes a minor appearance in one of Sapir's first publications, *Takelma Texts*, where Sapir, like Boas before him, carefully notates the many songs that are interspersed with ordinary speech in the context of narrative. This was followed several years later by a refined analysis of Paiute songs, which also appear during the recitation of myth, as the odd voices of characters channeled by the storyteller. Notable here is the careful attention to stylistic register, or the fine phonetic nuances of singing as opposed to speech and the linguistic peculiarities of the performance. Later, in his *Takelma Grammar*, Sapir even uses musical notation to describe the phenomenon of pitch accent in regular speech, not song, apparently drawing on his musical abilities to hone his ear for languages. Sapir's student Mary Haas would follow in her mentor's footsteps, drawing on her musical abilities to describe tonal languages with great accuracy.[45]

In Sapir's posthumously published *Psychology of Culture* we learn that he speculated endlessly about music in his classes. Like Lévi-Strauss, another musically inclined thinker who also came under the influence of Boas, Sapir used music in an analogical way, as an intellectual tool, as an exemplar of cultural patterning and a platform for comparison, especially given its obvious parallels to language.[46] In particular he points out that in language and music, much of the meaning—perhaps the deepest layer of meaning—is nonreferential, operating primarily in the social imagination.[47] Sapir also finds indexical layers of meaning in both language and music, in the sense that musical style—even as pure sound—can represent social status rather abstractly, as would be the case, for instance, with nearly any contemporary American musical genre, from folk to punk or Indigenous roots music.

Less well known is the musical interlude in Alfred Kroeber's long career in Native California ethnography. From Boas Kroeber clearly inherited a deep respect for music and a sense that this formed an important part of anthropological scholarship. Kroeber, however, published very little on this topic. Instead he spent much of his career scrupulously cataloging the musical traditions of native California, which stand out, on a structural basis, in terms of their strong sense of vocal polyphony, the use of microtones, and even polyrhythms. These are not easy to characterize in the standard notation developed for European classical music or even folk song, much as Boas had observed in his early work on sound perception.[48] As a consequence Kroeber struggled for decades to find an adequate system of notation before eventually giving up. At one point he

even hired professional musicologists to help him transcribe these texts, yet the music of this region was a challenge even to the great musicologist Herzog.

Fortunately Kroeber succeeded in documenting this rich musical tradition, cataloging thousands of songs and leaving behind a legacy that rivals John Peabody Harrington's linguistic work in terms of the sheer volume of unanalyzed archives.[49] The case of Ishi, the last speaker of the Yahi language, stands out in particular, given that Kroeber made extensive sound recordings without ever succeeding in cracking the semantic code that would shed light on the narratives behind Ishi's words, stories, and songs.[50] Even Sapir was unable to reveal the structures of Ishi's speech, leaving only a physical record of the sounds, which a gifted linguist, musicologist, or community member may partially decode someday, especially by drawing on comparisons to other related language in the area.[51] Of course this impressive record of Indigenous music must be seen as part of the Boasian legacy, given that Boas urged his students to take music seriously and to document it as an important part of both culture and expressive art. Now that we better understand the limitations of transcription for both language and music, the Kroeber corpus is even more impressive.[52]

Though most of Boas's students commented on music in their writings, Herzog was the principal specialist in this area, just as Sapir was the principal specialist in linguistics.[53] Herzog's ability was no less impressive than Sapir's, and Herzog is a legend in ethnomusicology, as Sapir is among linguists. Unfortunately Herzog's story is not as well known among anthropologists, though he deserves a place in the history of cultural anthropology and linguistics, alongside his primary area of ethnomusicology. Like Sapir and Lévi-Strauss, Herzog was also a committed comparativist, and in fact the field was called *comparative musicology* in his day, taking the name *ethnomusicology* only in the 1950s, when the focus was restricted to the study of music in specific cultural contexts.[54] From this platform of comparison, Herzog was one of the first anthropologists to discuss the place of culture areas in music, an insight he developed in his classic piece "Musical Styles in North America." In a truly Boasian fashion he was comfortable working with any musical tradition, carrying out original research on the music of West Africa, the U.S. Plains, and the U.S. Southwest, while also making thousands of sound recordings in these areas, which he was beginning to systematically transcribe during his brief teaching career at Indiana University in the late 1940s and early 1950s.[55] As his published record reveals, he was able to intuit the structure of any type of music, even grasping polyrhythms from West Africa

and the rapid-fire folk melodies of Eastern European folk music.[56] Like Boas and Sapir, he was an accomplished musician, primarily specializing in the piano—a good choice for an ethnomusicologist, given that multiple notes and parts can be played at once, across a range that rivals that of the human voice.[57] (The keys on the piano also correspond exactly to the "notes" in standard Western notation, unlike fingerings on a violin, for instance, which can easily play pitches above or below the standard value.) Unfortunately his career was cut short by mental illness.[58] Thus even in the case of northwestern California, Herzog never finished the analysis of the materials he collected while working with Sapir, which were full of challenging microtones, polyrhythms, and polyphonic singing. Even in his short career, however, Herzog succeeded in training the two principal scholars in the field of ethnomusicology, Bruno Nettl and Alan Merriam. Thus the influence of Boas can still be felt in contemporary ethnomusicology, given that two of its architects were trained by one of his own students.

Helen Roberts is another major figure in the early history of ethnomusicology, who, like Herzog and Sapir, was trained as a generalist. and so was not limited to any one geographical area or theoretical topic. In a fairly modern way she wrote musical ethnographies, covering Jamaica, Hawaii, and several areas of North America, from northern California to the American Southwest.[59] Like Boas, she was always sensitive to variation, personal style, and creative forces in Native society, all of which militate against simplistic ethnic stereotyping (essentialism). She was also one of the first voices in musicology to call for an analysis of music from an Indigenous (even a discursive) perspective.[60] Roberts also completed several papers on comparison. She was one of the first to apply the "culture area" model to the music of North America, following Herzog.[61] In another sense of comparison she wrote a groundbreaking piece on the circulation of songs across ethnic and linguistic boundaries in the American Southwest, where she found that even subtle changes in meter or accent could bear a strong ethnic mark, perhaps one that an outsider would not even notice.[62] Like Herskovits, she used comparison to ascertain the origins of a musical style, tracing the African roots of Jamaican songs.[63]

The Role of Comparison: The Case of Claude Lévi-Strauss

The question of comparison often comes up in relation to Boas. It is interesting to revisit this question in the light of his legacy on ethnomusicology, given that comparison was so central to his efforts in tracing the historical, linguistic, and cultural basis of the music. Thanks to Marvin

Harris (among others), many people believe that Boas was opposed to cross-cultural comparison, perhaps as a violation of the principle of cultural relativism, whereby each culture is understood on its own terms.[64] This is a myth, in the sense that the story continues to circulate without much critical scrutiny or even attention to the body of work produced by Boas and his students. Worse, this widely accepted narrative is a deliberate distortion on the part of those who sought to cut Boas down, suggesting that he was not theoretical. Skeptical, rather than nontheoretical, might be a more accurate assessment. As we have already seen, Boas frequently invoked comparison in his own work, in both identifying universals and in teasing out general tendencies; many of his students excelled at comparison.[65]

As Darnell points out, Lévi-Strauss was another inheritor of the Boasian legacy, even if he was a "self-incorporated Americanist," working himself into this tradition not as a student but as an admirer and eventual colleague.[66] Rather than being trained by Boas directly, Lévi-Strauss came under his influence rather heavily, especially during a brief period in the early 1940s when he, Boas, and Roman Jakobson were all living in New York. When he died, Boas collapsed into Lévi-Strauss's arms, in a sense passing on the tradition to the next generation. Like Boas, Lévi-Strauss wrote extensively about music and even dedicated the first volume of his masterpiece, *Mythologies*, simply "To Music."[67] Notably this book is structured around musical concepts, with musical titles for every chapter and section, as if the work were itself unfolding like a symphony in many parts, each one related to the whole. However, the pervasive reference to music is not merely a literary device or aesthetic choice but a reflection of Lévi-Strauss's claim that myth and music were profoundly similar at bottom,[68] both working with layered structures that come together to form coherent wholes, often in a highly unconscious way.

This premise is a recapitulation on one of the central themes Boas himself had laid out in *Primitive Art* nearly thirty-five years before, where he asserted that poetry, music, and myth were deeply related arts, perhaps emerging from the similar sound-symbolic processes, with parallel principles of rhythmic, melodic, and narrative structure. Over the course of his career Lévi-Strauss elaborated upon this theme, developing the idea in his own way, while augmenting the degree of comparison far beyond anything Boas himself had undertaken. Building on the discussion from *Primitive Art*, where Boas carefully considers the overlap among language, music, and oral literature, Lévi-Strauss once proposed a more elaborate scheme of analysis.[69] He went on to claim that music, in contrast to language, lacks the level of the word, or a sound pattern with a discrete

conceptual meaning; instead, he claimed, music proceeds directly to the level of the sentence, with a melody, thus generating a larger narrative meaning that is greater than the sum of its parts. That is, in music one goes directly from tonal units, which he calls "sonemes," to the sentence, presumably through a process of syntax or phrasal structure. While language clearly operates on both planes of sound and meaning simultaneously, sound takes center stage in music (meaning being secondary), while meaning dominates in myth (where sound is secondary).

In his work on the unconscious structures of human thought, Lévi-Strauss explicitly compared myth to music, for in both, he reasoned, the part echoes the whole, much as a prelude introduces themes that will be developed later on in a piece of music.[70] In a broadcast interview he revealed that he approached the difficult matter of comparative mythology much as a conductor would approach reading a musical score from top to bottom, reading all of the notated parts simultaneously (as lines going across the page):

> Therefore, we have to read the myth more or less as we would read an orchestral score, not state after stave, but understanding that we should apprehend the whole page and understand that something which was written on the first stave at the top of the page acquires meaning only if one considers that it is part and parcel of what is written below on the second stave, the third stave, and so on. That is, we have to read not only from left to right, but at the same time vertically, from top to bottom. We have to understand that each page is a totality. And it is only by treating the myth as if it were an orchestral score, written stave after stave, that we can understand it as a totality, that we can extract the meaning out of the myth.[71]

What better illustration could there be of the principle of holism, often considered one of the hallmarks of Boasian anthropology? Indeed with both myth and music, the part can be understood only in relation to the whole, much as a single tale must be placed alongside all other variations to comprehend its full significance as it might be understood within a culture, among those familiar with the full corpus. The metaphor was also a visual one for Lévi-Strauss; in a conductor's score, he noted, all of the parts are notated in parallel lines going across the page, but the conductor must read all of these lines simultaneously, as vertical columns on the page, measure by measure. The audience, for that matter, hears all of those parts simultaneously, even if the individual parts are written out separately. Myth, he reasoned, was a similar process.

The Boasian Legacy in Ethnomusicology

No one today would consider Lévi-Strauss a specialist in music—or even a specialist in comparative mythology. Like Boas, he was a generalist, working on the huge range of issues related to human cultural expression. However, as was the case with Boas, music played heavily into his thinking about humanity. Further, and again like Boas, his vision of music was holistic, not partitioned off from the rest of social life but very much a part of his effort to understand not only oral literature or myth but also the human mind. Interestingly the comparative element in Boas's work, which surfaces in his earliest writings on music and is carried through until the end, in *Primitive Art*, is carried on in the work of Lévi-Strauss in terms that were familiar to Boas—namely, in the comparative study of myth and music.

The Boasian Influence on Ethnomusicology

One is left to wonder: What would the field of ethnomusicology look like if Boas had never crossed the Atlantic or had taken up the comparative study of musicology? The case of Frances Densmore is instructive here, given that she was a contemporary of Boas and also worked in North America, but without anthropological training or the same level of interest in cultural context. Though she contributed massively to the scholarly record on North American Indigenous music, she was not trained by Boas (who taught at Columbia) but at Harvard, where Boasian relativism had not yet taken hold. Nor was her work ever as holistic as that of Boas and his students, often leaving out the social significance and ethnographic background of the music she was documenting. Late in his career Boas took aim at the technical side of Densmore's work, not surprisingly finding an absence of cultural relativism, in the sense that she had incorrectly analyzed some of the rhythms by hammering them into familiar European patterns, much as nineteenth-century amateur linguists had done with Native American languages.[72] Boas must have had a profound musical acumen since he was able to effortlessly assign these songs to challenging time signatures like 5/4 and 7/4, clearly revealing a regularity that Densmore had missed, despite all of her training in music. In other cases Densmore proposed a more complex pattern than the data called for in part because she was following the rhythm of the lyrics, which were out of step with the drum beat, as is often the case with Western music as well. Since Boas was equally at home in the realms of both language and music, this caused no confusion for him—which only underscores once more the importance of the holistic approach.

Even before the pioneering musicologist George Herzog immigrated to America, Boas and Sapir had already responded to Adler and Stumpf

in Europe, two major architects of ethnomusicology on the international scene. In one of Sapir's first reviews, published in 1912, he lays out an incisive critique of Stumpf's very formal approach to comparative musicology.[73] This piece also gives us insight into the Boasian critiques of other trends in comparative musicology. Echoing classic Boasian skepticism, Sapir commented that we could not easily reconstruct the history of humanity by making endless comparisons among present-day musical traditions, as one might trace the history of a linguistic family and construct a proto-stock through comparative inference. Where Sumpf, like other European musicologists, insisted on the study of modes and scales as the primary pursuit, Sapir pointed out that one could not neglect other aspects of music. Even on purely structural grounds, other features were being ignored, such as unusual time signatures, polyrhythm, microtones, and even atonal music! Of course, as a student of Boas, Sapir was quick to point out the obvious omission of the social context, which was largely treated as superfluous to musical analysis at the time.

Even far outside the halls of academia there is evidence that Boas had a significant influence on the development of musicology. Two of the legendary musicologists of the twentieth century frequently corresponded with Boas, namely Alan Lomax and Charles Seeger. Lomax studied at Columbia in the 1930s, working with two of Boas's students, Herskovits and Roberts; later he crossed paths with Mead, who mentored him on the premises of Boasian anthropology while they were both teaching at Columbia in the 1960s. In terms of his intellectual output, Lomax is probably most remembered for his cantometric methodology, which, despite the name, characterizes songs in terms of vocal quality.[74] This system is somewhat Boasian in spirit, in the sense that Boas was constantly underscoring the importance of perception, not structure alone, in the realms of both language and music.

A final question will have to remain unanswered: What would Boas think of contemporary ethnomusicology? Considering the central place of music in his early work, I imagine that he would wonder why cultural anthropology had turned away from music as a central pursuit, a necessary part of every ethnography or linguistic work. I suspect he would be pleased to find that linguistics in particular had come to embrace the scope of human languages, moving away from its insular Indo-European roots to the more abstract and comparative study of all languages and from the notion that some languages were "primitive." By the same logic I imagine Boas would be surprised that mainstream musicology—in contrast the smaller field of ethnomusicology—had not quite made room for all the world's musical traditions, much as linguistics has made room for

all languages, without exception. (While most ethnomusicologists argue that all music is ethnic, even Western classical music, the field of musicology as a whole still has not completely accepted this anthropological view.) Thus I suspect that Boas would be less than satisfied to find ethnomusicology still struggling to find a voice in mainstream anthropology and even musicology more generally. Certainly, as a founding figure in linguistics, he was not content to let the study of minority languages stand as a ghettoized field, at the margins of anthropology or mainstream linguistics. Instead he insisted that linguistics make room for the minority languages and treat them equally in intellectual terms. So, in a significant sense, anthropology is still in need of a complete Boasian revolution. Boas would probably insist that we analyze music in a holistic fashion, not partitioning it off as a separate specialization but including it alongside the study of language, culture, and social structure. In another sense he might have been surprised to witness the turn away from comparison, as the field went from comparative musicology to ethnomusicology.

Why music played a lesser role in linguistic and ethnographic work following Boas's death is something of a mystery, given that nearly all of his students in fact commented on the role of music at some point in their careers, generally working music into one of their major theoretical statements. What changed after his death? Does the turn away from music merely reflect the lesser focus on musical training in our own culture, perhaps as a result of the phonograph, the radio, and ultimately the television, which obviated the need for live performances in everyday life? While the phonograph played a heroic and revolutionary role in documenting music during Boas's time,[75] sadly it may have played a role in removing live music from the home and life during our own era. Or is the lesser emphasis on music a consequence of increasing specialization in anthropological training? Whatever the reason, there has been a noticeable turn away from Boas's more musical vision for the profession, wherein each anthropologist is responsible not merely for describing single cultures but also for making comparisons across cultures and drawing careful theoretical conclusions, as Boas did from the start.

Notes

1. See Boas, *The Central Eskimo*, 240–50; Boas, *Chinook Texts*, 150; Sapir, *Takelma Texts and Grammar*.
2. See Sapir, "Song Recitative in Paiute Mythology"; Roberts, "Chakwena Songs of Zuñi and Laguna"; Herzog "Speech-Melody and Primitive Music."
3. See Nettl, *Theory and Method in Ethnomusicology*; Merriam, *The Anthropology of Music*; Meyers, *Ethnomusicology: An Introduction*, 3.

4. See Nettl, *The Study of Ethnomusicology*; McLean, *Pioneers of Ethnomusicology*.
5. See Meyers, *Ethnomusicology: An Introduction*, 118–19; Jacknis, "Franz Boas and the Music of the Northwest Coast Indians"; Keeling, "Voices from Siberia"; McLean, *Pioneers of Ethnomusicology*, 115–16.
6. Meyers, *Ethnomusicology: An Introduction*, 3.
7. Meyers, *Ethnomusicology: An Introduction*, 118–19; Keeling, "Voices from Siberia," 284–85. See Jacknis, "Franz Boas and the Music of the Northwest Coast Indians."
8. "This is about the way I feel, dear Marie. The entire last part of the ninth symphony is going around in my head. Joy, only joy fills me. I do not know why I should be so happy today, but I am. If I were at home I believe I would indulge in all kinds of foolishness, I feel so merry . . . and I shall hurry as fast as I can to get home, but first to you. . . .

    "9 p.m. 'All day my mind has been full of music, especially 'Freude schooner Gotterfunken,' this uplifting music! I am longing to hear some good music, but since I cannot, I shut my eyes and think it. Later, when I shall be living a quiet, ordered life, I shall learn to play again. Then when my heart is full of happiness and love, you will be sitting at my side, and we will listen together to the unforgettable masterpieces. No other art moves me as deeply as music. It gives me the fullest expression to all my feelings.'" Franz Boas Correspondence, Arctic Expedition Diary (translation), 1883–1884, seven folders, box 2. I would like to thank Isaiah Wilner, who is deeply familiar with the contents of these diaries, for bringing this to my attention.
9. Boas, *The Central Eskimo*, 240–50.
10. Brady, *A Spiral Way*; Levine, *Writing American Indian Music*; Jacknis, "Franz Boas and the Music of the Northwest Coast Indians."
11. Meyers, *Ethnomusicology: An Introduction*, 118.
12. Cole, *Franz Boas: The Early Years*, 32.
13. Cole, *Franz Boas: The Early Years*.
14. See the following by Boas: "Poetry and Music of Some North American Tribes"; "Chinook Songs"; *Chinook Texts*; "Salishan Texts"; "Introductory"; "Notes on the Kwakiutl Vocabulary"; "Dance and Music in the Life of the Northwest Coast Indians."
15. Boas, "A Journey in Cumberland Sound," 271. What Boas describes here sounds a great deal like participant-observation, many decades before Malinowski advocated this revolutionary methodology, given that Boas lived among the Inuit long enough to learn their language and even understand their ceremonies and songs well enough to transcribe them. However, Boas does not use this expression, nor does he draw much attention to his methodology, which is far more sophisticated than he makes out, given that he was able to grasp the language, the culture, and the musical traditions well enough to document them during his short stay.
16. Boas, "Poetry and Music of Some North American Tribes," 385.

17. Boas, "Poetry and Music of Some North American Tribes," 383.
18. In "Umfang, Methode und Ziel der Musikwisssenschaft," Adler called for an all-encompassing field that would embrace not only the cultural underpinnings of music, in terms of its meaning within the community, but also the full range of musical expression in each society, including all of the genres one might find in a given society. Like Boas, he also called for a relativistic framework, taking local cultural values into consideration. See Nettl, *Nettl's Elephant*, 21.
19. Kroeber, "The Superorganic," 200.
20. Boas, *The Central Eskimo*, 240–50.
21. Roberts and Haeberlin, "Some Songs of the Puget Sound Salish"; Herzog, "The Yuman Musical Style"; Brady, *A Spiral Way*; Jacknis, "Franz Boas and the Music of the Northwest Coast Indians."
22. Boas, *The Central Eskimo*, 244.
23. See the following by Boas: "On Certain Songs and Dances of the Kwakiutl of British Columbia"; "Eskimo Tales and Songs"; "Songs of the Kwakiutl Indians"; "Chinook Songs"; "Salishan Texts."
24. Boas, "Poetry and Music of Some North American Tribes," 383–84.
25. Boas, "Eskimo Tales and Songs," 46.
26. See Harris, *The Rise of Anthropological Theory*, for a grossly distorted image of Boas.
27. Boas, "Introductory," 8.
28. Boas, *The Central Eskimo*, 140–50.
29. Boas, "On Alternating Sounds."
30. Boas, "The Occurrence of Similar Inventions in Areas Widely Apart," 65.
31. Jacknis, "Yahi Culture in the Wax Museum," 108.
32. See Wickwire, "The Grizzly Gave Them the Song," for the limitations even in Boas's careful approach.
33. See the following by Boas: "Dance and Music in the Life of the Northwest Coast Indians"; "On Certain Songs and Dances of the Kwakiutl of British Columbia."
34. Boas, *Primitive Art*, 299–300.
35. Lord, *The Singer of Tales*.
36. Boas, review of "A Study of Omaha Indian Music," 170.
37. Kroeber is the one student who, to my knowledge, took him up on this daunting task, endlessly documenting musical lore of the state of California, though that story is not well known.
38. Mead, *Coming of Age in Samoa*, 66.
39. Mead, *Growing Up in New Guinea*, 43.
40. Mead, *Growing Up in New Guinea*, 43–44, 181, 200.
41. Mead, *Growing Up in New Guinea*, 258–77.
42. See the following by Hurston: "Cudjo's Own Story of the Last African Slaver"; "Melodic Composition and Scale Foundations in Primitive Music"; *Their Eyes Were Watching God*.

43. See the following by Herskovits: "Negro Art"; "The Negro in the New World"; "Some Recent Developments in the Study of West African Native Life"; *The Myth of the Negro Past*; "The Southernmost Outposts of New World Africanisms"; "Problem, Method and Theory in Afroamerican Studies"; "The Contribution of Afroamerican Studies to Africanist Research"; "Anthropology and Africa: A Wider Perspective"; *The New World Negro*.
44. Quoted in Darnell, *Edward Sapir*, 153.
45. Victor Golla, personal communication, 1998; Haas, "Thai Word Games" and *Thai–English Student's Dictionary*.
46. Recent work in neuroscience sheds further light on the role music plays in cognition, suggesting primarily that playing music helps integrate brain functioning, strengthening communication throughout the brain's many centers. With professional musicians, a thickening of some brain regions is noticeable even on cursory inspection, especially the auditory cortex and the corpus callosum, which connects the two brain hemispheres, allowing for communication between the right and left sides. For this reason Oliver Sacks, a renowned physician and expert on neuroscience, even claims, "Anatomists today would be hard put to identify the brain of a visual artist, a writer, or a mathematician—but they could recognize the brain of a professional musician without a moment's hesitation" (*Musicophilia*, 94). Given that Sapir, Boas, and Lévi-Strauss all dedicated much of their private lives to their musical interests, it may be no accident that these scholars were all gifted generalists in their professional lives, able to make comparisons and see connections across a wide range of issues within the field. Music, in other words, may have primed not only their ears for language but also their brains for holistic, comparative thinking.
47. Sapir, *The Psychology of Culture*, 645.
48. Boas, "On Alternating Sounds."
49. Keeling, *A Guide to the Field Recordings* and *North American Indian Music*.
50. Jacknis, "Yahi Culture in the Wax Museum."
51. Consider the case of Jessie Little Doe Baird, who succeeded in reviving her ancestral language, Wampanoag, though no one had spoken it for over a hundred years when she started in the 1990s. She worked mostly from existing documentation, with the assistance of the linguist Ken Hale, which also involved drawing on the comparative record of related languages in the Algonquian family, where there were gaps in the record. Even Noam Chomsky doubted it was possible, until it came to pass.
52. In the decade following Kroeber's death another stealth Boasian, Alan Lomax, proposed a system of analysis known as cantometrics (*Folk Song Style and Culture* and *Cantometrics*) that was far better at characterizing these fine nuances of musical texture, including such subtle details as the tone of the speaker's voice and the use of counterpoint (see Keeling, *Cry for Luck*). Though not widely considered a Boasian, Lomax had come under Boas's

influence while at Columbia in the 1930s; to the extent that Lomax was concerned with documenting the cultural meaning of music, as well as with tracing its roots through careful comparison, Boas probably left his mark.

53. See Reed, "The Innovator and the Primitives: George Herzog in Historical Perspective"; Nettl, *Becoming an Ethnomusicologist*, 27–84.
54. Meyers, *Ethnomusicology: An Introduction*, 3.
55. See the following by Herzog, "Primitive Music"; "Plains Ghost Dance and Great Basin Music"; *Research in Primitive and Folk Music*.
56. Herzog, "Drum Signaling in a West African Tribe" and "Béla Bartók as a Folklorist-Composer."
57. Nettl, *Becoming an Ethnomusicologist*.
58. Nettl, *Becoming an Ethnomusicologist*, 27–84.
59. See the following by Roberts: "A Study of Folk Song Variants"; "Possible Survivals of African Song in Jamaica"; *Ancient Hawaiian Music*; "The First Salmon Ceremony of the Karuk Indians"; "Chakwena Songs of Zuñi and Laguna."
60. Roberts, review of *Teton Sioux Music* by Frances Densmore.
61. Roberts, *Musical Areas in Aboriginal North America*; Herzog, "Musical Styles in North America."
62. Roberts, *Musical Areas in Aboriginal North America*, 177–84.
63. Roberts, "Possible Survivals of African Song in Jamaica."
64. See Harris, *The Rise of Anthropological Theory*, 258–59.
65. See Sapir, *Time-Perspective in Aboriginal American Culture*; Herzog, "Musical Styles in North America"; Roberts, *Musical Areas in Aboriginal North America*; Benedict, *Patterns of Culture*.
66. Darnell, *Invisible Genealogies*, 282–89.
67. Lévi-Strauss, *The Raw and the Cooked*, vii; see Launay, "Myth and Music."
68. Boon, *From Symbolism to Structuralism*, 167–78.
69. Lévi-Strauss, *Myth and Meaning*, 45–47.
70. Lévi-Strauss, *The Raw and the Cooked*, 14–32.
71. Lévi-Strauss, *Myth and Meaning*, 40.
72. Boas, "Teton Sioux Music."
73. Sapir, review of *Die Anfänge der Musik* by Carl Stumpf.
74. Lomax, *Folk Song Style and Culture*.
75. See Brady, *A Spiral Way*.

References

MANUSCRIPTS AND ARCHIVES

APS. Franz Boas Papers, Mss.B.B61. American Philosophical Society, Philadelphia.

PUBLISHED WORKS

Adler, Guido. "Umfang, Methode und Ziel der Musikwisssenschaft." *Vierteljahrschrift für Musikwissenschaft*. 1 (1885): 5–20.

Benedict, Ruth. *Patterns of Culture*. New York: Harcourt, 1934.
Boas, Franz. *The Central Eskimo*. 1888. Lincoln NE: Bison Books, 1964.
———. "Chinook Songs." *Journal of American Folklore* 1.3 (1888): 220–26.
———. *Chinook Texts*. Bureau of American Ethnology, Bulletin 20. Washington DC: Government Printing Office, 1894.
———. "Current Beliefs of the Kwakiutl Indians." *Journal of American Folklore* 45.176 (1932): 177–260.
———. "Dance and Music in the Life of the Northwest Coast Indians of North America (Kwakiutl)." In Franziska Boas, ed., *The Function of Dance in Human Society: A Seminar Directed by Franziska Boas*, 7–18. 2nd ed. with new introduction. 1944. Brooklyn: Dance Horizons, 1972.
———. "Eskimo Tales and Songs." *Journal of American Folklore* 7.24 (1894): 45–50.
———. *Ethnology of the Kwakiutl Indians*. Memoirs of the American Museum of Natural History, Annual Report 35 (1913–1914), pt. 2, 795–1481. Washington DC: Government Printing Office, 1921.
———. "The Indians of British Columbia." *Journal of the American Geographical Society of New York* 28.3 (1896): 229–43.
———. "Introductory." *International Journal of American Linguistics* 1.1 (1917): 1–8.
———. "A Journey in Cumberland Sound on the West Shore of Davis Strait in 1883 and 1884." *Journal of the American Geographical Society of New York* 16 (1884): 242–72.
———. "Mythology and Folk-Tales of the North American Indians." *Journal of American Folklore* 27.106 (1914): 374–410.
———. "Notes on Mexican Folk-Lore." *Journal of American Folklore* 25.97 (1912): 204–60.
———. "Notes on the Kwakiutl Vocabulary." *International Journal of American Linguistics* 6.3–4 (1931): 163–78.
———. "The Occurrence of Similar Inventions in Areas Widely Apart: Museums of Ethnology and Their Classification." 1887. In George W. Stocking, ed., *The Shaping of American Anthropology, 1883–1991: A Franz Boas Reader*, 61–67. New York: Basic Books, 1974.
———. "On Alternating Sounds." *American Anthropologist* 2.1 (1889): 47–52.
———. "On Certain Songs and Dances of the Kwakiutl of British Columbia." *Journal of American Folklore* 1.1 (1888): 49–64.
———. "Poetry and Music of Some North American Tribes." *Science* 9 (1887): 383–85.
———. *Primitive Art*. 1927. New York: Dover, 1955.
———.. "The Relationships of the Eskimos of East Greenland." *Science* 30.772 (1909): 535–36.
———. Review of "A Study of Omaha Indian Music, by Alice Fletcher, Aided by Alice Fletcher, with a Report on the Structural Peculiarities of the Music by John Comfort Filmore." Archeological and Ethnological Papers of the Peabody Museum of Harvard University, vol. 1, no 5, Cambridge MA, June 1893. *Journal of American Folklore* 7.25 (1886): 169–71.

———. "A Revised List of Kwakiutl Suffixes." *International Journal of American Linguistics* 3.1 (1924): 117–31.

———. "Salishan Texts." *Proceedings of the American Philosophical Society* 34.147 (1895): 31–48.

———. "The Social Organization of the Tribes of the North Pacific Coast." *American Anthropologist* 26.3 (1924): 323–32.

———. "Some Traits of Primitive Culture." *Journal of American Folklore* 17.67 (1904): 243–54.

———. "Songs of the Kwakiutl Indians." *Internationales Archiv für Ethnographie* 9 (1896): 1–9.

———. "Stylistic Aspects of Primitive Literature." *Journal of American Folklore* 38.149 (1925): 329–39.

———. "Summary of the Work of the International School of American Archeology and Ethnology in Mexico." *American Anthropologist* 17.2 (1915): 384–95.

———. "Teton Sioux Music." *Journal of American Folklore* 38.148 (1925): 319–24.

———. "Traditions of the Tillamook Indians." *Journal of American Folklore* 11.41 (1898): 133–50.

———. "Traditions of the Ts'ets'ā'ut." *Journal of American Folklore* 10.36 (1897): 35–48.

———. "Vocabulary of the Kwakiutl Language." *Proceedings of the American Philosophical Society* 31.140 (1893): 34–82.

Boas, Franz, and Ella Deloria. "Notes on the Dakota, Teton Dialect." *International Journal of American Linguistics* 7.3–4 (1933): 97–121.

Boas, Franz, Helene Boas Yampolsky, and Zellig S. Harris. "Kwakiutl Grammar with a Glossary of the Suffixes." *Transactions of the American Philosophical Society*, n.s., 37.3 (1947): 203–377.

Boon, James A. *From Symbolism to Structuralism: Lévi-Strauss in a Literary Tradition*. Oxford: Blackwell, 1972.

Brady, Erika. *A Spiral Way: How the Phonograph Changed Ethnography*. Jackson: University Press of Mississippi, 1999.

Cole, Douglas. *Franz Boas: The Early Years, 1858–1906*. Seattle: University of Washington Press, 1999.

Darnell, Regna. "Camelot at Yale: The Construction and Dismantling of the Sapirian Synthesis, 1931–39." *American Anthropologist* 100.2 (1998): 361–72.

———. *Edward Sapir: Linguist, Anthropologist, Humanist*. Berkeley: University of California Press, 1990.

———. *Invisible Genealogies: A History of Americanist Anthropology*. Lincoln: University of Nebraska Press, 2001.

Densmore, Francis. *Teton Sioux Music*. Bureau of American Ethnology, Bulletin 61. Washington DC: Government Printing Office, 1918.

Haas, Mary. *Thai—English Student's Dictionary*. Stanford: Stanford University Press, 1964.

———. "Thai Word Games." *Journal of American Folklore*, 1957, 173–75.

Haeberlin, Hermann, and Franz Boas. "Mythology of Puget Sound." *Journal of American Folklore* 37.145–46 (1924): 371–438.

Harris, Marvin. *The Rise of Anthropological Theory*. New York: Thomas Crowell, 1968.

Herskovits, Melville Jean. "The Ahistorical Approach to Afroamerican Studies: A Critique." *American Anthropologist* 62.4 (1960): 559–68.

———. "Anthropology and Africa: A Wider Perspective. The Lugard Memorial Lecture for 1959." *Africa: Journal of the International African Institute* 29.3 (1959): 225–38.

———. "The Contribution of Afroamerican Studies to Africanist Research." *American Anthropologist* 50.1.1 (1948): 1–10.

———. "Drums and Drummers in Afro-Brazilian Cult Life." *Musical Quarterly* 30.4 (1944): 477–92.

———. *The Human Factor in Changing Africa*. New York: Knopf, 1962.

———. *The Myth of the Negro Past*. New York: Harper, 1941.

———. "Negro Art: African and American." *Social Forces* 5.2 (1926): 291–98.

———. "The Negro in Bahia, Brazil: A Problem in Method." *American Sociological Review* 8.4 (1943): 394–404.

———. "The Negro in the New World: The Statement of a Problem." *American Anthropologist* 32.1 (1930): 145–55.

———. *The New World Negro: Selected Papers in Afro-American Studies*. Bloomington: Indiana University Press, 1966.

———. "Past Developments and Present Currents in Ethnology." *American Anthropologist* 61.3 (1959): 389–98.

———. "The Present Status and Needs of Afroamerican Research." *Journal of Negro History* 36.2 (1951): 123–47.

———. "Problem, Method and Theory in Afroamerican Studies." *Phylon* 7.4 (1946): 337–54.

———. "The Significance of West Africa for Negro Research." *Journal of Negro History* 21.1 (1936): 15–30.

———. "Some Next Steps in the Study of Negro Folklore." *Journal of American Folklore*. Elsie Clews Parsons Memorial 56.219 (1943): 1–7.

———. "Some Recent Developments in the Study of West African Native Life." *Journal of Negro History* 24.1 (1939): 14–32.

———. "Some Thoughts on American Research in Africa." *African Studies Bulletin* 1.2 (1958): 1–11.

———. "The Southernmost Outposts of New World Africanisms." *American Anthropologist* 45.4.1 (1943): 495–510.

Herskovits, Melville J., and Frances Herskovits. *Suriname Folklore*. With transcription of songs and musicological analysis by Dr. M. Kolinski. Columbia University Contributions to Anthropology 27. New York: Columbia University Press, 1936.

Herzog, George. "Béla Bartók as a Folklorist-Composer." *Bulletin of the American Musicological Society* 11–13 (1948): 17–18.

———. "A Comparison of Pueblo and Pima Musical Styles." *Journal of American Folklore* 49.194 (1936): 283–417.

———. "Do Animals Have Music?" *Bulletin of the American Musicological Society* 5 (1941): 3–4.

———. "Drum Signaling in a West African Tribe." *Word* 1 (1945): 217–38.

———. "Expression in Primitive and Folk Music." *Bulletin of the American Musicological Society* 4 (1940): 25.

———. "General Characteristics of Primitive Music." *Bulletin of the American Musicological Society* 7 (1943): 23–26.

———. *Jabo Proverbs from Liberia: Maxims in the Life of a Native Tribe*. London: Oxford University Press, 1936.

———. "Musical Styles in North America." *Proceedings of the 23rd International Congress of Americanists*, 1930, 455–58.

———. "The Music of Yugoslav Heroic Epic Folk Poetry." *Journal of the International Folk Music Council* 3 (1951): 62–64.

———. "Note on Pima Moieties." *American Anthropologist*, n.s., 38.3.1 (1936): 520–21.

———. "Observations on Text and Melody in Primitive Music." *Bulletin of the American Musicological Society* 6 (1942): 9–11.

———. "On Primitive Music." *American Anthropologist* 34.3 (1932): 546–48.

———. "On the Phonemic Status of Pima-Papago *w* versus *v*, with a Note on Orthography." *International Journal of American Linguistics* 48.1 (1982): 86–87.

———. "Plains Ghost Dance and Great Basin Music." *American Anthropologist* 37.3.1 (1935): 403–19.

———. "Play-Party Song." *American Speech* 12.3 (1937): 215–17.

———. "Primitive Music." *Bulletin of the American Musicological Society* 1 (1936): 3–4.

———. *Research in Primitive and Folk Music in the United States*. Bulletin 24. Washington DC: American Council of Learned Societies, 1936.

———. Review of *Ancient Hawaiian Music* by Helen H. Roberts. *Journal of American Folklore* 41.159 (1928): 178–81.

———. Review of *Form in Primitive Music: An Analytical and Comparative Study of the Melodic Form of Some Ancient Southern California Indian Songs* by Helen H. Roberts. *American Anthropologist* 36.3 (1934): 476–78.

———. Review of *Jewish Cantillation and Song in the Isle of Djerba* by Robert Lachmann. *Jewish Social Studies* 3.4 (1941): 430–31.

———. Review of *Musical and Other Sound Instruments of the South American Indians: A Comparative Ethnographical Study* by Karl Gustav Izikowitz. *American Anthropologist* 42.2.1 (1940): 338–41.

———. Review of *Musik des Orients* by Robert Lachmann. *American Anthropologist* 33.2 (1931): 253–57.

———. Review of *The Musical Instruments of the Native Races of South Africa* by Percival R. Kirby. *American Anthropologist* 43.1 (1941): 105–6.

———. "Rhythmic Cadence in Primitive Music." *Bulletin of the American Musicological Society* 3 (1939): 19–20.

———. "Some Primitive Layers in European Folk Music." *Bulletin of the American Musicological Society* 9–10 (1947): 11–14.

———. "Speech-Melody and Primitive Music." *Musical Quarterly* 20 (1934): 452–66.

———. "Study of Native Music in America." *Proceedings of the Eighth American Scientific Congress* 2 (1942): 203–9.

———. "The Yuman Musical Style." *Journal of American Folklore* 41.160 (1928): 183–231.

Herzog, George, and Harold Courlander. *The Cow-Tail Switch.* New York: Henry Holt, 1947.

Hurston, Zora Neale. *Collected Plays.* Edited and with an Introduction by Jean Lee Cole and Charles Mitchell. New Brunswick NJ: Rutgers University Press, 2008.

———. "Cudjo's Own Story of the Last African Slaver." *Journal of Negro History* 12.4 (1927): 648–63.

———. "Folklore and Music." *Frontiers: A Journal of Women* 12.1 (1991): 182–98.

———. "Melodic Composition and Scale Foundations in Primitive Music." *American Anthropologist* 34.1 (1932): 79–110.

———. *Their Eyes Were Watching God.* 1937. New York: Harper-Collins, 2006.

Jacknis, Ira. "Franz Boas and the Music of the Northwest Coast Indians." In Laurel Kendall and Igor Krupnik, eds., *Constructing Cultures Then and Now: Celebrating Franz Boas and the Jesup North Pacific Expedition*, 105–22. Contributions to Circumpolar Anthropology 4. Washington DC: Arctic Studies Center, Smithsonian Institution, 2003.

———. "Yahi Culture in the Wax Museum: Ishi's Sound Recordings." In Karl Kroeber and Clifton Kroeber, eds., *Ishi in Three Centuries*, 235–74. Lincoln: University of Nebraska Press, 2003.

Keeling, Richard. *Cry for Luck: Sacred Song and Speech among the Hupa, Yurok, and Karok Indians of Northwestern California.* Berkeley: University of California Press, 1992.

———. *A Guide to the Field Recordings (1900–1949) at the Lowie Museum of Anthropology.* Berkeley: University of California Press, 1991.

———. *North American Indian Music: A Guide to the Published Sources and Selected Recordings.* New York: Garland, 1997.

———. "Voices from Siberia: Ethnomusicology of the Jesup Expedition." In Igor Krupnik and William W. Fitzhugh, eds., *Gateways: Exploring the Legacy of the Jesup North Pacific Expedition, 1897–1902*, 279–96. Contributions to Circumpolar Anthropology 1. Washington DC: Arctic Studies Center, Smithsonian Institution, 2001.

Kroeber, Alfred. *Configurations of Culture Growth.* Berkeley: University of California Press, 1944.

———. "The Superorganic." *American Anthropologist* 19.2 (1917): 163–213.

Launay, Robert. "Myth and Music: The Musical Epigraphs to *The Raw and the Cooked*." In Regna Darnell and Frederic W. Gleach, eds., *Histories of Anthropology Annual*, 7: 83–90. Lincoln: University of Nebraska Press, 2011.

Levine, Victoria Lindsay, ed. *Writing American Indian Music: Historic Transcriptions, Notations, and Arrangements*. Recent Researches in American Music, vol. 44. Music of the United States of America, vol. 11. Middleton WI: A-R Editions, 2002.

Lévi-Strauss, Claude. *Myth and Meaning*. 1978. New York: Routledge, 2001.

———. *The Raw and the Cooked*. New York: Harper and Row, 1964. Originally *Le Cru et le cuit*.

———. "Structuralism and Myth." *Kenyon Review* 3.2 (1981): 64–88.

———. "The Structural Study of Myth." In "Myth: A Symposium." Special issue of *Journal of American Folklore* 68.270 (1955): 428–44.

Lévi-Strauss, Claude, and Yves Cantraine. "Overture to *Le Cru et le cuit*." In "Structuralism." Special issue of *Yale French Studies* 6.37 (1966): 41–65.

Lomax, Alan. *Alan Lomax: Selected Writings, 1934–1997*. Ed. Ronald D. Cohen. Introductory essays by Gage Averill et al. New York: Routledge, 2003.

———. *Cantometrics: An Approach to the Anthropology of Music*. Berkeley: University of California Press, 1976.

———. *Folk Song Style and Culture*. With contributions by the cantometrics staff and with editorial assistance by Edwin E. Erikson. AAAS Publication 88. Washington DC: American Association for the Advancement of Science, 1968.

Lord, Albert B. *The Singer of Tales*. Cambridge MA: Harvard University Press, 1960.

McLean, Mervyn. *Pioneers of Ethnomusicology*. Coral Springs FL: Llumina Press, 2006.

McNutt, James C. "John Comfort Fillmore: A Student of Indian Music Reconsidered." *American Music* 2.1 (1984): 61–70.

Mead, Margaret. *Coming of Age in Samoa*. New York: Morrow, 1928.

———. *Growing Up in New Guinea*. New York: Morrow, 1930.

Merriam, Alan P. *The Anthropology of Music*. Evanston IL: Northwestern University Press, 1964.

Meyers, Helen, ed. *Ethnomusicology: An Introduction*. New York: Norton, 1992.

———, ed. *Ethnomusicology: Historical and Regional Studies*. New York: Norton, 1993.

Nettl, Bruno. *Becoming an Ethnomusicologist: A Miscellany of Influences*. Lanham MD: Scarecrow Press, 2013.

———. *Nettl's Elephant: On the History of Ethnomusicology*. Urbana: University of Illinois Press, 2010.

———. *The Study of Ethnomusicology: Thirty-one Issues and Concepts*. 2nd ed. Urbana: University of Illinois Press, 2005.

———. *Theory and Method in Ethnomusicology*. London: Free Press of Glencoe, Collier-Macmillan, 1964.

Nettl, Bruno, and Philip V. Bohlman, eds. *Comparative Musicology and Anthropology of Music*. Chicago: University of Chicago Press, 1991.

Pisani, Michael V. *Imagining Native America in Music*. New Haven CT: Yale University Press, 2005.

Reed, Daniel. "The Innovator and the Primitives: George Herzog in Historical Perspective." *Folklore Forum* 26.1–2 (1993): 69–92.

Roberts, Helen H. *Ancient Hawaiian Music*. Honolulu: The Museum, 1926.

———. "Chakwena Songs of Zuñi and Laguna." *Journal of American Folklore* 36.140 (1923): 177–84.

———. "The First Salmon Ceremony of the Karuk Indians." *American Anthropologist* 34.3 (1932): 426–40.

———. *Musical Areas in Aboriginal North America*. Yale University Publications in Anthropology 12. Ed. Edward Sapir and Leslie Spier. New Haven CT: Yale University Press, 1936.

———. "Musical Styles in Aboriginal North America." *Bulletin of the American Musicological Society* 2 (1937): 2–3.

———. "New Phases in the Study of Primitive Music." *American Anthropologist* 24.2 (1922): 144–60.

———. "Possible Survivals of African Song in Jamaica." *Musical Quarterly* 12.3 (1926): 340–58.

———. Review of *Teton Sioux Music* by Frances Densmore. *Journal of American Folklore* 32.126 (1919): 523–35.

———. "Spirituals or Revival Hymns of the Jamaica Negro." *Ethnomusicology* 33.3 (1989): 409–74.

———. "A Study of Folk Song Variants Based on Field Work in Jamaica." *Journal of American Folklore* 38.148 (1925): 149–216.

Roberts, Helen H., and Herman K. Haeberlin. "Some Songs of the Puget Sound Salish." *Journal of American Folklore* 31.122 (1918): 496–520.

Roberts, Helen H., and Morris Swadesh. "Songs of the Nootka Indians of Western Vancouver Island." *Transactions of the American Philosophical Society* 45.3 (1955): 199–327.

Sacks, Oliver. *Musicophilia: Tales of Music and The Brain*. New York: Knopf, 2007.

Sapir, Edward. "Blowing Winds." *Poetry* 30.4 (1927): 194.

———. "The Contribution of Psychiatry to an Understanding of Behavior in Society." *American Journal of Sociology* 42.6 (1937): 862–70.

———. "The Musical Foundations of Verse." *Journal of English and Germanic Philology* 20.2 (1921): 213–28.

———. "Note on French-Canadian Folk-Songs." *Poetry* 16.4 (1920): 210–13.

———. "Percy Grainger and Primitive Music." *American Anthropologist* 18 (1916): 592–97.

———. *The Psychology of Culture*. In Judith Irvine, ed., The Collected Works of Edward Sapir, vol. 10. Berlin: Mouton de Gruyter, 1993.

———. "Representative Music." *Musical Quarterly* 4 (1918): 161–67.

———. Review of *Die Anfange der Musik* by Carl Stumpf. 1912. In Regna Darnell and Judith Irvine, eds., *The Collected Works of Edward Sapir*, vol. 4: *Ethnology*, 141–46. Berlin: Mouton de Gruyter, 1994.

———. Review of *The Book of American Negro Spirituals* by James Weldon Johnson. *Journal of American Folklore* 41.159 (1928): 172–74.

———. "The Rival Whalers, a Nitinat Story (Nootka Text with Translation and Grammatical Analysis)." *International Journal of American Linguistics* 3.1 (1924): 76–102.

———. "Song Recitative in Paiute Mythology." *Journal of American Folklore* 23.90 (1910): 455–72.

———. "Southern Paiute Dictionary." In "The Southern Paiute Language." Special issue of *Proceedings of the American Academy of Arts and Sciences* 65.3 (1931): 537, 539–730.

———. *Takelma Texts and Grammar.* 1907. In Victor Golla, ed., *The Collected Works of Edward Sapir*, vol. 8. Berlin: Mouton, 1990.

———. *Time-Perspective in Aboriginal American Culture: A Study in Method.* Geological Survey Memoir 90, no. 13, Anthropological Series. Ottawa: Government Printing Bureau, 1916.

Seeger, Charles. "The Music Process as a Function in a Context of Functions." *Anuario* 2 (1966): 1–42.

———. *Studies in Musicology 1935–1975.* Berkeley: University of California Press, 1977.

Wickwire, Wendy. "The Grizzly Gave Them the Song: James Teit and Franz Boas Interpret Twin Ritual in Aboriginal British Columbia, 1897–1920." *American Indian Quarterly* 25.3 (2001): 431–52.

PART 2 Ethnography

7 Friends in This World

The Relationship of George Hunt and Franz Boas

ISAIAH LORADO WILNER

No man is an *Iland*, intire of it selfe;
every man is a peece of the *Continent*,
a part of the *maine.*

—JOHN DONNE, *Devotions upon Emergent Occasions*

From all the ends of earth we come!

—W. E. B. DU BOIS, "A Hymn to the People"

One hot night in Chicago in 1893 several thousand visitors to the World's Columbian Exposition crowded the decks of a ship called *Progress*, spilling out onto the gangway and nearby walkways. As they craned their necks toward a barge on the lagoon, the tourists expected to see a show in the style of the fair's global promenade, the Midway Plaisance, where Indigenous people served as "living exhibits," human artifacts of a vanishing past. But when an Indigenous dance troupe took the stage, whirling to a tense drumbeat, it was clear they planned to offer a different kind of drama—one that cast Indians as agents of their own destiny.[1]

Gasps rang out when a mustachioed impresario removed from his pocket a gleaming blade. Two dancers stripped off their shirts and bared their backs to the man, who flayed four strips of flesh from each with all the calm of a Chicago butcher. Quickly now, he passed ropes through the wounds and knotted the ends. The beat picked up and the dancers yanked the ropes, spilling what appeared to be blood from their backs. Women fainted. A man called out to stop the show. Moving deliberately, the maestro rolled up his sleeve. For a finale he presented his arm to a dancer, who jumped upward and—so it seemed—took a bite. The maestro displayed his arm to the crowd, revealing a red mark the size of a silver dollar.[2]

The next week's papers buzzed with outrage about "cannibals" at the world's fair.[3] But the show caused another set of reverberations in Brit-

ish Columbia, where friends and relatives of the dancers would laugh for decades about who fooled whom.[4] There were no cannibals on the lagoon. To the contrary, the dance troupe had made use of careful training in an intricate form of trompe l'oeil—techniques that took years to master and that, combined with complex rhythms, steps, songs, and props (much "blood," for instance, spilled from collapsible packets), allowed the performers to stage a political spectacle.[5] Banned by Canada from practicing dances that stood at the core of their civilization, the Kwakw<u>aka</u>'wakw people of Vancouver Island had elevated their struggle to a global stage.[6] With rope and blade, music and dance, they issued an Indigenous declaration of independence.

The Kwakw<u>aka</u>'wakw dance was an *emergent occasion*: an event without precedent that presaged and ultimately influenced a transformation of thought.[7] Hired to play out a colonial social script, the Kwakw<u>aka</u>'wakw invented a new role for themselves. They could not have done it without the star of the performance, also its choreographer. George Hunt, the Indian son of an English trader, had grown up among and married into the Kwakw<u>aka</u>'wakw, and with their help he was beginning to fashion an against-the-grain anthropology. Hunt had attracted a vast group of spectators that night, but, in retrospect, he was playing for an audience of one: the anthropologist Franz Boas, who eagerly scribbled notes about the Kwakw<u>aka</u>'wakw ceremonies that Hunt shared with him throughout that summer in Chicago—and whom Hunt invited to learn more in Canada.[8]

This essay presents a reading of Hunt's relationship with Boas, now recognized as a seminal partnership in the development of modernist anthropology.[9] Hunt is thought of as a Native "informant," but I argue that he was a thinker and teacher. More than a mediator between worlds, Hunt lived in one global world—and found a way to alter it. With Kwakw<u>aka</u>'wakw aid and support, he contributed to the formation of Boasian anthropology, providing colonized people an opportunity to speak back to their colonizers.

To recognize this history of Indigenous influence, we need to look beyond the texts Hunt published with Boas and the masks they collected to the letters that provide an intimate record of their interaction. Hunt's forty-year correspondence with Boas provides a historical template of friendship as a nexus—a site of interpersonal exchange where unexpected alterations in emotion and belief can bring about a transformation of values. Friendship is always an emergent occasion, a new event that may lead to new results. The study of friendship takes us beneath social structures toward a fine-grained analysis of con-

sciousness as a dynamic process, shaped and reshaped by the interaction of individuals. It was in friendship, through friendship, that Hunt exercised influence.

Chicago, the futurist metropolis altered by an Indigenous performance, recaptures the *event* of Hunt's appearance. Hunt reached Boas at a nadir: after eight years of periodic joblessness, Boas would shortly lose his position at the Field Museum and suffer the loss of his infant daughter. Exhausted and out of funds, he retreated to a cottage at Alma Farm on Lake George, where his wife's family had a summer estate.[10] It was at this time that he began to think seriously about a letter he had received from Hunt, who pointed him toward a different path. Cultivating the relationship they had begun in Chicago, Hunt urged Boas to continue their work together. "The Danak-toq Indian got Lot of fancy mask also, and if you want to get them its best for you to Let me know as soon as you can," Hunt wrote. "I hope you well Get me some thing to Do for you or some Body now my Dear Friend Dr Boas I ll trust Every thing to you."[11] Jobless, broke, but not out of hope, the anthropologist cobbled together funds for a trip to the Northwest Coast.

In November 1894, Boas rode south through the Queen Charlotte Strait aboard an old ship called the *Barbara Boskowitz,* headed for a rendezvous with Hunt.[12] His heart soared as he passed each waterfall cascading down from the peaks of the Coast Range. Boas knew that his boat would pass Hunt in Fort Rupert, but he did not know whether the captain would stop. The Strait was treacherous, and the *Boskowitz* came ashore only on calm days. But when the wind dropped the *Boskowitz* plowed ahead, and suddenly Boas found himself ashore. As the captain pulled the boat's whistle, Boas stood alone for a moment before he saw a lone man paddling toward him in a canoe. Hunt had seen the *Boskowitz* put in and had come to greet his friend.[13]

Two days later, Boas stood before a gathering of 250, dressed in a Hudson's Bay blanket, his head crowned with cedar. Hunt stood by his side. Three groups of Kwakw<u>aka</u>'wakw Indians had arrived, painted in red and black, wearing cedar bark cloaks and abalone jewelry. When the secret societies filed to their spot by the fire in the back of the house, the hall went silent. Several chiefs stood up to address Boas, who then learned his Kwak'wala name, Heiltsakuls, which has been translated as The One Who Says the Right Thing and also as The Non-Speaking One.[14] Each of the groups sang its songs, and Boas stood up to present them with gifts of hard tack and molasses, which Hunt had directed him to offer his hosts. The chiefs thanked Boas lavishly: "You are the loaded canoe that has anchored in front of a mountain from which wealth is rolling down

upon all the people of the whole world. You are the pillar supporting our world."[15]

Feeling the rhythm now, Boas declared to the assembly that he had wanted to visit for a long time. He then issued a personal greeting to the members of Hunt's dance troupe. To each of the dancers Boas presented a gift: a portrait photograph taken at the fair in Chicago. Tabulating the evening's fun, Boas considered it a bargain. "The whole thing lasted four hours and cost me $14.50," he wrote his wife, Marie, in New York. "I gained the good will of these people and received invitations to all the feasts."[16]

We are witnessing here, in Boas's letters home, the preparations for a local tour: (1) *the meeting on the beach*, allaying the traveler's anxieties and ushering him into a close relationship with his guide; (2) *the ceremonial summit*, a conference with the leaders of the society, arrayed in their most "authentic" attire, and choreographed by the guide, who directs the traveler in an exchange of gifts, cementing his relationship to the public; (3) *the granting of a name*, altering the identity of the traveler and providing him a provisional status in the host community; and (4) *the reciprocal gesture*, an exchange of sentiments expressing mutual gratitude and appreciation, which makes the visitor feel welcome in his temporary home and seals the new relationship.

By formalizing bonds between Boas and the Kwakwaka'wakw, Hunt did what is now handled with proposals and permission slips: he attained public consent for a collaborative research project. Hunt's endorsement lay behind Boas's actions not only because he directed Boas's movements but also because the Kwakwaka'wakw knew that he had invited Boas to stay with his family, sharing a house with his children.[17] When the Kwakwaka'wakw ratified the project, they raised the odds of a successful engagement.

The word *informant* does not describe Hunt's work here. While anthropologists have applied the term to their Indigenous partners and collaborators since the middle of the twentieth century, it continues to carry connotations from its use in colonial and criminal contexts. Among police an informant, or informer, is a stool pigeon, a "rat," someone who cannot be trusted within his own community. Hunt *built* trust. He established a healthy relationship between Boas and the Kwakwaka'wakw and then began the searching work of thinking about, interpreting, and bringing a foreign visitor to understand a way of life. A better word for this role would be *teacher* or *guide*.

For the next two weeks Hunt produced what we would now think of as a reality show. What he showed Boas was real but carefully managed. Hunt was an expert in this kind of intercultural collaboration. The

Indian son of an English trader for the Hudson's Bay Company and his high-born Tlingit wife, Hunt descended on his mother's side from Tlingit chiefs and fur traders. He, however, had grown up within his father's trading post, some 340 miles south, where Fort Rupert elders, captivated by the child's haunting eyes, named him Loon and encouraged him to attend their secret feasts.

Hunt had married into Kwakiutl society and become a member of the Fort Rupert community.[18] For him the winter ceremonials were a family affair, more secret now than ever because those engaged in them were maintaining Indigenous lines of political organization in defiance of Canada's potlatch ban. Hunt and his family were among those who defied the law. His eldest son, David, was the chief of all secret society initiates, who were together known as the Seals, and the senior member of the highest ranking society, the Hamatsa. Hunt, the sponsor of his son's ascent, stood in an ideal position to offer Boas a privileged view.[19] During the next two weeks he would take Boas on a mental tour of Kwakwaka'wakw religious belief, political practice, and social ceremony.

The next day David gave his first feast of the season, using sticks, spears, and long ropes to drive his guests to the party with the help of his fellow Seals. The society barred the door of the house with planks so no one could escape. David passed out platters of salmon and no fewer than ten barrels of berries drizzled with candlefish oil.[20] Displaying his wealth, he poured out so much grease that the fire roared to the house beams and attendants scurried upward to douse the roof. "You really should see me in my blanket, eating with a spoon out of a platter together with four Indians!" Boas wrote his wife. "Tomorrow I will have Hunt translate the speeches for me."[21]

Boas's diary from this time makes clear that he understood little of what he saw and less of what he heard. But his facility for language allowed him to make out unfamiliar sounds and write them down, even when he did not know what they meant. He therefore gave up the aim of interpretation and simply recorded what he could.[22] Aside from a few reportorial observations—an aside, for instance, on Kwakwaka'wakw sleight-of-hand techniques similar to what he had seen in Chicago—Boas's notes from this period, recorded in letters to his wife, are exceedingly bare.[23] If he did not understand something, he preferred not to guess.

The interpreter was Hunt, who worked one-on-one with Boas, translating the speeches and explaining the rituals. This was the first time Boas's work would depend so heavily on a single person, and he worried about being so reliant on one partner. Once, as Hunt translated a speech David had given, two steamers appeared at the beach, one carrying a seal

hunter who hoped to find wage labor and the other, more threateningly, an Indian agent. "I was trembling with fear that he wanted to engage Hunt," Boas wrote Marie. "Fortunately, though, he left this morning."[24] As the father of a Hamatsa initiate, Hunt was juggling quite a few responsibilities, which only increased Boas's nervousness. At times Boas sulked like a jilted lover. "George Hunt is so hard to get along with," he wrote Marie. "He acts exactly as he did in Chicago. He is too lazy to think, and that makes it disagreeable for me. I cannot change this, though, and have to make the best of it. He left at noon with some excuse and returned only after several hours. He knows exactly how I depend on him."[25]

By early December, as the whistles and cries of a Hamatsa who had returned from the forest echoed over the houses—a sign that the last society dances of the Fort Rupert gathering were about to begin—Boas thought he had witnessed the innermost aspects of the Kwakwaka'wakw winter ceremonies. In fact he had seen what Hunt saw fit to introduce to him. What he saw most clearly and understood most deeply concerned David Hunt. On the other hand, when the Hunts were absent, Boas learned little—a fact that he recognized when a Hamatsa dancer appeared on the beach, approaching a girl dressed as a supernatural spirit to dance around her body. This was a key moment of the ceremonies—the girl, Qominoqa, bore the responsibility of luring the Hamatsa back into the dancing house—but the meaning behind the movements eluded Boas. "Unfortunately George was not here," he wrote, "and so I did not know what was going on."[26]

Boas's reliance on Hunt, combined with his role as a "nonspeaking one" and his frequent tendency to translate individual actions into social patterns, produced what we might call a *displacement effect* in his papers. Hunt's name appears repeatedly in Boas's letters home, but the names of the chiefs, elders, and initiates whose dances and speeches Boas recorded—and who welcomed him within their community—rarely appear. In Boas's published volumes the displacement effect goes one step further: even the name of George Hunt is erased from the ethnographic text, replaced by Hunt's Indian names. By means of this displacement, Boas obscured the fact that the source and subject of his ethnographic project were the same individual.

We can correct the displacement if we view this history from the vantage point of the Columbian Exposition. As in Chicago, so in Fort Rupert, Hunt's exchange with Boas went beyond a one-on-one. In the person of Hunt the leaders of Kwakwaka'wakw society had found a spokesman who could attract a foreigner and thereby spread their outlook to the wider world.[27] The Kwakiutl of Fort Rupert symbolized this union in one

of their last dances of the season, when they took Hunt and Boas by the hand and tied them together with rope.[28]

By sealing Hunt to Boas, the Kwakw<u>aka</u>'wakw people took a considerable risk. It was Boas, not Hunt, who held the accoutrements of power: research funds, a European doctorate, and, beginning in 1896, a faculty position at Columbia University.[29] Boas exercised his power as patron, for it was he who gave the gifts. Hunt in turn treated Boas as a social superior, carefully expressing his gratitude when Boas sent him a breech-loading rifle, eyeglasses for nighttime reading, or dysentery medicines unavailable in Fort Rupert—items that traveled west as Hunt's manuscripts went east, enriching Boas's storehouse.[30]

But if power flowed through feeling, then feeling could also provide a form of power. When Marie Boas selected a silver bracelet for Hunt's wife, Lucy, Hunt thanked Boas profusely, writing, "She say that she will Keep it and the gold Ring till Death take her away from this World."[31] Reaching out to Boas through the mail, Hunt transformed a professional partnership into a personal comradeship, addressing Boas as his friend and reminding him of their mutual obligations. "Oh I was glad to here from you again for I thought there was something Rong with you for it was long since I here from you for you know that you are the only Help I got in this world," Hunt wrote Boas in 1896. "I thank you for sending the mony to me for you know what a Big famely I got to Work for."[32]

The result was Boas's great ethnography, *The Social Organization and the Secret Societies of the Kwakiutl Indians*. We have tended to view this work as a continuation of Boas's relativist research aims, but the report marked a departure from his previous efforts. Instead of depicting a static cultural array, Boas presented a dynamic portrait of a community in motion, creating and re-creating a way of life. This was a study of practice as a social process. Hard-edged, spare, factual, it gave the impression of documentary reality. The report convinced by its *intimacy*, a firsthand familiarity with two Kwakw<u>aka</u>'wakw practices: the winter dances and the potlatch speeches.

With an eye for performance and an ear for oratory, these passages epitomized the skills Boas prized in Hunt. That is why the report, published in the Annual Report of the U.S. National Museum, featured a double byline: "By Franz Boas, based on personal observations and on notes made by Mr. George Hunt."[33] Boas readily admitted his dependence on Hunt and in fact prefaced the book with a fuller statement: "The great body of facts presented here were observed and recorded by Mr. George Hunt, of Fort Rupert, British Columbia, who takes deep interest in everything pertaining to the ethnology of the Kwakiutl Indians and to whom

I am under great obligations. I am indebted to him also for explanations of ceremonials witnessed by myself, but the purport of which was difficult to understand."[34]

Here Boas simplified the story, defining Hunt as an observer but not a participant in the ceremonies he described. Laying that story bare would have exposed the rickety foundations of the emerging science of anthropology, a house of ideas propped atop reeds of personal happenstance. But Boas may have had another reason to minimize his reliance on Hunt. The ceremonies he described were illegal. By portraying Hunt as a scientist investigating Native customs rather than an Indian participating in them, Boas insulated his working partner from the reach of colonial oppression—although, as it turned out, not enough.

By stepping forward in Boas's book, Hunt knew that he was taking a considerable risk. Alfred Hall, a missionary who had lived in the Hunt family compound when Hunt was a child and who relied on Hunt's services to translate the King James Bible into Kwak'wala, was also the strongest advocate of repressing Kwakwaka'wakw ceremonies.[35] Hunt's Chicago performance had convinced Hall—quite correctly—that Hunt would be an obstacle to the colonization of the Kwakwaka'wakw. The book threw fuel on his missionary fervor. Soon after it was published, Hunt visited nearby Alert Bay on Cormorant Island, where he was mocked by some young men who lived at Hall's island mission and who opposed the potlatch. "They say here is he Who is finding out all our Dances then he go's and tell it to Dr. Boas," Hunt wrote Boas. "Now My Dear friend you see that the Hall's school Boys is Recking against us yet. But I inhopes that we will get the Best of them yet."[36]

In contrast the Kwakwaka'wakw elders who resisted the potlatch ban supported Hunt's work, though they monitored his affairs closely. Two years later, when a sensational Victoria newspaper article appeared, giving the impression to Kwakwaka'wakw elites that Boas had perpetuated old stereotypes about them by portraying them as cannibals, Hunt faced opposition from his community. A chief, Hemasaka, called Hunt to account at a feast, banning him from future ceremonials. "All the People told me that they Dont want you or me to see the Dance of any kind again," Hunt wrote Boas. "So you see that I know friend Even Mr Spencer and sisters are against me now. now you are the only one I have now. the only thing I am wishing for is for my life Be speard."[37]

Rumors that Kwakwaka'wakw ceremonialists were disturbing graves to make use of skeletons for their rituals played out against actual graverobbing, not by the Kwakwaka'wakw but by anthropologists.[38] Boas had begun a large excavation of Kwakwaka'wakw burial grounds that

violated, in spirit if not in letter, the ethic he and Hunt had established with the people potlatching at Fort Rupert in 1894. Hemasaka's pressure, while understandably frightening for Hunt, served its purpose to an extent. Boas did not send back the controversial fieldworker Harlan Smith, whose indiscretion had cast the partnership into doubt.

Hemasaka influenced Boas in another way: he politicized him. Minutely focused on extracting information from Indigenous communities, Boas began to modify his approach, beginning a transition away from physical anthropology. Equally important the Kwakwaka'wakw inspired a personal letter from Boas, who sent Hunt money to throw a feast on his behalf and read aloud a promise to Hemasaka. "The Kwakiutl have no better friend than I," Boas wrote. "Whenever I can, I speak for you."[39] This statement was truer in wish than in fulfillment, but in future years Boas would speak and write against the potlatch ban and attempt to influence colonial officials to put an end to it.[40]

Satisfied that Boas had sufficiently repaired the harm, Fort Rupert elites readmitted Hunt to their ceremonies—an event that brought Boas closer to the Kwakwaka'wakw while placing Hunt in grave danger. Tensions were rising between Hall and Hunt. In March 1900, as Hall's potlatch persecutions continued, his ally George Pidcock, the Indian agent at Alert Bay, accused Hunt of participating in a Hamatsa ceremony. Hunt was arrested, accused of cannibalism, and held for trial at Vancouver's assizes.[41] At last released to collect witnesses for his trial, he wrote Boas that he had hired a lawyer to construct a defense. "Now My Dear friend is there any thing comeing to me in money way," Hunt closed his letter. "If there is any would you Be kind Enough to send me Help as soon as you can. Pleas Do send some Help to Me / that is all / Geo Hunt."[42]

Hunt's arrest fostered a character test for Boas, even as it confirmed how closely these two men were linked. Boas acted immediately. He sent Hunt the funds that were due him, thereby contributing to the costs of a lawyer hired by Hunt's white brother-in-law, the cannery owner Stephen Allen Spencer. Boas also sent Charles F. Newcombe, a collector in Victoria who occasionally collaborated with Boas, a copy of *The Social Organization and the Secret Societies of the Kwakiutl Indians*, featuring Hunt's name in the front. Boas emphasized to both Newcombe and Spencer that the book should be displayed in court. "It would seem to me that in the opinion that any judge or jury would have in regard to this matter, the motive which induced George to go there would play a most important part," Boas wrote. "I believe that this book will go far to show that his interest is one which in no way can be considered as culpable, and that for this reason the production of the book in court may be of very mate-

rial assistance to him."[43] A crucial piece of evidence, the book established Hunt's status as a scientist investigating Native customs rather than an Indian carrying them out—a key argument of Hunt's defense.[44]

In his next letter to Boas, Hunt explained that he had faced three trials in Alert Bay. The next and last trial, in Vancouver, could result in a six-month sentence.[45] "I am very much disappointed that I shall not be able to have you with me during the summer," Boas coolly replied.[46] For six weeks Boas kept watch on the Canadian newspapers. On April 28 he read some good news, soon repeated in a telegram from Newcombe. "My dear George," Boas dictated to his secretary. "I am very glad to learn from Dr. Newcombe and also through the papers that your trial resulted in your acquittal, and I flatter myself that the book with your name on the titlepage was of material assistance in this matter. Will you please answer my last letter, in which I asked you if you could give me about half an hour a day during the month of July, and spare enough time to get some of the old people to keep me busy until you would be free."[47]

Having contributed to Hunt's incarceration and trial, Boas now drew him deeper into potentially dangerous explorations. As the Jesup Expedition expanded between 1897 and 1902 and Boas faced competition from his former employer, the Field Museum, the market for Indian artifacts rose, and so did the demand for bones. Boas in turn leaned on Hunt, encouraging him to enter burial sites to recover skeletons from the era before colonization and art free of Western influence.[48] Otherwise Hunt would not be paid.

Boas demanded new material constantly, often in a hectoring tone, and he was not above manipulating Hunt's financial condition in quest of myths and artifacts. "If you are successful in getting good old material from out of the various places where the Indians used to hide it, we shall go on collecting," Boas wrote Hunt in May 1901, "but if you cannot get the material, I shall not be able to get any more money for you." Having threatened Hunt with the possibility of losing his livelihood, he then switched tone, employing Hunt's customary salutation. "Now, my dear friend, you know that the whole success of this work is in your hands, and that it depends only upon your efforts and your success in collecting and in writing, how long we are going to continue it," he closed. "If you are able to satisfy the Museum during the present year, I feel sure that I can continue your employment for quite a number of years."[49]

Boas's exhortations spurred Hunt into his skiff, out of Fort Rupert, down the winding waterway of Kingcome Inlet, and back to Nimpkish Lake, where the explorer found graves, caves filled with skeletons, clam shell heaps filled with tools, stacks of bones, and an eight-inch chisel. He

worried his explorations would provoke further controversy in Alert Bay, so he asked Boas to write A. W. Vowell, British Columbia's superintendent of Indian affairs. "Would you be kind enough to see if you can send to Mr. Vowel and get a leaf from him for me to Have a Power to get some of the old grave from the nemges lake, for there is lots of it there in one cave," Hunt wrote Boas. "If you can do this I can send you lots of them, for the mission People would like to get me on another trouble if they can find out me Breaking into the graves. . . . Now I wants to know, will I send the Humen Bones all mixed or just as they are from the grave."[50]

Nearly three weeks later, in September 1901, Hunt had yet to receive a reply from Boas. He thought he might be arrested again. "The mission People are watching me very close," Hunt warned Boas. "That is How. I am wishing you to get Permision from Mr Vowel for me to have Power to go and git into the old graves. . . . The Indeans I know well let me go and get it. But the mission People telling them to lay complaint against me. so you see I got to look out what I am Doing that is all at Present."[51] It would be nearly three months before the Department of Indian Affairs granted permission for Hunt's work. By then it was Boas who begged for an update. Boas had received three skulls and one comb, neatly packed in a small box between layers of moss. He desperately wished for more. "I have not heard from you for a long time, and I am very anxiously awaiting news from you," Boas wrote Hunt. "Now please, my dear friend, let me hear from you what you have been doing."[52]

The skulls, skeletons, stone tools, masks of carved cedar, totem poles, and chiefs' seats that Hunt collected formed the basis of an extensive collection of Northwest Coast artifacts that were crated and sent to the American Museum of Natural History. Similar Hunt excavations in partnership with the photographer Edward S. Curtis and the collector George Heye would create Northwest Coast displays at the Burke Museum and the Museum of the American Indian.[53] By 1902 Hunt, along with others, had collected so many artifacts that Boas needed to rearrange his Hall of the North Pacific at the Museum of Natural History. The anthropologist asked Hunt to come to New York and help set up the exhibit.[54]

This would be the longest trip of Hunt's life, his only trip to the East Coast, and he did not wish to make it. He would be traveling alone, far from family and friends.[55] In January 1903 Hunt boarded a Canadian Pacific train that rumbled eastward. It was ten years since he had first traveled east to take part in the Columbian Exposition, six years since the publication of Boas's book. "And now I feel like if I was in the world unknown for I did feel like if I was daid man from all my relations or something like wounded duck with one wing broken no friend near to

Friends in This World 173

me," Hunt wrote in his diary. "Oh I thought how foolish I was to leave my near Relations to go and Pleas other man and that I only got a very short time to live in this world Oh I felt sorry but I at last made up my mind to go through with my trip."[56]

As it turned out, the trip to New York altered both Hunt and Boas in at least one way that neither could have predicted. When Boas had to visit the doctor, he arranged for Hunt to spend an evening with an associate named Harrington—most likely the departmental assistant and fieldworker Mark Raymond Harrington—who took Hunt to see what he called a "moveing Picture of on curtian." This was no mere treat for Hunt, an early experimenter in ethnographic photography, whose brother-in-law owned a photography studio in Victoria and who had already seen one film there. After his evening with Harrington he immediately wrote Boas a note, translating his Kwak'wala into English before he went to bed: "Now I thank you Friend for you have sent he Mr. Harrinton (name) to go and show By he to me to the theater (name) last night for that I was truly think it was good what they where Playing. this I think was good the moveing Picture of on curtian. Now I have seen that twice now the same thing. and what I saw at Victoria (Plase name). and it was Very good."[57] It is hard to tell from Hunt's phrase "the same thing" whether he had seen the same movie twice or merely the same kind of show, that is, a film. In any case he had seen at least two films and was clearly quite taken by the medium, perhaps even considering its possibilities for his own work. Within the next decade Hunt would go behind the camera, making *In the Land of the Headhunters* with Curtis, the first film to feature an Indigenous cast, almost a decade before *Nanook of the North*.[58] In 1930 Boas caught up to Hunt's innovation, bringing a camera to Fort Rupert to record games and dances—at last following through on the dynamic concept of culture that had begun to emerge from his work with Hunt during the potlatch season of 1894.[59]

The letters both men sent after Hunt's return suggest that their New York collaboration contributed to a deepening respect. In April 1903 Boas sent Hunt's sister, Annie Spencer, an express package of gifts, including traps, small shot, and instruments for preparing animal skins. "I enjoyed your brother's stay here very much, and I hope that he has only pleasant memories of his visit in New York," Boas wrote.[60] Eight years later, when Hunt met an anthropologist who informed him that Boas had left the museum and that the new curators planned to rearrange the Northwest Coast exhibit, he addressed a letter to Boas's secretary that expressed his opinion of the work they had achieved: "Every thing was Put in the Place where there Belong to while I was there at New york and here is one

thing I can say. that there is no man on Earth knows more than Dr Boas about the Kwagol tribes and where to Put the collection in there Places."[61]

Boas had left the American Museum of Natural History in 1905 to work full time at Columbia University, occasioning a research transition from the collection of objects to the manufacture of texts.[62] But a tight focus on institutions runs the danger of obscuring interpersonal causes for change, including the feedback loop between the desk in New York and the desk in Fort Rupert. When Boas left for Columbia he had not yet envisioned his famous "five-foot shelf," the attempt to create a set of Native language texts that would perpetuate Indigenous cultures and provide a database for their study. It was Hunt who set him on this path as the result of a personal experience.

The transition began in January 1900, when Hunt led Boas into a new area of research the anthropologist had not anticipated: an examination of Indian medicine practices. The pursuit began for a simple reason. Hunt's wife, Lucy, had taken ill, the first of several bouts that would plague her for the next eight years. In his efforts to heal Lucy, Hunt made use of Western medicines and also called upon shamanic forces and local fauna, which he soon began describing in detailed manuscripts for Boas.[63]

Delighted by the unexpected contribution, Boas took the research in a new direction. "The tale about the method of calling the northwest wind pleased me very much, and I beg to ask you to go ahead collecting this kind of material," Boas wrote, "that is to say, all sorts of charms, no matter what they may be used for,—for curing sickness or for obtaining the love of women, or for luck in hunting or for doing harm to one's enemies. Every thing of that kind will be very welcome, and the more you can get of it, the better."[64] For six years Boas continued to urge Hunt to send him spells.

Hunt, who was trained in the shamanic tradition, politely pushed back, reminding Boas that the shamans did not like to give those powers away to just anyone. "Now the things you wants me to write Down next. I think some of them will be Hard to find out," Hunt wrote. "That is to kill another By takeing Hair. or spetle from the man they wants to kill. for you know that it is a greatest secreat of all. Now I think I will coast me some thing to get a man to tell me this. yet I will let you know as soon as I can."[65]

Hunt's interchange with Lucy, brought on by the attempt to cure her illness, gradually blossomed into a long-running collaboration. He embarked on an exploration of Kwakwa̱ka'wakw culinary customs, with Lucy as his expert source (after all, she cooked for her husband). As he wrote about catching fish and picking berries, Hunt photographed the processes he

Friends in This World 175

discussed, for example, the Kwakw<u>a</u>ka'wakw method of gutting and broiling salmon.[66] Looking at the pictures Boas gained an understanding of Kwakw<u>a</u>ka'wakw ideas that words could not provide. Europeans considered hunting and cooking separate projects: the catching of food and the making of it—a killing operation performed by males followed by a female act of domestic assembly.[67] The Kwakw<u>a</u>ka'wakw viewed all aspects of finding and preparing food, from the construction of a fishhook to the leveling of a canoe, as deeply intertwined—in fact fundamentally one.

Hunt had a holistic mind, a fine eye, and a dogged endurance. When he wrote about the cooking of halibut, he began not with the preparation of the fish but with the assembly of the traps that the Kwakw<u>a</u>ka'wakw used to catch it, thereby depicting the place of halibut within Kwakw<u>a</u>ka'wakw culture. As Hunt explained it to Boas in one letter, he preferred to start "from How the Net is made" because "I think it is Best to Have Every thing Down from the Begining to the Last."[68] In such passages Hunt's letters offered Boas more than a glimpse of the Kwakw<u>a</u>ka'wakw worldview; they provided a portrait of George Hunt's mind. Once again he was making his life the subject of science.

Boas, however, misunderstood Hunt's holistic approach. He wondered why Hunt could not produce as many pages about sea slugs and sea urchins as he had on the speeches given at parties. He proposed to lower Hunt's wages from fifty cents to twenty cents a page, provoking their first major disagreement.[69] What appeared to be a labor dispute masked a cultural divide. Hunt hoped to give Boas a fuller understanding of Kwakw<u>a</u>ka'wakw cosmography, based on the prosaic matters that formed the material existence of his people. But it was difficult work. Hunt knew little about women's activities, so his research involved pulling together facts from numerous sources. He had difficulty expressing such problems to Boas, instead protesting various technical matters: he wrote in smaller script than before; the paper he used featured more lines per page; the drop from fifty cents to twenty seemed steep.

But Hunt felt most aggravated by the standard he set for himself—a scrupulous approach that forced him into a never-ending chain of research:

> And now you thinks that it's Easy thing to study all the Deffrent ways of the Indian geting food and cooking them. now it is a Hard on my Head to Do it in the Right way. Of cause some People would gave it to you in a short way. and you would only get it Half Done. . . . now I will send you about clam cooking. and after you Recieved them. then you will see for your self. what trouble it gave me in studying all the

in and outs of it. for I know that you are Learning lots of thing and words that you Did not know any thing about Befor."[70]

Several days later Hunt improved his bargaining position further, sending Boas some notes from an anthropologist at the Field Museum, which revealed the museum's attempt to procure a Mowachaht shrine before Boas could reach it. "I am not going to work for any Body But you," Hunt promised, "onless the Pay gets to low."[71] They settled on a dollar for every three pages—about three dollars a day.[72]

But soon their partnership faced another test. In the summer of 1907 Boas moved his family across the Hudson River to a new house of his design in Grantwood, New Jersey.[73] The postal service began delivering the few letters Boas found time to write Hunt in Fort Rupert to the town of Prince Rupert, just south of the Alaskan border, more than three hundred miles north.[74] Not hearing from Boas, Hunt went to work in a new copper mine at Fort Rupert. "I was Very much Pleased to get a letter from you, for I Begen to think that there was something Rong with you," Hunt wrote Boas after finally receiving a letter in August. "I Did not know where you was. and that is How I stop wrieting the Indian cooking."[75]

Months passed and Boas heard nothing more. "I think it very strange that I should not have heard from you for so long a time," he wrote Hunt in November. "I am also much disappointed that you do not go on with the work of writing on the subject of cooking, and that, notwithstanding my many requests, you have never sent me the photographs of the split trees. Will you not please go on with these matters?"[76]

Following so closely upon the disagreement over pay, Hunt's silence disturbed Boas. He assumed Hunt felt disillusioned by the lowering of his pay. Boas did not often show it in his letters, but he cared for Hunt. He had promised to match whatever pay Hunt could get in other work, and he had kept his promise. It had been four years now since they had last seen each other, and Boas believed time and distance contributed to their misunderstanding. "I rather think that the trouble in regard to our whole work is that we ought to meet again and talk over matters, and have once more a pleasant time around your own home," he wrote Hunt, "but I do not see at present how it will be possible for me to go out to British Columbia once more this year or next, although I think I ought to. Now, I hope that you will not wait any longer, and answer to my letter right away."[77]

Hunt wasn't sulking, though. His family had come down with the measles. He brought his children to his house to help them recover, an undertaking that slowed his work, but he kept up his writing, studying

Friends in This World 177

the ways of cooking eulachon. When his children improved, he began taking some photographs Boas had requested. Given the stresses on Hunt at this time, his reply to Boas attested to his commitment to their common work. "You wrote to me on your last letter. where you said that you might come out here this year if you Had the time to spear," Hunt wrote. "I told my famely about it they all say that they would like to see you out here once more. and I told my wife that I might take a trip to New york to see you there. that is if you call me there. wel she said if you are wanted there. you would Have to go. that is all at Present."[78]

Considering how lonely he had felt while traveling to New York, Hunt's letter presented a generous answer to Boas's gesture of friendship. Yet Boas failed to summon Hunt to New York, and their work was bogged down again. "According to your last letter, I expected to hear from you in February, but I have not had a letter from you since you said that you were going on with writing the cooking-matter," Boas wrote Hunt in March 1908, after waiting for word for a month. "I do not see exactly why it is, but it seems to me our work has been going on terribly slowly for the last year or two. You know, of course, that I am much interested in the work, and that both you and I would like to preserve everything that is worth knowing about the Indians; and at the same time you are able to make quite a nice little money out of work of this kind, if you would only keep at it."[79] Finding again a personal note, Boas closed, "I trust you are well, and I am looking forward to the time when we may meet again."

A few weeks later Boas finally learned the cause of Hunt's troubles. Lucy's health had declined. "It is true I am going on Very slow with my writing the cause of this is my Poor wife Has Been sick in Bed Ever since Last December," Hunt wrote Boas on April 13, 1908. "And today she is that weak that she could not swallow water. yet I have not gaven her up yet. . . . as soon as my wife get a little Better I will get all the Photos Ready."[80]

Hunt sent along some manuscript pages written in English, without any Kwak'wala terms—an unusual procedure, perhaps necessary because Lucy felt too ill to give him the Indigenous words that she used for various cooking techniques. Only eleven days later Hunt took up his pencil to write Boas an addendum: "I write you this few lines to let you know. that My Dear Wife Lucy Died yesterday Evening at 6.30. this is the Hardest trial I Ever went through. I Remain yours Very truly Geo Hunt."[81]

Unfortunately Boas had already written Hunt, who received a curt note from the anthropologist shortly after Lucy's death:

While the material you sent me is very interesting, I am sorry that you are writing it in English only. There are so many new words and

new phrases in your writing on the cooking, that I should much prefer to have it as you usually write it, with the Indian and English translation. Will you not please continue your writing in that way. I am looking forward anxiously for the photographs which you promised me; and since you were not able to get them to me in time, I hope you will use the opportunity during this spring and summer to get every thing pertaining to the cutting and preparing of the salmon when the salmon-run begins.

I am exceedingly sorry to hear that your wife is not well, but I hope that when this letter reaches you, she may be in good health again. [82]

Once he realized his error, Boas immediately corrected it, sending his condolences. "I hope very much to hear from you at an early day, because I am anxious to know how you and your children are getting along," he wrote Hunt. "I have been thinking of you very often, and it must be hard for you to get accustomed to the loss of your dear wife." But Boas's latest letter only further illuminated his obsessive focus on intellectual concerns, his fundamental discomfort with matters of emotion, and his tendency to squeeze out every last drop of Hunt's energy in his never-ending quest to grasp Kwakwaka'wakw ways. He closed:

Just now I am very anxious to get information on two points. I find that I have no record of the method of peeling the bark of the red cedar, of preparing it and splitting it. I need this very badly.

Then I find that I have no detailed information on the actual measurements and sizes of the different types of canoes. . . . Could you please get this for me?[83]

In the following weeks Boas would write Hunt twice more. He asked for a detailed explication of Kwakwaka'wakw canoe construction. He asked which dishes the Kwakwaka'wakw preferred to eat in the morning and which at night. After two years of miscommunication, he demanded more than ever from his partner in the time of his grief.[84]

Hunt did not seem to take offense. In fact he welcomed Boas's letters, which provided him a chance to share his feelings. In his next several notes Hunt took Boas into his confidence as never before:

Oh My Dear friend it is true what you say in your last letter. this is about the Hardest thing I Ever got. that is to lose my Dear loveing wife. who was a great Help to Both you and me in the work I have to Do for you. That Dreadfull Evening when she Died on the 23 of last

Friends in This World 179

month she seem to know Every thing till the last minutes. Poor thing she said george take care of our childrens. good Bye then she went to sleep when she said good Bye. that was the last Breath she Breathed. I am travelling in my Boat all the time for I could not stay in Fort Rupert. I am trying to get a tomb stone for her grave. for I wants to work for her once more to get it. But I will never forget her. [85]

Later that day Hunt sent Boas ninety-four pages of manuscript about the catching and cooking of kelp fish, the peeling of cedar bark, and the types of canoes Boas had asked about, including the high-bow war canoe. Boas's request for information had encouraged Hunt, reminding him of the part he had chosen to play in life—a pursuit neither criticism nor jail nor even the death of his wife could diminish. "Now My Dear friend I will try to Do all I can to work for you," he wrote Boas. "For My Poor childrens for there all seems to turn into little childrens Ever since there Poor Dear Mother left us in this world. I thank you and Mrs Boas. for I feel like if I got some friends in this world left to comfort me and my Poor childrens when I Read your letters."[86] Hunt closed his letter in Kwak'wala, extending to Boas an essential word that expresses hospitality and gratitude: *Gila'kasla*.

Thus began the most productive period of Hunt's life. Too depressed by thoughts of Lucy to remain at home, he closed the door of his house and sailed away from Fort Rupert in the summer of 1908. He settled with his children far to the north, in the cannery town of Rivers Inlet, where he embarked on a burst of creativity—finally writing the vast description of Kwakwaka'wakw food gathering he had promised Boas for years.

Beginning with "Porperses spearing from the Begining to the End," Hunt moved on through the forty-three names of northwest canoes, the spears, paddles, seat mats, and spearing lines associated with hunting, and the holes the Kwakwaka'wakw drilled through the canoes to make sure they constructed each part of the boat to the perfect diameter. He wrote about cedar bark peeling, the making of feasting dishes, hair-seal cooking, the cooking of beached whales and octopi, sea slugs, large red sea eggs, small green sea eggs, and sea urchins.[87] He dashed off hundreds of pages in just a few weeks. "I cant go in the House where my wife Died. so I seems to feel Better away for a while," he wrote Boas. "I am trying to write for you as wel as I can. that is all at Present."[88]

It is likely that Hunt overworked himself at this time, and indeed he soon fell ill. In November he checked himself into the Rivers Inlet hospital, but the doctors there were unable to help him. He walked out again, thinner than ever.[89] Three days later, realizing that Boas had not writ-

ten him for several months, Hunt jotted down a brief note, explaining that he had been too sick to finish his writings about the giant traps the Kwakw<u>aka</u>'wakw constructed to catch perch and how they cleaned and cooked the fish.

The letter showed how close Hunt had come to feel toward Boas, and how much he depended on their deepening relationship now that his wife was gone. "I write you thes few lines which I hope will find you wel," Hunt wrote. "For I Begin to think that you might Be sick again which I hope is not so. for In my mind since my Poor wife Died that you are the only liveing Friend I have in this world."[90] In such moments it was Hunt, the supposedly junior man in the partnership, who exhibited the superior knowledge. He sensed how much he meant to Boas, and how much Boas meant to him.

Between the death of his wife in 1908 and his recovery from grief and illness in 1910, Hunt wrote hundreds of pages of manuscript. His papers from this time form a love letter to the dearly departed. By sharing the knowledge that had once belonged to his wife with his friend in the East, Hunt transferred his energies from the past to the present, linking his life with a single woman to his love for the culture she inhabited and preserving the essence of both in the public mind.

Certainly the texts preserved important aspects of Kwakw<u>aka</u>'wakw life. But Hunt's letters achieved something more distinctive than that. It was Hunt's style, not his content, his methodical approach to thinking and writing about Kwakw<u>aka</u>'wakw customs that gave Boas—and everyone who has come to study the Northwest Coast since then—an inner view not of a people but of a *person*. Hunt's letters revealed to Boas the genius of one Indigenous intellectual. Sometimes intentionally and sometimes not, Hunt's insights took Boas in unpredictable directions, bringing him to subjects he had not known about and to approaches that he could not have considered without his friendship with Hunt. With the flick of a pencil stub Hunt cast into motion entire structures of thought merely by describing the personal story of his family.

Much as Boas relied on Hunt, he never thought to send him the more general pieces of writing that emerged from their work. In 1911, when Boas published his treatise on race and culture, *The Mind of Primitive Man*, Hunt did not even know where to find his friend. Boas sent Hunt several letters from Mexico, but they never made it north to Fort Rupert.[91] Hunt heard only rumors: that Boas had lost his position in New York; that he had moved to Chicago; that he would never be seen in British Columbia again. Finally Hunt gave up hope of hearing from Boas. He took work as a hunter, a trapper, and a translator, producer, scenarist, and guide for

Curtis, "takeing old fation Indean Dressed Photograph" but "Very few stories." Finally in 1913 a letter from Boas made it through. "Now to tell you the trueth," Hunt replied, "I have mised you."[92]

This feeling of closeness did not prevent Hunt from recognizing the power held by the man who paid him, printed his words, and asked for his thoughts. But the feeling remained and even strengthened—transcending time, background, and distance—because Hunt, as much as Boas, felt that he was altered and enriched by their exchange of views. When Boas informed Hunt that he was having the texts Hunt had written bound and preserved in Columbia's library, Hunt was deeply gratified by this, and he was careful to credit Boas for his sponsorship. "Now My Dear Dr F Boas. if you think it is Best to Put my name on the Book as you say it will Please me," Hunt wrote. "But you know that I could not have get these stories without your great Help to me. there for I say my work is only one third of it. to your two third. yet I thank you Very much for Puting my Humble name up. for truly your the only Help I got." After giving Boas the words a shaman sings to seek a killer whale's help in curing the sick—words Hunt likely recited in his unavailing ministrations to his wife—he closed the letter with his usual request to be remembered to Marie. "Good Bye to you Dear Friend and Master," Hunt wrote his collaborator. "I Remain yours as Ever and true Friend / George Hunt."[93]

In this case, as in so many others, it would seem that Hunt, more than Boas, recognized the intricate imbalance of their collaboration. But Boas left at least one hint that he grasped the pattern. He craved all things Kwakwa̲ka'wakw, and when Hunt hinted of an old mask or pole or shrine, Boas would unleash a barrage of letters, begging Hunt to send on the goods. In all the years he worked with Hunt, Boas never expressed a greater desire for a particular work of Kwakwa̲ka'wakw craftsmanship than when he asked Hunt to send him a post that held up the roof of a cedar house on Hope Island, just off the coast of the northern tip of Vancouver Island. The post stood on a stretch of rocky shore in the village of Newitti, where Boas had begun his work among the Kwakwa̲ka'wakw in 1886.[94]

The place meant a great deal to Boas, but so did the object. Its distinguishing feature was a large hole carved between two lips, forming the shape of a mouth. At a key moment of the potlatch, when the chief who owned the post sought to establish his connection to the founder of his lineage, he would step into the shadows, stand behind the post, and speak through the hole. His words projected across the room and echoed through the house as if the chief had been transformed into his

ancestor.⁹⁵ The chief who owned the speaking post did not wish to give it away, but Boas had to have it. Hunt did everything he could to lay his hands on the post and ship it to New York, even making use of a precious asset: his status in white society. He threatened the chief, claiming that he would go to jail if he refused to cooperate. "I told him if he tells me another lie that I will Have him Rested," Hunt wrote Boas, "so I think that he will Do it this time."⁹⁶

The chief gave in, and Boas got his post. It stands today in the Hall of the North Pacific in the American Museum of Natural History.⁹⁷ The post bears the imprint of an age when Indigenous Americans reached out to reshape the world. It recalls a time when European settlers reached beyond the confines of a racist mind-set to discover what the world might look like from inside someone else's mind. In the mind of Franz Boas, the post simply showed the importance of ancestry in Kwakwaka'wakw ceremony. But a rattle is what a rattle does, and even a silent post can carry a message.

Much like the Kwakwaka'wakw dance in Chicago, the post that obsessed Boas exercised a sleight-of-hand. It carried a message within the message. Boas grasped instantly the type of transformation the post evoked because he had experienced it in his relationship with Hunt. Ever since the Kwakwaka'wakw bound them together, Hunt had stood behind Boas, speaking through him. Boas's books were Hunt's speaking post. That is all at present.

Acknowledgments

I am grateful to Regna Darnell for providing the opportunity to participate in the stimulating meeting that led to this volume. This essay developed from research at the American Philosophical Society, the American Museum of Natural History, and the Peabody Museum at Harvard University. I thank the archivists and staff of these institutions and Gloria Cranmer Webster of Alert Bay, British Columbia, for their help accessing collections of letters, manuscripts, and records.

Notes

1. "Horrible Scene at the Fair," London *Sunday Times*, August 20, 1893, 3; "A Brutal Exhibition," *New York Times*, August 19, 1893; Helm, *Pioneers of American Anthropology*, 214–16; Raibmon, *Authentic Indians*, 15–16, 56–60.
2. "A Brutal Exhibition"; "Horrible Torture Dance," Milwaukee *Sentinel*, August 19, 1893; "Horrible Scene at the Fair"; Helm, *Pioneers of American Anthropology*, 214–16.

3. "No More Torture Dances, Please!," Chicago *Evening Post*, August 18, 1893; "A Brutal Exhibition"; "Horrible Torture Dance"; "Horrible Scene at the Fair"; "Stop the Horrid Torture Dances" *Chicago Daily Tribune*, August 20, 1893; "Torture Dances at the Fair," New Orleans *Picayune*, August 25, 1893.
4. Helm, *Pioneers of American Anthropology*, 214–16.
5. Boas, *The Social Organization and the Secret Societies of the Kwakiutl Indians*, 489, 495–97; Curtis, *The North American Indian*, 161–62, 173–79, 192, 201–4, 210–22; Ford, *Smoke from Their Fires*, 25, 114–16, 119–22, 186–90; "It Was All Jugglery," Portland *Morning Oregonian*, October 7, 1893.
6. Raibmon, *Authentic Indians*, 50–62.
7. Jay, "Historical Explanation and the Event," 564; Romano, *Event and World*; Benjamin, "Theses on the Philosophy of History," 264.
8. Boas, "The Exhibits from the North Pacific Coast," 122–36; Johnson, *A History of the World's Columbian Exposition*, 2: 331; Johnson, *A History of the World's Columbian Exposition*, 3: 422.
9. Cannizzo, "George Hunt and the Invention of Kwakiutl Culture"; Jacknis, "George Hunt, Collector of Indian Specimens," 177–224; Jonaitis, *Chiefly Feasts*; Berman, "'The Culture As It Appears to the Indian Himself'"; Briggs and Bauman, "'The Foundation of All Future Researches'"; Whitehead, "The Hunt for Quesalid"; Glass, "Conspicuous Consumption," 406–67; Wilner, "A Global Potlatch."
10. Cole, *Franz Boas: The Early Years*, 143–46, 157–68; BPP: Boas to Marie, October 3, 1894; Rohner, *The Ethnography of Franz Boas*, 149.
11. APS Boas Papers: Hunt to Boas, Hunt to Boas, January 15, 1894.
12. APS Boas Family Papers: Boas to Marie, November 12, 1894; Rohner, *The Ethnography of Franz Boas*, 175.
13. APS Boas Family Papers: Boas to Marie, November 15, 1894; Rohner, *The Ethnography of Franz Boas*, 176–77.
14. APS Boas Family Papers: Boas to Marie, November 17, 1894; Rohner, *The Ethnography of Franz Boas*, 177–78; Boas, "The Indians of British Columbia," 232.
15. APS Boas Family Papers: Boas to Marie, November 17, 1894; Rohner, *The Ethnography of Franz Boas*, 177; Boas, "The Indians of British Columbia," 233.
16. APS Boas Family Papers: Boas to Marie, November 17, 1894; Rohner, *The Ethnography of Franz Boas*, 177–79.
17. APS Boas Family Papers: Boas to Marie, November 15, 1894, November 17, 1894; Rohner, *The Ethnography of Franz Boas*, 177.
18. Boas, *Kwakiutl Ethnography*, 56–60; Curtis, *The North American Indian*, xii.
19. Wilner, "A Global Potlatch," 94–96; BPP: Boas to Marie, Nov. 19, 1894; Rohner, *The Ethnography of Franz Boas*, 180–81; Boas, *The Social Organization and the Secret Societies of the Kwakiutl Indians*, 545–58; Boas, *Kwakiutl Ethnography*, 183–223.

20. APS Boas Family Papers: Boas to Marie, November 19, 1894; Rohner, *The Ethnography of Franz Boas*, 180–82.
21. APS Boas Family Papers: Boas to Marie, November 19, 1894; Rohner, *The Ethnography of Franz Boas*, 180–82.
22. APS Boas Family Papers: Boas to Marie, November 19, 1894, November 21, 1894, November 22, 1894, November 25, 1894, November 27, 1894, November 28, 1894, December 1, 1894; Rohner, *The Ethnography of Franz Boas*, 177–89.
23. APS Boas Family Papers: Boas to Marie, November 27, 1894; Rohner, *The Ethnography of Franz Boas*, 185.
24. APS Boas Family Papers: Boas to Marie, November 21, 1894; Rohner, *The Ethnography of Franz Boas*, 182.
25. APS Boas Family Papers: Boas to Marie, November 22, 1894; Rohner, *The Ethnography of Franz Boas*, 183.
26. APS Boas Family Papers: Boas to Marie, December 1, 1894; Rohner, *The Ethnography of Franz Boas*, 188; Boas, *The Social Organization and the Secret Societies of the Kwakiutl Indians*, 398, 462.
27. APS Boas Family Papers: Boas to Marie, November 25, 1894; Rohner, *The Ethnography of Franz Boas*, 184.
28. APS Boas Family Papers: Boas to Marie, November 25, 1894; Rohner, *The Ethnography of Franz Boas*, 184.
29. Kroeber, "Franz Boas: The Man", 13; Cole, *Franz Boas: The Early Years*, 183.
30. APS Boas Papers: Hunt to Boas, April 30, 1896.
31. APS Boas Papers: Hunt to Boas, December 1, 1897.
32. APS Boas Papers: Hunt to Boas, July 9, 1896.
33. Boas, *The Social Organization and the Secret Societies of the Kwakiutl Indians*, 311.
34. Boas, *The Social Organization and the Secret Societies of the Kwakiutl Indians*, 315.
35. Gough, "A Priest versus the Potlatch," 75–89.
36. APS Boas Papers: Hunt to Boas, March 4, 1898.
37. APS Boas Papers: Hunt to Boas, January 10, 1899.
38. Stocking, *A Franz Boas Reader*, 125.
39. APS Boas Papers: Boas to Hunt, February 3, 1889; Boas to Chief Hemasaka, February 3, 1899.
40. Pinkoski, "Back to Boas," 156.
41. Halliday, *Potlatch and Totem*, 10.
42. APS Boas Papers: Hunt to Boas, March 15, 1900.
43. HCF: Boas to Spencer, March 29, 1900.
44. APS Boas Papers: Boas to Hunt, April 10, 1900.
45. APS Boas Papers: Hunt to Boas, March 27, 1900.
46. APS Boas Papers: Boas to Hunt, April 10, 1900.
47. APS Boas Papers: Boas to Hunt, April 28, 1900.

48. APS Boas Papers: Hunt to Boas, October 10, 1900; Boas to Hunt, January 7, 1901; Hunt to Boas, February 22, 1901.
49. APS Boas Papers: Boas to Hunt, May 1, 1901.
50. APS Boas Papers: Hunt to Boas, August 12, 1901.
51. APS Boas Papers: Hunt to Boas, September 6, 1901.
52. APS Boas Papers: Boas to Hunt, December 21, 1901.
53. Jacknis, "George Hunt, Collector of Indian Specimens," 177–224.
54. HCF: Boas to Hunt, November 5, 1902, December 1, 1902, December 18, 1902.
55. GW, January 24, 1903.
56. GW, January 24, 1903.
57. BML: Hunt to Boas, March 1, [1903].
58. Holm and Quimby, *Edward S. Curtis in the Land of the War Canoes.*
59. Boas and Holm, *The Kwakiutl of British Columbia.*
60. HCF: Boas to Annie Spencer, April 27, 1903.
61. APS Boas Papers: Hunt to to H. A. Andrews, January 31, 1911.
62. Jacknis, "The Ethnographic Object"; Berman, "'The Culture As It Appears to the Indian Himself'"; Darnell, "The Pivotal Role of the Northwest Coast"; Darnell, *Invisible Genealogies.*
63. APS Boas Papers: Boas to Hunt, January 27, 1900.
64. APS Boas Papers: Boas to Hunt, February 24, 1900.
65. APS Boas Papers: Hunt to Boas, January 9, 1900. See also Boas, *Kwakiutl Ethnography*, 121–25; Boas, *The Religion of the Kwakiutl Indians*, 1–56; Whitehead, "The Hunt for Quesalid."
66. APS Boas Papers: Hunt to Boas, March 27, 1900, May 22, 1906; Boas to Hunt, February 14, 1907, August 16, 1907.
67. Berman, "'The Culture As It Appears to the Indian Himself,'" 242.
68. APS Boas Papers: Hunt to Boas, March 10, 1908.
69. APS Boas Papers: Boas to Hunt, December 19, 1906.
70. APS Boas Papers: Hunt to Boas, January 18, 1907.
71. APS Boas Papers: Hunt to Boas, January 23, 1907.
72. APS Boas Papers: Boas to Hunt, February 14, 1907.
73. APS Boas Papers: Boas to Hunt, August 16, 1907.
74. APS Boas Papers: Hunt to Boas, November 30, 1907.
75. APS Boas Papers: Hunt to Boas, August 30, 1907.
76. APS Boas Papers: Hunt to Boas, November 16, 1907.
77. APS Boas Papers: Hunt to Boas, November 16, 1907.
78. APS Boas Papers: Hunt to Boas, January 6, 1908.
79. APS Boas Papers: Boas to Hunt, March 27, 1908.
80. APS Boas Papers: Hunt to Boas, April 13, 1908.
81. APS Boas Papers: Hunt to Boas, April 24, 1908.
82. APS Boas Papers: Boas to Hunt, April 27, 1908.
83. APS Boas Papers: Boas to Hunt, June 11, 1908.
84. APS Boas Papers: Boas to Hunt, June 17, 1809, June 18, 1908.
85. APS Boas Papers: Hunt to Boas, June 18, 1908.

86. APS Boas Papers: Hunt to Boas, June 18, 1908.
87. APS Boas Papers: Hunt to Boas, June 18, 1908, July 10, 1908, July 16, 1908, July 22, 1908, September 3, 1908, September 3, 1908, October 27, 1908, November 4, 1908.
88. APS Boas Papers: Hunt to Boas, July 22, 1908.
89. APS Boas Papers: Hunt to Boas, November 23, 1908.
90. APS Boas Papers: Hunt to Boas, November 23, 1908.
91. APS Boas Papers: Boas to Hunt, March 12, 1912, April 4, 1913.
92. APS Boas Papers: Hunt to Boas, March 20, 1913.
93. APS Boas Papers: Hunt to Boas, May 7, 1916.
94. APS Boas Papers: Hunt to Boas, February 7, 1898; Boas, "The Houses of the Kwakiutl Indians," 209.
95. APS Boas Papers: Boas to Hunt, April 30, 1897; Boas, "The Houses of the Kwakiutl Indians" 209; Boas, *The Social Organization and the Secret Societies of the Kwakiutl Indians*, 376, 379.
96. APS Boas Papers: Hunt to Boas, July 14, 1899.
97. Jonaitis, *Chiefly Feasts*, 216.

References

MANUSCRIPTS AND ARCHIVES

APS. American Council for Learned Societies Committee on Native American Research. Mss.497.3.B63c. American Philosophical Society, Philadelphia.

APS. Franz Boas Papers Mss.B.B61. American Philosophical Society, Philadelphia.

APS. Franz Boas Family Papers.Mss.B.B61f. American Philosophical Society, Philadelphia.

GHC. George Hunt Correspondence. Division of Anthropology Archives, American Museum of Natural History, New York.

GW. Diary of George Hunt. Personal Collection of Gloria Cranmer Webster, Alert Bay, British Columbia.

PM. Peabody Museum Director's Records. Peabody Museum Archives, Harvard University.

PUBLISHED WORKS

Benjamin, Walter. "Theses on the Philosophy of History." In Hannah Arendt, ed., *Illuminations: Essays an Reflections*, 253–64. Trans. Harry Zohn. New York: Schocken Books, 1968.

Berman, Judith. "'The Culture As It Appears to the Indian Himself': Boas, George Hunt, and the Methods of Ethnography." In George W. Stocking Jr., *Volksgeist as Method and Ethic: Essays on Boasian Ethnography and the German Anthropological Tradition*, 215–56. Madison: University of Wisconsin Press, 1996.

———. "Raven and Sunbeam, Pencil and Paper: George Hunt of Fort Rupert, British Columbia." Unpublished manuscript on file with the author, n.d.

Boas, Franz. "The Exhibits from the North Pacific Coast." In *World's Columbian Exposition Reports*, 86–142. Cambridge MA: Peabody Museum of Archaeology and Ethnology at Harvard University, Director Records, World's Columbian Exposition (8.5), 1893.

———. "The Houses of the Kwakiutl Indians." *Proceedings of the United States National Museum* 11 (1888): 197–213.

———. "The Indians of British Columbia." *Journal of the American Geographical Society of New York* 28.3 (1896): 229–43.

———. *Kwakiutl Ethnography*. Ed. Helen Codere. Chicago: University of Chicago Press, 1966.

———. *The Religion of the Kwakiutl Indians*. Part 2: *Translations*. Columbia University Contributions to Anthropology 10. New York: Columbia University Press, 1930.

———. *The Social Organization and the Secret Societies of the Kwakiutl Indians*. Report of the U.S. National Museum. Washington DC: Government Printing Office, 1897.

Boas, Franz, and Bill Holm. *The Kwakiutl of British Columbia*. DVD. 37 min. Seattle: University of Washington Press, 1973.

Briggs, Charles L., and Richard Bauman. "'The Foundation of All Future Researches': Franz Boas, George Hunt, Native American Texts, and the Construction of Modernity." *American Quarterly* 51.3 (1999): 479–528.

Cannizzo, Jeanne. "George Hunt and the Invention of Kwakiutl Culture." *Canadian Review of Sociology* 20.1 (1983): 44–58.

Cole, Douglas. *Franz Boas: The Early Years, 1858–1906*. Seattle: University of Washington Press, 1999.

Curtis, Edward S. *The North American Indian*. Vol. 10: *The Kwakiutl*. Norwood MA: Plimpton Press, 1915.

Darnell, Regna. *Invisible Genealogies: A History of Americanist Anthropology*. Lincoln: University of Nebraska Press, 2001.

———. "The Pivotal Role of the Northwest Coast in the History of Americanist Anthropology." In "Ethnographic Eyes," ed. Wendy Wickwire. Special issue of *BC Studies* 125–26 (2000): 33–52.

Donne, John. *Devotions upon Emergent Occasions*. Ed. John Sparrow. London: Cambridge University Press, 1923.

Du Bois, W. E. B. "A Hymn to the People." *African Methodist Episcopal Church Review* 28.2 (1911): 619.

Ford, Clellan S. *Smoke from Their Fires: The Life of a Kwakiutl Chief*. New Haven CT: Yale University Press, 1941.

Glass, Aaron. "Conspicuous Consumption: An Intercultural History of the Kwakwaka'wakw Hamat'sa." PhD dissertation, New York University, 2006.

Gough, Barry. "A Priest versus the Potlatch: The Reverend Alfred James Hall and the Fort Rupert Kwakiutl, 1878–1880." *Journal of the Canadian Church Historical Society* 24.2 (1982): 75–89.

Halliday, William. *Potlatch and Totem: The Recollections of an Indian Agent*. London: J. M. Dent and Sons, 1935.

Helm, June. *Pioneers of American Anthropology: The Uses of Biography*. Seattle: University of Washington Press, 1967.

Holm, Bill, and George Irving Quimby. *Edward S. Curtis in the Land of the War Canoes: A Pioneer Cinematographer in the Pacific Northwest*. Seattle: University of Washington Press, 1980.

Jacknis, Ira. "The Ethnographic Object and the Object of Ethnology in the Early Career of Franz Boas." In George W. Stocking Jr., ed., *Volksgeist as Method and Ethic: Essays on Boasian Ethnography and the German Anthropological Tradition*, 185–214. Madison: University of Wisconsin Press, 1996.

———. "George Hunt, Collector of Indian Specimens." In Aldona Jonaitis, ed., *Chiefly Feasts: The Enduring Kwakiutl Potlatch*, 177–224. Seattle: University of Washington Press, 1991.

Jay, Martin. "Historical Explanation and the Event: Reflections on the Limits of Contextualization." *New Literary History* 42 (2011): 557–71.

Johnson, Rossiter, ed. *A History of the World's Columbian Exposition*. Vol. 2: *Departments*. New York: D. Appleton, 1897.

———. *A History of the World's Columbian Exposition*. Vol. 3: *Exhibits*. New York: D. Appleton, 1898.

Jonaitis, Aldona, ed. *Chiefly Feasts: The Enduring Kwakiutl Potlatch*. Seattle: University of Washington Press, 1991.

Kroeber, A. L. "Franz Boas: The Man." In A. L. Kroeber, ed., *Franz Boas, 1858–1942*, 13. Memoirs of the American Anthropological Association 61. Menasha WI: American Anthropological Association, 1943.

Pinkoski, Marc. "Back to Boas." *Histories of Anthropology Annual* 7 (2011): 127–69.

Raibmon, Paige. *Authentic Indians: Episodes of Encounter from the Late-Nineteenth-Century Northwest Coast*. Durham NC: Duke University Press, 2005.

Rohner, Ronald P., ed. *The Ethnography of Franz Boas: Letters and Diaries of Franz Boas Written on the Northwest Coast from 1886 to 1931*. Introduction by Ronald P. Rohner and Evelyn C. Rohner. Trans. Hedy Parker. Chicago: University of Chicago Press, 1969.

Romano, Claude. *Event and World*. New York: Fordham University Press, 2009.

Stocking, George W., Jr. *A Franz Boas Reader: The Shaping of American Anthropology, 1883–1911*. Chicago: University of Chicago Press, 1974.

Thomas, David Hurst. *Columbian Consequences*. Vol. 3: *The Spanish Borderlands in Pan-American Perspective*. Washington DC: Smithsonian Institution Press, 1991.

Whitehead, Harry. "The Hunt for Quesalid: Tracking Lévi-Strauss's Shaman." *Anthropology & Medicine* 7.2 (2000): 149–68.

Wilner, Isaiah Lorado. "A Global Potlatch: Identifying the Indigenous Influence on Western Thought." In "The Settler Complex," ed. Patrick Wolfe. Special issue of *American Indian Culture and Research Journal* 37.2 (2013): 87–114.

8 The Ethnographic Legacy of Franz Boas and James Teit

The Thompson Indians of British Columbia

ANDREA LAFORET

In September 1894 Franz Boas, who was traveling through British Columbia gathering information on the physical attributes of Aboriginal people, wrote to his parents in Germany about his first meeting with James Teit, who lived a few miles above Spences Bridge, near the confluence of the Thompson and Nicola Rivers. He reported that he had met "a redheaded Scotsman . . . who is married to an Indian woman. He knows a great deal about the Indians and was especially kind. I engaged him right off. . . . Yesterday the Scotsman came down with horses and we visited the Indian tents. The Indians here irrigate the land and raise horses and cows on the irrigated pastures."[1]

By mid-December 1894, well before the inception of the Jesup North Pacific Expedition in 1897, Boas had asked Teit to write a report on the Nlaka'pamux, also known at that time as "the Thompson Indians," and to make the first of several ethnographic collections.[2] This was the beginning of a collaboration between Teit and Boas that continued in various ways, largely at a distance and through correspondence, for nearly thirty years, until Teit's death in 1922. By that time Teit had written ethnographic monographs on several peoples speaking Interior Salish languages, had written about the Athapaskan-speaking Tahltan and Kaska, had made ethnographic collections for the American Museum of Natural History, the Field Museum, the Smithsonian Institution, the British Columbia Provincial Museum, the National Museum of Canada, and the Peabody Museum at Harvard, and had assembled a significant body of unpublished notes.

Teit's role and ethnographic legacy are explored in the ongoing work of Wendy Wickwire and Judith Thompson, and his role as an activist working in collaboration with Aboriginal and non-Aboriginal colleagues to secure rights to land is detailed in work by Wickwire and Peter Campbell.[3] In this essay I focus on the construction and format of Teit's first descriptive monograph, "The Thompson Indians of British Columbia,"

and discuss certain of the implications of scholarly decisions made in the 1890s for the Nlaka'pamux today.

In the 1890s Teit lived among, worked among, and was most familiar with the Nlaka'pamux who lived along the Thompson River above and below Spences Bridge and those who lived along the nearby Nicola River. This is one region among several constituting the Nlaka'pamux homeland, which consists of several thousand square miles situated in the mountains and plateaus of southwestern British Columbia and Washington State. It is defined by three rivers that run through the middle of the Canadian portion, and in Washington by portions of the Skagit and Nooksack rivers. In Canada the Fraser and Thompson rivers and the Thompson and Nicola rivers intersect at points of topographical change and subtle shifts in climate, creating four river valleys: the steep, forested Fraser canyon that extends to a few miles below Lytton; the drier, somewhat more open mountains of the Fraser River valley above Lytton; the even drier Thompson River valley; and the lightly forested Nicola River valley. The river valleys now in Washington are flanked by forested mountains. All of these regions were cognitively mapped. Prior to the arrival of Europeans, the Nlaka'pamux economy depended entirely on the exploitation and use of both riverine and upland resources and lands, and in spite of the introduction of ranching, work for wages, and other occupations into the postsettlement Nlaka'pamux economy, both continued to be important in Teit's day. Teit estimated the Nlaka'pamux population as approximately two thousand in the mid-1890s and noted that, because of the smallpox epidemic of the early 1860s and the prevalence of other diseases in the settlement period, the population was considerably reduced from its level immediately prior to contact.

At the inception of Teit's work, Boas's mentorship and direction were crucial. Born in the Shetland Islands in 1864, Teit had come to British Columbia at the age of nineteen to work in his uncle's store. He had the relatively basic but effective education accorded in Scotland to intelligent young men of his class. When he met Boas he was just over thirty, married to Antko, a Nlaka'pamux woman, and making his living from the land. He brought to his work with Boas a familiarity with the Nlaka'pamux culture of the 1890s, fluency in the Nlaka'pamux language, and an ability to gather information and present it lucidly in writing. He had no university education or training in anthropology. Boas was thirty-six, had had his first ethnographic field experience in British Columbia in 1886, and, as 1894 drew to a close, was conducting research for the British Association for the Advancement of Science and living rather precariously on

contracts.[4] The appointment to the American Museum of Natural History that would secure his career began on January 1, 1896.[5]

Over the previous seven years Boas had been defining the approach to ethnology and the concept of culture that would be implemented and developed in various ways in the Jesup Expedition monographs compiled by ethnographers working under his direction. In a series of letters exchanged in *Science* with Otis Mason in 1887 Boas argued that objects assembled in museum collections were best understood within their social and historical context rather than within the evolutionary model Mason proposed.[6] His address at the conclusion of his term as president of the American Association for the Advancement of Science, titled "The Human Faculty as Determined by Race," saw the inception of his long-term endeavor to establish historical events rather than race as the primary factor in the shaping of human societies.[7]

In the preface to *The Social Organization and the Secret Societies of the Kwakiutl Indians* Boas emphasized the importance of history and context in studying Northwest Coast Aboriginal societies: "While a hasty glance at these people and a comparison with other tribes emphasize the uniformity of their culture, a closer investigation reveals many peculiarities of individual tribes which prove that their culture has developed slowly and from a number of distinct centers, each people adding something to the culture which we observe at the present day."[8]

The meeting between Boas and Teit in 1894 led to the creation of a voluminous, multifaceted body of work. The first Teit publication edited by Boas reflected Boas's ongoing interest in mythology. *Traditions of the Thompson River Indians* was published as a memoir of the American Folk-Lore Society. By 1898 Teit had submitted components of a comprehensive descriptive ethnography of the Nlaka'pamux for Boas's review.[9] "The Thompson Indians of British Columbia" was published in 1900.

Between 1900 and 1912 Teit went on to conduct ethnographic research organized along similar lines for the Lillooet, the Shuswap, and the Okanagan and Salishan peoples living in Washington State,[10] although the results of this last work were not published immediately. The last work published in this period was "Mythology of the Thompson Indians." Subsequently Teit worked on contract for Edward Sapir of the National Museum of Canada, making collections and developing information in the same spirit as that begun with Boas in the 1890s. During these years he expanded the geographic scope of his work, to include research among the Kaska and Tahltan and of northern British Columbia.[11]

In keeping with the practice of the day, all of the ethnographic collec-

tions Teit made were retrospective, representative of a time before contact. Where older material was no longer available, he commissioned new objects from people who had the requisite knowledge and skill. With the wax cylinders that came into use during his time he made audio recordings of Nlaka'pamux songs, accompanied by documentary notes that extended the ethnographic information published in "The Thompson Indians of British Columbia," and compiled extensive notes on basketry designs, Nlaka'pamux knowledge and use of plants, and face paintings. In an extended series of photographs he documented hair styles, again those customary prior to European settlement, buckskin and woven clothing, the construction of temporary dwellings, and activities such as root digging. He also photographed people, sometimes wearing traditional dress, at other times in contemporary clothing. He recorded the names of people who contributed the songs or whom he photographed. Teit also assisted Boas's student Herman Haeberlin in his basketry research, although this was hampered by Haeberlin's chronic illness. The paper, "Coiled Basketry in British Columbia and Surrounding Region," published by Boas after the deaths of Teit and Haeberlin, includes snapshot biographies of basket makers.[12] While it is not clear whether these were actually written by Teit or Haeberlin, Teit's interest in basketry and connection with Nlaka'pamux basket makers was likely crucial to their recording. Teit died at the age of fifty-eight, with a substantial volume of work still unpublished. After Teit's death Boas edited or saw into print Teit's "The Middle Columbia Salish," *The Salishan Tribes of the Western Plateaus*, and his paper "Tattooing and Face and Body Painting of the Thompson Indians, British Columbia," as well as his research materials on ethnobotany and coil basketry.[13]

Although generated within a period of less than thirty years, and fully representative of the time in which it was created, Teit's ethnographic legacy is susceptible to interpretation, reinterpretation, and use for various purposes by people whose grandparents were not born in his day. In considering how the components of this body of work are resonant with current interests I am thinking primarily of the work Teit did with the Nlaka'pamux, with whom he worked first and with whom he never stopped working as long as he lived.

Ironically the products of Teit's work that are most profoundly resonant with current community interests are those he never published: the song recordings that make it possible to hear an ancestor's voice, the notes on songs that provide narratives of encounters by different individuals with their *sneʔm*, or guardian spirit, and photographic portraits of people, that is, cultural materials that are less contained within a constructed expres-

sive framework and are explicitly connected to people and places within Nlaka'pamux country.[14] These are fairly readily integrated into local histories, family histories, and collective biography, particularly when combined with information about family history and individual experience that are held by families and by older individuals with knowledge accumulated across a broad spectrum, as well as parish records and census records. Of more generalized collective value are maps and ethnographic notes archived with the American Philosophical Society and the collections of objects housed in several museums, including the American Museum of Natural History, the Canadian Museum of History, the Royal British Columbia Museum, the Field Museum, and the Peabody Museum at Harvard University. As a whole these collections are a valuable component of Nlaka'pamux heritage. However, they resonate with the specific interests of twenty-first-century Nlaka'pamux in ways that are less comprehensive and more fluid. Stone pipes collected by Teit are of interest to the artist who makes pipes now; the baskets Teit acquired for several museums are studied by local historians in association with collections and photographs in the community in order to reconstruct the oeuvre of particular basket makers.[15]

"The Thompson Indians of British Columbia" is harder to penetrate and resonates much less directly with current concerns than the unpublished material. Self-contained and set in an antiquated form, it floats apart from present-day reality. The generalized, didactic character of the text obscures the identity of the people with whom Teit worked to record the information. Although Teit had extensive knowledge of the Nlaka'pamux society of the 1890s, "The Thompson Indians of British Columbia" is largely a description of a culture in past time, a time not actually specified by date but implied to be a moment prior to the arrival of settlers. As the sole comprehensive ethnography of Nlaka'pamux society, it carries substantial authority, yet it is also subject to criticism on the grounds that, like other "golden age" ethnographies, it tacitly claims legitimacy for a version of Nlaka'pamux society untouched by external influence at the expense of the reality that modern Nlaka'pamux, including those of Teit's day, have lived.[16]

The late 1890s were a very dynamic time for Nlaka'pamux society, both politically and socially. The Gold Rush and the establishment of the Crown Colony of British Columbia were forty years in the past; reserves had been laid out and reviewed twenty years previously, significantly reducing the land base accessible for the continued development of the Nlaka'pamux economy; the Nlaka'pamux had become wards of the Crown, subject to a system of governance administered by the Department of

Indian Affairs; epidemics and the movement of people to new areas to develop grazing and farm land had changed the demography; marriage patterns had been altered by Christian missionaries and intermarriage with settlers unfamiliar with the Nlaka'pamux kinship system; smallpox was not entirely eradicated but had been succeeded as a major threat to health by influenza and other illnesses; families contended with a high rate of child mortality; Nlaka'pamux educational practices were seriously compromised by the development of residential schools, at that time located just outside Nlaka'pamux country. Very little of this appears in "The Thompson Indians of British Columbia." Boas had other issues in mind. The content is entirely devoted to descriptions of an array of elements of culture and their relationship to one another, while the broader purpose is to gather indications of historical influences and define the Nlaka'pamux culture as a unit of comparison with neighboring cultures. In the conclusion to the book, which he authored separately, Boas is concerned with the degree of influence of Plains and Northwest Coast societies on Nlaka'pamux culture and the relative complexity of their ideas and institutions. Correspondence between Teit and Boas from 1894 to 1900 provides clues both to the manner of the construction of the ethnography and also to Teit as an ethnographer at that early period of his work.[17]

In the early stages of his work for Boas, Teit was working among people who were his neighbors. When Boas first approached him in 1894 he asked Teit to do something that would be quite difficult even in modern society: request Nlaka'pamux people in the vicinity of Spences Bridge (then Cook's Ferry) to allow themselves to be measured for his study of physical anthropology. To ask Nlaka'pamux men of that time to allow themselves to be measured by a stranger for purposes that were abstract, to say the least, must have been very difficult. To ask Nlaka'pamux women to allow this must have seemed virtually impossible. Nonetheless Teit did so, and in correspondence with Boas later that year he provided the names of those who generously complied.[18] They included Xluxluxpauz, an "old man" when measured by Boas in 1894, and his daughters, Neltko and Kwonkwonamtko, and Tcatius, also an "old man" in 1894 when measured by Boas, and his son, Snauts or Matthew Snots. Tcatius ("Chateuse") and Snots are enumerated in the 1881 Government of Canada census for Cook's Ferry as belonging to household 156; Xluxluxpauz ("Clokclokpowse") and his wife, Qulpansah, are in household 157; and in household 158 is "Hantko," who may be Teit's wife, Susannah Lucy Antko.[19] Antko is listed as a seventeen-year-old orphan in the census carried out in 1878 in conjunction with the federal provincial commission on Indian reserves.[20] Between 1894 and 1922 at least fifty Nlaka'pamux individu-

als contributed to the overall course of Teit's work. Many are included with other members of their families in the parish records of the Church of England mission to the Nlaka'pamux as well as successive censuses. Most lived in communities along the Thompson River between Nicomen and Ashcroft, or along the Nicola River, although some are recorded as members of the Lytton band and Spuzzum. These are the communities with which Teit was most familiar and from which he drew a large part of his knowledge.

In 1894 Teit was a knowledgeable layman. The ethnography he produced might have been close to a sojourner memoir based on observation of and participative presence in Nlaka'pamux society, had not Boas's direction and feedback turned the process of its production into a tutorial event. Teit began writing in October 1894; "The Thompson Indians of British Columbia" was published in April 1900. During most of this time Boas was in New York or elsewhere. He visited Spences Bridge again only for short periods in December 1894 and in 1897. They communicated with each other, on matters large and small, through letters.

Teit and Boas made complementary contributions to the production of the ethnography. Teit contributed the data, draft manuscripts, and additional information written in response to Boas's queries. In early February 1895 he sent Boas a paper 216 pages in length. Teit innocently believed this paper to be finished. In April he was responding to Boas on "some important points to be made subjects of future inquiry."[21] In November he was forwarding information on the construction of winter houses.[22] This exchange continued virtually until the moment of publication. By 1897 he was engaged in a formal revision of the paper. In April 1898 he undertook the first of two research trips to the Fraser Canyon, where he spent approximately two weeks, mostly at Spuzzum, the Nlaka'pamux village nearest the boundary of the Halkomelem-speaking people of the Fraser Valley. He followed this with a second trip to Spuzzum in June 1898, spending a few days at the end of the trip in North Bend, the site of another Fraser Canyon Nlaka'pamux village. During the course of this work he recorded fifty-two narratives and material for a paper on the Nlaka'pamux of the Fraser Canyon, which he sent to Boas in April 1899. Teit provided responses to Boas's continual requests for further information in spite of the pressure of other work and Antko's illness during the winter of 1899 and her death on March 2 of that year. As the book neared publication he also reviewed and revised proofs and galleys.

Boas's contributions were drawn from a different skill set. He provided a template for the focus and organization of the work that in many ways paralleled his own comprehensive ethnography, *The Central Eskimo*. Many

of the chapter headings in "The Thompson Indians of British Columbia," such as "Historical and Geographical Setting, Clothing and Ornaments, Subsistence," "Travel, Transportation and Trade," "Social Organization and Festivals," "Birth Childhood, Puberty, Marriage and Death," and "Religion," are reminiscent of those in *The Central Eskimo*. Both books emphasize the material and the visual and incorporate into the text line drawings illustrating objects in museums. This is a museographic approach to ethnography, following the museography of the late nineteenth century, in which objects served as both illustrations and exponents of culture. Boas also followed this practice in *The Social Organization and Secret Societies of the Kwakiutl Indians*. Information within each section of "The Thompson Indians of British Columbia" is illustrated with line drawings of Nlaka'pamux objects collected by Teit for the American Museum of Natural History during the time he was compiling the ethnography.

Although Teit continued to use the template developed for "The Thompson Indians of British Columbia" in the ethnographies he wrote for other Interior Salish peoples, not every Jesup Expedition ethnography followed this table of contents. John Swanton, who went to the field in 1900 as a graduate student with a letter of instructions from Boas about subjects to pursue, produced an ethnography of the Haida organized around quite different topics.[23]

From early 1895 to publication in 1900, Boas provided Teit with timely reviews of the drafts of the various chapters of "The Thompson Indians of British Columbia" as well as requests for additional information. A large part of his work was editorial. Teit wrote straightforward, lucid, and grammatical prose, with very few errors. He certainly understood that Boas was preparing his initial paper on the Nlaka'pamux living near the confluence of the Thompson and Nicola rivers for independent publication, and there is some indication that this was Boas's initial intention, but in 1899 he decided to combine it with the paper on the Fraser Canyon Nlaka'pamux.[24] Even as the book was in the final stages before press, Boas demonstrated assiduous concern for the inclusion of all possible detail. Between August 29 and September 27, 1899, he sent Teit no fewer than nine separate requests for supplementary information. Teit answered them all.

Boas assumed responsibility for the general organization of the book, including the merging of methods of manufacture into a single comprehensive chapter.[25] He also made two broad editorial changes to the text with lasting implications. Finding Teit's terms *NkamtcinEmux* and *Utamqt* cumbersome, he coined the terms *Upper Thompson* to refer to the NkamctinEmux and all other Nlaka'pamux people north of the Fraser Can-

yon, and *Lower Thompson* and *Lower division* to refer to the Nlaka'pamux of the Fraser Canyon. At the same time he decided to omit all of the Nlaka'pamux words Teit had included in his manuscripts, partly in order to make the text more accessible to readers and partly because he planned to publish, with Teit, a grammar and vocabulary of Nlaka'pamuxcin.[26] The grammar and vocabulary were not published.

Boas oversaw the preparation of the line drawings and engravings for the illustrations, and he prepared the map illustrating Nlaka'pamux territory himself. He wrote to Teit, "I am preparing a map of the location of the tribe for your paper, which I am compiling from Dr. Dawson's maps and from Brownlee's map of British Columbia. On these maps I enter the information contained in your papers."[27]

The ethnography Teit and Boas produced has certain distinctive features. Unlike either *The Central Eskimo* or *The Social Organization and the Secret Societies of the Kwakiutl Indians*, "The Thompson Indians of British Columbia" is written generally in the past tense, with certain exceptions. There are in fact three voices in this book: Boas's voice in the conclusion and the section on art, simply entitled, "Art," which he also authored separately, and two voices for Teit. For the most part Teit wrote in the past tense, but he shifted into the present tense to describe activities such as fishing, possibly on the basis of his own experience, to advocate better medical care, and to interpolate contemporary information. In a passage reminiscent of Boas's first comment about cattle raising, he wrote, "The young men of the Upper Thompson, especially those of the Spences Bridge and Nicola bands, affect the cowboy style of dress. Cowboy hats are the common head wear, and the horses are saddled and bridled in cowboy fashion."[28] Boas did not oppose the inclusion of contemporary information. In fact near the end of the research for the book he asked Teit to update a table outlining demographic facts for the Thompson River communities, and Teit complied.[29] In the text Teit's present-tense commentary on the situation of the Nlaka'pamux in the 1890s stands out as information that can be linked to a particular time.

"The Thompson Indians of British Columbia" is not explicitly a work of theory. No theoretical perspective or argument is proposed within the text, although the entire work can be seen as a component of a larger purpose in regard to the theory of the day. Darnell notes that Boas "insisted that there must be an ethnographic baseline before grand generalization could proceed."[30] As a broadly conceived professional goal, however, at this early point, at least, this was Boas's goal, not Teit's. Teit's interests were more specifically focused on compiling knowledge and developing his expertise, and he was enthusiastic in both endeavors. Their cor-

respondence is punctuated with Teit's requests for current ethnological publications and acknowledgment of those sent by Boas, including a copy of *The Social Organization and the Secret Societies of the Kwakiutl Indians*. Between 1896 and 1898 Teit wrote several times to James Fletcher, the Dominion botanist in Ottawa, seeking information about plants significant to the Nlaka'pamux.[31] At the outset he was not unlike James Swan and other nineteenth-century correspondents of the Smithsonian to whom ethnology offered an opportunity to have a career in science that was otherwise denied to them, although his eventual contribution was larger and better grounded than theirs.

Teit's methodology in this phase of his work is not entirely clear. He recorded the name of every person from whom he acquired the objects in the first collection he assembled and compiled lists of names of all the residents of the communities at Cook's Ferry and two villages farther up the Thompson River in 1893,[32] but the ethnography is written without reference to particular living people. Again this is likely following the lead of Boas, who wrote *The Central Eskimo* in generalized prose, reserving references to individuals for his personal diary and letters.[33] Also completely absent are accounts of particular observed events illustrating the Nlaka'pamux practices described in the various chapters, although retold accounts of past actions, such as raids, are included. Teit was writing nearly thirty years before Malinowski in *Argonauts of the Western Pacific* presented participant observation to a wide anthropological audience as a possible methodology, but the circumstances in which he lived and worked meet several of the criteria for participant observation set out by Kathleen Dewalt and Billie Dewalt: extended residence within the cultural context, knowledge and use of the language, active participation, use of everyday conversation as an interview technique, informal observation, recording observations in field notes, and use of both tacit and explicit information in analysis and writing.[34] Teit's involvement with the Nlaka'pamux of the Spences Bridge area met most of these criteria; the archived field notes are often brief and in secondary formats such as lists. Whether his methods constitute participant observation as it came to be understood later in the twentieth century is an open question. However, a key factor in anthropological participant observation is the use of the method with the intention to represent. He had begun writing within a few weeks of meeting Boas for the first time, and by early December 1894 had written fifty pages.[35] The timing suggests that this early manuscript cannot have been based on intentional participant observation or on field notes inscribed and transcribed,[36] but on knowledge acquired during past experience. In large part his writing represents

a summative form of distilled observation and, equally important, listening. Nevertheless as his work for Boas proceeded he did make notes on the basis of interviews. Following work with an elderly woman, "a veritable genealogist," he clarified information Boas had received during his initial visit in September 1894.[37] His accounts of his work at the Fraser Canyon village of Spuzzum specifically refer to "notes."[38] Notes archived from Teit's early work often provide information that supplements what was published; however, they are also often without information as to the specific context of their inscription. Narratives recorded after 1900, for example "Npal and Kolomastcut" and his "Notes on Songs of the Indians of British Columbia," have more contextual information and are clearly the result of inscription and transcription.

Neither Boas nor Teit saw the completion of the ethnography as other than the beginning of Teit's research. While he wrote the ethnography Teit also wrote the narratives that make up *Traditions of the Thompson Indians*; conducted two field trips to gather information on the Athapaskan-speaking Stuwixamux of the Nicola Valley; acquired through purchase and commission collections of Nlaka'pamux artifacts sent to the American Museum of Natural History in 1895, 1897, and 1898; compiled information on the Nlaka'pamux language; inaugurated research among the Lillooet (Stl'atl'imx), including a collection of narratives; and compiled a separate body of Nlaka'pamux narratives in the course of his research in Spuzzum, which eventually saw publication as "Mythology of the Thompson Indians."

Both Boas and Teit valued Nlaka'pamux knowledge and information about Nlaka'pamux cultural practice. The direct opposite of the kind of colonial resident lamented by Malinowski, one who "had lived for years in the place with constant opportunities of observing the natives and communicating with them, and yet hardly knew one thing about them really well,"[39] Teit was unusual among non-Aboriginal people in British Columbia in the 1890s. Although both Boas and Teit believed that this knowledge was unlikely to survive the forces of assimilation,[40] it is also important to remember that, notwithstanding the constructed frame of the untouched past in which it was presented, the knowledge was within the intellectual compass of people who were Teit's neighbors. The social and cultural milieu of the Nlaka'pamux had certainly changed over the previous century, with the introduction of the horse, Simon Fraser's visit, the arrival of fur traders at Kamloops not far outside Nlaka'pamux country in 1811, the distant echo of Christianity, and in 1858 the Gold Rush with all its consequences, but in the 1890s Nlaka'pamux concepts continued to provide an interpretive framework for the experience of

Nlaka'pamux people. The major precipitating event for the changes that had occurred, the Gold Rush, was barely forty years in the past. Anyone much over sixty in 1898 had benefited from a fully Nlaka'pamux education and had reached adulthood before the Gold Rush.

Much of the information in the monograph has been independently reaffirmed and augmented by Nlaka'pamux of succeeding generations, with concerns and sometimes outright disagreement expressed about certain arbitrary statements, but the form in which it is presented in the monograph does not resonate with present-day consciousness, either within anthropology at large or within Nlaka'pamux society in general. From both points of view there are also huge areas left unaddressed. In many ways it is a period piece.

Nonetheless working with "The Thompson Indians of British Columbia" becomes inescapable whenever issues arise that implicate Aboriginal title and rights. Since the late 1990s the ethnographies produced by the Jesup Expedition have taken on a relevance to contemporary political life that neither Boas nor Teit could have foreseen. The emergence of Aboriginal title as a concept with legal weight was launched by *Calder v. British Columbia* (1973). The meaning of Aboriginal rights in the light of Section 35(1) of the Constitution was defined at least partly in the Supreme Court decision in *Regina v. Sparrow* (1990). In 1996 the Supreme Court judgment in *Regina v. Van der Peet*, supplemented by judgments in *Regina v. N.T.C. Smokehouse Ltd.* (1996) and *Regina v. Gladstone* (1996), refined the concept, defining an Aboriginal right as "an element of a practice, custom or tradition integral to the distinctive culture of the aboriginal group . . . of central significance to the aboriginal society in question" and having "continuity with the practices, customs and traditions that existed prior to contact with European society." The Supreme Court of Canada decision in *Delgamuukw v. British Columbia* (1997) reiterated a test for Aboriginal title originally presented in the Federal Court of Canada judgment in *Hamlet of Bake Lake v. Minister of Indian Affairs and Northern Development* (1979). This test required that an Aboriginal society claiming title to lands demonstrate occupation at the time of sovereignty, that the occupation had been continuous since that time, and that it had been maintained in exclusion of occupation by other Aboriginal groups. Following a note by Justice Allan McEachern, the trial judge in *Delgamuukw v. British Columbia*, that European sovereignty had been established in British Columbia in 1846, the date of the Treaty of Oregon, 1846 has been presumed to be the critical date for establishing Aboriginal rights and title.[41] Thus by the beginning of 1998 claims to both Aboriginal title and Aboriginal right in British Columbia were required to be demonstrated

through reference to the culture of the Aboriginal society concerned as it was in the 1840s.

The wording of the Supreme Court decision in *Regina v. Van der Peet* (1996) suggests that culture is an assemblage of fixed attributes in a static array with a center and a periphery. There is no process here, no recognition of the contemporary conception of culture as "a system and a process" undergoing constant change,[42] and there is an underlying assumption that the only possible change is depletion of an original essence. A substantial literature on the shortcomings of this approach, which began to develop immediately following the first decision in *Delgamuukw v British Columbia* in 1991, includes anthologies edited by Frank Cassidy and Michael Asch and journal contributions by both legal scholars and anthropologists, for example Russel Lawrence Barsh and James Youngblood Henderson, Kent McNeil, John Borrows, and Brian Slattery.[43]

Asch states, "At heart the Court's approach is to ground recognition of Aboriginal rights on the basis of cultural 'distinctiveness'—a concept probably unique to its understanding."[44] In analyzing the concepts animating these judgments and their antecedents Asch adduces examples from introductory and classic works by Malinowski, Mair, Lévi-Strauss, and Marvin Harris. He does not mention Boas. Antonio Lamer's source is uncertain. A counsel for the defense in *Regina v. Van der Peet* indicated that the concept of culture was not part of the argument at trial.[45] Lamer may have come to his definition of culture independently and on the basis of his own resources.

A Supreme Court of Canada decision in *Tsilhqot'in Nation v. British Columbia* in 2014 resolved a long-standing issue regarding occupation of territory, a key criterion for Aboriginal title. In doing so the ruling referenced Aboriginal culture in a more open way, stating, "In determining what constitutes sufficient occupation, which lies at the heart of this appeal, one looks to the Aboriginal culture and practices, and compares them in a culturally sensitive way with what was required at common law to establish title on the basis of occupation" (2014 SCC 44). However, the ruling retained "the time of the assertion of European sovereignty" as the effective time frame for establishing the basis for Aboriginal title, with the implication that the relevant cultural practices are those of the early to mid-1800s.

The two vectors of culture and time have brought the Jesup Expedition ethnographies into focus as early comprehensive statements about the cultures of Aboriginal societies in British Columbia. They highlight cultural attributes, and although written at least fifty years after the Oregon Treaty they give the illusion of a description of a time before con-

tact. Their attraction is reinforced by the fact that 1846 is a difficult date to work with, particularly east of the Coast Mountains. There are a few journals by fur traders based in Kamloops and Fort Langley that provide fragmentary comments and the more extensive journal of Simon Fraser, whose time was spent exclusively on the Fraser River,[46] but to rely on these is to rely on the casual comments of a few sojourners, almost exclusively male, who were poorly placed to witness events beyond those of particular interest to themselves and even more poorly placed to understand fully what they saw.

The invocation of "The Thompson Indians of British Columbia" as a source of information on distinctive cultural attributes of Interior Salish societies followed the *Delgamuukw* decision very quickly. In 1998 a lawyer practicing in Vancouver drew on information presented in the monograph to defend clients charged with transporting tobacco illegally across an international boundary (*Regina v. Jacobs*). This was unsuccessful, but along the way to this conclusion several people gathered in a courtroom to argue about whether baskets of a certain shape had been used to carry tobacco or fish.

This first ethnography continues to be referenced fairly frequently. The resolution of Aboriginal title may be addressed in major undertakings such as the *Delgamuukw* litigation or treaty negotiation. Aboriginal title and rights are also addressed, and far more commonly, in the course of dealing with smaller, more geographically focused issues—the right to sell fish, as in the *Van der Peet* case, or proposals concerning industrial development on or near Aboriginal lands. In addressing these issues Aboriginal societies are constrained by the Supreme Court decisions to weigh ethnographic information from the original ethnographies very carefully. In this light the most casual comment in "The Thompson Indians of British Columbia" takes on great significance, far greater perhaps than Teit ever intended. This became apparent in 2009 in a case involving eligibility of the First Nation to be consulted in an industrial development.[47] As a complicating factor, the monograph lacks information about major sectors of Nlaka'pamux society and practice. One of the most problematic lacunae is the absence of documentation of the cognitive mapping and economic use of the upland areas on either side of the rivers in Canada and of the entire section of Nlaka'pamux country that lies south of the forty-ninth parallel. The standard Western European distinctions between culture and nature, habitation and wilderness are absent from concepts central to Nlaka'pamux thought in Teit's day and afterward,[48] but even within the Western perspective what is often still thought of as "wilderness," promoted by the government of British

Columbia as "Super, Natural British Columbia," is now the site of industrial development designed to facilitate resource extraction on a major scale or to provide support to expanding urban populations. These lands and their associated ecosystems continue to be defined by Nlaka'pamux and other Aboriginal societies as central to their identity. In the past several decades different upland areas significant to the Nlaka'pamux have become sites for a copper mine, two major hydro transmission lines, a waste dump for a city several hundred miles away, and a dam intended to facilitate the provision of electricity to Seattle. As legal interest in or opposition to these initiatives on the basis of Aboriginal title and Aboriginal rights is required to be grounded in data confirming the use of these areas in the mid-1800s, it is often necessary for the Nlaka'pamux to generate new information along the same channels in which Boas directed Teit's inquiry. While this information, once generated, is certainly valuable, it is possibly not the only information that might be wanted by a society with limited resources, facing now, as it did a century ago, challenges in regard to demographic change, housing, access to and preservation of resources, and education.

The decision taken in the early 1890s to focus "The Thompson Indians of British Columbia" on a reconstructed indefinite past was a methodological decision designed to further a particular intellectual goal. This decision had the consequence of marginalizing late nineteenth-century Nlaka'pamux culture, at least within the scope of the book. The book is now caught up in present-day judicial decisions that are also focused on an arbitrarily chosen "original moment," that is, the date of the assertion of British sovereignty. In this context the implications of Boas's decision have become magnified. The invocation of this ethnography as the primary source for interpreting Nlaka'pamux history in the light of the judicial decisions has the effect of marginalizing the entire modern history of the Nlaka'pamux and reinforcing the Supreme Court's reliance on a static concept of culture.

Like all other modes of cultural expression, ethnography is subject to changes in fashion, and within the discipline of anthropology those written according to methodologies and disciplinary goals that have long been superseded are historicized, with the label "classic" reserved for those few considered seminal. However, in the communities that furnished their subjects, ethnographies can have a long reach. The scholarly decisions that underlie the structure and content of ethnographies produced long ago can have implications in the present day that the authors cannot have foreseen and might well deplore. Neither Boas nor Teit was oblivious to the political issues of his day. A major issue fac-

ing the Kwakwaka'wakw with whom Boas worked was the law banning the potlatch, and he protested it in 1897 and joined Edward Sapir of the National Museum of Canada in a protest in 1915.[49] From 1908 on, Teit worked with Nlaka'pamux colleagues as well as Aboriginal political organizations to further the resolution of land claims.[50]

"The Thompson Indians of British Columbia" was an early expression of a methodological perspective that was to inform much of the work Boas supervised in British Columbia. When it was published it was the first stand-alone comprehensive description of an Aboriginal society in British Columbia. Even so it is unlikely that either Boas or Teit intended it to be relied on in perpetuity as the singular ethnographic authority concerning the Nlaka'pamux. The publication of "The Thompson Indians of British Columbia" in 1900 was a professional milestone for both Teit and Boas, but this first ethnography produced during their collaboration is best considered simply as the work it was intended to be: a broad, retrospective description of the understandings and customs of a particular people and an early exemplar of an approach to a concept of culture that was focused more on historical factors than on race and evolution.

Acknowledgments

My interest in this topic was stimulated by conversations with Chief Robert Pasco and Pauline Douglas of the Nlaka'pamux Nation Tribal Council, as well as conversations over the past several years with Nathan Spinks, John Haugen, Charles Brown, and the late Mandy Brown of Lytton. I began working with Annie York of Spuzzum, much in the Boasian tradition, in 1971. In the late 1980s, largely in collaboration with Nathan Spinks, I worked with Nlaka'pamux people in various localities in relation to the proposal of the Canadian National Railway to put a second track through the Fraser Canyon, and since 2009 I have worked with the Nlaka'pamux Tribal Council on several issues of current concern. I am also indebted to the late Clara Clare, originally of Spuzzum, who, during my first fieldwork in 1970, told me a "Jimmy Teit" story.

Notes

1. Quoted in Rohner, *The Ethnography of Franz Boas*, 140–41.
2. Rohner, *The Ethnography of Franz Boas*, 196.
3. See the following by Wickwire: "James A. Teit," "To See Ourselves as the Other's Other," "Beyond Boas?," and "'They Wanted Me to Help Them.'" See also Thompson, *Recording Their Story*; Campbell, "'Not as a White Man, Not as a Sojourner.'"
4. Wickwire, "'They Wanted Me to Help Them,'" 299.

5. Cole, *Franz Boas: The Early Years*, 184.
6. Boas, "The Occurrence of Similar Inventions in Areas Widely Apart"; Boas, "Museums of Ethnology and Their Classification."
7. Stocking, "Franz Boas and the Culture Concept," 870.
8. Boas, *The Social Organization and the Secret Societies of the Kwakiutl Indians*, 317.
9. Boas to Teit, January 4, 1898, Boas Correspondence, American Museum of Natural History Accession 1898-32.
10. Teit, "The Lillooet Indians" and "The Shuswap."
11. Teit, "Kaska Tales" and "Tahltan Tales."
12. Boas et al., *Coiled Basketry*, 431–54.
13. Boas, *Tattooing and Face and Body Painting*; Steedman, *The Ethnobotany of the Thompson Indians*; Boas et al., *Coiled Basketry*.
14. Wickwire, "James A. Teit"; Teit, "Notes on Songs of the Indians of British Columbia."
15. Bjerky, "First Nations Baskets."
16. Wickwire, "'They Wanted Me to Help Them,'" 313.
17. American Museum of Natural History Accession files 1895-32, 1897-2, 1898-32, 1899-48.
18. Teit, "Genealogy of NkamtcinEmux."
19. Census, 1881, 34.
20. " Summer Census of Indian Tribes, 1877–1878."
21. Teit to Boas, April 16, 1895, American Museum of Natural History.
22. Teit to Boas, November 9, 1895, American Museum of Natural History.
23. Boas to Swanton, June 5, 1900, American Museum of Natural History; Swanton, *Contributions to the Ethnology of the Haida*.
24. Boas to Teit, July 28, 1899, American Museum of Natural History.
25. Boas to Teit, July 31, 1899, American Museum of Natural History.
26. Boas to Teit, October 11, 1899, American Museum of Natural History.
27. Boas to Teit, July 31, 1899, American Museum of Natural History.
28. Teit, "The Thompson Indians of British Columbia," 320.
29. Boas to Teit, July 28, 1899, American Museum of Natural History; Teit, "The Thompson Indians of British Columbia," 176, 177.
30. Darnell, "Theorizing the Americanist Tradition," 49.
31. Teit, "Plant Names of Thompson Indians."
32. Teit, "List of Cooks Ferry Band of Indians,"
33. Sanjek, "The Secret Life of Fieldnotes," 193.
34. Dewalt and Dewalt, *Participant Observation*, 4.
35. Teit to Boas, October 29, 1894, December 6, 1894, American Museum of Natural History.
36. Clifford, "Notes on (Field)notes," 47.
37. Teit, "Genealogy of NkamtcinEmux."
38. Teit to Boas, April 6, 1898, American Museum of Natural History.
39. Malinowski, *Argonauts of the Western Pacific*, 5.
40. Silverman, "The Boasians and the Invention of Cultural Anthropology," 261.

41. Doherty, "Recent Developments in Aboriginal Rights and Title Cases."
42. Asch, "The Judicial Conceptualization of Culture," 129.
43. McEachern, *Reasons for Judgment*; Cassidy, *Aboriginal Title in British Columbia*; Asch, *Aboriginal and Treaty Rights in Canada*; Barsh and Henderson, "The Supreme Court's Van der Peet Trilogy"; McNeil, "Aboriginal Title and Aboriginal Rights"; Borrows, "Frozen Rights in Canada"; Slattery, "The Generative Structure of Aboriginal Rights."
44. Asch, "The Judicial Conceptualization of Culture," 120.
45. Louise Mandell, personal communication to Andrea Laforet, December 3, 2010.
46. Lamb, *Simon Fraser: Letters and Journals*.
47. O'Callaghan and Westgeest, *Nlaka'pamux Nation Tribal Council v. Griffin*.
48. Laforet and York, *Spuzzum Fraser Canyon Histories*, 61–63.
49. Rohner, *The Ethnography of Franz Boas*, 201; Canadian Museum of History, Marius Barbeau's Correspondence, folder Edward Sapir (1911–1920), Box B237 f. 6.
50. Wickwire, "'They Wanted Me to Help Them,'" 298.

References

MANUSCRIPTS AND ARCHIVES

Accession 1895-32. American Museum of Natural History, New York.
Accession 1897-2. American Museum of Natural History, New York.
Accession 1898-32. American Museum of Natural History, New York.
Accession 1899-48. American Museum of Natural History, New York.
Franz Boas Papers, Mss.B.B61. American Philosophical Society, Philadelphia.
Boas-Swanton Correspondence. American Museum of Natural History, New York.
Canada Report. "Lytton Band or Bands." Prepared by James Teit. Department of Indian Affairs, National Archives of Canada RG 10, vol. 11302, file 158/30. Ottawa, Ontario.
———. Marius Barbeau's Correspondence, folder Edward Sapir (1911–1920), Box B237 f.6.. Canadian Museum of History, Gatineau, Quebec. Census, 1881. Province of British Columbia, District No. 189, S. District Nekumcheen, Cook's Ferry, Pukayst, 33–37.
"Summer Census of Indian Tribes No. 2, 1877–1878." RG88, vol. 494. National Archives of Canada, Ottawa, Ontario.
Teit, James. "Genealogy of NkamtcinEmux." N.d. Boas Collection, files 59–61. American Philosophical Society, Philadelphia.
———. "List of Cooks Ferry Band of Indians or Wheestimneetsa's Band." January 1893. Boas Collection, 372.16. American Philosophical Society, Philadelphia.
———. "Notes on Songs of the Indians of British Columbia." N.d. Canadian Museum of History, Gatineau, Quebec.

———. "Npal and Kolomastcut." N.d. Boas Collection, file 61. American Philosophical Society, Philadelphia.

———. "Plant Names of Thompson Indians." N.d. Boas Collection, s1b3. American Philosophical Society, Philadelphia.

PUBLISHED WORKS

Asch, Michael, ed. *Aboriginal and Treaty Rights in Canada: Essays on Law, Equality and Respect for Difference*. Vancouver: UBC Press, Centre for Constitutional Studies, University of Alberta, 1997.

———. "The Judicial Conceptualization of Culture after Delgamuukw and Van der Peet." *Revue of Constitutional Studies* 5 (2000): 119–37.

Barsh, Russel Lawrence, and James Youngblood Henderson. "The Supreme Court's Van der Peet Trilogy: Naive Imperialism and Ropes of Sand." *McGill Law Journal* 42 (1996–1967): 993–1009.

Bjerky, Irene. "First Nations Baskets at the Langley Centennial Museum." Langley Centennial Museum, 2007. www.langleymuseum.org (accessed August 8, 2013).

Boas, Franz. "Art." In *The Thompson Indians of British Columbia*, by James Teit, 376–86. Memoir of the American Museum of Natural History 2 (1). Jesup North Pacific Expedition 4. New York: Knickerbocker Press, 1900.

———. *The Central Eskimo*. Washington DC: Bureau of American Ethnology, 1888.

———. "Conclusion." In *The Thompson Indians of British Columbia*, by James Teit, 387–90. Memoir of the American Museum of Natural History 2 (1). Jesup North Pacific Expedition 4. New York: Knickerbocker Press, 1900.

———. "The Human Faculty as Determined by Race." *Proceedings of the American Society for the Advancement of Science* 43 (1894): 301–27.

———. "Museums of Ethnology and Their Classification." *Science* 9 (June 17, 1887): 587–89, 614.

———. "The Occurrence of Similar Inventions in Areas Widely Apart." *Science* 9.226 (1887): 485–86.

———, ed. *The Salishan Tribes of the Western Plateaus*, by James Teit. Forty-fifth Annual Report of the Bureau of American Ethnology, 1927–1928. Washington DC: Smithsonian Institution, 1930.

———. *The Social Organization and Secret Societies of the Kwakiutl Indians Based on Personal Observations and on Notes Made by Mr. George Hunt*. Report of the U.S. National Museum under the direction of the Smithsonian Institution for the year ending June 30, 1895. Washington DC: Smithsonian Institution, 1897.

———, ed. *Tattooing and Face and Body Painting of the Thompson Indians, British Columbia, by James Teit*. Forty-fifth Annual Report of the Bureau of American Ethnology, 1927–1928. Washington DC: Smithsonian Institution, 1930.

Boas, Franz, H. K. Haeberlin, J. Teit, and H. Roberts. *Coiled Basketry in British Columbia and Surrounding Regions*. 41st Annual Report of the Bureau of

American Ethnology, 1919–1924. Washington DC: Smithsonian Institution, 1928.

Borrows, John. "Frozen Rights in Canada: Constitutional Interpretation and the Trickster." *American Indian Law Review* 22.1 (1998): 37–64.

Calder v. British Columbia. S.C.R. 313 (1973).

Campbell, Peter. "'Not as a White Man, Not as a Sojourner': James A. Teit and the Fight for Native Rights in British Columbia, 1884–1922." *Left History* 1994: 37–57.

Cassidy, Frank ed. *Aboriginal Title in British Columbia: Delgamuukw v. The Queen*. Fernie, British Columbia: Oolichan Books, Institute for Research on Public Policy, 1992.

Clifford, James. "Notes on (Field)notes." In Roger Sanjek, ed., *Field Notes: The Makings of Anthropology*, 47–70. Ithaca NY: Cornell University Press, 1990.

Cole, Douglas. *Franz Boas: The Early Years, 1858–1906*. Seattle: University of Washington Press, 1999.

Darnell, Regna. "Theorizing the Americanist Tradition: Continuities from the B.A.E. to the Boasians." In Lisa Philips Valentine and Regna Darnell, eds., *Theorizing the Americanist Tradition*, 38–51. Toronto: University of Toronto Press, 1999.

Delgamuukw v. British Columbia. 3 S.C.R. 1010 (1997).

Dewalt, Kathleen M., and Billie R. Dewalt. *Participant Observation*. Walnut Grove CA: Altamira Press, 2002.

Doherty, Michael P. "Recent Developments in Aboriginal Rights and Title Cases." Materials prepared for the Continuing Legal Education Society of British Columbia. Aboriginal Law Conference, June 2009.

Hamlet of Baker Lake v. Minister of Indian Affairs and Northern Development. 1 F.C. 48 (1979).

Lamb, W. Kaye, ed. *Simon Fraser: Letters and Journals, 1806–1808*. Toronto: Macmillan, 1960.

Laforet, Andrea, and Annie York. *Spuzzum Fraser Canyon Histories 1808–1939*. Vancouver: University of British Columbia Press, 1998.

Malinowski, Bronislaw. *Argonauts of the Western Pacific*. London: Routledge and Kegan Paul, 1922.

McEachern, Allan. *Reasons for Judgment: Delgamuukw v. B.C*. Smithers: Supreme Court of British Columbia, 1991.

McNeil, Kent. "Aboriginal Title and Aboriginal Rights: What's the Connection?" *Alberta Law Review* 36.1 (1997): 117–48.

O'Callaghan, Kevin, and Danielle Westgeest. 2009 *Nlaka'pamux Nation Tribal Council v. Griffin*. Aboriginal Law Bulletin. Fasken Martineau, September 2009. www.fasken.com (accessed December 2009).

Regina v. Gladstone. 2 S.C.R. 723 (1996).

Regina v. Jacobs. 3 C.N.L.R. 239 (1999). British Columbia Supreme Court.

Regina v. N.T.C. Smokehouse Ltd. 2 S.C.R. 672 (1996).

Regina v. Sparrow. 1 S.C.R. 1075 (1990).

Regina v. Van der Peet. 2 S.C.R. 507 (1996).

Rohner, Ronald, ed. *The Ethnography of Franz Boas: Letters and Diaries of Franz Boas Written on the Northwest Coast from 1886 to 1931*. Chicago: University of Chicago Press, 1969.

Sanjek, Roger. 1990 "The Secret Life of Fieldnotes." In Roger Sanjek, ed., *Field Notes: The Makings of Anthropology*, 187–270. Ithaca NY: Cornell University Press.

Silverman, Sydel. "The Boasians and the Invention of Cultural Anthropology." In Frederick Barth, Andre Gingrich, Robert Parkin, and Sydel Silverman, eds., *One Discipline Four Ways: British, German, French and American Anthropology*, 257–74. Chicago: University of Chicago Press, 2005.

Slattery, Brian. "The Generative Structure of Aboriginal Rights." *Supreme Court Law Review* 38.2 (2007): 595–698.

Steedman, Elsie Viault, ed. *The Ethnobotany of the Thompson Indians of British Columbia: Based on Field Notes by James Teit*. Forty-fifth Annual Report of the Bureau of American Ethnology, 1927–1928. Washington DC: 1930.

Stocking, George. "Franz Boas and the Culture Concept in Historical Perspective." *American Anthropologist* 68 (1966): 867–82.

Super, Natural British Columbia. "Destination B.C." 2013. www.hellobc.com (accessed August 8, 2013).

Swanton, John R. *Contributions to the Ethnology of the Haida. American Museum of Natural History Memoirs 8*. Jesup North Pacific Expedition 5. Leiden: E. J. Brill, G. E. Stechert, 1905.

Teit, James. "Kaska Tales." *Journal of American Folk-Lore* 30.68 (1917): 427–73.

———. "The Lillooet Indians." In Franz Boas, ed., *Memoir of the American Museum of Natural History* 2(5), 193–300. Jesup North Pacific Expedition. Leiden: E. J. Brill, 1906.

———. "The Middle Columbia Salish." *University of Washington Publications in Anthropology* 2.4 (1928): 89–128.

———. "Mythology of the Thompson Indians." In *Memoir of the American Museum of Natural History* 12(2), 203–416. Leiden: E. J. Brill, G. E. Stechert, 1912.

———. "The Shuswap." In Franz Boas, ed., *Memoir of the American Museum of Natural History* 2(7), 443–813. Jesup North Pacific Expedition. New York: G. E. Stechert, 1909.

———. "Tahltan Tales." *Journal of American Folk-Lore* 32 (1919): 223–53.

———. "The Thompson Indians of British Columbia." In Franz Boas, ed., *Memoir of the American Museum of Natural History* 2(1), 163–392. Jesup North Pacific Expedition 4. New York: Knickerbocker Press, 1900.

———. *Traditions of the Thompson River Indians: Memoir of the American Folk-Lore Society 6*. Boston: Houghton, Mifflin, 1898.

Thompson, Judith D. *Recording Their Story: James Teit and the Tahltan*. Vancouver: Douglas and McIntyre, Canadian Museum of Civilization, University of Washington Press, 2007.

Tsilhqot'in Nation v. British Columbia. SCC 44 (2014).

Wickwire, Wendy. "Beyond Boas? Re-assessing the Contribution of 'Informant' and 'Research Assistant' James A. Teit." In Laurel Kendall and Igor Krupnik, eds., *Constructing Cultures Then and Now: Celebrating Franz Boas and the North Pacific Expedition*, 105–22. Washington DC: Smithsonian Institution, 2003.

———. "James A. Teit: His Contribution to Canadian Ethnomusicology." *Canadian Journal of Native Studies* 8.2 (1988): 183–204.

———. "'They Wanted Me to Help Them': James A. Teit and the Challenge of Ethnography in the Boasian Era." In Celia Haig-Brown and David Nock, eds., *Good Intentions: Eurocanadians Working for Justice in Aboriginal Contexts*, 297–320. Vancouver: University of British Columbia Press, 2005.

———. "To See Ourselves as the Other's Other: Nlaka'pamux Contact Narratives." *Canadian Historical Review* 75.1 (1994): 1–20.

PART 3 Activism

9 Anthropological Activism and Boas's Pacific Northwest Ethnology

DAVID W. DINWOODIE

The dominant foci for anthropological activism by and on behalf of peoples of Aboriginal descent in North America today are land claims, repatriation, and language preservation and revival. Activism in these areas is predicated on the idea that enhanced status and improved living conditions follow from achieving political "recognition" (of Aboriginal title and rights, of culturally based property, and Indigenous languages). The level and intensity of anthropological activism has been considerable, and successes in gaining recognition have been tangible, though it is important to acknowledge that they have not been sweeping. Collective recognition and the coalitions leading up to it have consolidated Aboriginal middle classes for the groups in question. Availed of the opportunities presented to members of the middle classes generally, members of these Aboriginal middle classes have excelled in ways that have confirmed the validity of the principle of meliorism and belied racist preconceptions. Collective recognition, however, has not necessarily improved the lot of the poorer members of Aboriginal groups: for them it has not necessarily resulted in greater acceptance into mainstream society, nor to improved access to the most dynamic sectors of the economy, nor to improved political access.

The demand for "recognition," as Charles Taylor terms it, comes to the fore in a number of ways in today's politics on behalf of minority or "subaltern" groups."[1] By a demand for recognition, Taylor means that politics on behalf of minority or "subaltern" groups shifts from fighting discrimination to demanding that people be recognized for their differences. The rationale is that ostensibly neutral but biased-in-fact workings of liberalism, such as requiring subaltern groups to exercise legal and political rights only in the language of dominant groups, not only puts them at a tactical disadvantage but can also damage their sense of self-worth. Being politically acknowledged, and being in the process recognized for what distinguishes them as minorities, the thinking goes, not only includes people but enhances the authentic basis of their self-worth.[2]

Franz Boas's anthropology and activism centered not on "recognition," however, but on what K. Anthony Appiah calls "the great liberal struggle . . . to get the state to treat its members as individuals only, without favoring or disfavoring particular ethnic or religious or gender identities."[3] In George W. Stocking's words, "Equality of opportunity, education, political and intellectual liberty, the rejection of dogma and the search for scientific truth, and identification with humanity and devotion to its progress are all part of a single outlook—a single left-liberal posture which, as in the case of Rudolph Virchow, is at once scientific and political."[4] Boas's ethnology, including his and his colleagues' research on the Tsilhqut'in,[5] was meant to show the historical interdependence and essential unity of all of humanity. In his ethnology his effort was to show that past patterns of behavior that appeared to us to be abnormal or markedly inferior were neither isolated nor intrinsically chaotic nor primitive but were often widely shared elements of behavior, predicated on the same types of social and psychological categories as our own.

The approach he used was designed to challenge scientific racism and the latent racism of social evolutionary thought; it was not oriented to illuminate the modern historical processes by which such contemporary identities as ethnicity and nationality develop. While Boas was certainly aware that ethnic and national identity posed special analytic challenges for anthropology, he made no attempt to systematically address the historical circumstances and institutional factors widely recognized to contribute to them, whether colonial territorialization, missionization, literacy, print capitalism, public education, changes in way of life, or what have you.[6] And yet the Aboriginal ethnicities and ethnic nationalities of today (First Nations in Canada and the many subgroupings identifying as First Nations) have histories in colonial contact that extend back beyond anthropology's entry into the Pacific Northwest. For the Tsilhqut'in of what is now west-central British Columbia, a hinterland of the greater Pacific Northwest, the maritime fur trade arrived in the late eighteenth century.[7] For interior peoples like the Tsilhqut'in the main effect of the coastal trade was to intensify the flow of goods and people, expanding the scope of social-relational and material-relational possibilities. With the implementation of the interior trade in the Fraser and Columbia corridors from 1808 to 1846, however, system of posts and communications were established, and such roles as fur harvesters and intermediaries came to be allocated and reinforced within trading districts. Elements of a thin and narrow but nevertheless global infrastructure, the roles allocated and negotiated within trading districts put

peoples of the Pacific Northwest into a complex translocal set of relations. As suggested in Eleanor Burke Leacock's pioneering work, "The Montagnais 'Hunting Territory' and the Fur Trade," the fur trade stimulated territorialization of unprecedented scope.

In the Chilcotin region systematic missionization followed some time after the fur trade. A Jesuit visited bands identified as Tsilhqut'in in 1845, but systematic missionization began later, when missionaries followed a wave of gold miners and ranchers into the area in the 1860s, and intensified their efforts in the 1880s just prior to Boas's visit in the summer of 1897. The Oblates of Mary Immaculate, who eventually charged themselves with missionizing the Tsilhqut'in, were a reactionary Catholic order that arose in the conflicts surrounding the French Revolution to combat secular liberalism among the rural poor of Provence. After being drawn abroad to Quebec, the Oblates, ultramontane and influenced by the Jesuits, developed Pacific Northwest versions of the reductions of South America. The Oblates enforced geographical and linguistic isolation, social structural integration, and biblically based ideological opposition to liberalism.[8] Following the fur trade's locating of groups within hierarchical fields of social difference, the Oblates further consolidated linguistic and cultural integration, social structural centralization, territorialization, and ethnic identification.[9] Vis-à-vis the insecure and antipathetic settlers rushing into what would become the province of British Columbia, many recently from California, Tsilhqut'in people developed a sense of themselves as a distinctive ethnic group among other ethnic groups.

In appreciating the value of Boas's ethnological work for contemporary activism, two points are helpful to bear in mind. First, although his ethnology was not directed toward such processes as ethnic or national formation, it is rich in material useful for reconstructing cultural history. Using Boas's ethnological material for this purpose nevertheless requires critical reframing. Douglas Cole, the author of Boas's benchmark biography, argues that as a result of a personal intellectual crisis, Boas shifted from a scientific to a historical approach:

> At the conclusion of his Eskimo research, Boas was thrown into a personal intellectual crisis. The exact sciences, spectacularly successful in their discovery of natural laws, possessed an unquestioned significance and prestige. He had left that secure area for geography, what he called a "half-historical" field, and his then results cast doubt on its value. He wondered whether it was "worth it," whether his move

had not placed him in "an inferior scholarly position." Boas, after a period of "tortured" thought and "severe mental struggles," resolved his problem while in Berlin in 1885. His solution was to go the whole way, to personally repudiate the scientific approach by making his new field of geography an entirely "historical" discipline possessing a legitimacy equal to the sciences.[10]

Though Cole's biography is excellent in many ways, the proposal that Boas developed an "entirely" historical approach to ethnology is not persuasive, as Michel Verdon argues.[11] Through his work Boas pointed to the potential of a historical approach but failed to develop it himself. His historicist orientation to ethnographic documentation in the Pacific Northwest was not historical per se but rather, borrowing from Clifford Geertz, anti-antihistoricist. He marshaled evidence to demonstrate that the peoples of the Pacific Rim could not be studied effectively in accordance with crude assumptions regarding Asian versus American races, nor on the basis of any single "grand system of the evolution of society."[12] And while he proposed a "new" historical method "based on 'the careful and detailed study of local phenomena' within a 'well defined, small geographical area,' with comparisons limited to 'the cultural area that forms the basis of the study,'" out of which would "emerge 'histories of the cultures of diverse tribes,'" the method, I concur with Alexander Lesser, Alfred Kroeber, Paul Radin, Marion Smith, and Judith Berman, was not fully historical, and nor was it well-equipped for the study of the distinct cultural-political history of the Pacific Northwest.[13] George Stocking observes, "Boas seems . . . quietly to have acknowledged this by a change in one word of the reprinted version of his 'Limitations of the Comparative Method.' In 1896, induction involved a study of the 'actual history of definite phenomena'; in 1940, it involved the study of the 'actual relations of definite phenomena.'"[14]

Second, revisiting *Anthropology and Modern Life*, Boas's elaboration of his work and its political implications, we are reminded that recognition, while the predominant concern of our time, is not the only matter warranting activism on behalf of people of Aboriginal descent. For many such people the challenges today are very much as Boas saw them at the turn of the nineteenth and twentieth centuries, the challenge of identifying biases even in the workings of liberalism and the attitudes of the educated classes, the challenge of being accepted without regard for socioeconomic impoverishment and cultural difference, the challenge of gaining real access to the dynamic sectors of the economy and the upper echelons of the political system.

*Boas's Ethnological Approach in View of the
Course of His Intellectual Development*

Even as a young man Boas was clearly aware of the roles of commerce, empire building, and religion as factors in contemporary political dynamics. He followed the events of the Franco-Prussian War, at least insofar as he experienced them in Minden and beyond. The war broke out in the summer of 1871, as his family was holidaying at Clus. From their balcony, according to Cole, they observed Prussian soldiers marching toward France. Moreover the garrison city of Minden, according to Cole, was "greatly affected by the conflict," and Boas would certainly have followed a course of events shaped by republicanism, imperialism, and the defensive reactions of Prussians and others.[15]

Based on his Gymnasium curriculum vitae we also know that he read Friedrich Schiller's history of the Thirty Years War "until he knew much of it perfectly."[16] In it Schiller argues that religion and the reformation played a key role in the development of new political sympathies and the restructuring of the political world through which Europe "first learned to see herself as a community of nations." "All this was effected by religion," writes Schiller, but religion was not "the sole motive of the war." The emergence of the new political realities was shaped by not religion alone but rather by the close connection between religion and "private advantages" and such "political considerations" as "state interests."[17]

And we know that he was aware of the culture wars of the nineteenth century, for example, of the *Kulturkampf* of Bismarckian Germany.[18] *Kulturkampf* was a policy that promoted the cultural unification of the state over and against the traditional religious authority of the Catholic Church. Boas's mentor, Rudolph Virchow, had in fact "dubbed the *Kulturkampf*, leaving little doubt about Boas' immersion in the political movement."[19] While liberal and forward looking in many ways, this is the movement that revived the reactionary doctrine of ultramontanism among Catholics in nineteenth-century Germany by means of patent discrimination. And so we know he was aware of the lively interanimation of religion, economy, politics, and ideology.

Moreover during World War I, Boas wrote a very interesting series of articles and letters on nationalism, one of which Stocking reprinted, "American Nationalism and World War I," in his important 1974 reader.[20] In this series he reveals at times the very critical appreciation of the semi-artificial invention of nations later developed at great length by Eric Hobsbawm, Terence Ranger, and others.[21]

Nevertheless the course of intellectual development leading to his

Pacific Northwest ethnology is clear: Boas was trained in the sciences. He developed his methodology in order to fashion a kind of natural historical alternative to what he saw as the pseudo-science of social evolutionary anthropology. Later, as he developed more of an understanding of the workings of political ideology in the United States, he saw that the social evolutionary position had become entangled with the "malaise" of a national anthropological tradition.[22]

Boas's intellectual vision and his life have been reasonably documented at this point.[23] My goal is to identify the course of his education and of his intellectual development as an anthropologist. I rely heavily on Douglas Cole's wonderfully well researched if not entirely definitive biography.

The Boas family was from Minden, Prussia, in what is now Germany, a small administrative and military center located on the Weser River, just a few miles downstream from the gap in the Westphalian Mountains that formed the last barrier to the North Sea. They lived in town, but the surrounding country was readily accessible. Franz's mother, Sophie, provided them with sufficient time outdoors to become acclimated to it and sometimes to find inspiration in their natural surroundings.[24] The family were clothing and textile retailers and were part of a small community of Jewish merchants numbering roughly two hundred in 1850. They acquired their surname when Boas's great-grandfather, Bendix Feibes Aron, took the name Boas after the biblical figure "who married Ruth and became the great-grandfather of David." Bendix took the name to meet the requirement that Jews assume family names following the 1808 emancipation of the Jews in Westphalia. Though they were targeted at different clientele, Franz's mother's family and his father each operated clothing and textile stores.[25]

Franz was born in 1858, the third child and the first son of Meier and Sophie Boas. Minden was a bastion of liberalism during the mid-nineteenth century, a relatively liberal period in German history. According to Cole, Jews had been integrating into German society since the late eighteenth century, and by Boas's time the family had assumed the German ideal of *Bildung*, mental cultivation, as their own.[26] Julia Liss provides a more nuanced perspective on Boas's relationship to *Bildung*:

> Boas' worries about the development of taste and his interest in method and rational understanding reflect his problematic relationship to German culture and the ideal of *Bildung*. On the one hand, like many members of the middle class for whom the classical education of the *Gymnasium* provided entry into an elite, Boas shared the desire to develop correct taste and make appropriate distinctions in aesthetic

matters. But being also of "Hebrew origin," as he identified himself on the first page of his *Curriculum Vitae*, he was an outsider to the dominant culture. While the inculcation of *Bildung* facilitated the assimilation of Jews in the post-Enlightenment period of Jewish emancipation, Boas' concern with acquiring aesthetic judgment suggested that these distinctions did not come naturally to him and were, he thought, absent from his immediate (familial) environment. He felt himself on the margins of the world which by virtue of his education he was supposed to enter.[27]

After attending the Minden *Bürgerschule* for two years, between 1865 1867, Franz entered the Gymnasium at Minden, where he followed the academic program emphasizing history, geography, German literature, science, mathematics, and languages. He developed interests in plants, animals, and rocks, and due to current events, and the ongoing German response to French imperialism, an interest in such foreign destinations as Africa.[28]

Boas's academic record was apparently uneven. His mind was opening in many directions, and in periods of family distress and personal ill health his grades occasionally declined. During a sojourn at Jena he became acquainted with the custodian of the university herbarium and developed an interest in plant taxonomics. At the time he also began to read German literature on his own time. Though his results were not what he or his family had hoped, he passed his final Gymnasium exams in early 1877. His favorite subject had long been geography, but his only outstanding mark was in mathematics.[29]

Boas emphasized science at Heidelberg, where he began university. In the fall of 1877 he moved to Bonn and pursued sciences, geography, and botany. In fall of 1879 he moved on to the Christian-Albrecht University in Kiel and settled somewhat reluctantly into a dissertation in physics under Gustav Karsten, examining the factors influencing the color of water.[30]

The dissertation was passable but apparently somewhat indeterminate in its conclusions and hence unremarkable. Kiel was not known for physics at the time, and Karsten had limited influence. Boas sensed that his prospects in physics per se were poor and began to reevaluate his career plans. Along with cultivating his knowledge of the psychological influences on perception, he renewed an earlier interest in geography, possibly stimulated by the newsworthiness of exploration at that time. Following his military service at Minden, he moved to Berlin in hopes of developing an expedition of his own, centering on the study of the influence of the physical environment on Eskimo perceptions and con-

ceptions. In Berlin family connections introduced him to Dr. Johan Wilhelm Reiss, vice president of the Berlin Geographical Society. Reiss in turn began to incorporate Boas into the geographical and anthropological communities, and soon Boas was acquainted with Rudolf Virchow and the patriarch of German ethnology, Adolf Bastian of the Berlin Museum of Ethnology. Geography and anthropology were exciting fields at the time due to the extent of exploration, and in these circles Boas frequently met the prominent explorers of the day.[31]

Unable to secure funding for his expedition from conventional sources, Boas appealed to the owner of the *Berliner Tageblatt*, a major Berlin newspaper, promising that he would write stories on the exploration of unknown parts of Arctic America. Possibly unique among explorers, Boas's references were scientists, including Theobald Fischer (geographer), Benno Erdmann (philosopher), and Gustav Karsten (physicist). The paper agreed to advance money for fifteen promised articles, and the expedition was under way. The plan was to study a limited region for a year by following the model of explorer C. F. Hall, who had shown the benefits for arctic research of adopting the Eskimo way of life. Boas departed Germany for Baffin Island in June 1883 and exited the Arctic in September 1884. His Arctic exploration was of great interest at the time in Germany, and his research was well received.[32]

Unable still to secure permanent employment, Boas resolved to seek a more advanced degree, this time in geography, a relatively new field at the university level. He enrolled at Berlin, where the only professor of geography was Heinrich Kiepert, a senior professor specializing in the lands of classical antiquity. Kiepert had no interest in Boas's New World research, shaped as it was by Boas's modern naturalistic approach. Boas nevertheless went on to pass his exams, lecturing on Arctic ice for the faculty colloquium.[33] Though his continuing relationship with Bastian and Virchow kept him in contact with, if not directly involved in, the dynamic new field of anthropology, his habilitation in geography would be based on the publication of his Eskimo research and *not* on any systematic geographical training from Kiepert or anyone else.

Boas began to publish, but his employment prospects unfortunately did not improve. His uncle and lifelong benefactor, Abraham Jacobi, had moved to New York in 1853. Born in the neighboring village of Hartum, Jacobi attended the Minden Gymnasium and there came under the influence of Theodor Herzberg, a democratic and liberal thinker. After his time at the Gymnasium, Jacobi studied medicine. Further stimulated by the Revolution of 1848, Jacobi radicalized, befriending revolutionaries and promoting revolutionary socialism as Germany entered a period of

reactionary conservatism. In 1851 he was arrested and charged with high treason. Though he was acquitted of this charge, he was imprisoned on a lesser charge and held for two years. Afterward he departed for England, visiting Marx and Engels before emigrating to New York, where he established a successful medical career. In roughly 1854 Jacobi married Fanny Meyer, Boas's mother's sister and thereby became Boas's uncle.[34]

In various ways Jacobi encouraged Boas to consider a life in America. His success in New York provided some encouragement in and of itself. In 1881 he visited Boas in the company of the daughter of a fellow New York doctor and émigré of 1848, Marie Krackowizer, and Boas soon became entranced with her. He visited her in New York just after his Arctic expedition and began to seriously contemplate moving from Germany. In 1886 he visited her again in New York, and during the visit Jacobi encouraged him to attend the meetings of the American Association for the Advancement of Science (AAAS). There he met Horatio Hale and Frederic Ward Putnam, whom Boas quickly realized were professional contacts of great significance, and in fact each eventually provided employment to him in one form or another.[35]

In the context of his growing interest in America, as stimulated by his uncle, his love interest, dim employment prospects in Germany, and a deteriorating political climate in Germany, the Northwest Coast presented itself as an attractive new avenue of research, one that, as Cole explains, offered "an opportunity to expand his breadth as an Americanist and thus make him more marketable in the new world." A key factor in opening this possibility to view was his experience with an 1885 exhibition of J. Adrian Jacobsen's collections from Alaska and British Columbia. Hired by Bastian as a temporary assistant in the Royal Ethnological Museum, Boas's major assignment was cataloguing and installing Jacobsen's collections. In January 1885 Jacobsen brought to Berlin a touring group of nine Bella Coola Indians. Boas spent as much time as possible with them, got to know them quite well personally, and even conducted some linguistic research with them.[36]

In these circumstances of burgeoning interest in New World employment and fresh ties to Bella Coola people, Boas planned a research trip to British Columbia for the fall of 1886. The purpose of the trip was to map the distribution of tribes based on language and myth. He would fund the trip by collecting ethnic artifacts for resale to museums. In addition Uncle Jacobi lent him $500, and Jacobi's prominent friend Carl Schurz was able to bequeath a Northern Pacific rail pass. As in the case of the Baffin Island expedition, Boas received no support from foundations or other conventional sources. The trip lasted from September 1886 to

the end of the year. He spent three weeks in Victoria, forty years after its founding as a fur trading post, eleven days at the Kwakiutl village of Newitti, five weeks at Quamichan, Comox, and Nanaimo, then back to Victoria, and then over to Vancouver.[37]

Boas took six more research trips to the Northwest Coast in the early phase of his life. The second was from May to July 1888 and was supported by Horatio Hale and the British Association for the Advancement of Science (BAAS). Hale sought an ethnological map, a general outline of linguistic stocks, comparative vocabularies, grammatical outlines for a language of each stock, and preliminary work on physical anthropology.[38]

His third trip was in July and September 1889 and, like the previous one, was sponsored by Hale and the BAAS. Whereas Boas favored more in-depth work with the Kootenai and interior Salish, people less influenced by Europeans, Hale wanted more research on Kwakiutl, Salish, and Nootka to fill out a general ethnological survey, which was his ultimate goal. Boas had no choice but to acquiesce to Hale. It was on this trip that Boas began to work with George Hunt.[39]

Boas's fourth trip to the Northwest Coast was in July and August 1890 and was sponsored by the Bureau of American Ethnology and the BAAS. July he spent in places like the Siletz Reservation, Tillamook, Grand Ronde, Astoria, and Shoalwater Bay, which is now known as Willapa Bay, an enormously productive estuary. In August he was in and around the canneries of New Westminster, British Columbia. By this time he had taken a position in the anthropology program at Clark University and had begun teaching anthropology, which, we must remind ourselves, is a field in which he had no formal training. And not coincidentally, on this trip he initiated anthropometric studies in the Pacific Northwest.[40]

Boas's fifth research trip to the Northwest Coast was a two-month trip in the summer of 1891 to Bay City, Shoalwater Bay, to continue his work with the Chinookan speaker Charles Cultee.[41] He delegated his work among the Kootenai for the BAAS to Alexander Chamberlain and thereby avoided time in Canada, devoting his attention to work for the Bureau of American Ethnology.

For Boas's sixth and relatively long trip in the fall of 1894 he acquired support from the BAAS, the American Museum of Natural History, the AAAS, and the Bureau of American Ethnology (BAE). Each had their interests: the BAAS wanted to establish the relative position of the interior Salish; the AAAS wanted to remeasure southern Californian tribes; and the BAE wanted to support further work on Chinook.[42]

Boas's seventh trip took place from early June through July 1897. This

was the first season of research for the Jesup North Pacific Expedition, a study funded by Morris K. Jesup, president of the American Museum of Natural History since 1881. Its purpose was to investigate the ethnological relations between the races of America and Asia. The trip consisted of a horseback tour of interior British Columbia lasting thirty-eight days, a trip to Port Essington on the Skeena to "measure, make cases, and identify museum pieces," and two weeks with George Hunt among the Kwakiutl. In the mid- to late 1890s Boas was more creative and more successful at pitching his research to anthropological foundations and institutions. The Jesup North Pacific Expedition, along with the research proposal to study the Vanishing Tribes of North America, and his East Asian venture, were meant to dramatically reconfigure the agenda for American anthropology.[43] They were projects that addressed the changes in perception of human history resulting from the globalization of the nineteenth century. His eighth and last major trip to the Northwest Coast, in 1900, was a continuation of the Jesup North Pacific Expedition.[44]

Despite his early socialization into the Humboldtian worldview, Boas's Pacific Northwest research was not primarily historical in its methodological orientation but rather natural historical. In "The Limitations of the Comparative Method," which he read at the American Society for the Advancement of Science in Buffalo between his sixth and seventh field trips to the Pacific Northwest, Boas proposed that a safer alternative to the comparative method, favored by American anthropologists, was a "detailed study of customs in their relation to the total culture of the tribe practicing them, in connection with an investigation of their geographical distribution among neighboring tribes":

> Its application is based, first of all, on a well-defined, small geographical territory, and its comparisons are not extended beyond the limits of the cultural area that forms the basis of the study. Only when definite results have been obtained in regard to this area is it permissible to extend the horizon beyond its limits, but the greatest care must be taken not to proceed too hastily in this, as otherwise the fundamental proposition which I formulated before might be overlooked, viz: that when we find an analogy of single traits of culture among distant peoples the presumption is not that there has been a common historical source, but that they have arisen independently. Therefore the investigation must always demand continuity of distribution as one of the essential conditions for proving historical connection, and the assumption of lost connecting links must be applied most sparingly.[45]

"We have in this method a means of reconstructing the history of the growth of ideas with much greater accuracy than the generalizations of the comparative method will permit," Boas argued reasonably, but it would be a mistake to assume that this method was well equipped to address the dynamics of ideas in accordance with Pacific Northwest colonial history.[46] The direct historical method is designed to consider the possibility that a cultural element originated elsewhere. By tracking the flow of cultural elements, it is possible to identify the cultures that invent them and the cultures that borrow them, and in this way to reconstruct the historical relations of tribes to their neighbors.

Particularly in the Pacific Northwest Boas directed his ethnographic attention toward the compilation of Native language texts "direct from natives of a culture."[47] He "envisioned bodies of primary materials as scholarly resources comparable to the historical records and remains of civilizations of the Old World." As is well known, he prioritized the documentation of what he called myths and tales over all other texts. His reasoning was that they were the most self-contained and independent of European influence and therefore could provide the least biased evidence on the remote past.[48] While he also collected historical and personal narratives, he did so on a much smaller scale and not for the purpose of studying them in their own right; rather he collected them in order that we might better assess the character and quality of his sources. I believe that Judith Berman is correct when she observes that for Boas ethnology was a science dealing with mental phenomenon and that "his views on the methods and goals of ethnographic description, while developing somewhat over time, are nevertheless remarkably consistent in many ways from his first field trips in the 1880s."[49] His were methods trained for scientific questions regarding human mental development; they were not trained for emergent political subjectivities in Pacific Northwest colonial history.

The Russian fur trade opened on the Northwest Coast with Vitus Bering's trip of 1841. The British and American trades opened when Captain Cook visited the Northwest Coast on his third voyage, in 1778. His men bartered for a few furs that were later sold in China for astonishing prices. News traveled quickly and set in motion "a train of events of worldwide significance."[50] The interior fur trade began around 1800, and by the 1830s the Hudson's Bay Company, "by a bizarre quirk of logic," worked with the Catholic Church to support the mission work of Augustine Blanchet and Modest Demers that led to the Oblate entry into the Pacific Northwest.[51] The Oblates established their base of operations in British Columbia at

Saint Mary's in the 1860s and continued to missionize the hinterlands into the 1890s. In addition to cultural exchanges, then, this period saw the mobilization of the region's Indians relative to empire formation in the case of the Oregon question. Later the Oblates carried their restoration agenda to the hinterlands and built up structural bulwarks against secularization and liberalism.

Boas begins his research in the area in 1886, well after the heyday of the fur trade and well after the onset of Oblate missionization. His major Jesup North Pacific Expedition is in 1897. For Boas the Pacific Northwest first represented an opportunity to enhance his stature as an Americanist, which would in turn bolster his career opportunities in the United States. Once he had a foothold in America, he perceived the national character of the anthropology being practiced, and he attempted to democratize the field, as it were, by bringing to bear those counter-Enlightenment arguments that had been particularly well developed in the German intellectual milieu of his education. Nevertheless he did not fully reorient himself, as I believe Cole suggests he does, to history. Rather he oriented his research to demonstrate the limitations of a national anthropology by demonstrating the limitations of the comparative method. Hence his direct historical method was not fully historical. Rather it was meant to reveal historical genealogies that would belie comparative overgeneralizations. In this sense it was anti-antihistorical.

Predicated on the detailed study of customs in relation to the total culture of tribes practicing them and in connection with and investigation of their geographical distribution among neighboring tribes of a limited region, his method may have been sufficient to illuminate the shortcomings of the comparative method but was not conceived to comprehend ethnic formation in a region that as much as or more than any other had been—and was still in process of being—transformed in the violent dialectic of European economic globalization and counter-Enlightenment that Boas hoped to escape in immigrating to the New World.[52]

So while his ethnology represented an enormous documentary effort, while his texts, the supporting editorial apparatus, and his notes and correspondence contain such vital historical information as names, genealogies, places, dates, and occasionally event descriptions of considerable value for sorting through the historical complexities of cultural process, this material will only reach its full potential in researching matters of interest to the politics of recognition if it is marshaled critically alongside the larger cultural historical record, including especially, but not exclusively, the records pertaining to the fur trade and missionization, and alongside our best attempt to understand the cultural politics of the time.

Today the primary orientation of anthropological activism by and on behalf of people of Aboriginal descent is to cultural recognition. Such recognition has been encouraged in multicultural policy as an alternative to the enforced assimilation of unilateral paternalism. Cultural recognition is predicated on identifying contemporary populations of Aboriginal descent with putative precontact ethnolinguistic polities like those intimated in the linguistic maps of such publications as *Languages,* volume 17 of the *Handbook of North American Indians*, edited by Ives Goddard. Whether notions of political subjectivity predicated on common language and culture arose in the relations between creoles and people of Aboriginal descent in the structural circumstance of colonialism, as Benedict Anderson argues, or whether they were later borrowed directly from the thinking of Johan Gottfried Herder, political subjectivity predicated on shared language and culture was not indigenous to North America, or any other continent in any pure sense. The basis for recognition is the idea that "the proper foundation for a sense of collective political identity is not the acceptance of a common sovereign power, but the sharing of common culture," and abundant evidence suggests that it arose not prior to European colonial history but among people of European descent in the dialectics surrounding the quintessentially modern European Enlightenment, revolution, and subsequent imperialism—not in a state of nature prior to the modern history of imperialism and colonialism but in the midst of it.[53] Consequently maintaining it as a standard of recognition requires people to identify with an "impossible object of an authentic self-identity," in Elizabeth Povinelli's phrase.[54]

Of course ethnolinguistic subjectivities have arisen in many circumstances throughout contact history, and these histories are no less real for not antedating contact. In practice instances of recognition have facilitated the consolidation of new, semi-elite Aboriginal middle classes and in this way diversified Canadian middle classes and challenged intolerance. Anthropologists have played an important role in recognition in this sense, and there are good reasons for their continuing to do so in the future.

However, there are very real problems with orienting anthropological activism exclusively or even primarily toward collective recognition. First, collective recognition does not conserve culture for a population; it changes culture. And it changes culture by reference to modern European ideals. Second, the "two modes of politics, . . . both based on the notion of equal respect, [can] come into conflict," as Taylor recognized. For Taylor the concern is that procedural liberalism requires the accep-

tance of a hegemonic culture.[55] K. Anthony Appiah identified the reverse possibility, namely that collective recognition can undermine individual rights, as when individuals are effectively constrained to learn only heritage languages and culture. Though Appiah is a proponent of some forms of multiculturalism, he sees this sort of enforced culturalism as replacing one kind of tyranny for another.[56]

Thus, especially during this phase of prioritization of multicultural recognition, we might try to access not only the riches of Boas's ethnological record but also his commitment to "the great liberal struggle . . . to get the state to treat its members as individuals only, without favoring or disfavoring particular ethnic or religious or gender identities."

Acknowledgments

As Boas and his assistants were the first to conduct ethnological research among the Tsilhqut'in, their work has been invoked in subsequent ethnographic research there and in the Tsilhqut'in land claims case. The thoughts expressed in this paper have arisen in the context of the reframing of Tsilhqut'in ethnography—including my ethnographic research at Xeni, or The Nemiah Valley Indian Reserve—in expert testimony in *Tsilhqu'tin v. BC* (2007, BCSC 1700), and in continuing conversations with Tsilhqut'in and other parties involved in the case. (On the mobilization of Boas's Pacific North West Ethnology in the land claims context, see Dinwoodie, "Ethnic Community in Early Tsilhqut'in Contact History.")

In researching the legacy of Boas's research I am deeply indebted to Boas himself and to all those who have shared their insights into his life and his research, including especially Judith Berman, Robert Brightman, Regna Darnell, Raymond D. Fogelson, Herb Lewis, Julia Liss, Robert E. Moore, Michael Silverstein, and the late George W. Stocking Jr.

Finally I hereby register my deep gratitude to Regna Darnell, Joshua Smith, Adair Harper, and all the others who organized and supported the conference Franz Boas: Theorist, Ethnographer, Activist, Public Intellectual, December 2–5, 2010, in London, Ontario, and subsequent meetings and discussions.

Notes

1. Taylor, *Multiculturalism*, 25.
2. Silverstein, "The Whens and Wheres," provides an anthropological perspective on the phenomenon of recognition.
3. Appiah, *The Ethics of Identity*, 70. See also Bauman and Briggs, *Voices of Modernity*, 255–98; Stocking, *Race, Culture, and Evolution*, 149.
4. Stocking, *Race, Culture, and Evolution*, 149.

5. Boas, "Vocabulary of the Chilcotin Language"; Farrand, "The Chilcotin," "Traditions of the Chilcotin Indians," and "Tsilkotin"; Teit, "Notes on the Chilcotin Indians."
6. See Boas, *Anthropology and Modern Life*, 81–105, and below; Anderson, *Imagined Communities*; Armstrong, *Nations before Nationalism*; Gellner, *Nations and Nationalism*; Hobsbawm, *The Age of Empire*; Hutchinson and Smith, *Ethnicity*; Smith, *The Ethnic Origins of Nations* and *The Ethnic Revival in the Modern World*.
7. Gibson, *Farming the Frontier* and *Otter Skins, Boston Ships, and China Goods*; Merk, *The Oregon Question*.
8. Cronin, *Cross in the Wilderness*; Huel, *Proclaiming the Gospel*; Leflon, *Eugen de Mazenod*; McCarthy, *From the Great River to the Ends of the Earth*; Morice, *Histoire de L'Eglise Catholique* and *History of the Northern Interior of British Columbia*; Whitehead, *They Call Me Father*.
9. Dinwoodie, "Ethnic Community in Early Tsilhqut'in Contact History."
10. Cole, *Franz Boas: The Early Years*, 122.
11. Verdon, "Cultural History of the Present."
12. Boas, "Limitations of the Comparative Method," 276.
13. Lesser, "Franz Boas"; Kroeber, *"History and Science in Anthropology"*; Radin, *The Method and Theory of Ethnology*; Smith, "Boas' 'Natural History' Approach"; Berman, "'The Culture As It Appears to the Indian Himself.'"
14. Stocking, *A Franz Boas Reader*, 13.
15. Cole, *Franz Boas: The Early Years*, 20–21.
16. Cole, *Franz Boas: The Early Years*, 24.
17. Schiller, *The History of the Thirty Years War*, 2, 3.
18. Clark and Kaiser, *Culture Wars*; Stocking, "Anthropology as Kulturkampf," 94.
19. Stocking, "Anthropology as Kulturkampf," 96.
20. Stocking, *A Franz Boas Reader*.
21. Hobsbawm and Ranger, *The Invention of Tradition*; Hobsbawm, *The Age of Empire* and *Nations and Nationalism Since 1780*.
22. Lomnitz, "Bordering on Anthropology."
23. Bauman and Briggs, *Voices of Modernity*; Berman, "George Hunt and the Kwak'wala Texts" and "'The Culture As It Appears to the Indian Himself'"; Bunzl, "Franz Boas and the Humboldtian Tradition"; Cole, *Franz Boas: The Early Years*; Liss, "German Culture and German Science"; Orta, "The Promise of Particularism"; Stocking, *Race, Culture, and Evolution*, *A Franz Boas Reader*, and "Anthropology as Kulturkampf."
24. Lesser, "Franz Boas," 7; Liss, "German Culture and German Science," 156.
25. Cole, *Franz Boas: The Early Years*, 10–11.
26. Cole, *Franz Boas: The Early Years*, 14.
27. Liss, "German Culture and German Science," 162.
28. Cole, *Franz Boas: The Early Years*, 19–21; Liss, "German Culture and German Science," 157–60.
29. Cole, *Franz Boas: The Early Years*, 22–24, 27.

30. Cole, *Franz Boas: The Early Years*, 44–47, 51–52.
31. Cole, *Franz Boas: The Early Years*, 53, 65–67.
32. Cole, *Franz Boas: The Early Years*, 66, 71, 77–78, 86.
33. Cole, *Franz Boas: The Early Years*, 89, 93.
34. Cole, *Franz Boas: The Early Years*, 14, 15, 16.
35. Cole, *Franz Boas: The Early Years*, 99.
36. Cole, *Franz Boas: The Early Years*, 87, 96, 97.
37. Cole, *Franz Boas: The Early Years*, 99–100, 101.
38. Cole, *Franz Boas: The Early Years*, 111.
39. Cole, *Franz Boas: The Early Years*, 116–18.
40. Cole, *Franz Boas: The Early Years*, 149.
41. Cole, *Franz Boas: The Early Years*, 149–50.
42. Cole, *Franz Boas: The Early Years*, 169–72.
43. Cole, *Franz Boas: The Early Years*, 186, 189, 194, 204, 207–8.
44. Jacknis, "The Ethnographic Object," 190–91.
45. Boas, *Race, Language, and Culture*, 276–77.
46. Boas, *Race, Language, and Culture*, 276.
47. Berman, "'The Culture As It Appears to the Indian Himself,'" 215–18; Darnell, "Theorizing American Anthropology"; Valentine and Darnell, *Theorizing the Americanist Tradition*.
48. Berman, "'The Culture As It Appears to the Indian Himself,'" 218, 219; Dinwoodie, *Reserve Memories*, 30.
49. Berman, "'The Culture As It Appears to the Indian Himself,'" 218.
50. Cox, *The Columbia River*, xxi.
51. Burns, *The Jesuits and the Indian Wars*, 33.
52. Boas, *Race, Language, and Culture*, 276; Stocking, *A Franz Boas Reader*, 307.
53. Barnard, *Herder on Social and Political Culture*, 7; Anderson, *Imagined Communities*; Hobsbawm, *The Age of Empire*.
54. Povinelli, *The Cunning of Recognition*, 6.
55. Taylor, *Multiculturalism*, 43.
56. Appiah, "Identity, Authenticity, Survival," 163.

References

Anderson, Benedict. *Imagined Communities: Reflections on the Origin and Spread of Nationalism*. London: Verso, 1983.

Appiah, K. Anthony. *The Ethics of Identity*. Princeton NJ: Princeton University Press, 2005.

———. "Identity, Authenticity, Survival: Multicultural Societies and Social Reproduction." In Amy Gutmann, ed., *Multiculturalism: Examining the Politics of Recognition*. Princeton NJ: Princeton University Press, 1994.

Armstrong, John A. *Nations before Nationalism*. Chapel Hill: University of North Carolina Press, 1982.

Baker, Lee. *From Savage to Negro: Anthropology and the Construction of Race, 1896–1954*. Berkeley: University of California Press, 1998.

Barnard, F. M., ed. *Herder on Social and Political Culture: A Selection of Texts Translated, Edited and with an Introduction.* Cambridge, UK: Cambridge University Press, 1969.

Bauman, F. M., and Charles L. Briggs. *Voices of Modernity: Language Ideologies and the Politics of Inequality.* Cambridge, UK: Cambridge University Press, 2003.

Berlin, Isaiah. *Four Essays on Liberty.* Oxford: Oxford University Press, 1969.

Berman, Judith. "'The Culture as It Appears to the Indian Himself': Boas, George Hunt, and the Methods of Ethnography." In George W. Stocking Jr., ed., *Volksgeist as Method and Ethic: Essays on Boasian Ethnography and the German Anthropological Tradition,* 215–56. Madison: University of Wisconsin Press, 1996.

———. "George Hunt and the Kwak'wala Texts." *Anthropological Linguistics* 36.4 (1994): 482–514.

Bishop, Chuck. "Chilcotin Missionary." Roman Catholic Diocese of Kamloops. *Diocesan News,* 2000: 6.

Bishop, Chuck, and Frances Bishop. "Last Oblate Priest Leaves Chilcotin Country." Roman Catholic Diocese of Kamloops. *Diocesan News,* June 2007: 7.

Boas, Franz. *Anthropology and Modern Life.* 1928. New York: Norton, 1962.

———. "Limitations of the Comparative Method of Anthropology." In *Race, Language, and Culture.* 1940. Chicago: University of Chicago Press, 1982.

———. "Vocabulary of the Chilcotin Language." In *The North-Western Tribes of Canada.* Twelfth and Final Report of the Committee 4: Linguistics, 664–65. Report of the 68th Meeting of the British Association for the Advancement of Science, 1899.

Bunzl, Matti. "Franz Boas and the Humboldtian Tradition." In George W. Stocking Jr., ed., *Volksgeist as Method and Ethic: Essays on Boasian Ethnography and the German Anthropological Tradition,* 17–78. Madison: University of Wisconsin Press, 1996.

Burns, Robert Ignatius. *The Jesuits and the Indian Wars of the Northwest.* New Haven CT: Yale University Press, 1966.

Clark, Christopher, and Wolfram Kaiser, eds. *Culture Wars: Secular-Catholic Conflict in Nineteenth Century Europe.* New York: Cambridge University Press, 2003.

Cole, Douglas. *Franz Boas: The Early Years 1858–1906.* Vancouver: Douglas & McIntyre, University of Washington Press, 1999.

Cox, Ross. *The Columbia River.* Edited and with an introduction by Edgar I. Stewart and Jane R. Stewart. Norman: University of Oklahoma Press, 1957.

Cronin, Kay. *Cross in the Wilderness.* 1960. Toronto: Mission Press, 1976.

Darnell, Regna. "Theorizing American Anthropology: Continuities from the B.A.E. to the Boasians." In Lisa Philips Valentine and Regna Darnell, eds., *Theorizing the Americanist Tradition,* 38–51. Toronto: University of Toronto Press, 1999.

Dinwoodie, David W. "Ethnic Community in Early Tsilhqut'in Contact History." *Ethnohistory* 57.4 (2010): 651–78.

———. *Reserve Memories: The Power of the Past in a Chilcotin Community*. Lincoln: University of Nebraska Press, 2002.
Farrand, Livingstone. "The Chilcotin." *Report of the 68th Meeting of the British Association for the Advancement of Science, 1898*. 1899, 645–47.
———. "Traditions of the Chilcotin Indians." *Memoirs of the American Museum of Natural History* 4.1 (1900): 11–54.
———. "Tsilkotin." In Frederick W. Hodge, ed., *Handbook of American Indians North of Mexico*, 2: 826. Bureau of American Ethnology Bulletin 30. Washington DC: Government Printing Office, 1910.
Geertz, Clifford. "Anti-Anti-Relativism." *American Anthropologist* 86.2 (1984): 263–78.
Gellner, Ernest. *Nations and Nationalism*. Ithaca NY: Cornell University Press, 1983.
Gibson, James R. *Farming the Frontier: The Agricultural Opening of the Oregon Country 1786–1846*. Seattle: University of Washington Press, 1985.
———. *The Lifeline of the Oregon Country: The Fraser-Columbia Brigade System, 1811–47*. Vancouver: University of British Columbia Press, 1997.
———. *Otter Skins, Boston Ships, and China Goods: The Maritime Fur Trade of the Northwest Coast, 1785–1841*. Seattle: University of Washington Press, McGill-Queens University Press, 1992.
Goddard, Ives, ed. *Handbook of North American Indians*. Vol. 17: *Languages*. Washington DC: Smithsonian Institution, 1996.
Hobsbawm, Eric. *The Age of Empire 1875–1914*. New York: Pantheon Books, 1987.
———. *Nations and Nationalism Since 1780: Programme, Myth, Reality*. Cambridge, UK: Cambridge University Press, 1990.
Hobsbawm, Eric, and Terence Ranger, eds. *The Invention of Tradition*. Cambridge, UK: Cambridge University Press, 1983.
Huel, Raymond J. A. *Proclaiming the Gospel to the Indians and the Metis*. Edmonton: University of Alberta Press, 1996.
Hutchinson, John, and Anthony D. Smith, eds. *Ethnicity*. Oxford: Oxford University Press, 1996.
Jacknis, Ira. "The Ethnographic Object and the Object of Ethnology in the Early Career of Franz Boas." In George W. Stocking Jr., ed., *Volksgeist as Method and Ethic: Essays on Boasian Ethnography and the German Anthropological Tradition*, 185–214. Madison: University of Wisconsin Press, 1996.
Kroeber, Alfred L. "History and Science in Anthropology." *American Anthropologist*, n.s., 37 (1935): 539–69.
Leacock, Eleanor Burke. "The Montagnais 'Hunting Territory' and the Fur Trade." *American Anthropologist* 56.5, part 2 (1954): memoir 78.
Leflon, Jean. *Eugen de Mazenod: Bishop of Marseilles, Founder of the Oblates of Mary Immaculate 1782–1861*. Trans. Francis D. Flanagan. Vols. 1–4. New York: Fordham University Press, 1961–1970.
Lesser, Alexander. "Franz Boas." In *Totems and Teachers: Perspectives on the History of Anthropology*, 1–34. New York: Columbia University Press, 1981.

Liss, Julia E. "German Culture and German Science in the *Bildung* of Franz Boas." In George Stocking Jr., ed., *Volksgeist as Method and Ethic: Essays on Boasian Ethnography and the German Anthropological Tradition*, 155–84. Madison: University of Wisconsin Press, 1996.

Lomnitz, Claudio. "Bordering on Anthropology: Dialectics of a National Tradition." In Benoît de L'Estoile, Federico Neiberg, and Lygia Sigaud, eds., *Empires, Nations, and Natives: Anthropology and State Making*, 167–96. Durham NC: Duke University Press, 2005.

McCarthy, Martha. *From the Great River to the Ends of the Earth: The Missionary Oblates of Mary Immaculate*. Edmonton: University of Alberta Press, 1995.

Merk, Frederick. *The Oregon Question: Essays in Anglo-American Diplomacy and Politics*. Cambridge MA: Belknap Press of Harvard University Press, 1967.

Morice, A. G. *Histoire de L'Eglise Catholique Dans L'Ouest Canadien Du Lac Supérior au Pacifique (1659–1905)*. Vol. 3. Montreal: Granger Freres, 1915.

———. *History of the Northern Interior of British Columbia*. 1904. Smithers, British Columbia: Interior Stationary, 1978.

Orta, Andrew. "The Promise of Particularism and the Theology of Culture: The Limits and Lessons of Neo-Boasianism.'" *American Anthropologist* 106.3 (2004): 473–87.

Povinelli, Elizabeth. *The Cunning of Recognition: Indigenous Alterities and the Making of Australian Multiculturalism*. Durham NC: Duke University Press, 2002.

Radin, Paul. *The Method and Theory of Ethnology*. Westport CT: Bergin and Garvey, 1987.

Schiller, Friedrich. *The History of the Thirty Years War in Germany*. Trans. A. J. W. Morrison. Boston: Francis A. Niccolls, 1901.

Silverstein, Michael. "The Whens and Wheres—As Well As Hows—of Ethnolinguistic Recognition." *Public Culture* 15.3 (2003): 531–57.

Smith, Anthony D. *Chosen Peoples: Sacred Sources of National Identity*. New York: Oxford University Press, 2003.

———. *The Ethnic Origins of Nations*. Oxford: Blackwell, 1986.

———. *The Ethnic Revival in the Modern World*. Cambridge, UK: Cambridge University Press, 1981.

Smith, Marian W. "Boas' 'Natural History' Approach to Field Method." In Walter Goldsmidt, ed., *The Anthropology of Franz Boas*, 46–60. American Anthropological Association, Memoir 89, vol. 61, no. 5, part 2, 1959.

Stocking, George W. Jr. "Anthropology as Kulturkampf: Science and Politics in the Career of Franz Boas." In *The Ethnographers Magic and Other Essays in the History of Anthropology*, 92–113. Madison: University of Wisconsin Press, 1992.

———, ed. *A Franz Boas Reader: The Shaping of American Anthropology, 1883–1911*. Chicago: University of Chicago Press, 1974.

———. *Race, Culture, and Evolution: Essays in the History of Anthropology*. Chicago: University of Chicago Press, 1968.

Taylor, Charles. *Multiculturalism*. Edited and with an introduction by Amy Gutmann. Princeton NJ: Princeton University Press, 1994.

Teit, James. "Notes on the Chilcotin Indians." In *The Shuswap*, 759–89. American Museum of Natural History, Jesup North Pacific Expedition, Memoirs, vol. 2, pt. 7, 1909.

Valentine, Lisa Philips, and Regna Darnell, eds. *Theorizing the Americanist Tradition*. Toronto: University of Toronto Press, 1999.

Verdon, Michael. "Cultural History of the Present, or Obsolete Natural History?" *Journal of the Royal Anthropological Institute* 13.2 (2007): 433–51.

Whitehead, Margaret. *The Cariboo Mission: A History of the Oblates*. Victoria: Sono Nis Press, 1981.

———, ed. *They Call Me Father: Memoirs of Father Nicolas Coccola*. Vancouver: University of British Columbia Press, 1991.

10 Franz Boas, Wilson Duff, and the Image of Anthropology in British Columbia

ROBERT L. A. HANCOCK

In the past five decades anthropological research has emerged as a critical component of Aboriginal rights litigation in Canada. Anthropologists have been called upon to apply their knowledge and analyses on behalf of both Indigenous peoples and the Canadian state. Increased use does not necessarily mean sensitive application, however, as several cases have demonstrated that crucial elements of the anthropological project confound commonsense understandings of even the most learned of jurists. Most egregiously, in his judgment in the *Delgamuukw* case Chief Justice Allan McEachern of the Supreme Court of British Columbia cited the American Anthropological Association's then-current Code of Ethics, and its injunction upon anthropologists to protect the people with whom they worked, to discredit the expert witness testimony of Richard Daly on behalf of the Gitksan:

> With regard to Dr. Daly, he made it abundantly plain that he was very much on the side of the plaintiffs. He was, in fact, more an advocate than a witness. The reason for this is perhaps found in the Statement of Ethics of the American Anthropological Association which Dr. Daly cites at p. 29 of his report, as follows:
>
> "Section 1. *Relations with those studied*; In research, an anthropologist's paramount responsibility is to those he studies. When there is a conflict of interest, these individuals must come first. The anthropologist must do everything within his power to protect their physical, social and psychological welfare and to honour their dignity and privacy...."
>
> For these reasons, I place little reliance on Dr. Daly's report or evidence. This is unfortunate because he is clearly a well qualified, highly intelligent anthropologist. It is always unfortunate when experts become too close to their clients, especially during litigation.[1]

McEachern's fundamental misreading of the discipline's foundational ethical responsibilities—whether willful or not—and the responses to it demonstrated one aspect of the gulf between anthropological representations of Indigenous peoples and "commonsense" interpretations of these by nonspecialists.[2] This misunderstanding goes beyond the specifics of the representations of Indigenous peoples to include the character of anthropology as a discipline and its emergence over the past century and a half.

While nothing can be done to undermine misrepresentations in the wider world, anthropologists have a role to play both in challenging them and in creating alternative representations of the discipline's history. Our understandings of the discipline, of its contemporary state and its future possibilities, are constrained by misconceptions about its past, and these affect the ways our research and its engagement with the world are depicted and perceived. Anthropology has never been an objective, apolitical science, and its relationship to colonial projects is much more complicated than is usually assumed; it has always had a radically engaged component, as much as this has been downplayed by certain dominant trends in the self-understanding of anthropologists.[3] Shying away from a concerted engagement with the political elements of anthropological research has not protected its status as a science. Instead it has left the field open to people in positions beyond the discipline to define anthropology in their own terms and then critique this misrepresentation for what they perceive as its shortcomings. The solution for anthropologists is more engagement, not more stringent attempts at detachment. With this chapter, I seek to contribute to this process by analyzing two such misrepresentations in the historiography and arguing for a more nuanced understanding of anthropological engagement with political and legal issues.

The attacks on the very idea of an engaged anthropology extend to the academic arena as well. McEachern's critique, and the fundamental misunderstandings on which it is premised, are mirrored in the work of the policy analysts Frances Widdowson and Albert Howard. Their discussion of non-Indigenous involvement in Aboriginal rights litigation focuses on the role played by anthropologists—including, among others, Franz Boas and Wilson Duff—and rehearses the same tired defenses of evolutionary analyses and about the distinction between science and objectivity and the risk of "distorted research".[4] The power and reach of this representation is deep and wide and demonstrates the challenges faced by anthropologists seeking to change the perception and reception of the discipline in wider discourses.

Scholars from other disciplines read anthropological literature for spe-

cific purposes, looking to glean specific information useful in the construction of their narratives and analyses; in this sense anthropology is a tool and not an end in itself. We cannot expect researchers from other fields seeking to apply anthropological research in particular contexts to be sensitive to the complicated and nuanced contexts of its production, both theoretical and political, if these aspects continue to be neglected even by historians of anthropology. Regna Darnell, for example, has argued that "our history of anthropology must trace the anthropologists through their fieldwork back to the theoretical preoccupations within which they are intertwined."[5] It is not enough to know what Boas wrote about the Kwakwaka'wakw or Duff wrote about the Stó:lō, for example; we need to know how to contextualize their work in their wider theoretical and political projects. While we cannot prevent willful ignorance or intentional misrepresentation, we are obligated to consider the role our own representations of these theoretical and political contexts play in applications or misapplications of anthropological research.

While at first glance the juxtaposition of Boas and Duff might seem a bit jarring, I consider them together because their prominence in the research universe of the North Pacific Coast is not matched by a congruent understanding of the contexts of their research. Their respective contributions are vast, though on different scales, and scholars have tended to focus on one aspect abstracted from the others; I argue that these individual aspects need to be understood in relation to both the internal (disciplinary) and external (historical, political, social) contexts in which they undertook their work. Operating two generations apart, they remain the central figures in anthropological research on Indigenous peoples living on the northeastern coast of the Pacific Ocean. Boas's position and importance in the field is already well documented.[6] Less obvious, perhaps, is that Duff is the most direct inheritor of the Boasian legacy in this region, on three major counts. First, his Americanist intellectual genealogy traces directly back to Boas, through Erna Gunther, Duff's mentor at the University of Washington and the supervisor of his MA thesis.[7] Second, his career was Boasian in scope, comprising the acquisition of artifacts, the design of museum exhibits, the collection of linguistic and textual materials, the excavation of archaeological sites, and the analysis of art.[8] Third, Duff had a significant public profile and trained a number of students, a large proportion of whom were women.

The work of both has been subject to caricature and misrepresentation, and there is much to be done before the context of either man's work can be unpacked. As a result this chapter is historiographical in focus and more exploratory than explanatory in intent, gesturing toward the cre-

ation of frameworks suitable for analyzing these contexts. In the case of Boas, I ask three interrelated and overlapping questions: What was his project relating to the Indigenous peoples of the North Pacific Coast? How does his public engagement with legal debates around the potlatch, particularly his criticisms of the Canadian law banning it, fit into this? And how do both of these aspects—his academic research and his public commentary—fit into his wider project? This is not to say that Boas was committed only to one long-term project. Rather, to understand his work we need a macro-level perspective, the lack of which is at the root of the misunderstandings and misrepresentations of his work in British Columbia. At the same time, the issues raised by his work, and by its representations, are emblematic of those that arose in other periods and other facets of his career. Scholars have tried to find the best fit for his work in a limited number of boxes, but we have yet to find, or recognize, the right ones for him. That said, he also is not sui generis; his work has a context that it both builds on and responds to. In this sense what I originally framed as a basic, simple task—identifying the intellectual and philosophical context of Boas's work—in the end has to be understood as connected to a vast network of other concepts.

The same general questions can be asked of Duff's work, though obviously on a different scale. Duff's engagement with crucial questions and public debates of the day, most especially in his expert witness testimony in Aboriginal rights court cases, took a different approach than Boas's. While Duff's career was not as influential on an international level—although perhaps nobody will ever be able to rival the extent of Boas's impact—it remains central to the anthropological understanding of Indigenous peoples on the North Pacific Coast, to the history of Canadian anthropology, and to the emergence of Aboriginal rights discourses in Canadian jurisprudence. In their own particular ways the careers of Boas and Duff represent congruent approaches to the critical engagement of anthropology with dominant contemporary legal and political depictions of Indigenous peoples and have much to offer current debates about the roles anthropology can play in those fields today.

The Case of Franz Boas

This section focuses on three separate but related issues in this aspect of Boas's work and concludes with a discussion of the sort of research necessary to reconstruct his own vision. I begin with an examination of three representations of his North Pacific work, by Wendy Wickwire, Michael Harkin, and Charles Briggs and Richard Bauman. I then situate these in the relationship between politics and science in Boas's work

before moving to a preliminary consideration of how the wider context of Boas's work has been represented by anthropologists. I start with the work of Wickwire, Harkin, and Briggs and Bauman because it represents an interconnected (not to say self-referential) narrative of Boas's work and also because it constitutes my own introduction to this field: their works play a crucial role in my own intellectual genealogy and professional formation, one with which I continue to grapple in my attempts to think through and with Boas's work.

Wickwire sets the context for her detailed call for a new understanding of the history of Indigenous peoples in British Columbia by outlining what she sees as the ways Boas's work demarcated the boundaries for an emerging discourse:

> During the first decades of the twentieth century, British Columbia became the site of a major social scientific research project. Anthropologist Franz Boas (1858–1942) was the driving force behind much of this work. Concerned that the indigenous cultures of this region would not survive the onslaught of westernization, Boas established a rigorous field research program aimed at ethnographic rescue. He envisioned the published monographs as the key to cultural preservation. Armed with sufficient field data, he was confident that he could produce textual portraits of traditional cultures that would outlive the cultures themselves. That many of his so-called informants were horsepackers, miners, cannery workers, missionary assistants, and construction laborers several generations removed from his imagined pristine contact point did not deter him. Over the course of a few decades, he and his associates produced thousands of pages of written text framed against the backdrop of a Golden Age.[9]

Wickwire does not cite any other scholars in crafting this representation. It has become, or she is trying to make it appear to be, a hegemonic understanding of Boas's project among a certain segment of researchers working in British Columbia. Similarly, in an earlier paper, she emphasizes:

> The Boasian textual legacy exists in the form of a large number of monographs on countless topics published under the auspices of American museums. Only recently have scholars begun to question it—in particular, its narrow focus on the "pre-contact" past. Early scholars systematically mined the memories of "informants," mostly males, whom they considered best able to reconstruct for them the cultural traditions of their subjects' distant ancestors. Meanwhile, they ignored current

views and traditions, on the grounds that they were too Westernized for inclusion in their pristine ethnographic record.[10]

On one level it is clear that Wickwire is constructing Boas as a straw man independent of the historiography—the professional, foreign, metropolitan, hegemon—in order to provide a contrast to the main subject of her research, James Teit.[11] Her representations of Boas have a particular function in the context of her work on Teit and need to be understood in the context of defending local and amateur anthropologists against the perceived intrusion of Boas's entry into and control over the field.[12]

Wickwire orients herself by building on the critical analyses of Harkin and of Briggs and Bauman, among others. Both of these latter approaches occupy an explicit position between criticizing and attempting to contextualize Boas's ethnography and wider project but, for a variety of reasons, I will argue, fail. Harkin asserts:

> The textual view of culture denied the possibility that culture was something fluid, a continuing adaptation to a historical environment, which resisted codification. For Boas, any elements of flux or imperfect systematicity were products of postcontact history. His goal was to look behind the curtain of contact, to recover the untainted "genius" of the culture before it had been degraded by contact with Europeans. To the degree that he thought about it at all, Boas viewed post-contact history as a sordid tale of decline that threatened to eliminate Indian cultures altogether. . . . Not only was Boasian anthropology perforce a work of salvage, it identified its object with a sort of timeless Golden Age.[13]

In contrast with earlier attempts to portray Boas as nonscientific, if not antiscientific, in terms of objectivity and commitment, Harkin argues in favor of Boas's position as a scientist but cites disapprovingly its foundation on a sense of detachment.[14] Asserting that "social, temporal, emotional, and geographic distance is indeed essential to Boas' view of anthropology as a science," he observes that "Boas' emotional detachment is in great contrast to the other main observers of Native cultures, the missionaries, who were, if nothing else, engagé."[15]

Offering an approach diametrically opposed to the standard representation of Boas's project as idiographic or particularist, Briggs and Bauman offer a sweeping and wide-ranging condemnation of Boas's project and publications, on a variety of a not entirely consistent count. They assert that what concerns them "most directly was Boas's sense that anthropology was centrally concerned with the production of texts that docu-

mented the languages and traditions of Others and with their systematic comparison, including their systematic comparison, including their comparison to the discursive and cultural forms associated with 'civilized man.'" They go beyond Harkin's accusations of detachment and argue that in fact he was actively assimilationist: "In spite of his anti-racist convictions and his fight to establish the dignity of Native American cultures, Boas's construction of tradition as unconscious, affective, and inevitably disappearing in the face of science, conscious reasoning, and modernity rendered him complicit in naturalizing white control of Native American communities and the ideology of 'assimilation.'" In their view these aspects of Boas's project need to be understood as a product of his imbrication in "modernity" and his drive to assimilate Indigenous peoples into this "modernity." Engaged as they are in what they call an analysis of Boas's metadiscursive practices, they offer no citations to specific passages of Boas's work that, taken individually or collectively, lead them to conclude that he was engaged in a comparative project on a grand scale.[16]

In essence what they perceive as Boas's usurping of authority through the textualization of Indigenous cultures actually in their view "rationalizes the marginalization and disappearance of the very people that his writings celebrated." They argue:

> Our analysis suggests that Boas's metadiscursive practices likewise distressed the texts, removing traces of the colonial context in which they were produced—and thus of the modernity that was embedded in the "traditional." His metadiscursive practices thus played a role in constructing anthropology as a science of culture rather than of the colonial encounter, an historical mode of inquiry that rested on a principled effort to construct history as a pre-contact, romanticized past—one that carefully excluded the anthropologist from its purview.

They ultimately conclude, "In spite of Boas' relativist position, his work thus fit into the larger contours of colonial domination that increasingly deprived Native American communities of land, material wealth, and cultural and linguistic autonomy."[17]

Wickwire, Harkin, and Briggs and Bauman are united in their conceptualization of Boas's project as a colonizing one that either ignores the contemporary political context in favor of a quixotic salvage effort or actively participates in an assimilationist project. Interestingly even though they take as their period of concentration the last quarter of the nineteenth century and the first quarter of the twentieth, they offer no discussion of his public stance against the potlatch ban.[18] In contrast

Darnell argues that "both Boas and [Edward] Sapir were firm defenders of the right of the Indians to defend their traditional culture by preserving one of its core institutions—in spite of the dramatic changes in the potlatch system as a result of postcontact population decline and increasing wealth";[19] that is, Boas's position against government policy was not a result of a salvage drive to preserve precontact practices but was actually about the cultural, and therefore political, autonomy of Indigenous peoples.

Boas's public political engagements on behalf of Indigenous peoples against the potlatch ban is mentioned only once, as an aside, in the pieces I have been discussing—even though Wickwire's focus is the rehabilitation of James Teit's politically engaged fieldwork (see also Laforet, this volume).[20] Contrasting Boas with Alfred Kroeber's silence on government policy affecting California Indigenous peoples, Harkin writes, "Clearly Kroeber's failure to account for history and culture change . . . was a moral as well as an epistemological one. Boas's failing was not primarily moral, as he spoke out about Canadian government actions that were certainly less destructive than the California genocide. Nevertheless, his systematic ethnography, like Kroeber's, failed to take account of such matters in the way that others, less systematic but more sympathetic, did."[21] While Stocking mentions Boas's work against the potlatch law, and Berman presents Wayne Suttle's intriguing insight that Boas's representation of Hunt's identity might have been shaped by concerns about potential prosecutions under the law, it is remarkable, from a disciplinary perspective, that the most intense and prolonged engagement with this issue comes from a literary critic (Pinkoski 2008a, 2008b).[22]

What is at issue, the source of confusion in these representations of Boas's work on the North Pacific Coast, is a much wider question of the relationship of politics and science in Boas's project. The necessary first step appears to be the recognition that Boas's project was unified (which is not to say uniform) and based on an explicitly theoretical underpinning and then to demonstrate this in contradistinction to a dominant and widespread misrepresentation of his work. Stocking has argued, in a more limited context (specifically Boas's debates with Mason about causality; Pinkoski 2008a, 2008b), that "there is an internal consistency to Boas' anthropology, and that it may contribute to our historical understanding to view it in terms of this inner logic."[23] Similarly Berman contends that the commonsense view of Boas's project as a collection of ethnographic trivia "is a distortion. In collecting and compiling these texts, Boas was motivated by an important theoretical principle. Furthermore, the col-

lection process itself was structured and purposeful—though the structure and purpose are obscured by the texts' published form."[24]

Part of the issue appears to be that Boas was practicing a different kind of science, one whose objectivity came from its situatedness. Janine Hitchens points in this direction, although she still errs in downplaying the role of theory in his project, when she writes, "For Boas, the scientific quality of anthropology resided less with the capacity to postulate laws than with the faithful apprehension of cultural reality through fieldwork and historical reconstruction. This interpretation of Boas' scientific sensibility is consistent with his own emphasis on method over theory, and on detailed observation over speculation."[25] Crucially, and in a similar vein, Stocking locates Boas's conceptualization of science as distinct from both that of his contemporaries and that of "modern" philosophy of science.[26] In a slightly later piece Stocking makes explicit one of the most critical connections in Boas's work, one central not only to a historical understanding of his project but also to current dominant disciplinary conceptualizations of the role and function of anthropology:

> To Boas . . . any ethical and epistemological issues involved in the implicit opposition between what might be called the progressivist and the romantic anthropological attitudes never seemed a serious problem. Science for him remained always an ethically self-justifying activity. Retrospectively he saw his work as the expression of a unified scientific and political position: the scientific search for the "psychological origin of the implicit belief in the authority of tradition" would be fulfilled politically when, recognizing tradition's shackles, we were able to break them.[27]

Thus for Boas science was a form of critique, an attempt to understand the contingency of the world in order to conceptualize a different way of being or of relating to others.[28] Hitchens makes this connection explicit: "Boas brought to the field a rigorous and critical methodology which linked the unmasking of ethnocentric biases with the affirmation of alternative cultural possibilities. This represented both an invaluable corrective to nineteenth century evolutionist methodology and an innovation that paved the way for an anthropology better calibrated for normative critique of the relationship between Western and non-Western cultures."[29]

This political aspect of Boas's work, when it has been recognized, has been both celebrated and condemned. In the latter camp were scholars such as Murray Wax, who collapsed the distinction between critique and criticism and concluded with the complaint that "Boas' *forte* was criti-

cism. He was a master at exposing the generalization that was false to the phenomena, or that explained away a serious problem by reifying culture, or that was constructed in violation of the canons of scientific method. In so far as his targets were would-be scientists relying upon inadequate data and slipshod methods, his criticism was healthful for the growing discipline. But cultural anthropology also required positive leadership, and here Boas failed."[30] On the other hand, scholars of the same generation as Wax, such as Robert Murphy, drew a positive message from Boas's critical approach: "If Boas's influence long after his death is to be understood properly, we must see in his teaching a classic instance of what Weber called 'exemplary prophecy,' in which the prophet eschews a systematic theology of words and, instead, provides the conduct of his life as The Way. Boas left no Word, leaving his students very much on their own theoretically, but with a Way to follow . . . toward socially responsible science."[31] Boas's project escapes simplistic depictions: it was clearly not bereft of a theoretical component, but it did not attempt to be "scientific" in the ways some have tried to apply that term.

It appears that an underemphasized component of research on Boas's work is a consideration of its intellectual context. Stocking points in that direction in his consideration of the role of *Kulturkampf* in Boas's intellectual and professional formation:

> Fundamental to his viewpoint was the commitment—which Virchow had seen as basic to the *Kulturkampf*—to science and rational thought against the irrational authority of tradition. . . . In this context the political meaning of Boas' scientific life may be seen as a transvalued and dichotomized *Kulturkampf*: on the one hand, as a struggle to preserve the cultural conditions of the search for universal rational knowledge, and on the other, as a struggle to defend the validity of alternative cultural worlds.[32]

Both Briggs and Bauman and Harkin offer muddled representations of the relationship of Boas's work to its wider intellectual context, which remains largely misunderstood. For example, both offer confused accounts of the relationship between Boas's project and its philosophical underpinnings. In the space of two pages Harkin manages both to call attention to the counter-Enlightenment foundations of Boas's work and to claim that Boas's focus on myth "is a form of Neo-Kantian idealism."[33] Similarly Briggs and Bauman comment on Boas's reliance on "the Herderian legacy" without elaborating or citing Herder and outline "Boas' movement from an a priori, analytic to ethnographically relevant categories"

without identifying it as an anti-Kantian move. Ultimately they conclude, "While Boas's aesthetics runs counter to Kant's in terms of the emphasis that he places on the historical and cultural determination of aesthetic judgment, Boas is Kantian in locating artistic creativity beyond consciousness and cognition, apart from survival, necessity, and everyday life, and in opposition to collective experience."[34] Clearly further work is needed to untangle the contextual issue in terms of the philosophy undergirding Boas's scientific and political projects.

Some work has been done in this direction. Herbert Lewis has been offering important correctives to the commonsense representations of Boas's project and its place in anthropological understandings of the discipline for a decade and a half.[35] Darnell's work on what she calls the Boasian or Americanist text tradition and the formative role that the North Pacific Coast played in it offers another alternative understanding of Boas's project.[36] Matti Bunzl has sought to locate Boas firmly in a specific tradition, finding in his work at the end of the nineteenth century

> the theoretical currents of historicist Counter-Enlightenment thinking: first, the skepticism of finding natural laws governing human behavior; second, the rejection of a psychic unity of humanity, operating according to rational principles regardless of space and time; third, the focus on the individuality and diversity of phenomena as opposed to their similarity and universality; finally, the emphasis on actual historical development in place of conjectures and speculation, on induction as opposed to deduction.[37]

Finally, and most fruitfully for a discussion of Boas's science and politics, is Barbara Saunders's assessment of the concept of cultural relativism as applied to Boas. At the same time that she untangles Boas's project from the shibboleth of relativism later commentators hung on it, she outlines a radically political and ethical component of Boas's materialism, by demonstrating that he worked "in such a way as to oppose the entire field on which the patterns of universalism and relativism are played out and that he was attempting to shift the grounds of discourse in subtle ways—not least in that the 'alethically true' might itself be bound by time and prejudices. In other words, the universal might be regarded as unfixed, historical, and changing." She also offers a revised understanding of objectivity that emerged in his research, based on the relationships between the scientist and the subjects rather than from a position purportedly outside of the systems or structures being studied: "Investigation was objective in the sense that it transcended narrow attachments

and preconceptions in ongoing dialogue with others. Objectivity was thus a process of de-parochialization in which investigators transcended the congenial, the personal and conventional. This process required the dialectical engagement of open-ended framework, supplemented by enduring and developing relations with 'informants.'"[38]

Taken together these analyses constitute an important foundation for the sort of contextual framework that I am advocating. Their attention to the wider philosophical, intellectual, and institutional contexts of Boas's work models an approach that can be expanded to take in more elements and aspects of his career and can be applied, at a different scale, to Duff's work.

The Case of Wilson Duff

Today the anthropologist Wilson Duff (1925–1976) is perhaps best known in the anthropological literature for his innovative, insightful, and intense analyses of the Indigenous arts of the North Pacific Coast of North America.[39] Less well-known among anthropologists, however, is his pivotal research and testimony as an expert witness in Aboriginal rights litigation on behalf of several Indigenous groups in British Columbia. His most influential and significant contribution in this area has been his testimony in *Regina v. White and Bob*, which established that the agreements signed between Governor James Douglas and a number of Indigenous nations on Vancouver Island were binding treaties, and in *Calder v. Attorney General, British Columbia*, where a majority of Supreme Court of Canada justices found that the Nisga'a had Aboriginal title at the time of contact with Europeans. However, this influence and legacy have been overlooked by anthropologists; even a recent paper on the history of anthropology at the University of British Columbia mentions Duff only in passing.[40] In this section I hope to reshape perceptions of Duff's contributions to the discipline of anthropology among its practitioners, particularly the representations of Indigenous cultures and societies in his expert witness testimony which remain salient in the current political and legal context. Interestingly scholars working in other disciplines, such as history or law, are more likely to acknowledge this aspect of his career than anthropologists.[41]

Duff's life came to a tragic, early end, and a number of his colleagues and commentators identify this as the central aspect of his career and his legacy,[42] making inevitable his marginalization in the wider discipline. Even those scholars who focus on his actual work, such as Wayne Suttles, E. N. Anderson, Robin Ridington, and Michael Ames, neglect or severely downplay his contributions to Aboriginal rights efforts, especially his

work as an expert witness in the *White and Bob* and *Calder* cases. In fairness Ridington's tribute focuses on a different aspect of Duff's work,[43] but the articles by Ames, Suttles, and particularly Anderson, which at least attempt synopses of Duff's career, touch on this work only in passing. Suttles's only comment on the article by Thomas Berger in the Duff memorial volume, which explains the legal arguments in *Calder* and in *White and Bob*, is that "it is a fine account of the uses of historical documents and anthropological evidence."[44] Even more startling in this context is Anderson's 103-page "Introduction to Wilson Duff," which mentions Duff's work on "the Fort Victoria Treaties" without mentioning its connection with his testimony in *White and Bob*, and describes in passing his "instrumental" role helping the Nisga'a case to reach as far as the Supreme Court of Canada.[45] Textual and archival sources point to the importance of these projects in the context of his career.

The details of Duff's contributions to the *White and Bob* case, along with those of the provincial archivist at the time, Willard Ireland, are relatively well-known, at least in the legal community.[46] Their ethnohistorical and archival research, linking a sheet of paper with 159 X marks to the ancestors of Clifford White and David Bob Sr., demonstrating that that paper represented the "lost" fourteenth Vancouver Island treaty, which protected their rights to hunt and fish, was a masterpiece of scholarly investigation and was critical to the defense of the accused men. Less well known, however, is Duff's contribution to the legal argument making use of the evidence. In a letter to Berger, written the day after oral arguments in the County Court, Duff introduced a recent American precedent while critiquing the precedent that Berger had relied on in his arguments:

> I hope you will find time to examine the copy of the United States Court of Claims decision which I loaned to you. I think it contains the best description of the nature of native title. My impression is that your present conception of native title is based on usufruct, the right to *use* the products of the land. My conception is that native title is based on more than use, it is based on clearcut Indian concepts of *ownership* of the land. The Court of Claims decision makes that case very well, and it could apply equally to the northern coast tribes of British Columbia.[47]

Berger, of course, was relying on the definition of Indian title in the *St. Catherine's Milling* case, where the Law Lords of the Privy Council found, based on the Royal Proclamation of 1763, "that the tenure of the Indians was a personal and usufructuary right, dependent upon the good will of the Sovereign."

Duff expanded this analysis more generally in the introduction to his *Indian History of British Columbia,* volume 1: *The Impact of the White Man* (1965), which appears to have been entered as evidence in each of the courts that heard *Calder* (e.g., the passage below is cited as "material filed at the hearing" by Justice Judson in *Calder*).[48] He writes:

> At the time of contact the Indians of this area were among the world's most distinctive peoples. Fully one-third of the native population of Canada lived here. . . . Here, too, was the greatest linguistic diversity in the country, with two dozen languages spoken, belonging to seven of the eleven language families represented in Canada. . . . Most of all, their cultures were distinguished by a local richness and originality, the product of vigorous and inventive people in a rich environment.[49]

The next paragraph contains the crux of his argument and seems remarkable for having been written nearly five decades ago. While it appears simply to be the pronouncement of some basic anthropological verities, at least to somebody familiar with structural-functionalist theoretical models,[50] Duff is actually offering empirical evidence to undermine the legal rationale for the dismissal of Aboriginal rights claims, going back to *St Catherine's Milling*.

> It is not correct to say that the Indians did not "own" the land but only roamed over the face of it and "used" it. The patterns of ownership and utilization which they imposed upon the lands and waters were different from those recognized by our system of law, but were nonetheless clearly defined and mutually respected. Even if they didn't subdivide and cultivate the land, they did recognize ownership of plots used for village sites, fishing places, berry and root patches, and similar purposes. Even if they didn't subject the forests to wholesale logging, they did establish ownership of tracts used for hunting, trapping, and food-gathering. Even if they didn't sink mine shafts into the mountains, they did own peaks and valleys for mountain goat hunting and as sources of raw materials. Except for barren and inaccessible areas which are not utilized even today, every part of the Province was formerly within the owned and recognized territory of one or other of the Indian tribes.[51]

Duff expanded on this analysis with particular reference to the Nisga'a, under examination by Thomas Berger, counsel for the Nisga'a.[52]

Justice Gould, in writing his judgment in the British Columbia Supreme

Court, recognized Duff and Willard Ireland, the provincial archivist who also presented evidence, as "scholars of renown, and authors in the field of Indian history, and records," and found "that all witnesses gave their respective testimony as to facts, opinions, and historical and other documents, with total integrity. Thus, there is no issue of credibility as to the witnesses in this case."[53] In any event the judge rejected the Nisga'a claim to Aboriginal title over their homeland on the grounds that it had been extinguished by actions of the Crown in the time since the Europeans arrived.

In spite of Justice Gould's vouching for the credibility of the expert witness testimony presented at trial, Duff's evidence did not fare very well in the British Columbia Court of Appeal, where Chief Justice Davey asserted in his concurring Reasons for Judgment:

> Turning to the evidence in this appeal, in spite of the commendation by Mr. Duff, a well known anthropologist, of the native culture of the Indians on the mainland of British Columbia, they were undoubtedly at the time of the settlement a very primitive people with few of the institutions of civilized society, and none at all of our notions of private property. I am not overlooking Mr. Duff's evidence that the boundaries of the Nishga territory were well known to the tribes and to their neighbours, and respected by all. These were territorial, not proprietary, boundaries, and had no connection with notions of ownership of particular parcels of land. Also Mr. Duff said that on occasion a chief would earmark a particular piece of property for the exclusive use of a particular family, but I see no evidence that this practice was general; even if it was, it would only support claims of the particular occupant, and not claims to the communal use by the whole tribe over all its tribal territory.
>
> I see no evidence to justify a conclusion that the aboriginal rights claimed by the successors of these primitive people are of a kind that it should be assumed the Crown recognized them when it acquired the mainland of British Columbia by occupation.[54]

This evolutionary narrative was rejected by six of the seven justices of the Supreme Court of Canada. In his dissenting judgment Justice Hall quotes at length from Duff's testimony at trial and finds that "an interesting and apt line of questions by Gould, J., in which he endeavoured to relate Duff's evidence as to Nishga concepts of ownership of real property to the conventional common law elements of ownership . . . disclose that the trial Judge's consideration of the real issue was inhibited by a preoc-

cupation with the traditional *indicia* of ownership." After quoting that exchange and rejecting Justice Gould's ethnocentric conceptualization of title, Justice Hall concludes, "What emerges from the foregoing evidence is the following: the Nishgas are in fact and were from time immemorial a distinctive cultural entity with concepts of ownership indigenous to their culture and capable of articulation under the common law."[55] Justice Hall's colleague Justice Judson goes even further in rejecting the ethnocentric and evolutionary reasoning of the lower court judges. Justice Judson quotes the lengthy passage from Duff's book about "patterns of use and ownership" but mis-cites it and uses it to offer a striking defense of Nisga'a concepts of their title at the expense of that put forward in *St. Catherine's Milling*: "The fact is that when the settlers came, the Indians were there, organized in societies and occupying the land as their forefathers had done for centuries. This is what Indian title means and it does not help one in the solution of this problem to call it a 'personal or usufructuary right.' What they are asserting in this action is that they had a right to continue to live on their lands as their forefathers had lived and that this right has never been lawfully extinguished."[56] Even though six of the seven judges accepted Duff's conception of Aboriginal title and rejected the ethnocentrism of the lower courts, they split evenly over the question of the continued existence of that title; the seventh judge, Justice Pigeon, rejected the Nisga'a claim on a technicality without addressing the substantive issues. As a result the Nisga'a lost the appeal.

However, Duff's contributions to the judicial conception of Aboriginal title were important to the jurisprudential recognition of Aboriginal rights beyond this one context. His research and testimony were crucial in demonstrating to the courts that the Nisga'a, and other Aboriginal groups, had the ability to conceptualize and defend ownership of their territories. Hall's findings in this case, based in large part on Duff's evidence, influenced policymakers and set a precedent for other cases to follow. In the policy realm the *Calder* judgment led Prime Minister Pierre Trudeau to reverse his government's previous position and admit that "perhaps [Aboriginal peoples] had more legal rights than we thought when we did the White Paper,"[57] as embodied in the establishment of the Office of Native Claims, with the mandate to settle comprehensive claims. In the legal realm *Calder* was cited as a precedent the same year the judgment came down in two major cases elsewhere in Canada. In the Northwest Territories Supreme Court that September, Justice Morrow ruled in *Re. Paulette* that the Aboriginal title of the Dene, based on their prima facie ownership of the land, "constitutes an interest in land which can be protected by caveat under the Land Titles Act." In the Quebec Superior Court

that November, Justice Malouf accepted the notion of Aboriginal rights and title to land set out in *Calder*, even in using other facts to find that the Cree of northern Quebec had rights in their territory that would be irreversibly damaged by the construction of a series of dams by Hydro-Québec and granting them an injunction to stop construction.[58] In both cases the trial judgments were overturned, but they still led in a positive direction: when plans to build a massive gas pipeline along the Mackenzie Valley pipeline were announced, the recognition of Dene rights in *Re. Paulette* played a role in the creation of a public inquiry to assess its impact,[59] and the recognition of Cree rights led to a process culminating with the signing of the James Bay and Northern Quebec Agreement between the Cree and the governments of Quebec and Canada. In British Columbia, on the other hand, the significance of Duff's work lies mainly in how little influence it seems to have had on the legal understanding of Indigenous cultures in subsequent years.[60]

Less than thirty years after Duff demonstrated that the Indigenous peoples resident in the province had "cultures [that] were distinguished by a local richness and originally, the product of vigorous and inventive people in a rich environment," and less than twenty years after their rights were affirmed by six of seven judges in *Calder*, Chief Justice McEachern could write of the Nisga'a's neighbors, "It would not be accurate to assume that even pre-contact existence in the territory was in the least bit idyllic. The plaintiffs' ancestors had no written language, no horses or wheeled vehicles, slavery and starvation was not uncommon, wars with neighbouring peoples were common, and there is no doubt, to quote Hobbs [sic], that aboriginal life in the territory was, at best, 'nasty, brutish and short.'"[61] This representation is striking on a number of levels—not only because of what had changed since *Calder* (both in terms of the representation of Indigenous peoples and of the perception of anthropologists as expert witnesses) but also because of what remained the same. The return of evolutionary analyses was accompanied by the reemergence of denunciations of a particular (Boasian) stream of anthropological thought.

This rekindled opprobrium functioned at two levels: it challenged representations of Indigenous peoples that undermined state narratives of their primitive lawlessness, and it challenged representations of anthropology as a discipline suited to supporting Indigenous peoples in such confrontations with the state. The attacks on Boas and Duff as unscientific advocates took place on different scales but comprise analogous matters: they embody a profound misrepresentation of the character

of anthropological research through a misunderstanding of the wider political contexts of their respective projects while simultaneously eliding the reactionary and evolutionary politics obscured by the veneer of science. To recognize that Boas or Duff had political projects that were embodied in the stances they took and the research they undertook is at the same time to demand an accounting of the politics of those whose work argued against racial equality or Aboriginal rights.

That these profound models of engaged anthropological scholarship can be misunderstood both within and beyond the discipline speaks to an acute failure of the current historiography of the discipline. The division between historicism and presentism as outlined by George Stocking has been definitively undermined in the past decade.[62] Similarly the countervailing internal historical emphases on theory and on personalities or institutions have been collapsed. These parallel processes have created the conditions of possibility for a theoretically engaged and textually and archivally rich analysis of the histories of anthropology in their contemporary and present contexts, both intellectual and political. Such work is critical if anthropologists are to offer compelling alternative representations of the possible scope and contributions of their discipline to each other, to our students, to Indigenous communities, and to a public audience beyond the discipline.

Acknowledgments

This chapter is dedicated to the memory of Marjorie Halpin, who introduced me both to the life and work of Wilson Duff and to the possibility of a critical history of anthropology.

I have benefited greatly from feedback offered by Jaime Yard, Sarah Moritz, Joshua Smith, and Michael Asch, by the two anonymous reviewers, and by the participants at the 2010 meeting in London. In particular I am grateful to Regna Darnell for her patient and astute editorial interventions.

Notes

1. *Delgamuukw*, 50–51.
2. Asch, "Errors in *Delgamuukw*"; Furniss, *The Burden of History*.
3. Pinkoski, "American Colonialism at the Dawn of the Cold War" and "Julian Steward, American Anthropology, and Colonialism"; Asch, "Radcliffe-Brown on Colonialism in Africa"; Price, *Threatening Anthropology*.
4. Widdowson and Howard, *Disrobing the Aboriginal Industry*, ch. 2, 40.
5. Darnell, "The Importance of the Northwest Coast," 35.

6. Rohner, *The Ethnography of Franz Boas*; Darnell, "The Importance of the Northwest Coast."
7. Published as Duff, *The Upper Stalo Indians*. See Darnell, *Invisible Genealogies*.
8. Cole, *Captured Heritage*; Jacknis, *The Storage Box of Tradition*; Hawker, *Tales of Ghosts*; Jonaitis and Glass, *The Totem Pole*; Duff and Kew, "Anthony Island."
9. Wickwire, "Stories from the Margins," 453.
10. Wickwire, "'We Shall Drink from the Stream,'" 200.
11. For example Wickwire, "'We Shall Drink from the Stream,'" 201.
12. Maud, *Transmission Difficulties*.
13. Harkin, "Past Presence," 3.
14. For example Harris, *The Rise of Anthropological Theory*; White, *The Ethnography and Ethnology of Franz Boas* and *The Social Organization of Ethnological Theory*.
15. Harkin, "(Dis)Pleasures of the Text," 97.
16. Briggs and Bauman, "'The Foundation of All Future Researches,'" 483, 519, 484.
17. Briggs and Bauman, "'The Foundation of All Future Researches,'" 505–6, 504, 518, 516.
18. For example Boas, "Fieldwork for the British Association," 105.
19. Darnell, "The Importance of the Northwest Coast," 49.
20. Wickwire, "Women in Ethnography, "'We Shall Drink from the Stream,'" and "'They Wanted . . . Me to Help Them'"; Tennant, *Aboriginal People and Politics*, chs. 8–9.
21. Harkin, "(Dis)Pleasures of the Text," 95.
22. Stocking, *The Ethnographer's Magic*, 98; Berman, "'The Culture as It Appears to the Indian Himself,'" 230; Bracken, *The Potlatch Papers*.
23. Stocking, *A Franz Boas Reader*, 2.
24. Berman, "'The Culture as It Appears to the Indian Himself,'" 217.
25. Hitchens, "Critical Implications," 245.
26. Stocking, *A Franz Boas Reader*, 12.
27. Stocking, *The Ethnographer's Magic*, 97.
28. See Bunzl, "Boas, Foucault, and the 'Native Anthropologist'"; Foucault, *Ethics*, 315–16.
29. Hitchens, "Critical Implications," 242.
30. Wax, "The Limits of Boas' Anthropology," 74; see Sidky, *A Critique of Postmodern Anthropology*.
31. Murphy, "Anthropology at Columbia," 67.
32. Stocking, *The Ethnographer's Magic*, 96–97.
33. Harkin, "(Dis)Pleasures of the Text," 98, 99.
34. Briggs and Bauman, "'The Foundation of All Future Researches,'" 504, 507, 509.
35. See the following by Lewis: "The Misrepresentation of Anthropology," "'Boas, Darwin, Science, and Anthropology,'" "The Passion of Franz Boas," and "Franz Boas: Boon or Bane?"

36. See the following by Darnell: "Franz Boas, Edward Sapir, and the Americanist Text Tradition," "The Boasian Text Tradition," *And Along Came Boas*, *Invisible Genealogies*, "Text, Symbol, and Tradition," and "The Importance of the Northwest Coast."
37. Bunzl, "Franz Boas and the Humboldtian Tradition," 61.
38. Saunders, "Not a Cultural Relativist," 114, 116, 108, 116.
39. Duff, *Images* and "The World Is as Sharp as a Knife."
40. Whittaker and Ames, "Anthropology and Sociology," 162.
41. In history, see Ray, "Native History on Trial," 255n5 and *Telling It to the Judge*, 240n18. However, Ray incorrectly identifies *Calder* as "the first [Aboriginal rights case] to involve anthropological or ethnohistorical experts" (*Telling It to the Judge*, 154) rather than *White and Bob*. In law, see Berger, "Wilson Duff and Native Land Claims" and *One Man's Justice*. In "Anthropology and Aboriginal Claims Research" Peter Elias has written about *Calder* and its implications for other cases without mentioning the role of Duff; in fact there is not a single reference to Duff in the any of the other contributions collected in that volume, *Anthropology, Public Policy, and Native Peoples in Canada*, a startling omission given his position as the first anthropologist to offer expert witness testimony in Canada (Berger, "Wilson Duff and Native Land Claims").
42. For example Suttles, "The World Is as Sharp as a Knife," 87; Anderson, *Bird of Paradox*, 7.
43. Ridington, "The World Is as Sharp as a Knife."
44. Suttles, "The World Is as Sharp as a Knife," 85. See Berger, "Wilson Duff and Native Land Claims"; Abbott, *The World Is as Sharp as a Knife*.
45. Anderson, *Bird of Paradox*, 19, 20.
46. Lindsay, "Archives and Justice"; Berger, "Wilson Duff and Native Land Claims" and *One Man's Justice*, ch. 4; Calder and Berger, "A Conversation."
47. RBCMA, series M-2, file COR-1963-B, Duff to Berger, December 12, 1963.
48. *Calder* (1973), 149.
49. Duff, *The Indian History of British Columbia*, 8.
50. For example Asch, "Errors in *Delgamuukw*."
51. Duff, *The Indian History of British Columbia*, 8.
52. Quoted extensively in *Calder* (1973), 179–89.
53. *Calder* (1969), 63.
54. *Calder* (1970), 66–67.
55. *Calder* (1973), 179–89, 187, 189–90.
56. Duff, *The Indian History of British Columbia*, 8; *Calder* (1973), 149, 156.
57. Cited in Asch, "From *Calder* to *Van der Peet*," 432.
58. *Gros-Louis*; Hancock, "Historiographical Representations of Materialist Anthropology," ch. 4.
59. Berger, *Northern Frontier, Northern Homeland*; Hancock, "Historiographical Representations of Materialist Anthropology," ch. 5.

60. Asch, "From *Calder* to *Van der Peet*" and "*Calder* and the Representation of Indigenous Society."
61. Duff, *The Indian History of British Columbia*, 8; *Delgamuukw*, 13.
62. Stocking, *Race, Culture, and Evolution*; Darnell, *Invisible Genealogies*; Hancock, "Afterword."

References

MANUSCRIPTS AND ARCHIVES

RBCMA. Royal British Columbia Museum Archives. Museum Fonds. Royal British Columbia Museum, Victoria BC.

PUBLISHED WORKS

Abbott, Donald N. *The World Is as Sharp as a Knife: An Anthology in Honour of Wilson Duff*. Victoria: British Columbia Provincial Museum, 1981.

Anderson, E. N., ed. *Bird of Paradox: The Unpublished Writings of Wilson Duff*. Surrey BC: Hancock House, 1996.

Asch, Michael. "*Calder* and the Representation of Indigenous Society in Canadian Jurisprudence." In Hamar Foster, Heather Raven, and Jeremy Webber, eds., *Let Right Be Done: Aboriginal Title, the Calder Case, and the Future of Indigenous Rights*, 101–10. Vancouver: UBC Press, 2007.

———. "Errors in *Delgamuukw*: An Anthropological Perspective." In *Aboriginal Title in British Columbia: Delgamuukw v. the Queen*, 221–43. Lantzville BC: Oolichan Books, 1992.

———. "From *Calder* to *Van der Peet*: Aboriginal Rights and Canadian Law, 1973–1996." In Paul Havemann, ed., *Indigenous Peoples' Rights in Australia, Canada, and New Zealand*, 428–66. Melbourne: Oxford University Press, 1999.

———. "Radcliffe-Brown on Colonialism in Africa." *Histories of Anthropology Annual* 5 (2009): 152–65.

Berger, Thomas R. *Northern Frontier, Northern Homeland: The Report of the Mackenzie Valley Pipeline Inquiry*. 2 vols. Ottawa: Minister of Supply and Services, 1977.

———. *One Man's Justice: A Life in the Law*. Vancouver: Douglas and McIntyre, 2002.

———. "Wilson Duff and Native Land Claims." In Donald N. Abbott, ed., *The World Is as Sharp as a Knife: An Anthology in Honour of Wilson Duff*, 49–64. Victoria: British Columbia Provincial Museum, 1981.

Berman, Judith. "'The Culture as It Appears to the Indian Himself': Boas, George Hunt, and the Methods of Ethnography." In George W. Stocking Jr., ed., *Volksgeist as Method and Ethic: Essays on Boasian Ethnography and the German Anthropological Tradition. History of Anthropology*, 8: 215–56. Madison: University of Wisconsin Press, 1996.

Boas, Franz. "Fieldwork for the British Association, 1888–1897." 1899. In George W. Stocking, Jr. ed., *A Franz Boas Reader: The Shaping of Ameri-*

can *Anthropology, 1883–1911*, 88–107. Chicago: University of Chicago Press, 1974.

Bracken, Christopher. *The Potlatch Papers: A Colonial Case History*. Chicago: University of Chicago Press, 1997.

Briggs, Charles L., and Richard Bauman. "'The Foundation of All Future Researches': Franz Boas, Native American Texts, and the Construction of Modernity." *American Quarterly* 51.3 (1999): 479–528.

Bunzl, Matti. "Franz Boas and the Humboldtian Tradition: From *Volksgeist* and *Nationalcharakter* to an Anthropological Concept of Culture." In George W. Stocking Jr., ed., *Volksgeist as Method and Ethic: Essays on Boasian Ethnography and the German Anthropological Tradition*. History of Anthropology 8: 17–78. Madison: University of Wisconsin Press, 1996.

———. "Boas, Foucault, and the 'Native Anthropologist': Notes toward a Neo-Boasian Anthropology." *American Anthropologist* 106.3 (2004): 435–42.

Calder, Frank, and Thomas R. Berger. "A Conversation." In Hamar Foster, Heather Raven, and Jeremy Webber, eds., *Let Right Be Done: Aboriginal Title, the Calder Case, and the Future of Indigenous Rights*, 37–53. Vancouver: UBC Press, 2007.

Calder v. Attorney General of British Columbia. British Columbia Supreme Court. *Dominion Law Reports*, 3rd series, 8 (1969): 59–83.

Calder v. Attorney General of British Columbia. British Columbia Court of Appeals. *Dominion Law Reports*, 3rd series, 13 (1970): 64–110.

Calder v. Attorney General of British Columbia. Supreme Court of Canada. *Dominion Law Reports*, 3rd series, 34 (1973): 145–226.

Cole, Douglas. *Captured Heritage: The Scramble for Northwest Coast Artifacts*. Vancouver: UBC Press, 1985.

Darnell, Regna. *And Along Came Boas: Continuity and Revolution in Americanist Anthropology*. Amsterdam: John Benjamins, 1998.

———. "The Boasian Text Tradition and the History of Canadian Anthropology." *Culture* 17 (1992): 39–48.

———. "Franz Boas, Edward Sapir, and the Americanist Text Tradition." *Historiographia Linguistica* 17 (1990): 129–44.

———. "The Importance of the Northwest Coast in the History of Anthropology." *BC Studies*, nos. 125–126 (2000): 33–52.

———. *Invisible Genealogies: A History of American Anthropology*. Lincoln: University of Nebraska Press, 2001.

———. "Text, Symbol, and Tradition from Franz Boas to Claude Lévi-Strauss." In Marie Mauzé, Sergei Kan, and Michael Harkin, eds., *Coming to Shore: Northwest Coast Ethnology, Traditions, and Visions*, 7–22. Lincoln: University of Nebraska Press, 2004.

Delgamuukw v. Attorney-General of British Columbia. British Columbia Supreme Court. No. 0843, *Smithers Registry* (1991).

Duff, Wilson. "The Fort Victoria Treaties." *BC Studies* 3 (1969): 3–57.

———. *Images: Stone. B.C*. Vancouver: Hancock House, 1975.

———. *The Indian History of British Columbia.* Vol. 1: *The Impact of the White Man.* Victoria: Provincial Museum of Natural History and Anthropology, 1965.

———. *The Upper Stalo Indians of the Fraser Valley, British Columbia.* Victoria: British Columbia Provincial Museum, 1952.

———. "The World Is as Sharp as a Knife: Meaning in Northwest Coast Art." In Roy L. Carlson, ed., *Indian Art Traditions of the Northwest Coast,* 47–66. Burnaby BC: Archaeology Press, Simon Fraser University, 1983.

Duff, Wilson, and Michael Kew. "Anthony Island, a Home of the Haidas." In *Provincial Museum of Natural History and Anthropology Report for the Year 1957,* 37–64. Victoria: Department of Education, Province of British Columbia, 1957.

Dyck, Noel, and James B. Waldram, eds. *Anthropology, Public Policy, and Native Peoples in Canada.* Montreal: McGill-Queen's University Press, 1993.

Elias, Peter. "Anthropology and Aboriginal Claims Research." In Noel Dyck and James B. Waldram, eds., *Anthropology, Public Policy, and Native Peoples in Canada,* 233–70. Montreal: McGill-Queen's University Press, 1993.

Engels, Friedrich. *The Origins of the Family, Private Property, and the State.* Trans. Alick West. London: Penguin, 1972.

Foucault, Michel. *The Essential Works of Foucault, 1954–1984.* Vol. 1: *Ethics: Subjectivity and Truth.* Ed. Paul Rabinow. New York: New Press, 1997.

Furniss, Elizabeth. *The Burden of History: Colonialism and the Frontier Myth in a Rural Canadian Community.* Vancouver: UBC Press, 1999.

Gros-Louis et al. v. la Société de développement de la Baie James et al. Quebec Superior Court. *Quebec Practice Reports* 38 (1974).

Hancock, Robert L. A. "Afterword: Reconceptualizing Anthropology's Historiography." In Dustin H. Wax, ed., *Anthropology at the Dawn of the Cold War,* 166–78. London: Pluto, 2008.

———. "Historiographical Representations of Materialist Anthropology in the Canadian Setting, 1972–1982." PhD dissertation, University of Victoria, 2007.

Harkin, Michael E. "(Dis)Pleasures of the Text: Boasian Ethnology on the Central Northwest Coast." In Igor Krupnik and William W. Fitzhugh, eds., *Gateways: Exploring the Legacy of the Jesup North Pacific Expedition, 1897–1902.* Contributions to Circumpolar Anthropology 1: 93–105. Washington DC: Arctic Studies Center, National Museum of Natural History, Smithsonian Institution, 2001.

———. "Past Presence: Conceptions of History in Northwest Coast Studies." *Arctic Anthropology* 33.2 (1996): 1–15.

Harris, Marvin. *The Rise of Anthropological Theory: A History of Theories of Culture.* New York: Thomas Y. Crowell, 1968.

Hawker, Ronald W. *Tales of Ghosts: First Nations Art in British Columbia, 1922–61.* Vancouver: UBC Press, 2003.

Hitchens, Janine. "Critical Implications of Franz Boas' Theory and Methodology." *Dialectical Anthropology* 19.2–3 (1994): 237–53.

Jacknis, Ira. *The Storage Box of Tradition: Kwakiutl Art, Anthropologists, and Museums, 1881-1981*. Washington DC: Smithsonian Institution Press, 2002.

Jonaitis, Aldona, and Aaron Glass. *The Totem Pole: An Intercultural History*. Seattle: University of Washington Press, 2010.

Lewis, Herbert S. "'Boas, Darwin, Science, and Anthropology' and Comments." *Current Anthropology* 42.3 (2001): 381-406.

———. "Franz Boas: Boon or Bane?" *Reviews in Anthropology* 37 (2008): 169-200.

———. "The Misrepresentation of Anthropology and Its Consequences." *American Anthropologist* 100.3 (1998): 716-31.

———. "The Passion of Franz Boas." *American Anthropologist* 103.2 (2001): 447-67.

Lindsay, Anne. "Archives and Justice: Willard Ireland's Contribution to the Changing Legal Framework of Aboriginal Rights in Canada, 1963-1973." *Archivaria* 71 (2011): 35-62.

Maud, Ralph. *Transmission Difficulties: Franz Boas and Tsimshian Mythology*. Burnaby, BC: Talonbooks, 2000.

Murphy, Robert F. "Anthropology at Columbia: A Reminiscence." *Dialectical Anthropology* 16.1 (1991): 65-81.

Pinkoski, Marc. "American Colonialism at the Dawn of the Cold War." In Dustin H. Wax, ed., *Anthropology at the Dawn of the Cold War*, 62-88. London: Pluto, 2008.

———. "Julian Steward, American Anthropology, and Colonialism." *Histories of Anthropology Annual* 4 (2008): 172-204.

Price, David H. *Threatening Anthropology: McCarthyism and the FBI's Surveillance of Activist Anthropologists*. Durham NC: Duke University Press, 2004.

Ray, Arthur J. "Native History on Trial: Confessions of an Expert Witness." *Canadian Historical Review* 84.2 (2003): 253-73.

———. *Telling It to the Judge: Taking Native History to Court*. Montreal: McGill-Queen's University Press, 2011.

Regina v. White and Bob (1964). British Columbia Court of Appeal. *Dominion Law Reports*, 2nd series, 50 (1965): 613-66.

Re Paulette. Northwest Territories Supreme Court. *Dominion Law Reports*, 3rd series, 39 (1973): 45.

Ridington, Robin A. "The World Is as Sharp as a Knife: Vision and Image in the Work of Wilson Duff." *BC Studies* 38 (1978): 3-13.

Rohner, Ronald P. *The Ethnography of Franz Boas*. Trans. Hedy Parker. Chicago: University of Chicago Press, 1969.

Saunders, Barbara. "Not a Cultural Relativist: The Boasian Legacy and Burden." In Barbara Saunders and Lea Zuyderhoudt, eds., *The Challenges of Native American Studies: Essays in Celebration of the Twenty-Fifth American Indian Workshop*, 107-23. Leuven: University of Leuven Press, 2001.

Sidky, H. *A Critique of Postmodern Anthropology: In Defense of Disciplinary Origins and Traditions*. Lewiston NY: Edward Mellen Press, 2003.

St. Catherine's Milling and Lumber Company v. The Queen. Privy Council. *Appeal Cases* 14 (1888): 46.

Stocking, George W., Jr. *The Ethnographer's Magic and Other Essays in the History of Anthropology.* Madison: University of Wisconsin Press, 1992.

———, ed. *A Franz Boas Reader: The Shaping of American Anthropology, 1883-1911.* Chicago: University of Chicago Press, 1974.

———. *Race, Culture, and Evolution: Essays in the History of Anthropology.* New York: Free Press, 1968.

Suttles, Wayne. "The World Is as Sharp as a Knife." *BC Studies* 56 (1982-1983): 82-91.

Tennant, Paul. *Aboriginal People and Politics: The Indian Land Question in British Columbia, 1849-1989.* Vancouver: UBC Press, 1990.

Wax, Murray. "The Limits of Boas' Anthropology." *American Anthropologist* 58.1 (1956): 63-74.

White, Leslie A. *The Ethnography and Ethnology of Franz Boas.* Bulletin no. 6. Austin: Texas Memorial Museum, 1963.

———. *The Social Organization of Ethnological Theory.* Rice University Studies 52. Houston: Rice University Press, 1966.

Whittaker, Elvi, and Michael M. Ames. "Anthropology and Sociology at the University of British Columbia from 1947 to the 1980s." In Julia Harrison and Regna Darnell, eds., *Historicizing Canadian Anthropology*, 157-72. Vancouver: UBC Press, 2006.

Wickwire, Wendy. "Stories from the Margins: Toward a More Inclusive British Columbia Historiography." *Journal of American Folklore* 118.470 (2005): 453-74.

———. "'They Wanted . . . Me to Help Them': James A. Teit and the Challenge of Ethnography in the Boasian Era." In Celia Haig-Brown and David A. Nock, eds., *With Good Intentions: Euro-Canadian and Aboriginal Relations in Colonial Canada*, 297-320. Vancouver: UBC Press, 2006.

———. "'We Shall Drink from the Stream and So Shall You': James A. Teit and Native Resistance in British Columbia, 1908-1922." *Canadian Historical Review* 79.2 (1998): 199-236.

———. "Women in Ethnography: The Research of James A. Teit." *Ethnohistory* 40.4 (1993): 539-62.

Widdowson, Frances, and Albert Howard. *Disrobing the Aboriginal Industry: The Deception behind Indigenous Cultural Preservation.* Montreal: McGill-Queen's University Press, 2008.

11 Cultural Persistence in the Age of "Hopelessness"

Phinney, Boas, and U.S. Indian Policy

JOSHUA SMITH

John Collier, the Commissioner of Indian Affairs from 1933 to 1945, said of his candidacy, "Once I was publicly a candidate, I was supported by most of the Indian groups, by various individuals who knew Franklin Roosevelt, and by the Scripps-Howard press. *Opposition to my appointment came from Franz Boas*, dean of American anthropologists, and from Francis C. Wilson, of Santa Fe, whom . . . I once had removed from employment by me." Curiously Collier singles out two people and he does not give a hint as to why Boas might have opposed him. Collier further states, "In 1922, at Berkeley, I laid before Franz Boas the purpose of working for a restored tribal authority and the cessation of the allotment in severalty of Indian lands. Boas approved, but did not thereafter, until 1938, lend a helping hand."[1] In sorting out why Boas was critical of Collier's appointment, it is vital to briefly demonstrate the significance of Collier's appointment both within the history of U.S. Indian policy and the scholarly debates over his politics.

Historically Collier has become an enigmatic and elusive character in terms of what he tried to do politically as the most radically progressive, and longest serving, Indian commissioner in U.S. history. It is ironic and surprising that Boas did not endorse Collier, mainly because Collier's vigorously sustained criticism and activism against the paternal and colonial scope of the Bureau of Indian Affairs, not to mention U.S. Indian policy in general is arguably unparalleled. His main achievement, the Indian Reorganization Act, legislated in 1934, was neither approved of nor implemented to the extent that he strove for in its fully conceived, politically undiluted form.

Nancy Lurie astutely notes one of the problems with pinning down Collier as either an effective political activist on the anticolonial side of the political spectrum or as an unwitting political agent on the other side, complicit in the colonial enterprise. On the one hand, "Collier's plan was inappropriate: too 'Indian' for some tribes, not 'Indian' enough for others, and characterized by unwarranted urgency and hard sell in

some instances." On the other hand, "Indian people recognized in large measure that Collier really understood what their grievances were about even if his methods were sometimes less than satisfactory."[2] Vine Deloria Jr. and Clifford M. Lytle further underscore the immense scope and radical divergence from U.S. policy that Collier envisioned and endeavored to enact despite falling short with Congress and the majority of the U.S. government: "Collier did not visualize a single formula for tribal charters. He rather believed that the traditions of each group of Indians could be expressed within the organic documents, thus allowing the Pueblos and other Indian communities with an already strong governing tradition to articulate the particular principles upon which their governments would rest. In formulating a charter, Collier saw old values and customs transformed, not replaced or transmuted." To be sure, Deloria and Lytle put forth many apt criticisms of Collier, but they sustain a nuanced view of him, understanding the difficulties and hostilities he faced in attempting to change the course of U.S. Indian policy. Despite his shortcomings, Deloria and Lytle assert in no uncertain terms that Collier both "articulated a philosophy of self-government that was more powerful than any competing policy alternative and created administrative support for his beliefs." Moreover, just as Lurie noted Collier's "unwarranted urgency," Deloria and Lytle assert that he jeopardized his political ambitions by moving too quickly, which "made himself and his ideas vulnerable to Congress, the bureau, and the Indians all within a week's time, and he would later regret the speed with which he attempted to push through his radical revision of federal Indian affairs."[3]

The criticisms noted by Lurie and Deloria and Lytle are precisely the same criticisms Boas maintained regarding Collier's potential as an Indian administrator, but his were entirely unbalanced and lacking nuance. Yet it is surprising that Boas opposed him given his radical divergence from the status quo and his original intention to focus on each particular community's self-determination for self-government as the basis of U.S. Indian policy.

In campaigning against Collier, Boas wrote letters to the newly elected president Franklin Delano Roosevelt, Secretary of the Interior Harold Ickes, Roger Baldwin, the founder of the American Civil Liberties Union, and Collier himself regarding Indian policy. These letters reveal more than a simple preference for the position of commissioner of Indian Affairs. They contain remarkable and poignant evidence of Boas's personal thoughts on the political relationships between the U.S. government and Indigenous nations.

The question of Boas's concerns over the appointment of the Indian

commissioner has deeper roots and requires a step back. Boas corresponded directly with Collier's predecessor, Charles J. Rhoads, Indian commissioner from 1929 to 1933, just before Collier ascended the ranks to be a serious candidate and replacement for Rhoads. Boas, initiating the conversation, exchanged several letters with Rhoads in attempting to arrange a meeting in Washington. On April 7, 1931, Boas wrote to Rhoads outlining his intentions. In this first letter Boas tactfully puts forth four proposals. First, he denounces the theories and policies of assimilation by emphasizing the persistence of Indian culture:

> We are also convinced that although the Indians, to all outer appearances, may seem to live like whites of the neighbourhood *their old culture is very much alive and determines their attitude towards modern ways of living*. I believe that in the first serious attempt to do justice to the Indians, which was made under the administration of Carl Schurz, this point of view was overlooked and that therefore the very best and the most honest intentions did not work out for the benefit of the Indians.
>
> The important problem seems to us *how to make use of their present cultural background* with a view of giving them the opportunity to live not as common laborers or loafers, but to be able to lead a life that is worth living.[4]

Second, Boas recognizes that the daily struggles of most Indian communities are immensely challenging and troubling, but he asserts that the solution to overcoming these challenges is for the government to overturn U.S. policy by beginning to support Indigenous peoples' own cultures, as they themselves articulate and express them, as the best means for assisting them in overcoming what he calls this sense of "hopelessness." Third, Boas suggests where Rhoads might find people with the right expertise to shift policy in this direction. Fourth, Boas invokes the example of the Colonial Service of Great Britain in order to emphasize the importance for officials to understand Native law and Native customs, together with the Russian example of recognizing the rights and the ability of their Native peoples to develop in accordance with their own cultures.

Of course Boas overestimates the effects of both the British Colonial Service and Russian policies, but his tactics are to impress upon Rhoads the possibility of turning to Indigenous laws, particular to each community, as starting points to shift Indian policy to be in keeping with "the native point of view," that is, each community's political problem as they might define it on their own terms in keeping with their own legal systems, relational ontologies, and epistemologies. In essence Boas is imply-

ing that the relationship between the U.S. government and Indigenous peoples is similar to the relationship between, for example, Great Britain and its colonies—in a word, a colonial relationship.

These points are consistent in Boas's letters regarding Indian policy and the appointment of Collier as Indian commissioner. In his expressions of concern over Indian policy, Boas articulates "Indian" cultures as fluid entities that do *not* assimilate but persist, and these, he contends, ought to be supported instead of thwarted. Indigenous cultures, according to Boas, are the people's touchstones of survival and their means to resist the causes of what he refers to as their states of "hopelessness."

Rhoads's congenial but patronizing reply comes ten days later: "You doubtless know of some of our beginnings in an effort to build on the Indian's own culture, and particularly to have our superintendents, teachers, and other officers know more about the Indians they work with than they do. We have encouraged our Educational people to take work in summer sessions in the anthropology of the American Indian, and a few of them have done so."[5] Rhoads was intent on utilizing Boas's suggestions to further improve the system of carrying out a policy of assimilation, whereas Boas had suggested a turn to Indian culture as a move away from assimilating Indians to be "white citizens." In response Rhoads rephrased Boas's appeal and advice regarding Indian policy to mean "an effort to build on the Indian's own culture" in continuing a program of assimilation, as opposed to Boas's tactful suggestion to encourage cultural persistence as a means to cope with the realpolitik of oppressive U.S. Indian policy and settler encroachment. The language and attitude in Rhoads's response partially foreshadows both the reason for Boas's opposition to Collier's candidacy for Indian commissioner in 1933 and Boas's support for the political ideas of his student Archie Mark Phinney (1903–1949), a Niimíipu scholar.[6]

Boas wrote back to Rhoads on February 16, 1932, a year before Collier's appointment, with hopes of impressing upon the commissioner the views of Phinney: "I am taking the liberty to send you, enclosed a paper by Mr. Archie Phinney, a Nez Perce Indian who has been with me for about three years and who I believe has good judgment, in regard to the general situation." Boas qualified his recommendation of Phinney's thoughts regarding "tribal conditions" and their "particular difficulties" as being "clear" and based on "good judgment."[7] Phinney's paper included vast criticisms of as well as salient solutions to the colonial assimilationist agenda of U.S. Indian policy. He advocated for a revitalization of traditional governance largely directed through a tribal center, but most important, Phinney sought out the "enlargement of native, traditional

associations, beliefs and customs by accretions of the elements of civilized culture rather than the eradication of tradition."[8]

Shortly afterward Phinney left the United States to study in the Soviet Union. He wrote "Niimíipu among the White Settlers," "in late 1936 and early 1937 in Leningrad," where he "was completing a five year residency as a doctoral student at the Museum of Anthropology and Ethnography of the Soviet Academy of Science."[9] He had to return to the United States in 1937 due to the Stalinist Great Terror. This position piece provides a concise and adamant view of Phinney's perspective on U.S. Indian policy. The title is a provocation and indictment of U.S. Indian policy as well as settler encroachment, not as a historical problem but as a contemporary one in Phinney's time and as it still remains for us today. Phinney places the Niimíipu among white settlers as a challenge and a shift in perspective of the more commonly accepted and adventurous, if not romantic notion of the white anthropologist or adventurer among the tribe. He accentuates the sense of being surrounded and closed in by the white settlers.

A number of pertinent points Phinney argued continue to be of direct importance and relevance to colonialism in North America today and to Indian policy in both Canada and the United States. Yet Phinney's clearly articulated and acute critique is tempered by a sensitive and nuanced appreciation for colonial pressures. He addresses the hopelessness Boas refers to but also speaks to a profound sense of hope tied to the possibility of an impending day when the U.S. government might live in accordance with the treaty relationship. These writings help to explain how and why Boas identified with and vouched for Phinney's political views.

Phinney's treatise begins with a direct statement on the Dawes Allotment Act. Its main function, by design, was to continue to dissolve Indigenous sovereignty and jurisdiction, while absolving the United States of any treaty obligations: "The Dawes Allotment Act of 1887 divested all Indian tribes in the United States of all rights of 'sovereignty': 'No Indian nation or tribe within the territory of the United States shall be acknowledged or recognized as an independent nation, tribe or power with whom the United States may contact by Treaty.'" Phinney's elegant but cutting prose cuts to the core of the sense of hopelessness caused by "white encroachment":

> The pitiful plight of the Niimíipu at the end of the nineteenth century was that of a tribe rendered *helpless*. Their culture had been undermined and vitiated; their freedom and independence had been more than impaired, first by *illegal violations*, then by the crushing military blow administered by the government in the War of 1877, and later

by the Dawes Act. The economic situation of the tribe had become steadily worse through the years of white encroachment on the reservation. This region, once abundant with wild game, fish, berries, and roots, had been transformed into a settled territory, dotted with white town sites and farmsteads. The Indians could no longer derive a subsistence from hunting, fishing, and gathering in a region that was no longer wild, and the economic practices of the Indians, adapted to free range, now required frequent trespassing on the individual land holdings of the whites, and the lands occupied, in violation of a treaty of 1855 by which the Niimíipu had been given hunting rights in this buffalo country to extend for a period of ninety-nine years.

Next Phinney delineated how the Niimíipu had become "agency" Indians and a new class of land-poor Indians, as well as the consequences of these upon Indian life. He refers to the quality of life of his people, the Niimíipu, as being "land-poor" due to the Allotment Act, which had "made individual ownership of land mandatory, and also the sale of 'surplus' lands." Note Phinney's intentional use of scare quotes to frame the concept of "surplus lands" as erroneous. On the point of surplus land he states conclusively that "the Indian's conception of land ownership has never been consistent with the white man's property system"; thus he underscores the absurdity and falsehood that festers, even to this day, in the notions of surplus, unused, unowned, or empty land.[10]

Phinney's assertion of Indian conceptions of landownership challenges evolutionary and Eurocentric assertions that Indians did *not* have conceptions of landownership at all or had less evolved ones until their interaction with the European economies. Additionally Phinney makes two pertinent observations regarding governance and treaty obligations, which tie back into the notion of the "hopelessness" Boas used to characterize, in general terms, the state of being of Indigenous peoples in the 1930s. First, "the Niimíipu live under the jurisdiction of two systems of government—the local government of the state and county, and the central federal government," but "they regard themselves only as wards of the federal government and but vaguely as citizens of the United States" and "most of the interest and energy of the tribe today is directed toward gaining new or greater bounties from the federal government." The Niimíipu strive to actively live in accordance with their treaty relationship while continuing to reject other political interferences being imposed by settler encroachment: "Psychologically, with regard to both young and old, it is the *eternal hope* that the government will some day recognize their claims and make restitution for past injustices." There was no question

of the importance of this treaty relationship to the Niimíipu. Moreover Phinney, who worked for the U.S. government, also understood the government's distorted view of the treaty relationship. It is worth reading his perspective on this in his own words:

> These claims against the government, for treaty violations by the whites in the early years of the reservation, have been the liveliest issue before the Indians for a score of years. . . . It is not surprising that a judicial organ of the federal government, in reviewing these cases, must have only one eye on the justice and validity of Indian claims, because the other eye is on the financial interests and Indian policy of the U.S. Government. The government has not chosen simply to deny in one sweeping action all the numerous claims of U.S. Indian tribes—it has preferred to disallow each claim separately, and thus to keep each issue alive through long years of expensive adjudication. Thus the Niimíipu have clung to their hopes for reimbursements by the government.[11]

In his manuscript, written in the late 1930s, Phinney outlined two of the Niimíipu's claims: (1) a "claim for a reimbursement of 3.25 million for gold mined by the whites on reservation lands since 1855 in violation of Indian treaty rights" and (2) "a claim for the reimbursement of 18.5 million for having hunting grounds in Montana taken from them in violation of the treaty of 1855. This case was reviewed and dismissed by the Court of Claims a few years ago."[12]

What ties Phinney's eloquent analysis of the Niimíipu political context to U.S. Indian policy is the treaty relationship between the Niimíipu and the federal government, a relationship that, according to Phinney, was perceived by the Niimíipu to be both legal and moral. Their hopes were invested in this relationship and the imminent recognition of the injustices the U.S. government had committed in violating the treaties through its own policies of allotments and assimilation. These are the crucial points in understanding why Boas pressed Rhoads to engage with Phinney's political thought and also why he actively opposed Collier's appointment as Indian commissioner. Boas did not see Collier, any more than Rhoads, as being capable of pursuing this line of thinking, mainly because Boas saw him as someone who, on the one hand, wanted to be an administrator too badly and, on the other hand, was too impatiently focused on quick reforms to be capable of careful thought.

Once it is clear that Phinney and Boas are thinking of Indian policy in terms of treaty relations, sovereignty, and jurisdiction, the bulk of Boas's criticisms of Collier, whether or not they are well placed, are at least more

understandable, as are the letters he wrote regarding both Collier and the future direction of U.S. Indian policy. Nowhere does Boas use the terms Phinney uses, but they are implicitly endorsed given Boas's unwavering endorsement and encouragement of Phinney's political thought.

On March 17, 1933, one month before Collier would be appointed Indian commissioner, Boas wrote to Roosevelt in a tactful attempt to influence the course of U.S. Indian policy. Again he began by criticizing the policy of assimilation and the notion of institutionalizing "the Indian" into a "White Citizen" while emphasizing the ongoing importance of "old ways." Boas then pointed to the problem of an Indian commissioner being "hampered" by the imposition of "old laws." Next he advised against both Collier and E. B. Meritt as potential commissioners. The reasons for his disdain for Merritt are obvious, as Meritt would have maintained the racist status quo of assimilation as government policy.[13] But his advisement against Collier is surprising given Collier's altogether radically socialist slant and his anti-assimilation politics. Of all the known candidates he was the most politically progressive. He advocated against assimilation and was himself deeply influenced by Boas's work and ideas .

As noted, Collier invited Boas to participate in his political campaign to abruptly alter U.S. Indian policy and radically change the structure of American Indian governance. Collier wrote in his memoir, "In 1922, at Berkeley, I laid before Franz Boas the purpose of working for a restored tribal authority and the cessation of the allotment in severalty of Indian lands. Boas approved, but did not thereafter, until 1938, lend a helping hand." This raises the following question: In Collier's view, what did Boas do in 1938 to "lend a helping hand"? The answer is not yet certain. However, 1938 is, coincidentally, shortly after Phinney returned from the Soviet Union with his manuscript in hand. Moreover Phinney communicated complex and pragmatic feelings toward Collier and his policy initiatives. Phinney seems to endorse the much needed spirit and overall commitment Collier put forth to further self-government and mobilize U.S. Indian policy to facilitate and empower each Native American community toward self-government and persistence via Indigenous cultural and political terms.

Despite being cynical, calling Collier's "reformism" the "height of bourgeois liberality," Phinney expressed hope in the Indian Reorganization Act and quoted a speech Collier gave in order to "clearly reveal the spirit of the new Indian policy" that is not evident in the written form of the Act.[14] In consideration of Phinney's pragmatic but critical acceptance of Collier and his reforms, albeit not until 1937, together with Boas's affirmation of Phinney's political views on policy in his earlier letters to Rhoads, it seems that Boas's 1933 critique of Collier was aligned with

both Phinney's politics and his focus on treaty relations as the proper basis of U.S. Indian policy.

In his letter to Roosevelt, Boas criticized Collier on three counts, consistently sustained in all of Boas's correspondence regarding U.S. Indian policy: (1) Collier makes promises he is unable to follow through on; (2) he does not understand what is tactically possible for an administrator; and (3) he does not "reserve judgment until he knows the facts of each case." These qualities, in Boas's view, are the cause of immense conflict and agitation in or between communities. For Boas, Collier was too firmly set in implementing his vision and did not appreciate how much might be achieved by protecting the legal status of Indians (from their point of view) coupled with efforts to change U.S. government laws that hindered Indian communities as opposed to striving for changes in tribal governments. For example, the ways Phinney articulated the Niimíipu's own understanding of their treaty relationship with the U.S. government as one that continues to exist would be a more appropriate place to begin. This understanding is also a foundation of hope for the future. It is more than a curious coincidence that Boas's suggestions are generalizations of the specific concerns Phinney outlined in his manuscript.

Thus Boas advocated the appointment of two kinds of persons: a legal expert who would "safeguard the legal status of the Indian" and change laws detrimental to the Indian, and another who understands not only Indians but how their conditions are affected by contact with "modern life." By "legal status" Boas meant their relationship with the U.S. government. This is also the position Phinney takes: the treaties are the eternal basis for the relationship between the Niimíipu and the U.S. government and the obligations that the government has yet to fulfill. The emphasis Boas put on actionable reforms within and through the government excluded recommendations that suggested further reforms to be imposed directly upon Indigenous peoples. Instead the impetus to implement just and moral reforms lay, in Boas's view, on the U.S. government and not on Indigenous peoples, who, as Phinney demonstrated, continue to live in accordance with the treaty relationships.

Collier was well informed of Boas's positions through shared correspondences. Boas sent a strongly worded letter on March 18, 1933, to Secretary Ickes, Collier's friend, colleague, and superior in the Department of the Interior. Ickes showed the letter to Collier, along with the one Boas wrote to Roosevelt. Boas's letter to Ickes is more of a personal attack than the tactful critique he wrote to Roosevelt: "I consider his an evil influence in the relations between Indians and Whites. He is too much of an agitator, and I think his judgment is not always good."[15]

Yet Boas expresses the same crucial points that he had maintained since at least his first letter to Rhoads, such as his "opinion that simply giving civil rights to the Indians is no solution to their problem for the reason that there is too much over-hang of their old culture which would bring it about that they would become helpless victims of exploiters." In this letter Boas touches on the same concerns, but the strong indictment of Collier as being an "evil influence" between Indians and whites is a much bolder and personal message.

Collier responded to Boas's criticisms on January 27, 1933.[16] He was entirely levelheaded and civil considering how well informed he was regarding Boas's efforts to thwart his becoming commissioner. It is important to remember that both Collier and Boas were master politicians and intensely manipulative in terms of advancing their own principles and political goals. Indeed each was passionate about various issues of social justice. On February 20, 1933, Collier again invited Boas to participate in implementing his massive changes in Indian policy. This invitation, especially in comparison to Boas's encounter with Rhoads, is a precise example of why Boas, whether justified or not, is so irritated by Collier's politics:

> Your trained field experience is such to enable you to help us in this inquiry. We are therefore taking the liberty of enclosing the within questionnaire, relating to those aspects of Indian school organization which may be of particular importance in establishing Indian life on a more satisfactory economic basis than has thus far been generally achieved. We trust that you will be able to fill out this questionnaire to the extent, at least, that you will return your answer to us as speedily as possible.[17]

Boas distanced himself from Collier and was unsupportive of his campaign largely due to Collier's methods and personality as opposed to his general intentions. First, the language Collier used was too similar to the language of Rhoads when Boas had appealed to him only a few years previously. Collier's statement "We are anxious to build upon the potentialities . . . that exist today within the social organization of various Indian tribes and communities" is reflective, at least rhetorically, of the same social experimental attitude that Rhoads alluded to, whereby the project was described in terms of using Indian culture as a springboard for assimilative measures into American civil society. The second error Collier made in appealing to Boas was his use of a questionnaire and the emphasis on getting things done "speedily." Boas had repeatedly warned against approaching the problem with a civil liberties mind-set. When

he criticizes Collier for being too emotional and quick in judgment, he is referring to what he perceives to be Collier's cookie-cutter approach to the problems of Indian administration; this is precisely what Lurie, as well as Deloria and Lytle, pointed out regarding Collier's impatience! In soliciting his cooperation Collier was not appealing to Boas's values of understanding the problem in any relational depth, that is, the historical and particular contexts of each distinct Indigenous community in relation to the realities of colonialism and the experiences of colonialism. To Boas, Collier was implementing another experiment in Indian administration. This interpretation makes further sense in consideration of Merriam's possible candidacy.

Author of the 1923 independent inquiry into U.S. Indian policy titled *The Problem with Indian Administration,* Meriam was on various persons' shortlists as a possible commissioner (including Collier's), but he did not want the job. He stated, "I couldn't decline if that's what I were asked to do but I'd rather not wish on the Indians another experiment."[18] This is exactly the kind of attitude Boas believed was a requirement for the position.

In response to Collier's requests for anthropological consultation on how to proceed with reversing allotment and implementing changes in Indian policy, Boas wrote a lengthy but tactful letter on December 7, 1933. This was a continuation of his unchanging position toward Indian policy. While he recommended both Ruth Bunzel and Alexander Lesser as more qualified than Collier to inform the direction of U.S. Indian policy, he described Ella Deloria as "unusually qualified" and pointed out that Archie Phinney, who was still in Russia, was studying the problem and had already written a position paper on the situation.[19]

In this letter Boas suggests there is no one who could perform the job of Indian commissioner well and proceeds to recommend a program for Indian educators to assist them in understanding the economic problems. He also suggests that physicians and nurses should have a better understanding of what Indigenous peoples need. On this point Boas was clear that scientific anthropology was not as important as an understanding of the pertinent needs of Indigenous peoples. Ultimately this suggestion is intended to clear the way for nonacademically trained persons to be involved, such as "Indians" who intimately understand their problems in ways no one else can but otherwise would not have the required credentials to work for the government. Boas next ties the significance of tribal cohesion and the importance of social traditions to the necessity of dismantling the standardized "factory" education policy. He asserts that Indigenous education should be particular to each community and

based on each community's specific cultural tradition and political goals as they articulate them. Boas was thinking relationally in arguing, "The education of each particular group ought to be adjusted in such a way that they can become a connecting link between the tribe and the White population." He reiterated the problem from another angle and reinforced the importance of encouraging "Indian cultures" in young persons as a means for them to overcome their "sense of inferiority" and ultimately their hopelessness.[20] Altogether these recommendations, made by Boas in 1933, articulate and foreshadow some of the most fundamentally pertinent challenges of decolonization today.

Epilogue

Unsurprisingly the United States has continued a policy of legalized grift through narrow interpretations (through the very same means Phinney describes in his manuscripts) of the treaty relationship and the extent that it is obligated to protect Native Americans' rights to fish and water. Alexander Hays notes, "In March 2005, the Nez Perce Tribal Executive Committee agreed to waive in stream reserved water rights claims for salmon throughout the Snake River Basin in a settlement with the federal government, State of Idaho, and Idaho water users." Denying that the treaty right to fish included rights to water, this ruling was reached despite the fact that a 1983 ruling of "the Ninth Circuit held that a treaty impliedly reserved water to protect fishing rights. As Justice Stevens once noted, 'broadly interpreting . . . treaties in the Indians' favor binds together these and other treaty cases.'"[21]

Citing Phinney's *Nez Percé Texts*, which are Niimíipu myths and legends that Phinney recorded from his mother, Mary Lily Phinney (Wayi'latpu), in Niimiipuutímt with English translations, Hays notes:

> Water permeates the myths and history of the Nez Perce people. According to tribal legend, the Monster whose girth filled the arid plateau between the Cascade Range and the Bitterroot Mountains before the time of Indians lay dead through the devices of Coyote. His deed done, Coyote washed his hands and "with the wash-water (bloody) he sprinkled the land." The Nez Perce, a "powerful" and "manly" people, grew from the water and settled the Clearwater River country of Idaho, Washington, and Oregon.[22]

This is fitting in the context of today's colonial legal apparatus, for we see, embedded in the stories of the Niimíipu, the eternal potential of decolo-

nization. Indeed Anthony D. Johnson, chairman of the Nez Perce Tribal Executive Committee, testified regarding the Nez Perce—Snake River Water Rights Act, "Simply put, Nez Perce people defined, and define, themselves in terms of their association with, and relationship to, fish and water."[23] These stories are powerful agents of decolonization, and Boas deemed them significant not only to understanding Indigenous history and culture, but, in his own way, as intangible assets to Indigenous persistence and resistance.

Notes

1. Collier, *From Every Zenith*, 171, 216, emphasis mine.
2. Lurie, "Historical Background," 42.
3. Deloria and Lytle, *Nations Within*, 67, 189, 65.
4. APS, Boas to Rhoads, April 7, 1931, emphasis mine.
5. APS, Boas to Rhoads, April 7, 1931.
6. For more on Phinney, see Willard and Pearson, "Remembering Archie Phinney."
7. APS, Boas to Rhoads, February 16, 1932.
8. Janiewski, "'Confusion of Mind,'" 99, quoting Phinney, "Paper on the Nez Perces."
9. Phinney, "Niimíipu among the White Settlers," 21.
10. Phinney, "Niimíipu among the White Settlers," 22, 27, emphasis mine.
11. Phinney, "Niimíipu among the White Settlers," 28, 29, emphasis mine.
12. Phinney, "Niimíipu among the White Settlers," 29.
13. APS, Boas to Roosevelt, March 17, 1933.
14. Phinney, "Niimíipu among the White Settlers," 30, 39.
15. APS, Boas to Ickes, March 18, 1933.
16. APS, Collier to Boas, January 27, 1933.
17. APS, Collier to Boas, February 20, 1933.
18. Quoted in Kelly, "Choosing the New Deal Indian Commissioner," 276.
19. APS, Boas to Collier, December 7, 1933.
20. APS, Boas to Collier, December 7, 1933.
21. Hays, "The Nez Perce Water Rights Settlement," 72; United States v. Adair, 1410.
22. Hays, "The Nez Perce Water Rights Settlement," 875, quoting Phinney, *Nez Percé Texts*, 26.
23. Quoted in Hays, "The Nez Perce Water Rights Settlement," 875n35.

References

MANUSCRIPTS AND ARCHIVES

APS. Franz Boas Papers, Mss.B.B61. American Philosophical Society, Philadelphia.

PUBLISHED WORKS

Collier, John. *From Every Zenith*. Denver CO: Sage Books, 1963.

Dailey, David. *Battle for the BIA: G. E. E. Lindquist and the Missionary Crusade against John Collier*. Tucson: University of Arizona Press, 2004.

Deloria, Vine, Jr. and Clifford M. Lytle. *Nations Within: The Past and Future of American Indian Sovereignty*. New York: Pantheon Books, 1984.

Hays, Alexander V. "The Nez Perce Water Rights Settlement and the Revolution in Indian Country. *Environmental Law* 36.3 (2006): 869–99.

Janiewski, Delores E. "'Confusion of Mind': Colonial and Post-Colonial Discourses about Frontier Encounters." *Journal of American Studies* 32.1 (1998): 81–103.

Kelly, Lawrence C. "Choosing the New Deal Indian Commissioner: Ickes vs. Collier." *New Mexico Historical Review* 49.4 (1974): 269.

Lurie, Nancy. "Historical Background." In Stuart Levine and Nancy O. Lurie, eds., *The American Indian Today*, 25–46. Jacksonville FL: Convention Press, 1968.

Phinney, Archie. *Contributions to Anthropology*. Vol. 25: *Nez Percé Texts*. New York: Columbia University Press 1934.

———. 2002 "Niimíipu among the White Settlers." *Wicazo Sa Review*, Fall 2002, 21–42.

Pinkoski, Marc. "Julian Steward, American Anthropology, and Colonialism." *Histories of Anthropology Annual* 4 (2008): 172–204.

United States v. Adair. 723 F.2d 1394 (9th Cir. 1983).

Willard, William, and J. Diane Pearson, eds. "Remembering Archie Phinney, a Nez Perce Scholar." Special issue of *Journal of Northwest Anthropology* 38.1 (2004).

12 Franz Boas's Correspondence with German Friends and Colleagues in the Early 1930s

JÜRGEN LANGENKÄMPER

After fifty years of scientific life, in 1931 Franz Boas intended to donate his personal library to the Museum für Völkerkunde, the Ethnological Museum of Hamburg. A few days after the celebration of the fiftieth anniversary of Boas's dissertation, "Beiträge zur Erkenntnis der Farbe des Wassers" (Contributions to the Knowledge of the Color of Water) at the University of Kiel in 1881, the director of the museum, Georg Thilenius, wrote to Boas at the address of his sister Anna Urbach in Berlin.[1] The German American anthropologist used to stay there part of the time during his trips to Germany. Thilenius thanked Boas for his letter of August 7, 1931.[2] Boas enclosed a "supplementary catalogue" of his library. Furthermore he seems to have proposed that titles of his library that were already present at the Völkerkundemuseum or at other libraries in Hamburg should be given to the Notgemeinschaft, the Emergency Society in Aid of German and Austrian Science and Art, to distribute them to other institutions in Germany.

In fact "for practical reasons," as Boas wrote in a letter to his children, Helene Boas Yampolsky, Ernst P. Boas, and Franziska Boas Michelson, the library should have been sold for the symbolic sum of one dollar.[3] This act, almost at the end of the long scientific life of Franz Boas and at the end of his public engagement, was a gift to the country he had left more than forty years earlier to become a well-known ethnologist and the founder of modern cultural anthropology in the United States. It is consistent with his long-established patterns of scholarly activity. Since the end of World War I Boas had been actively engaged on behalf of the sciences and scientists in Germany and Austria that lacked funds for research and the acquisition of new books and magazines from abroad. He cofounded the Emergency Society and chaired it until 1927. He was constantly in search of money, not only among German Americans but also at foundations, to buy books in the United States and send them to Germany. He was well respected by German colleagues for this engagement, for which he was awarded an honorary doctorate by the University

of Graz in 1923.⁴ Honors continued in the early 1930s. How could there be a better way to express his deep affection for his homeland than to give his personal library to a German institution?

Less than two and a half years later, Boas wrote to his children that the contract for this donation had been abrogated and that "you shall inherit the library." What had happened to interrupt this transfer, to cut off the friendly relations to Germany and German scientists and institutions in such a vigorous way? Boas himself explains the reason: "the limitations imposed on the freedom of scholarly research in Germany, especially the prevention of free use of books in the Social Sciences and questions of race, inasmuch as they don't conform with partisan views of the current government."⁵

To explore the developments that led to this change of his attitude, we will have to examine Boas's professional correspondence during the decisive years, for both Germany and Boas, of 1932 and 1933. This essay analyzes and summarizes his correspondence with friends, colleagues, and others in Germany. The situation was fluid, and Boas responded actively to the deteriorating climate for science and for Jewish intellectuals.

Speech about "Race and Culture"

In the summer of 1930 Boas went to Germany and attended the celebration of the 400th anniversary of his Gymnasium at Minden, where he presented a donation by former Minden citizens in the United States to be used for the benefit of students.⁶ In July 1931 he returned for the fiftieth anniversary of his own dissertation. On July 30 he delivered a remarkable, almost programmatic speech at the University of Kiel: "Rasse und Kultur"("Race and Culture"), on the dangers of the racial theories that were popular at that time in Germany, but also in the United States. Boas singled out Hans Günther, the so-called Rasse-Günther, and Madison Grant. He concluded, "The adaptability of various types to the same cultural conditions may, in my opinion, be set up as an axiom. The behavior of a people is not significantly determined by its biological origin, but its cultural tradition. The realization of these principles will save the world and especially Germany, many difficulties."⁷ In retrospect the final sentence has a prophetic message. Boas, then president of the American Association for the Advancement for Science, seemed to be at the height of his public recognition as a scientist and public intellectual in both countries. This stature is reflected in his correspondence: the number of pages registered in the Professional Papers rose by almost 50 percent, from about 1,830 in 1930 to nearly 2,700 in 1931, only to halve the next year. In 1933 Boas's correspondence reached its

last peak, with almost 2,500 letters.[8] This professional recognition coincided with many personal setbacks in the same years. In December 1929 Boas's wife, Marie, was killed by a car whose driver fled. In December 1931, after a year of high personal engagement, Boas himself fell seriously ill.[9]

The Trip to Germany in Summer 1932

A week before his departure on June 6, 1932, to Germany, where he was to stay for three months, Boas wrote to his younger colleague Richard Thurnwald, who was teaching at Yale University at the time. The two men had been in close contact for more than a decade. Boas emphasized that professional forecasts were very difficult: "I believe the best thing I can do is to talk to some people of the Faculty in Berlin in regard to future prospects and I will write to you from there."[10] Some days earlier Thurnwald had written, "I am not blind for [*sic*] drawbacks in America. But I wonder if you do not think them to be less than in Berlin, particularly for me."[11] Thurnwald also feared the "political passions" in Berlin, obviously referring to the heated atmosphere between left and right parties before the forthcoming parliamentary elections in July.

Boas himself had been a target of such political passions, of hate and anti-Semitism in the spring of 1932. Bruno Oetteking, a German-born anthropologist at Columbia University who had evaluated the craniometrical data of the Jesup North Pacific Expedition, wrote a letter to the Nazi magazine *Der Angriff* complaining of the "bad taste" of an article written by a certain Karl Gräbert, published on April 29, 1932, under the title "Untergang der Spenglerei" (Decline of Spenglerism). Oetteking criticized the article because "in various places" the author had treated Boas contemptuously by adding his race in front of his name: "the American Jew Boas," "the Jew Boas," and "the Jewish-American researcher of race." Oetteking countered by noting how deeply Boas was rooted in the German popular character, "im deutschen Volkscharakter." He emphasized in particular Boas's role in the establishment of the Notgemeinschaft and the donation of "his great valuable library to a German university."[12]

After his arrival in Germany, Boas received one of his first letters from Ludwig Aschoff, professor of pathology at Freiburg and, like Boas, a member of the fraternity Alemannia. In view of his impending retirement in two years he asked Boas for advice regarding the use of his personal *Privatbibliothek*, worth about $5,500.[13]

One of the main purposes of Boas's trip was to find a publisher for the speech he had given in Kiel. In July he stayed in Jena, where the publisher Gustav Fischer brought out the monograph *Race and Culture* in a

very short time, "although it is currently quite difficult to obtain the necessary sales for such a small booklet."[14] The author and publisher agreed to split the proceeds. Boas obviously intended to distribute the speech among friends and colleagues because he ordered seventy-five additional copies over the twenty complimentary copies he received.[15]

The title *Rasse und Kultur* reflects the German translation of one of Boas's major works, *The Mind of Primitive Man*, published in German as *Kultur und Rasse* in 1914 and reprinted in 1922. In addition to the early publications on the Baffin Island expedition and research trips to the Northwest Coast, including the *Indianische Sagen*, and some essays from the 1920s, *Kultur und Rasse* was the only one of his major works accessible in his native German. His wish to publish his most recent major work, *Primitive Art*, could not be realized, although he had been trying to find a German editor since 1929.[16] That year Boas had declined an offer by the publisher Strecker & Schröder to put out a German edition if he would contribute $1,000 to the costs.[17]

Worrying news came from the son of Boas's late colleague and friend Karl von den Steinen, to whose widow and children Boas had felt obliged over years. Helmut von den Steinen saw no prospects for himself in Germany and wanted to conduct research in the Soviet Union. Up to this time his efforts to find a job from a distance had failed because of "the bureaucracy of the authorities."[18] Boas could help with letters of recommendation because he maintained excellent contacts with the Soviet anthropologists Waldemar Bogoras and Waldemar Jochelson and had known the late Lev Sternberg, who participated in the Jesup North Pacific Expedition that Boas had organized for the American Museum of Natural History at the turn of the century. He may have advocated for the son of his old friend and perhaps even made available funds for a rapid move. In any case, Helmut von den Steinen wrote a short time later from Leningrad, where he was impressed by the "work ethic and the enthusiasm of the Russians."[19]

Boas's personal experiences of the heated political situation around the elections on July 31, 1932, are not directly reflected in his correspondence of that summer. Only a small number of his own letters during those months have survived. But in an open letter to Reichs President Paul von Hindenburg he referred to the situation eight months later.[20]

In a letter to his son Ernst he wrote from Jena shortly before traveling to Berlin: "Of the political situation, we note here a little. I think the Nazis have reached the climax. If they cannot do with the success of a coup, the story will probably fade like at the time of Boulanger in

France. . . . It is strange how history repeats itself in France after 1870; it is even more acute as a result of the injustices of the Versailles Treaty and the economic situation."[21]

Boas wrote of more peaceful themes in a brochure presenting the sciences in Germany at the World's Columbian Exhibition in Chicago the following year under the motto "A Century of Progress" and in responding to numerous requests for financial assistance or advice, as in the case of the Americanist Paul Kirchhoff[22] Boas seems to have tried to convince Kirchhoff to continue the research of his late friend Karl von den Steinen. He also made efforts to publish von den Steinen's manuscripts.

On September 17, 1932, Boas boarded the *Europa* at Bremen, together with Bruno Oetteking, his daughter, Franziska Boas Michelson, and his three-year-old granddaughter, Gertrude Michelson.[23] He could not know, of course, that this would be his final farewell to Germany.

Back in the United States Boas began to handle requests from German colleagues and institutions, for example that of the anthropologist Hans Jensen at his old University of Kiel. Requests for financial assistance continued, as well as contacts with researchers and museums and German students in the field like Günter Wagner and Frida Hahn.[24] According to the American Philosophical Society Guide, Wagner corresponded with Boas from 1928 to 1938 and studied in Hamburg with Thilenius, at Columbia with Boas, in London with Malinowski, and in Berlin with Thurnwald and Diedrich Westermann. He contributed an article on Yuchi to the third volume of Boas's *Handbook of American Indian Languages*.[25] During World War II he worked for the Reichs Propaganda Ministry, although he did not support the Nazis and had tried to find a position abroad.[26]

Frida K. Hahn was in contact with Boas from 1929 to 1938. Information about her is very scarce. Born near Hamburg in 1903, she went to Columbia at the end of the 1920s. She followed her husband, Dietrich Husemann, whom she had met in New York, to China. In the fall of 1937 the couple fled from Nanking shortly before the massacre by Japanese troops and settled in Berlin.[27] In the 1940s Kathrin Husemann, as she now preferred to be called, wrote a dissertation about Liberia under Thurnwald and Westermann. Her husband was killed in Berlin at the end of the war. With her newborn daughter she fled to her family, worked as a librarian, and died near Hamburg in 1985. She never published the linguistic material she had gathered among the Ponca Indians of Oklahoma in 1933 and 1934 under the instruction of Boas.

At the end of 1932 anxiety grew after the so-called *Preußen-Schlag* by

the new chancellor von Papen. Thurnwald worried that the man at the Education Ministry in Berlin with whom Boas had spoken on his behalf the previous summer was no longer in office.[28] Boas had apparently kept his promise and advocated for Thurnwald, though without success.

The Berlin geographer Albrecht Penck thanked Boas for the sending a copy of *Race and Culture* and lamented the growing need for his help: "Hardly a day passes without my hearing from a distressed academic." This had dire implications for society. "Dark is our political development," he feared. "How strong has become the Hitler movement, you have seen in Berlin, it is a collection of malcontents, of whom there are very, very many, because after the war a very hopeless protection has been held. This fact must be kept in mind when we want to understand the strong anti-Semitism of Hitler's people. The fact that scholars make this a racial issue is silly."[29]

Despite these ominous restrictions on scholarly life, Boas still seemed to enjoy great esteem in his native Germany. The German consulate general in New York wrote to tell him that the president of the German Red Cross had awarded him a decoration in recognition of his services to support their work. The medal and a certificate were enclosed.[30]

At the end of the year a friend from the old days in Chicago and Worcester, the mathematician Oskar Bolza, supplied Boas with a report of the political situation: "The fact that Papen brought the nationalist victory run to a halt is a lasting, big merit. But otherwise he has done great harm with his authoritarian governance, the worst thing is that he has radicalized the Social Democrats, who had become so reasonable under Brüning, and drove them back into the arms of the Communists."[31]

Hitler's Ascension to Power

Attitudes became even more somber shortly after the handover of power to the Nazis on January 30, 1933. Boas heard from his oldest friend, Adolf Vogeler, who had taken his *Abitur* with him at the Minden Gymnasium in 1877 and, like Boas, was a member of the fraternity Alemannia at Bonn. An illness of the Hildesheim Gymnasium professor had prevented a reunion several times in the previous summer, until they finally were able to meet in Bremen. "Here in Germany," Vogeler wrote at the beginning of the New Year, "it looks pretty bleak, and you do not know what the next months will bring." He saw clearly problems in America as well. "To me it seems as if the whole world would fall into a state of uncertainty and inconsistency."[32]

Despite the growing melancholia and depression among his friends in Germany, Boas's correspondence continued as usual during the first

weeks of 1933. The Polish ethnomusicologist Mieczyslaw Kolinski, whom Boas had hired to analyze his songs from the Northwest Coast through the mediation of the director of the Berlin Phonogram Archive, Erich Moritz von Hornbostel, complained about the devaluation of the dollar.[33]

A dramatic turning point, certainly in conjunction with other news Boas was reading in the daily press at this time, was a letter from Aschoff: "As you have probably heard or will hear, a good number of active scientific and cultural workers will be removed in the near future, if they are members of the Jewish race." He defended the measure of Hitler's government: "Because of the strong *Überjudung* [overrepresentation of Jews—editor's note] in some areas of our culture this seems justified to me." This shocking anti-Semitic statement by a German intellectual was followed by some soothing words: that not the race but "the services that the person had shown for German culture" would count. What this could mean Aschoff showed, as he asked Boas to look for a job in the United States for the Jewish pathologist Karl Löwenthal, a World War veteran, honored with the Iron Cross, "field sub-surgeon, then as assistant and senior consultant at the army reserve out there." And he closed, "Yesterday was the formal opening of the Reichstag in Potsdam's Garrison Church. I have heard everything on the radio. It was a solemn historic act that will surely remain unforgettable to all participants. If it stays at this national movement in its purity and it is not charged by excesses in any direction, one can only really enjoy it."[34] Surely Boas would not have enjoyed this development, with its naïveté and national pathos drowning in obvious anti-Semitism.

The "Open Letter" to Reichs President von Hindenburg

"I've called myself a German time and again with pride, but things have gotten so far that I'm almost ashamed to be German," Boas wrote to Reichs President von Hindenburg on March 27, 1933. "Yet it appears very clear that free expression of opinions is suppressed in an unheard-of way and that even the most modest opposition, i.e. half of the population, is suppressed in the most brutal fashion. No impartial observer will see the latest election as a free expression of a people because it was an election during which only the National Socialists were allowed to have any campaign organization."[35]

Boas claimed his right to contact Hindenburg directly and personally from his commitment to Germany during the war. After the war he had collected donations for culture and science in Germany and Austria. In 1933 he also sent books across the Atlantic. "The creation of the Emergency Society and rebirth of the Germanistic Society as instruments to

help Germany were due to my efforts and without me would not have taken place," Boas pointed out. He closed his letter to von Hindenburg, "And I still can't relinquish hope that these signs of the times are but symptoms of a fever afflicting the body of sick people which, even though deeply wounded, shall recover, and I hope that the Germany which I know and love shall rise again. May the day of recovery come soon!"[36]

Reactions to the "Open Letter"

Boas sent copies of the letter to scientists and institutions throughout the world. The response was mixed. Support came particularly from Germans in the United States, where the letter was printed in German-language newspapers. "I would wish that more letters would be written as yours," wrote Thurnwald, at that time a visiting professor at Harvard. But he added skeptically, "So far I still do not see how the bustle of the unbridled passions can be tamed, when the crucial men seem to sympathize with it." He suggested, "You should organize mainly German non-Jews to protest."[37]

From Germany the first response came from Otto Aichel, director of the Anthropological Institute of the University of Kiel. In the previous year he had written to Boas about the honorary medical doctorate that he had proposed for him.[38] It is not known whether Boas ever received the honor. In the 1980s Ludger Müller-Wille found no official letters to or from Boas about the awarding of an honorary doctoral degree, but only a newspaper clipping from the *Kieler Zeitung* (July 31, 1931) reporting on Boas's lecture "Rasse und Kultur" and the awarding of his honorary M.D. in the university auditorium on July 30, 1931.[39] Now, however, Aichel showed open hostility. Contemptuously he asked why Boas had been silent during the revolution led by Kurt Eisner in 1919 and the assassination of hostages in Munich. On the reasons for anti-Semitism he wrote, "You look at some Jewish high school teachers only with regard to their achievements in the scientific field, but not that they covered Germany's honor with mud, to name just one example at the University of Kiel, Professor [Hermann] Kantorowicz." Finally Aichel accused Boas: "By your open letter to the Reichs President you have, dear colleague, only demonstrated that you lack the necessary insight to assess the situation and specific issues of political life in Germany objectively."[40]

Boas took an unusually long time to respond to Aichel's letter. Almost three weeks after receipt, and a lot of terrible news, he thanked Aichel for his "candid answer" without retreating one step from his position. "I am afraid we do not understand each other," he wrote. He further clari-

fied his criticism of the vulgarity and lies "in newspapers such as 'Der Angriff,' 'Voelkischer Beobachter,' 'Rote Fahne' and speeches such as by Mr. Goebbels, Hitler's mean personal attack at Hindenburg last summer." Wishing Aichel well, he wrote, "How a decent man can endure is incomprehensible to me." He mentioned a "number of young friends of *non*-Jewish ancestry who are stopped simply because they are not Nazis" and that "the best people in all professions are leaving." As a result of the paranoia, he painted the dismemberment of Germany quite prophetically, as it occurred twelve years later.[41]

Other anthropologists, such as the Hamburg eugenicist Walter Scheidt, criticized Boas with racist arguments and defended the new government: "In this state of things it is almost self-evident that a wise government eliminates the conflict in that it removes the Jews, except for a small, pro-rata from the relative strengths of the rest, of those key positions. Indeed sometimes it can happen that a good man must be replaced by another honest man."[42] The director of the Hamburg Museum of Ethnology, Georg Thilenius, also made use of anti-Semitic arguments, stereotypes such as that of a "vast immigration of dubious items from the East and Southeast," and in relation to lawyers and doctors "a quite extraordinarily high percentage of Jews . . . their superior talent and performance was not proved absolutely." Furthermore he criticized "a Bolshevism in art and literature . . . whose bearers were Jews." He praised the political events, "apart from individual estates bully," as a revolution "with the opposite sign," "unification of the administration of the empire" and "positive achievements, no one can minimize."[43]

Even Oskar Bolza wanted to place the Nazi operations "beside the greatest revolutions of all time." In his late response to the Hindenburg letter, he said Boas had to "admit that here it is ordered and received remarkably lightly." The elimination of the other parties he evaluated as "a masterpiece of statesmanship."[44]

Unlike the German institutions in the United States, daily newspapers in Germany ignored Boas's open letter. As an example, Fritz Klein, the editor of the *Zeitung' Deutsche Allgemeine* (DAZ), replied to the publisher Johann Jakob Augustin, whose firm in Glückstadt could print in special fonts, like Egyptian hieroglyphs and Boas's Kwakiutl and other Indian texts. Klein's answer began with an astonishing argument for his refusal to publish the letter: "I would have loved to publish the communication in the DAZ, but I must disregard it because the anti-German incitement abroad and especially in America has almost completely fallen silent."[45] Therefore Boas's open letter would no longer be on the agenda.

Paul Rivet's Report

In fact the wave of requests for assistance that reached Boas from Germany was just beginning. A good and objective report of the situation from an almost neutral perspective came from the French anthropologist Paul Rivet in a thirteen-page letter after a two-week trip to Germany.[46]

Rivet had traveled to Berlin with a certain skepticism about international press reports and also with a critical attitude concerning the policy of the French government toward Germany. After the trip, however, he wrote, "Tout est *vrai* dans ce que les journaux ont écrit." One example: he had found a quarter of small Jewish shops deserted during an evening stroll. He described as serious that he saw "*aucune* réaction" against the boycott of Jewish shops.

In Rivet's opinion the ethnologist Konrad Theodor Preuss did not understand Boas's open letter to Hindenburg: "Au fonds, la classe intelligente est elle aussi *anti-Semite*." He saw opportunism, so much so that even ethnologists accused each other of Jewish kinship and origin, as Preuss seems to have tried to do with Walter Lehmann—at least according to the latter—probably not without success, as Lehmann's professorship in Berlin ended in 1934. One victim of the Nazi Law for the Restoration of the Civil Service, passed on April 7, 1933, was Julius Lips, director of the Rautenstrauch-Joest-Museum and a professor at Cologne University, because of his socialist political views. He lived almost trapped in his home and his mail was opened. The following year Rivet would help his German colleague to continue his journey to the United States after a stay in Paris.[47]

First Cries for Help

Letters to Boas from German scientists who were seeking new academic positions abroad continued as usual at the beginning of 1933, but in April their tone and urgency changed dramatically. Hedwig Danzel wrote vividly that her husband, Theodor-Wilhelm Danzel, was threatened with forced retirement because he had a Jewish grandmother: "Therefore a small, reasonably secure job even if it does not correspond quite to the scientific range here, would be good for the beginning there." She also asked for assistance to immigrate to the United States.[48]

Boas was affected directly when Kolinski left "the limits of the Third Reich" and fled to Prague. He wrote, "The conditions there were for me as 'non-Aryan' so unpleasant that I preferred to move abroad in order to do my Kwakiutl job in peace. Against the departure from Berlin I had even less concern as Professor von Hornbostel has left Germany for the time being and is staying in Zurich."[49]

Through his son Ernst, Boas received his first overview of the extent of persecution from England. "It is a gigantic, cold pogrom," Benjamin Liebowitz wrote to Ernst. He suggested an international panel of researchers to support threatened scientists with funds from foreign universities and scholarships. Along with a reference to prohibitions for lawyers, he pointed out that the position of at least ten thousand Jewish doctors in Germany was made even worse by their exclusion from the system of health insurance.[50] Boas tried to find his colleagues jobs at Columbia University, the New School for Social Research in New York, and the University of Chicago. "Maybe there is for me at least a temporary teaching position, such as the one Thurnwald had at Yale University," the law researcher and ethnologist Leonhard Adam added by hand into his pleas for assistance. He explained that, "as the son of a mixed marriage," he had been put on leave.[51]

The Brothers of the Alemannia

Boas's brothers in the Alemannia also had to face the changed situation. There is no doubt that some, like Aschoff, welcomed it. Yet others showed a lot of understanding of and agreement with Boas's open letter. But from the Burschentag (the federal conference) in Eisenach blew a noticeable anti-Semitic wind, even if Alexander Pflüger said optimistically, "I have therefore no doubt that they [will] leave our Boas and other Jewish Old Men untouched."[52] Despite his rejection of National Socialism and a downright combative attitude, Kurt Schneider lamented a lack of *Bekennermut* (courage to confess), and stated with resignation, "It is quiet in recognition of the futility of any opposition to impulsive, unrestrained violence, it is hoped the moment of reflection." He did not want to go through total submission to the National Socialist state under the "leadership principle": "I can no longer follow."[53] Other fraternity members feared for the survival of the Alemannia. Otto Oppermann thought it was "currently impossible" to act against National Socialism with journalistic articles, "even in confidential communications as it is our 'Alemannia' newspaper."[54]

In early July Boas suspected that his honorary senatorship at the University of Bonn had been withdrawn. Pflüger tried to calm him, in addition to reporting his joy over thirteen "foxes," new young members. Only the neuropsychiatrist Otto Lowenstein and the dentist Alfred Kantorowicz had been "removed." The first was, in the eyes of Pflüger, "a pretty nasty Communist," the other "also half or entire Communist." "Really we weep no tears for both, because they were still very significant foreign elements, especially Lowenstein."[55]

Book Burnings and Censorship

After reading press reports in the beginning of May, Boas was worried that his books had been burned. Such a message had come from Julius Lips, who was seeking help.[56] But to Boas's letter to the University of Kiel, Dean Carl Wesle had replied, "None of your books have been burned in Kiel." Obviously, however, works of Boas, as of other professors, could not be read for a certain time "because one wanted to examine whether they contained any attitude hostile or harmful towards the national revolution." Wesle showed sympathy for the "mistrust" against Boas due to his open letter to Hindenburg. Otherwise Wesle absolved the Senate and the faculty, as the book burning was put into effect by a "campaign committee against un-German spirit" supported by the Reichs Propaganda Ministry and undertaken by the police. The letter, which might have enraged Boas even more, ended with the remark, "A revolution of such an extent that has happened so calm and harmless has hardly ever been in the history."[57]

The furor intensified a few days later in a letter from Vice Rector Wolfgang von Buddenbrock, who blamed Boas when the journal *Science* printed a letter to the editor incorrectly. In that letter, Rector Lothar Wolf had admitted openly that works of some authors were not available from the library because "Professor Boas had raised false accusations against Germany in the Jewish question in an open letter to the Reichs President von Hindenburg." This was preceded by the publication of the open letter on April 21 in journals at Kiel.[58]

As a consequence Boas changed his will. In the letter to his children in November 1933, cited earlier, he reported that he had asked the president of the Notgemeinschaft, Friedrich Schmidt-Ott, to cancel the contract that had been returned and which he kept at home. Nevertheless he did not give up hope for a change in Germany, for he wished that the agreement could be fulfilled. He wrote his children, "If, at the time of my death, if full scholarly teaching freedom has been re-established, i.e. if full freedom of learning and teaching at the universities has been restored; if the exclusion of Liberals and Jews from the teaching bodies of schools and universities has stopped, and when reading of works of both popular and academic science no longer is subject to control of a political party. If this should not be the case, the contract remains rescinded, and you shall inherit the library."[59]

Further Efforts

Boas's library never went to Germany because he died before the fall of the Nazi regime, on December 21, 1942. His correspondence with Germans

had continued throughout all these years. It still has to be fully located and analyzed for the light it sheds on the circumstances of German intellectuals in the early years of Nazi rule and on the contacts that German scholars were able to maintain with colleagues abroad.

Boas intensified his efforts to save German scientists as far as he could, although not always successfully. His two younger sisters, Anna Urbach and Hedwig Lehmann, were able to leave Germany before the Nazi government decided to exterminate all European Jews. Antonia Wohlauer, Boas's elder sister, died in Berlin in 1935 at the age of eighty.

As an old man Boas wrote to his niece Elizabeth Krackowizer Johnson, "There is the endless flood of scientists who are driven out of Germany. There is not a mail in which I do not get frantic appeals for help, but I am absolutely at the end of my resources. I mean we cannot find anything for them. It is the craziest and at the same time most tragic condition you can imagine."[60]

Acknowledgments

My thanks go to Ludger Müller-Wille (Montréal), who helped me with the translation into English, and to Uschi Bender-Wittmann (Minden), curator of the exposition "Zwischen den Welten. Franz Boas und die Wissenschaft vom Menschen" in 2008, for many discussions in recent years. This text is mainly based on Langenkämper, "Ich fuerchte nur, wir verstehen einander nicht."

Notes

1. APS, Thilenius to Boas, August 10, 1931.
2. Like most Boas letters written during his journeys to Germany at this time, the letter is not included in the APS collections.
3. Boas to children, November 20, 1933, quoted in Boas, *Franz Boas 1858–1942*, 37.
4. Weiler, *Die Ordnung des Fortschritts*, 381, n3.
5. S. note 3, APS, Boas to children, November, 1933.
6. APS, Carl Dieckmann to Boas, December 11, 1929, January 17, 1930; APS, Boas to Dieckmann December 26, 1929, cited in Bender-Wittmann, "Franz Boas (1858–1942)," 19, and Bender-Wittmann, "Boas in der Provinz," 314.
7. Boas, *Rasse und Kultur*, 19. "Die Anpassungsfähigkeit verschiedener Typen an dieselben Kulturbedingungen darf meines Erachtens nach als ein Axiom aufgestellt werden. Das Verhalten eines Volkes wird nicht wesentlich durch seine biologishe Abstammung bestimmt, sondern durch seine kulturelle Tradition. Die Erkenntnis dieser Grundsätze wird der Welt und besonders Deutschland viele Schwierigkeiten ersparen."
8. American Philosophical Society, *Guide to the Microfilm Collection*.

9. APS, Secretary of Boas to Karl George Frank and to Julius Bewer, January 11, 1932.
10. APS, Boas to Thurnwald, June 1, 1932.
11. APS, Thurnwald to Boas, May 26, 1932.
12. APS, Oetteking to *Der Angriff* (copy), June 3, 1932; cited in Weiant, "Bruno Oetteking," 675.
13. APS, Aschoff to Boas, June 26, 1932.
14. APS, Fischer to Boas, July 12, 1932.
15. APS, Fischer to Boas, August 2, 1932.
16. APS, Strecker & Schröder Verlagsbuchhandlung to Boas, August 29, 1929.
17. APS, Boas to Strecker & Schröder, October 2, 1929.
18. APS, Von den Steinen to Boas, July 17, 1932.
19. APS, Von den Steinen to Boas, August 26, 1932.
20. APS, Boas to Paul von Hindenburg, March 27, 1933, reprinted in Grandmann, *Franz Boas (1858–1942)*, 181–88; Rodekamp, *Ein amerikanischer Anthropologe aus Minden*, 92–95; in English, Boas, *Franz Boas 1858–1942*, 234f.
21. APS, Boas to Ernst Boas, August 13, 1932. Also in Boas Family Papers. Citation provided by Uschi Bender-Wittmann.
22. APS, Kirchoff to Boas, August 9, 1932.
23. APS, Oetteking to Boas, August 16, 1932.
24. APS, Boas to Wagner, October 14, 1931; APS, Wagner to Boas, November 2, 1932.
25. Wagner, "Yuchi."
26. APS, Wagner to Boas, July 22, 1933; Mischek, *Leben und Werk Günther Wagners*; Gingrich, "The German-Speaking Countries."
27. APS, Hahn-Husemann to Boas, February 10, 1938.
28. APS, Thurnwald to Boas, November 1, 1932.
29. APS, Penck to Boas, December 2, 1932.
30. APS, Karl von Lewinski to Boas, end of December 1932.
31. APS, Bolza to Boas, December 14, 1932.
32. APS, Vogeler to Boas, February 10, 1933.
33. APS, Kolinski to Boas, March 9, 1933.
34. APS, Aschoff to Boas, March 22, 1933.
35. Quoted in Boas, *Franz Boas 1858–1942*, 234n.
36. Quoted in Boas, *Franz Boas 1858–1942*, 234n.
37. APS, Thurnwald to Boas, March 30, 1933.
38. APS, Aichel to Boas, July 20, 1932..
39. Akten betreffend Jubelfeier akademischer Lehrer und sonstige Festversanstaltungen, September 1925–July 1934, Titel IX, Abschnitt B, No. 2, Band II, Abteilung 47, No. 1367, Landesarchiv Schleswig.
40. APS, Aichel to Boas, April 16, 1933.
41. APS, Boas to Aichel, May 13, 1933.
42. APS, Scheidt to Boas, April 19, 1933.
43. APS, Thilenius to Boas, May 17, 1933.

44. APS, Bolza to Boas, June 19, 1933.
45. APS Fritz Klein to Johann Jacob Augustin (copy), April 20, 1933.
46. APS, Rivet to Boas, April 27, 1933,.
47. Julius Lips corresponded with Boas from June 1933 to January 1941. See American Philosophical Society, *Guide to the Microfilm Collection*.
48. APS, Hedwig Danzel to Boas, April 23, 1933.
49. APS, Kolinski to Boas, April 24, 1933.
50. APS, Liebowitz to Ernst P. Boas, with a copy to Boas, May 4–5, 1933.
51. APS, Adam to Boas, May 15, 1933.
52. APS, Pflüger to Kurt Schneider, June 7, 1933.
53. APS, Schneider to Lohmann et al. (copy), June 26, 1933.
54. APS, Oppermann to Boas, June 29, 1933.
55. APS, Pflüger to Boas, July 15, 1933.
56. APS, Lips to Boas, June 12, 1933.
57. APS, Wesle to Boas, August 21, 1933.
58. APS, Wolfgang von Buddenbrock to Boas, September 1, 1933.
59. Quoted in Boas, *Franz Boas 1858–1942*, 238.
60. Quoted in Boas, *Franz Boas 1858–1942*, 257f.

References

MANUSCRIPTS AND ARCHIVES

Akten betreffend Jubelfeier akademischer Lehrer und sonstige Festversanstaltungen, September 1925–July 1934. Landesarchiv Schleswig.

APS. Franz Boas Papers, Mss.B.B61. American Philosophical Society, Philadelphia.

Boas Family Papers, Mss.B.B61f. American Philosophical Society, Philadelphia.

PUBLISHED WORKS

American Philosophical Society. *Guide to the Microfilm Collection of the Franz Boas Professional Papers*. 2 vols. Wilmington DE: Scholarly Resources, 1972.

Bender-Wittmann, Ursula. "Franz Boas (1858–1942): Begründer der Kulturanthropologie, Humanist und Demokrat." In Ursula Bender-Wittmann and Jürgen Langenkämper, *Franz Boas, 9.7.1858–21.12.1942*. Minden: Schriftenreihe der Münzfreunde Minden und Umgebung, 2008.

———. "Boas in der Provinz: Bericht über eine Ausstellung." In Hans-Walter Schmuhl, ed., *Kulturrelativismus und Antirassismus: Der Anthropologe Franz Boas (1858–1942)*. Bielefeld: Transcript-Verlag, 2009.

Boas, Franz. *Rasse und Kultur*. Jena: Gustav Fischer Verlag, 1932.

Boas, Norman F. *Franz Boas 1858–1942: An Illustrated Biography*. Mystic CT: Seaport Autographs Press, 2004.

Gingrich, Andre. "The German-Speaking Countries." In *One Discipline, Four Ways: British, German, French and American Anthropology*, 59–153. Chicago: University of Chicago Press, 2005.

Grandmann, Heinz. *Franz Boas (1858–1942. In Land und Leuten dienen. Ein Lesebuch zur Geschichte der Schule in Minden: Zum 450 jährigen Bestehen im Auftrag des Ratsgymasiums Minden.* Ed. Friedhelm Sundergeld. Minden: Bruns, 1980.

Langenkämper, Jürgen. "Ich fuerchte nur, wir verstehen einander nicht." In Friedrich Pohl and Bernhard Tilg, eds., *Franz Boas—Kultur, Sprache, Rasse: Wegen einer antirassistechen Anthropologie*, 131–49. Münster: LIT-Verlag, 2009.

Mischek, Udo. *Leben und Werk Günther Wagners (1908–1952)*. Gehren: Escher, 2002.

Rodekamp, Volker, ed. *Ein amerikanischer Anthropologe aus Minden*. Bielefeld: Verlag für Regionalgeschichte, 1974.

Wagner, Gunter. "Yuchi." In Franz Boas, ed., *Handbook of American Indian Languages*, 3: 293–384. Washington DC: Smithsonian Institution, 1933–1938.

Weiant, C. W. "Bruno Oetteking 1871–1960." *American Anthropologist* 62.4 (1960): 675–80.

Weiler, Bernd. *Die Ordnung des Fortschritts: Zum Aufstieg und Fall der Fortschrittsidee in der "jungen" Anthropologie*. Bielefeld: Transcript-Verlag, 2006.

13 Franz Boas on War and Empire

The Making of a Public Intellectual

JULIA E. LISS

To historians and anthropologists alike, it has become almost commonplace to consider Boas as a public intellectual, a "citizen-scientist" whose contemporary and historical importance come from outside the profession no less than from within it. Especially in establishing anthropology as an academic discipline and putting his mark on the study of race, Boas reached well beyond the academy. As some have also rightly noted, Boas's emergence "in public" is tied to his place in the academy rather than to an escape from the ivory tower.[1] His move to the university from the museum and government work is significant in both his public role and the stature it brought to anthropology as an academic discipline and scientific endeavor. Less well-recognized is the role of war—the two world wars of the twentieth century in particular—in providing the context, the impetus, and the particular shape of Boas's ascendancy as a public figure.[2] One could even argue, with only some exaggeration, that without the world wars it is hard to imagine what Boas's public reputation would have been. In part this is just an index of how formative the wars were in defining the social and intellectual conflicts and transformations of the twentieth century. It is also a reflection of how Boas's career intersected with these historic events: his exodus from museum to university before World War I and his retirement and end of life during World War II. But more than that, the wars also provided a unique opportunity for Boas to articulate anthropology to a broad audience. A dual relationship—the wartime context of Boasian anthropology and the way his anthropology reflected upon that context—provided an essential, meaningful foundation for Boas's importance as a public intellectual.

In the years preceding both world wars Boas developed his arguments about anthropology and war around a constellation of related issues: race, nationality, and nationalism. But the conflicts themselves increased the urgency and relevance of his positions, mobilized his critiques, and placed him in positions of significant public prominence, if not acceptance or respect. Boas used and honed his understanding of anthropology during

these conflicts, and these wartime roles in turn shaped his emergence as an activist and public intellectual. I use these terms to describe the prodigious work of intellectual dissemination and movement organizing in which Boas engaged in public venues—lectures, articles, letters to the editor—outside of specifically professional arenas and, increasingly, in articles that were written about his activities in these publications. Both his own writings and articles about him are evidence of his public profile and importance. Throughout, Boas's arguments and areas of interest were remarkably consistent: he reused, restated, and reiterated essential points he had articulated during World War I, and it was the changing political, social, and institutional context rather than the sheer force of his ideas or even his personality that explains his visibility as well as his stature and relevance. This is why, although Boas's positions were controversial and his standing challenged during World War I, in its aftermath and during World War II his public presence met with and was, in a sense, defined by defeat. By the time of his death in 1942 he had cemented what would become his fundamental legacy. This legacy included both formidable adherence to principle and continued nonconformity, controversy, and opposition.

World War I: Anthropology at War

As part of efforts to further world peace, in 1912 Boas published "An Anthropologist's View of War," a pamphlet for the American Association for International Conciliation. In this essay Boas presented an argument that he would draw upon in years to come as war lay closer on the horizon and became a contested fact of daily life.[3] He argued that conflicts like war stemmed from primitive social forms, in which relatively small-scale "hordes" had, in self-defense, considered all outsiders or strangers as potential threats and enemies. Over time the larger units of social organization, from tribes to nations and eventually international cooperation, aided by increased contact and diversification, led to greater interdependence and "unification." At this point Boas was optimistic about the possibilities for peace, even though he noted that "the modern enthusiasm for the superiority of the so-called 'Aryan race,' of the 'Teutonic Race,' and the Pan-German and Pan-Slavish ideals," perpetuated "the old feeling of specific differences between social groups in a new disguise."[4] His central analytical and rhetorical strategy inverted the social evolutionary move from primitive to civilized, a critical argument that was as much descriptive as it was designed to disrupt the complacency of bourgeois society. He would soon draw on this understanding of history, particularly the primitive roots of in-group/out-group conflict and

the misunderstanding and misuse of ideas of race, to explain and criticize the escalation of World War I.

As war came to Europe, Boas's analysis of the conflict challenged prevalent views of the role race placed in the war, and the very meaning of "race" itself. In this respect he was elaborating on arguments he had already been pursuing in anthropological circles and brought them to bear directly on issues of contemporary urgency. The conflict was not a "race war," "an unavoidable war of races, . . . an outcome of the innate hostility between Teutonic, Slav, and Latin peoples" that stemmed from "racial instinct." This interpretation confused local types with racial and linguistic groups. Moreover while race was misunderstood as a pure and innate form, "scientific investigation does not countenance the assumption that in any one part of Europe a people of pure descent or of a pure racial type is found, and careful inquiry has failed completely to reveal any inferiority of mixed European types."[5] Here Boas applied arguments he had already advanced to a new context of public interest and concern. There were three core principles of his scientific message on race that the war gave him the opportunity to explain: it was not to be confused with "local types" that developed historically; there were no pure races; and racial differences and mixture were not associated with inferiority or superiority. This complex of ideas made up the Boasian critique of race that he would repeat throughout his life; he had many chances to do so.

Elevated perhaps by the popular success of *The Mind of Primitive Man*, Boas sought new outlets to disseminate his views—and correct what he saw to be dangerous misconceptions—particularly those occasioned by the war. He now published in a range of periodicals with a wider audience than he had, for the most part, addressed before. In addition to spreading his correctives on race and his dissenting views on war, these newspapers and magazines identified Boas with these positions to a broader public—the readers of metropolitan newspapers such as the *New York Times*, the *New York Evening Post*, the *New York Evening Mail*, the (socialist) *New York Call*, and the *Springfield Republican*, of literary and topical periodicals such as the *Dial, Everybody's Magazine, The New Republic, Atlantic Monthly*, and the *Nation*, and the German-language press, including the *Illinois Staatszeitung*, the *Vossische Zeitung, Viereck's*, and the *New-Yorker Staatszeitung*. Some of these articles reprinted speeches or were reissued and recirculated as pamphlets. As the author of articles and letters to the editor, Boas appeared both as an authoritative expert and as a concerned citizen, identities that were sometimes in tension as the role of scientist and German American were in flux. Wartime provided an opportunity to disseminate anthropological knowledge and an obligation to do so, but

it also occasioned a vexed and public working out of professional and personal identities around the very issues raised by the war.[6]

To explain wartime antipathies, Boas turned to the close bonds of nationality, particularly but not consistently reinforced by linguistic solidarity. In "Kinship of Language a Vital Factor in War," a full-page spread in the Sunday *New York Times Magazine* in January 1915, Boas argued that these bonds (rather than "race") explained the emotional ties of nationalism that in turn explained the war. Unlike "race," which science refuted and history complicated, language had "deep emotional value," particularly when wedded to "political aspirations." On the one hand, this combination helped to explain the appeal of nationalist sentiments at work in the move toward war. Historically, Boas argued, nationalism did not develop uniformly and might lead to different relationships between national aspirations and linguistic identities. Linguistic nationalism in Germany, Russia, France, and England, for instance, varied: the dispersal of German speakers and the desire to preserve the language without political unification; the efforts to bring all Slavs—despite linguistic and religious heterogeneity—under Russian control; the French preoccupation with Alsace-Lorraine; and the English goals of a maritime, global empire. By differentiating race from language and culture and, in a relativist mode,[7] emphasizing the particular, distinctive ways each nation defined itself and its wartime objectives, Boas provided a dispassionate, anthropological analysis of a fraught conflict.

In this context Boas made a surprising admission, an unusual "intru[sion] upon the public [of] my own personal views regarding political matters."[8] Tellingly his remarks exposed the tension between his scientific vantage point and his own loyalties, revealing his desire to separate them even as they clearly informed each other. He spoke of the harsh anti-German sentiment that wounded him and other German Americans who hoped for reconciliation. Perhaps he anticipated that the revelation might be understood as a legitimate view of one who shared both German and American perspectives and as an intervention in the growing xenophobia and war fervor. In the intolerant climate, however, Boas's dissent only drew public criticism.[9] This criticism of the war would have been controversial enough, but Boas raised a longer-lasting disillusionment with his "admiration of American political ideals," an "intrusion" of his beliefs that also provided a striking critique of U.S. policy. He claimed that he had always assumed American ideals valued self-protection and coexistence and had considered "events like the great movement westward, and the Mexican war . . . rather as digressions from the self-imposed path of self-restraint." Against these original

expectations, he now declared, "a rude awakening came in 1898, when the aggressive imperialism of that period showed that the ideal had been a dream. . . . At the end of the Spanish war, these ideals lay shattered."[10] Having initially bracketed out the United States' own aggressive nationalism, Boas had come to see it as part of an ongoing imperialist project, a revelation that now occurred at a new moment of rupture.

The timing of this confession, for which I know of no original (1898) statement, is striking. No matter how accurate the recollection, it suggests the extent to which World War I impelled Boas to consolidate a public position against war and imperialism by creating a meaningful, consistent (and retrospective) narrative. It also shows a willingness to defy the pressure to conform that perhaps was at the root of the more personal pain of German Americanism. Boas used a critique of imperialism to legitimate nationality in general and German identity in particular. His own view, speaking "as an American of German birth," derived from this particular perspective, reinforced (in the 1916 retelling) by a revelation of a larger principle that differentiated "nationality" from aggressive nationalism.[11] Boas also elaborated on how imperialism violated a personal—and professional—ideal of understanding other points of view and not imposing one's own as superior and absolute.

This principled stand, embedded as it was in the objectification of personal loyalty, also disguised an interesting blind spot in Boas's anti-imperialism. While he expressed his loss of faith in American political ideals in the face of imperialism, he also championed the "keen insight of Carl Schurz,"[12] who took up the anti-imperialist cause and founded the American Anti-Imperialist League. Schurz's anti-imperialism, while based on an argument similar to Boas's about territorial acquisition as a break with precedent and national values (but without Boas's insight that this episode suggested a continuity with rather than departure from the past), also advanced a racialist argument about the unsuitability of the Philippines for American settlement and Filipinos for U.S. citizenship.[13] Schurz would seem a strange hero without a splitting of his anti-imperialist agenda from the reasoning that supported it. Boas turned to Schurz even though he drew on the very argument of racial difference that Boas took pains to refute. Throughout his life, however, Boas continued to stand up for Schurz's reputation as a leading figure in a generation of 1848ers who had opposed inequalities of all kinds and with whom Boas had personal and familial connections.[14]

The murkiness of Boas's position on imperialism, filtered through these personal ties, also extended to his views on professional opportunity. The fruits of U.S. conquest, including those from the 1898 con-

flict itself, were not off limits for scientific exploration, as his efforts to develop projects in the Philippines, Puerto Rico, and American Samoa demonstrated. This sort of opportunism was also not new or unique, implicating his earlier work in the Northwest Coast and later projects in the southwestern United States.[15] Even if these efforts were entangled with attempts to gather anthropological material that might undercut the assumptions of imperialist power or challenge the uncritical sense of superiority of powerful nations, they never brought these contradictions to the surface. When the crisis of World War I exposed the conflicts between science, personal loyalty, and the uses of knowledge, it did so selectively. Boas seems to have evaded these questions, even as he strengthened his critique of imperialism. These contradictions reveal unresolved conflicts that science itself was supposed to address, a relationship that became clearer as Boas used anthropology more bluntly to condemn colonialism in the wake of World War I and during World War II.[16] By the end of World War I his uses of anthropology had taken on a new urgency that sharpened his argument in the face of public criticism and emboldened war efforts. Three essays published in 1919 exemplify his developing approach to scientific knowledge and the role of the scientist in public life.

Whereas earlier he had focused on the salience of national identity, in the aftermath of the war he turned his attention more directly to the problem of nationalism. In "Nationalism," an essay in the *Dial*, Boas distinguished "nationality," a local and historical identity of a group, from "nationalism," an appeal to political power joined with a state that, he argued, exploited class interests for political ends. This use of power was even more apparent in nationalism's extreme form, imperialism, an "intolerant nationalism" that "taught not . . . the nationalism of ideas but the imperialistic nationalism of political and economic power."[17] It was just this sort of exploitation for economic gain through the use of force and destruction of native "industrial and social life" that Boas said "must be condemned." In "Colonies and the Peace Conference," published in the *Nation*, Boas both refuted the criticism of the German Empire advanced by the victorious imperial powers and launched his own attack on the "disastrous results of European invasion" throughout the world. Citing Germany's contributions to science, including its ethnological and natural history museums, and its relatively just treatment of local populations, he argued that the problems with colonialism—including "our own difficulties with the Indians"—were systemic and "not peculiar to one nation." The self-serving license to increase profit derived from the potent combination of political power, economic motivation, and sense

of cultural superiority: "The problem involves our attitude toward those branches of mankind whom we are pleased to call backward races, and also our assumption of the absolute value of our cultural standards." But this view only rationalized the imposition of economic exploitation legitimated through force. To bring home this (il)logic, Boas used a clever example of estrangement, but one that played on contemporary fears: "I think this problem will become clear if we imagine the Chinese coming here and finding square miles of land in northern New York and New England lying waste, owned but not used. Would they not be entitled, on the same grounds on which we base our colonial claims, to say that they have no land at home and that for the sake of the welfare of humanity they will till the soil that we do not know how to utilize? Or is it only not right for them because they have not the might to force us to acquiesce?" To prevent such a marriage of self-interest and egotism, Boas endorsed the English Labour Party program to provide "national protection of the colonies of all countries against exploitation, and their government in the interest of the natives and of humanity." It was too late to save "the native races" of the United States, Canada, Australia, or the Argentine Republic, he thought, but there was still hope for parts of Asia, Africa, and India. Nationalism, supported by conceits of cultural and racial superiority, were underlying factors of the war and obstacles to a more just peace. These obstacles themselves became the object of study and key to liberating people from the "horde" mentality that had brought about the war and continued to threaten the future.[18]

At the same time Boas clarified a position—as a scientist—that authorized him to speak on these matters. The earlier statement about war, imperialism, and dissent, "Why German-Americans Blame America," was notable, as Boas himself stressed, because typically he advanced a view of scientific truth that emphasized the disinterested pursuit of knowledge. It is important, in this respect, that he emphasized the crisis in political ideals and values, not science per se. The *Nation* letter to the editor, "Scientists as Spies," in which Boas charged anthropologists doing work for the war effort with violating their ethical responsibilities *as scientists*—a type of responsibility that other professionals (such as journalists and diplomats) did not have—is the most famous example of his public position on science and politics. Boas had several interlocking concerns: their collaboration in a conflict he saw as illegitimate (although he waited until its conclusion to come forward about their transgression); the contamination of science by political motives; and the secrecy that violated science as free inquiry and differentiated these actions from his own use of public venues to advance anthropological knowledge about the war.

None of Boas's concerns had much currency, however, because the incident (his letter and not the scientists' behavior) was used to silence him on explicitly political grounds that were fixed in wartime views on patriotism and enshrined in the Espionage and Sedition Acts. He was censured by the American Anthropological Association and forced to resign from the National Research Council. The accuracy of his claims was irrelevant to the charges against him, which were defined as a question of patriotism, pure and simple. This episode also indicates that Boas's status was uncertain and his views controversial. He stood for a faction, and he took public rebuke in this wartime climate in which intolerance against dissenting views and foreigners was acute. Nonetheless, and in contrast to many of his contemporaries, such as John Dewey and W. E. B. Du Bois, Boas did not come to regret his wartime statements or positions. His very consistency marked him as at odds with the tenor of his times.

The combativeness of Boas's wartime insights and activities created a pattern of responses and arguments about anthropology and war that would define his public image, intellectually and professionally. As the *Nation* incident indicated, these positions were as divisive and controversial as the war itself. It was by no means clear that Boas would emerge victorious from these conflicts, or even survive them. How would he, given these embattled beginnings, become such a noted and respected figure? Here Boas's position as a scientist and the particular issues on which he focused provided a mutually strengthening combination of practice and content. To Boas and his supporters this reinforcement was a powerful incentive, a moral imperative, to public engagement. But to his critics it also opened up lines of resistance: the limits of intellectual freedom and opposition to the egalitarianism of his message. Wartime provided a heated context for the battle over both of these, variously defined as liberatory or subversive.

The Interwar Years: From Race to Racism

Despite his very public rebuke at the end of the war, and perhaps because of it, Boas spent what turned out to be the interwar years pursuing very similar topics and lines of argument. This continuity is significant even though World War I also shifted the emphasis in Boasian anthropology to the problem of (irrational) prejudice and cultural configurations. On the one hand, the turn toward cultural configurations developed out of Boas's earlier emphasis on historical diffusion.[19] On the other, it gained relevance because World War I highlighted how important such configurations were—both the role of national identity and nationalism and their resistance to anthropology's efforts to guide a more enlightened

view. Despite this shift in his research program, Boas's public profile was remarkably persistent and consistent, even as he reached out to wider, more public constituencies. The work on "culture and personality" was done by Boas's students, notably Ruth Benedict and Margaret Mead, and contributed in significant ways to their participation in the war effort in the 1930s and 1940s, but it seems to have had little impact on Boas's own public positions or on his reputation.[20]

Boas took stands on seemingly all of the major debates of the 1920s. He refuted eugenics, nationalism, and immigration restriction and championed education, racial equipotentiality, and cultural diversity. *Anthropology and Modern Life*, which touched systematically on each of these issues, summarized his arguments and explained his anthropological project for a broad, reading public, much as *Mind of Primitive Man* had introduced his ideas in 1911. Also like that earlier work, *Anthropology and Modern Life* developed from lectures, in this case weekly speaking engagements that were advertised in local papers. Even though the frequency of his interventions in the local press decreased (papers stopped publishing his letters before the war was over), as had occurred during World War I, Boas continued to publish in a spectrum of publications with nonprofessional readership—the *American Mercury*, the *New York Times*, the *Nation*, the *Forum (later Forum and Century)*, the *World Tomorrow*, and *Current History*—and his activities and ideas were reported on in metropolitan newspapers such as the *New York Times*, the *Los Angeles Times*, and the *Chicago Defender*. The *Defender*, which emerged after the Great Migration as a paper with a national circulation, reported Boas's speeches on the fallacy of racial inferiority and race problems in the United States (April 2, 1921, and January 27, 1923) as well as his participation in a conference on interracial harmony and peace (March 29, 1924); the *New York Times* reported on his work for the World Unity Conference (October 7, 1927). Boas was emerging as a public spokesman for progressive, egalitarian causes.[21]

Consistency and exposure did not equal influence or success, however. Many of the positions Boas took continued campaigns begun in the years leading up to World War I, but the war itself fueled xenophobic, racist, and nationalist fervor that did not end with the conflict. Madison Grant's *Passing of the Great Race; or, the Racial Basis of European History*, originally published in 1916 and negatively reviewed by Boas in 1917, reappeared in new editions that became very popular in the 1920s.[22] Boas's public stands against eugenics were rebuked by the spread of racial integrity acts and the 1927 *Buck v. Bell* decision that enshrined Oliver Wendell Holmes's words that "three generations of imbeciles is enough."[23] Boas's

view of scientific practice as an international endeavor transcending national and other boundaries, something he pursued during and after the war on behalf of German and Austrian scientists, chafed against and perhaps even provoked the revived Ku Klux Klan's racialist nationalism and 100 percent Americanism that saw cosmopolitan modernism as the enemy.[24] His pathbreaking work, *Changes in Bodily Form of Descendants of Immigrants*, was foundational for the antiformalist challenge to the very idea of race and for the lone volume of the Dillingham Commission reports to argue against immigration restriction.[25] When the long-term efforts to restrict immigration finally succeeded in the 1921 and 1924 National Origins Acts, they racialized immigration law and the status of the legal immigrant and illegal alien.[26] Boas was on the losing side of all of these issues.

Even Boas's two public victories were ironic, each in its own way showing the defeat. As an expert witness in *U.S. v. Cartozian* (1925)—a case in which the court sought popular and not scientific expertise to decide whether Armenians qualified as "white" under the law—Boas helped turn the tide of the *Ozawa v. U.S.* (1922) and *U.S. v. Thind* (1923) decisions, which had denied citizenship based on determination of whiteness.[27] In *Ozawa* the court had said, in an argument with a Boasian ring, that race could not be determined by appearance because there was such a range in skin color that it did not reflect whether a person was white. "The test is racial," the *Cartozian* decision still declared, but it must also, along the lines of *Thind*, be determined by "common understanding," not entirely by "ethnological and scientific research." With this ambiguous endorsement, Boas testified as an expert witness that Armenians were of "European origin," originally from the "Alpine" area and of "Dinaric type," and had migrated to Asia Minor. His point, characteristically negative and cautious, was nonetheless taken as support of the "racial" test: "Dr. Boas affirms . . . that 'it would be utterly impossible to classify them [Armenians] as not belonging to the white race.'" Boas also confirmed that Armenian immigrants intermarried at the same rate as other first-generation immigrants, an argument he likely meant to indicate the lack of racial antipathy and the impermanence of racial categories but that the court took as confirmation of white racial identity. In conclusion the court found in favor of Armenian naturalization based on the racial test for citizenship, in line with Boas's testimony: "Armenians in Asia Minor are of the Alpine stock, of European persuasion; they are white persons . . . [and] they amalgamate readily with the white races, including the white people of the United States." Boas's views about the history of population migration, the mistaking of national and local populations

for racial categories, and the importance of mixture to diffuse the ideology of racial purity and superiority had been used to sustain the "racial test" of whiteness for citizenship, a test that would not be removed until 1952. This was an odd victory.

Conversely Boas's reputation seemed to win by losing when Clarence Darrow cross-examined William Jennings Bryan in Dayton, Tennessee, also in 1925. Questioning Bryan on biblical literalism, creation, and the deep history of antiquity, Darrow used Boas as a standard for modern, scientific knowledge. "Do you know there are thousands of books in your libraries on all these subjects I have been asking you about? . . . Did you ever read a book on primitive man? Like Tyler's [sic] Primitive Culture or Boaz [sic] or any of the great authorities?" Darrow asked. "I don't think I ever read the ones you mentioned," Bryan replied.[28] While this escapade is often seen as a real victory for modern intellect, it hardly killed either religious fundamentalism or antimodernism, much less altered the verdict against Scopes.[29]

Boas's spotty record—and his position as a public intellectual who was both defied and defined by these challenges—exemplifies the contentious, unresolved nature of modernity between the wars.[30] John Higham may not have intended his phrase "the tribal twenties" to have a double meaning, but the popular vogue of primitivism that boosted Margaret Mead's *Coming of Age in Samoa* and in part fueled white attraction to the Harlem Renaissance in the Jazz Age United States existed in dialectical relationship to the revolt against modernism embodied in the racist nationalism that Boas challenged, a challenge with which he was increasingly identified.[31] This opposition reveals how significant the rise of fascism and Nazism and ultimately World War II itself were in providing Boas with authority and legitimacy, even though he had been working toward peace, international relief, and racial understanding throughout the 1920s and his views would remain contested, enduring lightning rods for racist agendas continuing these battles.[32]

Boas's selection as president of the American Association for the Advancement of Science in 1931 represented a reconstituted, public recognition of his self-concept as scientist. It also connected him with scientists who were rethinking their public role in the context of the Depression and international crises.[33] As the *Los Angeles Times* remarked of the summer meeting in Pasadena, "Scientists, once burned at the stake for supposed witchery, are now the world's most useful citizens."[34] Among the most prominent were natural scientists with whom Boas would collaborate in significant political and public enterprises in the last decade of his life, including Harold Urey (Nobel Prize in Chemistry in 1934), Rob-

ert Millikan (Nobel Prize in Physics in 1923), and L. C. Dunn, a pioneering geneticist. Boas used his 1931 presidential address to pronounce his position on race mixture and equality and to criticize the view that, as reported in the *New York Times*, "war and race prejudice are selective processes" that contribute to progress. On the contrary, "war eliminates the physically strong; war increases all the devastating scourges of mankind such as tuberculosis and genital diseases; war weakens the growing generation." Moreover Boas reiterated his long-term and updated arguments about race and war: "race antipathy and race prejudice," rather than being "implanted by nature," are "the effect of social causes"; the history of racial mixture demonstrates the equal endowments of different races.[35] The wartime context helped put Boas's research agenda more prominently and effectively in the public eye, as his activities and arguments increasingly became newsworthy. One telling example of this boon is the revival of his research on head form, which the *New York Times* called "now almost classic," even though it failed to influence public policy.[36] The rise of Nazism must have seemed like the most awful of opportunities.

World War II: The Urgency of Nonsense, the Scientist as Activist

Boas had spent the 1920s refuting eugenic theories in the United States, theories that influenced Nazi ideas of racial purity and selection. Then Boas had chastised; now he charged (in *The New Republic*) that Madison Grant's recent book, *The Conquest of the Continent*, was "a book of Nordic propaganda," combining "dogmatic" assertions "that culture is determined by race," "careless handling of facts," "speculations," "wrong" assertions, " supposition" and "fantastic" claims.[37] In an article in the *American Mercury* he rehearsed his theories on race in response to claims of Aryan distinctiveness and superiority: "A judgment of the German policy [of exclusion] requires the answer to two questions: one, what, racially, are the so-called 'Aryans' and 'non-Aryans'?; the other, to what extent does the behavior of a single human being and of a people depend upon hereditary traits?" "Aryans," Boas pointed out, denote a "linguistic term and nothing else." The history of migrations indicates a long history of "mixing of tribes," leading, particularly in Germany, to extensive intermixture. The three groups that "roughly speaking" describe the range of "the population of Europe" are "local types" that are distributed over a wide geographical area. The distinction of types is analogous to the domestication of animals, which isolates individuals in a group and reproduces certain identifiable traits (blondness, black skin, curly hair). "It is a fiction to speak of a German race.... There is no 'German race';

there are only local types. . . . National groups and local types have nothing in common."[38] Even as Boas deployed his argument in a new set of circumstances, he was self-consciously also continuing battles he had waged for decades.

To the question of whether scientific activism changed science,[39] the answer for Boas was no. At the same time, his commitment to science as a source of universal knowledge about particular conditions and as a practice requiring free inquiry newly motivated his activism. Consistent with the boundaries between science and politics that he drew during World War I, Boas legitimated activism as a moral and pedagogical imperative. Unlike Benedict and Mead, for instance, who used their work on culture and personality as employees of the U.S. government,[40] Boas took his stand in a league of scientists in the service of internationalism and intellectual freedom with a distinct public but nongovernmental role. This position was also consistent with Boas's pacifism, implicit in his anthropological understanding of war but complicated by the rise of Nazism. In 1930 he had published a letter to the editor of the *New York Times* that consisted entirely of a quotation from Nietzsche's "Der Wanderer und sein Schatten" (The Wanderer and His Shadow; the title was untranslated) as an argument for peace that echoed his own views. The state claims of defense were only an excuse for conflict: "They assume bad intent of the neighbor and good intent of their own. This assumption is inhuman. . . . It is a cause of war and an incitement to war."[41] Boas himself acted on these insights as a member of the American Committee for the World Congress against War.[42] With the rise of Hitler the threat became more palpable and complicated. Boas expressed his distress in an open letter to Hindenburg that the *New York Times* excerpted: "I have always with pride called myself a German, but today things have happened that make it necessary for me to say that I am ashamed to be German."[43] Initially hopeful for some resolution, and anxious to distinguish Hitler from the German people, Boas eventually adopted a position of protest, joining others in asking Columbia University president Nicholas Murray Butler to refuse an invitation to the university in Heidelberg. Boas himself said "he would not go to any German university 'under any circumstances.'"[44]

The corpus of Boas's antiracialism needed to be restated, more than ever. He did attend to the particular claims of Nazi racial theory, emphasizing still the larger logic: "Since the Jews are considered as a thoroughly different element, we must define their racial position. There is no more a Semitic than there is an Aryan race, since both terms define linguistic groups, not human beings. . . . The Jews are not a uniform race. . . .

An attempt is being made by those who are in power in Germany to justify on scientific grounds their attitude toward the Jews; but the science upon which they are building their policies is a pseudo-science."[45] Two things are of note here. First, the crisis encouraged Boas to speak directly about Jews in the context of his racial theory, something he had done before but with some reluctance.[46] Second, he branded the opposing views "pseudo-science," a new emphasis, although it was implied in his refutation of arguments such as Grant's as without scientific basis. The use of the term here, however, suggests not just a "bad" or "mistaken" science but a false and therefore pernicious one. Boas was in a stronger position to defend and define scientific knowledge to a broader public as a professional in this highly charged moment. This is a significant shift in an argument that otherwise mirrors many he had made and would continue to make. He closed his essay "Aryans and Non-Aryans" with an explanation of particular nationalities and intermixture, but now referring specifically to cultural assimilation: "Just as the Germanized Slavs and French have become German in their culture, as the Frenchified Germans have become French, the Russianized ones Russian; so have the German Jews become German."[47] This was a most telling conclusion. Boas would continue, throughout the decade and until the end of his life, to reiterate his understanding of the "Jewish problem" in the context of his understanding of "race" more generally: the confusion of "race" and "nationality"; the more general problem of the social segregation of a racially defined group; and how racial prejudice was (mis)appropriated against Jews.[48] Upon his retirement in 1936 (just a few months after his photograph appeared on the cover of the May issue of *Time* magazine), he said, "With the present condition of the world I consider the race question a most important one. I will try to clean up some of the nonsense that is being spread about race these days. I think the question is a particularly important one for this country, too, as here also people are going crazy. The race question is so acute at this time that you can't speak about it too often."[49] The urgency belied the "nonsense," and Boas was as concerned with this crisis in the United States as abroad; this was a burden shared by all.

The charged urgency of the 1930s helps to explain the altered context of Boas's remarks and the reception of them. Not only did the rise of "Hitlerism" provide a target for Boasian ideas about race, but it helped also to press scientists to see their work as socially necessary.[50] An important, orienting framework for this was the broad coalition of the Popular Front that developed during the Depression and war and defined both issues and constituencies: progressive New Deal liberals; socialists; Com-

munists; organized labor; and civil rights activists. Boas fit snugly in this group: he announced he would vote for the socialist Norman Thomas in 1936 and FDR in 1940; he mobilized on behalf of Spain, teachers unions, civil rights, and intellectual freedom.[51] The 1930s provided an intellectual and social milieu more hospitable to his left progressive and radical views, especially those generated by World War I and its aftermath when he had elevated the masses over elites and targeted economic and political power and imperialism.[52] These were enduring concerns that now seemed in step with the times, even if still demanding change. Once again the crisis of war occasioned an expansion of his public presence, but now also in new, left-leaning publications created for these times (*Modern Thinker*, the *Anti-Nazi Bulletin* of the Anti-Nazi League, *American Teacher, New Masses, Equality, Friday*, and *PM*). In all of these cases Boas was vocal and persistent in making both principled and pointed claims, drawing on his long-standing arguments, particularly his correctives about race. After World War I the resistance of "race prejudice" to enlightenment had become a subject of scrutiny and critique. Now, in the context of the 1930s, this resistance took on an explicitly ideological cast. The invention of the word *racism* to mean an ideology of race differences linked to inferiority and superiority, in contrast to *racialism* and *race prejudice*, is indicative of the logic of the war years.[53] Boas's own writings reveal this shift, as demonstrated by his titles "Race Prejudice from the Scientist's Angle" and "Race and Race Prejudice"; he himself also used the word *racism*.[54]

This focus on ideology raised new questions about the relation of science to politics and the role of the scientist. There was a revealing tension here between the power of scientific knowledge as universal truth and the urgency of using that knowledge for political ends. In the article "Race and Race Prejudice" that appeared in the *Jewish Social Service Quarterly* in 1937, Boas began with a statement of the "serious friction" that arose from the close proximity of different social groups. "The public interest," he declared, "demands a clarification of their fundamental causes." The problem, however, was not just social conflict in the world crisis but also within scientific circles that were part of the international situation. Boas raised the unusual argument that "science" had contributed to "race prejudice" by stressing hereditary differences and the connection between mental and physical differences.[55] The battle—in the "public interest"—was to resolve the friction within science by advancing scientific knowledge about the causes of conflict. It also required a new view about scientists, which Boas pressed in language characteristic of the 1930s: "The organization of scientific workers is one of the indications

of our consciousness that scientists can no longer work remote from the social problems of our time, that it is necessary both for the commonweal and for the interest of science that we become more keenly aware of the impact of scientific discovery upon our social structure and of the influence of social life upon the progress of science."[56] Even as he stood fast by the pursuit of science as "the ice-cold flame of the passion for seeking the truth for truth's sake," Boas claimed that "a new duty arises. No longer can we keep the search for truth a privilege of the scientist."[57]

Boas was still scrupulous about separating his "scientific" from his "political" work, even as he brought one to bear upon the other. As a reviewer noted about his collection of essays *Race, Language and Culture*, despite Boas's "active part in the political struggle about race questions . . . there is nothing in the whole volume that touches the present political outbursts."[58] Ernst Boas, his son, acknowledged as much in his foreword to *Race and Democratic Society* when he said that the 1940 volume "illustrat[ed] and prove[d] the validity of his point of view of anthropology, in particular that an understanding of the culture and behavior of man under conditions fundamentally different from our own, can help us to a more objective and unprejudiced view of our own lives and our own society" and left his political writings and speeches for a separate, posthumous publication.[59] But Boas *did* bring to bear the insights of anthropology on his public statements about war and actively established his public role as a scientist. How did this come about?

A turning point came in 1938, a year in which he published "An Anthropologist's Credo" in the *Nation* and mobilized scientists around antifascism and intellectual freedom, causes that would define the remainder of his life. Aptly the first of these, part of a series titled "Living Philosophies," was a retrospective of a man of accomplishment toward the end of his life, while the second was a response to a contemporary necessity. This is the character of Boas's public prominence: an ambitious and self-conscious research program pursued over decades that intersected with war-driven crises providing a historic opportunity to bring those issues to the fore.

"An Anthropologist's Credo" was a public statement that explained both Boas's anthropological views and how "they came into being." This was more than a conventional autobiography, however, because Boas juxtaposed his own origins with his vision for anthropology, especially the recognition of "implicit belief in the authority of tradition" and the liberation from it. Even though he claimed to have been raised in a liberal family "devoted to science" and free from "religious dogma," he focused on "the question: how can we recognize the shackles that tradition has

laid upon us? For when we recognize them, we are also able to break them." Many of the points Boas brings to the reader's attention repeat those he had made earlier, beginning with World War I: the roots of war and power in primitive hordes and in-group/out-group conflict; the elusive goal of a widening circle to define the in-group; and the confusion of race, nationality, and "aggressive nationalism" that is used to justify exclusion of the outsider. All this needed to be repeated because "we do not observe any progress in the standards of human society." Three new points, however, suggest how the present (1938) moment affected Boas's rendition of his own philosophy in the context of anthropology's purpose: the role of the nonconformist in challenging tradition and "free[ing] us from the errors of the past"; a refutation of the misguided view that cultural differences should lead to "a relativistic attitude toward ethical standards"; and, in place of this, an argument for the value of the individual and an expansion of the "ethical point of view of the in-group, which must be expanded to all humanity" to protect the individual by preventing exclusions. These imperatives presented a broad philosophy of life, but they found particular currency "in the present time" because of the domination of national and racial groups, "hysterical claims of the Aryan enthusiasts," and the "unpardonable error" of the "racialists" in Germany and also in the United States and England. Embracing the position of the nonconformist, Boas concluded by explaining what motivated him to activism: "My ideals have developed because I am what I am and have lived where I have lived; and it is my purpose to work for these ideals, because I am by nature active and because the conditions of our culture that run counter to my ideals stimulate me to action." Boas represented himself as a special case, someone whose "tradition" was "atraditional," whose familial emphasis on science impelled him to scientific work, whose idealistic nonconformity made him act.[60] By the time these words were published in August, Boas had already embarked.

The impetus came from an article in *Nature*. Among the many missiles that Boas launched in the popular press during his lifetime, this incident is particularly important because of the substance of the controversy and the organizational movement that Boas initiated in its wake. These activities, and the public recognition of them, would cement Boas's wartime reputation and its legacy. In April *Nature* published a translation of an article by the Nobel Prize–winning German physicist Johannes Stark entitled "The Pragmatic and Dogmatic Spirit in Physics." Stark argued that "pragmatic" science was dominated by "Aryans, predominantly of the Nordic race," while "dogmatic," by which he meant theoretical, science was favored by Jews. This latter approach—and the scientists who pro-

duced it—needed to be purged. To this the *New York Times* editor quipped, "Pragmatic anthropologists long ago exploded the racial myth to which he clings.... Professor Stark prefers to dogmatize in behalf of pragmatism with Hitler and Streicher."[61] *Nature*'s editor, Sir Richard Gregory, distanced himself from the article, and there was almost no response to its publication. Boas, however, wrote to the *New York Times* about the paper's editorial.[62] He praised the editor for "justly expos[ing] the social dogmatism of the physicist who claims that Nordics alone have the inductive spirit, that Jews always wallow in the morass of speculative deduction. These claims, however, require a specific refutation." Boas then went on to list examples, by name and field, of "men of Jewish descent who contributed to empirical science" in the years of its revival in Germany. He noted the significance of men "who happen to be of Jewish descent" not to imply "that they are better men than their Aryan colleagues, but merely to point out the absurdity of the claim that racial descent predestines one group to deduction, another to empirical work.... These few examples selected almost at random prove that only blind prejudice can claim any intimate relation between racial descent and form of thinking." The editor strangely pointed out in an addendum to Boas's letter, "in justice to Professor Stark," that he spoke only of "frequency" and not innate or fixed ability.[63]

The American scientific community responded to this conflation of scientific practice and racial theorizing. The American Association for the Advancement of Science issued a statement in defense of intellectual freedom and internationalism. But "something more militant is needed," the *Times* editorialized. "Professor Franz Boas provides it in the form of a manifesto, published today, which is signed by 1,284 scientists.... It recognizes 'the moral obligation to educate the American people against all false and unscientific doctrines.'"[64] Another article identified Boas, "dean of American anthropologists and former president of the American Association for the Advancement of Science," as the spokesman of this new movement. "'The present outrages in Germany,' Professor Boas said, 'have made it all the more necessary for American scientists to take a firm anti-fascist stand.... The agents of fascism in this country are becoming more and more active, and we must join with all men of goodwill in defending democracy today if we are to avoid the fate of our colleagues in Germany, Austria and Italy.'"[65] Here the public responsibility was ethical and pedagogical, with "democracy" defined as a value, not a contest of political views. At the same time, while scientific authority legitimated these efforts, no one could be holier-than-thou. It could happen here, to paraphrase Sinclair Lewis.

This manifesto was the beginning of a larger and sustained movement

to which Boas dedicated the remainder of his life. He helped to organize and was the spokesman or president of numerous organizations defending academic freedom, freedom of speech, and civil liberties. The manifesto led to the organization of the Lincoln's Birthday Committee for Democracy and Intellectual Freedom, which, the *New York Times* reported, held "public meetings on university campuses and in cities throughout the United States."[66] This event generated the American Committee for Democracy and Intellectual Freedom, which sponsored lectures throughout New York and other cities. Boas spoke as part of a series titled "Science as a Social Force" in January 1939, for instance, and participated in "How the Scientist Can Combat Racism," a panel at the World's Fair.[67] Before a meeting of the National Emergency Committee, he distributed a list of bills pending before Congress that "threaten[ed] civil liberty."[68] To some extent these activities were similar to those Boas had engaged in during World War I, when he came to the defense of scholars who were penalized for their dissenting views and helped to formulate principles of academic freedom. They also extended his earlier efforts to mobilize scientists as a group both in alliance with scientists elsewhere in the world—the internationalism of scientific endeavors—and in defense of democracy and freedom, ideals that he thought particularly necessary to scientific inquiry. While his own contributions focused on the particular topics of race and racism, they were also part of a larger project couched in terms of democracy and freedom. As the *New York Times* editorialized about "Minute Men of science" in words that could have been Boas's own, science could not remain "purely national in character. It is the chief pride and glory of science that it accepts men of all creeds and races, that it promulgates its discoveries for the benefit of mankind and not of any particular nation."[69] In this respect antifascism combined the internationalism of scientific practice with the specific content of scientific knowledge. It now placed Boas in the public eye as never before.

Just what these ideals meant, however, was already contested, both from the outside and from the inside. Although we know about the wartime rise of anti-Communism in the United States, its effects on Boas's activities may still come as something of a surprise.[70] Two episodes in particular indicate prewar history, a history that targeted activists more broadly and would necessarily outlive Boas himself. The first involves the so-called Dies Committee, established in 1938 and named after the congressman from Texas who chaired the House Committee Investigating Un-American Activities (the precursor to HUAC). The second involves the split in the American Committee for the Defense of Intellectual Freedom (ACDIF) over Communists within the movement and its position on the

Soviet Union. Both of these involved Boas (and posthumously the ghost of Boas) in anti-Communist crusades.

Early on Boas was one of a group of sixty-two scientists, writers, and artists "in defense of the Bill of Rights," who opposed the suppression of dissent by the Dies Committee. In particular they objected to the incitement to violence against labor and radicals, "discriminatory and repressive measures" against the foreign-born, and efforts to suppress the Communist Party, which, they argued, mirrored earlier efforts in Europe that culminated in "the destruction of all freedom."[71] Such actions were, Boas wrote in an essay in the reform journal *Forum and Century*, focused on "opinions" rather than "acts of force" and therefore violate "a fundamental principle of American democracy . . . the demand for absolute freedom of opinion." The Dies Committee's charge to investigate "un-American propaganda," Boas argued,

> is vague, undefined, and undefinable. . . . On these grounds I opposed the continuance of the Dies committee, not on account of the universally recognized indefensible methods of its procedure but on principle. . . . I do not doubt that the timidity of many liberals, which becomes more and more manifest under the influence of the European war, is largely owing to the innumerable personal attacks of the Dies committee, with its arbitrary definition of what is American and what un-American. It is perhaps not possible to prove conclusively that the committee is agitating "subversively" for the entry of the United States into the war, but it is certain that the persecution of aliens, of whom Mr. Dies claims that he will drive seven millions out of the country (!), increases the war hysteria. . . . My opposition is . . . founded on my opinion that the appointment of a committee for the purpose of investigating propaganda—that is, free discussion—is undemocratic and (if you will permit) un-American.[72]

Boas turned the tables on those who charged "un-American" actions and subversion, including liberals who buckled under "personal attacks" rather than rising to the demands of the moment that required principled stands. Although many scientists conflated democracy and freedom with American science, Boas's distinctions were consistent with his pacifism and defense of unpopular, not just dissenting, views that he had endorsed since World War I. His critique of liberals and opposition to entry into the war also suggest his own disaffection, something he had articulated more boldly in the *Daily Worker* when, commenting on the outrages in Spain, he had said that the "ultimate solution" for the democratic strug-

gle "for intellectual freedom and economic security" is "to my personal way of thinking . . . Socialism."[73]

This combination of principle, free speech, and dissent also lodged in the controversy within the ACDIF. When the ACDIF split, partly from the efforts of John Dewey's Committee for Cultural Freedom, over the presence of Communists within the organization and its focus on Italy and Germany to the exclusion of Russia, Boas held to his defense of intellectual freedom in what might be called anti-anti-Communism. Reports specified that protest against the ACDIF was "not aimed at Boas," "whose sincerity in his devotion to democracy and freedom was not doubted."[74] This desire to excuse Boas is a striking indication of his special status, one not accorded him in 1919, but it did not protect him now from investigation or, after his death, the taint of innuendo. If his activities and affiliations became suspect, his defense of them on principle only fueled anti-Communist suspicions. As early as 1936 the FBI initiated a file on Boas, the bulk of it focusing on his activities after 1940, including support for civil liberties, evaluation of textbooks, and criticism of Bureau activities. In 1943–1944 Boas was also named in the FBI files tracking the activities of the anthropologist Bernhard Stern and the sociologist Robert Lynd, including their part in the ACDIF, the New York College Teachers Union, and their opposition to red-baiting within those organizations.[75] Boas's unqualified defense of intellectual freedom and civil rights would make him suspect and even dangerous in a climate where wartime policies censored evidence of race contact and mixture.[76] The peculiar combination of Boas's honorific status and increasing evidence of the suspicion of his views points to the illiberal impetus to countersubversion that the wars generated, even as they praised—and used— the language of freedom. That World War II simultaneously confirmed Boas as a public intellectual in the service of freedom and democracy and found those values contingent and threatening shows the contested nature of their meaning and the intolerance of dissent that actually motivated Boas, the self-proclaimed nonconformist.

In the fight for democracy and intellectual freedom, schools became a significant battleground, in terms both of curriculum and of the defense of teachers themselves. Under the auspices of the ACDIF Boas spearheaded an examination of discussions of race in school textbooks, finding them scientifically inaccurate, reinforcing white supremacy, and all too similar to Nazi anti-Semitic propaganda.[77] He also championed teachers, including teachers in radical unions, who had come under investigation of the Russ-Coudert Committee in New York. In 1939 he publicly stated that he had joined the New York College Teachers Union, a move as much of pro-

test as of solidarity and "to win over those he opposes."[78] The most famous of these investigations involved Bertrand Russell, but the committee also occupied itself with secondary school teachers and teaching materials.[79] In "Dies to Fight Reds to Highest Court" the *New York Times* reported that Emanuel Celler, an ally from the immigration fights of the 1920s, read a statement by Boas into the Congressional Record, protesting "investigation into the political and social affiliations of textbook writers to be an indefensible invasion into the rights of the individual." Dies responded that Boas and Celler were "misinformed" and that threats of Communist subversion would be upheld.[80] Apart from the entanglements of free speech and anti-Communism, these instances also demonstrate Boas's commitment to activism that joined both practice (education) and substance (curriculum) that he felt he had an obligation as a scientist to pursue.

One of the striking indications of how Boas's lifelong work on the problems of race and equality contributed to movement activism and visibility as a public intellectual is his participation in and recognition by the growing civil rights movement. This attention places his efforts, in turn, within the history of the "long civil rights movement," a history that itself has much to do with the relationship of wartime to civil rights struggles, during World War I and particularly during World War II.[81] In this respect one can also see how the context of Nazi racism drew attention to the problems of racial injustice in the United States, a self-reckoning that Boas had encouraged. For instance when Marian Anderson's performance at the National Cathedral was denied and organizers took the event to the Lincoln Memorial, Boas loaned his name to the movement that developed around this exposure of racism at home. Notably he also joined in efforts to examine and publicize those who denied school facilities for the event.[82] Free speech, racial equality, and education came together. That Boas supported these struggles is not surprising; that he had moved fully into a contested public realm is indicative of a shift of the late 1930s and 1940s that gave its growing momentum to him even as it used him as a resource. The consistent coverage of these activities in the *Chicago Defender* is also indicative of this wider movement. In 1937, for instance, Boas received an honorary doctorate from Howard University, reported in the *Defender* but not, as far as I know, in the white press.[83]

In lending his name in support of civil rights organizing, Boas's ideas were particularly significant, as African Americans used wartime rhetoric and expectations to advance a national civil rights agenda. An article in the *Chicago Defender* in April 1938, for instance, had the title "Franz Boas Blasts Pure Race Notion." The body of the article focused on his critique of Nazi racial theory:

> Another blast against Adolph Hitler's so-called "Aryan" or "Pure-race" theory was sounded this week by Dr. Franz Boas, internationally-famed scientist and professor of anthropology at Columbia university. . . . Scientists have known for a long time that there is no such thing as a "German race" or a "Jewish race," but all of us realize that fascism pays little attention to science or culture, and that their persecution of the Jewish people is merely part of their program of barbarism. . . . Some months ago . . . Hitler's Nazi government became so enraged at the famous anthropologist's explosion of the Nordic supremacy theory which hit at Negroes and Jews as a part of those minority groups whose elements are "inferior" to whites, that they included his books in a public burning in Berlin.[84]

Through the medium of the African American press (the *Chicago Defender* had a national circulation) readers learned of Boas's ideas in the context of antifascism and-Nazism. Those ideas—his sustained arguments against "scientific racism" (a term itself derived from 1930s perspectives)—combined with the egalitarian impulse he had also long defended but that now, in the context of World War II, became a national, civil rights movement. Under the headline "White Anthropologist Decries Race Prejudice, Pleads for Equal Rights," the *Chicago Defender* reprinted an article by Boas from the *New Masses* on the persistence of racial prejudice and the scientific meaning of "race," issues that, he said, were

> particularly applicable to the Negro race. What right have we to any judgment in regard to their ability or character when we first attempted to break their spirit in slavery and then continued oppression by economic discrimination and social ostracism? . . . How can we expect the Negro race to take its proper place in our culture as long as economic and social discrimination persist? We must demand equality, not equality on paper, but equal rights in life, equal opportunities for education, equal economic opportunities, and a breakdown of the social barriers that oppress even those who in character and achievement are often infinitely superior to those who will not acknowledge for them the claim that is so often heralded as the basis of our society, the claim that all men are born with equal rights.[85]

Boas was here invoked as a useful and authoritative voice and a sympathetic (white) outsider to the movement. The resonance of "we" and "our" along with the *Defender*'s title makes this clear. The *Defender*'s civil rights campaign also made visible another significant shift of Boas's

antiracism, especially as it moved into the public realm. His earlier arguments had emphasized misapplication of scientific ideas to conceptions of "race" and eventually argued against these as "pseudo-science." As "race prejudice" became understood as ideological, freighted in a worldview as "racism," it also stood out as a cultural rather than biological concept. The article reprinted from the *New Masses* had originally been titled "The Myth of Race," combining the idea of myth as falsehood and as a culturally embedded tale. A later article in the *Defender*, "The Inferiority Myth," began with Boas's closing words about equal rights and elaborated on them:

> These utterances should have added weight especially now that the Negro is fighting for complete integration into our social order. . . . Dr. Boas' contention should enlighten not only narrow-minded white folk, but should shed equal light to those Negroes who have no faith in the ability of our race to assimilate this culture, and who have refused to acquaint themselves with Africa's glorious past. . . . Woodson the historian, DuBois the sociologist, and now Boas the anthropologist and other scientists have all given documented testimonies of the Negro's glorious ancestral background. We must accept either their authentic appraisal or the unsupported opinion of the biased historian who condemns us to an inferior status.[86]

Neither these arguments about worth nor the scholars who advanced them were new,[87] but a mobilizing movement around civil rights with a national focus, the rhetorical influence of antifascism and anti-Nazism occasioned their revival and renewed recognition of Boas's work dating from at least the turn of the century.

Despite indications of what might have become deeper ideological schisms had Boas survived the expansion of domestic anti-Communism, his presence as a figure of enormous respect solidified in these early years of the war. This admiration seemed to transcend the principled and often consciously provocative positions that he held. Unlike during World War I, when he was marginalized as a figure representing controversial, unpatriotic, and progressive views, and in the interwar years, when he stood for them in honorific defeat, now his reputation, in the context of a different war, protected him. In 1939, on his eighty-first birthday, Boas was honored "for his leadership in organized efforts to make science serve humanity." He received individual messages from President Franklin Roosevelt, Secretary of Agriculture Henry A. Wallace, Secretary of the Interior Harold Ickes, and 136 other officials, scientists,

writers, and educators. Members of the ACDIF and the Council for Pan American Democracy, of which he was honorary chairman, sent him a "round robin letter," recognizing how, "in an hour of need, you have come forward to help the scientist take his rightful place among his fellow citizens in deciding what the future of our society will be—whether it will be aborted by the warmongering barbaric hordes or whether it will expand in peace for the benefit and happiness of all mankind."[88] In April 1940 he received "the annual award of the Teachers Union for 'outstanding services in the cause of education for democracy,'" given the year before to Eleanor Roosevelt.[89] The following year he was honored by the National Federation of Constitutional Liberties and the New York Conference for Inalienable Rights. In accepting the award, Boas said, "The greatest danger that threatens us is the lack of confidence in the mass of our people. A serene confidence in the loyalty of the people is a better protection in times of stress than unjustified suspicions and hysterical fear of a free expression of opinion."[90] Even though appeals to fighting barbarism increasingly characterized the war effort, Boas's remarks avoided the recourse to primitivism he had earlier seen as central to war fever and looked instead to democracy, free speech, and loyalty.

I have found no public statement by Boas on the U.S. entry into the war, no mention of Japan or of the ensuing war in Europe. Even taking into account his death a year after the United States entered the conflict, it is hard to know how to interpret that apparent silence. In July 1941 Boas joined with others in issuing a statement, signed by 130 "eminent in Science and the Arts," "calling for the 'utmost material assistance by our government to England, the Soviet Union and China.'" In this statement, as elsewhere, Boas connected the wartime crisis at home and abroad: "'There can be no victory over Hitlerism abroad,' said the statement, 'if democracy is destroyed at home. The protection of civil liberties and the rights of labor, the maintenance of adequate living standards, and the elimination of all forms of racial and religious discrimination from our public and private life—these are an integral part of the world-wide defense of human liberty.'"[91] These were all positions consistent with the popular front movements of which he had been a part. The coming war, then, provided opportunity and motivation for urging these ideals, even if he may have been ambivalent about war itself. In May 1942 he supported Vice President Henry Wallace's speech "The Price of Free World Victory" (retitled "The Century of the Common Man"), in which he gave rhetorical shape to the war as one between freedom and slavery. Boas was quoted in *PM* magazine on Wallace's "historic speech," describing the war as a "people's revolution."[92] Just before his death he

did speak against "colonization and exploitation . . . in the very widest sense," calling for international efforts to act in the interests of the "so-called primitive people" toward a "Commonwealth of Nations in which we all have equal rights."[93] Boas hoped no less clearly, but perhaps less optimistically, that the widening ethical circle of humanity could prevail. He also offered a tribute to Nebraska senator George Norris who, after a distinguished career on behalf of democratic rights, labor, civil rights, and other "unpopular" causes, was defeated in 1942. In expressing "sincere gratitude" for his service, Boas also was dismayed at the "timid citizens" who balked at his "independence of judgment."[94] Norris had cut his dissenting teeth in opposing U.S. entry into World War I, and Boas may well have felt a long-term affinity with him. Norris's defeat and Wallace's marginalization from the Roosevelt administration are also useful reminders that there were significant divisions even in the heated environment of antifascism and that Boas aligned himself with principled nonconformists.

The making of Boas as a public intellectual in wartime therefore drew on a charged context that fueled a particular kind of consciousness and heightened sense of social responsibility and possibility. If Boas's stature owed much to this context, which made his ideas, long in circulation, particularly salient, the history was a distinctive one, yoked to the crises of wars in the twentieth century. World War I had provided the initial occasion for these encounters of Boas's anthropology and public attention. It had provided the opportunity for disseminating his message on race and nationalism and for acting as an informed citizen and responsible scientist. Then the results had been more divisive, ambiguous at best, providing an example of dissent and its risks. The interwar years continued this path of a good fight for progressive causes more than matched by reactionary postwar populism. Boas's reputation continued to be defined defiantly, in relation to those who opposed him. It is tempting therefore to read the story of World War II only as triumph, even heroism. This is the story that Boas's many honors and awards tell, and it is not unjustified. Boas evidenced rare consistency and principled determination in the face of public rebuke, painful loss, and ideological intimidation. Nonetheless changing context and the mobilization of others gave Boas a responsive audience whom he doggedly pursued. His public stature and his legacy come from the intersection of his individual agenda with this historical moment.

The fortuitous timing ended midcourse, as it were, with Boas's death in 1942, but even then the rifts were apparent. One still wonders what Boas would have made of the destruction of Europe and the war in the

Pacific, including the atomic bombs, of the rapid and lasting deployment of the language of freedom in the service of the cold war, of the continuing role of scientists in that struggle, and of the decolonization movements that followed the war. It is difficult to reconcile the almost hagiographic praise heaped on Boas at the end of his life with his unpopular and even politically dangerous positions on each one of these issues. The FBI had him within their net of suspicion, and it is hard to imagine that the deference to him would have endured after the war. Similarly praise should not blind one to Boas's ongoing role as a lightning rod for reactionaries and racists for whom his egalitarianism is a threat and rallying point.[95] Part of Boas's "success" is that he generated this backlash, but it should also remind one of the perceived danger of his views and the enduring resistance to them. If the celebration of Boas's accomplishments erases that threat, it also disguises the dark underside of the realities of equality and freedom in the United States, values that have been both mobilized and jeopardized by a society at war.

Acknowledgments

I am very grateful to the U.S. Fulbright Commission for a senior lectureship at the University of Bologna in 2010 that enabled me to begin work on this essay.

Notes

1. Barkan, "Mobilizing Scientists against Nazi Racism" and *The Retreat of Scientific Racism*; Hyatt, *Franz Boas, Social Activist*; Stocking, "Anthropology as Kulturkampf"; González, *Anthropologists in the Public Sphere*; Raibmon, *Authentic Indians*; Darnell, "Franz Boas: Scientist and Public Intellectual"; Baker, *Anthropology and the Racial Politics of Culture*; Gilkeson, *Anthropologists and the Rediscovery of America*; Whitfield, "Franz Boas: The Anthropologist as Public Intellectual."
2. But see Stocking, "Anthropology as Kulturkampf"; Liss, "Diasporic Identities"; Weiler, "Thus Spoke the Scientist."
3. See also the following by Boas: "Freedom of Thought," "Patriotism," "Solidarity," and "The International State."
4. Boas, *An Anthropologist's View of War*, 5–6, 8, 10.
5. Boas, *Race and Nationality*, 3, 4, 5–6; Boas, "The Race-War Myth."
6. To some extent this appears to be a very local story, centered in metropolitan, particularly New York, circles. When Boas ventured farther, however, news coverage followed him, and his remarks also adapted to local circumstances. During a summer stay at the University of California in 1914, for instance, the *Los Angeles Times*, *San Francisco Chronicle*, and *New York Times* all reported on his lectures on race equality and, more shocking, his

acceptance of "intermarriage" and "mixing races," including Americans and Japanese, "whites and Hindus and other oriental races," or among "half-breeds" in Mexico. "No Race Is Inferior, Says World Authority," *Los Angeles Times*, June 26, 1914, 11; "Racial Intermarriage Right, Says Lecturer," *San Francisco Chronicle*, June 26, 1914, 1; "Favors Mixing Races," *New York Times*, June 27, 1914, 1.

7. Weiler, "Thus Spoke the Scientist."
8. Franz Boas, "Why German-Americans Blame America," *New York Times*, January 8, 1916, 8.
9. See "An Anthropologist on German-Americans," *New York Times*, January 10, 1916, 10; Pauline Provine Clinton, "In Reply to Prof. Boas," *New York Times*, January 16, 1916, 16.
10. Boas, "Why German-Americans Blame America."
11. Boas, "As an American of German Birth"; Boas, "Why German-Americans Blame America."
12. Boas, "Why German-Americans Blame America."
13. Schurz, "American Imperialism," 3–15; Kramer, *Blood of Government*.
14. "Hail Centenary of Schurz Today," *New York Times*, March 2, 1929, 20; "Schurz Relatives Fight Nazi Link," *New York Times*, January 21, 1935, 7.
15. Raibmon, *Authentic Indians*; Cotera, *Native Speakers*.
16. See the following by Boas: "Colonies and the Peace Conference"; "In the Occupied Area," *New York Times*, October 20, 1923, 14; "Rights of Invaded Regions," *New York Times*, November 4, 1923, section 9, p. 8; "An Anthropologist's Credo"; and "Exploitation Must Cease." .
17. Boas, "Nationalism," 232, 236, 237.
18. Boas, "Colonies and the Peace Conference," 247–49.
19. Liss, "Diasporic Identities"; Hegeman, *Patterns for America*, 15–31; Silverstein, "Boasian Cosmographic Anthropology."
20. Silverstein, "Boasian Cosmographic Anthropology"; Yans-McLaughlin, "Science, Democracy, and Ethics."
21. Baker, *From Savage to Negro*; Selig, *Americans All*; Gilkeson, *Anthropologists and the Rediscovery of America*.
22. Higham, *Strangers in the Land*.
23. Franz Boas, "Lo, the Poor Nordic," *New York Times*, April 13, 1924, 19; Boas, "The Question of Racial Purity"; Boas, "This Nordic Nonsense"; Dorr, "Arm in Arm."
24. Kuznick, *Beyond the Laboratory*, 178–79, 182–84; Evans, *Anthropology at War*, 107, 192–93; Evans, "The Klan's Fight for Americanism"; MacLean, *Behind the Mask of Chivalry*.
25. Stocking, "The Critique of Racial Formalism."
26. Ngai, *Impossible Subjects*, 21–55.
27. Jacobson, *Whiteness of a Different Color*; Ngai, *Impossible Subjects*.
28. Baritz, *The Culture of the Twenties*, 175.
29. Larson, *Summer for the Gods*.

30. Higham, *Strangers in the Land*; Hegeman, *Patterns for America*; Selig, *Americans All*.
31. Higham, *Strangers in the Land*; Hutchinson, *The Harlem Renaissance in Black and White*.
32. Baker, *Anthropology and the Racial Politics of Culture*, 156–219. A Google search for "Boas Buck v. Bell," for instance, calls up David Duke's website: http://www.davidduke.com/general/whatever-happened-to-eugenics_29.html (accessed June 12, 2011). Another good example of what Baker means by the "Boas conspiracy," but one that adds red-baiting, is Bullert, "Franz Boas as Citizen-Scientist."
33. Kuznick, *Beyond the Laboratory*; Barkan, "Mobilizing Scientists against Nazi Racism" and *The Retreat of Scientific Racism*; Hollinger, *Science, Jews, and Secular Culture*, 81; Gormley, "Scientific Discrimination and the Activist Scientist."
34. "Science World Centers in Southland Today," *Los Angeles Times*, June 16, 1931, A1.
35. "War and Prejudices Called Ill for Man," *New York Times*, June 16, 1931, 5; "Racial Difference," *New York Times*, June 21, 1931, 120.
36. "The findings were of sensational importance because they showed that the physical characteristics of a 'race' change under the influence of environment." Walter Dornfeldt had done new research with the same findings regarding Jews from the East in Berlin: "It is remarkable that a study such as this could have been made at all under Hitler." "The Evolving American," *New York Times*, January 22, 1934, 14. See also "Changes in Heads," *New York Times*, October 11, 1942, E9.
37. Boas, "Lo, the Poor Nordic"; Boas, "Nordic Propaganda."
38. Boas, "Aryans and Non-Aryans," 219, 220, 221. This essay was first published, in German, in 1933 and reprinted from 1934 to 1939 in German, English, and Spanish.
39. Wright, "The Political Awakening of American Science," 615.
40. Yans-McLaughlin, "Science, Democracy, and Ethics."
41. Franz Boas, "Nietzsche on Armament," *New York Times*, April 13, 1930, 57.
42. "Anti-War Group Formed," *New York Times*, July 15, 1932, 13.
43. "As Others See Her," *New York Times*, May 14, 1933, E4.
44. "Plan Appeal to Butler," *New York Times*, March 28, 1936, 17.
45. Boas, "Aryans and Non-Aryans," 221, 223. See also Boas, "Race Prejudice from the Scientist's Angle."
46. Boas, "Are the Jews a Race?"; Liss, "Franz Boas and the Problem of Jewishness"; Glick, "Types Distinct from Our Own."
47. Boas, "Aryans and Non-Aryans," 223.
48. Boas, "The Individual Counts," 25; Boas, "Race and Race Prejudice."
49. "Dr. Boas, 78, Quits in a 'Sick' World," *New York Times*, July 1, 1936, 26. See also Franz Boas, "Quotation Marks: The Race Question," *New York Times*, July 5, 1936, E8.

50. Barkan, "Mobilizing Scientists against Nazi Racism" and *The Retreat of Scientific Racism*; Kuznick, *Beyond the Laboratory*; Gormley, "Scientific Discrimination and the Activist Scientist."
51. "Professional Group Appeals for Thomas," *New York Times*, October 22, 1936, 12; Boas, "Boas Says He'll Vote for FDR, Because . . ."; Franz Boas, "The Popular Vote in Spain," *New York Times*, October 11, 1937, 20; "Open Letter," *New York Times*, October 4, 1937, 12; "Statement on Joining the New York College Teachers Union"; "Teachers Must Be Free to Educate Youth"; "The Responsibility of the Schools"; "Statement on Education"; "Race and Progress"; "An Anthropologist's Credo"; "The Myth of Race"; "Intellectual Freedom in Nazi Germany"; "Cultural Freedom Sought," *New York Times*, May 17, 1939, 22; "Intellectual Freedom"; "Role of Science in Democratic Society." Boas's participation on behalf of Spanish Loyalists was ongoing, seeing the war as an international conflict about fascism, one that jeopardized democracy and scientific truth. He presided over a meeting of the Columbia University Faculty Committee for Aid to the Spanish People (*New York Times*, October 21, 1937, 4) and participated in a call to lift the embargo against Spain, an interesting turning point on the question of whether and how to intervene (*New York Times*, May 6, 1938, 1, January 1, 1939, 11). A statement of the Spanish catastrophe in the *Daily Worker* provided one of his rare explicit endorsements of socialism (March 30, 1938, 4).
52. Boas, "The Mental Attitude of the Educated Classes."
53. The first use of the term *racism* was in 1932 in the *Christian Science Monitor*, which said, "It is altogether inaccurate to suggest that Europe is being indoctrinated with Fascism or Racism." This denial is strikingly ironic next to the larger sense of the link between Nazi fascism in particular with antiracist politics. By the end of the decade Boas's student Ruth Benedict was credited with writing in *Race: Science and Politics* in 1940, "Racism is an *ism* to which everyone in the world today is exposed." "Racism, n.," *Oxford English Dictionary*, 3rd ed., June 2008; online version March 2011, http://www.oed.com:80/Entry/15097 (accessed June 9, 2011).
54. Boas, "Racial Purity," 28. See also Boas, "Class Consciousness and Race Prejudice," 15.
55. Boas, "Race and Race Prejudice," 227.
56. Boas, "Role of Science in Democratic Society," 215.
57. Boas, "International Broadcast," 1–2.
58. Ernest Harms, "Franz Boas and the Aims of the Science of Man," *New York Times Book Review*, April 27, 1941, 22.
59. Ernst Boas, foreword to Boas, *Race and Democratic Society*, i.
60. Boas, "An Anthropologist's Credo," 201–4.
61. "'Nordic Science'," *New York Times*, May 29, 1938, 42.
62. In "Pragmatic and Dogmatic Physics," Aharon Loewenstein says that there was only one letter published in *Nature*. He mistakenly attributes the *New York Times* editorial to Boas, although this cannot be the case because

Boas wrote his own letter to the editor of the *Times in response to the editorial:* "Races in Science," *New York Times*, June 12, 1938, 71.

63. Boas, "Races in Science," *New York Times*, June 12, 1938, 71.
64. "Science Strikes Back," *New York Times*, December 11, 1938, 92.
65. "Nazi's Conception of Science Scored," *New York Times*, December 11, 1938, 50.
66. "Scientists to Open Drive for Freedom," *New York Times*, January 24, 1939, 21.
67. "Science as a Social Force," *New York Times*, January 1, 1939, 100; "The Fair Today," *New York Times*, October 14, 1939, 11. See also Kuznick, "Losing the World of Tomorrow."
68. "Some Threats to Liberty," *New York Times*, May 10, 1939, 22.
69. "Minute Men of Science," *New York Times*, February 12, 1939, 80.
70. Price, *Threatening Anthropology*.
71. "Warning Sounded on 'Witch-Hunting,'" *New York Times*, December 14, 1939, 18.
72. Boas, "Opinion Not Subject to Inquiry," 156–57.
73. "Noted Anthropologist Likens Fascists to Barbarians, Cold-Blooded' Killers," *Daily Worker*, March 30, 1938, 4.
74. "New Group Fights Any Freedom Curb," *New York Times*, May 15, 1939, 13.
75. Krook, "Clio's Fancy"; Price, *Threatening Anthropology*, 142; U.S. Federal Bureau of Investigation, Robert S. Lynd file and Franz Boas file.
76. Roeder, *The Censored War*; Burkholder, "From 'Wops and Dagoes and Hunkies' to 'Caucasian.'"
77. Boas, "Statement on Education"; "Declares School Books Teach False Race Views," *Chicago Defender*, July 29, 1939, 3; "School Control Assailed by Boas," *New York Times*, August 22, 1939, 13; "Fighting Race Prejudice," *New York Times*, October 8, 1939, 10; Selig, *Americans All*; Burkholder, "From 'Wops and Dagoes and Hunkies' to 'Caucasian.'"
78. Boas, "Statement on Joining the New York College Teachers Union"; "Boas Joins Union Led by Reds," *New York Times*, December 31, 1938, 17.
79. "Rally Will Protest Blows to Education," *New York Times*, April 7, 1940, 42.
80. "Dies to Fight Reds to Highest Court," *New York Times*, April 11, 1940, 24. See also Boas, foreword to *The Winter Soldiers*.
81. Hall, "The Long Civil Rights Movement"; Burkholder, "From 'Wops and Dagoes and Hunkies' to 'Caucasian,'" 330–31.
82. "Expect 50,000 to Hear Marian Anderson," *Chicago Defender*, April 8, 1939, 1.
83. "Honorary Degrees," *Chicago Defender*, July 3, 1937, 4.
84. "Franz Boas Blasts Pure Race Notion," *Chicago Defender*, April 16, 1938, 240.
85. "White Anthropologist Decries Race Prejudice, Pleads for Equal Rights," *Chicago Defender*, August, 2, 1941, 4; the original version is Boas, "The Myth of Race." Also see Boas, foreword to *The Winter Soldiers*.
86. "The Inferiority Myth," *Chicago Defender*, August 23, 1941, 14.

87. Liss, "Diasporic Identities."
88. "Tribute to Boas, 81, Led by President," *New York Times* July 10, 1939, 14.
89. "Dr. Boas Receives Teachers' Award," *New York Times*, April 21, 1940, 12.
90. "Dr. Boas Honored as Friend of Liberty," *New York Times*, March 13, 1941, 8.
91. "Full War Aid Urged," *New York Times*, July 28, 1941, 6. See also "Gravity Marks Labor Messages," *New York Times*, September 1, 1941, 32; "Russia's 'Scorched Earth' Calls to America's Green Fields!," *New York Times*, October 10, 1941, 15 (Boas was among "eminent Americans [who] ask your help on behalf of the Russian people").
92. "Franz Boas Note on Wallace's Speech on War Aims," *P.M.*, May 12, 1942, 12.
93. Boas, "Exploitation Must Cease."
94. "A Tribute from Franz Boas, Noted Anthropologist," *P.M.*, November 9, 1942, 24.
95. Baker, *Anthropology and the Racial Politics of Culture*, 156–219.

References

MANUSCRIPTS AND ARCHIVES

U.S. Federal Bureau of Investigation. Franz Boas file. Boas Family Papers, American Philosophical Society, Series II. Box 1.
———. Robert S. Lynd file. Parts 3, 5, and 7. Retrieved from vault.fbi.gov.

PUBLISHED WORKS

Baker, Lee D. *Anthropology and the Racial Politics of Culture*. Durham NC: Duke University Press, 2010.
———. *From Savage to Negro: Anthropology and the Construction of Race, 1896–1954*. Berkeley: University of California Press, 1998.
Baritz, Loren, ed. *The Culture of the Twenties*. Indianapolis: Bobbs Merrill Educational, 1970.
Barkan, Elazar. "Mobilizing Scientists against Nazi Racism, 1933–1939." In George W. Stocking, Jr., ed., *History of Anthropology*. Vol. 5: *Bones, Bodies, Behavior: Essays on Biological Anthropology*, 180–205. Madison: University of Wisconsin Press, 1988.
———. *The Retreat of Scientific Racism*. Cambridge, UK: Cambridge University Press, 1992.
Boas, Franz. "An Anthropologist's Credo." *Nation* 147 (August 27, 1938): 201–4.
———. *An Anthropologist's View of War*. New York: American Association for International Conciliation, 1912.
———. *Anthropology and Modern Life*. New York: Norton, 1928.
———. "Are the Jews a Race?" *World Tomorrow* 6 (1923): 5–6.
———. "Aryans and Non-Aryans." *American Mercury* 32 (1934): 219–23.

———. "As an American of German Birth . . . I Protest." *Viereck's* 10 (1919): 185.

———. *Changes in Bodily Form of Descendants of Immigrants*. New York: Columbia University Press, 1912.

———. "Class Consciousness and Race Prejudice." 1943. In *Race and Democratic Society*, 15–19. New York: J. J. Augustin, 1945.

———. "Colonies and the Peace Conference." *Nation* 108 (February 15, 1919): 247–49.

———. "The Death of Freedom." *Independent Journal of Columbia University* 5 (1938): 1, 4.

———. "Democracy and Intellectual Freedom." *American Teacher* 23 (1939): 9–10.

———. "Exploitation Must Cease." *P.M.*, January 25, 1943, 5.

———. Foreword. *The Winter Soldiers*. New York: Teachers Union, 1941.

———. "Freedom of Thought." 1917. In *Race and Democratic Society*, 178–84. New York: J. J. Augustin, 1945.

———. "The Individual Counts." *Nation* 143 (July 4, 1936): 25.

———. "Intellectual Freedom." *New Masses* 30 (1939): 17.

———. "Intellectual Freedom in Nazi Germany." *Anti-Nazi Bulletin* 5 (1938): 7.

———. International Broadcast over National Broadcasting Company Networks." September 27, 1941, International Conference on Science and the World Order of the British Association for the Advancement of Science. In *Race and Democratic Society*, 1–2 New York: J. J. Augustin, 1945.

———. "The International State." 1919. In *Race and Democratic Society*, 141–52. New York: J. J. Augustin, 1945. (Originally "Democracy and Electoral Reform")

———. "Inventing a Great Race: Review of Madison Grant's *The Passing of the Great Race*." *New Republic* 9 (January 13, 1917): 305–7.

———. "The Mental Attitude of the Educated Classes." *Dial* 65 (September 5, 1918): 145–48.

———. *The Mind of Primitive Man*. New York: Macmillan, 1911.

———. "The Myth of Race." *New Masses* 40 (1941): 6.

———. "The Myth of Racial Excellence." *German American* 1 (1942): 3.

———. "Nationalism." *Dial*, March 8, 1919, 232–37.

———. "Nordic Propaganda." Review of Madison Grant's *Conquest of a Continent*. *New Republic* 78 (March 7, 1934): 107–8.

———. "Opinion Not Subject to Inquiry." *Forum and Century* 8 (March 1940): 156–57.

———. "Patriotism." 1917. In *Race and Democratic Society*, 156–59. New York: J. J. Augustin, 1945. (Originally "Preserving Our Ideals")

———. "The Question of Racial Purity." *American Mercury* 3 (1924): 163–78.

———. *Race and Democratic Society*. Ed. Ernst Boas. New York: J. J. Augustin, 1945.

———. *Race and Nationality*. New York: Special Bulletin of the American Association for International Conciliation, January, 1915.

———. "Race and Progress." *Science* 74 (July 3, 1931): 1–8.
———. "Race and Race Prejudice." *Jewish Social Service Quarterly* 14 (1937): 227–32.
———. *Race, Language and Culture*. New York: Macmillan, 1940.
———. "Race Prejudice from the Scientist's Angle." *Forum and Century* 98 (August 1937): 90–94.
———. "The Race-War Myth." *Everybody's Magazine* 31 (1914): 671–74.
———. "Racial Purity." 1940. In *Race and Democratic Society*, 28–37. New York: J. J. Augustin, 1945.
———. "The Responsibility of the Schools." *American Teacher* 24 (1940): 11.
———. Review of Grant's *The Passing of the Great Race*. *American Journal of Physical Anthropology* 1 (1918): 363.
———. "Role of Science in Democratic Society." 1939. In *Race and Democratic Society*, 215–19. New York: J. J. Augustin, 1945.
———. "Science in Nazi Germany." *Survey Graphic* 26 (August 1937): 415–17.
———. "Scientists as Spies." *Nation* 109 (December 20, 1919): 797.
———. "Solidarity." 1917. In *Race and Democratic Society*, 125–32. New York: J. J. Augustin, 1945. (Originally "The Primitive Mind and the Present Hour")
———. "Statement on Education: The Very Foundations of a Healthy Democracy Are Threatened Today." *Friday* 1 (1940): 17–18.
———. "Statement on Joining the New York College Teachers Union." *American Teacher* 23 (1939), front cover.
———. "Boas Says He'll Vote for FDR, Because . . ." *PM*, October 25, 1940, 8.
———. "Teachers Must Be Free to Educate Youth." *American Teacher* 24 (1939): 12.
———. "This Nordic Nonsense." *Forum* 74 (July 1925): 502–11.
———. "What Is behind Race Theories?" *Modern Thinker*, August 1934, 121.
Bullert, Gary. "Franz Boas as Citizen-Scientist: Gramscian-Marxist Influence on American Anthropology." *Journal of Social, Political and Economic Studies* 34 (Summer 2009): 208–43.
Burkholder, Zoë "From 'Wops and Dagoes and Hunkies' to 'Caucasian': Changing Racial Discourse in American Classrooms during World War II." *History of Education Quarterly* 50 (August 2010): 324–58.
Cotera, Maria Eugenia. *Native Speakers: Ella Deloria, Zora Neale Hurston, Jovita Gonzalez and the Poetics of Culture*. Austin: University of Texas Press, 2005.
Darnell, Regna. "Franz Boas: Scientist and Public Intellectual." In Jill B. R. Cherneff and Eve Hochwald, eds., *Visionary Observers: Anthropological Inquiry and Education*, 3–23. Lincoln: University of Nebraska Press, 2006.
Dorr, Lisa Lindquist. "Arm in Arm: Gender, Eugenics, and Virginia's Racial Integrity Acts of the 1920s." *Journal of Women's History* 11 (Spring 1999): 143–66.
Evans, Andrew D. *Anthropology at War: World War I and the Science of Race in Germany*. Chicago: University of Chicago Press, 2010.
Evans, Hiram Wesley. "The Klan's Fight for Americanism." *North American Review* 123 (March–May 1926): 33–63.

Gilkeson, John S. *Anthropologists and the Rediscovery of America, 1886–1965.* Cambridge, UK: Cambridge University Press, 2010.

Glick, Leonard B. "Types Distinct from Our Own: Franz Boas on Jewish Identity and Assimilation." *American Anthropologist* 84 (September 1982): 545–65.

González, Roberto J. *Anthropologists in the Public Sphere: Speaking Out on War, Peace, and American Power.* Austin: University of Texas Press, 2004.

Gormley, Melinda. "Scientific Discrimination and the Activist Scientist: L. C. Dunn and the Professionalization of Genetics and Human Genetics in the United States." *Journal of the History of Biology* 42 (Spring 2009): 33–72.

Hall, Jacquelyn Dowd. "The Long Civil Rights Movement and the Political Uses of the Past." *Journal of American History* 91 (March 2005): 1233–63.

Hegeman, Susan. *Patterns for America: Modernism and the Concept of Culture.* Princeton NJ: Princeton University Press, 1999.

Higham, John. *Strangers in the Land: Patterns of American Nativism, 1860–1925.* 2nd ed. New Brunswick NJ: Rutgers University Press, 1988.

Hollinger, David A. *Science, Jews, and Secular Culture: Studies in Mid-Twentieth Century American Intellectual History.* Princeton NJ: Princeton University Press, 1996.

Hutchinson, George. *The Harlem Renaissance in Black and White.* Cambridge MA: Harvard University Press, 1996.

Hyatt, Marshall. *Franz Boas, Social Activist: The Dynamics of Ethnicity.* Westport CT: Greenwood Press, 1990.

Jacobson, Matthew Frye. *Whiteness of a Different Color: European Immigrants and the Alchemy of Race.* Cambridge MA: Harvard University Press, 1999.

Kramer, Paul A. *Blood of Government: Race, Empire, and the United States Government in the Philippines.* Chapel Hill: University of North Carolina Press, 2000.

Krook, Susan. "Clio's Fancy: Documents to Pique the Historical Imagination: Franz Boas (a.k.a. Boaz) and the F.B.I." *History of Anthropology Newsletter* 16.2 (1989): 4–11.

Kuznick, Peter J. *Beyond the Laboratory: Scientists as Political Activists in 1930s America.* Chicago: University of Chicago Press, 1987.

———. "Losing the World of Tomorrow: The Battle over the Presentation of Science at the 1939 New York World's Fair." *American Quarterly* 46 (September 1994): 341–73.

Larson, Edward J. *Summer for the Gods: The Scopes Trial and America's Continuing Debate over Science and Religion.* New York: Basic Books, 2006.

Liss, Julia E. "Diasporic Identities: The Science and Politics of Race in the Work of Franz Boas and W. E. B. Du Bois, 1894–1919." *Cultural Anthropology* 13 (May 1998): 127–66.

———. "Franz Boas and the Problem of Jewishness." Unpublished manuscript, n.d.

Loewenstein, Aharon. "Pragmatic and Dogmatic Physics: Anti-Semitism in *Nature*, 1938." http://www.technion.ac.il/technion/chemistry/staff/loewenstein/nature.pdf.

MacLean, Nancy. *Behind the Mask of Chivalry: The Making of the Second Ku Klux Klan*. New York: Oxford University Press, 1994.

Ngai, Mai M. *Impossible Subjects: Illegal Aliens and the Making of Modern America*. Princeton NJ: Princeton University Press, 2004.

Price, David H. *Threatening Anthropology: McCarthyism and the FBI's Surveillance of Activist Anthropologists.* Durham NC: Duke University Press, 2004.

Raibmon, Paige. *Authentic Indians: Episodes of Encounter from the Late-Nineteenth Century Northwest Coast*. Durham NC: Duke University Press, 2005.

Roeder, George H. *The Censored War: American Visual Experience During World War II*. New Haven CT: Yale University Press, 1993.

Schurz, Carl. "American Imperialism." Address delivered at the Twenty-seventh Convocation of the University of Chicago. January 4, 1899.

Selig, Diana. *Americans All: The Cultural Gifts Movement*. Cambridge MA: Harvard University Press, 2008.

Silverstein, Michael. "Boasian Cosmographic Anthropology and the Sociocentric Component of Mind." In Richard Handler, ed., *History of Anthropology*. Vol. 10: *Significant Others: Interpersonal and Professional Commitments in Anthropology*, 131–57. Madison: University of Wisconsin Press, 2004.

Stocking, George W., Jr. "Anthropology as Kulturkampf: Science and Politics in the Career of Franz Boas." 1979. In *The Ethnographer's Magic and Other Essays in the History of Anthropology*, 92–113. Madison: University of Wisconsin Press, 1992.

———. "The Critique of Racial Formalism." 1968. In *Race, Culture, and Evolution*, 161–94. Chicago: University of Chicago Press, 1982.

U.S. v. Cartozian. 6 F 2d 919 (District Court, D. Oregon 1925). U.S. Dist. LEXIS 1183.

Weiler, Bernd. "Thus Spoke the Scientist: Franz Boas' Critique of the Role of the United States in World War I." In Sven Eliaeson and Ragnvald Kalleberg, eds., *Academics as Public Intellectuals*, 65–86. Newcastle, UK: Cambridge Scholars, 2008. http://scholar.google.com/scholar?cluster=8222893292647038016&hl=en&as_sdt=0,5.

Whitfield, Stephen J. "Franz Boas: The Anthropologist as Public Intellectual." *Society* 47 (September 2010): 430–38.

Wright, David E. "The Political Awakening of American Science." *Reviews in American History* 16 (December 1988): 612–16.

Yans-McLaughlin, Virginia. "Science, Democracy, and Ethics: Mobilizing Culture and Personality for World War II." In George W. Stocking Jr., ed., *History of Anthropology*, 4: 184–217. Madison: University of Wisconsin Press, 1986.

PART 4 The Archival Project

14 Anthropology of Revitalization

Digitizing the American Philosophical Society's Native American Collections

TIMOTHY B. POWELL

The role of archives in the history of anthropology is usually seen as somewhat passive, the final resting place for the papers of preeminent scholars. The American Philosophical Society (APS) houses one of the finest collections of linguistic and anthropological collections of Native American, Native Alaskan, and First Nations (hereafter referred to as Indigenous) cultures in the world. And while there is a certain sepulchral stillness to a collection that dates back more than two centuries, the APS has recently initiated a highly dynamic new phase of its long and distinguished history by working in close partnerships with anthropologists and Indigenous communities of origin on a new initiative called "digital knowledge sharing." This singularly successful program has generated more than $1.3 million in grant funding and produced a series of remarkable outcomes that include working to revitalize languages, to save ancestral homelands, and to protect culturally sensitive materials. The APS is currently raising the endowment for a new Center for Native American and Indigenous Research (CNAIR) so that this important work can continue into the future. CNAIR's partnership with scholars working on the Franz Boas Papers Documentary Edition (FBP) and those Indigenous communities where the archival documents originated is an exemplary instance of how digital knowledge sharing can play a dynamic role in what I call the "anthropology of revitalization."

The Franz Boas materials at the APS have remarkable transformative powers. In this essay, I begin by recounting how in 1945 the accessioning of Boas's work revitalized the APS's collecting of Indigenous cultures, which had been moribund for a century. The second section documents how the digitization of several generations of Boas's intellectual heirs, specifically materials from the papers of Frank Speck and A. I. Hallowell, have been used by Passamaquoddy and Anishinaabe communities to reawaken their traditional culture. The essay concludes with a glance forward at the plans for how the digitization of Boas materials at the

APS, in collaboration with scholars working on the FBP project, is beginning to revitalize some of the Kwakw<u>aka</u>'wakw communities where Boas himself worked more than a century ago.

Situating Boas in the History of the American Philosophical Society

Although the history of the Native American collections at the APS is an oft-told tale, it is worth reviewing quickly in order to document the impact that the Boas collections have had on its long and distinguished history of collecting Native American cultures. The Society's commitment to attaining Native American and First Nations materials dates back to when Thomas Jefferson served as president of the APS, 1797–1815, overseeing the collecting of vocabulary lists of Indigenous languages—a tradition that is very much alive to this day. In 1815 Jefferson helped establish the Historical and Literary Committee, "one of the most active committees in the Society's history."[1] Jefferson's vision was carried on by Peter Stephen du Ponceau, who served as the first secretary of the Historical and Literary Committee and later president of the APS (1827–1844). Jefferson and du Ponceau laid the foundation for the Society's development into one of the premier centers for the study of Native American languages, publishing more than a hundred papers in the field between 1840 and 1900. As Regna Darnell notes, before the professionalization of anthropology in the late nineteenth century, "the American Philosophical Society . . . served as the central institution for the collection of data about the American Indian."[2]

After du Ponceau stepped down as APS president in 1844, the collection of Indigenous materials went moribund for one hundred years. A renewed commitment to the preservation of the Indigenous languages was galvanized by the acquisition of the American Council of Learned Societies Committee on Native American Languages (ACLS) in 1945. The ACLS was formed in 1927 under the initiative of Boas, Edward Sapir, and other academic linguists and contains Boas's field notes along with a wealth of material solicited by and sent to Boas from fieldworkers and Indigenous "informants." The ACLS collection, in a very real sense, represents Boas's vision for American anthropology and profoundly shaped APS's collection policy for Indigenous materials following World War II. The collection was so valuable that even before the gift was formally made a special committee was convened to oversee the care and arrangement of the collection. During the summer of 1943 Zellig S. Harris and C. F. Voegelin, two of the leading linguists of the time, created an inventory. The following year Harris was named library research associate, with the special assignment of arranging the collection. When the ACLS

collection, which Harris refers to as "the Boas Collection," was accessioned, Harris wrote in "American Indian Linguistic Work and the Boas Collection," "The Boas Collection of manuscripts in American Indian Linguistics, which was acquired this year by the American Philosophical Society, represents one of the most valuable collections of unpublished materials in this field."[3]

Boas's vision, as represented by the ACLS collection and the acquisition of his papers in 1961, has had a profound impact on the APS that continues to the present day. In 1948 Harry Miller Lyndberg wrote an article in the *Proceedings of the American Philosophical Society* that described the flood of new materials donated to the library as a result of Boas's work in the ACLS collections:

> In December 1946 Miss Ruth Benedict presented her study of Chehalis folklore. Papers from Edward Sapir were given by Dr. Morris Swadesh. More than a hundred notebooks were turned over by Dr. A. L. Kroeber, gatherings made in the field by Dr. [Pliny E.] Goddard, studying the Athabaskan Indians of Canada under Dr. Boas. . . . In February 1947 Miss Muriel Rukeyser made a preliminary study of the Boas papers in connection with her biography of Dr. Boas. . . . Since the acquisition of the Boas Papers, the number of other sources has amounted to fully a hundred and fifty.[4]

Whereas Boas's own research focused predominantly on the Northwest Coast of North America, subsequent acquisitions provided geographic and cultural balance to the APS collections. Voeglin, who succeeded Harris as special library research associate, supervised W. D. Preston's gathering of materials among the Shawnee Indians. Jane E. Willets's collection of Ottawa manuscripts and audio recordings came into the APS in 1950. Harris in turn undertook a linguistic study of the Eastern band of the Cherokee to strengthen the Society's holdings in Iroquoian languages.

The impact of Boas's vision would continue throughout the rest of the twentieth century as three generations of Boas's students donated their papers to the library, creating one of the finest anthropological collections of Native American, Native Alaskan, and First Nations cultures in the world. The first generation, who studied with Boas, is represented by the papers of Frank Speck, Elsie Clews Parsons, Paul Radin, Ella Deloria, and Edward Sapir, among others. Their students, the second generation of the Boas legacy, are represented by Voegelin (trained by Alfred Kroeber and Robert Lowie), Harvey Pitkin (Kroeber), Mary Haas (Sapir), John Alden Mason (Sapir), Morris Swadesh (Sapir), A. Irving Hallowell

(Speck), and Anthony F. C. Wallace (Speck). The third generation includes Floyd Lounsbury (Swadesh) and Dell Hymes (Voegelin).[5] The process of acquiring the ACLS collection also profoundly influenced other parts of the APS. In 1944, the year before the ACLS came to the APS, the Committee on the Library made a decision to rededicate a large donation, given by Henry Phillips Jr. in 1892, to fund "the study of, and the gathering of source material on, the speech of native peoples of the Americas."[6] Today the Phillips fund committee, headed by Regna Darnell, continues to distribute grants in support of linguistic and ethnohistorical research and is the single most productive method of adding to the collections, given that recipients are asked to donate work done under the auspices of the grant to the APS.

Today the Boas and ACLS collections span more than 172 linear feet. Taken together these are the most important and most widely used collections of Native American materials at the APS. Obviously to undertake a documentary editing project for the Boas Papers is a formidable task that will take generations of scholars to complete. We are very fortunate to have Darnell, one of the most distinguished historians of anthropology and an APS member, to head a project that will undoubtedly continue to impact the work of the APS for decades to come. In light of this historical overview, the question at hand is how the digitization of the Boas Papers at the American Philosophical Society might create a second revitalization movement wherein the archival documents are returned, in digital form, to communities like the Kwakwaka'wakw First Nations, where Boas and George Hunt collected an enormous amount of material just before Potlatch ceremonies were banned and the residential school system drastically reduced the number of fluent speakers.

Digitization and Revitalization at the American Philosophical Society

Beginning in 2007 the APS launched a major new initiative to move its storied Native American collections forward into the digital age. That year the Society received a Getty Foundation grant to gain intellectual control of the more than 100,000 images of Indigenous cultures in its library. More than one thousand images were digitized in the process. The creation of this digital archive fostered stronger ties to Indigenous communities. As part of the Getty project, the APS created a Native American advisory board to ensure that no culturally sensitive images would inadvertently be placed on the website. This recognition of Native peoples as partners in the stewardship of the APS collection constituted a historical turn, on which the APS has continued to build.

In 2008, for example, the APS received a grant from the Andrew W.

Mellon Foundation to digitize more than a thousand hours of linguistic material, songs, stories, and oral histories. The word *digitize* is used loosely here. Some of the obsolete forms—wax cylinders, wire recordings, aluminum disks, and so on—had already been digitally transferred to recordable digital audiotape, but because this form of digital technology still involves a tape moving over a head, it is subject to deterioration. The first APS Mellon grant was, then, primarily for preservation purposes. The grant funded a conference at the APS in May 2010 entitled Building Bridges between Archives and Indian Communities. This gathering represents the first time in the APS's long and distinguished history that Native Americans were invited to study and advise on the collections that originated from their communities. Representatives from thirteen bands, tribes, and First Nations attended: Eastern Shawnee tribe of Oklahoma, Eastern Band of Cherokee Indians, Cherokee Nation, Penobscot Nation, Passamaquoddy tribe, Pueblo of Isleta, the Confederated Tribes of Grand Ronde, Abenaki tribe, Leech Lake band of Ojibwe, Akwesasne Mohawk Nation, Sandy Bay First Nation, Poplar River First Nation, and Nanticoke Lenni Lenape. Distinguished anthropologists such as Darnell and Ives Goddard attended, along with archivists from the National Museum of the American Indian, the National Museum of Natural History, the National Anthropological Archives, the Folklife Center of the Library of Congress, and the Newberry Library. One of the unique qualities of the conference was that the Indigenous participants came from such a diverse array of backgrounds, including academically trained linguists and historians, chiefs, tribal historians, language teachers, elders, and pipe carriers. The conference began with Watie Akins, a Penobscot elder, performing a traditional greeting song. Larry Aitken, a pipe carrier from the Leech Lake band of Ojibwe, then conducted a pipe ceremony in the Ojibwe language. To conclude the opening ceremonies, Chief Glenna Wallace of the Eastern Shawnee tribe of Oklahoma spoke to the historical importance of the gathering and expressed hope for future collaboration that would endure beyond the end of the conference, which indeed it has.

The opportunity for Indigenous people to do research in the archives at the time of the conference was augmented with funding from the Getty Foundation grant, which allowed Native American fellows to come to the APS a week in advance of the conference. One of these fellows, the Passamaquoddy Historical Preservation Officer Donald Soctomah, studied the Frank G. Speck photographic and audio recordings collections. He was provided with funding to digitize photographs and recordings that he deemed beneficial to ongoing cultural revitalization projects in his community. What was frankly surprising to the APS staff was the depth

and quality of the knowledge that Soctomah possessed about the photographs. When we realized how valuable this knowledge was to both the Passamaquoddy and to the APS, I arranged to have my special assistant Keara Duggan interview Soctomah on a digital recorder. The results of this collaborative effort exerted a profound influence on the APS and became a template for the second successful Mellon Foundation grant.

This recording of Soctomah's reflections is now part of the digital archive and is featured in a special exhibit on the APS website. Below are a few passages from that interview, which highlight the exciting new opportunities that can arise from what the APS is calling digital knowledge sharing. Looking at a series of photographs of Passamaquoddy women wearing peaked caps with beadwork designs from the Speck collection, Soctomah interpreted the meanings woven in beads:

> The reason I was looking at the hats, the peaked caps, is because of the designs on them. And each peaked cap in the collection here . . . had a really unique design that I've rarely seen before. And some of them were really breathtaking. And to really understand it, you have to analyze the design, because the designs represent . . . it could represent many things . . . but this one before us right here [ID 2943] with the sweetgrass double swirls. The front of the cap is like a double curve. And the way the curve is represented is symbolic of either a chief ceremony or a chief death or a coming together ceremony.[7]

Soctomah utilizes and embellishes Speck's famous ethnographic description of the double-curve motif and goes on to describe what these photographs will mean to the Passamaquoddy people back in Maine: "We have a lot of women in our community who do beadwork and they're always looking for new designs. Well, I'd want to say new designs but these are old designs. They're always looking for old designs to utilize in their work. So the ones I saw, that would be something coming back that hasn't been done for many years." Soctomah concluded the interview with an eloquent summation of the conference's goal of collaboration and sharing that, in part, provided the impetus for the APS to apply for a second Mellon grant: "There's just so much history here. It's just amazing. And it's good that it's coming back. It was good that it was collected. But there's so much more to do. And I think forming a partnership with APS, with Mellon . . . is important too. Because they opened up their doors for us to come and say here's our collection and look at it. And I think this might be the start of something really good."[8]

This exchange, and the recognition that Soctomah is a highly knowl-

edgeable expert on the culture that Speck studied, led to many of his insights being incorporated into the metadata of the APS catalogue. Soctomah identified unlabeled recordings as being Maliseet and recognized several important people in Speck's photographs, whose names had not previously been known to the APS. He also raised fascinating questions about how the material might be catalogued if it were one day incorporated, as he hoped, into an Indigenous digital archive maintained by the Passamaquoddy. "How are you going to organize it? By family? By regalia? By artifact? By time period? And I want to make it so it's easy and accessible to the community. But it's hard trying to figure that out. So I'm probably going to go along with family, but part of me wants to do a separate section just based on regalia and time period."[9] As someone who works to help establish digital archives in Indigenous communities, I am very interested in these kinds of questions: How should the material be conceptualized so that a complex navigation system can be easily managed by community members with limited experience researching on the web, but with a deeper knowledge of traditional ways of interpreting the content of the database? It is an intriguing if still unanswered question: What would an Indigenous archive look like if traditional knowledge could be translated into digital designs?[10] What kind of team would need to be put in place to accomplish such collaborations between programmers and elders? Where would such a complex and simple database be housed so that it could be technically maintained and still be readily accessible to community members? These questions, as we will see, are beginning to be addressed by Boas scholars and Indigenous community members working with materials collected by George Hunt and Franz Boas.

Following the Building Bridges between Archives and Indian Communities conference, the American Philosophical Society successfully applied for a follow-up grant from the Mellon Foundation (2011–2014).[11] The central focus of this project is to expand the digital archive of Native American materials by completing the digitization of the audio recordings, bringing the total number of hours to three thousand. Although Boas's recordings are not housed at the APS and thus are not part of the archive, his legacy is well represented by his students' work. Another innovative feature of the second Mellon grant is a partnership formed with wisdom keepers and scholars from four Indigenous communities: Ojibwe, Eastern Band of Cherokee Indians, Tuscarora, and Penobscot. The grant established a Native American fellowship program that, unlike the APS Library Fellows program, did not require that the fellows hold a doctorate in order to do research in the library. Although only recently under way, this fellowship program has already produced

extremely promising results, which I highlight in the second case study considered here.

There are a plethora of examples of digitization stimulating revitalization projects in Indigenous communities. The most striking, perhaps, is how the A. Irving Hallowell collection at the APS is being used in a UNESCO World Heritage Site grant application that seeks to preserve more than forty thousand square kilometers of boreal forest in northern Manitoba and Quebec. This project is being undertaken by the Pimachiowin Aki corporation, a partnership that includes the Bloodvein River First Nation, Little Grand Rapids First Nation, Pauingassi First Nation, Pikangikum First Nation, Poplar River First Nation, the provincial governments of Manitoba and Quebec, and the Canadian government. It is the first time that the Canadian government has put forth a UNESCO World Heritage Site application on behalf of Indigenous people. In the Ojibwe language, Pimachiowin Aki means "the land that gives life."[12] Sophia Rabliauskas, the former chief of Poplar River First Nation and current spokeswoman for the project, originally conceived the initiative after watching massive, industrial, clear-cut logging to the south and hydropower development on boreal rivers to the north of Poplar River. From her perspective the Pimachiowin Aki initiative is not new but a revitalization of Poplar River First Nation's traditional mandate to protect the land and its resources.[13]

Pimachiowin Aki contacted the American Philosophical Society in 2009 about using photographs from the Hallowell collection that had recently been digitized as part of the Getty project. The collection contains more than 250 photographs of the land and culture of four Ojibwe First Nations in what Hallowell called the Berens River area. The photographs are quite striking in that the wry smiles of the subjects reflect a level of comfort with the photographer or anthropologist that is unusual among the more than 100,000 images of Native people at the APS. Hallowell documented places adorned with petroglyphs, religious practices such as the Shaking Tent ceremony, hunting technologies, and maps of trap lines. The thoughtful subject matter of the photographs has enabled scholars working on behalf of the Pimachiowin Aki project—Jennifer S. H. Brown, Maureen Matthews, Roger Roulette, and Iain Davidson-Hunt, among others—to fashion an innovative argument that the "cultural landscape" of the area needs to be preserved along with the boreal forest. Papers are forthcoming at the Pimachiowinaki website. In this sense the photographs that Hallowell took in the 1930s have been reunited with contemporary wisdom keepers from these First Nation communities. The project enlivens traditional Ojibwe knowledge about, for example, fighting underground fires in the layers created by the permafrost of boreal

forests that is still valuable to ongoing efforts to maintain the physical and cultural landscape of the region.

To my mind, what is particularly interesting about this case study is the way the innovative efforts of these dynamic First Nation communities have become part of a recent revitalization of Hallowell's reputation in anthropological circles. Jennifer S. H. Brown deserves a great deal of credit for this resurgence of interest in "Pete" Hallowell, whose reputation had diminished as a result, Brown writes, of "an overall declining interest in Native American ethnography and 'a changing disciplinary milieu' in the late twentieth century" that "left him less prominent than other leading anthropologists of his day."[14] Brown was able to resurrect Hallowell's monograph, *The Ojibwa of Berens River, Manitoba: Ethnography into History*, a manuscript that was lost in transit to Holt, Rinehart and Winston in 1967. Working in collaboration with Susan Elaine Gray, Brown has recently published two important collections of Hallowell's writings: *Memories, Myths and Dreams of an Ojibwe Leader: William Berens* and *Contributions to Ojibwe Studies: Essays, 1934–1972*. Brown is currently involved in the Pimachiowin Aki project, writing white papers to present the argument for a cultural landscape along with Maureen Matthews, a decorated Winnipeg journalist and anthropologist, and Roger Roulette, a fluent speaker of Ojibwe and a linguist at the University of Manitoba. Matthews and Roulette are an important part of the latest Mellon project at the APS, building on the work carried on by Ojibwe communities for thousands of years, documented by Hallowell, and expanded by Brown and Gray—an intellectual continuum that we hope will continue to be passed on to new generations of scholars and Indigenous wisdom keepers.

The circulation of ever accumulating knowledge constitutes one of the primary goals of the Native American fellows program at the APS, supported by the latest Mellon grant initiative. As a result of the APS's collaboration with Pimachiowin Aki's UNESCO World Heritage Site proposal, Maureen Matthews has agreed to donate her collection of more than seven hundred hours of audio recordings to the newly established digital archive. What is significant about the Matthews collection is how her work with the Ojibwe linguist Roulette revisits Hallowell's collaborative work with William Berens, his longtime collaborator and the chief of the Berens River band of Ojibwe from 1917 to 1947. Matthews and Roulette have followed Hallowell and Berens's path through the boreal forest, interviewing elders descended from Berens and other Ojibwe wisdom keepers with whom Hallowell worked sixty to seventy years earlier. This work is featured in a series of radio documentaries for the Canadian Broadcasting Company, academic articles, and white papers cowritten

for the Pimachiowin Aki project. Matthews, for example, photographed Berens's son, Percy Berens, and his granddaughter, Margaret Simmons, looking at Hallowell's photographs. Matthews then recorded Simmons interviewing Percy Berens in the Ojibwe language. Matthews and Roulette also interviewed Ojibwe elders from the Berens River region talking about thunderbirds and the healing powers of drums, stories that date back to the late 1900s. "The Thunderbird does exist," Roulette translates for Charlie George Owen, pointing to his cousin Jacob Owen wearing an eagle feather in one of Hallowell's photographs, "In order for a person to be a champion warrior," Owen asserts, "you must have the power of Thunderbirds with you. . . . The sign of this is when people wear the feather. . . . Those are the one who receive the gift. . . . Those are the one that have the power."[15]

In the winter of 2011 Matthews and Roulette spent several weeks at the APS transcribing and translating these interviews between fluent Ojibwe speakers well versed in traditional knowledge. The Hallowell photographs, Matthews audio recordings, and Roulette translations were just recently presented to Fond du Lac Tribal and Community College, where they are being integrated into the curriculum and used by Ojibwe community members. Another important outlet for returning these recordings to Ojibwe communities is the website Gibagadinamaagoom: An Ojibwe Digital Archive, which I edit with Larry Aitken, the Leech Lake tribal historian, and which is used by Ojibwe high school and tribal college students across northern Minnesota for language preservation and cultural revitalization.

These contemporary cycles of revitalization, circulating traditional knowledge through both Ojibwe communities and the academy, constitute an important turning point in the history of anthropology. Writing at the end of his career, in an essay entitled "On Being an Anthropologist," Hallowell described his anthropological training with his mentor Speck at the University of Pennsylvania in the 1920s: "He was engaged in 'salvage anthropology' among the Indians of the eastern United States."[16] Today the ideology of salvage anthropology is deemed to be problematic because of its view that Indigenous peoples were on the brink of extinction and that the job of anthropologists was to preserve their culture since Native people would not be around to maintain it themselves — a version of the myth of the vanishing Indian still taught in far too many American elementary school classes to this day. It is interesting, however, that in the same essay Hallowell makes note of Speck's deep-seated respect for the Native people with whom he worked, who were contemporary keepers of traditional knowledge systems. "Speck's self-involvement

with the study people and their problems," Hallowell writes, "was perhaps greater than that of other anthropologists of the period. He was always extolling the sovereign virtues of the Indians and proclaiming the intrinsic values of their culture. . . . I imitated my mentor for a long while. I, too, identified myself with the Indians." Interestingly Hallowell sees Speck's interests as being closely related to those of his teacher, Franz Boas: "Anthropology in all aspects was the overarching thing and Boas was king, for Speck had been not only a student of Boas but also a deeply rooted follower."[17]

Throughout the course of his career Hallowell would articulate an exceedingly important counternarrative to salvage anthropology that can perhaps be seen as a precursor to the anthropology of revitalization. His open acknowledgment of Berens's role in preserving and perpetuating Ojibwe culture, for example, has become an intellectual touchstone for the American Philosophical Society. It is therefore worth quoting a passage from the beginning of Hallowell's *The Ojibwa of Berens River, Manitoba,* at some length:

> I have given considerable prominence here to one of my chief informants, William Berens, and his family, because in his direct ancestry there were persons who exemplified in microcosm the kinds of changes that were occurring among the Indians over a wide area, simultaneously with a tendency towards conserving the native culture of the past. The life histories of William Berens' fore bearers, as well as that of Berens himself, exhibit the historical process in concrete and personal form. This is a page often left blank because the Indians themselves left no records which can be correlated with those of the historian. . . . What I propose to do, therefore, is to introduce members of the Berens family and other Indians as observers of or participants in historic events.[18]

Here it is not the anthropologist but Berens who acts as a participant-observer. Hallowell's recognition that Berens and his family "exemplify in microcosm the kinds of [historical] changes" taking place in the world, without seeing the Ojibwe as doomed by the encroachment of modernity, opens up a new theoretical space that recognizes their key role in "conserving the native culture of the past." The next important step in the APS digital knowledge sharing initiative will be the collaboration with the Franz Boas Papers Documentary Edition project and the Dzawada̱'enux̱w First Nation of the Kwakwa̱ka'wakw. As the director of the new Center for Native American and Indigenous Research (CNAIR) at the APS, I have been working closely with Ryan and Deanna Nicolson of Dzawada̱'enux̱w

on establishing a collaborative relationship.[19] In the summer of 2014, I traveled to the village of Dzawada'enuxw with Darnell and members of the FBP project to present an exact replica of one of George Hunt's notebooks to Deanna Nicolson, the great-great-granddaughter of George Hunt. Darnell then provided the funding for Ryan and Deanna Nicolson to come to the APS, where they identified a highly valuable, unpublished Hunt notebook from the ACLS collection. CNAIR has digitized the notebook and made one hundred copies that were distributed at a Potlatch ceremony in March 2015. This exemplary instance of the anthropology of revitalization was the idea of Ryan Nicolson, who will distribute digital copies to traditional leaders of the Kwakwaka'wakw First Nations. The hope is that doing so will contribute to the process of revitalizing traditional forms of governance embodied by Potlatch ceremonies. As Nicolson explained, when Boas first came to the Kwakwaka'wakw, he held a Potlatch to explain his work. For the APS and FBP to follow in Boas and Hunt's footsteps, under the guidance of Ryan and Deanna Nicolson, is a great honor, particularly because this time the intent is revitalizing the community rather than removing materials from the community. Although we are at the very first stage of a much larger project that, if successful, will continue on for decades, there is great hope for the future as the digitization process again awakens the transformative powers of Boas's work. As these cycles intersect, reflect, and reconnect in complicated patterns, we are only beginning to understand the movement away from salvage anthropology toward the anthropology of revitalization, enlivening old stories, dances, and songs but also changing the way we see the work of anthropologists like Boas and Hunt through the historic lens of the digital age, looking back in order to move forward.

Notes

1. Du Ponceau Collection.
2. Darnell, *And Along Came Boas*, 86.
3. Harris, "American Indian Linguistic Work and the Boas Collection," 96.
4. Lydenberg, "The Society's Program in American Linguistics and Archaeology," 125.
5. See Darnell, *Invisible Genealogies*, for a more detailed account of this intellectual genealogy.
6. Lydenberg, "The Society's Program in American Linguistics and Archaeology," 124.
7. Soctomah, "Through Indigenous Eyes."
8. Soctomah, "Through Indigenous Eyes."
9. Soctomah interview.
10. See Powell and Aiken, "Seven Directions"; Powell, "Encoding Culture."

11. Powell, "Building Bridges."
12. Pimachiowin Aki World Heritage Project, "The Land That Gives Life."
13. The Goldman Environmental Prize, "Prize Recipient: Sophia Rabliauskas."
14. Brown in Hallowell, *The Ojibwa of Berens River*, xix.
15. Matthews, "Thunderbirds," 4.
16. Hallowell, "On Being an Anthropologist," 3.
17. Hallowell, "On Being an Anthropologist," 3.
18. Hallowell, *The Ojibwa of Berens River*, 3.
19. Nicolson, "Contemporary Revitalization."

References

MANUSCRIPTS AND ARCHIVES

Peter Stephen Du Ponceau Collection. 1781–1844. http://www.amphilsoc.org/collections/view?docId=ead/Mss.B.D92p-ead.xml;query=Stephen%20du%20Ponceau;brand=default (accessed November 6, 2011).

Gibagadinamaagoom: An Ojibwe Digital Archive. http://ojibwearchive.sas.upenn.edu/ (accessed November 6, 2011).

Donald Soctomah. Interview transcript. 2010. American Philosophical Society Archives, Philadelphia.

———. "Through Indigenous Eyes." http://www.amphilsoc.org/library/exhibit/indigeyes/passamaquoddy (accessed November 6, 2011).

PUBLISHED WORKS

Berens, William, as told to A. Irving Hallowell. *Memories, Myths and Dreams of an Ojibwe Leader*. Ed. Jennifer Brown and Susan Elaine Gray. Lincoln: University of Nebraska Press, 2009.

Darnell, Regna. *And Along Came Boas: Continuity and Revolution in Americanist Anthropology*. Philadelphia: John Benjamins, 1998.

———. *Invisible Genealogies: A History of Americanist Anthropology*. Lincoln: University of Nebraska Press, 2001.

The Goldman Environmental Prize. "Prize Recipient: Sophia Rabliauskas, 2007 North America." http://goldmanprize.org/node/607 (accessed November 6, 2011).

Hallowell, A. Irving. *The Ojibwa of Berens River, Manitoba*. Ed. Jennifer Brown. New York: Harcourt, Brace, Jovanovich, 1992.

———. "Prologue: On Being an Anthropologist." In Jennifer Brown and Susan Elaine Gray, eds., *Contributions to Ojibwe Studies: Essays, 1934–1972*, 1–15. Lincoln: University of Nebraska Press, 2010.

Harris, Zellig. "American Indian Linguistic Work and the Boas Collection." *American Philosophical Society Report on Committee on Library* 96 (1945).

Lydenberg, Harry Miller. "The Society's Program in American Linguistics and Archaeology." *Proceedings of the American Philosophical Society* 92 (1948): 124.

Matthews, Maureen. "Thunderbirds." Transcript. Canadian Broadcasting System, 1995.

Nicolson, Ryan. "Contemporary Revitalization Using Boasian Texts." Paper presented at Franz Boas: Ethnographer, Theorist, Activist Conference, London ON, December 2–5, 2010.

Pimachiowin Aki World Heritage Project. "The Land That Gives Life." http://www.pimachiowinaki.org (accessed November 6, 2011).

Powell, Timothy B. "Building Bridges between Archives and Indian Communities." *News from the American Philosophical Society* 12 (2010): 1–2.

———. "Digital Repatriation in the Field of Indigenous Anthropology." *Anthropology News* 52.7 (2011).

———. "Encoding Culture: Building a Digital Archive Based on Traditional Ojibwe Codes of Conduct." Amy Earhart and Andrew Jewell, eds., *The American Literature Scholar in the Digital Age*, 250–74. Ann Arbor: University of Michigan Press, 2011.

Powell, Timothy B., and Larry Aiken, eds. "Seven Directions." Gibagadinamaagoom: An Ojibwe Digital Archive. http://ojibwearchive.sas.upenn.edu/seven-directions (accessed September 7, 2014).

Soctomah, Donald. "Through Indigenous Eyes." Digital exhibit. Passamaquoddy Designs and Images. American Philosophical Society. http://www.amphilsoc.org/library/exhibit/indigeyes/passamaquoddy (accessed November 6, 2011).

Wallace, Anthony F. C. *The Death and Rebirth of the Seneca*. New York: Vintage Books, 1972.

———. "Revitalization Movements." *American Anthropologist* 58 (1956): 264–81.

15 "An expansive archive . . . not a diminished one"

The Franz Boas Papers Documentary Edition Project

MICHELLE HAMILTON

In partnership with the American Philosophical Society (APS) and the University of Nebraska Press, this volume initiates an ambitious project to digitize and critically edit the Franz Boas papers. We anticipate approximately twenty-five volumes that will thematically and chronologically explore the contemporary legacies of Boas's career between 1881, when he obtained his doctorate in physics from the University of Kiel, and 1942, the year of his death in New York City. While Boas has been pronounced the father of American anthropology, our project also focuses on the Canadian context of his ethnographic oeuvre, a context of his fieldwork that has been largely ignored by U.S.-based scholars. Grounding the appropriate parts of the documentary edition in Canadian scholarship will ensure redress, both within Canadian public consciousness and more broadly in the history of North American anthropology and intellectual life. Because Boas's scholarship was so wide-ranging, extending far beyond Canada in both geographic scope and implication, we have assembled an interdisciplinary and international team of scholars, including Aboriginal researchers and partners, in order to capture its breadth.

This documentary editing project further aims to co-create knowledge and to intellectually repatriate information derived from Boas's fieldwork in order that communities may use it for purposes of revitalization. At the same time the team recognizes the duality of digital repatriation; while it increases accessibility, it also creates ethical issues. Information recorded in Boas's papers may be considered to fall under intellectual if not legal copyright or may not be culturally appropriate for knowledge exchange or publication. By referring to similar projects as models for discussion and adaptation (see Powell, this volume), and with advice from our Indigenous Advisory Council, however, the team anticipates building a documentary archive that serves diverse audiences among scholarly and Native communities and the general public.

The Project

The APS holdings include Boas's family and professional correspondence, field notebooks and diaries from the Northwest Coast and the Arctic, almost three thousand photographs and sketches of ethnographic material culture, anthropometric data collected on reserves throughout North America, numerous maps of Kwakw<u>a</u>ka'wakw and Inuit territories, and public talks and academic lectures, all of which were produced between 1862 and 1942. Letters from Boas also appear in APS collections authored by his students and colleagues, as they do in archives elsewhere in North America. Additional manuscripts at the APS include the Franz Boas Collection of Materials for American Linguistics (via the American Council of Learned Societies), much of which was recorded or directly supervised by Boas.[1]

The Boas Papers at the APS are organized alphabetically by correspondent, allowing the reader to grasp a sense of Boas's individual relationships with his family, students, and peers. The microfilm version in 44 reels is largely organized chronologically, which provides an alternative perspective, that is, how Boas's career developed over time. Both organizational schemes make it difficult to understand his contributions to specific subfields within anthropology and history. Therefore the documentary edition will group Boas's work and correspondence thematically into the projected volumes. Because Boas's work encompassed ethnography, museology, archaeology, physical anthropology, folklore, ethnomusicology, ecology and health, linguistics, Afro-American and women's studies, and contemporaneous social issues such as anti-Semitism, no one scholar can sufficiently match his breadth of scholarship, making it more effective to cover his career by subdiscipline and thematic focus. In this sense the preceding chapters act as an introduction to the potential scope of the forthcoming documentary volumes and suggest potential revisions of our inherited images of Boas.

The Canadian Context and the Archival Papers

An important focus of the documentary edition is the Canadian contributions and legacies of Boas, which Darnell (this volume) argues have been relatively ignored by scholars who view him exclusively as an Americanist, narrowly defined. In 1883–1884, as part of his postgraduate studies, Boas conducted fieldwork among the Inuit on Baffin Island, part of the Arctic islands that had been transferred from Britain to Canada just three years earlier. Seeking to understand the impact of the environment on various aspects of Inuit culture and life, Boas mapped part of his study

area, recorded ethnographic and linguistic information, and collected material culture. His notes from these trips later evolved into his habilitation thesis "Baffin Land" in 1886 and his first monograph, *The Central Eskimo*, published in 1888. Despite being intrigued by Inuit culture, Boas never returned to the Arctic, instead choosing to focus most of his future fieldwork on the peoples of the North Pacific Coast.

Back in Berlin, while working at the Royal Ethnological Museum, Boas decided to visit the Northwest Coast and spent three months in the Canadian province of British Columbia in the fall of 1886. There he attended ceremonies, raided a few cemeteries, investigated linguistic diversity, mapped territories, and recorded and collected ethnographic objects and information.

Several years earlier, in 1884, the British Association for the Advancement of Science (BAAS) had met with Canadian scholars in Montreal and established the Committee on the North-Western Tribes of Canada.[2] Officially supervised by E. B. Tylor in England, the actual work in Canada was directed by Horatio Hale, a lawyer and self-trained avocational anthropologist; George Mercer Dawson, a geologist employed by the Geological Survey of Canada; and Daniel Wilson, a professor at the University of Toronto. In 1888 Hale wrote to Boas asking him to conduct ethnographic fieldwork in British Columbia. Though he was only a peripatetic researcher for the BAAS, Boas disagreed with Hale's prescriptive methodology and chafed against his control.[3] Likewise Dawson disagreed with Boas's view of culture and was perhaps territorial over fieldwork in the province where Dawson had begun his own studies in the 1870s.[4] Nevertheless Boas frequently corresponded with Dawson in the 1880s and 1890s, and with Hale until he died in 1896.

Boas would return numerous times to British Columbia for the BAAS. During his first trip he met George Hunt, who became his primary informant on Kwakwaka'wakw culture and eventually an anthropologist in his own right.[5] Their correspondence in the Boas papers spans almost four decades, though oddly it begins only in the early 1890s, several years after Boas met him.

In 1899, while employed by the BAAS, Boas joined Clark University in Worcester, Massachusetts, as an instructor in anthropology. His first graduate student was Alexander Francis Chamberlain, a Canadian who had moved south to obtain a doctorate, an impossibility in Canada at that time. Chamberlain had been educated in modern languages at the University of Toronto but had come under the influence of Daniel Wilson, who taught courses in history and ethnology. Chamberlain also

joined the Canadian Institute in Toronto, the preeminent emerging professional society for archaeology and ethnography in late nineteenth-century Canada. Through his Institute membership he met and assisted its curator, David Boyle, in fieldwork and writing the *Annual Archaeological Reports of Ontario*.[6] The first person to obtain a doctorate in anthropology in North America, Chamberlain eventually became a full professor at Clark University, where he remained until his early death in 1914. The two men kept in contact after Boas left Clark, and Boas wrote Chamberlain's obituary for the *Journal of American Folklore*.

In 1891 Frederic Ward Putnam, the head of Harvard's Archaeology and Ethnology Museum Department, hired Boas to prepare physical anthropology exhibits for the upcoming Chicago World's Fair. Boas envisioned this project as compiling thousands of measurements of individual Natives across North America and Greenland.[7] While he asked missionaries, Indian agents, and others to assist him, during the summers of 1891 and 1892 he personally collected information in Native communities in southern Ontario, Saskatchewan, Manitoba, and British Columbia, notes of which are held by the APS. Boas also arranged for Hunt to send Kwakwa̱ka'wakw objects for display at the fair and to bring a group of Kwakwa̱ka'wakw to camp at the fairgrounds as a living exhibit for visitors.

In 1894 Boas returned to his fieldwork on the coast and in the interior of British Columbia, this time for a number of sponsors, including the BAAS, the Bureau of American Ethnology, the American Museum of Natural History, and the U.S. National Museum. On this trip he met James Alexander Teit, a Scottish immigrant who lived in Spences Bridge, a small town in the interior of the province. Though a rancher by trade, Teit was interested in ethnology, collected objects, and spoke several Native languages. He thus became a useful informant and liaison for Boas and, like Hunt, an anthropologist in his own right.[8] Although letters from their first years of friendship are missing from the Boas papers, the existing correspondence is still voluminous.

In 1896 Boas was appointed assistant curator at the American Museum of Natural History in New York. One year later he would return to British Columbia as the scientific director of the Jesup North Pacific Expedition, organized by the museum.[9] Again he worked with Teit, and with Harlan Ingersoll Smith, who would also become important to Canadian anthropology.

The position at the American Museum was a joint one with Columbia University. There Boas attracted a number of students in anthropology who would go on to affect the development of the discipline in Canada. Edward Sapir, who had enrolled at Columbia in 1901, became the head

of the new anthropology division of the Geological Survey of Canada in 1910. Reginald Brock, the director of the Survey, specifically consulted Boas about this position, for which Boas strongly recommended Sapir. Employees of the Survey had long collected folklore and ethnographic and archaeological objects during their geological surveys, but it was not until 1910 that it organized a professional division for anthropology. In 1912 the Survey opened the Victoria Memorial Museum (now the Canadian Museum of History) in Ottawa to showcase its material culture collections, including objects related to Indigenous peoples.[10] In turn Sapir hired Boas's colleagues Teit and Smith as the head of archaeology, and as ethnologists, two of his former students, Alexander Goldenweiser and Frank Speck.[11]

Beyond correspondence with Dawson, Brock, Sapir, Teit, and Smith, the APS holdings include numerous letters from other employees of the Geological Survey, including the paleontologist Henry Ami and the geologists Robert Bell and Joseph B. Tyrell, all of whom were interested in Native peoples. These individuals also left behind boxes of their own correspondence, largely held at the Canadian Museum of History archives or at Library and Archives Canada.

In 1927 Boas and Sapir established the Committee on Native American Languages of the American Council of Learned Societies in order to record endangered Native languages.[12] Grants administered by Boas, Sapir, and Alfred Kroeber allowed them and many other individuals to document languages throughout North America, primarily during the 1920s and 1930s. Held by the APS, this fonds represents about 166 languages and totals about eighty linear feet.

Among others, repositories such as the archives at Harvard, Yale, and Columbia universities, the New York Public Library, the Smithsonian Institution, the Royal British Columbia Museum, the Peabody Museums, the American Museum of Natural History, and the Field Museum, which received the exhibits of the Chicago World's Fair, hold fieldwork notes and letters to and from Boas. With the assistance of the editorial board members Michi Knecht, Matthias Harbeck, Jürgen Langenkämper, Andre Gingrich, and Ranier Hatoum, we will locate and select documents from archives in Germany. The project team anticipates including select material from these repositories where judged editorially appropriate.

The Project Team

Although no single scholar, institution, or discipline could amass the geographical and anthropological scope and skill sets to implement this project single-handedly, the team, through its intersecting collaborations,

aspires to recapitulate the public range and impact of Boas himself. The interdisciplinary expertise of team members from the University of Victoria, Dalhousie University, the University of Western Ontario, the Université de Montreal, the American Philosophical Society, the University of Nebraska Press, and various Native communities includes archaeology, cultural and physical anthropology, ethnography, ethnomusicology, linguistics, law, history of anthropology, Native and environmental studies, Indigenous knowledge, museology and material culture, scholarly editing, public history, and archival practice. To produce the forthcoming volumes the Victoria and Dalhousie team members (Michael Asch, Peter Stevenson, Nancy Turner, Brian Noble, Robert Hancock, Marc Pinkoski) and Robert Wishart (University of Aberdeen) will take the lead on British Columbian ethnography and on the public engagement of Boas and his early students in Canada, while the Western and Montreal teams (Regna Darnell, project director, Michelle Hamilton, Susan Hill, John Leavitt) will take primary responsibility for editing, archival management, and the history of anthropology.

The project is supported by the Social Sciences and Humanities Research Council of Canada through its Partnership Grant Program, with substantial contributions from the partners. The Partnership Program aims, in part, to facilitate mutually beneficial relationships between scholars and other publics in order to co-create and exchange knowledge and to increase its accessibility outside of academe. Thus in addition to staff from the APS and the University of Nebraska Press (spearheaded by Martin Levitt and Matthew Bokovoy, respectively), who contribute technical expertise, participation by Aboriginal scholars and communities is fundamental to the management, research output, and increased accessibility of the Franz Boas Papers documentary editing project. The Kwakw<u>a</u>ka'wakw (Ryan Nicolson) and Nuu chah nulth (Johnny Mack) are represented on the research team, and the Musgamagw Dzawad<u>a</u>'enu<u>x</u>w Tribal Council is a formal partner. Further collaboration or formal partnership will be extended to additional communities and organizations as locally relevant materials are identified and as researchers establish ongoing relationships with them. An Indigenous Advisory Council is being established to guide editing and publishing decisions.

The core research team is primarily Canadian due to our objective of foregrounding Boas's Canadian impact, especially of his ethnographic work, and facilitating First Nations access to and use of the papers and editorial research. Nonetheless Boas's work, like the scholarship that has evolved from it, is far from restricted to Canada. Therefore the Editorial Advisory Board is international, to ensure due weight to non-Canadian

materials largely held in American and to a lesser extent German institutions.

Access and Digital Knowledge Sharing

As Elizabeth Edwards argues, while Indigenous communities are not often part of an institution's local constituency, they are part of "a wider ethical community" and have rights to the collections held by that institution.[13] Kimberly Christen, who has worked with Plateau groups in the Northwest, believes that Indigenous access to archival collections is a way to put political sovereignty into cultural practice.[14] A key aim of the Boas documentary edition is to increase Native community access to Boas's fieldwork notes, linguistic texts, and correspondence (Powell, this volume). These ethnographic materials have been rendered largely inaccessible to their source communities by physical and cultural distance, and yet they contain materials of critical importance for linguistic and cultural revitalization. Our research will emphasize digital knowledge sharing to relevant communities, information concerning their own culture and history that has been lost in the too often interrupted transmission of oral tradition. For example, Boas's early studies of Kwakwaka'wakw customs and traditional knowledge record matters no longer remembered within the community. Contemporary efforts to revitalize and reinstate ceremonies and their accompanying knowledge depend on evidence from earlier records produced in collaboration between Boas and his Native collaborator Hunt. Photographs, sketches, maps, and other illustrative materials also serve as stimuli to memory and thus the regeneration of knowledge.[15] Further, ethnographic fieldwork documents that became part of the colonizing record can be transformed into sources for family and clan histories.[16]

Many of the project team members approach their own scholarship and archival practice from the perspective of public engagement, whether in activist anthropology, public history, co-creation of knowledge with Native communities, the anthropology of revitalization, or various methods of repatriation. Further, both the American Philosophical Society and the University of Nebraska Press have strong mandates to link scholarship and service, especially to Native American publics. In his discussion of several digitization projects, Powell (this volume) demonstrates that the APS recognizes Native communities as partners in the stewardship of its holdings that relate to their history. This partnership has revealed that community members still hold deep knowledge about the materials held by the APS. Others can identify so-called anonymous individuals in photographs. Collaborative practice has resulted in the co-creation and

exchange of knowledge that benefits the institution, Native communities, and the researchers who use these materials.

In the United States the term *repatriation* is strongly associated with the 1990 Native American Graves Protection and Repatriation Act (NAGPRA), which requires federally funded museums to physically return items defined as sacred, of cultural patrimony, and from graves. Archival materials, such as the Boas Papers, however, are not covered by NAGPRA, although in the spirit of the legislation's intent, some institutions have returned documents and photographs that relate to human remains.[17] More often archives refer to professional ethical codes, such as the *Protocols for Native American Archival Materials* that were established in 2006 by a group of scholars, archivists, and Native American representatives. Addressing Native American concerns over the treatment of archival materials, the *Protocols* emphasize the importance of consultation with relevant communities in balancing public access to records with the need to restrict sacred, secret, or culturally sensitive materials; respect for Indigenous intellectual and cultural property rights that may not fall under Western copyright law; provision of historical context around the acquisition and archival description of records now considered culturally inappropriate or even offensive; recognition of community-initiated research protocols; and sharing, digital or otherwise, of certain materials.[18] Various groups, such as the Union of British Columbia Indian Chiefs, have adopted the *Protocols* as their own guidelines.

Canada has no national legislation comparable to NAGPRA. Nevertheless there are ethical statements and other models in Canada that allow the project team to conceptualize the goals and potential methods of handling archival material and its intellectual or digital repatriation. In 1992 the Assembly of First Nations and the Canadian Museums Association coauthored a task force report called *Turning the Page*, which advocated improved access to collections, repatriation of certain types of items, and the portrayal of Aboriginals as living peoples who had a significant role in Canadian history rather than as extinct and primitive societies. In 1996 the report of the Royal Commission of Aboriginal Peoples echoed many of these recommendations.

Since these ethical statements have been issued, larger museums and archives in Canada follow their principles and many have moved toward virtual, visual, digital, or intellectual repatriation. Of course the increasing ubiquity of the Internet and digital technology has exponentially increased access and opportunities for collaboration, exchange of knowledge, and repatriation. For example, the Algoma University Archives, the Children of Shingwauk Alumni Association, and the National Resi-

dential School Survivors' Society have created the award-winning Shingwauk Project, which collectively gathers, preserves, and interprets the records of Indian residential schools, partly for the purpose of knowledge exchange and healing. Its Remember the Children project brings residential school photographs to community members in order to identify the people portrayed in them, and many are now available online through the Survivors' Society.[19]

Library and Archives Canada in Ottawa initiated a similar project in 2001. Called Project Naming, it sought Inuit input to identify the individuals captured in the thousands of photographs taken between the late 1800s and the mid-twentieth century that now reside in the archives. Like the Boas papers, the photograph collection is housed at a dissuasive distance from the communities it depicts. Digitization of the collection made it more readily accessible to community members, although the archives also hosted Inuit students from the Nunavut Sivuniksavut Training Program, a postsecondary institution for youth in Ottawa, who then took the digital photos home on computers to foster connections with the elders of their communities. In this way Project Naming aimed to revitalize the traditional knowledge-sharing relationship between older and younger members of their communities.[20] The resulting database, along with a web exhibit, is accessible on the Library and Archives Canada website.

More holistic examples that combine archival records, objects, art, accession record information, and photographs include the Reciprocal Research Network (RRN) at the University of British Columbia Museum of Anthropology and the Great Lakes Research Alliance for the Study of Aboriginal Arts and Cultures (GRASAC) at the University of Ottawa. Codeveloped with the Musqueam Indian band, the Stó:lō Nation/Tribal Council, and the U'mista Cultural Society, the RRN provides a virtual space in which Native communities and organizations holding ethnographic collections can access, share, and create digital information about items held at their institutions. At the time of writing the RNN hosted nineteen institutions, and the database included over 400,000 objects and almost 250,000 photographs.

Partnered with the Woodland Cultural Centre and the Ojibwe Cultural Foundation, the GRASAC Knowledge Sharing Database focuses on items from Great Lakes peoples held in Canadian and international museums and archives, with over two hundred researchers. Indigenous communities can access collections and associated information online and contribute their own understandings of these collections. As Ruth Phillips, a key initiator of both projects, writes, GRASAC is "a project of reclamation and recovery, reconnection and reintegration," which "mitigates the

separation of people from heritage and the enforced losses of traditional knowledge that continue to have serious consequences for Aboriginal identity and spiritual and mental health."[21]

Documentary editing predates the previous projects that could be achieved only by digital technology. According to the historian and editor Gregory Massey, the first volume of the Thomas Jefferson papers, produced in 1950, symbolized the beginning of "modern" documentary editing because it stimulated President Harry Truman to reestablish the National Historical Publications Commission. The Commission selected individuals thought to be important in the development of the United States, gathered information about surviving papers in archives that could be edited, and awarded grants for publication.[22] Over the next few decades its support resulted in documentary editions of the papers of Benjamin Franklin, Alexander Hamilton, James Madison, Jefferson Davis, Margaret Sanger, Elizabeth Cady Stanton, and Susan B. Anthony, among others. Many of these multivolume projects have extended over several decades. The Association for Documentary Editing was founded in 1978 to gather together scholars interested in methodological and ethical issues in the field; it publishes the journal *Scholarly Editing* (previously called *Documentary Editing*).

In Canada historical editing has few comparable examples and certainly no national agency or professional organization. One of the first large historical editing projects that partially dealt with Canadian material was the seventy-two-volume series of the *Jesuit Relations and Allied Documents*, published in the United States between 1896 and 1901. Partnered with the historian Adam Shortt, the national archivist Arthur G. Doughty edited and produced several volumes on the early constitutional history of Canada, which were published between 1918 and 1935. In the 1960s an abortive project by the national archives to publish the papers of numerous prime ministers resulted only in two volumes addressing John A. Macdonald. That decade also saw the beginning of the *Documents on Canadian External Relations*, which now consists of over twenty volumes produced by the Department of Foreign Affairs and International Trade.[23] Most prominently the Champlain Society began editing historical documents in 1905.[24]

As with museums, technology has allowed documentary editing to now involve the public. Projects such as the University College London's *Transcribe Bentham* database in the United Kingdom and the just-emerging John A. Macdonald papers project by Library and Archives Canada and the Champlain Society utilize crowd-sourcing in order to transcribe and edit the massive archival holdings created by these historical figures.[25]

To increase accessibility the Franz Boas papers will be available both digitally and in print editions. A digital edition allows for easy searching across thematic volumes; as our Native partners will first be interested in the history of their own communities, they will be able to search for individual names and ultimately for community and clan names, for example. The digital materials will be available for use first by the Native communities with an ongoing proprietary stake but also by academic and archival institutions, including museums. Further, use of the Free Knowledge Project (FKP) website, developed by Marc Pinkoski, and the Boas Project website at Western will increase access to our research and our ability to exchange information with Native communities and other interested researchers. The FKP website already allows for the co-creation of knowledge through digital technology such as podcasts, and we expect to develop other dialogical avenues as our Native partners advise. As an activist and public intellectual, Boas brought greater visibility to anthropology during his lifetime. It is fitting, then, for the documentary editing project to aim to increase the accessibility of materials that will engage the general public with antiracial and gender issues, many of which have direct contemporary social and political salience. Other activist issues treated by Boas set the stage for contemporary treatments and continue to offer methodological, ethical, and theoretical models.

Documentary and Intellectual Property Challenges

Like the Franz Boas papers, most archival holdings related to Indigenous peoples were produced by non-Native individuals, many of whom collected ethnographic information under the ubiquitous nineteenth- and early twentieth-century paradigms of salvage ethnography and cultural evolution. Further, scholarly editing is a Western practice. In addition to the approach to "read beyond words" our partnership with Native communities will allow the inclusion of Indigenous knowledge and interpretations in editorial annotations and research.[26] These can produce a counternarrative or a more multilayered understanding of archival documents. The Yale Indian Papers Project that publishes New England source materials and the Plateau Centre for American Indian Studies at Washington State University, which gathers together materials from different institutions, for example, designed databases that allowed for multiple layers of annotations to be added. Both scholars and Native individuals were invited to add descriptions, oral stories, and interpretative comments; the goal was not to overwrite the academic voice but to augment it with Native interpretations.[27]

As these and other projects have correctly noted,[28] the digitization of

archival materials has raised issues of intellectual copyright and access to and treatment of culturally sensitive materials. Web 2.0 technologies and the digitization of records or photographs, while having the advantage of instantaneity and accessibility, also make it harder to control the copying, appropriation, and (re)interpretation of sources. Web 2.0, which places primacy on user-generated content, allows digital sources to be used in mash-ups to produce something new. While the Western world usually privileges intellectual freedom to access records and the idea that records are held by institutions for the public trust, Indigenous societies often restrict information based on age, gender, and clan or society membership, among other factors. Further, while Western museums often define "objects" and their reproductions in sketches or photographs as inanimate, Indigenous communities often consider them to be alive, other-than-human beings who need be treated with specific rituals or who cannot be seen by all members of society without harmful repercussions. Last, while archival records may not fall under Western copyright law because of the lapse of time since they were produced, Native communities, families, or individuals retain ethical rights to copyright and ownership of certain materials or information recorded in those materials. Strict upholders of the public trust doctrine often argue that archival and museum materials are held for the benefit of *all* humankind and thus oppose restrictions made by so-called special interest groups. But under the public trust doctrine, dissemination of digital copies can easily violate Indigenous protocols and copyright even if it is well-meaning and unintentional. Through consultation with Native advisors, many of these collaborative projects have built numerous layers of access into their digital databases or even created Indigenous-derived categories of in-group records to make them more meaningful to communities.

Boas's fieldwork, like that of many other anthropologists in the past, included matters now considered culturally sensitive, under Indigenous intellectual property copyright, and potentially inappropriate to share with non-Native communities or among different groups of a Native community. Our documentary research and the dissemination of its results will necessarily proceed collaboratively with the Indigenous Advisory Council to establish effective protocols for achieving shared goals by consensus and compromise. Veto power over which documents are presented and who has access to them will be given to the Indigenous Advisory Council.

An Expansive Archive

Our documentary editing project brings a digital and print accessibility to the Boas papers that is balanced with Native concerns, uses a

multilayered approach to provide scholarly and community interpretations, respects Indigenous intellectual copyright issues, and repatriates knowledge back to the source communities and families at the center of Boas's fieldwork. As they deem appropriate, such documentary and illustrative material can be used by the associated communities to build local archives of knowledge, flesh out family and individual histories, stir memories for oral transmission of stories, revive and teach languages, and revitalize ceremonies and other traditions. Further, we anticipate both a co-creation and an exchange of knowledge from our research and editing process, both of which will be disseminated through scholarly and community channels. To expand on Christen's phrase, the Franz Boas Papers project team envisions an "expansive archive . . . not a diminished one."[29]

Notes

1. Leeds-Hurwitz, "The Committee on Research in Native American Languages."
2. Avrith, "Science at the Margins."
3. Gruber, "Horatio Hale and the Development of American Anthropology"; Nock, "The Erasure of Horatio Hale's Contributions."
4. Avrith-Wakeam, "George Dawson, Franz Boas and the Origins of Professional Anthropology in Canada."
5. Berman, "'The Culture as It Appears to the Indian Himself'"; Briggs and Bauman, "'The Foundation of All Future Researches'"; Cannizzo, "George Hunt and the Invention of Kwakiutl Culture"; Jacknis, "George Hunt, Collector of Indian Specimens" and "George Hunt, Kwakiutl Photographer"; Wilner, this volume.
6. Hamilton, *Collections and Objections*; Killan, *David Boyle*.
7. Cole, *Franz Boas: The Early Years*.
8. Laforet, this volume; Wickwire, "James A. Teit" and "Women in Ethnography."
9. Kendall and Krupnik, *Constructing Cultures Then and Now*.
10. Vodden, *No Stone Unturned*; Richling, "Archaeology, Ethnology and Canada's Public Purse"; Zaslow, *Reading the Rocks*.
11. Thompson, *Recording Their Story*; Dyck, "Toward a History of Archaeology."
12. Leeds-Hurwitz, "The Committee on Research in Native American Languages."
13. Edwards, "Talking Visual Histories," 83.
14. Christen, "Opening Archives." 194.
15. Phillips, *Museum Pieces*.
16. Edwards, "Talking Visual Histories."
17. Underhill, "Protocols for Native American Archival Materials," 143.

18. Underhill, "Protocols for Native American Archival Materials"; *Protocols for Native American Archival Materials*.
19. McCracken, "Hidden No Longer."
20. Greenhorn, "Project Naming."
21. Phillips, *Museum Pieces*, 295.
22. Massey, "The Papers of Henry Laurens."
23. Donaghy, "Documenting the Diplomats."
24. Heidenreich, *Champlain and the Champlain Society*.
25. Causer and Wallace, "Building a Volunteer Community"; Causer et al., "Transcription Maximized."
26. Brown and Vibert, *Reading beyond Words*.
27. Grant-Costa et al., "The Common Pot"; Christen, "Opening Archives."
28. Christen, "Gone Digital" and "Opening Archives"; Hennessy, "Virtual Repatriation and Digital Cultural Heritage"; Phillips, *Museum Pieces*.
29. Christen, "Opening Archives," 210.

References

Assembly of First Nations and the Canadian Museums Association. *Turning the Page: Forging New Partnerships between Museums and First Peoples*. Ottawa: n.p., 1992.

Avrith, Gale. "Science at the Margins: The British Association and the Foundations of Canadian Anthropology." PhD dissertation. University of Pennsylvania, 1987.

Avrith-Wakeam, Gale. "George Dawson, Franz Boas and the Origins of Professional Anthropology in Canada." *Scientia Canadensis: Canadian Journal of the History of Science, Technology and Medicine* 17.1–2 (1993): 185–203.

Berman, Judith. "'The Culture as It Appears to the Indian Himself': Boas, George Hunt, and the Methods of Ethnography." In George W. Stocking Jr., ed. *Volksgeist as Method and Ethic: Essays on Boasian Ethnography and the German Anthropological Tradition*, 215–56. Madison: University of Wisconsin Press, 1996.

Briggs, Charles, and Richard Bauman. "'The Foundation of All Future Researches': Franz Boas, George Hunt, Native American Texts, and the Construction of Modernity." *American Quarterly* 51.3 (1999): 479–528.

Brown, Jennifer S. H., and Elizabeth Vibert, eds. *Reading beyond Words: Context for Native History*. Toronto: University of Toronto Press, 2009.

Brown, Jennifer S. H., and Elizabeth Vibert, eds. *Report of the Royal Commission of Aboriginal Peoples*. Vol. 3: *Gathering Strength*. Ottawa: Canada Communication Group, 1996.

Canadian Archaeological Association. Statement of Principles for Ethical Conduct Pertaining to Aboriginal Peoples. 1996. www.canadianarchaeology.com/ethical.lasso (accessed February 3, 2013).

Cannizzo, Jeanne. "George Hunt and the Invention of Kwakiutl Culture." *Canadian Review of Sociology and Anthropology* 20.1 (1983): 44–58.

Causer, Tim, Justin Tonra, and Valerie Wallace. "Transcription Maximized; Expense Minimized: Crowdsourcing and Editing the Collected Works of Jeremy Bentham." *Literary and Linguistic Computing* 27.2 (2012). http://llc.oxfordjournals.org/content/early/2012/03/28/llc.fqs004.short?rss=1 (accessed February 6, 2013).

Causer, Tim, and Valerie Wallace. "Building a Volunteer Community: Results and Findings from *Transcribe Bentham*." *Digital Humanities Quarterly* 6.2 (2012). http://www.digitalhumanities.org/dhq/vol/6/2/000125/000125.html (accessed February 6, 2013).

Christen, Kimberly. "Gone Digital: Aboriginal Remix and the Cultural Commons." *International Journal of Cultural Property* 12.3 (2005): 315–45.

———. "Opening Archives: Respectful Repatriation." *American Archivist* 74 (2011): 185–210.

Cole, Douglas. *Franz Boas: The Early Years, 1858–1906*. Vancouver: Douglas and McIntyre, 1999.

Donaghy, Greg. "Documenting the Diplomats: The Origins and Evolution of Documents on Canadian External Relations." *Public Historian* 25.1 (2003): 9–28.

Dyck, Ian. "Toward a History of Archaeology in the National Museum of Canada: The Contributions of Harlan I. Smith and Douglas Leechman, 1911–1950." In P. J. Smith and Donald Mitchell, eds., *Bringing Back the Past: Historical Perspectives on Canadian Archaeology*, 114–34. Mercury Series, Archaeological Survey of Canada Paper 158. Gatineau: Canadian Museum of Civilization, 1998.

Edwards, Elizabeth. "Talking Visual Histories: Introduction." In Laura Peers and Alison K. Brown, eds., *Museums and Source Communities*, 83–97. London: Routledge, 2003.

Free Knowledge Project. http://freeknowledgeproject.wordpress.com (accessed February 8, 2013)

Grant-Costa, Paul, Tobias Glaza, and Michael Sletcher. "The Common Pot: Editing Native American Materials." *Scholarly Editing* 33 (2012). http://www.scholarlyediting.org/2012/pdf/essay.commonpot.pdf (accessed February 8, 2013).

Greenhorn, Beth. "Project Naming: Always on Our Minds." In J. Trant and D. Bearman, eds., *Museums and the Web 2005: Proceedings*. Toronto: Archives and Museum Informatics Museums, 2005. http://www.museumsandtheweb.com/mw2005/papers/greenhorn/greenhorn.html (accessed February 6, 2013).

Gruber, Jacob W. "Horatio Hale and the Development of American Anthropology." *Proceedings of the American Philosophical Society* 111.1 (1967): 5–37.

Hamilton, Michelle A. *Collections and Objections: Aboriginal Material Culture in Southern Ontario, 1791–1914*. Montreal: McGill-Queen's University Press, 2010.

Heidenreich, Conrad E. *Champlain and the Champlain Society: An Early Expedition into Documentary Publishing*. Toronto: Champlain Society, 2006.

Hennessy, Kate. "Virtual Repatriation and Digital Cultural Heritage: The Ethics of Managing Online Collections." *Anthropology News* 50.4 (2009): 5–6.

Jacknis, Ira. "George Hunt, Collector of Indian Specimens." In Aldona Jonaitis, ed., *Chiefly Feasts: The Enduring Kwakiutl Potlatch*, 177–224. Seattle: University of Washington Press and American Museum of Natural History, 1991.

———. "George Hunt, Kwakiutl Photographer." In Elizabeth Edwards, ed., *Anthropology and Photography, 1860–1920*, 143–51. New Haven CT: Yale University Press, 1992.

Kendall, Laurel, and Igor Krupnik, eds. *Constructing Cultures Then and Now: Celebrating Franz Boas and the Jesup North Pacific Expedition*. Washington DC: Arctic Studies Center, National Museum of Natural History, Smithsonian Institution, 2003.

Killan, Gerald. *David Boyle: From Artisan to Archaeologist*. Toronto: University of Toronto Press, 1983.

Leeds-Hurwitz, Wendy. "The Committee on Research in Native American Languages." *Proceedings of the American Philosophical Society* 129.2 (1985): 129–60.

Library and Archives Canada. "Project Naming." http://www.collectionscanada.gc.ca/inuit/index-e.html (accessed February 6, 2013).

Massey, Gregory D. "The Papers of Henry Laurens and Modern Historical Documentary Editing." *Public Historian* 27.1 (2005): 39–60.

McCracken, Krista. "Hidden No Longer: Keeping Indigenous Heritage Alive." *Muse*, November–December 2011, 35–45.

Nock, David. "The Erasure of Horatio Hale's Contributions to Boasian Anthropology." In Julia Harrison and Regna Darnell, eds., *Historicizing Canadian Anthropology*, 44–51. Vancouver: University of British Columbia Press, 2006.

Phillips, Ruth B. *Museum Pieces: Toward the Indigenization of Canadian Museums*. Montreal: McGill-Queen's University Press, 2011.

Protocols for Native American Archival Materials. 2007. http://www2.nau.edu/libnap-p/protocols.html (accessed February 11, 2013).

Richling, Barnett. "Archaeology, Ethnology and Canada's Public Purse, 1910–1921." In P. J. Smith and Donald Mitchell, eds., *Bringing Back the Past: Historical Perspectives on Canadian Archaeology*, 103–14. Mercury Series, Archaeological Survey of Canada Paper 158. Gatineau: Canadian Museum of Civilization, 1998.

Thompson, Judy. *Recording Their Story: James Teit and the Tahltan*. Vancouver: Douglas and McIntyre, 2007.

Underhill, Karen J. "Protocols for Native American Archival Materials." *RBM: A Journal of Rare Books, Manuscripts, and Cultural Heritage* 7.2 (2006): 134–45.

Vodden, Christy. *No Stone Unturned: The First 150 Years of the Geological Survey of Canada*. Ottawa: The Survey, 1992.

Wickwire, Wendy. "James A. Teit: His Contribution to Canadian Ethnomusicology." *Canadian Journal of Native Studies* 8.2 (1998): 183–204.

——. "Women in Ethnography: The Research of James A Teit." *Ethnohistory* 40.4 (1993): 539–63.

Zaslow, Morris. *Reading the Rocks: The Story of the Geological Survey of Canada, 1842–1972*. Toronto: Macmillan of Canada with the Department of Energy, Mines and Resources, and Information Canada, 1975.

Contributors

CHRISTOPHER BRACKEN is the author of *The Potlatch Papers* (University of Chicago Press, 1997) and *Magical Criticism* (University of Chicago Press, 2007). His recent articles include "Lebhaftigkeiten, Die Lebenden und die Lebendigen," in *Re-Animationen*, edited by Höppner, Mangold, and Hanstein (Böhlau, 2012) and "'In This Separation': The Non-Correspondence of Joseph Johnson," in *Theorizing Native Studies*, edited by Simpson and Smith (Duke University Press, 2014).

J. EDWARD CHAMBERLIN is Professor Emeritus of English and Comparative Literature at the University of Toronto. He was senior research associate with the Royal Commission on Aboriginal Peoples and is an Officer of the Order of Canada. His books include *If This Is Your Land, Where Are Your Stories? Finding Common Ground* (Knopf, 2003) and *Horse: How the Horse Has Shaped Civilizations* (Knopf, 2006).

REGNA DARNELL is Distinguished University Professor of Anthropology and First Nations Studies at the University of Western Ontario. She is the general editor of the Franz Boas Papers: Documentary Edition and a member of the American Philosophical Society. She has published widely in history of anthropology, linguistic anthropology, and Native American/First Nations studies.

DAVID W. DINWOODIE is the author of "The Canadian Anthropological Tradition and Land Claims (*Histories of Anthropology Annual*, 2010), *Reserve Memories: The Power of the Past in a Chilcotin Community* (University of Nebraska Press, 2002), and other pieces on the historical dynamics of aboriginal voices and political subjectivities. He received his PhD at the University of Chicago.

MICHELLE HAMILTON is an associate professor and the director of public history at the University of Western Ontario. As a public historian and former museum curator of ethnology, she is interested in the history of museum anthropology, contemporary issues in First Nations—museum relations, Indigenous cultural property, and repatriation.

ROBERT L. A. HANCOCK (Metis) is the LE,NONET academic coordinator in the Office of Indigenous Affairs and an adjunct assistant professor of anthropology and environmental studies at the University of Victoria.

A specialist in the ethnography and material culture of British Columbia First Nations, ANDREA LAFORET (PhD UBC 1974) retired as the director

of ethnology and cultural studies at the Canadian Museum of Civilization in 2009 and continues to work independently with First Nations on current issues relating to ethnography and history.

JÜRGEN LANGENKÄMPER studied history, philosophy, and sociology at the University of Bielefeld and at the École des Hautes Études en Sciences Sociales in Paris. His interests include the Popular Front in France, political economy in the early eighteenth century, and sumptuary laws in early modern northwestern Germany.

HERBERT S. LEWIS, a cultural anthropologist, conducted fieldwork in the West Indies, Ethiopia, Israel, and Wisconsin. His works include *Jimma Abba Jifar: An Oromo Monarchy* (University of Wisconsin Press, 1965), *After the Eagles Landed: The Yemenites of Israel* (Westview Press, 1989), *Oneida Lives: Long-Lost Voices of the Wisconsin Oneidas* (University of Nebraska Press, 2005), and *In Defense of Anthropology: An Investigation of the Critique of Anthropology* (Transaction, 2014).

JULIA E. LISS is professor of history at Scripps College in Claremont, California. She earned her PhD at the University of California, Berkeley. An intellectual and cultural historian, her work focuses on Franz Boas and cosmopolitanism, particularly Boas's role in antiracism and the institutionalization of anthropology in New York.

SEAN O'NEILL is a linguistic anthropologist who specializes in oral literature (including song) in multicultural and multilingual settings. Early in his career he contributed to the *Collected Works of Edward Sapir* (Mouton de Gruyter, 2001). O'Neill is author of *Cultural Contact and Linguistic Relativity among the Indians of Northwestern California* (University of Oklahoma Press, 2008).

TIMOTHY B. POWELL is the director of the Center for Native American and Indigenous Research at the American Philosophical Society and a senior lecturer in the Religious Studies Department at the University of Pennsylvania. He is working on a book entitled *Digital Ethnography: Building Partnerships between Scholars, Archives, and Indigenous Communities*.

MICHAEL SILVERSTEIN is Charles F. Grey Distinguished Service Professor of Anthropology, Linguistics, and Psychology and the director of the Center for the Study of Communication and Society at the University of Chicago. Long-term work on languages and cultures of the North American Northwest has sharpened his appreciation of Boas and the Boasian project.

JOSHUA SMITH is the associate editor of the Franz Boas Papers at the University of Western Ontario. His doctoral research assesses the political philosophies and cultural (re)productions of engaged anthropological research methods with an emphasis on Sol Tax's action anthropology.

ISAIAH LORADO WILNER is a PhD candidate in history at Yale University. His article "A Global Potlatch: Identifying the Indigenous Influence on

Western Thought" appeared in a special issue on settler colonialism in the *American Indian Culture and Research Journal* and was awarded the 2014 Canadian Aboriginal History Article Prize by the Canadian Historical Association. He is a fellow at the Freie Universität in Berlin (2014–2015).

Fig. 18. The research team. *Back row*: David Dinwoodie, Tim Powell, Ted Chamberlin, Michael Silverstein, Christopher Bracken, Isaiah Wilner, Rob Hancock, Tim Bisha. *Middle row*: Aaron Glass, Michelle Hamilton, Barbara Saunders, Herb Lewis, Marianne Nicolson, Sean O'Neill, Matt Bokovoy, Mark Pinkoski, Ryan Nicolson. *Front row*: Regna Darnell, Judith Berman, Julia Liss, Andrea Laforet. Photograph by Joshua Smith.

The Franz Boas Papers Project Team

GENERAL EDITOR
 Regna Darnell (University of Western Ontario)

ASSOCIATE EDITOR
 Joshua Smith (Western)

MANAGING EDITOR
 Timothy Bisha (Western)

PROJECT AND OFFICE MANAGER
 Adair Harper (Western)

COMMUNITIES LIASON
 Marc Pinkoski (Western)

CO-INVESTIGATORS
 Michael Asch (Victoria)
 Michelle Hamilton (Western)
 Susan Hill (Western)
 John Leavitt (Montreal)
 Brian Noble (Dalhousie)
 Peter Stephenson (Victoria)

COLLABORATORS
 Robert L. A. Hancock (Victoria)
 Nancy Turner (Victoria)
 Robert Wishart (Aberdeen)

EDITORIAL ADVISORY BOARD
 Lee D. Baker (Duke University)
 Christopher Bracken (Alberta)
 Quetzil Castañeda (Open School of Anthropology)
 J. Edward Chamberlin (University of Toronto)
 David Dinwoodie (University of New Mexico)
 Andrea Laforet (Canadian Museum of Civilization)
 Andre Gingrich (Vienna)
 Mathias Harbeck (Humboldt University, Germany)
 Rainer Hatoum (Freie Universitat Berlin)
 Ira Jacknis (Berkeley)
 Sergei Kan (Dartmouth College)
 Jürgen Langenkämper, Mindener Tageblatt
 Michi Knecht (Humboldt University, Germany)
 Herbert Lewis (University of Wisconsin)
 Julia Liss (Scripps)

Sean O'Neill (University of Oklahoma)
Nancy Parezo (University of Arizona)
Jarrad Reddekop (Western)
Barbara Saunders (Leuven)
Michael Silverstein (University of Chicago)
*George W. Stocking Jr. (University of Chicago)
Isaiah Wilner (Yale University)

*deceased

Index

Page numbers in italics indicate illustrations

abduction, 86
Aboriginal title and rights, 202, 204, 240, 248, 252, 270; *Calder v. British Columbia* (1973), 202, 248–50, 252–53; definition of, 202; *Delgamuukw v. British Columbia* (1997), 74, 202, 203, 204, 237; fish and water, 274, 275; *Hamlet of Baker Lake v. Minister of Indian Affairs and Northern Development* (1979), 202; hunting, 269; landownership, 268; litigation, 237, 240, 248; *Paulette Caveat* (1973), 252, 253; *Regina v. Sparrow* (1990), 202; *Regina v. Van der Peet* (1996), 202, 203; *Regina v. White and Bob* (1965), 248, 249; *St. Catherine's Milling and Lumber Co. v. Regina* (1888), 249, 250, 252; *Tsilhqot'in Nation v. British Columbia* (2014), 203; treaty, 204, 267–69, 271, 274. *See also* land claims
Abrams, Meyer Howard, 71
acculturation, 31, 37
activism, xxii, 5, 215–35, 244; motives for, 309; science as, 304–28
Adam, Leonhard, 287
Adler, Guido, 133, 146, 150
Africa, 59, 140 143; Bushmen in, 137; Khoikhoi, 68; and music of West Africa, 142
African Americans, 5, 72, 73, 140, 314, 346; folklore of, 139–40; music of, 137, 139; in the press, 314, 315; stereotypes of, 137; scholarship about, xxii
Aichel, Otto, 284–85
Aitken, Larry (Leech Lake Ojibwe), 335, 340
Akins, Watie (Penobscot), 335
Alemannia fraternity (Bonn), 279, 282, 287
Alert Bay BC, 43

American Anthropological Association (AAA), xv, 19, 65, 120, 300; code of ethics of, 237
American Anthropologist, 6
American Anti-Imperialist League, 297
American Association for the Advancement of Science (AAAS), xv, 193, 223, 224, 225, 278, 303, 310
American Committee for Democracy and Intellectual Freedom, 311, 313, 317
American Committee for the Defense of Intellectual Freedom (ACDIF), 311
American Council of Learned Societies, Committee on Native American Languages (ACLS). *See* American Philosophical Society (APS)
American Folklore Society, xv, 54
Americanist tradition. *See* Boasian anthropology, school of
American Mercury, 73
American Museum of Natural History, 47, 76, 193, 195, 224, 225, 348; Jesup North Pacific Expedition exhibit in, 136, 172, 191, 198, 202, 203, 225, 227, 279, 280, 348
American Philosophical Society (APS), 5, 106, 107, 195, 331–42, 345, 351; Indigenous fellowship program, 337; Center for Native American and Indigenous Research at, xxii, 331, 341, 342; and Committee on Native American Languages of the American Council of Learned Societies, 349; digitization by, 331, 334, 337, 342, 355–56; and Endangered Languages partnership, xxiii; Franz Boas Papers at, xii, xiv, 278–79, 346; Mellon Foundation grant to, 334–36; metadata, 337; motto of, xxiii; Native

American Philosophical Society (APS) (*cont.*)
American fellows program, 339; protocols of, xxiii. *See also* American Council of Learned Societies
Americanist tradition of anthropology, 4
Ami, Henry, 349
Anderson, Benedict, 228
Anderson, Marian, 73, 314
Antgulilibix [Mary Johnson] (Gitxan), 74–75
An Anthropologist's Credo (Boas), 308
anthropology: modernist, 164; subdisciplines of (biological, cultural, linguistic, archaeology), xii, 4, 129; as salvage effort, 195, 340, 341
Anthropology and Modern Life (Boas), xvi, 33, 46, 218, 301
anthropometry, 6, 196, 224, 348
anti-Communism, 311, 313, 314, 316
anti-racism, xxii, 3, 5, 243
anti-Semitism, xxii, 21, 72, 279, 282, 283, 284, 286, 313
Antko [Susannah Lucy] (wife of Teit) (Nlaka'pamux), 196
Appiah, K. Anthony, 216, 229
Aristotle, 46, 56
Aron, Bendix Feibes, 220
art for art's sake, 78
Asch, Michael, 203
Aschoff, Ludwig, 279, 283, 287
Assembly of First Nations, 352
assimilation, 21; Jewish, 21; Native American, 243, 269–70, 272
Association for Documentary Editing, 354
audio recordings, 335, 337, 339, 340; on wax cylinders, 194

Baffin Island, Nunavut, xii, xix, 9, 45, 106, 112, 135, 222, 280
Baffinland. *See* Baffin Island, Nunavut
Baird, Jessie Little Doe (Wampanoag), 151
Baker, Lee, xxii
Baldwin, Roger, 264
the *Barbara Boskowitz*, 43, 165
basketry, 32, 194
Bastian, Adolf, 12, 24, 112, 113, 222, 223

Bauman, Richard, 242–43, 246
Beethoven, Ludwig von, 20–21
Bell, Robert, 349
Bella Coolas (Nuxalk), 223
Benedict, Ruth, 19, 65, 71, 301, 305, 333; *Patterns of Culture,* 19
Berens, Percy (Ojibwe), 340
Berens, William (Ojibwe), 339, 341
Berens River (Manitoba), 338
Berger, Thomas, 249, 250
Bering, Vitus, 226
Berlin, Isaiah, xv, 6
Berliner Tageblatt, 222
Berlin Geographical Society, 222
Berlin Museum of Ethnology, 222, 345. *See also* Königliches Museum für Völkerkunde (Royal Museum of Ethnology)
Berman, Judith, xv, 218, 244–45, 254, 366
Bildung, 220
Bill of Rights (U.S.), Boas's defense of, 312
Bishop, Hebert R., 47
Blenkinsop, George, 44
Bloomfield, Leonard, xviii, 98, 101, 113, 122 123
Boas, Ernst P., 277, 280, 287, 308
Boas, Franz: and alternating sounds, 11, 102; and authorship, 171; and Central Eskimos, xiv; as citizen scientist, 293; and debates with Mason, 244; diaries of, 131; early life of, 220–21; as editor, 196–99; education of, 108, 219, 221, 222; epistemological standpoint of, 5; and FBI, 313, 319; fieldwork of, 241, 332; as geographer, 9, 218, 221, 222; as German Jew, 8, 21–22, 221; on grave robbing, 170, 172, 173, 347; and Heiltsakuls, Kwak'wala name, 165; on human types, 7; Kathlamet notebook of, *115;* Lower Chinook notebook of, *114;* and map illustration, 199; and metadiscursive practice, 243; on North Pacific Coast, 43–64, 163–89, 191–206, 223–25, 280; on Northwest Coast, xiv; pacifism of, 305, 312; personal library of, xxii, 277, 278, 288; and point of view, xvi, 3, 11, 13; as public intellectual, xi, xiii, xiv, xv, xxi, xxii, 293, 303,

370   *Index*

313, 314, 318; and science *vs.* history, 217; shorthand of, 107; and status as immigrant, 13; as textualist, 57; as theorist, xvii, 144

Boas, Franz, works of: *An Anthropologist's Credo*, 308; *Anthropology and Modern Life*, xvi, 33, 46, 218, 301; *The Central Eskimo*, 197–99, 347; *Changes in Bodily Form of Descendants of Immigrants*, 302; *Eskimo Tales and Songs*, 110; *Handbook of American Indian Languages*, 105; *Houses of the Kwakiutl Indians*, 47–48; *Introduction to the Handbook of American Indian Languages*, xiii, 4, 11; *The Mind of Primitive Man*, xiii, xvi, 3–17, 32, 46, 71, 77, 295, 301; *Primitive Art*, 58, 136, 144, 146, 280; *Race, Language, and Culture*, xvi, 6, 14, 308; *Rasse und Kulture*, 278, 279–80, 284; *Social Organization and the Secret Societies of the Kwakiutl Indians*, 57, 193, 198–200; *The Study of Geography*, xvii, 9, 20, 27

Boas, Marie Krackowizer, 131–32, 149n8, 166, 168, 169, 223, 279

Boas, Sophie Meyer, 20, 97, 220

Boasian anthropology, school of, 131

Bogoras, Waldemar, 280

Bokovoy, Matthew, 350, *366*

Bolza, Oskar, 282, 285

Boyle, David, 348

Bradley, Andrew Cecil, 65

Briggs, Charles L., 242–43, 246

British Association for the Advancement of Science (BAAS), 192, 224, 345, 347; Committee on the North-Western Tribes of Canada, 347

Brock, Reginald, 349

Brown, Jennifer S. H., 338, 339

Bryan, William Jennings, 303

Buck v. Bell (1927), 301

Buddenbrock, Wolfgang von, 288

Bunzel, Ruth, 30, 32, 273

Bunzl, Matti, 247

Bureau of American Ethnology. *See* U.S. Government

Bureau of Indian Affairs. *See* U.S. Government

Burgum, Edwin B., 71

Burke Museum (Seattle), 173

Butler, Nicholas Murray, 305

Campbell, Peter, 191

Canadian Broadcasting Company (CBC), 339

Canadian Institute (Toronto), 348

Canadian Museum of History, 195, 206, 349

Canadian Museums Association, 352

cannibalism, 32, 163–64. *See also* Chicago World's Fair (1893)

cantometrics, 147, 151

Cassidy, Frank, 203

Cassirer, Ernst, 69

Celler, Emanuel, 314

census, Government of Canada, 196

The Central Eskimo (Boas), 197–99, 347

Chamberlain, Alexander Francis, 224, 347, 348

Champlain Society, 354

Changes in Bodily Form of Descendants of Immigrants (Boas), 302

Chautauqua circuit, 87

Chicago World's Fair (1893), 136, 163–64, 168, 183, 281, 348, 349; living exhibits at, 163, 348. *See also* cannibalism

Chinookans, *105*, 107, 114–16, *114*, 134, 224. *See also* Kathlamets

Christen, Kimberly, 351

civilization, 11, 12; primitive people's capacity for, 7; universals of, 9

civil rights, 272, 311, 313, 314, 317

Clark University, 224, 347

Coiled Basketry in British Columbia and Surrounding Region (Teit), 194

Cole, Douglas, xiii, 4, 102, 113, 132, 217–20, 223, 227

Collier, John, xxi, 76, 263–76; and Indian Reorganization Act, 263

colonialism, 200–205, 228, 243, 263, 266, 298, 299, 351; contexts of, 70; and settler colonialism, xvii, 267. *See also* imperialism

Columbia University, xii, xviii, 27, 71, 139, 279, 287, 305, 348; libraries of, 107

Committee for Cultural Freedom, 313

Comox BC, 224

comparative historical linguistics, 94, 103
comparative literature, 73, 74; Comparative Literature Society, 76
comparative methods, xv, 14, 54, 129, 139, 225, 226, 227
comparative musicology, 130, 131, 142, 148
comparative mythology, 145
concordances, 94; grammaticosemantic, 113; lexicosemantic, 113
Cook, James, 226
Cook's Ferry. *See* Spences Bridge
Council for Pan American Democracy, 317
Crees of northern Quebec, 253
Cultee, Charles, 224
culture: area, 143; concept of, 11, 13 205; and culturally sensitive materials, xxii, 331; diffusion of elements of, 31, 226; dissemination of, 54; dynamics of, 31, 226; and environment, 13; landscape of, 338; and personality, 301; relativism of, xxii, 4, 13, 129, 132, 144, 146, 169; textual view of, 242
Curtis, Edward S., 173, 174, 181–82; *In the Land of the Headhunters*, 174

Dalhousie University, 350
Daly, Richard, 237
Danzel, Theodor-Wilhelm and Hedwig, 286
Darnell, Regna, xi, 83–84, 144, 199, 239, 244, 247, 332, 334, 342, 350, *366*
Darrow, Clarence, 303
Darwin, Charles, 22, 23, 27, 28, 69, 77
Davidson-Hunt, Iain, 338
Dawson, George Mercer, 347
decorative art, 136–37
Deloria, Ella, 273, 333
Deloria, Vine, Jr., 264, 273
Denes, 252, 253
Densmore, Frances, 146
Department of Indian Affairs (Canada), 44; Indian agents of, 44, 45, 49, 51, 168, 171, 348
Derrida, Jacques, 56–57, 59
descendant communities, xx, xxii
Dewalt, Billie R., 200
Dewalt, Kathleen, 200

Dewey, John, 21, 300, 313
Dickinson, Emily, 68
Dies Committee, 311, 312, 314
diffusion, historical, 300
Digital Knowledge Sharing (DKS), xxiii, 331, 334, 336, 341, 351, 353
Dillingham Commission, 8, 302
documentary editing, xvi, xxiii
Documents on Canadian External Relations, 354
Dorsey, J. Owen, *109*
Dossetter, Edward, 47
Douglas, James, 248
DuBois, W. E. B., 72, 73, 78, 300, 316
Duff, Wilson, xxi, 239, 248–53; expert witness testimony of, 240; and juxtaposition with Boas, 239
Duggan, Keara, 336
Dunn, Leslie Clarence, 304
du Ponceau, Peter Stephen, 332
Durkheim, Emile, 26
Dzawada'enuxw BC, 342. *See also* Musgamagw Dzawada'enuxw Tribal Council

Eastern Band of Cherokees, 333
Eastern Shawnee Tribe of Oklahoma, 335
Edwards, Elizabeth, 351
Einstein, Albert, xv
Eliot, T. S., 68, 70
Emeneau, Murray B., 84
Emergency Society in Aid of German and Austrian Science and Art, 277, 279, 283, 288
empiricism, xvii, 27; radical, 27
Enlightenment, xviii, 11, 85, 228; Counter-Enlightenment, 247
environmental determinism, 8
environment and culture, xv, xvii
epistemological relativism, 3
Erdmann, Benno, 102, 222
Eskimos, Greenlandic, 108, 112
Eskimos of Baffin Island, 221, 222. *See also* Inuit of Baffin Island
Eskimo Tales and Songs (Boas), 110
Ethical Culture, Society for, 22
ethnocentrism, xviii, 245, 252

ethnomusicology, xix, 129–60, 283
ethnography, as salvage effort, xxii, 241, 243, 355
ethnopoetics, 66
eugenics, 5, 301
evolution, critique of, 4
expressive culture, xviii, 136

Fechner, Gustav, 36
Field Museum (Chicago), 165, 172, 177, 191, 195
Fischer, Gustav, 279
Fischer, Theobald, 102, 222
Foley, John Miles, 69
Fond du Lac Tribal and Community College, 340
Fort Rupert BC (Tsaxis), 51, 52, 54, 167, 177
Franco-Prussian War, 219
Franz Boas Papers project (FBP), xi, 331, 345–61; collaboration with the Musgamagw Dzawada'enuxw Tribal Council, 341; Indigenous Advisory Council, 350; and Library and Archives Canada, 353; research team, 366; website, 355
Fraser, Simon, 201, 204
Fraser Canyon BC, 197, 198, 199, 201, 206
freedom, 36; academic, xii, 21, 288, 311; and democracy, 311; intellectual, xii, 21, 36, 313; research, 278; science as, xvi, 6; of speech, 311; spiritual, 21, 36; from tradition, 308
Freud, Sigmund, 10, 58
Fröbel, Friedrich Wilhelm August, 97
Fröbel kindergarten. *See* Boas, Sophie Meyer
fur trade, 217, 227; maritime, 216; Russian, 226

Gamio, Manuel, 6
Geertz, Clifford, 218
gender roles, music and, 138–39
Geological Survey of Canada, 349
Germanistic Society, 283–84
Gesamtgeister, 25
Getty Foundation, 334
Gibagadinamaagoom: An Ojibwe Digital Archive, 340
Gilkeson, John, xv

Gitk_sans, 237
Glick, Leonard B., 21
Goddard, Ives, 228
Goddard, Pliny E., 333
Goethe, Johann Wolfgang von, 20, 65, 70, 73
Goldenweiser, Alexander, 12, 349
Gold Rush of 1858, 195, 201, 202, 217
Goldschmidt, Walter, 34, 37
Government of Canada, Department of Indian Affairs. *See* Department of Indian Affairs (Canada)Grant, Madison, 278, 301, 304
Grantwood, New Jersey, 177
Grassmann, Hermann, 94, *95,* 98
Grassmann's Law, 98
Gray, Susan Elaine, 339
Great Lakes Research Alliance for the Study of Aboriginal Arts and Cultures (GRASAC), 353
Gregory, Richard, 310
Grimm's Law, 98
Grube, Wilhelm, 113
Grünwedel, Albert, 113
Gūdō'yōs (Kwakwa̱ka'wakws), 52
Gunther, Erna, 239
Günther, Hans, 278

Haas, Mary R., 84, 141, 333
habilitation, 347
Haeberlin, Herman, 32, 194
Hahn, Frida K. *See* Husemann, Kathrin
Hale, Horatio, 223, 224, 347
Hale, Ken, 151
Hall, Charles Francis, 222
Hallowell, A. Irving, 333, 338–41; and revitalization, 339
Halpin, Marjorie, 254
Hä'masaqas (Kwakwa̱ka'wakws), 53
Handbook of American Indian Languages (Boas), 105
Handbook of North American Indians (Goddard), 228
Harcourt, Brace and Company, 72
Harkin, Michael, 242, 243, 246
Harlem Renaissance, 73, 303
Harper, William Rainey, 87, 88–94, *88, 89, 90, 91, 93, 95, 96*

Harrington, Mark Raymond, 174
Harris, Marvin, xiv, 143–44
Harris, Zellig S., 332–33
Harvard University, 28, 146, 284, 348, 349; Peabody Museum at, 183, 191, 195
Hawthorn, Audrey, 50
Hebrew Correspondence School, 87, *88–91*
Heidegger, Martin, 46
Herder, Johann Gottfried, 69, 228, 246
hermeneutic circle, 70
Herskovits, Melville, 73, 139, 140–41
Herzberg, Theodor, 222
Herzog, George, 142–43
Heye, George, 173
Hill, Susan (Mohawk), 350
Hindenburg, Paul von, xxii, 280, 283–84, 288, 305
historicism, 3, 6; *versus* presentism, xvii, 254
historiography, xiii, 238, 239, 242
Hitchens, Janine, 245
holism, 129, 132, 145, 175, 176
Holmes, Oliver Wendell, 301
Hope Island BC, 43, *49*, 182
hopelessness, age of, 265, 267, 268, 274
Hornbostel, Erich Moritz von, 283, 286
House Committee Investigating Un-American Activities, 311–12
Houses of the Kwakiutl Indians (Boas), 47–48
Howard University, 314
Hudson's Bay Company, 226
humanism, secular, 22
Humboldt, Alexander von, 28, 69, 102, 225
Humboldt, Wilhelm von, 28, 69, 225
Hunt, George (Tlingit/Kwakw*aka*'wakw), xix, xx, 51, 76, 120, 163–89, 224, 225, 337, 342, 347; and coauthorship, xx
Hunt, Lucy (Kwakw*aka*'wakw), 169, 175, 178–81
hunting and gathering, 137
Hurston, Zora Neale, 73, 139
Husemann, Kathrin (Frida K. Hahn), 281

Ickes, Harold, 264, 271, 316
Imanuel, Siegmund, 108
immigrant, head form of, 8, 304

immigration laws: *Ozawa v. U.S.* (1922), 302; policy on, 301, xxii; *U.S. v. Cartozian* (1922), 302; *U.S. v. Thind* (1923), 302
imperialism: in American Samoa, 298; in the Philippines, 297–98; in Puerto Rico, 298. *See also* colonialism
indeterminacy, 68
Indian Act, Section 114. *See* potlatch
Indianische Sagen (Boas), 280
Indian Reorganization Act, 270
Indo-European philology, xviii
induction, 86, 218; and deductive method, xvii; and epistemology, 85; as method, 86, 92, 94
inductivism, 319; epistemological, 94; linguistic pedagogical, 108; philological, 108; text-focal, 87
intellectual property, 345; and culturally sensitive materials, xxii, 331, 356
International Journal of American Linguistics, 135
In the Land of the Headhunters (film), 174
Introduction to the Handbook of American Indian Languages (Boas), xiii, 4, 11
Introduction to the Study of Indian Languages (Powell), 102
Inuits, 45, 106, 132, 134, 135, 346. *See also* Eskimos of Baffin Island
Inuktituts, 108
Ireland, Willard, 249, 250
Ishi (last Yahi speaker), 142

Jacobi, Abraham, 20, 222–23
Jacobsen, J. Adrian, 223
Jakobson, Roman, 35, 144
James, William, 25, 27, 28, 36
Jefferson, Thomas, 332, 354
Jensen, Hans, 281
Jesuit Relations and Allied Documents, 354
Jesup, Morris K., 225
Jewitt Island, 76
Jochelson, Waldemar, 280
Johnson, Anthony D., 275
Johnson, Elizabeth Krackowizer, 289
Jousse, Marcel, 69

Judaism, 8
Judson, Wilfred, 252

Kalmar, Ivan, 24
Kant, Immanuel, 247
Kantorowicz, Alfred, 287
Karsten, Gustav, 221, 222
Kaskas, 191, 193
Kathlamet (Chinookan) language, *105, 111, 115, 116*
K'ēxs (Kwakw*aka*'wakws), 52
Kiel, Germany, 279
Kiel University, 84, 102, 221, 281, 284, 288, 345; Boas speech at, 278–79
Kiepert, Heinrich, 222
Kirchhoff, Paul, 281
Klein, Fritz, 285
Kolinski, Mieczyslaw, 283, 286
Komena'kulu (Kwakw*aka*'wakw), 47–50
Königliches Museum für Völkerkunde (Royal Museum of Ethnology), 103, 112, 347
Kootenai, 224
Krackowizer, Marie. *See* Boas, Marie Krackowizer
Kroeber, Alfred L., xvi, 22, 31, 34, 84, 133, 244, 333; and music, 141–42; superorganic, 34
Kuhn, Thomas, normalizing, xiii, 97
Kulturkampf policy, 219, 246
Kwakiutls, xvii, xix, 30, 32, 51–53, 57, 104, 120, 136, 167–89, 193, 198–200, 224, 225. *See also* Kwakw*aka*'wakw
Kwakw*aka*'wakws, xv, xvii, xx, 30, 47, *48*, 51, 76, 104, 163–89, 206, 239, 332, 334, 341, 348; culinary customs of, 175–76; Koskimo (G*u*sgimukw), 51; Nakwoktak (Nakwaxda'*x*w), 51; Nkomgilisala band, 43; police dance of, 43–64; and speaking post, 183; Tłat'łai*k*wala (Tlatlaiskikwala) band, 43, 44, 50. *See also* Kwakiutl
Kwak'walas, 104

La Flèche, Francis (Omaha), *109*
Lā'gulag'ilis (Kwakw*aka*'wakw), 53
Lamer, Antonio, 203
land claims, 206, 215, 229; in James Bay and Northern Quebec Agreement, 253; in *Tsilhqu'tin v. BC*, 229. *See also* Aboriginal title and rights
land ownership, concepts of, 268
laws, 5; of culture, possibility of, 31; of mental development, 8; natural, 217; of sound change, 97–99
Lazarus, Moritz, 24
Leacock, Eleanor Burke, 217
League of the Iroquois (Morgan), 33
Lehmann, Hedwig (Boas), 289
Lehmann, Walter, 286
Lepsius, Richard, 104
Lesser, Alexander, 273
Lévi-Strauss, Claude, 9, 131, 140–46, 151, 203
Levitt, Martin, 350
Lewis, Herbert, 247
liberalism, 215, 216, 220; procedural, 228; secular, 217
Liebowitz, Benjamin, 287
Lillooet (Stl'atl'imx), 193, 201
linguistics, synchronic *vs.* diachronic, 87, 101
Linguistic Society of America, xv
Lips, Julius, 286, 288
Liss, Julia, 20, 220, *366*
literature, definition of, 69, 133
Lō'Xoaxstaaku (Kwakw*aka*'wakw), 53
Lomax, Alan, 139, 147, 151–52
Lowell Institute, 5
Lowenstein, Otto, 287
Löwenthal, Karl, 283
Lowie, Robert, xvi, 24, 333
Lubbock, John, 77
Lurie, Nancy, 263, 264, 273
Luschan, Felix von, 112–13
Lynd, Robert, 313
Lyndberg, Harry Miller, 333
Lyons, Scott, 50
Lytle, Clifford M., 264, 273

Mack, Johnny (Nuu chah nulth), 350. *See also* Franz Boas Papers project
Malinowski, Bronislaw, 68, 70, 83, 149, 200, 203, 281
Maliseets, 337
Malouf, Albert, 253

Index 375

Mann, Horace, 98
Mason, John Alden, 333
Mason, Otis T., 23, 193, 244
Massey, Gregory, 354
Matthews, Maureen, 338–40
McEachern, Alan, 74–75, 79, 202, 237, 238, 253
McLuhan, Marshall, 67
Mead, Margaret, xvi, 138–39, 301, 303, 305
medicine, traditional, 175
Mencken, H. L., 72, 73
Menominis (Menominee, Mamaceqtaw), 122
Meriam, Lewis, 273
Meritt, Edgar Briant, 270
Merriam, Alan, 143
metonymy, 56
Meyer, Fanny, 223
Michelson, Franziska (Boas), 136, 277, 281
Michelson, Gertrude, 281
middle class, Aboriginal, 215, 228
Minden, Germany, xxi, 97, 219, 220, 221, 222, 278
Minden Gymnasium (Germany) 219, 220, 221, 222, 278, 282
The Mind of Primitive Man (Boas), xiii, xvi, 3–17, 32, 46, 71, 77, 295, 301
missionization, 196, 217, 227
modernism, xviii, 65
modernity, 243, 303
monogenesis, *vs.* polygenesis, 29
Montagnais, 217
Morgan, Lewis Henry, *League of the Iroquois*, 33
Morrow, William G., 252
Mowachaht shrine, 177
Mr. Cheap. *See* Komena'kulu (Kwakwaka'wakw)
Müller-Wille, Ludger, xiv, 284, 289
Murphy, Robert, 246
museum: arrangement, 23; exhibit, 239; pedagogy, 9; public trust doctrine, 356
Museum für Völkerkunde, Hamburg, 277, 285
Museum of the American Indian, 173
Musgamagw Dzawada'enuxw Tribal Council. *See also* Dzawada'enuxw BC., xv, 341, 350

music, and myth, 144
Musqueam band, 353
mythology, 58, 226; comparative, 145
Mythology of the Thompson Indians (Teit), 193

Na'witi, Cape Sutil BC, 43; attacks on, 43–44
NAACP (National Association for the Advancement of Colored People), 72
Nahwitti (Nahwittee, Newette, Newitti, Nawitty), Hope Island BC, 43, 47, 49, 224. *See also* Xwamdasbe' (Humdaspe)
Nanaimo BC, 224
Nanook of the North (film), 174
The Nation, Boas letter to, 299–300
National Anthropological Archives, 106, 107
National Federation of Constitutional Liberties, 317
National Historical Publications Commission, 354
National Museum of Canada. *See* Canadian Museum of History
National Origins Acts, 302
National Research Council, 300
national traditions, xii
National University of Mexico, 6
nationalism, 293, 296–303, 309, 319; Jewish, 21; linguistic, 296; *vs.* nationality, 298; during World War I, 219
nationality, 296, 297, 298, 309
Native American Graves Protection and Repatriation Act (NAGPRA), 352
native point of view, xix, 3, 14, 86, 133, 265
natural selection, 8; and "selective processes," 304
Nemiah Valley Indian Reserve BC, 229
neo-evolutionary theory, xiv
neogrammarianism, 99, 100
neuroscience, 151
New Criticism, xviii, 65, 66
New Critics, 65–81
New School for Social Research, 71, 287
New York Conference for Inalienable Rights, 317
Newcombe, Charles F., 171
Newitti (Hope Island), 224

Nez Percés, xxi, 274, 275. *See also* Niimíipus
Nez Percé Texts (Phinney), 274
Nicolson, Deanna (Dzawada'enux̱w First Nation of the Kwakwaka'wakw), 341. *See also* Franz Boas Papers project
Nicolson, Marianne (Dzawada'enux̱w First Nation of the Kwakwaka'wakw), xv, *366*. *See also* Franz Boas Papers project
Nicolson, Ryan (Dzawada'enux̱w First Nation of the Kwakwaka'wakw), xv, 341, 342, 350, *366*. *See also* Franz Boas Papers project
Nietzsche, Friedrich W., 10, 58, 305
Niimíipus, xxi, 266, 267, 268, 269, 271, 274
Nisga'as, 248, 250–51
Nlaka'pamux (Thompson River Salish), xx, 136, 191–212; hydro lines of, 205; mines of, 205; as wards of the Crown, 195–96
Nō'Lq'auLEla (Kwakwaka'wakw), 51
Nootkas, 117, *119*, 224
Norris, George, 318
North/Northwest Pacific Coast, xiv, xix, xxi, 43–64, 163–89, 191–206, 216, 223–26
Notes on Songs of the Indians of British Columbia (Teit), 201
Notgemeinschaft der Deutschen Wissenschaft, 277, 279, 283, 288
Nū'lē Mrs. (Kwakwaka'wakw), 51
Nunavut Sivuniksavut Training Program, 353

objectivity, 247, 248
Oblates of Mary Immaculate, 217, 226, 227
Oetteking, Bruno, 279, 281
Ojibwe Cultural Foundation, 353
Okanagans, 193
Omaha language, *109*
Ong, Walter, 67
ontology, 103; relational, 265
Oppermann, Otto, 287
oral tradition, 69
organology, 135
Owen, Charlie George (Ojibwe), 340
Owen, Jacob (Ojibwe), 340

Paiutes, 141
Parsons, Elsie Clews, 26, 71, 333
participant-observation, 149, 200, 341

Passamaquoddys, 331, 335, 336
Patterns of Culture (Benedict), 19
Pearson, Karl, 65
Peck, Harry Thurston, 72
pedagogy: of "great books," 76; language, 87; museum-based, 6
Peirce, Charles Sanders, 27, 86
Penck, Albrecht, 282
People's Institute, 76
Pestalozzi, Johann Heinrich, 96–97, 108
petroglyphs, 338
Pflüger, Alexander, 287
phenomenology, 66
Phillips, Henry, Jr., 334
Phillips, Ruth, 353
philology: anthropological, 83; comparative, 85, 97; epistemological, 85; inductive, 85, 94, 96, 103
Phinney, Archie Mark (Nez Percé), xxi, 266–71, 273; *Nez Percé Texts,* 274
phoneme, 100
phonograph, 136
physics, 221; pragmatic and dogmatic, 322
Pidcock, George, 171
Pimachiowin Aki Corporation, 338, 339
Pinkoski, Marc, 366; and Free Knowledge Project (FKP), 355
Pitkin, Harvey, 333
plasticity, xvi, 4–8
Plateau Centre for American Indian Studies, 355
poetry, 137; scope of, 135
Poncas, 281
popular front, 317–18
positivism, postwar, xiv
postmodernism, 68, 139
potlatch: ceremony, 43–64, 169, 342; law (ban on), 44, 167, 206, 240, 243, 244, 334
Powell, Israel Wood, 44, 47, *48*
Powell, John Wesley, 45, 102, 106; *Introduction to the Study of Indian Languages,* 102
pragmatism, 27; American philosophy of, xvii
Preston, W. D., 333
Preuss, Konrad Theodor, 286
Preußen-Schlag, 281–82

Index 377

Primitive Culture (Tylor), 55
Primitive Art (Boas), 58, 136, 144, 146, 280
primitives, 32, 58–59, 136, 147, 251, 294, 309; and "civilized," 3
primitivism, 303
progressivism, 245, 306, 307, 318
Protocols for Native American Archival Materials, 352
Psychology of Culture (Sapir), 141
Pueblos, Keresan, 66, 68
Putnam, Frederic Ward, 223, 348

Quamichan (Kw'amutsun, Qu'wutsun), 224

Rabliauskas, Sophia (Poplar River First Nation), 338
race: Aryan, 10, 294, 304, 305, 309, 315; concept of, 29; critique of, 295, 305, 310; inadequacy as a biological concept, xvi; Jewish, 305, 306, 310, 315; and nationality, 306, 309; Negro, 315; and prejudice, 307; and pseudo-science, 306; and racism, 300–304; and war, 304
race, language, and culture, 10; as classification variables, 4
Race, Language, and Culture (Boas), xvi, 6, 14, 308
racialism, 305, 307
racism, 5, 6, 300–304; concept of, 307; and race prejudice, 316; stereotypes and, 137, 310; and warfare, 313, 314. *See also* anti-racism; scientific racism
Radcliffe-Brown, A. R., 84
Radin, Paul, xvi, xvii, 10, 12, 20, 33, 218, 333
Ransom, John Crowe, 70, 71
Rasse und Kulture (Boas), 278, 279–80, 284
rationalism, 27
Reciprocal Research Network (RRN), 353
recognition: collective, 228; cultural, 228; demand for, 215
register, definition of, 134
Reiss, Johan Wilhelm, 222
relativism, 243, 247, 309; epistemological, 3; ontology of, 85
repatriation, 251, 345, 352, 357

Resek, Carl, 26–27
residential schools, 196, 334, 353; and National Residential School Survivors' Society, 353
revisionism, xii, xix, xxiii, 345; historical, xviii
revitalization, 345; anthropology of, 331–44; and language preservation, 215, 332, 340, 349; of tribal governance, 226
Revolution of 1848, 20, 222; 1848ers, 297
Rhoads, Charles J., 265, 266, 269, 272
Ricoeur, Paul, 70
Rig-Veda, 94, 95
Rink, Hinrich, 108, *110*, 112
Rivet, Paul, 286
Roberts, Helen, 143
Rohner, Ronald, xiv
Romanticism, 20, 65, 245
Roosevelt, Eleanor, 317
Roosevelt, Franklin D., 264, 270, 271, 307, 316, 318
Rothenberg, Jerome, 66
Roulette, Roger, 338–40
Royal British Columbia Museum, 195
Royal Commission on Aboriginal Peoples, 352
Royal Museum of Ethnology, 103, 112, 347
Royal Proclamation of 1763, 249
Rukeyser, Muriel, 333
Russ-Coudert Committee, 313
Russell, Bertrand, 314

Sacks, Oliver, 151
Salish, Interior, 191, 198, 224
The Salishan Tribes of the Western Plateaus (Teit), 194
Sanskrit, 96
Sapir, Edward, xviii, 6, 67, 69, 113, 117–19, 193, 206, 244, 333, 348–49; and music, 140–41; Nootka notebook of, 117, 119; *Psychology of Culture,* 141; *Takelma Texts,* 141; *Time Perspective in Aboriginal American Culture,* 11; and Wishram (Kiksht), 117, *118*
Saunders, Barbara, 247
Saussure, Ferdinand de, 59, 122
Scheidt, Walter, 285
Schiller, Friedrich, 219

Schneider, Kurt, 287
school of Boasian anthropology, 131
Schurz, Carl, 35, 265, 297
science: as activism, 304; as critique, 245; as disinterested pursuit, 299; empirical, 97; and ideology, 307; inductive, 97, 104; as international effort, 302; philological, 84, 101; and politics, 240, 244; pragmatic *vs.* dogmatic, 309–10; and pseudo-science, 220, 306, 316; as social force, 311; as a value, xii
scientific racism, 6, 216. *See also* racism
seawater: optical properties of, 84, 131, 221, 277
Seeger, Charles, 147
self-government, 264
Shaking Tent ceremony, 338
Shingwauk Project, 352–53
Shuswaps, 103
Simmons, Margaret, 340
skepticism, 147
Smith, Charles Sprague, 75–77
Smith, Harlan Ingersoll, 348
Snake River Basin, 274
social evolution, 28, 216, 220, 294
socialism, 313
Social Organization and the Secret Societies of the Kwakiutl Indians (Boas), 57, 193, 198–200
Social Sciences and Humanities Research Council (SSHRC), Partnership Grant Program, xi, 350
Society for Documentary Editing, x
Soctomah, Donald (Passamaquoddy), 335–37
song texts, 129
sound change, 97
sound patterning, in music, 135
sovereignty, 269
Soviet Union, 267
Spanish Revolution, 322
Spanish-American War, 297
Speck, Frank, 331, 333–37, 340, 341, 349; beadwork collection of, 336
Spencer, Herbert, 28

Spences Bridge (Cook's Ferry) BC, 191, 196–97, 200, 348
Spingarn, Joel Elias, xviii, 71–73, 76
Spinks, Nathan, 206
Spuzzum BC, 197, 201
Stark, Johannes, 309, 310
Steinen, Helmut von den, 280, 281
Steinen, Karl von den, 280
Steiner, George, 70–71
Steinthal, Heymann, 24, 103, 104
Stern, Bernhard, 29, 313
Sternberg, Lev, 280
Stocking, George W., Jr., xiii, 4, 9, 35, 216, 218, 244, 245, 246
Stól:ō (Lower Fraser Salish), 239, 353
The Study of Geography (Boas), xvii, 9, 20, 27
Stumpf, Carl, 146–47
subaltern, 215
Survey of California Indian Languages, 84
Swadesh, Morris, 333
Swanton, John, 198

Tahltan, 191, 193
Takelma Texts (Sapir), 141
Tarde, Gabriel, 26, 32, 36
target sounds, 100
Taylor, Charles, 215
teachers union, 313, 317, 322
Teit, James Alexander, xx, 32, 191–212, 242, 244, 348; ethnographic legacy of, 194
Teit, James Alexander, works of: *Coiled Basketry in British Columbia and Surrounding Region,* 194; *Mythology of the Thompson Indians,* 193; *Notes on Songs of the Indians of British Columbia,* 201; *The Salishan Tribes of the Western Plateaus,* 194; *The Thompson Indians of British Columbia,* 191–206; *Traditions of the Thompson River Indians,* 193
textual studies, 58, 92; criticism of, 94; Hebrew, 87; legacy of, 241
Thilenius, Georg, 277, 285
Thomas, Norman, 307
Thompson, Judith, 191
Thompson Indians. *See* Nlaka'pamux (Thompson River Salish)

The Thompson Indians of British Columbia (Teit), 191–206
Thurnwald, Richard, 279, 281, 282, 284, 287
Time Perspective in Aboriginal American Culture (Sapir,), 11
Tlingits, 76
Tō'qoamalis (Kwakwa*ka*'wakw), 53
Traditions of the Thompson River Indians (Teit), 193
Treaty of Oregon, 202, 203
treaty relationships, 269
trickster: in literature, 71; poetic, 67
Tsilhqut'ins (Chilcotins), 216, 217, 229
Tsimshians, 106
Tylor, Edward B., 55, 70, 347; *Primitive Culture,* 55
Tyrell, Joseph B., 349

U'mista Cultural Society, 353
ultramontansim, 217, 219
unconscious, 145, 243
UNESCO, 338–39
Union of British Columbia Indian Chiefs, 352
U.S. Census Commission, 8
U.S. Congress Joint Immigration Commission. *See* Dillingham Commission
U.S. Government: Bureau of American Ethnology, 45, 112, 224; Bureau of Indian Affairs, xxi, 76, 263
U.S. Indian policy, 263, 264, 270; *Dawes General Allotment Act,* 267, 268
U.S. National Museum, 348; *Proceedings of the United States National Museum,* 47
universalism, 247
universals, 13; of civilization, 9; cultural, 12; linguistic, xix; music as, xix, 130
University College London, 354
University of Aberdeen, 350
University of Berlin, 222
University of British Columbia Museum of Anthropology: Reciprocal Research Network (RRN), 353
University of California, Berkeley, 84
University of California Publications in Linguistics, 84

University of Chicago, 77, 287
University of Kiel, 84, 102, 221, 277, 284, 288, 345: Boas speech at, 278–79
University of Ottawa Great Lakes Research Alliance for the Study of Aboriginal Arts and Cultures (GRASAC), 353
University of Pennsylvania, 340
University of Victoria, 350
University of Western Ontario, xi
Urbach, Anna Margaret (Boas), 277, 289
Urey, Harold, 303

Vancouver Island treaty (14th), 249
Vaughan, Henry, 68
Verdon, Michel, 218
Victoria Memorial Museum. *See* Canadian Museum of History
Virchow, Rudolph, 35, 216, 219, 222, 246
Voegelin, Charles F., 332–34
Vogeler, Adolf, 282
Völkerpsychologie, 24
Volksgeist, 25
Vowell, Arthur W., 173

Wagner, Günter, 281
Wallace, Glenna (Eastern Shawnee), 335
Wallace, Henry, 317–18
Wampanoags, 151
Washington State University: Plateau Centre for American Indian Studies, 355
Washington, Booker T., 72
Wax, Murray, 245–46
Wesle, Carl, 288
Westermann, Diedrich, 281
White, Hayden, 55
White, Leslie, xiv, 22, 23
Whitney, William Dwight, 96, 117
Whorf, Benjamin, 12, 67, 69
Wickwire, Wendy, 191, 241–42
Widdowson, Frances and Albert Howard, 238
Willet, Jane E., 333
Williams, William Carlos, 68
Wilson, Daniel, 347
winter ceremonial, 53, 57, 167, 169; Hamatsa, 53, 167, 168, 171

Wishart, Robert, 350
Wissler, Clark, xvi
Wohlauer, Antonia (Boas), 289
Woodland Cultural Centre, 353
Woodson, Carter G., 316
World Congress against War, 305
World Unity Conference, 301
World War I, xxii, 293–28; and interwar years, 300–304; and nationalism, 219
World War II, 293–328; and GI Bill, xiv; and interwar years, 300–304; as watershed, xvi

World's Columbian Exhibition. *See* Chicago World's Fair 1893
Wundt, Wilhelm, 36

xenophobia, 296, 301
*X*wamdasbe' (Humdaspe), 43, 44, 47, *48*, *49*, 52. *See also* Nahwitti BC

Yale Indian Papers Project, 355
Yampolsky, Helene (Boas), 277
York, Annie (Nlaka'pamux), 206
Yuchi, 281
Yutlinuk band, 43

In the Franz Boas Papers Documentary Edition series

The Franz Boas Papers, Volume 1: Franz Boas as Public Intellectual—Theory, Ethnography, Activism
Edited by Regna Darnell, Michelle Hamilton,
Robert L. A. Hancock, and Joshua Smith

To order or obtain more information on these or other University of Nebraska Press titles, visit nebraskapress.unl.edu.

THE FRANZ BOAS PAPERS DOCUMENTARY EDITION

THE FRANZ BOAS PAPERS, VOLUME 1